THE APPRAISAL OF REAL ESTATE

FOR EDUCATIONAL PURPOSES ONLY

THE APPRAISAL OF REAL ESTATE

Eighth Edition

American Institute of Real Estate Appraisers
430 N. Michigan Avenue · Chicago, Illinois

Foreword

A number of years ago my daughter presented me with a cherished gift: a copy of the 10-volume set of pamphlets entitled *Real Estate Appraising,* which was published by the National Association of Real Estate Boards in 1927. The 56-year-old NAREB manuscript, which was intended by its editor Arthur Mertzke "for the use of individual Realtors® or study groups organized in firms or member boards," was a forerunner of *The Appraisal of Real Estate,* the 8th edition of which you now hold. The American Institute of Real Estate Appraisers was founded in 1932 and published its first lesson text booklet in 1935.

The second edition of the Appraisal Institute's *The Appraisal of Real Estate* was published in an "MAI green" cover in 1951 and immediately became the standard appraisal text and reference. Subsequent editions were published in 1960, 1964, 1967, 1973; the 7th edition was published in 1978.

Over the decades, appraisal education has been evolving, as did education for earlier maturing professions. For example, would-be lawyers now neither read the law nor attend pre-law school. Rather, they obtain a liberal arts background and then attend graduate school to learn the law. Increasingly, appraisal education is available within university curricula. This 8th edition of *The Appraisal of Real Estate* is the first appraisal text specifically designed for use as a university textbook for upperclassmen and graduate students. This book differs markedly from the 7th edition in several respects. First, it is of wider scope in that it includes seven new chapters:

Real Estate Markets

Collection and Analysis of General Data

Money Markets and Capital Markets

Highest and Best Use

Collection and Analysis of Specific Data

Evaluation

Appraisal Specialties

Second, the source work for the 8th edition, in addition to previous Appraisal Institute publications, included a manuscript for each of the 26 chapters, which was specifically prepared for the 8th edition by a contributor selected on the basis of a reputation for particular expertise. In a few instances, more than one such expert was asked to contribute a manuscript. This method allowed much of the information in the book to reflect contemporary appraisal literature, judicial determination, and economic experience, all of which strengthen the practical specialized knowledge and experience on which these contributions are founded.

The third salient feature of the 8th edition is that it is developmental: each chapter builds on the preceding chapters.

Fourth, the work of the contributors was reviewed by one or more experts who then suggested additions and deletions to promote consistency, provide completeness, and eliminate dogma. Even so, the text includes opinions with which many appraisers will competently disagree; and so be it. No member of the American Institute of Real Estate Appraisers should subordinate personal competence to textbook adherence.

The final distinction of the 8th edition is that it was professionally written by Sheila F. Crowell, an educator-turned-writer, who throughout the process worked to ensure that the book would fulfill the defined educational objectives. Karla L. Heuer directed the project; the writing was enhanced by the copyediting of Marilyn Litvin; and Gretchen Messer managed the production process. We are grateful for their dedication and their performance.

During the making of this book, five members of the Appraisal Institute were in committee positions entailing an unusual degree of personal responsibility. They are Harold D. Albritton, MAI; Jerome N. Block, MAI; Max J. Derbes, Jr., MAI; Peter F. Korpacz, MAI; and Judith Reynolds, MAI.

The work of the following organizers, contributors, and reviewers is also gratefully acknowledged: Charles B. Akerson, MAI; Richard M. Betts, MAI; Peter D. Bowes, MAI; James H. Boykin, MAI; James H. Bulthuis, MAI; William H. Coulter, MAI; David W. Craig, MAI; Max J. Derbes, Jr., MAI; Gene Dilmore, MAI; John D. Dorchester, Jr., MAI; S. Grant Edwardh, MAI; J. B. Featherston, MAI; Jean C. Felts, MAI; James P. Gaines, Ph.D.; James E. Gibbons, MAI; Thomas Gillentine, MAI; James Graaskamp, Ph.D.; Henry S. Harrison, MAI; Wayne D. Hagood, MAI; Karla L. Heuer; Harvey P. Jeffers, MAI; James C. Kafes, MAI; William N. Kinnard, Jr., MAI; Richard L. Lodge, MAI; A. Scruggs Love, Jr., MAI; Kenneth M. Lusht, Ph.D.; Patricia J. Marshall, MAI; Robert J. McCarthy, MAI; James J. Mason, MAI; Bill Mundy, MAI; Terrell R. Oetzel, MAI; John O'Flaherty, MAI; Ronald L. Racster, Ph.D.; Judith Reynolds, MAI; Richard M. Rhodes, MAI; Thomas M. Rule, MAI; Jared Shlaes, MAI; Halbert C. Smith, Ph.D.; Walstein Smith, Jr., MAI; H. Grady Stebbins, MAI; H. Bruce Thompson, Jr., MAI; Julian Utevsky, MAI; Robert E. Ullman, MAI; and Timothy Warner, MAI.

Anthony Reynolds, MAI
1983 President
American Institute of Real Estate Appraisers

Table of Contents

Part I
Introduction

Chapter 1

Real Property Appraisal

Under all is the land. More than a physical reality is implied in this statement. Land is the surface of the earth and the major source of all mineral, vegetable, and animal substance; it is the foundation for the social and economic activities of people; it is a commodity and the wellspring of wealth.

Because land is essential to human existence and society, it is the subject of study of various disciplines, including geography, law, sociology, and economics. Each of these disciplines has somewhat different concepts of real estate. Geography focuses on describing the physical elements of land and the distribution and activities of people who use it. Law considers land as the subject of ownership. Sociology concentrates on the dual nature of land: as both a resource to be shared by all people and a commodity to be owned, traded, or used by individuals. In economics, land is regarded as one of the four agents in production (along with labor, capital, and coordination). Land represents all natural elements of a nation's wealth, and the concept of land value is an economic concept. The link among these disciplines is a common understanding of the attributes of land:

1. Each parcel of land is unique in its location and composition.

2. Land is physically immobile.

3. Land is durable.

4. The supply of land is finite.

5. Land is useful, and thus valuable, to people.

Along with geographers, lawyers, sociologists, and economists, real estate appraisers recognize these attributes of land. Real estate appraisers are concerned with the concepts of land from these disciplines because the concepts provide the basic common perceptions upon which real estate value ultimately rests. The particular emphasis of real estate appraisal is on real estate markets, which result from the actions of people as they respond to and often are directed or limited by all the important attributes of land that are delineated in the disciplines of geography, law, sociology, and economics.

Concepts of Land

Geographic

A sense of land begins with recognizing its diverse physical characteristics and the significance of the combination of these characteristics in a particular area. Developing a sense of land also includes an awareness of the effect of physical characteristics on the use of land.

Land is affected by a number of processes. Ongoing physical and chemical processes modify the land's surface; biological processes affect the distribution of all life forms; and socioeconomic processes direct human habitation and activity on the land. Together, these processes influence land capability and, therefore, land use.

Land may be used for many purposes, including agriculture, commerce, industry, residence, and recreation. Land-use decisions are influenced by climate, topography, and the distribution of natural resources, population centers, and industry. In addition, land use is determined by economic conditions, population pressures, technological practices, and cultural influences. The degree of influence of each of these varies, depending on the geographic area.

These subjects of geographic study are particularly significant for appraisers. The importance of land's physical characteristics—climate, geology, soils, water, and vegetation—is obvious. Just as important are the distribution of people and their facilities, as are services and the movement of goods and people. With its emphasis on such matters as resources and resource bases, industrial location, and actual and potential markets, the geographic concept of land forms much of the background knowledge about land that is required in any real estate appraisal.

Legal

A society's cultural, political, government, and economic attitudes are partly expressed in its body of law. When considering land, the law shifts the focus away from physical characteristics to the rights and obligations associated with various interests in land. While maintaining the right of individuals to own land and to use it for material gain, the law also protects the rights of all inhabitants in their shared use of land. Thus, the law recognizes the conflicts between private ownership and public use.

The ancient maxim "Whose is the land, his it is, to the sky and the depths" is undoubtedly the basis for the following legal definition:

Land includes not only the ground, or soil, but everything that is attached to the earth, whether by course of nature, as are trees and herbage, or by the hand of man, as are houses and other buildings. It includes not only the surface of the earth, but everything under it and over it. Thus, in legal theory, a tract of land consists not only of the portion on the surface of the earth, but is an inverted pyramid having its tip, or apex, at the center of the earth, extending outward through the surface of the earth at the boundary lines of the tract, and continuing on upward to the heavens.[1]

Seemingly implied in this definition is also full and complete ownership from the center of the earth to the periphery of the universe. But, in practice, ownership is limited. For example, Congress has declared that the U.S. government has complete and exclusive sovereignty over the nation's airspace and that every citizen has "a public right to freedom of transit in air commerce through the navigable air space of the United States."[2] Because ownership can be limited, own-

---

[1]Robert Kratovil and Raymond J. Werner, *Real Estate Law*, 7th ed. (Englewood Cliffs, N.J.: Prentice-Hall, Inc., 1979), p. 5.

[2]The Air Commerce Act of 1926 (formerly 49 USC 171 *et seq.*); the Civil Aeronautics Act of 1938 (formerly 49 USC 401 *et seq.*); and the Federal Aviation Act of 1958 (see 49 USC 401).

ership rights are the subject of law; the value of these rights is the subject of appraisal.

U.S. laws that govern the use and development of land are based on according an owner the fullest possible freedom in deciding land use. This right of enjoyment can be restricted only insofar as it unreasonably harms the rights of others. The definition of reasonable use has been tested in many legal-use cases.

Some legal matters of particular concern to appraisers are easements and access regulations, various use restrictions, and title recording and conveyance. Appraisers must be familiar with local and state laws because jurisdiction over lands is vested primarily in local and state, not federal, governments.

Social

As physical characteristics and legal limitations increasingly affect land use, many different groups in society become concerned with how land is used and how rights are distributed. Because the supply of land is fixed, the demand for land in modern American society causes pressure for its more intensive use. Conflicts often arise between groups whose views on land's proper use differ. Certain people believe that land is a resource to be shared by all. They want to preserve the land's scenic beauty and important ecological functions. Other persons view land primarily as a marketable commodity and believe that society is best served by private, unrestricted ownership. The fact that land is both a resource and a commodity prevents clear-cut solutions to these group conflicts.[3]

Both groups have won support for their beliefs. As a resource, land is protected for the good of society. Because land is also a marketable commodity, its ownership, use, and disposal are regulated so that unjust infringement on individual rights is precluded.

The government's right to regulate "the manner in which [a citizen] shall own his own property when such regulation becomes necessary for the public good" was established in 1876 by the U.S. Supreme Court, which repeated the words of England's Lord Chief Justice Hale: "When private property is 'affected with a public interest,' it ceases to be *juris privati* only."[4]

Even earlier, land ownership had been recognized as fundamental to America's institutions. John Adams wrote, "If the multitude is pos-

---

[3]Richard N. L. Andrews, *Land in America* (Lexington, Mass.: D. C. Heath and Company, 1979), p. ix.

[4]94 U.S. 113 (1896). Quoted in Richard F. Babcock and Duane A. Feurer, "Land as a Commodity 'Affected with a Public Interest' " in Andrews, *op. cit.,* p. 110.

sessed of real estate, the multitude will take care of the liberty, virtue, and interest of the multitude in all acts of government."[5]

The restrictions that society may fix in the public interest include building restrictions, zoning and building ordinances, development and subdivision regulations, and environmental controls. The latter include provisions to prohibit the pollution of air and bodies of water through dumping wastes, emitting dirt and chemicals, and causing excessive noise. Concern for preserving the natural state has made possible certain regulations that protect wetlands, beaches, and navigable waters.

Economic

Land is a physical substance imbued with ownership rights that can be legally limited for the good of society. Further, land is a major *source* of wealth. In economic terms, wealth is measured in relation to money value or exchange value. Land and its products are of economic value only as they are converted into goods or services that are useful to, and desired and paid for by, consumers. The economic concept of land as a source of wealth and object of value is central to appraisal knowledge and inquiry.

Appraisal

The geographic, legal, social, and economic concepts of land all are germane to the real estate appraiser's concept of land. Land, as defined legally to include everything attached to it, constitutes real estate. The appraiser studies the value of physical real estate and its accompanying ownership rights, but is always aware that real estate must be used to benefit the entire society. The potential uses of land are influenced by geographic, legal, social, and economic considerations. These considerations form the background against which appraisal activities are conducted.

Discipline of Appraisal

Because so much private, corporate, and public wealth lies in real estate, its proper use is essential to the social and economic well-being of society. The orderly growth and development of cities, suburbs, and rural areas are appraisal concerns. Proper estimates of real estate value

[5]Andrews, *op. cit.*, p. 31.

and competent evaluations of other real estate-related issues help produce sound judgments about the disposition and use of real estate. Accurate and realistic value estimates help to stabilize real estate loans and investments, which in turn help to promote widespread and socially desirable uses of real estate. Because decisions about the use and disposition of real estate and the rights inherent in its ownership depend on solid real estate knowledge, appraisers can provide great assistance to those who make such decisions.

The discipline has become increasingly sophisticated in response to new challenges. Appraisers use the most current techniques for gathering, analyzing, and applying information pertinent to property values and uses. Their professional opinions, backed by training and knowledge, inspire confidence and influence the decisions of people who own, manage, sell, purchase, invest in, and lend money on the security of real estate.

Real Estate, Real Property, and Personal Property

When beginning the study of real estate appraisal, one must recognize the important distinction between the concepts of real estate and real property. These concepts are different, although the statutes of certain states hold that the two are synonymous. Both concepts are significant in the discipline of appraisal.

Real estate is the physical land and appurtenances including structures affixed thereto. Real estate is immobile and tangible. Legally defined, real estate includes land and all things that are a natural part of it (e.g., trees and minerals) and all things that are attached to it by people (e.g., buildings and pavement). All permanent attachments to a building, such as plumbing, electrical wiring, and heating installations, as well as such items as built-in cabinets and elevators, are usually held to be part of the real estate.

Real property includes the interests, benefits, and rights inherent in the ownership of physical real estate. Real property includes the "bundle of rights" that is inherent in the ownership of real estate.

In the bundle of rights theory, ownership of real property is compared to a bundle of sticks. Each stick represents a distinct and separate right, which may be the right to use real estate, to sell it, to lease it, to enter it, to give it away, or to choose to exercise more than one or none of these rights. Although subject to certain limitations and restrictions, private enjoyment of these rights is guaranteed by law under the U.S. Constitution.

It is possible to own all of the rights in a parcel of real estate or only a portion of them. A person owning all of the rights is said to have fee simple title. *Fee simple title is regarded as an estate without limita-*

tions or restrictions. Less than complete estates result from partial interests that are created by selling, leasing, or otherwise limiting the bundle of rights in the fee estate. An appraisal assignment may require the appraisal of fee simple title or any partial interest such as a leasehold interest or an easement.

All estates in real property are subject to four powers of government: taxation, eminent domain, police power, and escheat.

Taxation is the right to take money from owners of valuable goods, products, and rights. Because the U.S. Constitution effectively precludes the federal government from directly taxing real property, the right of taxation is reserved for state and local governments.

Eminent domain is the right of the sovereign government to take private property for public use upon the payment of just compensation. This right can be extended to an entity acting under a government's authority, such as housing authorities and public utilities. Condemnation is the act or process of carrying out the right of eminent domain.

Police power is the right to regulate property so that the public's safety, health, morals, and general welfare are protected. Examples of this power are zoning ordinances, building codes, air and land traffic regulations, and sanitary regulations.

Escheat is the right to have titular ownership of a property return to the state if the owner dies and leaves no will and no known or ascertainable heirs.

The government also controls overflight, through which publicly chartered private aircraft may cross an owner's property, provided that the property's occupants suffer no inconvenience beyond established standards.

In addition to government restrictions on property, legal private agreements may also impose limitations. One type is a restriction inserted in a deed. Such restrictions can limit the use or manner of development, or even the manner in which ownership can be conveyed. The purchaser of a property so encumbered may be obligated to use the property subject to such restrictions. Other private restrictions include certain easements, rights of way, and party-wall agreements.

The rights in the bundle, subject to government limitations and private restrictions, can be sold, leased, transferred, or otherwise disposed of individually. Certain parcels of land afford owners a number of options. For example, one property owner could sell or lease mineral rights and still retain the rights to use the surface area. Another could lease surface rights to one party and lease subsurface rights to another. Still another could sell or lease air rights for construction or avigation. Thus, the ownership of certain rights may be severed from the ownership of the rest of a property by their being sold, leased, or given as a gift to other parties.

Just as appraisers understand the distinction between real estate and real property, so do they differentiate between real estate and personal property.

Personal property is, generally, movable items—that is, those not permanently affixed to and part of the real estate. Thus, personal property is not endowed with the rights of real property ownership. Examples of personal property are furniture and furnishings that are not built into the structure, such as refrigerators and freestanding shelves.

Although personal property generally consists of tangible items (in law, called chattels personal), an intangible personal property right, chattels real, may be created by a lease.[6]

Sometimes it is not clear whether an item should be considered personal property or real estate. Often, court opinions have been required to resolve the conflict. Such situations gave rise to the Law of Fixtures, which provides the following definition of a fixture. *A fixture is an article that was once personal property, but that has been installed in or attached to land or a building in some more or less permanent manner, so that such article is regarded in law as part of the real estate.*[7] Thus, a fixture is endowed with the rights of real property ownership.

Whereas fixtures are real estate, trade fixtures are not. *A trade fixture, also called a chattel fixture, is an article owned and attached by a tenant to a rented space or building for use in conducting a business.* Thus, trade fixtures are not real estate and are not endowed with the rights of real property ownership. Such personal property is movable and usually tangible. Examples are office furniture and equipment, livestock and farm machinery, and bowling alleys. A trade fixture is to be removed by the tenant unless this right has been surrendered in the lease. In apartments or rented homes, under specific lease terms, such items as bookshelves and venetian blinds may be installed by the tenant and remain personal property to be removed at the termination of the lease.

In deciding whether an item is a trade fixture, and therefore personal property, or is real estate, courts use the following criteria:

1. The manner in which the item is affixed. Generally, but with exceptions, an item remains personal property if it can be removed without serious injury either to the real estate or to itself.

---

[6]Historically, personal property also included ownership rights to real estate for a fixed number of years, such as a tenant's interest. These were called chattels real, to distinguish them from movable personal objects, which were called chattels personal. In most states today, it is more common to refer to a lessee's interest as an interest in or right to real estate.

[7]Kratovil and Werner, *op. cit.*, p. 10.

2. The character of the item and its adaptation to the real estate. Items specifically constructed for use in a particular building or installed to carry out the purpose for which the building was erected are generally considered permanent parts of the building.

3. The intention of the party who attached the item—that is, whether to leave it permanently or to remove it at some time (frequently revealed by the terms of a lease).[8]

Appraisers should know whether an item is personal property or a fixture. If an item is classified as a fixture, thereby becoming part of the real estate, its contribution to value is included in the value estimate; if it is classified as personal property, it contributes nothing to the real estate value. Thus, appraisers may decide which items will be included in or excluded from a property on the basis of their classification as real estate or personal property. Because differentiation is not always obvious, an appraiser should know how the Law of Fixtures is customarily applied in a given location.

Definition of Appraisal

In our complex society, professional real estate appraisers perform a variety of functions and services, including estimating several types of defined value and consulting and participating in decisions about real estate.

An appraisal is an unbiased estimate of the nature, quality, value, or utility of an interest in, or aspect of, identified real estate. An appraisal is based on selective research into appropriate market areas; assemblage of pertinent data; the application of appropriate analytical techniques; and the knowledge, experience, and professional judgment necessary to develop an appropriate solution to a problem.

The nature of a particular real estate problem indicates whether the appraisal is a valuation or an evaluation. *Valuation is the process of estimating market value, investment value, insurable value, or other properly defined value of an identified interest or interests in a specific parcel or parcels of real estate as of a given date.* Examples of valuation assignments are market value estimates of property owned in fee simple or of preservation easements or leasehold estates. *Evaluation is a study of the nature, quality, or utility of a parcel of real estate or interests in, or aspects of, real property without reference to a value estimate.* Examples of evaluation assignments are land utilization studies, supply and demand studies, economic feasibility studies, highest and best use analyses, and market-

---

[8]Kratovil and Werner, *op. cit.,* pp. 10-11.

ability or investment considerations for a proposed or existing development.

In valuation assignments, the appraiser communicates to the client an estimate of real property value that reflects all pertinent market evidence. In evaluation assignments, current market activity and evidence provide the basis for a conclusion other than a specified value conclusion. For both valuation and evaluation assignments, the conclusion is derived by appropriate data analysis in conformity with standards of professional practice.

The application of appraisal procedures and the final report of the appraiser's conclusions are guided by the nature of the assignment. Therefore, to avoid any confusion between the client and the appraiser, it is important to determine if the assignment is valuation or evaluation.

Purpose and Use of an Appraisal

The purpose of an appraisal is to estimate the defined value of any interest in real property or to conduct an evaluation study pertaining to real property decisions. The purpose is established on the basis of the question of the client, and it points to the information the client needs to answer specific questions pertaining to real property. If the questions are understood, the purpose of the appraisal can be clearly and fully stated in terms of the information requested by the client.

When an estimate of value is required in an appraisal, the particular type of value is defined at the outset. The defined value may be market value, insurable value, going-concern value, liquidation value, assessed value, use value, or investment value. (Distinctions among these terms are discussed in Chapter 2.)

The use of an appraisal is the manner in which the client employs the information in the appraisal report. The use is determined by the client's needs. A client may need to know the market value of a residence to avoid paying too much or accepting too little for its sale. Corporate clients may need to ascertain the rent levels or demographic trends in an area to help determine the advisability of locating there. Insurance companies and private citizens may wish to know the insurable value of buildings. A developer may need to know the conditions of supply and demand in a community before constructing an apartment complex.

Because an appraisal provides the basis for a decision concerning real property, the use of an appraisal depends on the nature of the decision the client wishes to make. Therefore, in defining the problem, the appraiser should develop an understanding of the client's requirements that is clearly acceptable to both client and appraiser and is consistent with accepted professional appraisal standards.

An appraisal may be requested in any of the following situations:

1. Transfer of ownership
   a. To help prospective buyers decide on offering prices
   b. To help prospective sellers determine acceptable selling prices
   c. To establish a basis for exchanges of real property
   d. To establish a basis for reorganization or for merging the ownership of multiple properties
   e. To determine the terms of a sale price for a proposed transaction
2. Financing and credit
   a. To estimate the value of security offered for a proposed mortgage loan
   b. To provide an investor with a sound basis for deciding whether to purchase real estate mortgages, bonds, or other types of securities
   c. To establish the basis for a decision regarding the insuring or underwriting of a loan on real property
3. Just compensation in condemnation proceedings
   a. To estimate market value of a property as a whole—that is, before the taking
   b. To estimate value after the taking
   c. To allocate market values between the part taken and damage to the remainder
4. Tax matters
   a. To estimate assessed value
   b. To separate assets into depreciable (or capital recapture) items, such as buildings, and nondepreciable items, such as land, and to estimate applicable depreciation (or capital recapture) rates
   c. To determine gift or inheritance taxes
5. To set rental schedules and lease provisions
6. To determine feasibility of a construction or renovation program.
7. To facilitate corporation or third-party company purchase of the homes of transferred employees
8. To serve the needs of insured, insurer, and adjuster
9. To aid in corporate mergers, issuance of stock, or revision of book value
10. To estimate liquidation value for forced sale or auction proceedings
11. To counsel a client on investment matters, including goals, alternatives, resources, constraints, and timing
12. To advise zoning boards, courts, and planners, among others, regarding the probable effects of proposed actions
13. To arbitrate between adversaries
14. To determine supply and demand trends in a market
15. To determine the status of real estate markets

Although this list does not include all uses for appraisals, it indicates the broad scope of the professional appraiser's activities.

The Importance of the Appraiser to the Community

The professional appraiser provides essential services that contribute to the growth and stability of a community or a city. Decisions concerning substantial investments are based on valuations and evaluations, including feasibility opinions. These studies, including the research on which an appraiser's opinions are based, are essential for new construction, large renovation or development programs, and major changes in land use.

To serve their clients and the general public properly, real estate appraisers must continue their educational activities throughout their professional years. They must keep pace with the vast expansion of the database, which is made possible by computer technology; the rapidly growing knowledge base of appraisal theory and practice; and the continuing refinement of appraisal methods and techniques. Only by being involved in this continuing process will an appraiser be able to render a sound appraisal analysis, opinion, or conclusion.

Summary

Appraisal is founded on an understanding of land, including geographic, legal, social, and economic concepts of land. Contingent on these concepts are the important distinctions made between real estate and real property. Real estate is the physical land and appurtenances, including structures affixed to it. Real property includes the interests, benefits, and rights inherent in the ownership of physical real estate.

It is possible to own all of the rights in a parcel of real estate or only a portion of them. Yet they are all subject to taxation, eminent domain, police power, and escheat—the powers of government. In addition, legal private restrictions may limit rights of ownership. Subject to such limitations, ownership rights can be sold, leased, transferred, or otherwise disposed of, in total or individually. Such disposition of ownership rights often necessitates an appraisal.

An appraisal is an unbiased estimate of the nature, quality, value, or utility of an interest in, or aspect of, identified real estate. The particular problem of the appraisal indicates whether the appraisal is valuation or evaluation. Valuation is the process of estimating market value, investment value, insurable value, or other properly defined value of an identified interest or interests in a specific parcel or parcels of real estate as of a given date. Evaluation is a study of the nature, quality, or utility of a parcel of real estate or interests in, or aspects of, real property, without reference to a value estimate.

Chapter 2

Foundations of Appraisal

Value is the principal subject of inquiry in appraisal. Therefore, real estate appraisers should understand value theory; anticipation and change, which are fundamental in appraising value; the principles and their related concepts, which explain shifts in value; the forces that influence value; and the factors that create value. Such comprehension provides the foundation necessary for a competent appraisal and use of the tools for an objective, systematic analysis of events and motivations that affect real property value.

History of Value Theory

Throughout history, numerous individuals, groups, and disciplines have developed theories about value in keeping with their philosophical premises and with their era's social and political conditions and state of technology. Contemporary appraisal theory is at once an outgrowth and an advancement of these theories. Because appraisers must understand the complexity of value concepts and interpret them in relation to real property, a brief review of the history of value thought is included here.

Early Economic Thought

Commerce, including the transfer of real estate ownership, is as old as civilized man. Indeed, the history of mankind may be traced through economic, as well as social, or military, behavior. As an economic concept, value received little attention during the Greek and Roman empires. Values of goods and services were considered absolute and fixed either by the owner or by general decree. A static value concept fit well in the sociopolitical fabric of these times when most states were governed by autocratic rule.

The flourishing commerce of the ancient world was eventually disrupted, which gave birth to the medieval period. Medieval economic life was dominated by the manor, a self-sufficient economic unit. Much of medieval literature centers on discussions of a just price for goods and criticisms of usury. The only real contribution to value theory during this time was made by St. Thomas Aquinas, who taught that value is a moral concept and leads to just or fair value. The fairness of the value of an item, however, was related to the social standing of the owner rather than to the item's quality. Nevertheless, the notion of fairness has survived; today the phrase *fair market value* is sometimes used.

The fifteenth century signaled the beginning of world exploration, conquest, and colonization, and commerce regained some measure of respectability. During the next 300 years, two schools of thought with conflicting ideas emerged. The first, mercantilism, dominated economic thought and most national policies well into the eighteenth century. Mercantilism provided economic doctrine to nations aspiring to world power.

According to the doctrine, world power could be achieved by amassing great national wealth through a favorable balance of trade and strong, central economic controls. A nation's wealth increased by selling goods to other nations for a profit, thereby bringing gold, the chief medium of exchange, into the selling nation's treasury. Mercantilism's chief contribution to value theory was its emphasis on the exchange relationship between an item and its worth, measured in gold, which was based on the supply of and demand for the item. Mercantilist theories on national wealth and power continue to influence national policies to this day, as seen in continued, widespread foreign trading.

By the middle of the eighteenth century, the second, rival school of economic thought, the Physiocrats, appeared. The Physiocrats, composed primarily of Frenchmen with Francois Quesnay as their major spokesman, objected to the commercial and national economic emphasis of the mercantilists. Instead, they proposed an individualistic, agrarian-based concept of economic behavior. Physiocrats opposed centralized economic controls because they believed that the "natural order" of human behavior would cause things to work as they should. The phrase *laissez-faire* (let it alone) was coined by the Physiocrats and underscores their individualistic approach.

Physiocrats asserted that value is based on utility, or usefulness. Agricultural productivity, not gold, was the source of wealth, and land was the fundamental productive agent. These concepts greatly influenced the major political movements of the day, including the American and French revolutions. Equally important was their influence on Adam Smith and the early classical economists.

Classical School

In 1776 Adam Smith, a Scottish philosophy professor, published *The Wealth of Nations*. In it, he expanded the basic tenets of the Physiocrats into an organized school of thought.

Smith believed that value was derived from the productive combination of land, labor, and capital (which Smith called stock). The final ingredient of production—coordination—was only briefly acknowledged. For Smith, value was objective and arose when the agents in production were brought together to produce a useful item. Consequently, an item sold for its natural price—that is, how much it cost to produce. The item was assumed to have utility; otherwise, it would not be produced. Moreover, to have exchange value, the item must be relatively scarce. Smith's concept is called the cost of production value theory and is basic to the classical school of economic thought.

The cost of production theory has influenced the cost approach, one of the important approaches used in appraising real property. The premise of the cost approach is that the market value of a property equals the value of the land plus the current cost of improvements less any accrued depreciation. The contemporary application of the cost approach also stresses entrepreneurial profit, an important part of coordination, which Smith touched on only lightly.

Other classical economists made important contributions to value theory. At the beginning of the Industrial Revolution, when land and factory owners began their struggle, David Ricardo developed a theory of rents while studying the relationship between wages, prices, and rents. He agreed with Smith that value was a function of an item's relative scarcity and its cost of production. His concept of land rent was derived from noticing that certain parcels of land generated surplus productivity.

Ricardo theorized that the increased demand for food caused the most fertile lands to produce revenues above the costs of labor and capital necessary for farming. Moreover, less fertile lands would be devoted to raising food so long as the land's productivity sufficiently covered the costs of production. Land that provided no surplus revenues was called marginal land. Land rent, therefore, equaled the surplus revenue (productivity) a parcel of land could generate relative to marginal land, which generated no surplus and consequently had no rental value.

Thus, Ricardo viewed land rent as an unearned increment that does not result from the efforts of landowners. Land was regarded as the last agent in production, and its owners were entitled to a return on land only after all other agents were paid. Landowners and landlords obtained surplus revenue by virtue of their monopoly positions. This residual concept of land rent is carried into the concept of highest and best use and the land residual technique of the income capitalization approach today. The land residual technique is based on the assumption that income to land will be paid only after returns are paid to other agents in production.

Thomas R. Malthus, another classical economist, asserted that relative scarcity causes value. Malthus is best remembered for his *Essay on the Principle of Population* (1798), wherein he predicted impending mass starvation based on calculations of the rate of population growth relative to the rate of growth in food supply. According to Malthus, land values would increase due to population increases, thus creating an even greater demand to grow more food.

Karl Marx and John Stuart Mill made their contributions to value theory in the mid-nineteenth century, and their ideas continue to influence world events. Both men differed with Adam Smith on separate, important issues. Mill's *Principles of Political Economy* (1848) reformulated Smith's ideas and replaced *The Wealth of Nations* as the basic economic text for the next half century. Mill argued for government intervention in the distribution of wealth. His best-known argument is that government should confiscate increases in property values as unearned benefits created by population and industrial growth. Mill stressed value as being purchasing power in exchange.

Marx zealously espoused that all values are the direct result of labor; therefore, all wealth should be owned by workers. While Smith referred to rational, economic man, Marx focused on human involvement and toil. Both Mill and Marx assumed that increased wages to labor would lower capitalistic profits, thereby leading to inevitable struggle between the two classes. However, Marx predicted an inevitable, violent clash, while Mill believed that such a clash could be avoided by system modification.

The Austrian (Marginal Utility) School

In the late nineteenth century, a number of Austrian, American, and English economists, working independently but employing similar logic, formed the marginal utility, or Austrian, school of economic thought. In direct opposition to classical economists, proponents of marginal utility reasoned that cost of production has little influence on value. Instead, they saw value as functionally related to the utility of and demand for the marginal (last) unit of an item. According to the Austrian school, the value of every unit is determined by the value of the marginal unit. If there is one more unit than needed (demanded), the whole market becomes diluted. At that point, the cost of production is irrelevant. W. Stanley Jevons, one of the founders of the Austrian school, declared that "labor once spent has no influence on the future value of any article: it is gone and lost forever."[1] Value, then, is a function of demand prices, and utility is the fundamental precept.

To understand the difference between the classical and the marginal utility theories, consider the value of a new bathroom. According to classical theory, a bathroom that costs $8,000 to construct would add exactly $8,000 to the value of the house. But the marginal utility theory would show that the room's value would be determined by buyers in the market who would relate the value of the room to its relative utility. If it were the first (and only) bathroom, it might have utility (value) greater than $8,000. On the other hand, if it were the fourth bathroom in a three-bedroom house, its marginal utility might be worth substantially less than its $8,000 cost. Marginal utility is the theoretical basis for the concept of contribution. This concept and its relation to the principle of balance are discussed later in this chapter.

The Neoclassical School

In the late nineteenth and early twentieth centuries, the neoclassical school of economics emerged. Of all schools of economic thought, it has had the most profound influence on current appraisal value theory. Alfred Marshall laid the foundation for neoclassicists by combining the supply-cost approach of the classicists with the demand-price theory of the Austrian school. Through this combination, the concept of value was again formulated. Marshall believed that value is influenced

[1]W. Stanley Jevons, *The Theory of Political Economy*, 5th ed. (New York: Augustus M. Kelley, 1965), p. 164.

by conditions of both supply (primarily reflecting cost of production) and demand (reflecting utility).

Marshall echoed Adam Smith's natural value concept. He reasoned that, in the long run, market prices (values) move toward equilibrium, at which point they equal the cost of production. Marshall's perfect economic market would form in the long run, when price, value, and cost all would be equal. In the short run, with supply relatively fixed, value is a function of demand.

Marshall's theories helped form the basis of appraisal's three established methods of value estimation—the sales comparison, income capitalization, and cost approaches.

Contemporary Value Theory

Appraisal methods and techniques owe much of their foundation to all schools of economic thought, and they continue to develop as economists build on value theory. Older economic theories, while rarely rejected completely, often are not relevant to changing conditions and contemporary events. New theories are often needed to provide additional, up-to-date insights.

Thus, value theory is still developing, but whether a new school of systematic thought is emerging is not clear. Economists today usually place little credence in Ricardian rent theory, which treats land income as a residual, unearned surplus. The relationship between cost of production and value is no longer regarded as absolutely fixed; it is now viewed as a general, long-term tendency. In modern value theory, land is regarded as an equal agent in production with labor, capital, and coordination. Its value is determined in its own market, not in those of the other agents as classical theory implies. Land income is neither residual nor exploitative. It is determined by the land's productivity in relation to the demand for that productivity.

This brief history of value theory demonstrates that the concept of value has always had significance, but that it has been interpreted differently at various times. Current appraisal theory of real property value builds on historical interpretations and recognizes that value theory changes in response to external influences. Much of current value theory derives from classical and marginal utility schools of thought and from neoclassical economics, which combined supply costs and demand utility into a unified concept. Appraisers today recognize that the interaction of supply and demand affects property value. However, they also recognize that supply and demand are affected by numerous other influences in the market.

Value Influences

Appraisals require the study of all value influences. Change and anticipation are fundamental in this study. They characterize human collective action and value judgments, and appraisers study them by analyzing appraisal principles and related concepts, forces that influence value, and factors that create value. Appraisers examine the creation or diminution of value in terms of these elements. In a specific assignment, an appraiser successively narrows the study of a property by ascertaining the ways in which anticipation and change, principles, forces, and factors external to the property operate to affect its value.

The appraisal principles—supply and demand, substitution, balance, and externalities—help to explain shifts in value. In turn, trends in anticipation and change, which are revealed by an analysis of the principles, can be studied more particularly through the analysis of four forces—social, economic, government, and environmental—that influence people and value. This analysis provides a more detailed understanding of the causes of value trends and also aids in forecasting their strength and duration. An appraiser can then study characteristics of specific properties and people who constitute a market for them in terms of four factors—utility, scarcity, desire, and effective purchasing power—that are essential for the creation of value in a particular item or a collection of items.

This progressive study enables an appraiser to analyze trends on the general level of economic activity and to trace the results of those trends through the external influences on individuals who make up specific and different markets for real property. This systematic, yet constantly overlapping, analysis forms the basis of all appraisal inquiries.

Anticipation

Anticipation means that value is created by the expectation of benefits to be derived in the future. In the market, the current value of a property is not based on historical prices or cost of creation; it is based on what market participants perceive to be the future benefits of acquisition.

In the case of owner-occupied properties, value is primarily based on expected future advantages, amenities, and pleasures of owning and occupying a particular property. For income-producing real estate, value is based on anticipated future income flows produced by the property. Hence, real property appraisers must be knowledgeable about local, regional, and national real estate trends that affect buyer or seller perceptions and anticipations of the future. Historical data concerning the property or the market are relevant only insofar as they aid in the interpretation of current market anticipations.

Change

Change is the law of cause and effect at work. It is inevitable and constantly occurring, although the process may be almost indiscernible due to its often gradual evolution. The pervasive quality of change is evident in the dynamic character of the real estate market. Social, economic, government, and environmental forces that affect real estate are in constant, inevitable transition. Because these forces undergo continual change, so do individual property values. Appraisers attempt to identify current and anticipated changes in the market that could affect current property values. Because of the inevitability of change, appraisal value estimates are valid only for the time specified by the appraiser.

Appraisal Principles

Appraisal principles, which are founded in general economics but are applied in an individual context relating to the unique physical and legal characteristics of a particular parcel of real property, are (l) supply and demand, (2) substitution, (3) balance, and (4) externalities. The result of the proper accord of these principles is highest and best use, a concept of great significance to real property appraisal.

Supply and Demand

The principle of supply and demand is that price varies directly, but not necessarily proportionately, with demand, and inversely, but not necessarily proportionately, with supply. Thus, increasing supply or decreasing demand tends to reduce the price obtainable in the market. The opposite is also true, although in either case the relationship may not be directly proportional. The interaction of the supply of and demand for an item is fundamental to all economic theories. This interaction of suppliers and demanders—sellers and buyers—constitutes a market.

  Usually, property values vary inversely with changes in the supply. That is, if properties for a particular use are abundant relative to the past relationship, the value declines; by contrast, if properties are in short supply relative to the past relationship, value increases. The supply of and demand for commodities always tend toward equilibrium. At this theoretical point, market value, price, and cost are equal.

  Supply is the schedule of the various amounts of a commodity, good, or service made available for sale at different prices. Typically, more of an item will be supplied at higher prices and less at lower prices. Thus, the supply of an item at a particular price, at a particular time, and in a particular place refers to that item's relative scarcity—a basic factor of value. The supply of real estate is a function of the capital necessary to bring a parcel of land to a given use relative to the current price for existing properties providing such uses. For example, as the price of houses increases, builders may find it profitable to build on land previously considered too expensive to develop.

Because real property is both a physical good and a service, the supply of real estate refers to the amount of service (use) space as well as the quantity of physical space. Consequently, a primary concern of those involved in real estate activities is the supply of land suitable for a specific use rather than only a total number of acres available. As such, the supply of real estate incorporates both the *quality* and *quantity* of service space provided. Quality of space may affect property values even more than quantity. Quality is a function of the tangible attributes of a property (size, shape, condition, and so forth) and the intangible attributes of the property (amenities). Proper comparisons can be made only between properties that are similar qualitatively and quantitatively.

The quantity of space supplied for a given real property use is generally slow to adjust to changes in price levels. The length of time needed to bring new structures into existence, the high capital requirements, and government regulations often delay a supplier's ability to meet changes in the market. The quality of service space supplied, however, can change rapidly through such actions as converting nonproductive space to alternative uses, deferring maintenance, partitioning existing usable space into smaller physical units, and the like.

Demand is the schedule of the various amounts of a commodity, good, or service that will be purchased at different prices. Typically, less of an item will be demanded at higher prices, and more at lower prices. Property values tend to vary directly with shifts in demand; that is, prices tend to increase if demand increases and other factors remain constant. As with supply, the relationship with price usually is not fixed. A changing relationship is described as the elasticity of demand.

Because the supply of real property for specific uses is difficult to adjust, especially immediately, values are most affected by current demand. Demand, like supply, can be motivated by the desire for real estate in terms of both quantity and quality. Demand supported by purchasing power results in effective demand, which is the relevant market consideration. Typically, there is a direct (although usually not directly proportional) relationship between demand and price. If demand increases relative to previous levels and supply remains constant, prices tend to increase; if demand falls relative to previous levels, prices tend to fall. Appraisers, therefore, interpret market behavior in order to judge the existing relationship between the supply of, and demand for, the type of property being appraised.

Competition.   Competition is a concept related to the principle of supply and demand. *Competition is the active demand by two or more market participants for an item in short supply.* Thus, it is fundamental to the dynamics of supply and demand in a free enterprise, profit-maximizing economic system.

Competition causes continual shifts in the levels of commodities available and therefore affects the levels of demand for those commodities. Buyers and sellers of real property operate in a competitive market setting. In essence, each property competes with all others suitable for the same use: a profitable motel faces competition from newer motels close by; existing residential subdivisions compete with new subdivisions; central downtown retail properties compete with suburban shopping centers.

Over time, competitive market forces tend to reduce unusually high (excess) profits. While profit encourages competition, excess profits tend to breed detracting competition. For example, the first store in a new and expanding area generates profit in excess of what is considered "typical" for that type of enterprise. Owners of similar retail enterprises, however, gravitate to the area to compete for the surplus profits. Eventually, there may not be enough business to support all the stores. One or a few may earn "normal" profits, but others may fail. The effects of competition and market trends on profit levels are especially important in helping an appraiser formulate accurate income projections through the income capitalization approach.

Substitution

The principle of substitution states that when several similar or commensurate commodities, goods, or services are available, the one with the lowest price attracts the greatest demand and widest distribution. This principle assumes rational, prudent market behavior with no undue cost of delay. According to the principle, a buyer would not pay more for one property than for another that was equally desirable.

Property values tend to be set by the cost of acquiring an equally desirable substitute property. The principle of substitution allows for the fact that buyers and sellers of real property have other options, that other properties are available for similar uses. The substitution of one property for another may be in terms of use, structural design, or earnings. The cost of acquisition may be the cost of acquiring a similar site and constructing a building of equivalent utility, assuming no undue cost of delay (the basis of the cost approach), or it may be the price of acquiring an existing property of equal utility, again assuming no undue cost of delay (the basis of the sales comparison approach).

The principle of substitution applies equally to properties purchased for amenity-producing capabilities and for income-producing capabilities. For income-producing properties, substitution refers to alternate investment properties that produce equivalent investment returns with equivalent risk. The limits of prices, rents, and rates tend to be set by the prevailing prices, rents, and rates for equally desirable substitutes. Substitution is therefore fundamental to all three traditional approaches to value—sales comparison, income capitalization, and cost.

Opportunity cost.   Related to the principle of substitution is the concept of *opportunity cost, the sacrifice of opportunities not chosen or the cost of options foregone.* Opportunity cost is especially significant when estimating rates of return required to attract capital. By analyzing and comparing the prospective rates of return for alternative investment opportunities, appraisers can judge the appropriate rate of return for a property being appraised.

Balance

The principle of balance is that value is created and sustained when contrasting, opposing, or interacting elements are in a state of equilibrium. Balance thus affirms that a proper economic mix of types and locations of land uses in an area creates and sustains value. The relationships between the entire property and its environment, and those among the various property components, constitute applications of the principle of balance. Concepts related to balance are (1) conformity, (2) contribution, and (3) surplus productivity.

Conformity.   *A property's external conformity refers to the relationship between the property and its surroundings.* The property values of an area are maximized when there are reasonable degrees of architectural homogeneity and compatibility of land uses in that area. Local zoning ordinances are the government's effort to regulate conformity by restricting land uses. The standards of conformity are market standards and are therefore subject to change. Zoning codes tend to set conformity in basic property characteristics, including size, style, and design. A particular market also sets standards of conformity, especially in terms of price. Usually, the value of an overimproved property will decline (regress) toward the value level of surrounding, conforming properties, while the value of an underimproved property may increase (progress) toward the prevailing market standard.

A *property's internal conformity occurs when the four agents in production—labor, capital, coordination, and land—are appropriately combined in the property.* For most real properties, the critical combination is land and building. The point of economic balance is achieved at the optimal combination of land and building—that is, at the point at which no marginal benefit (utility) is achieved by adding another unit of capital. Larger amounts of the agents in production produce greater net income up to a certain point (the law of increasing returns). At this point, the maximum value is developed (the point of decreasing returns). Any additional expenditures do not produce a return commensurate with the additional investment (the law of decreasing returns).

The fertilization of farmland provides a simple example of internal conformity. Applying fertilizer increases crop yield only up to a point. The optimum amount of fertilization is achieved when the value of the land's crops does not increase with any additional expenditures for fertilizer. This would be the point of balance.

Contribution.   When appraisers apply the principle of balance to component property parts, they study the concept of contribution. *Contribution states that the value of a particular component is measured in terms of its contribution to the value of the whole property or by how much that part's absence detracts from the value of the whole.* Accordingly, cost does not necessarily equal value. A swimming pool that costs $10,000 does not necessarily cause the value of a residential property to increase by $10,000. Instead, the pool's dollar contribution to value is measured in terms of how valuable its benefit or utility is in the market. Its contribution to value might be lower or higher than its cost. Thus, in some cases, a property's market value may not increase even if its physical attachments have additions, alterations, or modifications, or if they have been rehabilitated.

Existing improvements may not reflect the proper balance for the total property. Especially for properties in areas of rapid transition, present use may represent underutilization of the land. Nevertheless, an existing, suboptimal use, called interim use, will continue until it is economically warranted for a developer to absorb the costs of converting the property, including razing or rehabilitating the existing improvements.

Surplus productivity.   *Surplus productivity is the net income that remains after the proper costs of labor, capital, and coordination have been paid.* The surplus is imputable to land rent and tends to fix land value. The concept of surplus productivity is the basis for the residual concept of land returns and thus for residual valuation techniques.

The principle of balance and its related concepts are highly interwoven and are crucial when estimating highest and best use and market values. The related concepts of balance form the theoretical foundation for estimating all forms of depreciation in the cost approach, for making adjustments in the sales comparison approach, and for calculating expected earnings in the income capitalization approach.

Externalities

The principle of externalities is that external economies or diseconomies result from goods, products, or conditions that have a positive or negative effect on people other than those who produce or own the goods or products, or who create the conditions. For example, an external economy occurs when one group of ticket purchasers for a concert pays a price higher than the cost of its seats so that others may attend at a lower, subsidized price. When external economies affect great numbers of people, the product or service will probably be provided by government. Bridges, highways, police and fire protection, and other commonly needed services are provided more cheaply per user through common purchase by the government than through separate purchase by each individual.

External diseconomies occur when costs or inconveniences are imposed on other people by an individual or a firm. For example, a person who litters imposes the cleanup costs on other people. A business firm that erects an unattractive sign imposes the cost of offensive visual sensations on people who see the sign.

Real estate is affected by externalities more than any other type of economic good, service, or commodity. Its physical immobility subjects it to many types of external influences. Such influences emanate from all levels—international, national, regional, community, and neighborhood. The influences may be as broad as international currency and gold prices or as narrow as a neighbor's standard of maintenance. An appraiser should be knowledgeable about, and analyze the impacts of, all such influences on a parcel of real estate.

At the international and national levels, such influences as international trading policy, manufacturing efficiency, interest rates, and socioeconomic priorities affect real estate values greatly. For example, the combination of these influences caused many U.S. real estate values in the early 1980s to fall or to increase less rapidly than in previous years. Foreign imports tended to depress certain U.S. industries. Old plants and equipment tended to make U.S. manufacturing operations less efficient than certain foreign counterparts. High interest rates tended to depress home buying and industrial expansion. Moreover, a lesser emphasis on homeownership as a national priority resulted in competition for credit. Borrowers who wanted to buy a home had to compete with government and industry.

At the regional level, real estate values during these years prospered better in some areas than in others. Generally, the population migration to the Sunbelt tended to enhance values there at the expense of older, northern regions, where values tended to stabilize or decline. Industrial areas with manufacturing operations most susceptible to foreign competition suffered more than areas less reliant on such industries.

At the community and neighborhood levels, property values are affected by local laws, local government policies and administration, property taxes, economic growth, and social attitudes. Differential trends in property values often are noted among communities in the same state or region and among neighborhoods in the same community. An appraiser should be familiar with such external events and be able to assess their impacts on individual property values.

Highest and Best Use

Highest and best use is a basic premise of value. As with value, highest and best use is not an absolute fact; it reflects an appraiser's opinion of the best use of a property based on an analysis of prevailing market conditions. Highest and best use is defined as:

The reasonable and probable use that supports the highest present value, as defined, as of the effective date of the appraisal.

Alternately:

The use, from among reasonably probable and legal alternative uses, found to be physically possible, appropriately supported, financially feasible, that results in highest land value.

Because the use of land can be limited by the presence of improvements, highest and best use is determined for (1) the land or site as though vacant and available to be put to its highest and best use; and (2) the property as improved.

The first reflects the fact that land value is determined by potential land use. Indeed, land has no value unless there is a present or anticipated use for it, and the amount of value depends on the nature of the anticipated use (according to the concept of surplus productivity). Among all reasonable, alternative uses, the use found to yield the highest present land value, after allowing for payments to labor, capital, and coordination, is generally regarded as the highest and best use of land as though vacant.

For the purpose of analysis, the appraiser assumes that the parcel of land being analyzed is vacant. Even a site with a large building can be made vacant by demolishing the building. The question to be answered in this context is, If the land were vacant, what new improvement should be constructed on the site?

Highest and best use of the property as improved refers to the optimal use that could be made of a property including existing structures. The implication is that the existing improvement should be retained as is or renovated so long as the improvement has some market value or until the return from a new improvement will more than offset the cost of demolishing the existing building and constructing a new one. For example, a large, old house could be continued in single family residential use, or it could be converted to apartments or offices. The decision, of course, depends on the rents or prices that may be charged for the existing property under the alternative uses and their relationship to the costs of conversion. Even though an existing improvement does not represent the highest and best use of a site as though vacant, it should not necessarily be demolished.

Highest and best use of land as though vacant is useful for land or site valuation. Highest and best use of an improved property provides a decision regarding continued use or demolition.

The relationship between the supply of, and demand for, land adaptable to a particular use is significant in determining highest and best use. If the more profitable use must be delayed because of insufficient present demand, the *interim use* will continue until or unless the value of the land as if vacant plus the cost of demolishing the existing improvements exceeds the total value of the improved property at its current use.

Properties devoted to a temporary, interim use give rise to a related concept, *consistent use*. According to this concept, *land cannot be valued on the basis of one use while valuing the improvements on the basis of another*. Improvements must contribute to the land value to have any value attributed to them. Improvements that do not represent the land's highest and best use, but do have substantial remaining physical lives, may have an interim use adding temporary value or may have no value at all (or even negative value if substantial removal costs would be incurred).

Forces that Influence Real Property Values

The value of real property reflects and is affected by the interplay of basic forces that motivate human activities. These forces are considered in four major categories: *social* ideals and standards, *economic* conditions, *government* controls and regulations, and *environmental* conditions. Each force is dynamic, as it exerts pressure on certain human activities and is in turn affected by them. The interaction of all the forces influences the value of every parcel of real estate in the market.

Therefore, an appraiser interprets the ways the market views the property. The scope of investigation is not limited to static, current conditions. The appraiser analyzes trends in the forces that influence value in regard to the direction, speed, duration, strength, and limit.

Social Forces

Social forces are exerted primarily by population characteristics. The demographic composition of the population reveals the potential basic demand for real estate services; therefore, proper analysis and interpretation of demographic trends is imperative in real property appraisal. Real property values are affected not only by population changes and characteristics but also by the entire spectrum of human activity. Accordingly, among the more important value influences appraisers consider to be social forces are (1) total population, (2) rate of family formations and dissolutions, and (3) age distributions.

Economic Forces

Economic forces are significant to real property value. The appraiser analyzes the fundamental relationships between current and expected supply and demand conditions and the economic ability of the population to satisfy its wants, needs, and demands by its purchasing power. Among the many specific market characteristics considered in the analysis of economic forces are employment, wage levels, industrial expansion, the economic base of the region and community, price levels, and the cost and availability of mortgage credit. Most of these are considered demand-side economic characteristics. Supply-side economic characteristics include (1) the stock of available vacant and improved properties, (2) new development, (3) occupancy rates, (4) rent and price patterns of existing properties, and (5) construction costs. Other economic trends and considerations may be necessary as the analysis focuses on successively smaller geographic areas.

Government Forces

Government-political-legal actions at all levels may strongly influence property values. The legal climate at any particular time or place may overwhelm the natural market forces of supply and demand in affecting values. The government also provides many necessary facilities and services that are important elements in land-use patterns. Thus, appraisers must be diligent in identifying and examining the potential value influences of (1) the provision of such public services as fire and police protection, utilities, garbage collection, and transportation networks; (2) the extent and nature of local zoning, building, and health codes, especially in light of their obstruction to or support of land use; (3) national, state, and local fiscal policies; and (4) special legislation that influences general property values—for example, rent control laws, statutory redemption laws, forms of ownership allowed or restricted (condominiums, timeshare arrangements, and the like), homestead exemption laws, environmental legislation regulating new developments, and legislation affecting mortgage lending institutions (types of loans, loan terms, investment powers, and so forth).

Environmental Forces

Environmental forces, both natural and man-made, also influence real property values. Typical environmental-physical forces that are analyzed for real estate appraisal purposes include (1) climatic conditions, such as snowfall, rainfall, temperature, and humidity; (2) topography and soil; (3) natural barriers to future development, such as rivers, mountains, lakes, and oceans; (4) primary transportation systems, including federal and state highway systems, railroads, airports, and navigable waterways; and (5) the nature and desirability of the immediate area, or neighborhood, surrounding a property.

Environmental forces that affect specific real estate values may be best understood in relation to a property's location. *Location is the time-distance relationship between a property and all other possible origins and destinations of people and goods going to or coming from the property.* Time and distance are measures of relative access. An analysis of locational forces involves identifying linkages between the property and the important points or places outside of it, and measuring time and distances by the most commonly used types of transportation. Depending on the area and the property type, the appraiser investigates the property's access to public transportation, schools, stores, service establishments, parks, recreation, cultural facilities, places of worship, sources of employment, product markets, suppliers of production needs, processors of raw materials, and so forth.

Understanding all value-influencing forces is fundamental to the appraisal of real property. Although the four forces are discussed separately here, they work together to affect property values. Study of the forces creates a background against which appraisers view any parcel of real property being appraised.[2]

Factors of Value

Value is extrinsic to the commodity, good, or service to which it is ascribed; it is created in the minds of people who constitute a market. The relationships that must exist to create value are complex, and values change with changes in the factors that are most influential. Typically, four interdependent economic factors must be present to create value. They are (1) utility, (2) scarcity, (3) desire, and (4) effective purchasing power. All four factors must be present for a property to have value.

Utility

Utility is the ability of a product to satisfy a human want, need, or desire. All properties must possess utility to tenants, owner-investors, and owner-

---

[2]See Chapters 6, 7, and 12 for expansion and particularization of this discussion in the context of gathering and analyzing general, neighborhood, and specific data.

occupants. Residential properties fulfill people's need for shelter; the useful benefits of these properties are called amenities. Usually, the value of these amenities is related to their desirability and utility to the owner-occupant, but they also can be converted to income in the form of rent. The benefits from income-producing properties can usually be measured in dollar flows. The influence of utility on value is therefore relative to the characteristics of the property itself. Size-utility, design-utility, location-utility, and other specific forms of utility significantly influence property value.

The benefits of real property ownership derive from the bundle of legal rights that an owner possesses. Restrictions imposed on ownership rights may inhibit the benefit flows and thereby lower a property's value. Consequently, for a property to achieve its highest value, it must have the legal capacity to perform its most useful function. Environmental control regulations, zoning codes, deed restrictions, or any other limitations on the rights of ownership can enhance or detract from a property's utility and value.

Scarcity

Scarcity is the present or anticipated supply of an item relative to the demand for it. In general, if demand is held constant, the scarcer a commodity is, the more valuable it becomes. Land, for instance, is still generally abundant in total. Useful, desirable land, however, is relatively scarce and therefore has greater value. No object, including real property, can have value without scarcity coupled with utility. Consider air, which possesses a high level of utility yet typically has no definable economic value because of its abundance.

Desire

Desire is a purchaser's wish for an item to satisfy human needs (e.g., shelter, clothing, food, companionship) or individual wants beyond essential life support needs. Desire, along with utility and scarcity, are considered in relation to purchasing power.

Effective Purchasing Power

Effective purchasing power allows an individual who wants a commodity to participate in the market—that is, to acquire the item. A valid estimate of the value of a property includes an accurate judgment of the capability in the market to pay for the property.

Utility, scarcity, desire, and effective purchasing power are the four economic factors of value. Their complex interaction must be studied to provide a basis for decisions concerning the value of individual parcels of real property.

Value Definitions for Real Property Appraisal

Because of the wide variety of assignments and the many different purposes and uses of appraisals, different types of value must be understood.

Market Value

Market value is the major focus of most real property appraisal assignments; developing an estimate of market value is the purpose of most appraisal assignments. The current definition of market value was first formally identified by Adam Smith and has been continually refined.[3]

A current definition of market value is

The most probable price in cash, terms equivalent to cash, or in other precisely revealed terms, for which the appraised property will sell in a competitive market under all conditions requisite to fair sale, with the buyer and seller each acting prudently, knowledgeably, and for self-interest, and assuming that neither is under undue duress.

Fundamental assumptions and conditions presumed in this definition are

1. Buyer and seller are motivated by self-interest.

2. Buyer and seller are well informed and are acting prudently

3. The property is exposed for a reasonable time on the open market.

4. Payment is made in cash, its equivalent, or in specified financing terms.

5. Specified financing, if any, may be the financing actually in place or on terms generally available for the property type in its locale on the effective appraisal date.

6. The effect, if any, on the amount of market value of atypical financing, services, or fees shall be clearly and precisely revealed in the appraisal report.

---

[3]Most definitions of market value are based on a decision by the California Supreme Court in an eminent domain case (*Sacramento Railroad Company* v. *Heilbron*, 156 Calif. 408, 1909). That definition reads: "The *highest* price in terms of money which a property will bring in a competitive and open market under all conditions requisite to a fair sale, the buyer and seller each acting prudently, knowledgeably, and assuming the price is not affected by undue stimulus" [emphasis added].

The essence of this definition of market value relies on the prerequisite factors of utility, scarcity, desire, and effective purchasing power and expresses value as a result that should prevail if the parties to the transaction are under no undue influences, motivations, or conditions not typical of the market. The definition is sufficiently broad to encompass most transactions. In reviewing value estimates, federal and state court decisions have resulted in definitions of market value that are worded differently even though they are generally predicated on the same "willing buyer, willing seller" concept as the definition above. Appraisers must always be familiar with the specific definition applied in a particular situation.

The definition that was proposed by Richard U. Ratcliff, that *market value is the most probable selling price,* is sometimes used. Note that no idealized market conditions are required. Even if a buyer must buy or a seller must sell under duress, and even if financing is not available at typical market terms, the price that is expected to occur is the market value, according to Ratcliff.

Because of varied decisions in different legal jurisdictions, there is no "universal" definition of market value. Each definition carries its own parameters and presumptions. Obviously, different definitions of market value can result in different value estimates, and appraisers should be careful to state the definition they use in an appraisal.[4]

Market value, or value in exchange, is the purpose of most valuations. A market value estimate reflects the appraiser's interpretation of the actions of buyers and sellers in the marketplace.

Distinctions among Market Value, Price, and Cost

Appraisers make important distinctions among the terms *market value, price,* and *cost.* By traditional definition, market value and price are equal only under conditions of a perfect market. *Market value, as applied to real estate, represents an expected price that should result under specific market conditions.* Price, commonly referred to as a sale or transaction price, is an accomplished fact. *A price represents what a particular purchaser agreed to pay and a particular seller agreed to accept under the particular circumstances surrounding their transaction.*

Presumptions requisite for market value—rational behavior by buyer and seller and no undue duress or pressure—are not implicit in any actual sale price. Neither is there a presumption that the transaction was typical in the market. Without making an appraisal, an appraiser does not know whether a price actually paid or received

---

[4]See Halbert C. Smith, "Value Concepts as a Source of Disparity among Appraisals," *The Appraisal Journal,* April 1977, pp. 203-09.

equaled the property's market value. Although actual prices can provide strong evidence of market value, the appraiser must analyze specific transaction prices carefully before reaching a market value conclusion.

Cost, as used in appraisal procedures, applies to production, not exchange, and is not synonymous with either value or price. *Cost is the total dollar expenditure for labor, materials, legal services, architectural design, financing, taxes during construction, interest, contractor's overhead and profit, and entrepreneurial overhead and profit.* Cost is either a retrospective fact or a current estimate. It may or may not have a direct relationship to the utility (present or future) of the property created. Consider, for instance, the classic example of the luxury hotel built in an unpopular location. The hotel might cost much to build but have little value because of the lack of business.

Appraisal procedures provide the means to refine conclusions about whether the cost to construct a property equals the property's market value. Such market conditions as oversupply, undersupply, or poor design cause market values to fall below the current cost of duplicate development. Cost will equal market value if the new building represents the highest and best use of the land as though vacant; that is, if there is no accrued depreciation. Value can exceed cost only to the extent that buyers are willing to avoid the delay of constructing a duplicate.

Market Value Estimates

A market value estimate is based on the market parameters that are identified and examined by the appraiser; that is, the appraiser must identify and be familiar with the market conditions that prevail when the property is offered for sale. Conditions or terms generally available are subject to wide variations both in the same market and across markets. What is typical in today's market may have precedent or may differ from what was usual or typical in the past. In a depressed real estate market, seller financing, junior mortgages, zero interest mortgages, balloon mortgages, wraparound mortgages, instruments calling for variable or renegotiated interest rates, or other "creative" financing devices are widely used. Market value is generally based on payment in cash or its equivalent; however, market value might be estimated for a property based on specific financing terms. In either case, appraisers should specify financing terms.

Market value appraisals represent an appraiser's interpretation of the actions of buyers and sellers in the marketplace. Because the methods used for estimating market value constitute essential tools for all appraisal assignments, these methods are the major focus of this text.

However, appraisers are often called on to estimate other types of value and to conduct evaluation studies.

Other Values

Because the word *value* can be so easily misunderstood, and because there are many types of value, the professional appraiser should be careful to define the value involved in a particular assignment. Market value represents value in exchange for interests in real property and reflects the consensus of buyers and sellers in the market. However, certain appraisal assignments require an estimate of other types of value.

Use Value

Use value is the value a specific property has for a specific use. It is a value concept based on the productivity of an economic good. The concept of use value centers on the contributory value of the real estate to the enterprise of which it is a part without regard to highest and best use or what might be financially realized upon its sale. It may vary, depending on management of the property and such external conditions as changes in the business. For example, a manufacturing plant designed around a particular assembly-line process may have one use value prior to a major change in assembly technology and another value afterwards.

Many real properties have a use value *and* a market value. An old-fashioned factory still in use by the original firm, for example, may have considerable use value to that firm, but only a nominal market value for another use.

Representative use-value appraisal assignments are going-concern valuations including real property, for mergers and acquisitions or security issues. This type of assignment is particularly prevalent in appraising industrial real estate when existing business enterprises include real property.

In addition, court decisions or specific statutes may create the need for use-value appraisals. Many states, for example, specify agricultural-use appraisals of farmland for property tax purposes rather than value estimates based on highest and best use. The Tax Reform Act of 1976 added section 2032A to the Internal Revenue Code, which allows property of qualified, closely held corporations to be valued for estate tax purposes according to its use value.

Special Problems in Defining Value.   When a property being appraised is of a type not commonly exchanged or rented, it may be difficult to determine whether a market or a use value estimate is called for. Such properties, called limited market properties, can cause special

problems for the appraiser. *A limited market property is a property for which, at a particular time, there are relatively few potential buyers.* Large manufacturing properties, for example, typically appeal to relatively few potential purchasers.

Many limited market properties have structures with unique physical designs, special construction materials, or layouts that result in a highly restricted level of utility—that being the use for which they were originally built. These properties usually have limited conversion potential. Consequently, such properties are often called special purpose or special design properties. Examples of such properties include churches, museums, schools, public buildings, and clubhouses.

Limited market properties may be appraised for market value based on their current use or the most likely alternative use. The relatively small market and the sometimes lengthy market exposure period typical for this property type may result in sparse evidence to support a market value estimate. Nonetheless, if a market exists, an appraiser must search diligently for the limited, but available, evidence of market value.

However, if a property's current use is so specialized that there is no demonstrable market for it, but the use is viable and likely to continue, the appraiser may render an estimate of use value. Such an estimate should not be confused with a market value estimate.

Investment Value

Closely related to use value is investment value. As employed in appraisal assignments, *investment value is the value of an investment to a particular investor based on his or her investment requirements.* In contrast to market value, investment value is value to an individual, rather than value in the marketplace.

Investment value is the subjective relationship between a particular investor and a given investment. When measured in dollars, it is the highest price an investor would pay for an investment in view of its perceived capacity to satisfy a desire, need, or investment goal. In colloquial use, investment value may refer to the "reasoned value" of a given investment from the viewpoint of a typical, rather than actual, investor. In all appraisals that estimate investment value, specific investment criteria must be known.

Investment value appraisals are fairly common when the appraiser is employed by a potential purchaser of an existing investment or income-producing property, or by a developer of a new property.

Going-Concern Value

Going-concern value is the value existing in a proven property operation, considered as an entity with business established. This value is distinct from the value of real estate only—that is, ready to operate but without an ongoing business. Going-concern value includes an intangible enhancement of the value of an operating business enterprise associated with the process of assembling the land, building, labor, equipment, and marketing operation, all leading to an economically viable business that is expected to continue.

Common going-concern appraisals are conducted for hotels and motels, restaurants, bowling alleys, industrial enterprises, retail stores, and similar property uses. For these property types, the physical real estate assets are integral parts of an ongoing business such that market values for the land and building are difficult, if not impossible, to segregate from the total value of the ongoing business.

Insurable Value

Insurable value is based on the concept of replacement and/or reproduction cost of physical items subject to loss from hazards. *Insurable value designates the amount of insurance that may or should be carried on destructible portions of a property to indemnify the owner in the event of loss.*

Liquidation Value

Liquidation value is a price that an owner is compelled to accept when the property's sale must occur with less-than-reasonable market exposure.

Assessed Value

Assessed value is a value according to a uniform schedule for tax rolls in ad valorem taxation. The schedule may not conform to market value, but usually has some relation to a market value base.

Summary

Because value is appraisal's major subject of inquiry, appraisers must understand value theory and the external influences that affect real property value. With such an understanding, they have the foundation necessary for appraisal. They also possess the tools for an objective, systematic analysis of events and motivations that affect real property value.

Throughout history, individuals, groups, and disciplines have developed theories about value in keeping with their philosophical premises and with their era's social and political conditions and state of technology. Contemporary appraisal theory is at once an outgrowth and advancement of the earliest economic thought and the classical school of value, the Austrian school of value, and the neoclassical school of value. Of all schools of economic thought, the latter influenced current value theory the most because its theories helped form the basis of appraisal's three established methods of value estimation—the sales comparison, income capitalization, and cost approaches.

Appraisers study all influences at work in markets for real property. In a specific assignment, an appraiser successively narrows the study of a property by ascertaining the ways in which influences external to the property operate to affect its value. The appraiser studies the realities of anticipation and change, which characterize human actions and value judgments in terms of the appraisal principles—supply and demand, substitution, balance, and externalities—that help explain shifts in value.

The result of the proper accord of these principles is highest and best use, a concept of great significance to real property appraisal. Highest and best use is determined for (l) the land, or site, as though vacant and available to be put to its highest and best use; and (2) the property as improved. Trends in anticipation and change that are revealed by an analysis of the principles are studied more specifically through analysis of the four forces—social, economic, government, and environmental—that influence people and value. The appraiser then studies characteristics of specific properties and people who constitute a market for them in terms of four factors—utility, scarcity, desire, and effective purchasing power—that are essential for the creation of value. Such systematic analysis forms the basis of all appraisal inquiries.

An estimate of market value, or value in exchange, is the purpose of most valuation assignments. Such an estimate reflects the appraiser's interpretation of the actions of buyers and sellers in the marketplace and the conditions that prevail when the property is offered for sale.

In estimating market value, appraisers understand important distinctions among the terms *market value, price,* and *cost.* Market value represents an expected price that should result under specific market conditions. Price represents what a particular purchaser agreed to pay and a particular seller agreed to accept under the circumstances surrounding their transaction. Cost applies to production, not exchange, and is the total dollar expenditure for building a structure.

Certain assignments require an estimate of other types of value, including use, investment, going-concern, insurable, liquidation, and assessed values. Therefore, appraisers must be sure that the type of value being estimated is always defined.

Chapter 3

The Valuation Process

The valuation process is a systematic procedure employed to provide the answer to a client's question about real property value. This process leads an appraiser from fully identifying the particular problem to reporting its solution to the client.

Each real property is unique, and many different types of value can be estimated for any single property. The most typical appraisal assignment is undertaken to estimate market value, and the valuation process contains all steps appropriate to that type of assignment. However, the valuation process also provides the framework in which the estimation of any other defined value is accomplished. Further, conclusions in evaluation assignments often necessitate the derivation of value estimates through application of the valuation process.[1]

The valuation process is accomplished by following specific steps,

---

[1] Evaluation assignments are discussed in Chapter 24.

the number of which depends on the nature of the appraisal assignment and the data available to complete it. In all cases, however, the valuation process indicates the pattern to be followed in performing market research and analysis of data, in applying appraisal techniques, and in integrating the results of these analytic activities into an estimate of defined value.

Research and analysis of data begin with the examination of trends found at all market levels—international, national, regional, community, and neighborhood. The purpose of this examination is twofold. First, it leads to an understanding of the interrelationships of the principles, forces, and factors that affect real property value in a specific area. Second, it provides raw information from which to extract numerical measurements of market trends. These might include such measures as positive or negative percentage changes in property value over a number of years, the percentage of population movement into an area, or the numbers of employment opportunities and their effects on the purchasing power of the most likely users of property. These figures are employed in appraisal techniques to estimate a defined value.

Appraisal techniques are the specifics of the three appraisal approaches that are traditionally used to derive separate indications of real property value. One or more approaches may be used, depending on their applicability to a particular appraisal assignment.

In assignments to estimate market value, the ultimate goal of the valuation process is a well-supported conclusion that reflects the appraiser's study of all influences on the market value of the property being appraised. Therefore, the appraiser studies the property from each of the applicable viewpoints reflected in the three approaches:

1. The value indicated by recent sales of comparable properties in the market (the sales comparison approach)

2. The value of a property's earning power based on a capitalization of income (the income capitalization approach)

3. The current cost of reproducing or replacing the improvements, less loss in value from depreciation, added to land value (the cost approach)

The three approaches are interrelated, and each involves the gathering and analysis of sales, income, and cost data in relation to the property being appraised. Each approach is discussed briefly in this chapter and illustrated in detail later in the text. From the approaches, the appraiser derives separate indications of value for the property being appraised. One or more approaches may be used, depending on their applicability to the particular appraisal assignment.

To complete the valuation process, the appraiser integrates the information drawn from the market research and analysis of data and from the application of appraisal techniques in the three approaches to form a conclusion. This conclusion may be an estimate of value or a range in which the value may fall. An effective integration depends on an appraiser's skill, experience, and judgment.

The valuation process is presented graphically in Figure 3.1.

Figure 3.1   The Valuation Process

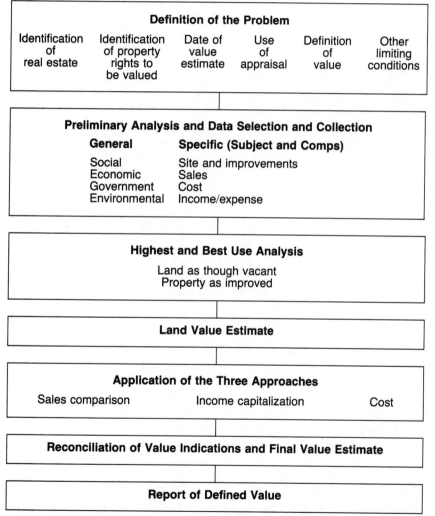

Definition of the Appraisal Problem

The first step in the valuation process is to develop a concise statement of the problem. This sets the limits of the appraisal and eliminates any ambiguity about the nature of the assignment and identifies the

1. Real estate to be appraised

2. Property rights involved

3. Date of the value estimate

4. Use of the appraisal

5. Definition of value

6. Other limiting conditions

Identification of Real Estate

A property is first identified by means of a common address, a location, or other descriptive data, which enables someone to locate it or to refer to it by recognized landmarks. At this point in the appraisal, the property is only identified; its physical description is dealt with at a later point. One succinct way to identify property is by using an outline:

Reference:	The Kennedy Building, commercial offices
Common Address:	2600 South Zephyr Denver, Colorado
Identity of the *Physical Entity:*	Lots 7-10, inclusive, Sterns Addition, 5th Filing, City and County of Denver, Colorado

If the property is identified by a legal description, the accuracy of the description is the client's responsibility and should be prepared by a surveyor or another qualified individual. Legal descriptions of real estate are basically derived from land surveys and are preserved in public records in accordance with local or state laws. The appraiser should be familiar with the specific system or systems commonly employed in a particular area. Systems of legal description are the metes and bounds system, the rectangular or government survey system, and the lot and block system.

Identification of Property Rights to Be Valued

A valuation of real property includes both physical real estate and rights that one or more individuals, partnerships, or corporations may have or contemplate having in the ownership or use of land and improvements. Therefore, an appraiser may be estimating the value of the fee simple estate or value of partial interests created by severance or division of ownership rights. Special attention is given to any limitation of ownership rights, such as easements, encroachments, liens, or leases. The specific rights to be valued must be ascertained at the outset of the assignment because the complexity of valuing these rights determines the procedures, skills, and time required to complete the assignment.

The fee simple estate is often valued before partial interests. However, the dollar estimate of the fee simple value is not necessarily equal to the total of the values of all partial interests because the value of a separate partial interest may differ from its contribution to the whole. For instance, a one-half interest may have a value significantly less than 50% of the fee simple value, and this lower value could be a direct result of the fee simple estate's being divided. In a market value estimate for a partial interest in real property, direct market evidence is usually sought to reflect market attitudes toward the particular aspects of that partial interest.

Date of Value Estimate

A specific date for a value estimate is necessary because of the constantly changing influences on real property value. Although conditions observed at the time of the appraisal may remain operative for a considerable time after that date, an estimate of value is considered valid only for the exact time for which it is estimated. Therefore, value influences reflect economic conditions at that time, and changes in the business and real estate markets can abruptly and dramatically influence values.

Most appraisals require current value estimates. In some cases, however, a valuation is required as of some date in the past. Retrospective appraisals may be required for inheritance tax (date of death), insurance claims (date of casualty), income tax (date of acquisition), law suits (date of loss), and other reasons. Frequently, it has been necessary to estimate a property's value as of March 1, 1913, the date of the inception of the federal income tax, to establish the capital gain on property owned since that date.

In condemnation appraising, the appraiser estimates value as of the date of filing the declaration or petition to condemn, the date of trial, or some other date either stipulated by the parties or fixed by the court.

Because historical market data often are available, estimates of market value can be made retrospectively. However, it is impossible to support an estimate of market value as of a future date in the same way. Comparable rents, expenses, construction costs, sale information, and so forth, as of a future date are, of course, unknown. However, trend projections leading to opinions of future price may be made by appraisers and used by owners, buyers, and other clients to make real estate-related decisions. Such projections are not market value appraisals.

Use of the Appraisal

The use of an appraisal is the manner in which a client employs the information in an appraisal report. The use is decided by the client, who specifies it when requesting an appraisal. Because an appraisal provides the basis for a decision, the nature of the decision affects the character of the assignment and the subsequent report. Examples of uses for which a value estimate may be needed are to determine the

1. Price at which to buy or sell

2. Amount of loan to make

3. Basis for taxation

4. Basis for a lease

5. Value of real property assets in financial statements

6. Basis for just compensation in eminent domain proceedings

   To avoid misdirected effort, the appraiser and the client must have the same understanding of the use and ownership of the appraisal report and its conclusions.

Definition of Value

The purpose of valuation is to estimate value; therefore, the specific type of value and the interests involved must be clearly defined. Examples of types of value appraised are market value, use value, going-concern value, investment value, assessed value, and insurable value.

   Although market value appraisals are most frequently requested, other value estimates often are needed. If the owners of an industrial concern require an appraisal for negotiating a merger, the appropriate value may be use value or going-concern value. If the same owners wish to sell the property, market value would be estimated.

   A written statement of the defined value to be estimated is included in the appraisal report. Such an exact statement delineates the question to be answered for the client, the appraiser, and all other readers of the report. It explains the choice of data considered and the methods employed to analyze the data, thus supporting the logic and validity of the final value estimate.

Other Limiting Conditions

Identification of the real estate and property rights to be appraised, effective date, use of the appraisal, and definition of value are limiting conditions in that they govern the appraisal. There are other limiting conditions as well. For example, the report might state that the valuation of subsurface oil, gas, or mineral rights is not part of the appraisal. One limiting condition might be that court or hearing testimony or attendance in court is not required by reason of rendering the appraisal, unless such arrangements are made a reasonable time in advance. Another limiting condition might be that no engineering survey has been made by the appraiser. Except as specifically stated, data relative to size and area were taken from sources considered reliable.

Preliminary Analysis and Data Selection and Collection

Defining the problem prepares an appraiser for the preliminary analysis of the character and scope of the assignment and of the amount of work that will be required to gather the necessary information. The preliminary analysis and work plan largely depend on the assignment and the type of property being valued. For example, much more information is required in the valuation of a large apartment building than in the valuation of a single family residence.

The efficient application of time and effort needed to complete an assignment requires the orderly planning and scheduling of all steps in the valuation process. How much time and personnel are needed vary with the amount and complexity of the work. Some assignments may require only a few days; more complex situations may warrant weeks or months for gathering, analyzing, and applying all pertinent data.

For some assignments, an appraiser can perform all the work of an appraisal individually. For others, the appraiser will need assistance from other staff members or appraisal specialists. The assistance of specialists in fields other than appraisal is sometimes necessary. A report's findings may have to be augmented by the professional opinion of a soil engineer, for example. The ability to recognize when work can or must be delegated improves efficiency and final accuracy.

A planned schedule of work is helpful, particularly for large, complicated assignments. A clear and definite understanding of individual responsibilities helps to expedite an assignment. Because the appraiser acts as a supervisor with ultimate responsibility, he or she must see the assignment both in terms of its total context and its numerous details. With this complete view, the appraiser can recognize the type and volume of work entailed and be able to schedule and delegate work properly.

Survey of an appraisal problem should lead to a definite work plan, which usually involves an outline of the proposed appraisal report. The outline delineates the report's main divisions and notes the data and procedures pertinent to each division. Such an outline permits intelligent and orderly assembling of data and the judicious allocation of time to each step in the valuation process.

Data gathered for appraisals are of two types: general and property specific. General data include information on principles, forces, and factors that affect property value. All social, economic, government, and environmental influences that affect property in a particular area are considered by the appraiser, who analyzes them to determine which are most germane to the problem.

Property-specific data are gathered for the property being appraised and for properties being compared to it. These include physical, locational, cost, and income and expense information about the properties as well as details of the sale transactions of comparables. Financial arrangements that could affect selling prices are also considered.

The amount and type of data collected for an appraisal are influenced by the approaches employed to estimate value. These, in turn, depend on the appraisal question. An appraisal performed to estimate the value of a property for insurance purposes might require emphasis on data pertinent to the cost approach. The most relevant consideration in the appraisal of a property taken by eminent domain usually is comparison to sale prices and characteristics of similar properties. Income data from the market are particularly indicative in the appraisal of income-producing investment properties.

Meaningful data are collected to be used for a purpose. Influences, pertinent facts, and deductions about trends are pointed out clearly in a report and are related specifically to the property being appraised. Because the data form the basis for the appraiser's judgments, a thorough explanation of the significance of the data assures the reader's understanding of the judgments.

Highest and Best Use Analysis

Highest and best use analysis (1) of the land as though vacant and (2) of the property as improved is essential in the valuation process.[2] Through highest and best use analysis, an appraiser identifies the use conclusion upon which the final value estimate is based.

In the valuation process, there are two functions in analyzing the land as though vacant. The first function is to help identify comparable properties. A property being appraised is always compared with similar properties that have sold recently in the market. All comparable properties should have a highest and best use of the land as though vacant similar to that of the subject property. Potential comparable properties that do not have similar highest and best uses may be eliminated from further analysis in the valuation process.

The second function is to identify the use of the land that would produce maximum income to the land after property income is first allocated to the improvements. In some appraisal methods (the cost approach and certain income capitalization techniques), a separate value estimate of the land is required. Thus, estimating the land's highest and best use is a necessary part of deriving that estimate.

There are also two functions in analyzing the highest and best use of the property as improved. The first function is the same as that of highest and best use of land as though vacant—to help identify comparable properties. Comparable improved properties should have the same or similar highest and best uses as the subject property.

The second function of highest and best use of the property as improved is to decide whether the improvements should be demolished, renovated, or retained in their present condition. The property as improved should be retained as long as the improvements have some value and the return from the property is greater than the return on the capital that would have to be invested in a new use, including demolition costs of the old building and construction costs of a new building. Identifying the existing property's most profitable use is crucial to that determination.

Land Value Estimate

Land value is tied directly to highest and best use. This relationship between highest and best use and land value causes the appraiser to question whether an existing use is the highest and best use of the land.

---

[2]A detailed discussion of highest and best use analysis is presented in Chapter 11.

Land value may be a major component of total property value. Appraisers often estimate land value separately even when estimating the value of properties that have extensive building improvements. Land value may change at a different rate than building value, which is almost always subject to depreciation (after the effects of inflation are removed). For many appraisals, an estimate of land value alone is required.

Although a total property value estimate is often derived without separation of land and improvement values in both the sales comparison and the income capitalization approaches, it may be necessary to estimate a land value separately in order to see clearly the contributory value of the land to the total property. For these reasons, it may be beneficial, and even necessary at times, to estimate the land value separately. In the cost approach, the value of the land is estimated separately and is specifically stated.

The land value estimate in the valuation process is a separate step, which is accomplished through the application of the sales comparison or income capitalization approach techniques. The most reliable procedure for estimating land value is by the application of the sales comparison approach. Sales of similar vacant parcels are weighed, compared, and related to the land being appraised. When few sales are available for comparison, or when value indications through sales comparison need substantiation, other procedures that are helpful in the valuation of land are

1. *The allocation procedure.* Sales of improved properties are analyzed, and the prices paid are allocated between land and improvements. This allocation is used either to establish a typical ratio of land value to total value, which may be applicable to a property being appraised, or to derive from the sale an allocation of either land value or building contribution for use in comparison analysis.

2. *The development procedure.* The total value of undeveloped land is estimated as if the land were subdivided, developed, and sold. Development costs, incentive costs, and carrying charges are subtracted from the estimated proceeds of sale, and the net income projection is discounted over the estimated period required for market absorption of the developed sites.

3. *The land residual procedure.* The land is assumed to be improved to its highest and best use, and the net income imputable to the land after all expenses of operation and return attributable to the other agents in production is capitalized to derive an estimate of land value.

Application of the Three Approaches

The valuation process is employed to develop a well-supported estimate of a defined value, which is based on consideration of all pertinent general and specific data. Toward this goal, an appraiser analyzes a property by applying specific appraisal procedures that reflect three distinct methods for analyzing data mathematically—sales comparison, income capitalization, and cost analyses. One or more of these approaches is used in all estimations of value, depending on the type of property, the use of the appraisal, and the quality and quantity of data available for analysis.

All three approaches are applicable to the solution of many appraisal problems. However, in specific assignments, one or more of the approaches may have greater significance. In some appraisal assignments, fewer than three approaches are used. For example, the cost approach may be impractical in the valuation of properties that include substantial accrued depreciation. The sales comparison approach is inapplicable for very specialized property, such as a garbage disposal plant; only rarely is the income capitalization approach helpful in the valuation of an owner-occupied home or other user-occupied properties. It is often unreliable when there is a two-tier market in which user-occupants compete with investors for commercial and industrial properties.

Sales Comparison Approach

The sales comparison approach is most viable when an adequate number of properties of similar type have been sold recently or are currently for sale in the subject property market.[3] The application of this approach produces a value indication for a property through comparison with similar properties, called comparable sales. The sale prices of properties judged to be most comparable tend to set a range in which the value indication for the subject property falls.

An appraiser estimates the degrees of similarity and difference between the subject property and comparable sales on the basis of six elements of comparison:

1. Conditions of sale

2. Financing terms

3. Market conditions (time)

4. Location

---

[3]A detailed discussion of the sales comparison approach is presented in Chapter 13.

5. Physical characteristics

6. Income characteristics

Dollar or percentage adjustments are then made *to the sale price of each comparable sale property.* Positive adjustments are made for deficiencies in the comparable property relative to the subject property. Negative adjustments are made for superior characteristics of the comparable property relative to the subject property. Through this procedure, the appraiser derives a logical estimate of the probable price for which the subject property could be sold on the date of the appraisal. This is the indication of value by the sales comparison approach.

Income Capitalization Approach

By using the income capitalization approach, appraisers measure the present value of the future benefits of property ownership.[4] Income streams and values of property resale (reversion) are capitalized (converted) into a present, lump-sum value. Basic to this approach are the formulas

Income ÷ Rate = Value
Income x Factor = Value

The income capitalization approach, like the cost and sales comparison approaches, requires extensive market research. Specific areas that an appraiser investigates for this approach are the property's gross income expectancy, the expected reduction in gross income from lack of full occupancy and collection loss, the expected annual operating expenses, the pattern and duration of the property's income stream, and the anticipated value of the resale or other real property interest reversions. When accurate income and expense estimates are established, the income streams are converted into present value by the process of capitalization. The rates or factors used for capitalization are derived by the investigation of acceptable rates of return for similar properties.

Research and analysis of data for the income capitalization approach are conducted against a background of supply and demand relationships. This background provides information on trends and market anticipation that must be verified for data analysis by the income capitalization approach.

The investor in an apartment building, for example, anticipates an acceptable return on the investment in addition to return of the

---

[4]A detailed discussion of the income capitalization approach is presented in Chapters 14-17.

invested funds. The level of return necessary to attract investment capital fluctuates with changes in the money market and with the levels of return available from alternate investments. The appraiser must be alert to changes in investor requirements as revealed by evidence in the current market for investment properties, and to changes in the more volatile money markets that may indicate a forthcoming trend.

Cost Approach

The cost approach is based on the premise that the value of a property can be indicated by the current cost to construct a reproduction or replacement for the improvements minus the amount of depreciation evident in the structures from all causes plus the value of the land and entrepreneurial profit.[5] This approach to value is particularly useful for appraising new or nearly new improvements and for providing an alternative to the sales comparison and income capitalization approaches. In addition, cost approach techniques are employed to derive information needed to apply both the sales comparison and income capitalization approaches to value.

Current costs for constructing improvements are derived from cost estimators, cost estimating publications, builders, and contractors. Depreciation is measured by market research and through the application of specific mathematical procedures. Land value is estimated separately.

Reconciliation of Value Indications

The final analytical step in the valuation process is an appraiser's reconciling the indications of value into a single dollar figure or into a range in which the value will most likely fall. The nature of the reconciliation depends on the number of approaches that have been used and on the reliability of the value indications derived from the approaches.

When all three approaches have been used, the appraiser examines the spread among the three separate indications. A wide spread may indicate that one or more of the approaches is not applicable to the appraisal problem. The appraiser always considers the relative dependability and applicability of each approach in reconciling the value indications into a final estimate of defined value.

A well-presented valuation analysis is concise and enables the reader to understand the problem and the factual data, and to follow the reasoning that leads to the appraiser's conclusion of value. This

[5] A detailed discussion of the cost approach is presented in Chapters 18-20.

value estimate is the appraiser's opinion, reflecting the application of experience and judgment to the study of all assembled data.

Report of Defined Value

With the final estimate of defined value, the appraiser has achieved the purpose of the valuation process. However, the assignment is not complete until the conclusion is stated in a report that will be presented to the client. Usually, a report is written and includes all data considered and analyzed, the methods used, and the reasoning followed in achieving the final value estimate. An appraisal report is the tangible expression of the appraiser's service. When an appraiser prepares a report, he or she should be particularly careful about the manner in which it is written, its organization and presentation, and its overall appearance.

Summary

The valuation process is a logical procedure to answer a specific economic question pertaining to real property. The valuation process begins with a concise statement of the problem. In defining the problem, the appraiser must identify the real estate to be appraised, the property rights involved, the date of the estimate, the use of the appraisal, the definition of the value to be estimated, and any other limiting conditions.

Then, the appraiser makes a preliminary analysis of the appraisal's character and scope, and collects and analyzes data. The type of value to be estimated, the use of the appraisal, the type of property, and the data available all influence the decision of the approach or approaches to be used. Data collected include general data, such as regional influences and community characteristics, and specific data about the subject property and the comparable sales.

The appraiser analyzes the highest and best use of the land as though vacant and of the property as improved. Closely related to highest and best use of the land as though vacant is the land value, which can be a major component of total property value. Land value is estimated primarily by the sales comparison approach, and sometimes by the allocation procedure, development procedure, and the land residual procedure.

Separate value indications are derived by applying the three approaches to value: the sales comparison approach, the income capitalization approach, and the cost approach. In different assignments, one or more of the approaches may have greater significance or reliability. To conclude the valuation process, the separate value indications derived from the approaches are reconciled. A final estimate of value and the data and analyses on which it is based are communicated to the client in an oral or written report.

Part II
Influences on Value

Chapter 4

Real Estate Markets

The real estate market is the interaction of buyers and sellers in exchanging real property rights for other assets, such as money. This type of interaction occurs in different areas, for different reasons, and in relation to different types of property. Thus, the real estate market is divided into categories, based on the differences among property types and their appeal to corresponding markets. The markets for these categories of real estate are further divided into submarkets that are based on the preferences of buyers and sellers. These divisions facilitate the study of real estate markets.

All real estate markets are influenced by the attitudes, motivations, and interactions of the buyers and sellers of real property, which in turn are subject to many social, economic, government, and environmental influences. Real estate markets may be studied in terms of geographic, competitive, and supply and demand characteristics as they relate to overall real estate market conditions.

Delineating real estate markets and submarkets is an important aspect of appraisal. Many evaluation studies concentrate on determining the characteristics of markets for investors and developers. In valuation, particularly in estimations of market value, an appraiser's understanding of the market characteristics for a specific property provides the criteria with which to judge the comparability of other properties. For each market value assignment, the appraiser identifies and analyzes the pertinent market or markets that influence the subject property. To provide credible evaluation conclusions and estimates of market value, the real estate appraiser must thoroughly understand the real estate market or markets relevant to the assignment.

Characteristics of the Real Estate Market

Economists study markets by comparing a hypothetical, efficient market with the actual, inefficient market. The perfect market concept is based on assumptions about the behavior of buyers and sellers and the characteristics of products. The real estate market, however, is not an efficient market. Contrasting the characteristics of an efficient market with those of the actual real estate market illustrates how the characteristics of real estate prevent its market from attaining a high degree of efficiency.

The goods or services in an efficient market are essentially homogeneous items that can be readily substituted for one another.

Each parcel of real estate is unique and its location is fixed. No two parcels of real estate are physically identical. Although certain parcels may be economically similar and substitutable, they differ at least geographically.

In an efficient market there is a large number of buyers and sellers who create a competitive, free market, and none of these participants has a large enough share of the market to have a direct and measurable influence on price.

In real estate, usually there are only a few buyers and sellers acting at one time, in one price range, and at one location for any type of property. Also, the high relative value of real estate requires high purchasing power. The real estate market is extremely sensitive to changes in wage levels, the stability of income, and the number of individuals employed. Construction costs, housing costs, and rent levels are affected by the ability of market participants to pay.

In an efficient market, prices are relatively uniform, stable, and low. They are often the primary consideration in purchase or sale decisions because quality tends to be uniform at a set price.

In the real estate market, prices are relatively high, and very few purchasers have enough money to pay cash for property. Thus, types of financing, the amount of mortgage money available, interest rates, the requirements for a down payment, and typical loan duration affect the decision to purchase real estate. Generally, if a property cannot be favorably financed, it will not be bought. An investor will be less likely to buy income-producing property if the debt service exceeds a certain percentage of gross income.

An efficient market is self-regulating. There are very few government restrictions on open and free competition.

The real estate market is not self-regulating. Federal, state, county, and local regulations govern the ownership and transfer of real estate. Contractual and deed restrictions further regulate the sale and purchase of property. For example, deed restrictions may require houses in a subdivision to contain at least 2,000 square feet.

Supply and demand are never far out of balance in an efficient market because the market tends to move toward balance through the effects of competition.

Although the supply of and demand for real estate also tend toward equilibrium, this theoretical point is seldom achieved. The supply of real estate for specific uses is slower to adjust to market demand than is the supply of less durable commodities. Further, shifts in demand may occur during the time needed to supply new real estate units, which results in an oversupply rather than in market equilibrium.

However, units of real estate that are comparable in size and quality do tend to sell at comparable prices, and if supply and demand are in relative balance, real estate prices tend to be stable. But if demand for real estate increases suddenly, an additional supply cannot be provided quickly. If demand decreases suddenly, any excess supply cannot be removed quickly from the market.

In the real estate market, supply and demand *are* considered causal factors; price is the result of the interaction of supply and demand. Price changes usually are preceded by changes in market activity. Often there is a period of no activity or of increased activity when supply or demand shifts suddenly.

Buyers and sellers in an efficient market are knowledgeable and fully informed about market conditions, the behavior of others, past market activity, product quality, and product substitutability. Any information needed on bids, offers, and sales is readily available.

Buyers and sellers in the real estate market are not always well informed about the product. Most people do not buy and sell real estate frequently, so they are not very familiar with the procedure or how to judge a property. Information on bids, offers, and sales on a particular property or similar properties is not readily available to a buyer or a seller.

Buyers and sellers in an efficient market are brought together by an organized market mechanism, such as the New York Stock Exchange, and it is relatively easy for sellers to enter into the market in response to market demand.

In the real estate market, however, demand may be volatile. There can be a sudden shift of population either in or out of a locality. A sudden influx of population results in high prices because it can take months or years to construct buildings or develop an area. A sudden migration caused by economic conditions could result in an oversupply relative to previous periods and, therefore, in lower prices.

Finally, in an efficient market, goods are readily consumed, quickly supplied, and easily transported.

Real estate, however, is a durable product and, as an investment, may be relatively unmarketable or illiquid. Real estate usually is not sold quickly because the process involves the exchange of large sums of money and the appropriate financing cannot always be readily secured. Also, the supply of real estate is relatively inflexible, and because it is fixed in location, the supply on a national or regional level cannot be adjusted quickly.

Thus, the real estate market does not meet the tests of an efficient market. Due to the real estate market's imperfections, such as lack of product standardization and time requirements for the production of a new supply, it is difficult to predict its behavior accurately. However, recognizing that the real estate market does not operate under premises similar to markets for other commodities leads an appraiser to analyze the significant aspects of market activity that are indicated by the market's inefficient nature. The focus of real estate market analysis, then, is on the motivations, attitudes, and interaction of market participants as they respond to the particular characteristics of real estate and to external influences on its value.

Types of Real Estate Markets

Real estate's different markets are created by their participants' needs, desires, motivations, locations, ages, and so forth, and by property types, locations, designs, zoning restrictions, and the like.

Five broad categories of properties have corresponding markets. They are

1. Residential

2. Commercial

3. Industrial

4. Agricultural

5. Special purpose

Each market for a particular property type can be further subdivided into smaller and more specialized markets, called submarkets. Submarkets for urban, suburban, and rural residential properties may be divided by a purchaser's preference for high-, medium-, or low-priced properties. Offices, stores, loft buildings, parking garages, motels, hotels, and shopping centers—all commercial properties—usually appeal to different groups of buyers and sellers. Industrial properties include factories, warehouses, and mining operations. The market for agricultural properties could be divided into markets for pasture, timber, crop, orchard, or ranch lands. Special-purpose properties include parks, gasoline stations, cemeteries, churches, clubs, golf courses, historic or recreational government properties, and public utilities.

The process of identifying and analyzing submarkets of a larger market is called *market segmentation.* A submarket can be created by developments in the demand side of the market, such as a type of property in demand by a particular group. Families looking for residences and companies in need of warehouses may be considered real estate markets. However, any type of real estate in which a market may be interested is heterogenous; that is, residences and warehouses can be large or small, old or new, well designed or poorly designed. Therefore, a market can be separated into a number of smaller, more homogeneous submarkets by recognizing the differing product preferences among buyers and sellers. These preferences include building size and design, price range, and property location.

Real estate appraisers identify and research market segments by locational, demographic, socioeconomic, psychological, and product-related characteristics. The professional appraiser may use survey research techniques to discover, quantify, analyze, and draw conclusions about the composition of particular submarkets.

Approaches to Market Study

Three major elements affect and help form real estate markets: location, competition, and the demand unit. An appraiser studies a market from these three viewpoints to understand the positions of the market participants; their actions reveal patterns that can be employed to identify trends in market behavior.

Location

A real estate market can be identified by its location. An appraiser ascertains a market for a particular property by delineating the surrounding physical or political boundaries within which related economic decisions are made. This market area should be delineated in terms of time and distance from common destinations and origins.

A property can have an international, national, regional, state-wide, urban, rural, district, and neighborhood market. In appraising a large industrial plant, an appraiser might study the national, or even international, market for this type of property. The real estate or space involved, the price level or price range of the properties, and the current or intended use of the space help determine the geographic extent of the market for that property. For example, the geographic extent of the market for office buildings in major commercial cities is far broader than that for single family residences in a rural community.

Competition

Real estate transactions occur in a competitive environment. This competitive environment is a function of two interrelated components: the number of available properties that appeal to potential purchasers and the number of potential purchasers (or renters) who constitute the market for those properties. Competition influences the behavior of market participants. It is a function of supply and demand and, as such, can be studied in terms of the availability and prices of similar properties. However, competition also results from the behavior of market participants. Buyers compete to obtain the most personally satisfying or useful property at the most advantageous price. Sellers compete to sell at the price most advantageous to them.

Because prices also are affected by the supply of and demand for properties, an appraiser studies the number of available properties and, generally, the number of buyers and sellers in a market during a particular time period. If there are few properties for sale and many potential buyers, it is called a seller's market and prices tend to increase. If there are many properties for sale and few buyers, it is a buyer's market, and prices tend to decline. Price is considered a credible value indicator when several similar, competing parcels of real estate are offered for sale and several competing, competent buyers are available to purchase such units. Thus, alternative or competitive choices influence the competition of market participants.

An appraiser also studies market competition by noting the prices asked by sellers, offered by buyers, accepted by sellers, and paid by buyers. The appraiser may find that parcels of real estate comparable in size, condition, and desirability of location tend to sell or rent for similar prices at a given time in a particular community or neighborhood. Such equalizing of prices is due to competition between sellers or lessors. However, properties of different sizes and conditions and in dissimilar locations tend to sell or rent for different prices because adjustments are made by the people in the market.

Demand Unit

A market is also viewed in terms of economic units that are eligible, or may become eligible, to express demand for the product. The basis of all demand for real estate and its resources is people, and the rate of increase in the number of potential buyers in a particular market or submarket is a determinant of future demand. An appraiser looks at the number of potential buyers in a specified population who are financially capable of purchasing or leasing particular types of real estate. The potential market for retail space is determined by an accurate assessment of the number of people who are likely to shop in an area or at a particular store or shopping center. People with money or credit create value by demanding a service or good, and people with financial resources create effective demand.

Demand can be affected by changes in (1) the level of property prices or rents, (2) expectations of consumers, (3) prices of competing budget items, (4) net new family or household formations, (5) net inmigration or outmigration, (6) family preferences, (7) typical ages within the population, (8) asset holdings or savings, and (9) growth in real income.

Market Analysis

Market analysis is the identification and study of a pertinent market. From a market study or analysis, an appraiser can develop an overview of the demand for real estate and an analysis of the general market demand for a single type of real estate, such as shopping centers, office buildings, condominiums, or multifamily apartments. The analysis identifies the present and probable supply of and demand for a property type.

Market analysis is important in evaluation assignments. The evaluation of a proposed real estate venture involves both a marketability study and a feasibility study. In a marketability study, the present and future demand for a particular property and its absorption rate are studied; the goal of such a study is to determine whether the property can be marketed, based on competition in price, quality, and the like. The likelihood of a property's financial success or failure is analyzed in a feasibility study, which should encompass the findings of a properly analyzed market study. A property could have many marketable attributes, such as location, type of soil, and so forth, but its financial success may depend on economic conditions that make its purchase or use unfeasible.

A market is delineated and identified for the appraisal assignment after study of the area and the influences that help create a market. Because people generally acquire or use real estate for specific purposes, such as personal occupancy, the market can be delineated by type of use, such as single family residential, commercial, or light industrial. Further, purchases of these properties may be motivated by investment goals or speculation. To designate a particular market or submarket, the appraiser determines such matters as the following:

1. Where are the properties located?

2. What kinds of properties are competitive with and similar to the subject?

3. What is the geographic range of properties that can effectively compete with the subject?

4. How will the principle of substitution apply to the comparable properties?

An appraiser also determines whether the scope of the market for the property is international, national, regional, or local. Single family residences, smaller commercial and industrial properties, and small farms and ranches usually appeal to local and regional markets. Large apartment projects, industrial plants, regional shopping centers, and government parcels often appeal to an international, national, or regional market. Once the scope of the market is determined, an appraiser studies such characteristics of market participants as income range, age, interests, and the like.

Raw land presents a special problem in the delineation of a market. It can appeal to segments of several markets. Raw land often is purchased by subdividers or developers who may be real estate brokers, construction contractors, or speculators. If the land is subdivided, it is platted into lots; if it is developed, streets and utilities are installed. Land often is developed for industrial parks, mobile home parks, shopping centers, strip centers, institutional and recreational uses, and residential subdivisions. As with most real estate, land in good locations may be in short supply and in great demand, but the high price of land and high construction costs can diminish development activity. In delineating a market for raw land, an appraiser is aware not only of the effects of costs, but also of the local zoning laws and state and federal land use restrictions that can affect land availability for specific uses.

Many buyers purchase land to hold for resale without further improvement. This type of investment, known as speculation, is based on the potential for land appreciation. Although speculators often purchase unimproved land, such as prairie or forestland, land in agricultural use, vacant urban lots, and even parking lots, this market cannot be delineated by property type. Speculators also purchase residential, commercial, industrial, and special-purpose properties in anticipation of obtaining profit by resale.

Given the subject property and the location and available supply of similar, competitive properties, an appraiser can analyze the market and determine the appropriate submarket primarily on the basis of the competitiveness and location of the properties and the supply of and demand for the property type.

An accurate market analysis is also necessary in an appraisal to estimate market value because conclusions pertaining to a property's value are drawn from the market. In conducting a market analysis for such a valuation, an appraiser designates the market area of the subject property and then studies the impact of market conditions within the delineated market area by analyzing both supply and demand.

The market conditions examined by an appraiser relate to the subject property and its use. For example, a manufacturing property is examined in terms of labor, transportation, raw materials, power, utilities, taxes, government regulations, and sales territory for its products. An apartment complex requires a study of population growth and trends for the community, wage levels in certain age groups, the percentage of population owning and renting homes, employment data, the existing supply of competitive rent levels, and the availability of financing at given interest rates.

General market conditions are studied in relation to the market for the subject property and its location. Although the market for some properties usually is local, increasing numbers of out-of-state and foreign buyers are participating in the market. Although international and national market conditions may have strong effects on the value of a subject property, these same conditions probably would have an equivalent effect on comparable properties. Thus, even when the market for a property is broad, an appraiser's emphasis usually is on local community and neighborhood analyses.

In all appraisal assignments, a knowledge of the components of supply and demand helps an appraiser investigate a particular community, region, or state. The analysis of the supply of competing properties includes a study of the following items:

1. Volume of new construction

2. Availability and price of vacant land

3. Construction costs

4. Current offerings of available houses or other properties (new and old)

5. Competition

6. Standing stock

7. Owner occupancy versus tenant occupancy

8. Causes and number of vacancies

9. Conversions to alternate uses

10. Special economic conditions and circumstances

11. Availabilty of mortgage money and financing

12. Impact of building codes, zoning ordinances, and other regulations on construction volume and cost.[1]

The study and investigation of demand is a study in demography: the number of people, ages, sex, households, disposable income, preferences, and behavior patterns are involved. The major factors in any analysis of demand are

1. Demographic data relating to population, rate of increase or decrease, and age distribution

2. Income and wages

3. Employment types; rate of unemployment

4. Geographic factors, such as climate, topography, natural or man-made barriers

5. Financial aspects, such as savings and lending

6. Land use and city growth

7. Cultural institutions

8. Educational facilities

9. Health and medical facilities

10. Fire and police protection

11. Transportation facilities and highway system; costs of transportation

12. Tax structure administration

Summary

Real property appraisal depends on information about the markets for real property. Because the real estate market *is* the interaction of buy-

---

[1] Jerome Knowles, Jr., "City and Neighborhood Data and Analysis," *The Appraisal Journal,* April 1967, p. 261.

ers and sellers in the exchange of real property, an appraiser must study the behavior of market participants to find patterns and trends. However, because the characteristics of the real estate market make it inefficient, and therefore unpredictable, an appraiser delineates the particular market that is available for a property or properties.

Many types of real estate markets are created by the needs, interests, and motivations of buyers and sellers. The five most general markets reflect five broad categories of properties: residential, commercial, industrial, agricultural, and special purpose. These markets can be further divided into submarkets—smaller and more specialized markets that are identified by the preferences of the market participants concerning price, location, and so forth.

To identify and describe a market or submarket, an appraiser studies it in terms of location, competition, and demand unit to see how that market is formed and to understand the actions of its participants. The appraiser locates a market for a particular property by determining the boundaries in which relevant economic decisions are made. The market area is delineated by the time and distance from common destinations and origins.

An appraiser studies the prices proposed, offered, accepted, and paid by buyers and sellers. The competition of market participants leads to competitive choices in the market. Because the basis of all demand for real estate is people, the appraiser studies the rate of population increase in a market area to ascertain effective demand for a property type and to determine possible future demand.

Market analysis is accomplished by researching market segmentation and by studying the influences that affect and form the market. An appraiser delineates the market and analyzes it in terms of competitiveness for the property, the location of both the market and the property, and the operation of supply and demand in that market. From this market analysis, the appraiser can identify the present and probable supply of and demand for a property type. Throughout the analysis, the appraiser uses collected market data to discern patterns of behavior and trends in the market. The information derived in market analysis may be used as a basis for value estimates and evaluation conclusions.

Chapter 5

Money Markets and Capital Markets

In business, money is the exchange medium employed in the sale and purchase of goods and services. Parties to a transaction agree on the value of the object of the transaction, which is expressed in terms of money. Each nation has a monetary currency that may be hard (such as gold, silver, copper, and the like), or paper, or a combination of the two. Through international banking agreements and trading, relative values are established for currencies. Because real estate is priced in terms of money, the value of money influences price; therefore, appraisers must understand monetary values.

The term *money* is difficult to define. Economists define the term variously. Some believe that money is "currency in the hands of the public plus demand deposits at commercial banks"; others believe that it is "currency plus demand and time deposits (i.e., those for which notice of withdrawal must be given) at commercial banks"; and still others think that it is "currency plus demand and time deposits plus

the liabilities of non-bank financial intermediaries."[1] By far, the largest
monetary element is checking account balances. In our economic and
commercial systems, checks are thoroughly accepted and used as
money. Whether the money supply is defined as currency or account
balances or both, its value is influenced by its availability.

The Supply of and Demand for Money

Supply and demand relationships set the cost, or price, of money. In
relation to any level of demand, when money is plentiful, the price is
modest, but when it is scarce, the cost rises. The price of money is
expressed as an interest rate—the cost to hire funds. This fact is particularly important in real estate because investments are created by combining debt and equity funds. Tight supply-demand monetary situations tend to increase capital costs, or interest rates, and thus affect
real property values.

One can see a significant difference between money and other
commodities on the supply side of the pricing formula. While the demand for money is a product of natural economic forces, the supply of
it is mechanically regulated by the Federal Reserve. It follows that the
manager of supply has the power to regulate general interest rate levels, which strongly influence the selection of discount rates employed
in real estate valuation. Thus, it is frequently said that realty values are
established in money markets rather than in real estate markets.

Trading Funds

*A money market is the interaction of buyers and sellers in trading short-term
money instruments.* These short-term instruments generally mature in
one year or less and include federal funds; Treasury bills, Treasury
notes, and other government securities; repurchase agreements and reverse repurchase agreements; certificates of deposit; commercial paper; bankers' acceptances; municipal notes; and Eurodollars. Although
called a market, a money market is not formally organized, as is the
New York Stock Exchange. It is an "over-the-counter" operation, but it
also provides accurate and readily available national and international
trading information due to computerization. Because the Federal Reserve System regulates the money supply, it influences trading in a
money market daily. This, in turn, greatly influences the real estate
market, in which short-term financing is essential for construction and

---

[1]Howard R. Vane and John L. Thompson, *Monetarism—Theory, Evidence and Policy* (New
York: Halsted Press, 1979), p. 49.

development activity. The availability of money and the cost of materials regulates the industry's magnitude and pace.

A capital market is the interaction of buyers and sellers in trading long- or intermediate-term money instruments. These instruments usually mature after more than one year and include bonds or debentures, stocks, and mortgages and deeds of trust. Although stocks are capital market items, they are equity investments and have no maturities. The distinction between money markets and capital markets is not sharp because both involve trading in funds for varying terms and are sources of capital for all economic activities, including real estate.

In money markets and capital markets, observable relationships between various instruments stem from differing interest rates, maturities, and investment qualities. In periods called "normal," an investor who puts money in a long-term instrument is viewed as assuming greater risk than one who invests in a short-term instrument. The former investor is compensated by receiving higher yields than the latter investor. Thus, in "normal" periods, long-term instruments offer higher yields than short-term instruments. This situation illustrates a normal yield curve.

The relationship can be reversed. In highly inflationary periods, investors usually do not take long-term positions. They fear erosion of capital caused by escalating interest rates and try to stay in short-term instruments. But the Federal Reserve, seeking to combat inflation, causes interest rates to rise. This action is intended to be temporary, lasting only long enough to dampen inflationary expectations. Short-term yields are then greater than longer-term yields, and the yield curve is said to be "inverse."

Fractional Reserve Banking

When a commercial bank makes a loan to a business or an individual, it credits that business or personal checking account with the amount of the transaction. It has been said that the banks manufacture money through this loan process because by monetizing debt they create money. Essentially, banks fund large loan volumes by entering the money market. They raise the cash to do so by selling their paper, such as certificates of deposit, to a broad group of investors. Of course, banks are constrained in their money creation activities and are required to maintain reserves equal to specified percentages of their deposits. Thus, if a bank has a 20% reserve requirement, for each dollar of its reserve it could support four dollars of deposits, which could be created by extending four dollars in loans and crediting them to their borrowers' accounts. This arrangement has been called fractional reserve banking, and it pervades the operations of central banking systems throughout the world.

Federal Reserve System

In 1913, Congress passed the Federal Reserve Act, which created a central bank to control monetary affairs. Framers of the act studied central banking in other countries and intended to provide a banking system that was characterized by efficient facilities but avoided either political or private hegemony. Thus, they created an independent banking system—the Federal Reserve System (Fed)—that over time has broadened its scope to manage money and credit to promote the economy's orderly growth. The system's independence distinguished it from the central banks of other countries because it was intended to function within the general structure of the U.S. government. Thus, it was to act in accordance with rational, economic policies while having the power to exercise its judgment independently.

Rather than having a single central facility, the Fed comprises 12 regional banks, which serve the 12 Federal Reserve regional districts, and numerous member banks, which include all nationally chartered commercial banks and a significant number of state chartered banks. It is directed by a seven-member board of governors who make policy and who are appointed by the president and confirmed by the Senate of the United States for 14-year terms. Members are selected with regard to geographic distribution and to occupation. So that no region is overrepresented on the board, no more than one member of a particular region can serve at any one time. To avoid conflict of interest, no member can be an officer, director, or stockholder of any banking institution.

Credit Regulation

Reserve requirements, discount rates, and the Federal Open Market Committee are three credit regulation devices employed by the Fed to promote the orderly growth of the economy. Because the Fed regulates money supply and credit, an appraiser should be familiar with its money and credit regulation devices.

Reserve Requirements

Within statutory limits, the Federal Reserve Board can fix the amount of reserves that member banks must maintain. One requirement of membership in the system is that member banks cannot make all of their deposit liabilities available for business loans but must agree to keep part of them frozen in reserve accounts at Federal Reserve banks. The Federal Reserve changes the amount of the reserve requirement from time to time; such a change expands or contracts the volume of money and credit. If the Fed wants to restrict the money supply, it increases deposit reserve obligations; if it wants to increase the supply, it lowers the obligations. In recent years, demand deposits have been subject to an approximate 15% reserve requirement and time funds of 3% to 8%.

Federal Discount Rate

Another major credit regulation tool is the discount rate. One advantage members in the Reserve System have is their ability to borrow from the Fed, which enables them to obtain funds for their customers during periods of great demand. In return, member banks agree to pay the Federal Reserve discount rate. The borrowing privilege is not unrestricted, however. The Fed denies loan requests whenever it believes that borrowing is not in the best interests of the economy. The phrase used to describe such an action is "the discount window is closed." Thus, the borrowing privilege is a vehicle for expanding the monetary supply, and its curtailment is a vehicle for contracting the supply and thus for restricting credit.

Federal Open Market Committee

The third credit regulation tool is the Federal Open Market Committee (FOMC). The FOMC is probably the most extensively used and most potent of the Federal Reserve's credit regulating devices. The committee comprises the Federal Reserve Board of Governors, the president of the New York Federal Reserve Bank, and four district reserve bank presidents who serve one-year terms on a rotating basis. The FOMC buys and sells U.S. government securities in the open market, thereby exerting a powerful influence on interest rates. In fact, these daily operations reasonably maintain short-term money rates at committee-selected target levels. When the committee buys securities, it causes credit to be infused to an amount approximately six times the purchase amount. The committee buys securities with Federal Reserve checks, which bond dealers deposit in the commercial banking system. These checks increase member bank reserve accounts, which permits greater loan activity and increases the money supply in the form of checking account balances. Thus, economic growth and expansion are encouraged. By contrast, when the committee sells securities, it causes funds to be removed from member banks and causes the supply of money and credit to be reduced. Thus, economic growth is discouraged.

Usually, FOMC meets once a month, at which time it sets monetary policy strategies. The meeting's minutes remain secret for 30 days, after which time they are published. During the time of secrecy, money dealers watch the committee's activities and infer current policy from them. Money dealers and financial operators are aided by the opinions of experts, called "Fed watchers," who often analyze the committee's activities successfully. Thus, real estate investors and appraisers, whose function is market interpretation, carefully follow the information provided by Fed watchers.

Fiscal Policy

While the Fed determines monetary policy, the Department of the Treasury manages the government's financial activities. The Treasury's strategies comprise the nation's fiscal policy. Essentially, the Treasury raises funds and pays bills. To raise funds, the Treasury generates currency, collects taxes, and borrows money. Expenditures are made pursuant to congressional appropriations for national projects and activities.

A desirable, but rare, condition occurs when income matches or exceeds spending. This condition promotes balance throughout the economy. When outflow exceeds collections, the result is a federal deficit, which requires funding.

Heavy spending not covered by taxes produces deficits that are financed by the sale of such public debt instruments as bonds, bills, and notes. The Treasury manages these affairs. When deficits are monetized by selling large amounts of debt, the Fed is tacitly expected to cooperate by supplying the banking system with sufficient reserves to accommodate the sales program and still leave reasonable credit for the private sector.

In theory, expenditures should expand the economy, increase government tax collections, and finally lead to an operating surplus that permits government debt reduction. In practice, spending has grown much faster than revenues, producing deficits and severe inflation. Throughout this experience, the Fed has supplied the money necessary to fund resulting deficits. Financial institutions are concerned that excessive Treasury borrowing might so use up credit supplies that private sector needs would be short-changed and smaller borrowers would be "crowded out." This is meaningful to the real estate industry, which can be deprived of long-term mortgage capital because of the volatility of money markets and capital markets.

Money Market Instruments

Prices that are established in a money market determine investment yields. These yields include stated interest rates and earned discounts or premiums from a security's stated price. Money cost has often been called an interest rate because when a borrowing instrument is created, it carries that day's market interest level for the maturity involved. If a six-month-term instrument is sold when it is three months old, and prevailing interest rates are higher than when the instrument was created, a buyer will not be satisfied with the face, or coupon, rate. To make a deal, a seller must discount the paper; the investment yield to the buyer will then be the face rate plus the discount. If lower levels of interest rates prevail at the time of sale, a buyer cannot purchase at the coupon rate. A seller will demand a premium. Yield to the buyer will then be the rate reduced by amortization of the premium. These conditions are mirrored in real estate market activities where, as of the date of any transaction, a buyer prices property to provide good prospects for a competitively attractive yield on the equity investment.

Money markets are especially important to real estate development activities. Construction loans are short-term mortgages that have variable interest rates tied to market indexes. For example, the market might evidence borrowing costs of two to four percentage points above the floating prime rate, which is the best commercial bank short-term loan rate and is offered only to favored customers. It is not unusual for building loan rates to be adjusted monthly without a cap or upper limit, but with a floor, or minimum, instead. When demand for short-term money is intense and supply is limited, market interest rate levels must escalate and thereby make construction funds exceedingly expensive. Resulting real estate project cost increases can destroy economic feasibility and cause failures and bankruptcies. The outlook for cost and availability of short-term funds is a key consideration for developers, and their perceptions cause real estate activity to expand or recede.

In money markets, a wide variety of instruments and arrangements are employed. They are offered by the federal government, banks, corporations, and local governments. Certain important ones, covered in the following discussion, are federal funds, Treasury bills, Treasury notes, other government securities, repurchase and reverse repurchase agreements, certificates of deposit, commercial paper, bankers' acceptances, municipal notes, and Eurodollars.

Federal Funds

When member banks experience intense loan demand, they usually fall below the Federal Reserve System's required reserve balances. To increase their reserves, the banks can borrow from either the Fed at its "discount window" or from other banks that have experienced slack demand and thus have excess reserves that can be loaned short term. The borrowed or loaned money is called federal funds because it is employed to meet Federal Reserve requirements. To obtain federal funds, banks deal directly with each other or employ brokers to arrange the transactions.

The federal funds rate is influenced by any or all Federal Reserve credit regulation devices. It is a key rate and its movements generate sympathetic trends in money markets and capital markets. Changes throughout all markets vary largely because of the differences in investment qualities and maturities; but general trends are always influenced by the varying rates of Federal Reserve funds.

Treasury Bills

Treasury bills are short-term, direct debt obligations of the U.S. government, usually having maturities of three months, six months, or one year, and issued in denominations of $10,000, $15,000, $100,000, $500,000, and $1 million. These instruments do not bear a coupon interest rate but are sold at a discount, which provides investor earnings. Yield is calculated on a 360-day year but maturities are based on a 52-week year.

Bills are backed by the full faith and credit of the U.S. government and are sold at auction frequently. In preparing bids, purchasers are influenced by the recent levels and movements of the federal funds rate, which are examined to determine monetary policy direction. This plainly demonstrates the close interrelationship between these money rates.

Treasury bills greatly influence the activities of the real estate industry. In the early 1980s, banks and savings and loan associations received regulatory permission to sell six-month savings certificates at yields equal to or 25 basis points above the six-month Treasury bill yield established at the most recent auction. The arrangement was intended to make these institutions competitive in attracting the savings funds, which they usually channel into home mortgage loans. Without the thrift industry's having this capacity, mortgage fund shortages were expected to occur. The plan's success has been primarily negative; experience has demonstrated that as interest rate levels moved higher, results were poorer.

Other Government Securities

Although U.S. Treasury notes have longer maturity terms than typical money market instruments, they are traded in money markets. They are backed by the full faith and credit of the U.S. government and are issued in maturities of one to ten years. Many issues, however, fall in the two- to four-year range. Denominations are $1,000, $5,000,

$10,000, $100,000, and $1 million. They are interest bearing and carry a face rate.

After issue, Treasury notes are traded freely, and deals are priced to reflect current market yields. In these transactions, remaining maturities are usually short and indicate rates that fit typical money market patterns for similar-quality investments.

Because of their maturities, Treasury note earning rates influence real estate "bridge" mortgage rate requirements. These are real estate loans for a two- to four-year period during which an owner might be waiting for a more favorable, longer-term financing climate, or might be converting a rental property to a condominium or cooperative ownership plan.

Other government securities are the obligations of such U.S. government-sponsored bodies as the Federal National Mortgage Association, the Federal Farm Credit System, the Federal Home Loan Bank, the World Bank, and the Federal Land Bank. The instruments created by these agencies are backed by the full faith and credit of the United States, have maturities of 5 to 20 years, and are interest bearing. The securities are freely traded over the counter.

Repurchase Agreements and Reverse Repurchase Agreements

Repurchase agreements (repos) and reverse repurchase agreements (reverse repos) are short-term financing arrangements made by securities dealers, banks, and the Federal Reserve System. A repurchase agreement occurs when a person who needs funds for a short period uses his or her portfolio of money market investments as collateral. The person sells an interest in the portfolio with the obligation to repurchase it, with interest, at a specific future time. The person then achieves the needed liquidity and the securities provide the lender good collateral. Individuals and business organizations with excess short-term cash invest in repurchase agreements. The future time to repurchase ranges from overnight to up to several months.

The Fed has used this procedure in fine tuning money markets to achieve selected interest rate levels. By executing a purchase from a securities dealer who is obliged to repurchase in a few days, the Fed temporarily creates additional bank reserves because the dealer deposits transaction proceeds in a commercial bank. A reverse repurchase agreement is created when the Fed sells securities to dealers with an obligation to buy back with interest. The Fed temporarily withdraws reserves from the banking system because the dealer will pay by a check drawn on the commercial bank account.

Repurchase agreements enable corporations to lend excess cash for short periods. This is especially important because these business organizations cannot engage in Federal Reserve funds trading, which is usually restricted to banking organizations. Interest rates in repos are a function of the prevailing supply-demand conditions in short-term money markets. They are, of course, influenced by the quality of collateral, which usually is excellent.

Certificates of Deposit

Certificates of deposit (CDs) are financial instruments that represent time deposits with banking organizations. They may be for one month, three months, six months, one year, or up to seven years. The most typical large denominated certificates ($100,000 and up) are for one or three months. A CD is a contract between a bank and a lender by which the bank agrees to pay negotiated rates of interest in return for the depositor's agreement to maintain the deposit for a fixed period of time. A CD is backed only by the credit of the issuing banking institution. Many CDs are negotiable and can be traded.

Although a CD interest rate is negotiated, constraints have been imposed by Federal Reserve Regulation Q. The thrust of regulatory changes in the early 1980s, however, was to liberalize and remove such limitations. Congress established the Depository Institutions Deregulation Committee, which works toward eliminating Regulation Q to ensure equality among all institutions.

Commercial Paper

Commercial paper is the use of a corporation's promissory notes to borrow short-term funds for current operations. It is a device through which organizations with excess cash lend to those in need of money. This money market sector is well organized. Transaction data, including prices and interest rates, are widely and quickly disseminated by computer facilities. Dealers specializing in commercial paper "make markets" and have the ability to consummate deals quickly and efficiently. Because commercial paper is backed only by the credit of issuing corporations, none but the largest, soundest companies use it. Due to the vagaries of money supply-demand conditions, commercial paper rates are frequently less expensive than bank loan costs; hence, large corporations benefit from the ability to use the paper.

In real estate, commercial paper is important in raising short-term construction funds. For example, an REIT (Real Estate Investment Trust) might issue its commercial paper to acquire the money with which it funds construction loans. For the REIT, the key consideration is that commercial paper interest rates be sufficiently below construction mortgage rates to provide the trust with earnings adequate to handle expenses and to provide satisfactory profit.

Bankers' Acceptances

Bankers' acceptances are similar to commercial paper in that an acceptance is a bank's obligation or promise to pay. The main difference between the two is that only the corporation's credit backs paper, but both corporation and bank stand behind acceptances. Thus, the latter eliminates a certain amount of risk, which causes the yield on acceptances to be often less than that on commercial paper.

Acceptances are short-term, noninterest-bearing notes that are sold at discount and redeemed at par or face amount, as are Treasury bills. Most bankers' acceptances are created in the course of foreign trading. Large banks with foreign departments operate in this market. These instruments are not immediately related to real estate operations, but they mirror trends in short-term interest rates for varying investment qualities.

Municipal Notes

Municipal notes are short-term obligations of villages, cities, counties, and so forth, that finance current operations and bridge the period required to obtain satisfactory long-term funds. Because these instruments are exempt from federal and state taxation, they are favored by investors. The tax advantage has caused the interest rates to be relatively low. Earning rates provide clues to investor requirements for after-tax yields. Although real estate investments are generally longer term, the rates observed do offer some useful insights on investment strategies.

Eurodollars

Eurodollars are dollars deposited outside the United States. This monetary element has grown enormously since World War II. The growth has been aided by U.S. trading deficits being paid in dollars, world oil bills being settled in dollars, and increasing numbers of multinational business operations using and requiring dollars. Banks and businesses that require short- to intermediate-term financing have profitably employed this capital.

In the expanding days of the REIT industry, many trusts secured Eurodollar loans to fund mortgage lending operations. Eurobond and debenture issues of five to seven years have been employed but maturities of one to six months are more common. When supply-demand conditions generate favorable interest levels, Eurodollar loans can provide the real estate industry with bridge financing.

Yield Levels

In following the money market for indications of monetary value, an appraiser usually reads daily financial reports. These reports provide information on the various instruments and their yield rates, which indicates the general state of the economy and may affect the real estate industry. Figure 5.1 is a sample from the *New York Times* daily financial section; it shows yield levels as evidenced in the day's trading. Other publications provide this and additional information.

Capital Market Instruments

Descriptions of traditional capital market operations are presented in this section, but one must keep in mind that conditions for long-term, fixed-interest rate instruments are subject to many changes. An ap-

Figure 5.1
Key Rates in Percent

Key Rates
In Percent

	Yesterday	Previous Day	Year Ago
PRIME RATE	10.50	10.50	16.00
DISCOUNT RATE	8.50	8.50	12.00
FEDERAL FUNDS	8.75	8.50	13.75
3-MO. TREAS. BILLS	8.15	8.07	12.20
6-MO. TREAS. BILLS	8.14	8.07	12.28
7-YR. TREAS. NOTES	10.25	10.17	13.75
30-YR. TREAS. BONDS	10.55	10.47	13.49
BELL SYSTEM BONDS	12.03	11.94	14.90
MUNICIPAL BONDS	9.99	9.92	13.67
6-MONTH SAVINGS CERTIFICATES*	8.663		

*Maximum rate

Salomon Brothers estimates for bellwether issues

© 1983 by The New York Times Company. Reprinted with permission.

Figure 5.2
New Bond Issues

New Bond Issues
MONDAY, MARCH 7, 1983

UTILITY BONDS

Issues	Moody's Rating	Current Bid&Asked	Chng	Yield
So.west Bell 16⅛$21	Aaa	120⅜-120⅝	−⅛	13.35
Louis P & L 13¼$13	Baa3	101-101½	−⅛	13.05
Georgia Pwr 13¼$13	Baa1	102-102½	−½	12.91
CORPORATE BONDS				
Arco 12½$12	Aaa	105½-106	−¾	11.77
Genl Foods 7$11	Aa2	62¾-63¼	−¾	*11.37
INTERMEDIATE NOTES				
DuPont 12⅞$92	Aa2	106⅞-107⅜	−¾	11.57
CBS 14½$92	Aa2	113¼-113¾	−¾	11.99
Du Pont 6$01	Aa2	58½-59	−1⅛	11.31
Com Ed 14¼$92	A2	109¼-109¾	−¼	12.46
INTERNATIONAL ISSUES				
Hydro Que 13⅜$13	A1	105-105½	...	12.66
Ontario 11½$13	Aaa	98⅝-99⅛	−½	11.60
Hydro Que. 11¾$89	A1	102¼-102¾	−⅝	11.10

Source: First Boston Corp.

© 1983 by The New York Times Company. Reprinted with permission.

praiser, as any market analyst, must be aware of these changes and how they affect the financing arrangements discussed next.

Bonds

Bonds are capital market instruments issued with a fixed-face interest rate and with maturities of one year or more. Among those who issue bonds to raise long-term capital for operations and developments are the U.S. government, business corporations, states, and municipalities. Earnings from government-issued bonds are not free from federal, but are often free from local, taxation. Generally, short-term funding is used for project development periods with the intention of converting it, upon completion, into long-term arrangements.

Bonds are usually sold with a par value of $1,000; if an issue offers a face interest rate of 12%, each bond will earn $120 per year. A buyer will receive this earnings rate, and at maturity, of say 20 to 30 years, will be repaid the $1,000 principal amount.

The bond market is closely related to real estate investment activities. Real estate is normally bought with a mixture of equity capital and medium- to long-term debt funds, called mortgage money. Most real estate deals have been structured with a substantial amount of low-cost mortgage money and with a smaller input of higher earning equity, or venture funds. Institutional investors with long-term capital usually survey bond markets, then examine mortgage opportunities, and finally make investment decisions that are intended to secure the best earnings for the risk qualities involved. The correlation of bond market yields and mortgage capital costs proves an intriguing study. Until the excessive inflation of the 1970s and early 1980s caused money market volatility, there was a close correlation between good-quality mortgages and AA-rated utilities bonds.

The financial conditions of those years reduced the availability of long-term, fixed-interest capital, which required a rethinking of real estate investment analyses as methodologies. As an outgrowth of those years, the traditional mortgage-equity combination involves debt funds with variable costs, and property feasibility studies factor in expected rate changes. This operation requires an interest rate forecast that covers the projected investment terms.

Municipal bond yields evidenced in daily trading reflect investors' current after-tax earnings requirements. A popular proxy for these bonds, found in the financial press, is the Bond Buyers Index. To illustrate maturities, risk ratings, and daily price changes, Figure 5.2 provides an example from "New Bond Issues," a regular feature of the *New York Times*. The quoted yields are calculated on indicated pricing, interest rates, and a full payment at maturity. Certain bonds are traded on such organized exchanges as the New York Stock Exchange, but many are handled over the counter.

Stocks

A stock corporation is a common legal entity. Investors provide organizational capital by subscribing to shares, which represent ownership and a right to all proprietary benefits but are subject to prior claims of operating expenses and debt service on capital raised through the sale of bonds, debentures, and other money market instruments. Shareholder benefits consist of any cash or stock dividends declared, augmented by share price appreciation or diminished by depreciation.

Marketing mechanisms in the form of stock exchanges, such as the New York Stock Exchange and the American Stock Exchange (Amex), were organized to provide ventures with ready access to capital sources and with flexibility and ease in trading shares. Through the continued refinement of exchange operations, orderly market conditions have been established, including regular publication of share values.

Mortgages and Deeds of Trust

Mortgage loans traditionally have supplied most of the capital employed in real estate investments. Essentially, they are secured borrowings. A borrower gives a lien on real estate to a lender as assurance that the loan will be repaid. If the borrower fails to make payment, the lender can foreclose the lien and acquire the real estate, thereby offsetting the loss of loan repayment. Mortgage loans were traditionally made for long terms, such as 20 to 30 years, and carried fixed interest rates. A level-payment mortgage, which requires the same dollar amount of payment to be made each month for the entire loan term, has been a popular contract. The payment is calculated to pay interest at the selected rate and to fully amortize the loan over its term so that less of each payment is required for interest and more is available for debt reduction. Other payment arrangements have been used. Parties are generally free to contract in any fashion they desire, subject only to such matters as usury and public policy.

A borrower may pledge real estate to more than one lender, thereby creating several liens; in such cases the issue of lien priority is important. The first loan contract executed and recorded is the first mortgage, which has priority over subsequent transactions. Second and third mortgages are sometimes referred to as junior liens, and they clearly involve more lending risk than first mortgages, which is demonstrated by the higher rates of interest charged for secondary financing.

Mortgages fall into three major categories. They are guaranteed, insured, and conventional. Veterans' Administration (VA) home mortgages are the most notable example of guaranteed mortgages, but other state and national government agencies have also provided guarantees. Federal Housing Authority (FHA) mortgages are the most extensively used insured loans, but again, other government bodies and private insurance companies offer loan insurance. Conventional mortgages are neither insured nor guaranteed. In most states, institutional lenders are limited to a 75% to 80% conventional loan-to-value ratio. But regulations vary from state to state.

Mortgage terms are set by contractual agreement between lender and borrower, subject to usury limitations. In the early 1980s, the Fed's monetary policy generated such high interest rates that usury ceilings had to be either raised or erased. Without these actions, mortgage money would have become unavailable. Congress sets interest rate limits for FHA and VA mortgages. In rapidly changing money markets, the change procedure operates slowly, and a practice of paying points has emerged. The lender is paid, up front, a fee measured as a percentage of the total loan amount. This compensation to the lender enhances the loan yield to make it competitive with other current capital market rates.

Effects of competition for capital are clearly seen in mortgage markets. In the early 1980s, yields soared and changes occurred so frequently that investors preferred to stay in short-term investments, which offered generous rates and maximum flexibility for changing positions. In such a climate, investors resist long-term positions and fixed-rate instruments because they provide poor inflation protection. Reaction to changed conditions has generated the creation of such contracts as variable rate mortgages, adjustable mortgages, rollover mortgages, and so forth. Essentially, they provide periodic adjustments in interest rates to keep yields competitive with current capital market conditions. The contract may cover a long period of years, but the payment requirements change at frequent intervals, and a real estate owner cannot budget fixed debt service. In managing property, an owner might arrange leasing programs that permit rapid rental adjustments to offset increases in mortgage payments caused by money market fluctuations.

Nonmoney Credit Instruments

Land contracts, frequently called installment sale contracts, are instruments that provide for the future delivery of a property deed to a buyer after certain conditions are met. A buyer finances the acquisition of property by paying for it over a period of time but receives the title only after completing the series of payments. In the event of defaults on an installment, the buyer is subject to forfeiture of all payments made. A seller benefits by being able to defer tax consequences of a gain and also by being able to evict a defaulting buyer quickly without the delay and expense of foreclosure. Because these contracts are not recorded, a buyer usually makes sure that the agreement contains provisions of protection against liens or encumbrances filed against the property prior to the buyer's receipt of the deed.

The purchase-money mortgage is similar to the installment sale contract and is a common real estate financing device. Through this instrument, a buyer finances all or much of a property's cost by arranging for the seller to accept a purchase-money mortgage as part of the purchase price. The contract specifies the required interest rate and amortization payments, and a date for final and full payment. To facilitate a transaction, a seller often takes back a purchase-money mortgage so that the buyer does not have to obtain funds from other mortgage and equity sources. The buyer thus takes title immediately and becomes the property owner. If the buyer defaults on a payment or some other requirement, the seller may foreclose. When used for land acquisition, a purchase-money mortgage should contain release clauses that specify the principal payments to be made so that parts of the property are released from the lien of the mortgage. Other procedural matters are included, such as the order in which lots may be released.

Relationships between Money Market and Capital Market Instruments

Rates

By following daily trading over a period of time, one can observe relationships among rates on instruments traded in money markets and among rates on instruments traded in capital markets. For example, one might observe a relatively constant spread of 50 percentage points between yields on three-month and six-month Treasury bills. However, market volatility can cause the spread between yields to increase or decrease for a period of time. For instance, the spread between three-month and six-month paper could widen to 70 percentage points and remain constant at that level for 6 to 12 months.

The federal funds rate, the one rate directly controlled by the Fed, is a foundational rate, the fluctuations of which cause great concern in money markets and capital markets. Another key investment yield, Treasury bills, are auctioned weekly. Because these instruments represent top credit quality and short maturity, their yields establish the base for short-term money rates. Money market and capital market rate relationships are products of the prime investment considerations of borrower's credit, the term of a loan, and the financial supply-demand conditions.

Pattern of Rates

Long-term instruments have usually provided the most generous yields. In the early 1980s, however, financial markets reflected an inverse yield curve, in which short-term rates exceeded longer-term investment returns. Stiff debt service requirements, created by high interest rates, may drain business earnings and thus leave poor equity returns. Consequently, many real estate ventures in those years lacked economic feasibility, and development activity was abated.

Cycles, Trends, and Inflation

Money market and capital market conditions are cyclical. As the economy expands, competition for capital intensifies, costs increase, inflation appears, and the Fed then tightens money and credit until it achieves an economic slowdown. Subsequently, the demand for funds subsides, interest rates decline, and finally economic conditions appear sufficiently stable for business organizations to begin new expansion. When the frequency of the cycle accelerates and its amplitude increases, business and money conditions change rapidly, thereby creating an unattractive economic environment for long-term investments.

Inflation is often described as price escalations occurring throughout the economy; when goods and services become increasingly expensive, inflation is said to be accelerating. Inflation is also described as the proliferation of monetary units—a currency expansion. Both views are inextricably related. As monetary units proliferate, with no growth of underlying wealth, the value per unit declines; more units are required in exchange for goods and services, and price levels escalate.

One good illustration of how inflation affects real estate can be seen in the single family residence market. In the late 1970s, the supply of money in the United States expanded sharply; simultaneously, median prices of new and used dwelling units also escalated sharply, which was supported by a healthy housing demand.

Traditional real estate investment practices involve the use of two types of capital, debt and equity, and a typical venture is structured with a substantial mortgage and a smaller equity contribution.

Before the inflationary period of the 1970s and early 1980s, the major suppliers of mortgage funds were thrift institutions (savings banks and savings and loan associations) and life insurance companies. But the period's high interest rates negatively affected these organizations' mortgage portfolios. Their investment yields became inadequate, liquidity diminished, and mortgages would be repaid with funds cheaper than those originally loaned. High interest rates caused these traditional mortgage lenders to experience deposit withdrawals that impaired their ability to offer loans. The term *disintermediation* describes this condition.

Business and Real Estate Cycles

The economic volatility of the early 1980s emphasized the way in which money market and capital market activities and trends were related to the real estate industry. The post-World War II years (1946-1966) were characterized by discernible patterns in real estate and general business cycles. As business prospered, inflation tended to accelerate. Finally, an oversupply of goods and services was generated. Then, monetary policy and other economic strategies were used to slow the pace. A recession usually emerged, and Congress developed economic revival programs. Invariably, the industry selected to provide economic stimulation was real estate, particularly home building. Programs to provide abundant, moderately priced mortgage money were developed. Usually they involved loan insurance or guarantees to induce capital managers to participate. Because there was a substantial housing demand, the programs were well received. As residential development expanded, employment increased in all economic sectors. Manufacturers of hardware, supplies (heating, plumbing, and electrical), paints, furniture, equipment, and so forth, experienced business improvement. The economy revived, inflation accelerated, and so on—all as before; the cycle was repeated. Real estate prospered when loan insurance and guarantee programs supplied inexpensive, long-term capital.

Volatile economic conditions preclude reliance on the repetition of these traditional cycles and the periodic availability of abundant, moderately priced mortgage money. It is not clear whether real estate can prosper in a climate of short-term variable rate financing, but traditional relationships between business and real estate cycles will undergo change. Recognizing the reality of change and analyzing its effects are basic to the practice of real estate appraisal.

Sources of Capital for Real Estate

The real estate industry employs two major capital types: equity and debt. The different aspirations of equity and debt investors are revealed in their market actions. The debt investor, whether in bonds or mortgages, usually pursues conservative paths, seeking certainty of income and repayment of principal. Such an investor expects a priority claim on the earnings of the investment and often looks for security in the form of a lien on assets involved. A debt investor is relatively passive. By contrast, an equity investor is active. Such an investor is more willing to assume risk; hence the funds used for equity investment have come to be known as venture capital.

Inflation reorders traditional investor attitudes. Institutions that traditionally restrict their real estate positions to debt (mortgage) become dismayed as they realize that interest rates of return they bargained for, and once deemed adequate, are woefully low. They also realize that expensive dollars loaned will be repaid with cheap inflated dollars. In the early 1980s, these conditions impelled institutions to alter investment policies and seek real estate equity positions, believing them to be reasonable hedges against damaging inflation. One cannot be sure how far such a trend will go. In those years, certain authorities believed that a significant amount of long-term, fixed-interest rate, debt capital would prove to be a thing of the past.

Equity

Investors in equity realize that their earnings are subordinate to a project's operating expenses and debt service requirements. Equity income earnings are called dividends, but they are only one part of the total return that the investor expects. Investors also expect that the value of their original investment will increase. However, equity investors take the risk that the value of their investment will not increase and may even decline. When such investors believe that ventures have potential, they are willing to forego such items as lien priority and collateral security. Their position is proprietary and all value increases are theirs.

Trusts

In amassing equity funds for real estate investment, trust entities are used extensively. A form frequently employed is the Massachusetts business trust, which provides holders of shares of beneficial interest with immunity from personal liability for the trust's actions. Usually, this protection is achieved by using a corporate form of entity. In addition, the trusts afford shareholders immunity from the double income taxation incurred in the use of corporations. A corporate entity is taxed on its earnings, and with its after-tax net income it distributes dividends to its shareholders, who are then personally taxed on that income. A trust's earnings, however, are passed through to beneficial shareholders with no income tax paid by the trust and only a single tax paid by the shareholders. The investing public has been greatly attracted by this income and tax pass through.

Real Estate Investment Trusts (REITs) were successful in pooling funds of small investors to acquire real estate investment positions that could not be handled by these people individually. REITs offer shareholders freedom from personal liability, the benefit of expert management, and the transferability of shares. To qualify for tax pass through, an REIT must pay dividends of not less than 90% of net income. Because of complicated income-measuring practices, trusts attempted to pay almost *all* net income. They are, therefore, precluded from establishing reserves for possible losses.

Partnerships

A common vehicle for pooling real estate equity funds is a partnership. A partnership is a business arrangement between two or more persons whereby they co-own the business and share in profits and losses. There are two kinds of partnerships. A general partnership is an arrangement in which all partners share gains, and each is fully responsible for all liabilities. A general partner's complete liability for the acts of, and responsibility for debts incurred by, the other partners in business operations is one deterrent to this type of business arrangement. General partners can legally participate in full active management. A partnership's most attractive feature is the pass through to partners of real estate investment tax shelter, depreciation, and interest.

A limited partnership is an arrangement in which one partnership class is labeled general and the other is called limited. The general partners manage the business and assume full liability for partnership debt. The limited partners are so named because liability is limited to their partnership capital contributions. Limited partners may not manage; they must remain passive, and failure to do so will bring on general partner liabilities. Limited partnerships are popular because they permit an uneven distribution of tax shelter benefits. While a limited partner's financial liability is restricted to capital contribution, a partner may receive tax benefits in excess of that amount.

Syndicates

A popular arrangement for raising real estate equity capital is a syndication. This is simply a partnership that pools funds for acquisition or development of real estate projects. Syndications are both private and public. Private syndications are limited to small groups of investors, who enjoy relative freedom from government regulation. Public syndications involve large groups that operate interstate and are subject to Security Exchange Commission (SEC) registration regulations. Because of their large groups, public syndications have amassed large equity funds, gathering contributions from people whose individual resources were not large enough to handle an entire equity investment.

Often a syndication organizer is the general partner, having full financial liability for the partnership's activities. The other syndicate investors are limited partners. To attract investors, syndication agreements provide for an unequal distribution of investment benefits, with a major share of the tax shelter going to syndicate-share purchasers, not the general partner. The choice of the legal entity employed in a syndication can vary with the type of real estate interest involved and the objectives of the investment group.

Joint Venture

A joint venture is a combination of two or more entities that undertakes a specific project. Although a joint venture often takes the form of a general or limited partnership, it differs from them in that it is not intended to continue indefinitely. The parties may later embark on other ventures, but each venture is the subject of a separate contractual agreement. General and limited partnership arrangements are popular in real estate joint ventures because they permit uneven pass through of tax shelter benefits, giving the largest portion to the partner best able to benefit by it. Tenancy in common is another legal form of joint ownership, usually employed for small properties.

A joint venture is frequently used in large projects. One part, usually a financial institution, supplies most of the required capital, and the other provides building or management expertise. Life insurance companies and pension trusts join with entrepreneurial building entities in a joint venture to develop large offices, shopping malls, and other major real estate projects. If the financial partner requires the restricted liability of a limited partnership, it must be willing to forego active project management. Another common example of the joint venture is the teaming up of home or condominium builders with service corporations of savings and loan associations. The combinations have produced a substantial volume of housing facilities.

Pension Funds

Private and government-operated pension funds are a huge and rapidly growing source of investment capital.

Usually, pension contributions from employer and employee are placed with a trustee, who is obliged to invest and reinvest prudently, accumulate funds, and pay plan benefits to retirees. The trustee may be a government body, a trust company, an insurance company, or an individual. In the performance of these duties, the individual trustee may employ trust departments of commercial banks, insurance companies, and other financial institutions. In the early 1980s, it was estimated that total U.S. pension funds exceeded $600 billion, and if they continued to grow according to the rates at the time, they would soon aggregate $1 trillion. A capital source of these proportions can have major investment impact. Pension trusts are the only group that can feasibly consider longer-term situations because of the long-term characteristics of their fund collections and pension benefit payouts.

Traditionally, pension funds have gone into such securities investments as stocks and bonds. The development of Government National Mortgage Association pass-through securities has made it easier to invest in mortgages, and pension trusts have taken sizable positions. Pension trusts have also been willing to invest in real estate equities. This has been accomplished by using real estate equities held by life insurance companies and commercial banks. Banks and life insurance companies acquire high-quality real estate equities, pool the investments, and, for a fee, supply the necessary management. Pension trusts commit funds to the accounts and share in earnings, which consist of income returns and sales profits.

Life Insurance Companies
Through normal insurance operations, life insurance companies develop large amounts of investable funds that are placed in diverse fields. Besides being large mortgage lenders, insurance companies make substantial real estate equity investments, both on their own account and as managers of separate accounts. Investment officers regard equities as attractive earnings situations that provide reasonable protection against capital erosion.

International Equity Capital
Equity capital is brought into the real estate industry through investment activities of foreign individuals, countries, financial institutions, pension funds, and the like. These "off-shore" capital sources have become increasingly important in U.S. real estate. They often take a longer-term investment view than do domestic investors, which is demonstrated by their bidding up prices, accepting relatively low initial cash flow returns, and looking to future income and value growth to supply the major share of anticipated total equity return. These investors often do not hesitate to make 100% equity acquisitions when properties are attractive and have exciting growth potential. Many of these investors undoubtedly mortgage at a time when monetary conditions generate interest rates that permit positive leveraging.

International capital comes from many sources, such as oil-rich nations of the Middle East and financial institutions and individuals of Western Europe. Although these entities have supplied important equity capital to U.S. realty ventures, they still represent a very small fraction of total U.S. real estate investment.

Debt

As noted, the traditional real estate investment has been structured with a large amount of mortgage funds and a smaller input of equity. Since mortgage money is so important to real estate, investors, appraisers, and counselors must be familiar with sources and costs of capital.

Savings and Loan Associations

Along with mutual savings banks, life insurance companies, credit unions, and others, savings and loan associations are financial intermediaries. This means they receive savings deposits, lend them at interest, and distribute dividends to depositors after they pay operating expenses and establish appropriate reserves.

Savings and loan associations are both state and federally chartered. Federal associations are supervised by the Federal Home Loan Bank Board (FHLBB), a U.S. agency created in 1932 to provide credit to thrift and home financing institutions. FHLBB's main functions are to relieve liquidity problems and to provide the savings and loan industry with even funds flows. Savings and loan association objectives are to promote thrift, pool savings, and invest them in home mortgages.

The relationship between the health of savings and loan associations and residential real estate is close. When short-term interest rates are high, savers withdraw funds and reinvest in higher-yielding, short-term money market instruments and funds. Because associations are financial intermediaries, the funds outflow has been labeled disintermediation. The high interest rates reduce mortgage funds availability and escalate cost.

Commercial Banks

Commercial banks are privately owned institutions, offering businesses and individuals a broad variety of financial services. They may be state or federally chartered. They are managed by boards of directors, who are selected by stockholders but are subject to government regulation.

Commercial banks have traditionally supplied construction and development loans, consistent with their role as short-term lenders. They usually require construction borrowers to obtain commitments from long-term permanent lenders, obliging them to take out a loan when the project is completed. Commercial banks make a limited volume of permanent mortgage loans. In small communities, they also supply customers with home loans.

An important commercial bank real estate credit function is warehousing mortgages for mortgage bankers and other financial institutions. This consists of short-term loans to mortgage bankers, which is secured by their mortgage inventories. The arrangement provides a mortgage banker with liquidity to continue lending operations during the time the bank is seeking to sell the accumulated mortgages to a permanent lender.

Life Insurance Companies

Life insurance companies are large suppliers of real estate mortgage credit and are of two principal types: mutual or stock. Mutual companies are owned by policyholders who share in net earnings by receiving dividends that can be used to reduce their premium expenses. In stock companies, profits belong to shareholders who may or may not be policyholders.

Real estate has always been a major life insurance company investment outlet. Activities have included both mortgage lending and property ownership. Most real estate positions acquired are long term and relate well to the life insurance business in which policy premiums are often collected over extended periods.

Mortgage investments made by life companies cover the full range of realty types, including residences, apartments, offices, shopping malls, hotels, and industrials. Because many organizations have grown to great size, they have been important in mortgage lending on large income-producing properties. The companies prefer loans on offices and shopping malls and have less interest in rental apartments.

Life insurance companies acquire full ownership of real estate (1) for their own investment account, and (2) for separate investment accounts in which they manage funds for pension trusts. Although real estate ownership for their own account may amount to only 3% to 5% of assets, a large dollar investment position is involved because major life companies are of multibillion-dollar size.

Mutual Savings Banks

Mutual savings banks are very similar to mutual savings and loan associations. They promote thrift and invest substantial amounts of these savings in real estate mortgages. In general, their investment powers are broader than savings and loan associations; in the early 1980s they began to expand their scope, which equaled that of commercial banks. Mutual savings banks have grown substantially; they control assets of more than $100 billion dollars. They are located in 17 states and are regulated by the various state banking departments and the Federal Deposit Insurance Corporation (FDIC).

Savings banks have been important mortgage lenders on local and national levels. When the FHA became dominant in home mortgage lending, savings banks participated extensively. Like savings and loan associations, they have supplied large amounts of mortgage funds for the one- to four-family residential real estate market. While savings banks have long enjoyed reasonably broad investment powers, they have emphasized mortgages. These investments are often 65% to 75% of a bank's assets. Other fund outlets are government bonds, corporate bonds, and, to a minor degree, real estate and stock equity investments.

Thrift institutions have been in the unenviable position of borrowing short and lending long. This means that their deposits are of the demand type but are invested in long-term mortgages. When unusual withdrawals occur, liquidity is a major concern and banks must borrow at high cost to meet obligations. The earnings squeeze results from the trend to deregulate interest rates paid on savings. With ceilings lifted, banks and savings and loans pay high, competitive dividend rates to retain the funds they traditionally received and invested in low-yield, fixed-rate mortgages. Such a situation causes net worth erosion of significant proportions. For the real estate industry, such conditions point to poor mortgage money availability; any that is found costs a great deal. When interest rates escalate, fewer aspiring home purchasers qualify as acceptable credit risks because debt service takes too much of their disposable income.

Junior Mortgage Originators

Real estate investments are structured with not only first mortgages, but with seconds, thirds, fourths, and so on. Junior mortgages have been used to raise substantial amounts of mortgage funds and have been employed to achieve various investment goals, such as (1) creating additional leverage and (2) facilitating sales in money markets not conducive to refinancing first mortgages. In most legal jurisdictions, loans must be recorded to establish their priority. The first lien recorded takes priority over those subsequently filed. This means that when a mortgagor defaults, junior lien holders must keep senior positions financially current or run the risk of being cut off by foreclosure of the prior liens. Obviously, junior mortgages entail greater risks than senior liens; hence, they command higher interest rates.

Law and regulations usually preclude banks, savings and loan associations, and life insurance companies from making junior mortgage loans except in very limited amounts. Essentially, such institutional lending is illegal, but various regulatory "leeway" or "basket clauses" permit these loans to be made in amounts that are not to exceed 3% or 4% of institutional assets. Other private lenders offer secondary financing as a regular line of business. Among this group are REITs, financing companies, factoring organizations, and the like. They offer expensive secondary financing in the form of junior mortgages or subordinated land purchase-leasebacks, and are not supervised in a way similar to banks and life insurance companies.

Secondary Mortgage Market

When intense competition causes ensuing capital shortages to curtail mortgage market activities, government and monetary authorities often believe that housing activity can most effectively improve the situation. Therefore, government and private organizations stimulate home building by creating facilities known collectively as the secondary mortgage market. This market enables mortgagees to sell a package of mortgages at prices consistent with existing money market rate conditions. The sales-free capital creates liquidity and permits mortgagees to return to lending when they might otherwise lack funds.

Federal National Mortgage Association. One major influence on the secondary mortgage market is the Federal National Mortgage Association (FNMA). The FNMA's principal purpose is to help the housing industry by purchasing mortgages from primary mortgage markets, thus increasing liquidity among primary mortgage lenders. It issues long-term debentures and short-term discount notes to raise most of its funds. Two important FNMA programs are the over-the-counter program, in which the FNMA posts prices it will pay for the immediate delivery of mortgages, and the free market system commitment auction, in which there are separate but simultaneous auctions for FHA, VA, and conventional mortgages.

Mortgage Corporation. The Federal Home Loan Mortgage Corporation (FHLMC) was created in 1970 to increase the availability of mortgage funds and to generate greater flexibility for mortgage investors. The organization is directed by the Federal Home Loan Bank Board. The FHLMC facilitates the expansion and distribution of capital for mortgage purposes by conducting both purchase and sales programs.

In its purchase programs, the FHLMC buys single family and condominium mortgages from approved financial institutions. The selling organization gains liquidity in times of credit stringency and can continue to make mortgage funds available for housing. While FNMA programs emphasize insured and guaranteed mortgages, the main thrust of the FHLMC is in conventional mortgage fields. Both whole mortgages and participations are purchased by the corporation.

In its sales programs, the FHLMC sells its mortgage inventories and thus acquires funds from organizations that have excess capital. By its purchases, the FHLMC supplies these funds to others having shortages. Because its operations are conducted nationally, the FHLMC generates mortgage capital availability throughout all regions.

Government National Mortgage Association. Another major secondary mortgage market influence is the Government National Mortgage Association (GNMA). Its operations have made much mortgage capital available to housing markets. While FNMA is a private corporation, GNMA is a government organization that gets financial support from the U.S. Treasury. GNMA provides special assistance in mortgage programs involving loans that could not be handled without extraordinary support. It also manages and liquidates certain mortgages acquired by the government. But its most potent role in the secondary market is in the Mortgage Backed Security Program.

GNMA is authorized to guarantee timely payment of principal and interest on long-term securities that are backed by pools of insured or guaranteed mortgages. The most popular security is called pass through because it is based on mortgage payments being passed on to the holder of the security. In this program, mortgage originators pool loans in groups of $1 million or more, issue covering securities, and obtain a GNMA guarantee. Through the program, investors lacking mortgage-originating capacity can still be involved in home finance markets. Because of excellent investment attributes, GNMA securities trade extensively. Money and capital market investors regard the indicated investment yields as current return on top-quality liquid paper.

Private. Although the greatest secondary mortgage market activity has been generated by FNMA, GNMA, and FHLMC, substantial private sector dealings also have occurred. Banks and insurance companies that have mortgage-originating capacity often sell loan portfolios, or participations, to private or institutional investors. REITs have been purchasers of mortgages from other institutions, thereby supplying sellers with the liquidity necessary to continue lending programs.

The development and growth of private mortgage insurance programs has facilitated private secondary mortgage activity. In the residential field, these programs have been successful in insuring mortgage loan increments that exceed legal ratios. This has encouraged private secondary market operations, which would not have occurred without the insurance.

Debt and Equity Relationships

In money markets and capital markets, when risks are comparable, funds flow to the investment that offers the optimum prospective yield. Risks are related to rewards; if capital is to be attracted, competitively attractive yield must be offered. Debt and equity investments have different characteristics and appeal to different investors. A survey of these investment attributes is presented here to clarify a real estate venture's mortgage and equity components.

Equity yield is a combination of cash flow or dividend income that is augmented by growth or is diminished by depreciation. This is true whether the investment is a real estate equity or a common stock. For most of the period 1955-1980, real estate appraisers and analysts largely depended on real estate market data to form opinions about competitively attractive equity yields. Throughout most of the period, capital was readily available at modest and stable costs.

Inflation slowed down real estate investment activities, reducing the availability of market data for appraisal purposes. The information that was gathered was difficult to interpret because the rapidity of monetary changes quickly impaired its market relevance. For example, when more than 10 general interest rate changes occur in a year, it is difficult to attach much importance to a capitalization rate that has been extracted from a sales transaction completed as recently as six months ago. Adjustments too large to be comfortable are required.

In such circumstances, an appraiser is well advised to search money markets and capital markets for data as general support of conclusions developed from real estate data. Daily transactions in financial markets number hundreds of thousands, which reflects the discounting of economic futures by well-informed investors. The composite picture should provide useful guidance and enlightenment for investment analysts.

The largest equity market is trading in common stocks. Transactions are reported daily, showing share prices and current dividend rates. Most substantial newspapers carry full details. In addition, other financial publications offer abundant information about corporate earnings records and other general business conditions related to numerous commercial and industrial organizations. Such data provide the basis for risk rating of securities. The rating task is often performed by professional organizations, such as Standard & Poor's and Moody's, whose opinions are widely published. Other information is furnished by securities analysts of major financial institutions, brokerage companies, and the investment banking industry. Their opinions are readily available to the investment community. Analysts generally follow groups of companies, examine their business affairs in detail, and forecast prospects for earnings and growth.

Analyst reports and the financial press do not reveal calculations of prospective stock yields. However, they provide information from which investment indexes can be drawn. Because value may be expressed as the combined present worth of future income and reversion, a key element is anticipated appreciation or depreciation. In stocks, securities analysts are the best sources of the in-depth information on which the investment world bases its growth or depreciation forecasts. In this regard, their function parallels that of the appraiser in the real estate field, who may seek support for value estimates by discounting market-supported income and reversion forecasts.

The second and larger real estate investment element is its debt capital segment, or mortgage funds. Again, capital markets offer abundant information concerning investor yield requirements for a great variety of debt instruments, which covers a wide assortment of maturities and risk ratings. The bond and debenture markets experience tens of thousands of daily transactions that involve hundreds of millions of dollars. Each transaction represents an investor's discounting of future economic conditions as the investor perceives them. The entire volume affords an excellent picture of well-informed anticipations for debt capital performance.

There are differences in the characteristics of investment yields from debt and equity instruments. In debt, the original lender is entitled to an interest rate bargained for, whether fixed or variable, and full payment of the loan amount at maturity. The arrangements may involve payments of interest only, as in the case of many bonds; or, as in the case of most mortgage loans, it may involve payments that combine interest and debt reduction. However, an original lender may sell an investment during its contractual term. If money market conditions are tight, and interest rates are higher than when the loan was originated, the lender sells the position at a discount. If money is freer and rates are lower, the lender may be able to sell at a premium. The purchaser collects interest in the original contract dollar amount, but as an earnings rate it is related to the new investment basis. Upon loan repayment at maturity, the purchaser receives the full face amount, which includes the earning of any discount involved in the acquisition or loss of any premium paid. Investment yield comprises interest plus or minus any gain or loss realized at the loan's maturity and repayment.

Relationship to Valuation Process

The various instruments and facilities described in this chapter should not be thought of as isolated elements. All are interrelated and exhibit sympathetic interest rate or yield movements. Certain rates—for example, those of federal funds and Treasury bills—are foundational. They are closely followed by traders and investors whose movements set rate levels and velocity throughout money markets.

In the real estate industry, development and construction sectors employ short- and medium-term funds, the cost of which largely influences a project's economic feasibility. Because this financing is priced on a variable-rate basis, with its cost tied to such an index as the commercial bank prime lending rate, cost estimating and project budgeting require interest rate forecasts covering the development period. Thus, it is critical that a real estate appraiser be familiar with money markets and their activities.

Sales Comparison Approach

When mortgage financing is readily available at moderate cost, real estate markets function freely. They tend to slow to a halt when funds become scarce or unobtainable. It has been noted that using high interest rates as an inflation antidote usually generates disintermediation in the thrift and life insurance industries. Scarce, expensive mortgage money causes market slowdowns. This prompts efforts to find alternative financial arrangements, such as "creative financing," to keep some sales volume alive.

In the residential field, sellers are often compelled to take back purchase-money mortgages in amounts and at rates buyers can afford.

If sales are structured around existing low-interest rate mortgages, not callable on sale, secondary mortgage financing must be sought from sellers or other financial sources. When large, high-quality commercial properties are involved, buyers capable of paying all cash can and do preempt the market. This crowds out buyers who require mortgage financing, which is scarce and expensive. For the intermediate commercial grade and more modest properties, the investment market dries up and dies. Use of a high interest rate cure for inflation clearly diminishes availability of comparables for use in the sales comparison approach.

In such situations, not merely a decline in general interest rates is needed to improve mortgage capital availability; there must be proper relationships between certain money rates. For example, if commercial bank certificate of deposit rates maintain a significant margin over U.S. Treasury bill rates, most savers will be persuaded to place their money in money market investment funds rather than in thrift institutions. None of this money will find its way into mortgage loans.

Drastic money fluctuations and lack of rate predictability are negative factors, retarding mortgage activity and slowing real estate investment activity. Under these conditions, lenders are constrained to keep very liquid, investing their available funds in high-quality, short-term debt instruments, rather than in long-term, fixed rate mortgages.

Income Capitalization Approach

The income capitalization approach is based on anticipation. Value may be expressed as the present worth of anticipated future benefits, and valuation involves a discounting of these benefits. One key element is the selection of an appropriate discount rate. One view is that the rate is basically a weighted average of the costs of the mortgage capital and equity funds used to create the investment. Credit stringency causes intense capital competition and high rates; credit ease loosens the market and tends to moderate rates. Changes of this sort clearly affect the basic capitalization rates.

Although the capitalization rate may be a key valuation element, the forecast of investment benefits is of equal importance. An investor looks for income earnings during an investment's term and hopes to realize reversionary profits upon its disposition. These benefits are clearly influenced by monetary conditions, particularly those related to inflation. The income capitalization approach requires that an appraiser forecast for the future. It should be accomplished with the support of the most complete real estate and capital and money market information obtainable, and by employing logical, sophisticated methodologies.

Cost Approach

Money market and capital market activities are important in the cost approach because they affect land values, cost estimates, and accrued depreciation.

Land Values

A holder of land for sale usually capitalizes such ownership costs as debt service, taxes, and so forth. Because the owner expects to recapture these outlays when the investment is sold, he or she tends to build up asking prices. In this connection, inflationary interest rate escalations certainly cause mortgage debt service increases. Cities, towns, and counties also incur higher capital borrowing costs in providing municipal services; this brings about substantial increases in real estate tax burdens.

Because markets fluctuate so widely in periods of great economic change, it is not always possible to realize asking prices. In such times, many owners vigorously hold on and wait for more favorable markets.

Cost Estimates

Proper cost estimates, whether for reproduction or replacement, necessitate interest rate forecasts covering the contemplated building period. Many real estate projects are sufficiently large that two to three years are required to complete construction and to achieve full occupancy. To finance these operations, construction funds are acquired through building loan contracts having variable costs (interest rates) tied to an index, such as the commercial bank prime lending rate.

Although certain loans include rate float ceiling and floor limitations, the more common arrangement provides for unlimited movement. Because building loan interest is the major element in "soft," or indirect, construction costs, its proper estimation calls for an interest rate forecast covering the development period. In view of interest rate volatility flowing from the Federal Reserve's monetary moves, the task is difficult but necessary.

Hard construction costs, such as materials and labor, also are influenced by interest rate variations. Price escalations of this nature have come to be called "cost-push" inflation. Again, a rate forecast is clearly a must in construction cost estimation.

Accrued Depreciation

Accrued depreciation is often described as the difference between reproduction or replacement cost and value. During inflationary periods, when money costs escalate sharply, construction costs rise rapidly; therefore, a building's cost base from which depreciation is subtracted shows substantial growth. The influence of inflation on accrued depreciation varies.

In income properties, such as rental housing, revenue growth often lags behind operating expense increases, which erodes net earnings. At the same time, capitalization rates rise in response to interest rate escalations. This results in a reduction in investment values, and with rising replacement costs the measure of accrued depreciation grows substantially.

In other types of income properties, such as shopping centers and office buildings, leases may call for rent escalations and overages that match and sometimes exceed growth of operating expenses. In these cases, accrued depreciation does not experience inflation-related growth.

Summary

The value of all money influences the price of real estate. Monetary values throughout the world are established through international banking agreements and trading. To help estimate a property's market value, an appraiser must thus acquire a knowledge of money and the value of a nation's currency. The supply of and demand for money sets the cost, or price, of money, which is expressed as an interest rate. The supply of money in the United States is regulated by the Federal Reserve. The demand for money may be discerned by studying money markets and capital markets. The activities of the Federal Reserve and of money markets and capital markets affect real estate value.

Because the Federal Reserve regulates U.S. money supply and credit, an appraiser must also understand money and credit regulation devices. Reserve requirements, the federal discount rate, and the Federal Open Market Committee are employed by the Federal Reserve to regulate credit. However, financial activities of the U.S. government are managed by the Department of the Treasury through its fiscal policy. Because its duties are to raise funds and to pay bills, the Treasury affects the monetary activity of the country and thus its activities affect the real estate market.

The money market is an informally organized operation, in which participants trade funds through such instruments as federal funds; Treasury bills, Treasury notes, and other government securities; repurchase and reverse repurchase agreements; certificates of deposit; commercial paper; bankers' acceptances; municipal notes; and Eurodollars. They are known as short-term instruments because they generally mature in one year or less. In real estate, short-term financing is the basis of construction and development activity. Both the availability of money and the cost of materials regulates the construction industry's magnitude and pace.

The capital market is an operation in which participants trade funds through instruments that generally mature after one year. These instruments include bonds, debentures, stocks, and mortgages. Both money market and capital market operations involve trading funds for terms of varying lengths and are sources of capital for real estate, as well as other economic activities.

The direct sources of capital for the real estate industry are debt and equity. The actions of debt and equity investors reveal investors' expectations in terms of earnings requirements. Investors in equity earn dividends and look for investment growth. The types of arrangements for amassing equity funds include trusts, partnerships, syndicates, pension funds, life insurance companies, joint ventures, and investment activities of the international community.

Traditional real estate investments have been structured with a large amount of mortgage funds. The sources of debt capital include savings and loan associations, commercial banks, mutual savings banks, junior mortgage originators, and the secondary mortgage market (FNMA, mortgage corporations, GNMA, and private sources).

All of the instruments and organizations that provide funds to or indirectly affect the real estate market are interrelated and exhibit interrelated interest rates, or yield movements. The importance, then, of yield rates and the money market to real estate cannot be ignored by an appraiser.

Chapter 6

Collection and Analysis of General Data

General data include information on social, economic, government, and environmental forces that affect property value. Such information is part of the store of knowledge with which appraisers approach each appraisal problem. All general data are ultimately understood in terms of their effect on the economic climate in which real property transactions occur. In general data analysis of property values in an area, appraisers examine the operation of appraisal principles by studying the interaction of the four forces. Although each force provides a convenient category for examining general data, it is its interaction with the three others that ultimately affects property value by creating an economic climate in which property values at a specific time and in a specific place increase, decrease, or remain stable.

Types of Data

Data useful in real property appraisal are both general and specific. *General data are items of information on influences that derive from the four forces originating outside a property and that affect the property's value.* General data are different from specific data. *Specific data are details about the property being appraised, comparable sale and rental properties, and relevant local market characteristics.* The specific data gathered and analyzed by an appraiser are discussed in Chapters 8, 9, and 12.

General data are classified as primary or secondary; they can be further divided into macrodata and microdata. Primary data are original elements of information generated by an appraiser. For example, an appraiser may conduct interviews and gather information pertaining to the number of housing units available in a particular neighborhood.

Many primary data studies are conducted for publication by groups and agencies. When these studies are published, they then become secondary data for use by the public. Appraisers obtain secondary data from such published sources as U.S. Census publications; state directories of manufacturing firms; studies prepared by planning commissions, other government agencies, or private research firms; and information reported by chambers of commerce. Secondary information sources often report broad underlying influences on value, such as the increase in the proportion of elderly households in the nation or the expectation of continuing high rates of interest and inflation. General data are most often obtained from secondary sources. Secondary sources of general data are discussed in detail later in this chapter.

Macrodata comprise information on aggregate phenomena, such as total employment at the national, regional, and local levels; national and regional income or product growth or decline; interest rates; or the balance of trade. Macrodata are typically general data obtained from secondary sources.

Microdata are less aggregated observations. The supply of new apartment units in the community, the vacancy rates in a housing submarket, the number of local households in the $25,000 to $49,999 income bracket, and the comparable sale properties used in the sales comparison approach are all examples of microdata. Microdata may be obtained from a primary source, such as a sample of vacant units taken from the local apartment market, or from a secondary source, such as the number of persons employed locally in manufacturing as reported in the *United States Census of Population*.

Uses of General Data

General data are essential in valuation because they (1) provide a background against which to place specific properties being appraised; (2) supply information from which possible trends affecting land values can be inferred and figures for appraisal calculations within the three approaches can be derived; and (3) form a basis for judgments about highest and best use, reconciliation of value indications within the approaches, and the final estimate of defined value.

An appraiser should have an understanding of all elements that contribute to the market price and market value of all types of real estate. An awareness of social, economic, government, and environmental trends allows an appraiser to interpret specific market phenomena. The interaction among value-influencing forces creates a situation or situations in which property values in a specific area at a specific time advance or decline.

In estimating value using sales or cost data, an appraiser uses prices and costs that have been determined in the market and, therefore, are the products of the interaction of all value determinants. Similarly, the income capitalization approach to value requires estimation of market-determined rents, interest rates, capitalization rates, and financing terms. When the methodology of the income capitalization approach requires an appraiser to make explicit forecasts of future income or reversion value at the end of an assumed investment holding period, these forecasts are conditioned by judgments concerning the effects of the basic determinants of value embodied in general data.

An appraiser uses general data in evaluation studies, such as market and feasibility analyses, marketability studies, and investment analysis. An appraiser may perform market analyses for clients who are contemplating new developments. Marketability studies may be performed to improve the acceptability of the project in the marketplace. Feasibility and investment analyses may help developers and investors determine if a proposed project is profitable enough and suggest the optimum development, financing, ownership, and management plans.

For certain assignments, an appraiser must forecast levels and trends of value determinants. Such forecasts demand extensive analysis of the general forces affecting property values. Analyzing the highest and best use of a vacant site, appraising land under an anticipated program of use, or counseling a client concerning the characteristics of a proposed development may require an appraiser to interpret value trends. Analyzing future housing demand and supply and assigning probabilities to different levels of rents, vacancies, or operating expenses in an investment analysis also require forecasts of critical economic, demographic, and social factors.

An appraiser also may do a quantitative analysis in which he or she reports the level, changes, and trends in general data; then applies the quantitative data to the problem under consideration; and finally shows the relative importance of the data trends. For example, the comparison of two local economies among markets for various types of real estate, or the analysis of comparable sales data from a given market, requires analysis of relative trends and cross-sectional differences in the variables appropriate to the problem. The significance of a 2% population increase in one city depends on the population increases in other cities. The demand for apartments must be considered relative to the demand for detached, single family houses. The selection of comparable properties depends on their competitiveness and substitutability with the subject property.

The following discussion of general data is focused on the types of information an appraiser uses in an assignment. The interpretation and use of data require careful judgment, and the usefulness of general data ultimately depends on the appraiser's ability to judge their significance in relation to the specific appraisal problem.

Economic Trends

A trend may be defined as a series of related changes brought about by a chain of causes and effects. These changes are studied to extrapolate an historical trend, which in turn forms the basis for forecasting a future trend. A forecast suggests whether the trend might be expected to continue exactly as indicated by its historical pattern. For example, extrapolation of a trend might suggest that property values have gone up 5% per year. But a forecast might indicate that property values are likely to increase 8% in the current year, level out to 5% in the following year, and continue at 4.5% for several subsequent years. These extrapolations and forecasts involve the judgment of an appraiser, who considers all pertinent factors affecting future conditions.

Recognizing and understanding economic trends that affect the value of real property are prerequisite to an appraisal analysis. It is not enough to know that changes have occurred in the economic situation. The probable direction, extent, and impact of the changes are studied additionally to identify and reasonably forecast a trend.

When changes in the forces that affect property values occur in a predictable manner, a trend may be extrapolated or a future condition may be forecast. Thus, the population increase in a market may be extrapolated, and the number of households in the market for condominium units may be forecast. The demand for condominiums largely depends on observed trends in the formation of one- and two-person households and of households headed by a person over 45 years of age.

The particular trends that concern appraisers vary with the type of problem and the type of real estate being appraised. The market value estimate of a shopping center, for instance, depends on forecasted income from the base rent and overage rent under a percentage lease. The total gross potential income depends on trends in the number of households in the trade area, their incomes, and their typical expenditures on the goods and services supplied by the center, in addition to the availability of alternative shopping facilities.

International Economic Trends

In the economy, trends at any level can affect all levels. In the world economy, the economic well-being of one nation may directly and indirectly affect many nations. The extent of foreign investment in U.S. real estate, for instance, is partly due to the relatively low prices for land and the stability of the U.S. government, which gives a foreign investor some measure of protection. Thus, inflation and political instability in other countries affect the demand for and value of real estate in the United States.

The greater the intensity and duration of an economic trend, the wider its influence. For example, the energy crisis that began in the 1970s generated far-reaching effects on real estate in the United States. High gasoline costs affected the value of fringe-area residences and may have prompted resurgence of inner-city neighborhoods. High energy costs also made energy-conserving features desirable. The presence or absence of such features sometimes affects a property's market value.

Basic trends in national and international economic indicators, such as the balance of foreign trade, rates of foreign exchange, commodity price levels, wage levels, interest rates, industrial production levels, and the volume of retail sales, also merit consideration.

National and Regional Economic Trends

The state of the national economy is basic to any appraisal analysis. National economic conditions can be observed in the gross national product, national income, the balance of payments to other nations, price level indexes, interest rates, aggregate employment and unemployment statistics, housing starts, building permits issued, the dollar volume of construction, and other general data. Time series of economic indicators may reveal fluctuations around a longer-term trend and help place current statistics in perspective.

Federal programs and tax policy can affect the value of favored real estate. Until deregulation of financial institutions, for instance, the mortgage interest rate for home financing was sheltered; this helped support the demand for homeownership and the value of owner-occupied housing. The need for financial institutions to compete for loanable funds with each other and with the money market mutual funds has increased lending rates and has resulted in an adjustment of demand in the market. Tax policy established in the 1981 Economic Recovery Tax Act permits accelerated cost recovery for buildings held for the production of income or used in one's trade or business. Investment tax credits for rehabilitation of older nonresidential real estate and for historic preservation projects enhance the profitability of investment property and ultimately affect value.

The national economy reflects the economic condition of the nation's geographic regions. A region's economic health depends on the status of economic activity. These activities, in turn, are the aggregate of the economic activities of individual areas and communities in the region's geographical boundaries. However, minor disruptions in the economic growth of a community may not appreciably affect the region if the regional and national economies are strong.

The extent to which an appraiser is concerned with the economy of a nation or region, in addition to the economy of the city or neighborhood, depends on matters such as the size and type of property being appraised. For example, a large regional shopping center that serves a trade area of 500,000 people, or an automobile assembly plant that employs 5,000 workers, is more sensitive to the general state of the economy than is a medical-dental office building or a retail service operation in a suburban residential area.

Local Economic Trends

Analysis of a local economy often focuses on trends in population, employment, and income. Population change, net household formation, the diversity of employment that constitutes the economic base of the community, the level and stability of employment, wage rates, and household or family income are indicators of the basic economic strength of a community.

The conditions and prospects of a local economy are relevant for most appraisal assignments. The value of real estate in a community is affected by the strength of demand for its use. This demand for the services provided by many types of real estate is dependent on the population in the market that the real estate serves, the income of the population, and the purchasing power that the income represents. The economic condition of the community is a fundamental determinant of the value of residential real estate in the market and of the value of office buildings, retail properties, and other types of real estate that serve the resident population.

Employment and Economic Base Analysis

Population and income in a region or a community depend on the employment that constitutes the economic base of the area. The economic base, in turn, is determined by the area's comparative advantage, which causes it to be relatively more productive in providing certain products or services than other areas. The comparative advantage may be due to its proximity to commodity markets, the presence or availability of natural resources, the existence of a trained work force, climate, or a government decree that has established the community as a county seat or state capital. As a result of the advantage, a community's work force may largely be engaged in the production of durable goods, such as automobiles and appliances, or involved in assembly and distribution. The community may include a significant amount of government employees or a diverse mix of occupations.

The character of employment in a community or region can affect population growth, the level and stability of income, the willingness of the population to spend disposable income, and the risk associated with investments in the area. These characteristics affect the demand for and value of real estate of all types. A community that has a diversified economic base with a variety of employment is more attractive to investors than is a single-industry town. The stability of a diversified local economy can reduce the risk of a real estate investment and, all else being equal, increase the property's value.

City Origins and Growth Patterns

An appraiser recognizes that urban growth and change in a community can affect neighborhoods and areas differently. An awareness of the forces contributing to urban growth patterns is essential in analyzing the neighborhood or district where the subject property is located insofar as the area affects the quantity, quality, and duration of the stream of future income or amenities that create value.

The structure of urban land uses in a community usually reflects, to some extent, the origin of the settlement, known as its *siting factor*. Some cities in the United States were established where a break in transport was necessary, such as at a seaport, a river crossing, or an intersection of trade routes. Other cities were founded at power sources needed for manufacturing, and still others were located for defensive, commercial, or political reasons. As the national standard of living improved, climate and other natural advantages became the siting factors responsible for the development of retirement and recreational communities. From its initial site, community growth radiates outward; this growth is influenced by the nature and availability of developable land, the evolution of technology, and the government's ability and willingness to provide essential public services.

Communities that experience a scarcity of land, such as San Francisco and New York, may have an increase in the density of land use. Development corridors can channel new construction to usable land. Advancing technology in building materials and construction methods makes possible construction of high-rise buildings in cities lacking bedrock or in those subject to earth tremors.

Transportation improvements and the advent of the automobile have shaped today's cities. Improved transportation permits urban settlements to grow in size and to serve larger markets. At the same time, the structure of city growth is influenced by the local transportation network; growth moves outward from the central city along major transportation routes, and greater dispersion is experienced due to the advent of the freeway system.

Local Market Considerations

An appraiser should be aware of the geographic distribution of economic activity. After other pertinent facts have been analyzed, an economist may conclude that an expected net increase in households in a particular region would tend to raise rents and prices. A real estate appraiser working in a community in that region, however, may conclude that the community will not benefit from the regional trend and, in fact, may suffer an outmigration of households, which may depress property values.

To understand how national and even international economic demographic trends influence value, an appraiser studies how the region and community will respond. The appraiser should be knowledgeable about the economic structure of the region and the community, the comparative advantages that each possesses, and the attitudes of government and residents toward growth and change. For instance, the increasing number of elderly households nationally is less significant to property values in Minnesota than to values in Sun Belt states, which have a comparative advantage in attracting these residents. However, a Florida community with a no-growth policy may not benefit from the additional increase in population.

Demographics

Population and its geographic distribution are basic determinants of the need for real estate. Households must have shelter, and the production and distribution of goods and services require plants, stores, hotels, hospitals, warehouses, and offices. An appraiser should be aware of the potential for change in the aggregate population and in the demographic attributes of the population that constitute the market for the subject property. Population growth is affected by birth and death rates and by migration. These determinants of aggregate population, in turn, reflect the rate of household formation, the age distribution of households, improved medical technology, the standard of living, social mores, and regulations imposed on inmigration.

Aggregate population growth is distributed among regions in response to changing economic opportunities. Past decades saw a migration from the South to the North and Northeast, and from rural to urban areas. The flow to north and northeastern regions has been reversed. The move to suburban areas has slowed because of transportation costs and the expense of providing municipal services and utilities to these outlying areas. As a result, there is an increasing demand for housing in older, close-in neighborhoods in some cities.

Real estate improvements are provided in response to the demand generated by a population with effective purchasing power. Households, which are the basic demanders of housing units, must have income to transform their needs into effective demand. (A household is a single person, or a group of persons with a recognized head who live together, in a housing unit.) Knowledge of trends in the formation of households and household characteristics is crucial to an analysis of a local housing market. The demand for luxury condominiums in an exclusive neighborhood near the central business district is dependent on the number of households who find such housing attractive. A household's age, size, income, and so forth must be considered when analyzing the demand for housing.

The demand for commercial and industrial real estate derives from a population's demand for goods and services to be produced or distributed at these sites. An appraiser must be aware of changes in the characteristics and distribution of the population that consumes the goods and services, and of changes in the work force that produces them. A changing population coupled with technological advance can alter the demand for services provided by the physical property, which can affect property value.

Government Regulations and Societal Attitudes

General data include information about society's attitudes and government regulations and actions that embody these attitudes in land use regulation or in the provision of public services, such as transportation systems and municipal utilities. An appraiser accumulates information on zoning, the master plan, environmental impacts, the transportation system, the local annexation policy, and other data that reveal government policies and societal attitudes affecting real estate.

Local zoning ordinances regulate land use and the density of development. In some instances, zoning is retroactive and attempts to remove uses that are nonconforming at the time of zoning by giving the owner time to alter the property's use. Zoning also can be used to preserve the architectural character of an area. With varying success, communities attempt to use zoning to stop growth, to slow growth, and to coordinate new development with the expansion of capital improvement programs, such as sewage treatment facilities, fire stations, streets, and public recreation facilities. Zoning is used to enforce the community's master plan. The master plan typically is based on economic growth projections and is sometimes modified for political reasons. The appraiser should be aware of the assumptions underlying the plan and the potential for revision.

Environmental goals have prompted increased regulation of land development at state and local levels. Zoning ordinances and building codes have long imposed additional costs on developers. Concerns about the quality of the environment require developers to consider the impact of larger developments on the ecology of a particular area and on the larger environmental system. Developers may be required to improve public roads, construct sewage treatment facilities, preserve natural terrain, or take other steps to conform to the recommendations of local, regional, or state planning agencies. These regulations can add significantly to the time·required to complete the development, and thus to its final cost.

The creation or modification of a transportation system is a government action based on an analysis of the direct and indirect impacts of the system on users and nonusers. An improvement in the transportation system can affect the accessibility of a site and thus its value. Improved transportation routes often generate areas to be developed and affect the value of other sites that must compete with the increased supply. To a great extent, the suburbanization of an urban population results from improvements in the transportation system, via highways, railroads, and bus and airplanes routes.

The movement of commercial and retail enterprises to the suburbs has adversely affected property values in many central business districts. The highway system has opened certain regions to development and has altered the comparative advantage of regions by decreasing the cost of transporting products to markets.

A municipality's willingness to annex outlying areas and to provide public services to these areas can affect the direction and amount of development. Sewer moratoriums have been effective in controlling local growth. These restrictions can increase the value of developments already in place if demand is pressing on a limited supply.

An appraiser should understand the government regulations and actions that affect the subject property to estimate value properly. Comparable properties are selected if they are similar to the subject property in terms of zoning, accessibility, and other characteristics. The value of subdivision land is obviously influenced by environmental regulations, which can affect the amount of time required to develop and sell the sites.

Purchasing Power

Households receive personal income from wages and salaries, yields on savings and other investments, profits from businesses, and private and government pensions. Many American households get a significant proportion of their personal income in the form of government transfer payments, such as social security, unemployment compensation, and farm subsidies. Personal income after taxes is disposable income, which is spent or saved. Housing competes with other goods and services for the household's consumption dollar.

The demand for housing depends on the level of household income, the propensity to consume, the price of housing relative to other goods and services (including the cost and availability of credit and tax advantages afforded homeownership), and the consumer's tastes and preferences. The amount of disposable income spent on all goods and services indirectly determines the demand for other types of real estate, such as shopping centers, industrial plants, office buildings, and warehouses.

Price Levels

Price-level changes affect the quantity of goods or services that can be purchased for a dollar. Nominal prices that have been adjusted for a changing price level are called "real" prices. The sale prices, rents, operating expenses, construction costs, and interest rates used by an appraiser in estimating market value, and the final value estimate, are typically expressed in nominal dollars, unadjusted for changes in price level.

Investments vary in their ability to retain a constant real value in inflationary periods. Owners of income-producing real estate often attempt to keep the real value of their property constant by including escalator clauses in leases. These clauses adjust rents according to an inflation index, so that the tenant pays increases in operating expenses.

Lenders are increasingly unwilling to accept the risk of changing price levels and are attempting to obtain some protection against that portion of inflation that may not be fully priced in the mortgage interest rate. In the early 1980s lenders on income properties began to ask for not only a mortgage rate of interest that contains a premium for anticipated inflation, but also equity participation in the income and, in some instances, a portion of the sale price if the property is sold by the borrower. Other lenders use a floating rate tied to the prime rate, or some other interest rate. Such provisions affect the net operating incomes and before-tax cash flows of properties, and thus the value indications derived through the income capitalization approach.

Building Fluctuations

Housing starts and the construction of commercial and industrial properties fluctuate in response to business recessions and booms, wars, and the cost and availability of financing. These fluctuations occur around the long-term trend of new construction, which has been on an upward course. These short-term fluctuations can depress rents and prices as the result of temporary misallocations of supply.

The standing stock of housing units at any point in time comprises units occupied by households and vacant units. The stock is continually altered by the construction or conversion of units in response to developers' perceptions of the demand for new households and by the need to replace existing units. Six months to two years can pass between the time the developer decides to supply units and the time the units enter the market. During this period, changing conditions may reduce demand. Units coming on the market may remain unrented and unsold, and the vacancy rate may increase. Developers may continue to produce additional units for some time, even in the face of rising vacancies. Once produced, this excess supply of units remains on the market and can depress rents or prices until demand becomes sufficient to remove the surplus. When the market tightens, the supply response lags behind the increase in demand, resulting in abnormally low vacancy rates and upward pressure on rents and prices. Ultimately, supply materializes as developers respond.

These fluctuations in construction can occur because of war, credit stringency, or changing business conditions. Fluctuations in supply and demand on the local level are influenced by regional and national conditions. Therefore, an appraiser looks for trends on these larger levels that may indicate a positive or negative change in property values at the local level. Although all regions may not experience the same downturn in construction, a tight monetary policy affecting the cost and availability of mortgage credit exerts a moderating influence even in a booming region.

Commercial real estate is affected by business conditions and the cost and availability of financing. Business firms pass the high financing costs on to consumers, which may restrict residential construction. If the demand for the goods and services produced or supplied remains strong, the business firm can raise prices and continue to add new plants or offices even though credit is tight and interest rates are high.

An appraiser estimates market value as of a specific date, which may fall during a fluctuation in building activity. Because market value is influenced by the balance of supply and demand at the time of the appraisal, the appraiser should be certain that the client understands the economic conditions in the market that affect the subject property's value at a specific time.

Building Costs

The cost of reproducing a building tends to follow general price levels established over a long period. However, these price levels vary from time to time and from place to place. Building costs generally decline in times of deflation and increase in periods of inflation. Building costs are affected by material and labor costs, construction technology, architect and legal fees, financing costs, building codes, and such other public regulations as zoning ordinances, environmental requirements, and subdivision regulations.

The cost of construction can alter the quantity and character of demand and, therefore, the relative prices in real estate submarkets. The high cost of new buildings increases the demand for and prices of existing structures. Rehabilitation of existing buildings can become economically feasible when the cost of new structures increases. High building costs increase prices in the single family residential submarkets and thus affect the demand for rental units and their prices. The size and quality of the dwelling units demanded are reduced by building costs that increase more rapidly than purchasing power.

Taxes

Real estate taxes are based on the assessed value of real property, hence the term *ad valorem* (according to value) taxes. The assessed value is based on but not necessarily equivalent to the market value of a property. If, for example, the tax rate is $60 per $1,000 of valuation, and the assessed value is equal to market value and taxes are based on 50% of assessed value, then the real estate tax equals 3% per year of assessed value:

$$\frac{60}{1,000} \times 50\% = 3\%$$

If assessed value is not consistent with market value, the formula must be modified to reflect the inconsistency.

If the gross annual rental income of another property is 12.5% of the market value and annual real estate taxes are 2.5% of market value, one-fifth of the gross income must be allocated for payment of taxes. Where ad valorem real estate tax assessments bear an established or probable relationship to market value, appraisal services may be required in the resolution of tax appeals.

In some communities, the trend in real estate taxes is an important consideration. In cities where public expenditures for schools and municipal services increase, a heavy burden of taxation may adversely affect real estate values. Under these circumstances, new construction may be discouraged.

Although income taxes are not treated as an expense in appraisal calculations, except in certain specialized situations, they can influence property value. The homeowner's ability to deduct mortgage interest and property tax when itemizing deductions in computing ordinary taxable income influences the overall price level of single family residences and condominiums. The 1981 Economic Recovery Tax Act permits rapid recovery of costs in calculating the taxable income of investment properties and properties used in trade or business. Rehabilitation of older commercial buildings and historic preservation have been encouraged by investment tax credits. The beneficial reductions in taxable income that result from these laws affect the market's perception of the value of benefited properties.

Differing levels of sales taxes and earnings taxes can also affect the relative desirability of properties. Although these taxes may be uniform within a state, properties in different states are often in competition with one another. For example, for several years Vermont imposed relatively low taxes and attracted many more new residents and industries than surrounding New England states. This increased demand probably enhanced property values in Vermont relative to values in surrounding states.

Financing

As discussed in Chapter 5, the cost and availability of financing help determine the demand for and supply of real estate and therefore affect real estate values. The cost of financing includes the rate of interest on the mortgage instrument, deed of trust, or installment contract, and any points, discounts, equity participations, or other charges that the lender requires to increase the effective yield on the loan. The availability of financing includes all nonprice determinants that affect the ability of the borrower to obtain financing, including the loan-to-value ratio, the housing expense-to-income ratio required by a lender on single family homes, and the debt-service coverage and breakeven ratios required by a lender on income-producing properties. The cost and availability of financing typically move together; that is, high interest rates and other costs usually are accompanied by a decrease in the availability of credit.

The cost and availability of credit for real estate financing affect both the quantity and quality of the real estate demanded and supplied. In times of high interest rates and limited availability of mortgage funds, households that would have been in the homeownership market find that their incomes cannot support the required housing expense. Purchases are delayed and smaller homes with fewer amenities are bought. The cost of land-development financing and construction financing is reflected in the higher prices asked for single family homes; the result is a further reduction in the quantity demanded. The rental market is affected by the demand pressures of households that remain as renters and by the high cost of supplying new units, which in part results from financing costs. Occupancy rates and rents rise under these conditions. Businesses attempt to pass on their higher occupancy costs to customers by increasing the prices of products or services. If they are unable to recover the increased occupancy cost fully, the quantity of commercial and individual space demanded is reduced. The effects of financing costs on the demand for and supply of real estate ultimately are reflected in the value of the properties.

Secondary Sources of General Data

General data necessary for the appraisal of real property are available from a wide variety of sources. A substantial amount of information is compiled and disseminated by agencies of the federal, state, and local governments. Other sources include trade associations and private business enterprises.

The largest body of data comes from the federal government. The *Economic Report of the President,* published by the Council of Economic Advisors, includes data and analysis of housing starts, financing, and so forth. The *Federal Reserve Bulletin* and *Historical Chart Book,* published by the Federal Reserve Board, give information on the gross national product, national income, mortgage markets, interest rates, and other financial statistics; installment credit; sources of funds; business activity; labor force, employment, and industrial production; housing and construction; and international finance. The National Office of Vital Statistics compiles statistics on birth and death rates.

The U.S. Department of Commerce, Bureau of the Census, publishes the *Census of Population,* the *Census of Housing,* the *Census of Manufacturers,* the *Census of Agriculture,* the *Annual Housing Survey,* the *Statistical Abstract of the United States,* and various series on current population, population estimates, and population projections; consumer income; and housing completions, housing authorized by permits, and other housing statistics. These publications provide detailed characteristics of population and housing for the nation, states, counties, standard metropolitan statistical areas (SMSAs), municipalities, census tracts, and blocks in metropolitan areas. They also include interim reports on selected population, income, and housing data.

U.S. Department of Commerce, Bureau of Economic Analysis, publishes the *Survey of Current Business.* This is a source for such data as the consumer price index, the wholesale price index, mortgage debt, and the value of new construction. The U.S. Department of Housing and Urban Development issues reports on FHA starts, financing, and housing programs administered by the department. It also disseminates FHA post office vacancy surveys for selected metropolitan areas. The U.S. Department of Labor, Bureau of Labor Statistics, publishes the *Monthly Labor Review,* which lists the consumer price index, wholesale prices, and monthly and annual employment and earnings.

On the state and local levels, departments of development, local and regional planning agencies, and regional or metropolitan transportation authorities can provide an appraiser with data on population, households, employment, master plans, present and future utility, and transportation systems. They also have directories of manufacturers that include, by county, the names of firms, their products, and their employment figures.

Each state's *Bureau of Employment Service* is a source of county data on employment, unemployment, and wage rates. Chambers of commerce provide a variety of information on local population, households, employment, and industry, which they often obtain from other secondary sources such as the census.

Trade associations can also be very useful data sources. The National Association of Realtors compiles information on existing home sales for the nation as a whole and for separate regions. Its numerous publications, as well as those of its affiliates, provide numerous data useful to appraisers. The National Association of Homebuilders disseminates information on new housing starts and prices, construction costs, and financing.

Sales and Marketing Management Magazine, Survey of Buying Power, gives information on households, income distribution, and retail sales by county and selected cities.

Other useful data can be gathered from such private sources as banks, utility companies, university research centers, private advisory firms, multiple listing services, and cost services such as E. H. Boeckh and Marshall Valuation Service. These can be used for a variety of information on bank debt; department store sales; employment indicators; land prices; corporate business indicators; mortgage money costs; wage rates; construction costs; deeds; mortgage recordings; and the installation of gas, electrical, and water meters.

General data are an important component of an appraiser's office files. Cataloging and cross-indexing data obtained from sources such as those listed above provide rapid access to important information. In addition, some general data, including multiple listing information and census data, are amenable to computer storage and retrieval. Local or regional planning and development agencies may have computerized information on housing inventory, housing vacancies, demolitions and conversions, commercial construction, household incomes, new land use by zoning classification, population and demographics, and housing forecasts by geographic area.

Appraisers may avail themselves of computerized data in several ways. Some offices are equipped with sophisticated computer equipment and extensive software. Often, software packages containing data required for a specific assignment can be purchased from a central data source. The census data for a specific geographic area relevant to a housing demand analysis, for instance, might be purchased from a depository of that data. Appraisers who do not own computer systems can arrange to timeshare both hardware and software.

Summary

General data can be primary or secondary data and microdata or macrodata. Data collected by an appraiser from original sources are primary data; data obtained from published sources or prior studies are secondary data. When the information concerns national or local income, population, and employment figures, it is macrodata and is usually obtained from secondary sources. When the information is disaggregated—concerned with targeted portions of a population or community—it is microdata.

General data reflect the influences on property value that result from the social, economic, government, and environmental forces operating outside the property. These influences include the demographic characteristics of the population; government and societal attitudes affecting land use, transportation, and the environment; conditions influencing city growth and structure; and economic trends at the international, national, and local levels.

Appraisers should understand the various elements that contribute to market price and market value. In the estimation of market value, an appraiser examines rents, prices, operating expenses, rates of return on investment and equity, mortgage interest rates and terms, the reproduction cost of the structure, and other market-determined variables that reflect the impact of social, economic, government, and environmental forces. These data are objective and relatively precise. The final appraisal conclusion should reflect all elements that have a demonstrable impact on the appraisal problem and exclude any that are conjectural, remote, biased, or speculative. Accurate appraisal conclusions depend on an appraiser's ability to interpret data and judge its applicability to the appraisal problem.

The nature of the appraisal problem dictates the scope of the data included in the value estimate. Although appraisal conclusions should rely only on data that have a reasonably direct bearing on the subject property, it is important to understand the general economic climate in which realty transactions occur. To understand how national and global trends affect value, an appraiser studies how the region and community will participate in these trends. General data on the local and regional economy are most significant when the property competes in a restricted geographic market.

Chapter 7

Analysis of Neighborhoods and Districts

Neighborhood analysis provides a bridge between the analysis of general influences on all property values and the study of a particular subject property. The goal of neighborhood analysis is to determine how the operation of social, economic, government, and environmental forces influence property values in the specific area in which the subject property is located.

Neighborhood boundaries are identified by determining the area in which the forces operate on properties in the same way that they operate on the property being appraised. Although a neighborhood may be seen as a grouping of properties within physical boundaries, these physical boundaries are less significant than are the boundaries of influences on property values, even though influences may end at observable physical points.

The area most closely surrounding the subject property, whether it contains residential properties only or a mixture of commercial and residential properties, is called a *neighborhood*. A neighborhood may also designate an area comprised solely of commercial or industrial properties, although the term *district* is often used for these properties. Consequently, a specific definition of *a neighborhood or a district is a grouping of complementary land uses affected by similar operation of the four forces that affect property value.*

To identify the neighborhood boundaries of a subject property, an appraiser investigates the property's surroundings. Such an investigation begins with the subject property and proceeds outward to ascertain all relevant actual and potential influences on the property's value that can be attributed to its location. The appraiser extends the geographic search far enough so that all influences the market perceives as affecting the value of the subject property become included in the boundaries. This search reveals the proximate and relevant influences on the property being appraised and it shows how influences on the property are related to the same influences operating on other properties in the neighborhood. At the physical points where the appraiser's investigation reveals no value-affecting influences on the subject and surrounding properties, the subject property's neighborhood effectively ends. Conclusions regarding a neighborhood's impact on the subject property's value are significant only when the neighborhood boundaries are properly delineated in terms of the extent of value influences on the subject property. Thus, neighborhood analysis must be adequately thorough so that an appraiser can make meaningful conclusions about the neighborhood's relative desirability, value trend, and impact on the subject property's future desirability and, thus, present value.

Neighborhood analysis provides a framework, or context, in which property value is estimated. It identifies and limits the area for analysis and establishes potential limits of search for data to be used in applying the three approaches to value. Identification of the neighborhood enables the appraiser to determine whether comparable properties to be used in the valuation process are located in or outside the neighborhood. The sale prices of comparable properties in the neighborhood usually require little or no adjustment for location.

Neighborhood analysis also helps an appraiser to determine change or stability in an area. The analysis provides a basis for determining the stage that properties may be at in a neighborhood's life cycle and may indicate future land uses and value trends for the properties.

Objectivity in Neighborhood Analysis

An appraiser must be objective when identifying and discussing neighborhood conditions and trends that enhance or detract from property values. The appraiser should describe specifically and impartially any special amenities or detrimental conditions. For example, general reference to a presumed "pride of ownership" (or the lack thereof) is too vague and subjective to be indicative of an actual effect on property values. Such a reference requires the ascribing of motives and attitudes to people, which should be avoided by appraisers.

An appraiser's findings concerning neighborhood conditions and their effects on property values are considered by buyers, sellers, brokers, lenders, courts, arbiters, public officials, and other decision makers or advisers. Thus, the appraiser is often called on to provide specific evidence of neighborhood conditions and trends and to explain the findings in a written report. By using photographs and detailed field notes, an appraiser can recall important evidence and verify the facts in the analysis.

An appraiser should avoid making generalizations about the desirability of particular types of neighborhoods. Older urban neighborhoods, as well as newer suburban subdivisions, can attract a variety of residents. Neighborhood trends are responsive to a variety of influences; each should be analyzed thoroughly and objectively.

Neighborhoods

A neighborhood is an area that usually has distinguishing characteristics. A neighborhood may be a section of a community or an entire community. One subdivision may be one neighborhood, while another neighborhood may be comprised of all or parts of two or more subdivisions. In larger towns and cities, the neighborhood usually consists of a portion of the larger urban area, whereas the entire community may constitute the neighborhood in small towns and cities. Neighborhood occupants usually have an observable commonality of interests. Obviously, no grouping of inhabitants, buildings, or business enterprises can possess identical features or attributes; therefore, a neighborhood is *relatively* uniform. That is, a neighborhood exhibits a greater degree of commonality than the larger area.

Boundaries

A neighborhood's boundaries map the physical area that exerts relevant influences on a subject property's value. The boundaries may coincide with changes in prevailing land use, occupant characteristics, or physical characteristics, such as structures, street patterns, terrain, vegetation, and lot sizes. Because changes in natural or physical features often coincide with the change from one neighborhood area to another, features such as transportation arteries (highways, major streets, railroads), bodies of water (rivers, lakes, streams), and changes in elevation (hills, mountains, cliffs, valleys) often constitute neighborhood boundaries.

The neighborhood of a house in a homogeneous subdivision usually ends when the land uses change to commercial, apartment, or industrial. However, houses in the same subdivision that are in closer proximity to these different land uses may be influenced by them, and therefore the neighborhood of these houses might not end at these points.

Within a neighborhood are often minor differences that define a smaller area—the immediate neighborhood. The subject property ordinarily cannot be isolated from the characteristics of the most proximate properties. Therefore, an appraiser should pay special attention to the subject property's immediate neighborhood while analyzing the larger neighborhood.

Properties in closest proximity to one another tend to exert the greatest influence on value. Any property, even one that is commercial, that is on the fringe of a residential district and near attractive, well-maintained, and desirable properties tends to progress in value. The same property, near less attractive, well-maintained, and desirable properties tends to regress in value.

Because legal, political, and economic jurisdictions collect data for standardized or statistically predefined areas, information about income and educational levels may be available for cities, counties, tax districts, census tracts, or special enumeration districts. Although such data may be relevant, they rarely conform to neighborhood boundaries that are identified for property valuation. An appraiser who uses secondary data to help identify neighborhood boundaries should verify and supplement the data by primary research.

An appraiser should follow several steps when identifying a neighborhood's boundaries.

1. *Inspection of the area's physical characteristics.* An appraiser should drive around the area to develop a sense of the area, particularly the degree of similarity in land uses, types of structures, architectural styles, and maintenance and upkeep. On a map of the area, an appraiser should note points where these characteristics show perceptible changes and should note any physical barriers, such as major streets, hills, rivers, and railroads, that coincide with such changes.

2. *Drawing preliminary boundaries on a map.* An appraiser should draw lines that connect the points where physical characteristics change. The appraiser should identify the streets, hills, rivers, railroads, and so forth, that coincide with or that are near the shifts in physical characteristics.

3. *Testing preliminary boundaries against socioeconomic characteristics of the area's population.* If possible, an appraiser should obtain accurate data concerning the ages, occupations, incomes, and educational levels of neighborhood occupants. Such data are collected every 10 years by the Bureau of the Census, U.S. Department of Commerce. U.S. Census of Population data that pertain to population and housing characteristics, employment, and earnings are available.

Reliable data may also be available from local chambers of commerce, universities, and research organizations. In unusual cases, the appraiser may also consider sampling the population of the area to obtain an indication of the relevant characteristics.

The appraiser may informally interview neighborhood occupants, business persons, brokers, and community representatives to determine their perceptions about how far the neighborhood extends.

Districts

Multifamily, commercial, and industrial areas are generally referred to as districts, not neighborhoods. Apartment, commercial, and industrial districts are usually clearly recognizable by homogeneous land use. Each district is subject to value influences that are different from those for other districts or for single family neighborhoods. Sometimes an appraiser may have to identify a district more precisely than what is suggested by the boundaries created by land use alone. Variations in the type of the dominant land use, in rent and occupancy levels, in the credit strength of occupants, and in the ages of buildings can signal the need to establish more limited boundaries for the subject property's relevant neighborhood.

Change

An appraiser conducts a neighborhood analysis to determine how value trends in the subject property may be similar to or different from value trends in the neighborhood. When value trends in the neighborhood are moving upward, an appraiser must determine whether the subject property's value can be expected to exceed, lag, or be about equal to the neighborhood trend. The appraiser also analyzes the value of the subject property relative to stable or downward neighborhood value trends.

In analyzing neighborhoods, appraisers are guided by all appraisal principles. The principles and the concept of highest and best use tend to explain the way in which neighborhoods form, develop, stabilize, or decline in size, desirability, and relative values.

In using a neighborhood analysis, an appraiser recognizes the propensity for change and attempts to determine how a neighborhood may be changing. Appraisers usually consider historic trends of urban growth and composition when analyzing patterns of change in neighborhoods. Just as a dwelling is influenced by the surrounding residential neighborhood, the neighborhood is influenced by the surrounding community or metropolitan area. Each urban area responds to its own local demands for urban space. A careful analysis can reveal the general trends and directions of growth, decay, and renewal.

Stages of a Neighborhood

A neighborhood's life cycle usually consists of stages:

1. Growth—a period during which the neighborhood gains public favor and acceptance

2. Stability—a period of equilibrium without marked gains or losses

3. Decline—a period of diminishing demand

4. Revitalization—a period of renewal, modernization, and increasing demand

Although the stages describe a neighborhood's evolution in a general way, they should not be overemphasized as providing guidelines to neighborhood trends. Many neighborhoods are stable for very long periods of time, and decline is hardly imminent in all older neighborhoods. Unless caused by the advent of some specific external influence—a new highway that changes traffic patterns, for example—decline may be at a barely perceptible rate and subject to interruption by changing use or revival of demand. Thus, there is no definite life expectancy for a neighborhood. Moreover, the stages are not always sequential. At any time in the cycle, major changes can occur, which interrupt the order of the cycle's stages. For example, a neighborhood that is in a stage of growth may decline precipitously rather than stabilize.

After a period of decline, a neighborhood may undergo a period of transition to other land uses or its life cycle may begin again due to revitalization. Neighborhood revitalization often results from organized rebuilding or restoration. It may also be the result of a natural rekindling of demand. The rebirth of an older inner city neighborhood, for example, may occur simply because of changing preferences and lifestyles without a planned renewal program.

Evidence of Change

An appraiser often detects neighborhood change, or transition, by variations within the neighborhood. For example, a neighborhood in which some homes are well maintained and others are not may indicate that the neighborhood is in the process of decline or of revitalization. The introduction of different uses, such as rooming houses or offices, into a single family residential neighborhood indicates a possible change. These new uses may indicate potential increases or decreases in the neighborhood's property values.

The changes in one neighborhood are usually influenced by changes occurring in others and in the larger area of influence. In any relatively stable city, for example, the rapid growth of one neighborhood or district may adversely affect a competitive neighborhood or district. A city's growth may reach the point where accessibility to the center from the more remote districts is difficult. In such instances, the establishment of new, competing business centers may better serve the needs of the outlying neighborhoods. Thus, commercial subcenters come into being; the city's pattern becomes complex.

Suburban business centers may adversely affect the central business district. Newer residential areas may affect the old. The added supply of new homes may induce shifts from old to new, thereby placing older homes on the market. This increased supply may affect the market value of all homes in the area. If the location of a neighborhood makes it ripe for conversion to a more intensive use, the existing improvements may undergo extensive remodeling or may be torn down to make way for redevelopment.

The growth of the city results in changes in the utility of both vacant and improved parcels of real estate. Utility may be increased or decreased, and changes in value may result. No neighborhood is absolutely static. Changes may be proceeding at a slow pace (which is usual), but they are always present.

Gentrification and Displacement

A relatively recent neighborhood phenomenon, whereby middle- and upper-income families and single persons purchase properties and renovate or rehabilitate them and existing residents become displaced, is called *gentrification*. The existing residents are often lower-income

Distinct change in land use with arterial and natural boundaries

groups, who moved into certain older neighborhoods in various cities when middle- and upper-income groups either left or did not move in because they found the neighborhoods unappealing and unattractive. Often two or more households would occupy what was formerly a single family residence. Such neighborhoods often became blighted.

Gentrification appears to be the result of the preponderance of smaller families and single persons in metropolitan areas and especially those who enjoy living in proximity to urban activities.

Analysis of Value-Influencing Forces

Appraisers analyze neighborhoods by examining the forces that influence value, which are manifested in analogous characteristics of the neighborhood. Thus, such characteristics reveal the influences that have affected value trends in the past and may affect values in the future.

Social Considerations

Although race, religion, color, and national origin are social characteristics, they have no relationship to real estate values. Social considerations in neighborhood analysis involve characteristics of neighborhood

Variety of land uses in residential neighborhood

occupants that rarely affect value. Relevant characteristics may be the availability and quality of services, including recreation and shopping.

The motivations occupants have for living or working in the area may help reveal the neighborhood's scope. Occupants are attracted to a locale for reasons such as status, physical environment, availability of services, affordability, and convenience.

Although a certain degree of similarity is typical in neighborhoods, occupants of some neighborhoods prefer much social heterogeneity. Such occupants may share a preference for social interaction with persons of different economic and social backgrounds. A changing society does not contain a universal set of social standards. Considerations that are relevant in one neighborhood may be irrelevant in another. Thus, in performing a neighborhood analysis, an appraiser identifies relevant characteristics and influences that are reflected in market actions.

The appraiser may identify and even describe a neighborhood's social characteristics. The appraiser should be aware that it is extremely difficult to determine the characteristics that have the greatest influence on property values in the neighborhood, inasmuch as they tend to overlap. The relative overall desirability of the social characteristics of the subject neighborhood with those of other, competing neighborhoods is, of course, found in their respective price levels.

The important social characteristics that the market considers in neighborhood analysis include

1. Population density, particularly important in commercial neighborhoods

2. Occupant educational levels, particularly important in industrial districts

3. Occupant age levels, particularly important in residential neighborhoods

4. Occupant employment types, including types of unemployment

5. Extent or absence of crime

6. Extent or absence of litter

7. Quality of educational, medical, social, recreational, cultural, and commercial services

8. Community or neighborhood organizations (e.g., improvement associations, block clubs, crime watch groups)

It is difficult, if not impossible, to ascertain and quantify accurately the social preferences of the many people who comprise a given market and to attempt to relate the preferences to an effect on value. Accordingly, an appraiser should not place too much reliance on social influences when arriving at a value conclusion. From an appraiser's viewpoint, the social characteristics of a residential neighborhood are significant only insofar as they are considered by the buying public and can be objectively and accurately analyzed by the appraiser. An appraiser is sensitive to social changes but performs an unbiased neighborhood analysis.

Economic Considerations

Economic considerations involve the financial capacity of a neighborhood's occupants to rent or own property, to maintain it in an attractive and desirable condition, and to renovate or rehabilitate it when needed. The economic characteristics of the occupants and the physical characteristics of the area and of individual properties may indicate the relative financial strength of area occupants and the extent to which the strength is translated into neighborhood development and upkeep.

Ownership and rental data provide clues to such financial capability. Income levels also are revealed by recent census information, newspaper surveys, and private studies. Such information indicates the price levels occupants can afford for the rental or purchase of property.

Vacancy statistics are frequently compiled by newspapers, the U.S. Postal Service, and other fact-finding agencies. Other significant statistics include the quantity of classified newspaper advertising of properties for rent or sale. Such data help an appraiser to estimate the strength of demand and the extent of supply.

The existence of vacant lots or acreage suitable for development may forecast construction activity or indicate a lack of demand. Current construction creates trends that affect the value of existing improvements. A careful study of the trends helps an appraiser to rate the probable future desirability of an area.

Block-by-block information helps pinpoint directional trends of growth. A neighborhood may be developing, static, declining, or in a period of revitalization. The trend may be a local phenomenon or may affect the entire community. A change in the economic base on which a community depends (e.g., the addition or loss of a major industry) is frequently reflected in the rate of population growth or decline. Sales demand and rental occupancy levels tend to remain strong when population is growing and to lag when population is declining.

In analyzing a neighborhood's economic characteristics, an appraiser modifies the general analytic procedure to include the identification and analysis of economic trends—preferably over a three- to five-year period. The appraiser then decides which economic variables significantly determine value differences among neighborhoods, and finally compares current economic characteristics between competing neighborhoods.

Economic characteristics that an appraiser may consider include

1. Income levels

2. Extent of occupant ownership

3. Rent levels of rental properties

4. Property value levels

5. Vacancy rates for various types of property

6. Development and construction

7. Effective ages of properties

8. Changes in property use

Government Considerations

Government considerations involve the laws, regulations, and taxes impinging on a neighborhood's properties. They also include administration and enforcement activities that are associated with such constraints. Certain buyers desire neighborhoods that are subject to effective zoning laws, building codes, and housing and sanitary codes. The property tax burden relative to benefits provided and relative to taxes and benefits provided in other neighborhoods are also considered. Enforcement of the various codes, regulations, and restrictions should be equitable and effective. An appraiser gathers data pertinent to government characteristics in the neighborhood and compares them with those in other, competing neighborhoods.

Tax burdens can vary significantly among areas, and variations in taxes are significant in making comparisons. Sometimes, special assessment levels in a certain location become so heavy that they seriously affect the marketability of property. Benefits that result from special assessments may not enhance the obtainable sale price in proportion to their cost; nevertheless, the cost must be offset. As a rule, properties that are otherwise comparable to those not subject to special assessments can be expected to bring a lower sale price. For example, assume that two identical properties, located in the same block on different streets, are each worth $75,000 if free of encumbrances. If, however, one were subject to a $1,000 special assessment lien, its market value, subject to the lien, may be $74,000 despite that an uninformed buyer might not discount for the lien.

Divergent tax rates may also affect market value. Local taxes may favor or discriminate against certain property types. Thus, it is advisable for an appraiser to examine the local structure of assessed values and tax rates to compare the burdens created by various forms of taxes and their apparent effect on the values of different types of real estate.

Counties or cities may have authority to impose such optional taxes as sales and earnings taxes on residents. When variations exist among competing communities in the sales and local earnings taxes, the relative desirability of the communities may be affected. Such variations are often more significant to commercial and industrial real estate marketability, and therefore values, than are real estate taxes.

Most communities have enacted detailed zoning ordinances, which are designed to implement an area's comprehensive plan. Zoning laws typically identify zones or districts in which certain land uses are permitted and others are prohibited. The broadest categories of zones are residential, which might be indicated by R; commercial, indicated by C; and industrial, indicated by I. The categories are further divided into subcategories, such as Rla for only detached, single family residences that must be constructed on lots of a specified minimum size, shape, and frontage. Rlb may allow smaller lots, while R2 may allow duplexes. R3 might designate low-density apartments. The zoning code for a moderate-sized city may contain several hundred pages identifying and explaining the various zones. An appraiser should examine the relevant zoning requirements for the neighborhood and attempt to assess their adequacy and enforcement provisions.

Somewhat similar to certain government regulations are private restrictions that are placed on land use by private owners through provisions in deeds or plat recordings. Such restrictions deal with lot and building sizes in a subdivision, architectural style, uses, and other matters. An appraiser should make certain that private restrictions do not limit property uses inordinately, as compared with other neighborhoods. In the absence of zoning, an appraiser should determine if the restrictions are adequate to protect long-term property values.

Government characteristics to be considered include

1. Tax burden relative to services provided, as compared with other neighborhoods in the community

2. Special assessments

3. Zoning, building, and housing codes

4. Quality of fire and police protection and other government-provided services

Environmental Considerations

Environmental considerations consist of any natural or man-made features that are contained in or affect the neighborhood and the neighborhood's graphic location. Important environmental considerations include building size, type, density, and maintenance; topographical features; open space; nuisances and hazards emanating from nearby facilities such as shopping centers, factories, and schools; adequacy of public utilities, such as street lights, sewers, and electricity; existence and upkeep of vacant lots; general maintenance; street pattern, width, and maintenance; and the attractiveness and safety of routes that enter and exit from the neighborhood. An appraiser should be aware of all such physical features.

Due to excessive or deficient cost, quality, or size relative to their sites and surrounding properties, certain buildings may be overimprovements or underimprovements. For example, a six-bedroom, four-bathroom house in an area of three-bedroom, one-bath houses might be an overimprovement, or it might be the first of a trend toward larger homes in the area. Overimprovements usually are worth less than cost new. Thus, an appraiser should consider whether the subject property is overimproved or underimproved.

Topographical features can have positive or negative impacts on neighborhood property values. The presence of a lake or river, a bay or swamp, or a hilly area in or contiguous to a neighborhood may endow an area with a scenic advantage uncommon in other sections. A hill may mean little in a mountainous area, but an elevated or wooded section in a predominantly flat area could enhance property value.

Physical environmental features

Such features may also be disadvantageous. A river subject to severe flooding would cause the value of homes along its banks to reflect the risk from such a hazard. Topographical conditions can endow a neighborhood with protection against or can expose it to damage from wind, fog, or flood. A river, lake, or park may serve as a buffer between a residential district and commercial or industrial enterprises.

An excessive volume of vehicular traffic or odors, smoke, dust, and noise from commercial or manufacturing enterprises limits a residential neighborhood's desirability.

Provisions for gas, electricity, water, telephone service, and storm and sanitary sewers are essential to meet the standard of living in municipal areas. A deficiency in any of these services tends to decrease values in a neighborhood. The availability of utilites affects the direction and timing of new neighborhood growth or development.

A neighborhood's environmental characteristics cannot be judged on an absolute scale. They must be judged in comparison with those of other, competing neighborhoods. Do the terrain, vegetation, street pattern, structural density, property maintenance and upkeep, public utilities, and so forth, of one neighborhood render it more or less favorable than other neighborhoods? Further, what is the relative desirability of the neighborhood's location?

Location is the time-distance relationships, or linkages, between a property or neighborhood and all other possible origins and destinations of people going to or coming from the property or neighborhood. Time and distance are measures of relative access. Usually, all neighborhood properties have the same or highly similar locational relationships with common origins and destinations. Such relationships are graphically depicted in Figure 7.1.

To analyze the impact of location in a neighborhood, an appraiser must identify the important linkages and measure their time-distances by the most commonly used types of transportation. The most suitable type of transportation largely depends on the preferences and needs

Figure 7.1 Locations of Neighborhood Properties

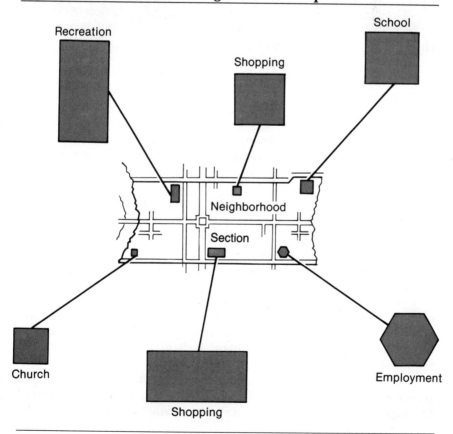

of neighborhood occupants. It is not enough to note that transportation exists; the type of service provided and how it relates to the needs of occupants must be considered.

Linkages must be judged in terms of how well they serve the typical users of real estate in the neighborhood. For example, in analyzing a single family residential neighborhood, an appraiser considers the places to which typical occupants need to commute. If adequate facilities are not available for certain necessary linkages, such as schools or shopping, the neighborhood would not be regarded as favorable relative to competing neighborhoods that have better linkages. For single family residential neighborhoods, linkages with schools, grocery stores, and employment centers are usually the most important. Linkages with recreational facilities, houses of worship, restaurants, and stores that do not sell food are usually somewhat less important. When current zoning ordinances do not restrict change from the present land use, or when change in the predominant land use is evident, an appraiser may need to determine linkages in terms of the current and the anticipated predominant land use in the neighborhood.

Public transportation is crucial for the numerous people who do not own automobiles or prefer not to use them during the day or week. Thus, residential properties in remote sections or areas that have slow and infrequent public transportation may command lower rentals and prices than do properties that are more conveniently located or that have better service.

Distance from public transportation is considered in relation to the people who are to be served by it. Although in the past, public transportation was not a primary consideration in areas where most families own two or more cars, high energy costs and emphasis on public transportation's ecological advantages and convenience make it a potentially important consideration in such areas. Urban apartment dwellers usually prefer to be within convenient walking distance of public transportation.

An appraiser's study of neighborhood transportation facilities considers the territory through which users must pass. People dislike poorly lighted streets and rundown areas. Generally, the closer a property is to good public transportation, the wider is its market.

An appraiser also compares linkages of the subject neighborhood with those of other, competing neighborhoods. In this way, the appraiser determines how favorably or unfavorably the subject neighborhood compares with similar neighborhoods whose properties would be in the same market.

Market perceptions regarding the desirability of location in different neighborhoods can be studied through an analysis of comparable sales. Dollar and percentage differences among sale prices for similar properties in different locations can provide a basis for this analysis.

Important environmental characteristics that an appraiser considers in a neighborhood analysis include

1. Land use pattern

2. Lot size and shape

3. Terrain and vegetation

4. Street patterns and width

5. Density of structures and open space

6. Property maintenance and upkeep

7. Availability and quality of utilities

8. Nuisances and hazards, such as odors, noises, vibrations, fog, smoke, or smog

9. Access to public transportation

10. Access to schools

11. Access to stores and service establishments

12. Access to parks and recreation areas and facilities

13. Access to houses of worship

14. Access to work places

Neighborhood Analysis in Form Reports

Certain organizations and business firms have developed their own appraisal forms. The forms often contain sections in which the appraiser rates and summarizes various elements believed to enhance or detract from value. Probably the most widely used is the FHLMC and FNMA form for appraisals of properties for which these agencies may purchase the mortgage paper. The section of the form concerning neighborhood analysis is shown in Figure 7.2.

Note that the FNMA-FHLMC form contains a number of items with boxes at their left. By checking the appropriate boxes, an appraiser describes and rates a neighborhood. Although the form includes a number of considerations, it does not report as complete or thorough an analysis as can be accomplished by a narrative report. It is usually fully adequate, and the FNMA-FHLMC form provides space

Figure 7.2 Neighborhood Analysis Section (FHLMC Form 70/FNMA 1004)

NEIGHBORHOOD

Location □ Urban □ Suburban □ Rural
Built Up □ Over 75% □ 25% to 75% □ Under 25%
Growth Rate □ Fully Dev. □ Rapid □ Steady □ Slow
Property Values □ Increasing □ Stable □ Declining
Demand/Supply □ Shortage □ In Balance □ Over Supply
Marketing Time □ Under 3 Mos. □ 4–6 Mos. □ Over 6 Mos.

Present Land Use ____ % 1 Family ____ % 2–4 Family ____ % Apts. ____ % Condo ____ % Commercial
____ % Industrial ____ % Vacant ____ %

Change in Present Land Use □ Not Likely □ Likely (*) □ Taking Place (*)
(*) From _____ To _____

Predominant Occupancy □ Owner □ Tenant ____ % Vacant
Single Family Price Range $ _____ to $ _____ Predominant Value $ _____
Single Family Age _____ yrs to ____ yrs Predominant Age _____ yrs

	Good	Avg.	Fair	Poor
Employment Stability	□	□	□	□
Convenience to Employment	□	□	□	□
Convenience to Shopping	□	□	□	□
Convenience to Schools	□	□	□	□
Adequacy of Public Transportation	□	□	□	□
Recreational Facilities	□	□	□	□
Adequacy of Utilities	□	□	□	□
Property Compatibility	□	□	□	□
Protection from Detrimental Conditions	□	□	□	□
Police and Fire Protection	□	□	□	□
General Appearance of Properties	□	□	□	□
Appeal to Market	□	□	□	□

Note: FHLMC/FNMA do not consider the racial composition of the neighborhood to be a relevant factor and it must not be considered in the appraisal.

Comments including those factors, favorable or unfavorable, affecting marketability (e.g. public parks, schools, view, noise) for additional comments. It does not contain any provision for an analysis other than that applicable for the subject neighborhood, but appraisers are obligated to extend the neighborhood analysis beyond the provisions of the form whenever appropriate.

Districts

Apartment, commercial, industrial, agricultural, and other special districts have unique characteristics that require special considerations. The following sections deal with special considerations that are pertinent to district analysis.

Apartment Districts

In large cities, an apartment district usually covers an extensive area; in smaller cities, the district may be dispersed or limited in size. Apartment design may be multistory, garden, row, or townhouse. Units may be privately owned as cooperatives or condominiums.

Although apartment districts differ somewhat from single family residential areas, they are subject to many similar influences. Thus, an appraiser can outline the characteristics and amenities that affect an apartment district in a manner similar to that applied to a single family residential neighborhood, but with a change of emphasis. In an apartment district, desirability and value may be influenced by

1. Access to work places

2. Transportation service

3. Access to shopping centers and cultural facilities

4. School facilities

5. Neighborhood reputation

6. Residential atmosphere, neighborhood appearance, and protection against unwanted commercial and industrial intrusion

7. Proximity to parks, lakes, rivers, or other natural features

8. Supply of vacant apartment sites that are likely to be built up, with the potential effect of making present accommodations either more or less desirable

9. Parking for tenants and guests

10. Economic status of tenants

11. Vacancy and tenant turnover rate

Such characteristics and other pertinent data form the background for an appraiser's study of rental housing property. In certain cities, statistics are available concerning the supply of apartments, vacancy, and rent levels. When statistics are not available, an appraiser gathers data from primary research.

Commercial Districts

The grouping of stores that influences the use and value of a commercial property being appraised is called a commercial district. A commercial district may be a local grouping along a business street or freeway service road; a development adjacent to a public transportation intersection; a regional or neighborhood center; or a downtown central business district (CBD).

When analyzing a commercial district, an appraiser identifies a commercial district's trade area; that is, the area the stores serve. The commercial district and its property values are affected by influences on the values of the properties surrounding it. The type and character of land uses in close proximity, therefore, affect the commercial district.

Over the past 30 years, trends in population growth, suburbanization, and use of private automobiles have made shopping centers important sources of commercial activity. Until the mid-1970s, inexpensive energy encouraged outward urban development. The commercial activities of large regional shopping centers and community centers began to replace those of many central business districts. Commercial establishments in shopping centers often have gained from an association with complementary establishments, while those in downtown areas and in strip developments have not fared so well. Commercial activity in many downtown areas has declined, although in certain cases this has led to a CBD being brought into the revitalization stage.

Since the mid-1970s, characterized by increased energy costs, outward urban development has slowed. Most new shopping centers have been constructed in smaller cities. The commercial activities in CBDs of certain cities have been revitalized. In an analysis of a commercial district's trade area, an appraiser focuses on the quantity and quality of purchasing power available to the shopping area.

An appraiser also considers other elements, which are

1. Locational considerations, such as time-distance from potential customers, access, highway medians, and traffic signals

2. The 100% location or core of store groupings

3. Direction of visible growth

4. Retailers' inventory, investments, leasehold improvements, and enterprise

5. Availability of land for expansion and customer parking

6. Buying power of trading area; economic trends of contributing residential neighborhood

7. Character and location of existing or anticipated competition

8. Pedestrian or vehicle traffic count

9. Physical characteristics, such as visibility, attractiveness, quality of construction, and property condition

When analyzing local retail groupings that are not in shopping centers, an appraiser also examines the zoning policies that govern the supply of competing sites, studies the reasons for vacancy and business failure, and considers the level of rents compared to current rent levels for stores in new buildings.

Central Business Districts

Central business districts (CBDs) have not experienced the same pattern of growth and development as other commercial areas. Business surveys conducted by the U.S. Department of Commerce show that CBDs have lost commercial establishments and have experienced smaller increases in sales than the average for all commercial districts.[1] Although appraisers should be aware of the general trends for CBDs, they should recognize the efforts toward revitalization of many of them. Downtown merchants, often through downtown development associations, have attempted to revitalize CBDs through improved public transportation, larger parking areas, better access, and coordinated sales promotion programs.

CBDs usually contain several types of operations that reflect several types of land use—retail stores, offices, financial institutions, and entertainment facilities, for example. Retail clothing stores tend to serve the employees of offices. Financial institutions tend to locate in areas containing other financial institutions, and retail establishments of all types tend to locate where large numbers of people work, shop, and reside. Major entertainment and cultural facilities tend to be located in or near CBDs to be accessible to the greatest number of residents of and visitors to a metropolitan area.

An appraiser should recognize that shifting functions in a CBD

---

[1] *Survey of Current Business* (Washington, D.C.: U.S. Department of Commerce, monthly). Biennial supplement is *Business Statistics*.

can lead to changes in land uses and potential increases in real estate values. For example, a shift from commercial to office and entertainment uses may generate additional restaurants, art galleries, and specialty shops in a downtown area.

In assessing the viability of a CBD, an appraiser must consider the sales potential for various commercial products and services and whether the CBD's establishments can attract a particular share. In assessing the viability of a location in a CBD, an appraiser considers which use—office, hotel, retail, entertainment, and so forth—is the most appropriate, based on the subject property's location in the CBD. In many cases, the existing use will be the highest and best use.

Regional Shopping Centers

A regional center contains 40 to 100 or more stores, an extensive parking facility, and more than 250,000 square feet of gross leaseable area. Major tenants of such centers are department stores that offer a full range of merchandise. Regional centers also contain a greater variety and number of the types of stores found in a neighborhood center. A regional center may also have banks; service establishments; medical, dental, and business offices; and theaters.

A regional center's trade area may include several neighborhood centers. Despite competition for certain segments of economic support, neighborhood centers provide services to their immediate areas and may be considered supplementary to, rather than competitive with, the major shopping services provided by a regional center.

Regional centers generate a substantial value for the land occupied and significantly influence the values of surrounding sites and tracts. Generally, they affect adjacent or nearby land favorably by creating a demand for satellite stores, office buildings, and other commercial uses. Moreover, regional centers increase the demand for new single or multifamily residential development.

Community Shopping Centers

A community center is part of the neighborhood it serves. It contains establishments that sell convenience and shopping goods, such as furniture, clothing, and specialty items, and may also contain professional offices (e.g., medical, dental), financial services, and recreational facilities. The principal tenant in such a center usually is a variety or junior deparment store.

A community shopping center usually contains 100,000 to 250,000 square feet of gross leaseable area, which is between the sizes of regional and neighborhood centers.

A community center's customers are usually from an area having a time-distance radius of 10 to 20 minutes' driving time. The viability of such a center depends on the sales potential for the various products and services it offers. The potential is allocated by the market among the various competing establishments in the service area. Sales potentials may be estimated from various surveys of consumer buying patterns, which are conducted by the U.S. Department of Commerce, certain universities, and private and trade organizations. Studying historical patterns and changes in the number and types of competing establishments helps an appraiser to determine the market share of a particular center.

Neighborhood Shopping Centers

A neighborhood shopping center usually contains 10 or more stores, parking, and up to 100,000 square feet of gross leaseable area. The centers serve the day-to-day needs of a limited surrounding and supporting area, and thus contain supermarkets, drug and variety stores, and service establishments. Therefore, such centers are seldom affected seriously by a new regional center. Neighborhood shopping centers must provide easy access and adequate parking. They also should be in a good location and be on or near public transportation routes.

Office Districts

Office districts may consist of several small office buildings or numerous large office buildings in a large city. They may contain offices that primarily house one profession (e.g., medicine, law) or that serve a variety of tenants. They may range from the executive suites of multinational corporations to back offices for small service companies. Many new offices are being developed in office parks.

Professional Office Parks

Office parks that cater to certain industries are popular with firms and customers because they provide good location, easy access, physical attractiveness, and functionalism.

Office parks may contain offices that house members of one or more professions. Service employment has become relatively more important in recent years, and thus office areas for service firms are becoming increasingly popular.

Industrial Districts

Land and building values in an industrial district are influenced by the nature of the district, the labor supply, transportation, the economics of bringing in raw material and of distributing finished products, the political climate, and the availability of utilities. To arrive at an informed conclusion about the value of any industrial property, an appraiser must obtain the pertinent data.

District Characteristics

Industrial districts range from those containing the operations of heavy industry, such as steel plants, foundaries, and chemical companies, to those that serve assembly or other "clean" operations. In most urban areas, heavy- to light-use districts are established by zoning ordinances, which may limit uses and place controls on air pollution, noise levels, and the operations that occur outside buildings.

So-called manufacturing or warehouse districts include older districts, in which obsolete multistory elevator buildings are typical and parking and expansion areas are limited, and newer districts and parks, with modern, one-story buildings. Each such district has a value pattern that reflects the reaction of the market to its location and the characteristics of sites and improvements.

One important influence on land value in such districts is the availability of public utilities, including sanitary and storm sewers and municipal (or well) water. Prevailing levels of real estate and personal property taxes also influence desirability and may be reflected in real estate values.

Availability of labor.   An appraiser ascertains whether a district has an adequate and suitable labor supply and assesses the costs of the supply. A district is desirable only if it can be filled with an adequate and suitable labor supply. The dependence of industry on such a labor supply is reflected by many districts being located near residential areas of workers. Workers are often attracted to a particular plant by special inducements, such as a company cafeteria, other employee facilities, or social activities. The plant's parklike atmosphere may also attract workers.

Availability of materials.   Manufacturing operations require a convenient and economic source of raw or semifinished materials, and facilities for convenient and economic distribution of manufactured products. The desirability of a district or a site largely depends on the means of access to unprocessed raw material.

Distribution facilities.   The size, weight, and nature of a commodity and the distance of shipment determine how the commodity is shipped—by air, rail, truck, or water. Accessibility to major highways, adequate ingress and egress, and on-site parking and maneuver areas are crucial considerations for most manufacturing or warehouse operations.

Agricultural Districts

Although agricultural districts may extend over large areas, their occupants usually share the commonality of socioeconomic characteristics that distinguish neighborhoods. In fact, the extent of social interaction may approach or even exceed that of urban neighborhoods. Agricultural neighhorhoods vary in size, ranging from a portion of a township to several counties.

The most important value-determining influences relate to an individual property rather than an agricultural district because of the distances that separate farms. Nevertheless, the physical features of a district usually are representative of an individual farm and contribute to its desirability. An appraiser considers soil type, crops grown, typical land use, the size of a typical operation in the district, and whether the operation is run by an owner or a tenant to help define an agricultural district.

Grain farm districts usually are characterized by soil types and topography conducive to the growing and harvesting of grain crops, such as corn and wheat. Orchards and groves are another type of farming in which soil and climate combine to create certain crops.

Areas that are not capable of producing cash crops may be adapted to the growing of certain grasses. The boundaries of such areas are related to altitude and climate. Generally, grasslands are used for livestock production.

Dairy neighborhoods are found near the soil that is best for the growing of pasture grasses and hay. Such areas are traversed by highways that lead to marketing centers for farm products. As in any neighborhood, the standard of the farm community depends on government services, such as roads and schools, availability of utilities, and proximity to cultural institutions, markets, and shopping centers.

Specialty Neighborhoods and Districts

Certain areas that contain specialized activities qualify as neighborhoods or districts. An area may be regarded as a district or a neighborhood if it contains a commonality of functions, land uses, or the socioeconomic characteristics of occupants. Although the procedures for analyzing all neighborhoods or districts are similar, the specific characteristics that contribute to desirability and value vary according to function.

Medical Districts

An entire district may be comprised of hospitals, related facilites, and physicians' offices. Medical districts may contain one or more hospitals with related facilities, such as a parking lot and patient services buildings, a number of physicians' offices, and pharmacies. The districts can be found in highly dense urban areas or in less dense, parklike settings.

The desirability and value of a particular property, such as a physicians' office building, depend on whether it is modern and in close proximity to hospitals and other medical offices. In addition to the quality of professional personnel and availability of modern equipment, location and access are also important considerations.

Research and Development Parks

A number of research and development parks contain the research and development departments of larger firms, such as drug, chemical, and computer companies. Other parks cater to firms that completely or partly specialize in research activities. Such firms are usually small and specialize in identifying and developing new products that are typically sold to other firms. Occasionally, a small research firm will retain, develop, and market a new product with considerable success, but in such cases the nature of the firm must shift from research to marketing.

Research and development parks are often sponsored and promoted by universities. Research-oriented firms, or divisions of firms, find that proximity to a university helps provide a convenient source of technical expertise and qualified employees. Universities may be able to sell excess land, provide employment for students and consulting for faculty, and raise an area's level of economic activity.

High Technology Parks

Firms that are engaged in high technology activities often locate in the same area as one another or in parks for the technical expertise that may be available from a university or a research park. Electronics and computer firms have dominated such parks, but firms dealing with space equipment, drugs, cosmetics, and aviation also have offices in them.

Education Districts

Local schools, colleges, and universities may constitute a district if they have more than one building or facility or if they are considered part of the surrounding residential neighborhood. Educational districts may contribute economically, as well as socially and culturally, to the surrounding community. Colleges and universities often attract students far from the local community. The students bring income to the community, and thus contribute to its economic base. Certain universities and colleges in towns and smaller cities provide nearly the entire economic base. Such a district should be easily accessible to the surrounding residential neighborhood.

Summary

An appraiser analyzes neighborhoods and districts to determine how the operation of social, economic, government, and environmental forces influence property values in the specific area in which the subject property is located. The area most closely surrounding the subject property, whether it contains residential properties only or a mixture of commercial and residential properties, is called a neighborhood. A neighborhood may also designate an area comprised solely of commercial or industrial properties, although the term *district* is often used for such properties.

Neighborhoods and districts are characterized by similarity in land use. Further, neighborhoods have distinguishing characteristics. Neighborhood occupants usually have common values and interests. A neighborhood's physical characteristics are usually similar.

The specific variables that contribute to desirability and value differ among the types of neighborhoods and districts. Depending on the type, variables may include population growth; economic status; occupations; community interests; convenience to transportation and to educational, religious, and recreational facilities; road patterns; municipal services; employment opportunites; and business centers. The relative importance of such characteristics changes over time, which reflects changes in lifestyles, social customs, and economic conditions.

Thus, neighborhoods differ greatly and change over time. As neighborhoods change, their utility may increase or decrease, which results in changes in property values. A neighborhood analysis should recognize and interpret such changes. The form and depth of an analysis may vary, but the objective of any analysis is to represent fairly and accurately the considerations of the market.

Chapter 8

Land or Site Description and Analysis

An appraisal assignment may be undertaken to estimate the value of land only or the value of land and improvements. In either case, an appraiser must make a detailed description and analysis of the land. Land itself can be raw or improved. Raw land can be undeveloped or in agricultural use. It might be on an urban fringe and ready for development to residential, commercial, or industrial use, or it might be within a city's limits and have development potential. *When land is improved to the extent that it is ready to be used for the purpose for which it was intended, it is known as a site.* A site can have off-site improvements only, such as sewers, utility lines, access to roads, and so forth, that make it ready for its intended use or development, or it can also have on-site improvements, such as buildings, landscaping, driveways, and the like.

Regardless of the type of property to be appraised, an appraiser describes and analyzes the land or site. *A land or site description is a detailed listing of factual data, including a legal description, other title and record data, and information on pertinent physical characteristics.* A land or site analysis goes further. *A land or site analysis is a careful study of factual data in relation to the neighborhood characteristics that create, enhance, or detract from the utility and marketability of the land or site as compared with competing comparable land or sites.*

To estimate the value of improved real estate, an appraiser analyzes two distinct entities: the land and the improvements. Although the two are joined physically, it is often desirable and even necessary to value them separately. Such separate valuations may be required by the appraisal procedure or for specific purposes, such as

1. Local tax assessments

2. Estimation of building depreciation

3. Application of specific appraisal techniques

4. Establishment of ground rent

5. Eminent domain proceedings

6. Estimation of casualty loss

7. Valuation of agricultural land

One principal objective of a land or site analysis is to gather the data that tend to indicate the highest and best use of the land or site as though vacant and to estimate land value in terms of that use.[1] Whether valuing a site or raw land, an appraiser must assess the highest and best use. When the highest and best use is for agriculture, an appraiser analyzes and values the land for that use principally through applying the sales comparison and income capitalization approaches. When the land's development to urban residential, commercial, or some other use seems likely, an appraiser may use both sales comparison analysis and special techniques of the income and cost approaches.

Purposes of land or site description and analysis are to provide

1. A description of the property being appraised

2. A basis for an analysis of comparable sales

3. A basis for allocating values to land and improvements

4. An understanding of the property being appraised and its present use

5. A foundation for determining the property's highest and best use

This chapter focuses on the description and analysis of the land

---

[1]See Chapter 11 for a full discussion of highest and best use.

component of real property.[2] However, because appraisers typically deal with land that has been improved to some degree, *site* is the term used throughout this chapter except when raw land is specified. The information required for a full site description and analysis is noted and explained, and sources for obtaining this information are presented.

Legal Descriptions

When boundaries of land are created for ownership, the land within the boundaries is often referred to as a parcel, lot, plot, or tract. These terms may refer to all types of improved and unimproved land.

A parcel of land generally refers to any piece of land that may be identified by a common description in one ownership. Thus, every parcel of real estate is unique. To identify parcels adequately, an appraiser uses legal descriptions. A legal description identifies a property in such a way that it cannot be confused with any other property. Because it specifically identifies and locates a parcel of real property, a legal description may be included in an appraisal report. A legal description is usually entered on a deed and may be obtained from a deed held by the owner of the property or from county records.

Three principal methods are used for legally describing real property in the United States. They are the metes and bounds system, the rectangular survey system, and the lot and block system. An appraiser should understand these forms of legal description and should be familiar with the form or forms accepted in the area where the appraisal is done.

Metes and Bounds

Metes and bounds is a survey system that measures and identifies land by describing property boundaries. The system is centuries old, dating back to when property transfers were accomplished by a buyer and a seller walking a property's perimeter and establishing landmarks to identify boundaries. In America, in 1640, a procedure was added: a notice of conveyance was to be publicly disclosed and recorded.

---

[2]Throughout this discussion, the property being appraised is the primary reference. However, the same type of detailed inspection and data gathering are necessary for all comparable properties used in appraisal analysis.

Because the system was used for land transfers when the original 13 colonies were settled, it has continued to be the primary method of describing real property in those 13 states, and eight others have also adopted the method. States using metes and bounds descriptions are Connecticut, Delaware, Georgia, Hawaii, Kentucky, Maine, Maryland, Massachusetts, New Hampshire, New Jersey, New York, North Carolina, Pennsylvania, Rhode Island, South Carolina, Tennessee, Texas, Vermont, Virginia, parts of Ohio, and the District of Columbia.

A metes and bounds description of a parcel of real property describes the property's boundaries in terms of reference points. In following a metes and bounds description, one starts at the point of beginning (POB), the primary survey reference point and one that is tied to adjoining surveys, and moves clockwise through several intermediate reference points until finally returning to the POB. The return is called *closing*, which is necessary to ensure the survey's accuracy.

Bounds describe the POB, which is also the point of return, and all intermediate points. Points are also called monuments, which are reference points such as marked stones, trees, a creek, another property corner, or simply a survey point.

Metes describe the direction one moves from one reference point to another and the distances between points. One moves from one point to another by knowing the *courses* of each point. Courses are degrees, minutes, and seconds of angle from north or south. Thus, when one moves from one point to another, one is moving from the vertex of one angle to the vertex of another.

Distances between angles are measured linerally in feet or meters. Sometimes, though, this measurement between angles is found to be in error. When this happens, the actual distance between points or monuments is measured. Thus, in such cases, actual distance takes precedence over angle measurement, especially in boundary disputes and the like.

Modern times have witnessed more accurate determinations of points, directions, and distances. Uncertainty with regard to points of beginning has largely been eliminated through the use of established benchmarks, which are survey markers set in heavy concrete monuments.

In addition to being the primary method of describing real property in 21 states, the metes and bounds system is often used as a corollary to a system used in other states, the rectangular survey system, especially when describing unusual or odd-shaped parcels of land that cannot be adequately described by the rectangular survey system. (The rectangular survey system is discussed in this chapter, beginning on page 156.)

An example of a metes and bounds description is provided in Figure 8.1.

Figure 8.1   Metes and Bounds System

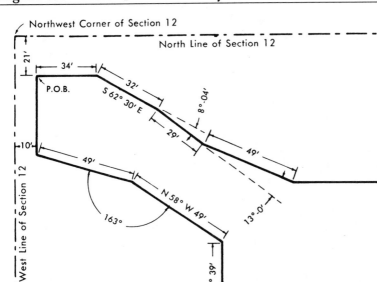

Description of Tract: Commencing at the Northwest corner of Section 12 thence South along the section line 21 feet; thence East 10 feet for a place of beginning; thence continuing East 34 feet; thence South 62 degrees, 30 minutes East 32 feet; thence Southeasterly along a line forming an angle of 8 degrees, 04 minutes to the right with a prolongation of the last described course 29 feet; thence South 13 degrees, 0 minutes to the left with a prolongation of the last described line a distance of 49 feet; thence East to a line parallel with the West line of said Section and 180 feet distant therefrom; thence South on the last described line a distance of 65 feet; thence due West a distance of 82 feet; thence North 1 degree West 39 feet; thence North 58 degrees West a distance of 49 feet; thence Northwesterly along a line forming an angle of 163 degrees as measured from right to left with the last described line a distance of 49 feet; thence North the place of beginning.

Land Grants

A title to land and the resulting legal description ordinarily flow from the land's original recognized ownership.

Land ownership in the various areas of the United States can usually be traced back to the foreign countries that took part in this country's exploration and colonization (England in much of the Atlantic seaboard; France in the Great Lakes region and along the Mississippi River; Russia in Alaska; the Netherlands and Sweden in New York and Delaware, respectively; and Spain in Florida and in large parts of the Southwest and West).

Subsequent land transfers from one government or crown to another were conveyed through wars, treaties, and uncontested annexations. Because proof of title often must go back to the origination of some form of transferable title on the property, studying historical documents has often been the first step in researching land descriptions.

Eventually, land in the United States could be privately owned by individuals and companies. They were given or sold patents or land grants by the various crowns or governments. The descriptions of land contained in many of the patents and grants are still recognized as basic legal descriptions.

Certain land was acquired by private parties who occupied it for long periods and attained squatters rights, referred to legally as adverse possession. These titles usually have been formalized by later patents, decrees, or other operations of law.

One example of a land grant is a Spanish land grant, whereby the king of Spain gave large tracts of land to individuals in what is now the southwestern United States. These grants often had their bases in metes and bounds descriptions. Many of the original grants were made in uninhabited territory, which lacked facilities for detailed suveying. In modern times, the agreed or adjudicated boundaries of these grants have been established and many have been divided into lots. The lots may represent large agricultural tracts or smaller town-type lots and blocks. The rectangular survey system has been extended into some, but not all, land grant areas.

Rectangular Survey System

As the United States began to expand its borders south and west, a newer system of description was needed to facilitate rapid sale of the large tracts of land that the federal government had gained through purchases or through treaties, often secured after war. The government needed to sell the land quickly to create much-needed revenue, and wanted to transact sales in a simple and orderly fashion. Thus, the U.S. Rectangular Survey System was created.

The rectangular survey system, also known as the government survey system, was established by an ordinance of the Second Continental Congress that was passed May 20, 1785. The first public land surveys in the United States were made in Ohio the next year. The system became the principal survey system in most lands west of the Ohio and Mississippi rivers. Also included in the system were the states of Florida, Alabama, and Mississippi. Any land that was settled or colonized prior to the act was not included.

Initial reference points from which to start government surveys were established by the commissioner of the U.S. General Land Office. From each initial point, true east-west and north-south lines were run.

These lines are called the base lines and the principal meridians, respectively. Each meridian has a unique name and is crossed by its own base line. Thus, the base lines and the principal meridians were established to locate land accurately.

The land surveyed under the rectangular survey system is divided by north-south lines, six miles apart, called range lines, and by east-west lines, also six miles apart, called township lines. When the lines intersect, they create rectangles, which are called townships. The standard township is six miles square and contains 36 square miles. When applied to surveying, *township* has two meanings. It is a location on a line north or south of a base line, and it is a square of land that measures six miles by six miles.[3]

The intersection of the base line and the principal meridian is the starting point from which to count east or west on the range lines and north or south on the township lines to locate the desired township in the legal description. Ranges are numbered east and west from the principal meridian, and townships are numbered north and south from the base line.

In Figure 8.2, the shaded township is called Township 4 North, Range 3 East. It is four township rows north of the base line and three range lines east of the principal meridian. If this property were located in northern California, it would be called Township 4 North, Range 3 East, Mt. Diablo Base and Meridian. This would be abbreviated to read T.4N, R.3E., M.D.B.&M.

Townships are further divided into 36 sections. Each standard section is one mile square and contains 640 acres. For a more specific description of a parcel, a section may be divided into quarter-sections and fractions of quarter-sections (see Figure 8.3). Due to the spherical shape of the earth, additional lines called guide meridians are run every 24 miles east and west of the principal meridian. Other lines, called standard parallels, are run every 24 miles north and south of the base line. These correction lines are used to adjust the rectangular townships to fit the curvature of the earth.

Sectioned land descriptions are easily understood and commonly used. The proper writing of the legal description goes from the specific to the general. That is, a legal description begins with the exact site and ends with the base and meridian. The township illustrated in Figure 8.2 was the third one east and the fourth one north from the principal base and meridian; it is called Township 4 North, Range 3 East. Similarly, the proper legal description of the 20-acre parcel located in the southeast part of the section that is illustrated in Figure 8.3 is as follows: The west half of the northeast quarter of the southeast quarter

---

[3]In some states, *township* denotes a political subdivision similar to a county.

Figure 8.2   Government Survey System

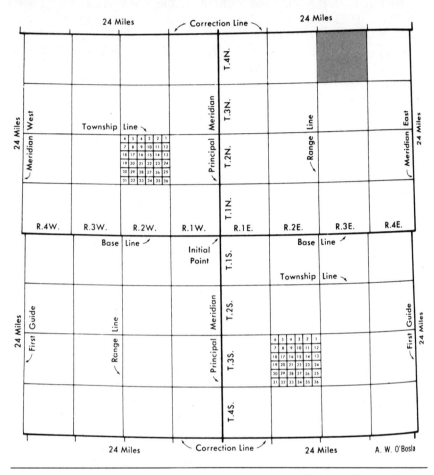

Source: John S. Hoag, *Fundamentals of Land Measurement* (Chicago: Chicago Title Insurance Company, 1976), p. 8. Reprinted through courtesy of Chicago Title Insurance Company.

of Section 10, Township 4 North, Range 3 East, Mt. Diablo Base and Meridian. If this were a full-sized section, the described property would contain 20 acres. However, because many townships are adjusted for the curvature of the earth and some sections are oversized or undersized and do not contain precisely 640 acres, this section may not contain exactly 20 acres.

In addition, the township's northern boundary is not exactly six miles long, due to the curvature of the earth and to the convergence of the meridians. This discrepancy and any others due to errors in measurement are allowed for in the most westerly half-mile of the

Figure 8.3 Division of a Section of Land

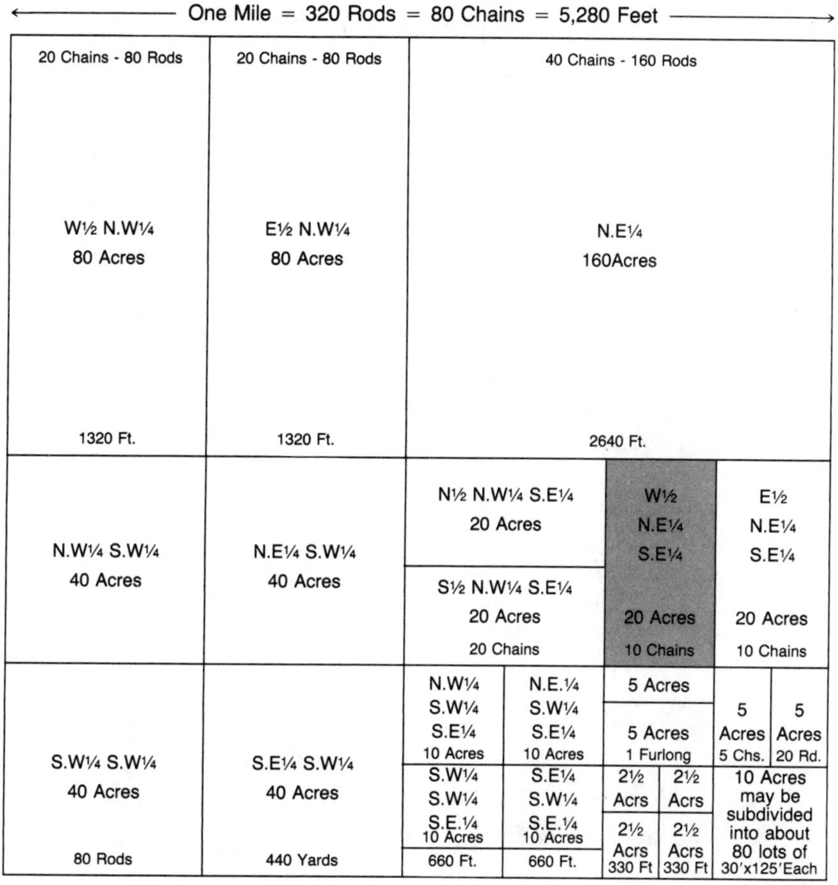
One Mile = 320 Rods = 80 Chains = 5,280 Feet
20 Chains - 80 Rods
20 Chains - 80 Rods
40 Chains - 160 Rods
W½ N.W¼
80 Acres
E½ N.W¼
80 Acres
N.E¼
160Acres
1320 Ft.
1320 Ft.
2640 Ft.
N.W¼ S.W¼
40 Acres
N.E¼ S.W¼
40 Acres
N½ N.W¼ S.E¼
20 Acres
S½ N.W¼ S.E¼
20 Acres
20 Chains
W½
N.E¼
S.E¼
20 Acres
10 Chains
E½
N.E¼
S.E¼
20 Acres
10 Chains
S.W¼ S.W¼
40 Acres
80 Rods
S.E¼ S.W¼
40 Acres
440 Yards
N.W¼
S.W¼
S.E¼
10 Acres
N.E.¼
S.W¼
S.E¼
10 Acres
S.W¼
S.W¼
S.E.¼
10 Acres
S.E¼
S.W¼
S.E.¼
10 Acres
660 Ft.
660 Ft.
5 Acres
5 Acres
1 Furlong
2½
Acrs
2½
Acrs
2½
Acrs
2½
Acrs
330 Ft
330 Ft
5
Acres
5 Chs.
5
Acres
20 Rd.
10 Acres
may be
subdivided
into about
80 lots of
30'x125'Each

township. Other causes for irregular townships are preexisting land grants and boundaries of navigable waters.

Shortages and overages in acreages of sections are usually found in the north and west corners of townships. Fractional sections and government lots are also found where adjustments were necessary.

Geodetic Survey System

As part of the government survey system, the U.S. Department of the Interior Geological Survey maintains a geodetic survey system and publishes detailed topographic maps. These maps, called quadrangles, ordinarily contain the base lines and principal meridians, section lines, and most major topographic features, including towns, roads, bodies of

Figure 8.4   U.S. Department of the Interior Geological Survey

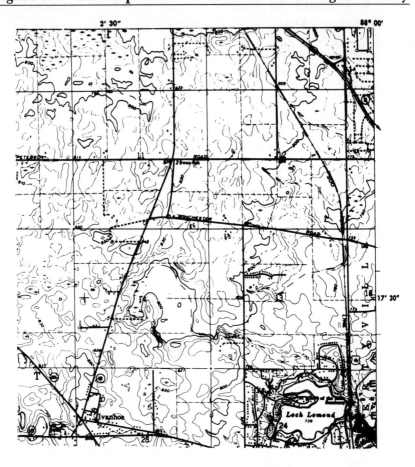

Mapped, edited, and published by the Geological Survey
Control by USGS and USC&GS

Topography by photogrammetric methods from aerial
photographs taken 1958. Field checked 1960

Polyconic projection. 1927 North American datum
10,000-foot grid based on Illinois coordinate system, east zone

This Map Complies with National Map Accuracy Standards
For Sale by U.S. Geological Survey, Washington, D.C.
And by the State Geological Survey, Urbana, Illinois

A Folder Describing Topographic Maps and
Symbols is Available on Request

Reduced from original scale 1:24,000
Contour Interval 10 Feet
Dotted Lines Represent 5-Foot Contours
Datum is Mean Sea Level

APPROXIMATE MEAN
DECLINATION, 1960

water, and contour lines and elevations of land. The maps also include coordinates that are based on latitude and longitude, which are used by engineering surveyors who operate according to national and regional systems of surveying. In addition, benchmarks have been physically placed throughout the country and are accurately depicted on the maps. Figure 8.4 illustrates a topographic map of the geodetic survey system.

Lot and Block System

The lot and block system originated either as an outgrowth of the rectangular survey system or out of the necessity to simplify the locational descriptions of small parcels.

The system began when land developers subdivided land in the rectangular system and provided lot numbers that identified individual sites within blocks. Lots and blocks were numbered in a fashion similar to that in Figure 8.5. The maps of the subdivisions were then filed with local government to establish a public record of their precise locations. Each block could be identified precisely by ground survey or established monuments.

Using the lot and block system in old, unsurveyed communities helped to denote each owner's site or parcel of land. Typically, a surveyor located the boundaries of streets on the ground and drew maps

Figure 8.5   Lot and Block System

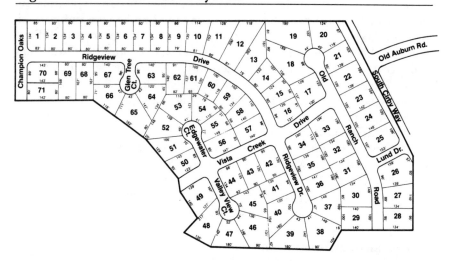

Woodridge Unit #1. Owner: Sunrise Properties, Sacramento, Calif.; engineer: Morton & Pitalo, Sacramento, Calif.

outlining the blocks. Then, by agreement among owners, lot lines were established. Although a precise, measured description was established for each lot, each had a number or a letter that could be referred to, thus simplifying routine transactions.

For example, the description of a lot in a rectangular survey area might be as follows: Lot 5 of Block 18 of Adam's Orangegrove Colony, a Subdivision of the southwest quarter of Section 10, Township 3 North, Range 3 East, Mt. Diablo Base and Meridian.

Tax Parcels

A variation of the lot and block system is the system of laying out tax parcels by various government taxing authorities. Typically, the system of laying out tax parcels works by using a numerical reference to coded map books, which are maintained by the assessing authority. These descriptions then become tax parcels with numbers referring to the map book, the page, the block, and the parcel number. Even though few jurisdictions permit a tax parcel to be used as a legal description of a property for a conveyance, the parcel often serves as a description an appraiser can use when gathering data.

Other Title and Record Data

Prior to making an on-site inspection, an appraiser should accumulate the necessary property data by inspecting published material and public documents. Most jurisdictions have a public office or depository for deeds so that transactions can be documented and made public. This process, known as constructive notice, ensures that interested individuals are able to research and, when necessary, to contest deed transfers. Most county recorder's offices keep index books for land deeds and land mortgages from which the book and page on which the deed is recorded may be found. An appraiser might also find pertinent information in an abstract of title. Official county plat books may also be available in a county auditor's office.

Sometimes, public records do not contain all information about a particular property. Although official documents are the most dependable sources of information, they may be incomplete or not suited to an appraiser's purposes. Helpful support data can be found in land registration systems, land data banks, and assessors' maps.

Ownership Information

A property's legal owner and type of ownership can be ascertained from public records, which are maintained by a county clerk and recorder. Local title or abstract companies may also provide the information.

The most common form of property ownership is ownership in fee simple. If a property is not appraised in fee simple, the elements of title that are to be excluded are to be indicated and carefully analyzed. When an appraiser is asked to estimate the value of a fractional ownership interest, he or she must understand the exact type of legal ownership so that the property rights to be appraised will be accurately defined.

An appraiser also must find out if the property has any outstanding rights, which may affect the property's value. Thus, the appraiser must know the ownership status of surface and subsurface rights. He or she may have access to a title report, abstract of title, or other documentary evidence of property rights to be appraised. Title data indicate easements and restrictions, which may limit the use of the property, and special rights and obligations, such as air rights, water rights, mineral rights, obligation for lateral support, easements for common walls, and others.

Easements, rights-of-way, and private and public restrictions affect property value. Easements may be provided for such uses as electrical transmission lines, underground sewers or tunnels, flowage, aviation routes, roads, walkways, and open space. Some easements or rights-of-way acquired by utilities or public agencies may not be built on for many years. Thus, an appraiser's physical inspection of the property may not disclose any evidence of such use, and he or she should search diligently for information pertaining to any such limitations on ownership rights.

Restrictions cited in the deed may limit the type of building or the types of business that may be conducted or permitted on the property. One typical example is the prohibition of the sale of liquor or gasoline in a certain place. Often, a title report will not go into the details of private restrictions. A copy of the deed or other conveyance should be obtained for thorough identification of the limitations imposed on the property.

Zoning and Land Use

Government regulation on land use and development may originate at the city or county level, but is often subject to regional, state, and federal controls.

An appraiser analyzing zoning matters considers all current regulations and any likelihood of a change in zoning. Usually, a zone calls for a general use, such as residential, commercial, or industrial, and then specifies a more detailed type or density of that use. In addition, regulations may control the height and size of buildings and lot coverage, the number of units allowed, parking requirements, sign requirements, building setbacks, plan lines for future street widenings, and other factors of utmost importance to the highest and best use of the site.

Zoning codes usually identify and define the uses to which a property may be put without reservation or recourse to legal intervention, and then describe the process necessary to obtain nonconforming use permits, variances, and zoning changes, if permissible. Even though zoning ordinances and maps are public records, which are available at zoning offices, an appraiser frequently requests the assistance of planning and zoning staff to help understand the impact of zoning regulations. Often, an appraiser must contact several agencies. Many zoning and land-use restrictions are not listed in a recorded title to a property. Confirmation by controlling agencies may be necessary.

In areas subject to floods, seismic disturbances, and other natural dangers, special zoning regulations impose controls on buildings. Other zoning restrictions govern building location and design in coastal and historic districts.

Probable changes in government regulations are also considerations. For example, a building moratorium or a cessation of land-use applications may be enforced for a stated period, thus possibly delaying the highest and best use of sites in the area.

Public land use or government programs in an area can also affect land uses and values. For example, construction of public parking garages may enhance or detract from a property's value. Requirements for the provision of mixed low- and high-cost housing directly affect land use.

Any reasonable probability of a zoning change must be considered. If the highest and best use of a site requires a zoning change, an appraiser investigates the probability of such a change. An appraiser may obtain pertinent information by interviewing planning and zoning staff or elected officials. An appraiser may also consult a study of patterns of zoning changes to draw conclusions about the likelihood of a change in a particular instance. If a highest and best use recommendation relies on the probability of a zoning change, that probability must be supported by three elements. They are physical practicality, economic feasibility, and political/legal probability.

Assessments and Taxes

Real property taxes in all jurisdictions are based on ad valorem assessments. The records of a county assessor or tax collector provide details pertaining to a property's assessed value and annual tax load. Often, an appraiser obtains the property inventory on which the property assessment is based before conducting the physical inspection and inventory of the property.

Taxation levels are important in considering a property's potential uses. Obtaining the present assessments and tax rate as well as a short history of these rates can help in forming a conclusion about the probable trend in the tax burden. However, assessed values are rarely useful as direct indicators of market value; mass appraisals tend to equalize the application of taxes rather than produce realistic appraisals of market value. Furthermore, because local authorities can adjust revenue needs by changing tax rates rather than assessed values, assessment figures may not be current.

Physical Characteristics

In site description and analysis, an appraiser describes and interprets the value influences of all physical characteristics of a site, including the physical relationship of the improvements to the land and to neighboring properties. Important physical characteristics to be considered are size and shape, corner influence, plottage, excess land, topography, utilities, site improvements, location, and environment.

Size and Shape

A size and shape description includes a site's dimensions, street frontage, width, depth, and any advantages or disadvantages caused by these physical characteristics. An appraiser describes the site and analyzes the effects of size and shape on property value. Special attention is given to any characteristics that are unusual for the neighborhood. The effects of size and shape vary according to the probable use of the property. For instance, an odd-shaped parcel may be appropriate for a dwelling but unacceptable for certain types of commercial or industrial use.

Land size is expressed in different units according to local custom and land use. Land suited for agriculture is described in acres, as are large industrial tracts. Other large tracts may be described in miles and sometimes in rods and chains. Residential and commerical sites are usually described in square feet, although acreage may be used. Dimensions are expressed in feet and tenths for easy calculation. However, metric system measurements, including square meters and hectares, are sometimes used in describing land size. Table 8.1 shows forms of measurement.

Frontage is the measured footage of a site that abuts a street, stream, railroad, or other facility. The frontage may or may not be the same as the width of the rest of the property. For instance, a property might be wider in the center than at the front.

Often, a site that is larger or smaller than normal size will not

Table 8.1 Measures

The English System

Linear Measure

12 inches	= 1 foot
3 feet	= 1 yard
5.5 yards	= 1 rod
40 rods	= 1 furlong
8 furlongs	= 1 mile

Square Measure

144 square inches	= 1 square foot
9 square feet	= 1 square yard
43,560 square feet	= 1 acre
640 acres	= 1 square mile

Surveyor's or Land Measure

1 link	= 7.92 inches
1 rod (or pole) = 25 links	= 16½ feet
1 chain = 100 links = 4 rods	= 66 feet
1 furlong = 40 rods = 10 chains	= ⅛ mile
1 mile = 320 rods = 80 chains	= 5,280 feet
1 acre = 160 square rods	= 43,560 square feet
1 square mile = 640 acres	

Engineer's Chain

12 inches	= 1 link
100 links or 100 feet	= 1 chain
52.8 chains	= 1 mile

Metric System

1 meter	=	39.37 inches	
1 kilometer	=	0.62137 mile	
1 foot	=	0.3048 meter	
1 centimeter	=	{ 3.28083 feet	
		1.0936 yards	
		1 centiare	
1 inch	=	{ 0.3937 inch	
		2.54 centimeters	
		25.4 millimeters	
1 millimeter	=	{ 0.03937 inch, or	
		approximately	
		¹⁄₂₅ in.	
1 yard	=	0.9144 meters	
1 rod	=	5.029 meters	
1 mile	=	1.6093 kilometers	

1 meter = 39.37 inches
1 kilometer = 0.62137 mile
1 foot = 0.3048 meter
1 centimeter = { 3.28083 feet
                1.0936 yards
1 inch = 2.54 centimeters
1 millimeter = { 0.3937 inch
                25.4 millimeters
                { 0.03937 inch, or
                approximately
                ¹⁄₂₅ in.
1 yard = 0.9144 meters
1 rod = 5.029 meters
1 mile = 1.6093 kilometers

1 square meter = { 10.764 square feet
                  1.196 square yards
                  1 centiare
1 square yard = 0.836 square meter
1 square foot = 0.0929 square meter

1 square centimeter = 0.155 square inch
1 square inch = { 6.452 square centimeters
                645.2 square millimeters
1 square rod = 25.29 square meters

1 square millimeter = 0.00155 square inch

1 acre = 0.4046 hectares
1 square mile = 259 hectares

Cuerda   3,930.40 square meters   0.97123 acres
Hectare   10,000 square meters   2.471 acres
Are   100 square meters   119.6 square yards
Centiare   1 square meter   1,550 square inches

have the same square foot or acreage value as neighboring sites. These differences can affect value and are considered in a site analysis. Because the functional utility of a site often results from an ideal or optimum size and frontage-to-depth ratio, an appraiser should recognize value tendencies to appraise sites that are not of optimum size or frontage-to-depth ratio. These tendencies can be observed by studying market sales or leases of lots of varying sizes.

Corner Influence

Frontage on two or more streets sometimes creates a higher unit value than is found for neighboring properties with frontage on only one street. However, the advantage of the easier access to such sites may be diminished by the loss of privacy to residential sites. An appraiser must find out whether the local market considers corner location favorable or unfavorable.

Corner sites can have utility not possessed by inside properties because they allow flexibility in the layout of building improvements and in the subdivision of large plots. Residences situated on corner sites may allow for a rear garage or carport with fewer driveways, which usually reduces the number of abutting owners to two instead of three. For commercial properties, a corner influence provides both added exposure and the ease of rear service entrance. For any drive-in service, a corner is usually advantageous for ingress and egress.

However, corner sites also can have disadvantages. The original cost of off-site improvements is more for corner sites. In practice, even though part or all of side-street costs are apportioned to all lots, a developer frequently demands and gets a higher price for corner sites. For residential properties, corner sites can create more traffic noise and danger and provide less security because of exposure. There may also be a higher cost for front-footage sidewalks and assessments. The side street setback may affect the permitted size of the house.

For mass appraisal work, such as ad valorem taxation, assessors and others have developed various tables that provide mathematical formulas to compute corner influence. Such tables are depth tables, corner influence tables, and size adjustments based on mathematical curves. However, using the values derived through these formulas alone may lead to unsound value estimates. More accurate adjustments for depth, corner influence, and size can usually be made by a careful analysis of market data pertaining to local attitudes and land-use patterns.

Plottage

Plottage is the process of assembling two or more sites under a single ownership in such a way that a value increment is derived from greater utility. Plottage value refers to an increment in value that results from assembling two or more parcels of land under single ownership or control. If the combined parcels have a greater unit value than they did separately, plottage value results. Plottage value may also refer to the value of an existing site of abnormal size or special shape that has greater utility than average lots of more conventional, smaller size. Analysis of neighboring land uses and values will indicate whether the appraised property has a plottage value.

Plottage is significant in agricultural land because properties of less-than-optimum size have lower unit values because they cannot support the expensive modern equipment needed to produce maximum profits.

Excess Land

The portion of land area that provides a typical land-to-building ratio with the existing improvements may be considered an economic unit. Excess land is the portion of a property that is not necessary to serve existing improvements. Assuming that the excess land is marketable or has value for future use, its market value as vacant land constitutes an addition to the estimated value of the economic entity. Therefore, excess land is typically valued separately.

Topography

Topographical studies include information about land's contour, grades, natural drainage, soil conditions, view, and general physical usability. Particular sites may differ in value because of these characteristics. Steep slopes often preclude building construction. Natural drainage can be advantageous or disadvantageous, the latter particularly if a site is "downstream" from other properties that have a right to direct excess flows onto it. Adequate storm drainage systems may offset topographic and drainage problems that would otherwise inhibit the development of such a site.

The terminology an appraiser uses for describing topography must be consistent with that used in the area. What is described as a steep hill in one part of the country might be described as a moderate slope in another. In certain instances, the descriptions of a property's topography may be taken from published sources, such as contour maps.

Surface soil and subsoil conditions are important for improved properties as well as for agricultural land. Soil suitability for building foundations is important for all types of structures and is a major consideration when the construction of large, heavy buildings is contemplated. The need for special pilings or floating foundations has a major impact on the adaptability of a site for a particular use, and therefore on its value.

Agronomists and soil scientists measure agricultural qualities of soil. Engineering qualities are tested by engineers who are trained in soil mechanics. Subsoil conditions frequently are known to local builders, developers, and others. However, when there is doubt about soil-bearing capacity, an appraiser should inform the client of the need for soil studies. The resolution of such doubts is essential for a successful highest and best use analysis.

Utilities

An appraiser investigates all utilities and services available to a site. Off-site utilities may be publicly or privately operated, or there may be a possibility of on-site utility systems, such as septic tanks and private water wells. Major utilities to be considered are sanitary sewers; domestic water; types of raw water for commercial, industrial, and agricultural uses; natural gas; electricity; storm drainage; and telephone systems.

Although a neighborhood analysis gives a general idea of the utility systems that are available in an area, a site description and analysis provide a detailed description of the utilities that are available to the appraised site. Any limitations that result from a lack of utilities are important in a highest and best use analysis, and all possible alternative sources of utility service must be investigated.

The rates for utility services and the burden of any bonded indebtedness or other special utility costs are considered. For commercial and industrial users, the quality and quantity of water and its cost; the costs and dependability of energy sources; the adequacy of sewer facilities; and any special utility costs or surcharges that might apply to certain businesses are especially significant.

Accurate information on public utilities can be obtained from local utility companies or agencies, local public works departments, and providers of on-site water and sewage disposal systems.

Site Improvements

In doing a site description, an appraiser describes off-site improvements and analyzes their effect on value. The quality, condition, and adequacy of sewers, curbs, access to utility hookups, and so forth, influence the use and value of a site. An appraiser also describes and analyzes land improvements, including landscaping, fences, curbs, gutters, walks, roads, and other man-made land improvements.

The location of existing buildings on a site must also be described and analyzed. An appraiser often makes a plot plan, which shows all major buildings in relation to lot lines. Land-to-building ratios are quite significant. In a residential area where buildings typically cover one-half of the lot, an 80/20 building-to-land ratio may diminish a property's value. Similarly, for commercial buildings, the space allotted for parking influences the value for business and commercial use. Therefore, the parking space-to-building ratio is analyzed.

An appraiser also indicates on-site improvements that add to or detract from a property's probable best use. For example, a commercial-zoned lot may be improved with an 18-unit apartment building that is too valuable to demolish. If the lot could accommodate a 24-unit building, but the present structure blocks access to any possible location for additional units, an appraiser may conclude that the site is under-improved and not being used at its highest and best use.

Location

Analysis of location focuses on the time-distance relationships between the site and common origins and destinations. An appraiser describes and analyzes all forms of access to and from the property and neighborhood. In most cases, private automobile parking and the location and condition of streets, alleys, connector roads, freeways, and highways are important to land use. Industrial properties are affected by rail and freeway access, docking facilities, and the like. Industrial, commercial, and residential areas are influenced by the location of airports, freeways, mass transportation, and railroad services.

After noting the access facilities available and their conditions, an appraiser analyzes the effects of the facilities on the site and the uses to which the site can be put. For instance, residential sites are influenced by the ease with which persons can go to and from work, school, shopping, recreation, places of worship, and so forth. The adequacy of the transportation facilities to serve the needs of property owners in the area is analyzed.

The volume of traffic may be either disadvantageous or advantageous to a site, depending on other conditions that affect its highest and best use. High-volume local traffic in commercial areas is usually an asset. Heavy through traffic can be deleterious to most retail stores, except those serving travelers. The volume of traffic passing the property is determined by a traffic count, which can usually be obtained from a local or state road department. The counts indicate average daily traffic, peak hours, and directional flows. Observing the actual vehicles and their speeds and turning movements helps an appraiser form an opinion about traffic effects on highest and best use.

Noise, dust, and fumes that emanate from a heavily traveled artery or freeway are detrimental to nearly all low-density residential lots. However, advertising values of these major arteries can benefit offices and shopping centers unless traffic chokes free-flowing movement. The visibility of a commercial property from the street is an advertising asset. It is most valuable when a customer in a vehicle can easily exit from traffic and directly approach the property.

A median strip, a left-turn restriction, a one-way street, or an access restriction may limit the potential uses of a parcel. The site analysis should test any probable uses in relation to the effects of traffic flows. Any planned changes in access should be verified with the appropriate authority and be considered in the appraisal.

Environment

An appraiser should analyze climatic conditions in terms of land use. For instance, certain sites are influenced by wind exposure, their direction in relation to the sun, and so forth. A very windy location can be disastrous to a resort but beneficial to a fossil-fuel power plant. The sunny side of the street is not always best for retail shops. In hot climates, the shady side ordinarily gets more pedestrian traffic and creates greater sales, thus producing higher rents and higher land values.

An analysis of the environment focuses on the interrelationships between the appraised site and neighboring properties. The effects of any hazards or nuisances that neighboring properties cause are considered. Particularly important are safety matters—the safety of employees and customers, of occupants and visitors, of childern going to and from school, and so forth.

Important amenities created by developments on adjoining sites, such as parks, fine buildings, and compatible commercial buildings, influence a site's value. The types of structures on, and the activities of the users of, lots surrounding the property being appraised can greatly influence its value.

Agricultural and Resource Land

In addition to many of the characteristics discussed in this chapter, special attention is directed to the following for agricultural resource lands.[4]

1. Soil. Precise soil surveys that indicate the soils found on properties,

---

[4]For a thorough discussion of the methods for describing and analyzing these and other significant characteristics of land used for agricultural production, see *The Appraisal of Rural Property* (Chicago: American Institute of Real Estate Appraisers, 1983).

appropriate crops, and expected production often are available. These survey subjects are useful in comparing properties.

2. Drainage/irrigation. The long-term dependability and cost of adequate drainage and supplies of water are investigated and analyzed.

3. Climate. General climatic conditions and growing seasons affect crop production and the subsequent land value.

4. Possible crops. Crops grown on any property are related not only to climate, soil, and irrigation, but also to the availability of labor, transportation, and markets to make, transport, and sell the products produced from crops.

5. Environmental controls. Cropping patterns are subject to regulations on herbicides, insecticides, access to special equipment, air and water pollution standards, and wildlife protection.

6. Other considerations. Locations of minerals, wildlife habitats, and streams and lakes; distances from populated areas; recreational land uses; and many other considerations are analyzed. Special tax situations, such as reduced taxes on agricultural or resource properties, are studied.

Summary

In estimating the value of any site, an appraiser provides a detailed description and analysis of the land only or the land and improvements. Site description is a detailed listing of factual data, including a legal description, other title and record data, and information on pertinent physical characteristics. Site analysis is a careful study of these data in relation to the neighborhood characteristics that affect the utility and marketability of the site as compared with comparable sites.

The three principal methods used to describe real property in the United States are the metes and bounds system, the rectangular or government survey system, and the lot and block system. The metes and bounds system describes property boundaries in a clockwise direction from the point of beginning. Established benchmarks, or survey markers, which are set in heavy concrete monuments, indicate a point of beginning. The metes and bounds system is especially useful for irregularly shaped parcels of land.

In the rectangular survey system, the federal Land Office established official points of beginning from which east-west, or base, and north-south, or principal meridian, lines were run. From each initial reference point, north-south lines called range lines and east-west lines called township lines are run. They are spaced at six-mile intervals, forming 36-square-mile rectangles known as townships. Townships are, in turn, divided into one-square-mile sections, which may be subdivided into even smaller parcels.

The lot and block system is a simplified way of locating small parcels by assigning a number or letter to individual sites or by laying out tax parcels.

Before making an on-site inspection, an appraiser gathers title and record data on the property. Most of this information can be obtained from published material and public documents. Legal ownership and type of ownership can be found in public records maintained by the county clerk and recorder. It is imperative that appraisers know the exact type of legal ownership so that the property rights to be appraised can be accurately defined. They must also search carefully for information on any limitations on ownership rights. Other legal items an appraiser looks for include zoning and land use restrictions and assessment and tax information.

The value influence of a site's total physical characteristics is also an important determinant of land use and value. Natural qualities, such as the size and shape of a parcel, frontage width, possible corner influence, and topography, are described, and their effects on land use and value are interpreted. However, man-made improvements, both off-site utilities and on-site structures, are also part of the site's physical makeup. The land-to-building ratios are significant—for example, an 80/20 building-to-land ratio in an area where most buildings cover only one-half of the lot may diminish the property's value.

Although not an integral part of the land itself, location influences land value. Locational analysis centers on the time-distance relationships between the site and common origins and destinations. Means of access to and from the site and forms of transportation available are important to land use. Parking space-to-building ratio is the key concern in commercial properties.

The appraiser also looks at the subject property in relation to the environment to assess its compatibility with its surroundings. Climatic conditions are analyzed in terms of their effects on land use. The effects of any hazards or nuisances presented by neighboring properties are considered, and the types of structures on lots surrounding the property and the activities performed on those lots can influence the value of the subject property.

Chapter 9

Building Description

An important part of every appraisal is the description of buildings on the site. An appraiser describes each building's design and layout and its construction details, which include structural components, materials, and mechanical systems. The appraiser also determines building size and the condition of each element described. A building description provides the basis for comparisons between the subject property's improvements and improvements typically accepted in the subject property's market.

An appraiser needs accurate building descriptions to select comparable properties for use in the sales comparison approach. Building descriptions are also necessary for calculating the reproduction or replacement cost and all forms of depreciation for the cost approach to value. The descriptions also provide important information for use in the income capitalization approach.

General Description

An appraiser begins a building description by providing a general description, which cites the property's current use or uses and any apparent alternate uses. These are analyzed in depth in the highest and best use portion of the appraisal. The description of the improvements provides important background information for estimating the highest and best use of the property as improved. Therefore, the adaptability of improvements for various alternative highest and best uses should be included in the building description if relevant.

Use Classification

Real estate is usually divided into five major use groups. They are residential, commercial, industrial, agricultural, and special purpose. The planning, construction, and use of buildings are directed by various laws, codes, and regulations. These controls are enacted at all levels of government to protect the public health, safety, and welfare.

Zoning regulations primarily control a property's use. Existing and potential property uses must be checked against zoning regulations to determine if they are conforming or nonconforming uses. When a use does not conform to current zoning regulations, an appraiser should consider how this fact might potentially decrease the property's value.

Building design and construction are controlled by building, plumbing, electrical, and mechanical codes. When violations exist, the cost to correct them must be estimated and then considered to judge its effect on value.

Codes

Building codes are enacted at local, state, and federal levels. Over half the states in the United States have codes that control various classifications of the buildings constructed within their borders. Federal regulations ensure occupational health and safety, environmental protection, pollution control, and consumer protection. Generally, building codes establish requirements for the construction and occupancy of buildings and contain specifications for materials, methods of construction, and mechanical systems. They establish standards of performance and deal with such considerations as structural strength, fire resistance, adequate light, and ventilation.

To provide an adequate description of a building, an appraiser should have knowledge of all codes in the area and should examine whether the building complies with all applicable codes. A building that does not probably has less value than a similar building that does comply. Bringing a building up to the standards set forth in the code may produce additional expenses for owners of a noncomplying building and may limit the building's future use.

Due to the lack of uniformity in the establishment and enforcement of codes, industrial and professional groups have developed model codes, which have been slowly accepted throughout the country, especially in larger communities.

Size

In each building description an appraiser must determine the building's size. No standard national methods were available to measure a building until standards for measuring a residential property were developed by the FHA, the VA, the FNMA, and the FHLMC. The standards of these agencies have provided the standards for millions of appraisals.

The agencies developed the terms gross living area (GLA) and gross building area (GBA) for a single family residence and a multifamily building, respectively. Other national agencies are developing standard measuring systems for various types of buildings. Gross leaseable area (GLA) is commonly used for shopping centers. Industrial buildings are generally measured on a gross building basis.

Office buildings present special problems for appraisers because they are measured differently in various areas.[1] Office building descriptions should include gross building areas, finished building areas, and rentable building areas. In measuring office buildings, the trend is away from net rentable area (the area actually occupied by a tenant) and toward measurement methods that include the total area of an office floor except vertical openings such as elevator shafts, stairwells, and air ducts in the leaseable area. These methods assign to each tenant a pro rata portion of the restrooms, elevator lobbies, and corridors. Another method includes a pro rata portion of the ground floor main lobby in each tenant's leased area. Measurement methods used by office building management sometimes vary between a single-tenant floor and a multiple-tenant floor; because these measurements fluctuate with various occupancies, a consistent floor-by-floor rentable area of the building should be calculated by an appraiser.

An appraiser uses the system of measurement that is customary in a particular area and includes a description of the system in the appraisal report. The various measurements of a building can be calculated from the plans, when available. However, these measurements should be checked against the actual measurements of the building be-

---

[1]The Building Owners and Managers Association International (BOMA) has established a system of measuring offices, which is widely used.

cause alterations and additions often are made subsequent to the preparation of the plans.

It is necessary to know building sizes for the sales comparison approach. This is especially true when the subject and comparable properties vary in size. To adjust for size differences, the common practice is to reduce the total properties to units that are representative of the whole, such as square feet of building area or square feet of living area.[2]

Building size is also important in estimating effective rent in the income capitalization approach. Comparable rentals rarely reflect buildings that are exactly the same size. Therefore, size differences must be adjusted to indicate the market rent of the appraised property. Often, comparable rental information is converted to rent per square foot. The rent for the property being appraised is obtained by multiplying the selected reconciled rent, based on the comparable data, by the number of square feet of rentable area. Expenses obtained from market data also are converted to square foot units. These are often the same units that are used for income analysis.

The calculations used in the cost approach require measurements of the entire building and certain components. Two similar buildings that have the same square footage will have different costs if the linear feet of their exterior or interior walls are different. All other significant differences must be accounted for when the cost of a comparable building is used to estimate the cost of the building that is being appraised.

Description Format

A complete building description includes information about the details, including the condition, of a building's exterior, interior, and mechanical systems. However, there is no proscribed method for describing all buildings. The following outline is useful for establishing a format to describe a specific building.

1. Exterior description
   a. Substructure: footings, slabs, piles, columns, piers, beams, and foundation walls, whichever exist
   b. Superstructure
      (1) Framing
      (2) Insulation
      (3) Ventilation
      (4) Exterior walls
      (5) Exterior doors

[2]Units of comparison are discussed in Chapters 12 and 13.

    (6) Windows, storm windows, and screens
    (7) Facade
    (8) Roof and drain system
    (9) Chimneys, stacks, and vents
   (10) Special features

2. Interior description
   a. Interior walls
      (1) Doors
   b. Division of space
      (1) Storage areas
      (2) Stairs, elevators, and the like
   c. Interior supports
      (1) Beams and columns
      (2) Flooring system
      (3) Ceilings
   d. Painting, decorating, and finishing
      (1) Basement
      (2) Floor covering
      (3) Molding and baseboard
      (4) Fireplaces
   e. Termite protection
   f. Miscellaneous and special features

3. Equipment and mechanical systems
   a. Plumbing system
      (1) Piping
      (2) Fixtures
   b. Energy systems
      (1) Hot water system
      (2) Heating system
         (a) Warm or hot air
         (b) Hot water
         (c) Steam
         (d) Electricity
      (3) Heating system fuels
         (a) Fuel oil
         (b) Natural gas
         (c) Electricity
      (4) Air-conditioning and ventilation system
      (5) Electrical system
   c. Miscellaneous equipment
      (1) Fire protection
      (2) Elevators, escalators, and speed ramps
      (3) Signal, alarm, and call systems
      (4) Unloading facilities

Exterior Description

When giving a building's exterior description, an appraiser provides information about the details of the building's substructure and superstructure. When giving a description of a group of buildings or a complex, the appraiser may also have to include details about the infrastructure. The infrastructure is the core of development in a group of buildings or in a complex, and serves as the common source of utilities or support services. A boiler and an electrical system that service more than one structure are examples of what the infrastructure provides.

Substructure

Substructure usually refers to a building's entire foundational structure, which is below grade, or ground, and includes such foundation supports as footings, slabs, piles, columns, piers, and beams. Piers, however, do extend above ground. The foundation or substructure provides a support base upon which the superstructure rests.

Footings

Footings are support parts that prevent excessive settlement or movement. The most common form of footing is a perimetric base of concrete that rests on undisturbed earth below the frost line. It distributes the load of the walls over the subgrade. Some common types of footings are plain footings, which are unreinforced and are intended to carry light loads, and reinforced footings, which contain steel to increase their strength. Spread footings are used frequently where the soil has poor load-bearing capacity.

Because footings are visible only when a building is under construction, an appraiser gets information about them from plans or from architects, contractors, or builders. Improperly designed and constructed footings often cause settling and excessive wall cracks. An appraiser determines any structural problems and judges their effect on the property's value. When the problems can be corrected, the cost to do so is estimated. Certain defects are ignored by the market or have little effect on a property's value, while others result in substantial decreases in value.

A building's foundation is made of natural or prepared material. Most foundations today are made of poured concrete walls or concrete or cinder block walls that rest on concrete footings. Many older foundations are made of cut stone or stone and brick. Mat and raft foundations, known as floating foundations, are used over soils that have low load-bearing capacity. They are made of concrete slabs that are heavily reinforced with steel so that the entire foundation acts as a unit.

Pile foundations are made of columnlike units (made of concrete, metal, or wood) that transmit loads through soil with poor load-bearing capacity to lower levels of soil with adequate load-bearing capacity. They serve as a substitute for footings. Columns, piers, and grade beams are other types of foundation supports that can be used separately or can be combined with other foundation supports.

Superstructure

Superstructure usually refers to the portion of the building above grade. However, in multipurpose buildings, parts that are not used for habitable space but are above grade, such as a parking garage, are often considered part of the substructure.

Framing

A structural frame is the load-bearing skeleton of a building. A building's exterior and interior walls are attached to the frame. The structural frames of most houses in the United States, including many that have brick veneer siding, are made of wood. The three most common types of wooden frame construction are platform, balloon, and post and beam. Of the three, platform framing is the most common.

In platform construction, only one story of a building is constructed at a time and later serves as a platform for the next story. Studs are cut at the ceiling height of the first story, horizontal plates are then laid on top, and more studs are cut for the second story.

In balloon framing, which was popular in older multistory brick buildings, long studs run from the top of the foundation wall to the roof. They are notched to receive a horizontal framing member at each upper floor level. Balloon framing is rarely used today because the long studs that are needed cost a great deal and because the framing has poor fire resistance.

Post and beam framing is made of beams that are spaced up to eight feet apart and are supported on posts and exterior walls. Its framing members are much larger and heavier than those used in the other framing systems. The post and beam system was used in colonial houses and barns and regained popularity beginning in the mid-1970s.

One relatively recent method of framing has panels of framing members and siding or subflooring that are prefabricated at a mill or are built on site. Construction begins on the ground and later materials are lifted as a unit and installed in place. Some buildings are constructed with solid masonry exterior walls, which act as part of the framing system. Often, interior framing is made of steel beams or reinforced concrete. Older masonry buildings had interior framing made of wood beams and posts.

The form of industrial buildings has changed substantially in the past century. At the turn of the century the most popular form was the multistory mill building, which had exterior masonry walls and large post and heavy beam framing systems that were often supported by solid interior masonry walls and columns. After 1900, steel began to replace timber framing; by 1910, many multistory industrial buildings were built of reinforced concrete with rectangular columns and beams and heavy slab floors. By 1920, round, mushroom-capped columns under rectangular areas of heavier slab floors were generally used. Several other types of integral beam and slab construction, such as the tee-beam floor design with hollow tile between the tee-beams or the use of pans to form beams or waffle patterns, became common, especially in buildings that required lower live loads.

Large residential, commercial, and industrial buildings today often have steel beams or reinforced or precast concrete framing systems. Precast units that frequently use prestressed, reinforced steel are widely employed. Tilt-up construction uses precast concrete slabs, which can be lifted to a vertical position to become exterior bearing or curtain walls. The interior frame may consist of precast and prestressed concrete beams and columns with lighter precast slabs that constitute the structural roof.

There has been a trend toward more functional, single-story horizontal buildings for industrial plants. The framing for this type of building usually is made of steel. Bays are becoming increasingly larger; those that are 30 to 50 feet are quite common. Certain aircraft plants have been built with over 100 feet clear span between columns. When the frame also supports heavy cranes, the weight and size of the structural steel members are increased.

When wood framing systems are defective, they cause walls to crack immoderately, exterior walls to bulge, windows to stick, doors not to open or close properly, and the space between the wall siding and masonry chimneys to be excessively wide. Steel framing is usually less expensive than precast or reinforced concrete and is easier and faster to erect. But it has one major disadvantage. Unless it is encased in heat-resistant, fireproof material such as plaster or concrete, it will buckle and bend from the heat of a fire, thereby pulling adjacent members out of position and greatly increasing fire damage to the building. Reinforced and precast concrete framing is the most expensive and difficult to construct. It has a high resistance to damage by fire.

Insulation

Insulation is as important in warm climates to keep out the heat as it is in cold climates to keep out the cold. Insulation has become increasingly essential due to increasing fuel costs, which have generated the necessity to conserve energy. Any building without adequate insulation is considered substandard.

Prior to World War II, most buildings were constructed without special added insulation materials, although the heavy building materials that were then used provided some insulation. Many newer buildings are more energy efficient than similar older buildings, many of which are being renovated with energy efficiency in mind. Thus, insulation is added to many of these older buildings. Insulations are classified according to their form, which can be loose fill, flexible, rigid, reflective, or foamed in place.

Loose-fill insulations are poured or machine-blown into structural cavities. They are manufactured from mineral wool (rock, slag, or glass wool) or cellulosic fiber (recycled newsprint, wood chips, or other organic fibers).

Flexible insulations are manufactured in batt and blanket form from mineral wool or cellulosic fibers in three forms. They can be wrapped with Kraft paper on the edges and a vapor barrier on one or both sides; faced with a vapor barrier on one side only; or friction-fit without any covering because the interlaced fibers have sufficient resilience to remain upright in the cavity. Flexible insulations are generally used in areas where it is not practical to install loose fill or where attached foil or Kraft paper facing is desired as a vapor barrier.

Rigid insulations have become more popular and can be used in many parts of a building. They come in four forms. They are structural wall insulation, fiberboard, structural deck insulation, and rigid board insulation.

Reflective insulation is made of foil so that it can reflect heat, which is transferred by radiation. It should face an air space of at least three-quarters of an inch and should remain free of dust or other materials that could reduce its reflective qualities.

There are two basic types of foamed-in-place insulations. They are urethane foam and urea-formaldehyde foam. Each type is created by a chemical reaction that first expands the mixture to about 30 times its original size and then solidifies it in about 24 hours.

On April 2, 1982, the Consumer Product Safety Commission issued a rule that banned urea-formaldehyde foam insulation (U.F.F.I.) in residences and schools. The ban, which became effective August 1982, applies to all U.F.F.I. that is manufactured for use in residences or schools in the United States.

The ban results from the commission's investigation of the effects of formaldehyde gas released from the insulation, which can be at very high levels, especially immediately after installation. The stated basis of the ban is that the use of U.F.F.I. presents an unreasonable risk of injury from "irritation, sensitization, and cancer that can occur when consumers are exposed to formaldehyde gas that is released from the product into the interiors of buildings."[3]

The ban is not retroactive and does not affect the approximately 500,000 homes that had U.F.F.I. installed prior to its issue. Appraisers, therefore, must recognize the potential effects of U.F.F.I. on the market value of any structure in which it has been installed. Extreme caution should be used by appraisers in the valuations of properties known to have or formerly to have had U.F.F.I. The obligation of disclosure is imposed on property sellers, real estate brokers, and salespersons representing a seller. Failure to fulfill this obligation could constitute a breach of an employed warranty of habitability or could entitle the buyer to rescind his or her contract of sale or rental agreement or to recover damages occasioned by the breach.

The ability of all insulation materials to resist the flow of heat is measured in R values. R value[4] is the resistance to heat flow and is derived by measuring the British thermal units (Btus)[5] that are transmitted in one hour through one thickness of the insulation. The higher the R value, the better the insulation. There is no universal standard for the amount of insulation required. The amount varies according to the climate and the type of building. For example, overceiling or underroof insulation with an R value of 13 in a mild climate might be satisfactory if there is gas or oil heat and no air-conditioning. In colder or hotter climates, or in places where there is electric heat or air-conditioning, an R value of 24 might be necessary. There has been a growing trend toward superinsulation in which much higher R values are used.

Insulation provides a number of benefits. The two major ones are helping to economize on fuel and providing comfort. Others are reducing noise transmission and impeding fire from spreading. The adequacy of a building's insulation and other energy conservation features are noted by an appraiser in a building description.

Ventilation

In many buildings, ventilation is required to reduce heat in closed-off areas such as attics, basementless spaces, and spaces behind walls. It

---

[3]U.S. Consumer Product Safety Commission, "Ban of Urea-Formaldehyde Foam Insulation," vol. 47, no. 64, April 2, 1982, p. 14366.

[4]"The R value is computed by taking the reciprocal of its conductivity, k, $(1/k)$. Resistance (R) represents the ability of a material to retard heat flow." In Harold B. Olin, John L. Schmidt, and Walter H. Lewis, *Construction—Principles, Materials, & Methods*, 4th ed. (Chicago: The Institute of Financial Education and the Interstate Printers and Publishers, 1980), pp. 105-9.

[5]A Btu is the quantity of heat required to raise the temperature of one pound of water one degree Fahrenheit at or near 39.2 degrees Fahrenheit.

also prevents the condensation of water that collects in unventilated spaces, which causes building materials to rot and decay. When water condensation seeps into insulation, it reduces the R rating. Ventilation can be accomplished by providing holes that range in size from one inch to several feet in diameter. These holes should be covered with screens to keep out vermin. Ventilation can also be increased by the use of fans.

Exterior Walls

The two basic types of exterior walls are load bearing and nonload bearing. Load-bearing walls are often made of solid masonry, such as cement block, brick, or a combination of the two. Load-bearing walls are also made of poured concrete, prestressed concrete, steel beams covered with siding material, and wood framing heavy enough to support the weight of the roof and the upper stories. Load-bearing walls can be strengthened with masonry pilasters, the columns being attached to the exterior side of the wall.

Nonload-bearing walls are common, especially in larger buildings, and are attached to the framing system. Common wall materials are porcelain enamel, steel, aluminum, precast aggregate concrete slabs, or glass. For industrial buildings, less handsome but serviceable materials are available, such as corrugated iron, tilt-up precast concrete slabs, asbestos board, fiberglass, and metal sandwich panels. When the quality of the exterior wall is below the standard for buildings in the same market, the property may suffer a loss in value.

Exterior Doors

Exterior doors are typically made of solid wood, metal, or glass. Hollow wood exterior doors usually signal poor-quality construction. There are a variety of special-purpose doors, many with automatic door openers. Commercial and industrial buildings often have large steel truck doors. Special automatic doors must be described by an appraiser. The use or lack of energy-conserving materials, such as weatherstripping, around doors is also noted by the appraiser. Air leakage through cracks at door bottoms can be stopped with door shoes, weatherproof thresholds, and sweeps that are attached to the door bottom.

Windows, Storm Windows, and Screens

Wood was the first material used for windows and is still the most common material used in houses. It has good insulating properties, is readily available, takes either natural or painted finishes, and is easy to install and repair. Other popular window materials are aluminum and steel, but they are usually used in larger residential, commercial, and industrial buildings. When describing a building, an appraiser notes the type of window and the material. Various window types include single and double hung, casement windows, horizontal sliding windows, clerestory, fixed, awning, hopper, center pivot, and jalousie windows.

Because windows are major sources of heat and cooling loss, the way they are designed and installed has become increasingly important. There is a growing trend toward reducing the size of windows and constructing them higher to conserve energy and also to increase security. Windows should be tightly sealed, with caulking at the joints and between the wall and the window. In addition, the use of insulated glass, multiple glazing, and storm sashes helps keep cold air out and heat in. An appraiser describes these energy-saving features in a building description.

Storm doors and windows provide good insulation. They can save the owners of a typical house between 10% and 20% of fuel costs. They also result in fuel savings when used in office buildings. Storm doors and windows are used in commerical and industrial buildings that are found in climates with extreme weather conditions. Modern storm doors and windows are often made of aluminum and are permanently installed, with screens. Wooden storm doors and windows, which are removed and stored during the summer, are becoming obsolete. Appraisers find it difficult to judge how much storm windows and doors add to the value of a building in certain markets. However, analyzing what is typically expected in an area is helpful.

In nearly every part of the country, screens are needed in windows that open. Most screens have aluminum frames and screening material. In residences, screens are often combined with storm windows. An appraiser counts all removable window and door screens, noting if any are missing.

Facade

Many houses, stores, office buildings, and industrial buildings have a facade, or front, that differs from the design and construction of the rest of the building. Frame houses often have extra masonry veneer on the front or contrasting types of siding. Retail stores often have elaborate fronts that consist of glass and other decorative materials. Even certain industrial buildings have fronts that are more elaborate than their exteriors. An appraiser describes the special fronts and considers their cost and their effect on the property's value.

In modern industry and commerce, public image is important. An attactive store, warehouse, industrial plant, or office building has valuable advertising and public relations value to the occupant. Ornamentation, identification signs, lighting, and landscaping all contribute to a building's attractiveness.

Roof and Drain System

A roof is designed and constructed to support its own weight in addition to the weight of pressures from snow, ice, and wind. A roof also provides a base for its finish materials. There are a variety of common roof types, such as flat (used extensively in industrial and commerical buildings and much less extensively in houses), shed, gable, saltbox, gambrel (popular in barns and in Cape Ann and Dutch colonial houses), hip, and mansard.

The most typical systems of roof construction that are found in houses are trusses, joists, joists and rafters, post and beams, and panels. In commerical and industrial construction, the roof structure may be of steel or wood trusses, glued wood beams, or a steel or concrete frame with wood joists or purlins or with steel bar joists. These systems support a variety of roof sheathings, which may be plywood, steel roof deck, lightweight precast concrete slabs, reinforced concrete slabs, or insulated sheathing in large sheets.

Roof covering prevents the entrance of moisture. In most regions of the United States, asphalt shingles are typically used for residential roofing. They are available in various weights and often have cemented tabs that protect against wind damage. Other common residential roof coverings are shingles and shakes made of wood (usually cedar), asbestos, and cement. Fiberglass shingles have recently been introduced. Metal, clay tiles, slate, and built-up or membrane roofs are also found in houses.

Many types of residential roof coverings are also used in commercial and industrial buildings. Flat roofs are very common in nonresidential buildings. They are built-up layers of felt or composition material that are nailed to the sheathing and covered with tar. Gravel or other surfacing helps keep the roof from drying out and cracking. Membrane roof assemblies are becoming popular for commercial and industrial buildings.

In roofs, joints are created by the intersection of two different roof slopes or the roof and adjoining walls or projections, such as chimneys, pipes, and ventilation ducts. All of these joints must be flashed. Flashing is usually accomplished by first nailing metal strips (usually galvanized iron or copper) across or under the point, then applying a waterproofing compound or cement, and finally applying the roofing material over the edges to hold it permanently in place.

An appraiser closely observes the condition of a roof to determine its remaining useful life. Most roofs need to be replaced at least several times during a building's life. A roof's condition and age are considered in the valuation process.

Water that falls on the roof must be directed to the ground or into a drain system. Gutters and downspouts provide a means for controlling water disposal from roofs. This prevents damage and the unsightly appearance of walls when roof overhangs are not provided. Gutters or eave troughs catch rainwater as it reaches the edge of the roof and carry it to downspouts or leaders, which are vertical pipes that carry water to the ground and sometimes into sewers, dry wells, drain tiles, or splash pans. In large buildings, storm water is collected by roof drains, which are connected to storm drains by pipes in the building. Even so-called flat roofs are often pitched enough to direct water to drains and gutters. Materials used for gutters and downspouts are galvanized iron, aluminum, and copper.

Chimneys, Stacks, and Vents
Chimneys, stacks, and vents should be constructed and installed to be structurally safe, durable, and smoketight, and to be capable of withstanding the action of flue gases. The efficiency of any heating system, except one fueled by electricity, depends on its chimney, stack, or vent. Chimneys and stacks with cracked bricks, loose mortar joints, or any kind of leak may constitute a serious fire and health hazard. The construction of chimneys, stacks, and vents ranges from simple metal vents and flues to complex masonry fireplaces, industrial chimneys, and ventilation systems. These items and their apparent condition are described in an appraisal report.

Special Features
Certain buildings have special features that must be carefully described and considered in the valuation process. Examples of such items are artwork, ornamentation, exterior elevators, solar and wind equipment, unique fenestration, special masonry work and exterior materials, and other features required for the commercial or industrial use of buildings. When these items are unique to one building, they present a difficult valuation problem. An appraiser must decide if the item or items add market value or if they are of value only to the current user. In the latter case, the item or items add use value but little or no market value. Such items can even have a negative effect on market value if any future owner would be likely to remove them.

Interior Description

Interior description includes all information about the interior walls and the spaces between them, including how the space is divided and finished.

Interior Walls

In residences, most interior walls are made of wood studs that are covered with such materials as gypsum board, wood panels, ceramic tile, plywood, and hardboard. Plaster was once popular but is used less frequently now. Masonry houses often have masonry interior walls. Commercial and industrial buildings have interior walls that range from simple wire partitions to solid masonry walls, which provide fire protection. Glass, wood, plywood, hardboard, metals, tiles, concrete, brick, and a number of other products are used for wall construction. Interior walls can be painted, wallpapered, or covered with decorative products.

Doors

Many types of interior doors are considered part of the real estate. They include simple, hollow-core doors, which are used in most residential construction; complex, self-closing, fire-resistant doors, which are found in commercial and industrial buildings; specialty self-opening and closing doors, which are used in offices and commercial buildings; and special purpose doors, such as those used in bank vaults. The hanging of doors is complex and often improperly done, which often causes a door to stick or to have uneven openings.

Division of Space

In a building description, a complete list of the number of rooms, their uses, and sizes is provided. For residential properties, the differences in the number of bedrooms and baths usually influence the market for and the market value of the property. The number of units in an apartment building and the types and sizes of the rooms that constitute the units significantly influence the property's income-producing potential. Similarly, the amount of office space in industrial properties may affect the value of those properties, as may the interior partitioning in office suites.

In certain parts of the United States, basements are found in all types of buildings. In such areas, the value of buildings without basements may be substantially less than similar buildings with them. In areas where basements are not common, they may add little or no value to a building.

Storage Areas

An appraiser describes and considers the adequacy of storage areas. One common complaint homeowners express (especially those whose homes are without basements) is about the lack of adequate storage space, especially in kitchens. Good cabinets, closets, and other storage areas help solve the problem. Storage problems also exist in commercial and industrial buildings.

Stairs, Ramps, Elevators, Escalators, and Hoists

To design and construct even the most simple staircase is complicated. Codes for buildings that are used by the public often regulate where stairs are located, how they are designed and constructed, and how they are enclosed to provide fire protection. In a residence, a well-planned stairway provides safe ascent and adequate headroom and space for moving furniture and equipment. Railings should be installed around the open sides of all interior stairwells, including those in an attic and a basement where they are often omitted.

Elevators and escalators are mechanical systems that move people and freight. Whether they are adequate must be considered by an appraiser. Many elevators and escalators in multistory buildings are inadequate and do not meet current market standards. Curing the deficiency often proves too expensive or impossible.

Relatively recent laws provide handicapped persons access to public buildings and require that ramps be installed inside and outside a building. An appraiser does not assume that a building complies with these requirements, especially because the enforcement of such requirements can be triggered by a change in use or through a title transfer.

Special elevators and hoists are often considered part of a building, although they are sometimes studied under the category of equipment (see page 202). They must be carefully described and their contribution to the value of the building must be estimated.

Internal Supports

A building description takes into consideration a building's internal supports, which include beams and columns, the flooring system, and ceilings.

Beams and Columns

Most houses and many commercial and industrial buildings have basements or crawl spaces that are too large for the first floor joists or subfloor system and cannot be supported by the foundation walls alone. Therefore, in large buildings, foundation walls are an important part of the main framing system and are designed to support heavy loads. Bearing beams that rest on columns of wood, masonry, or steel provide additional support. Cracks in or sagging of the beams may be early warnings of more serious problems in the future. When an appraiser observes these signs, he or she should consider and report them.

Flooring System
The purpose of subflooring is to provide safe support for floor loads without excessive deflection and adequate underlayment for the support and attachment of finish floor material. Bridging stiffens the joists and prevents them from deflecting sideways.

Ceilings
In residences with gypsum walls, ceilings are often made of the same material. In other buildings, tiles are popular. Sometimes the underside of the upper story is an adequate ceiling. Ceiling height must be described and considered by an appraiser. Ceilings that are too low or high for the current highest and best use of the property as improved may be an item of functional obsolescence, which decreases the property's value.

Painting, Decorating, and Finishing

The primary purpose of interior painting and decorating is to give the building an attractive appearance. A building is usually decorated many times during its useful life. An appraiser reports the condition of the painting and decorating and when they will have to be redone.

What constitutes attractive painting and decorating is subjective. Many new owners and tenants redecorate to suit their personal tastes. Unusual decorations and nonstandard colors may have limited appeal and may detract from a building's value. The quality of decoration sometimes is an important consideration in the value of a restaurant, store, or other commercial building.

Basements
Especially in residences and some commercial buildings, basements may be finished and used for purposes other than just storage. When these uses are well accepted and typical in the area of the building being appraised, they add significant value to the building.

Dampness, often a problem in basements, may be caused by poor foundation wall construction, excess ground water not properly carried away by ground tiles, poorly fitted windows or hatches, poor venting of equipment, and poorly constructed or operating roof drains that allow water to enter. Signs of a wet basement are the presence of a powdery white mineral deposit a few inches off the floor, stains along the lower edge of the walls and columns and on equipment that rests close to the floor, and the smell of mildew.

Flooring and Floor Coverings

A wide variety of flooring is available. Certain flooring materials are selected primarily for their low cost and durability. Sand, packed-down dirt, bituminous paving, brick, stone, gravel, concrete, and other similar products are suitable for many industrial buildings, warehouses, garages, and basements. The floors in many commercial and industrial buildings require special thicknesses or extra reinforcment to support work that uses heavy equipment. Terrazzo flooring (made of colored marble chips that are mixed into cement and then ground smooth) is used for high traffic areas, such as public building lobbies.

Wood in various forms continues to be a popular material for floors. Planks and blocks are used for industrial floors, and many commercial buildings use wood floors to conform with their design and overall decorations. Wood planks and hardwood strips are found in many residences, although other types of flooring have become even more popular. A wide variety of resilient, ceramic, and quarry tiles are used in all types of buildings. Resilient flooring, usually composed of a combination of vinyl and asphalt, is also produced as sheet goods.

Carpeting was once considered a luxury for residences, offices, stores, commercial buildings, and other appropriate places. Today it is widely used in all types of buildings. An appraiser considers whether floor coverings will stand up to wear and tear and how they conform to a building's design and decoration.

Molding and Baseboards

In the past, architects often designed a unique molding for a building; today, moldings are standard size and shape and their use is decreasing. Beautiful, restored molding adds value to older houses. Simple baseboards are widely used in many types of buildings to protect the walls from damage by cleaning equipment and furniture.

Fireplaces

Fireplaces are still popular and are found in many houses and certain commercial buildings, including restaurants, inns, specialty stores, and so forth. Most fireplaces do not provide a building's primary source of heat. In fact, because of their design, many have little heating power. There are attempts to make fireplaces better sources of heat. One example is the Heatolator, which returns hot air into the room.

The most typical type of fireplace has a single opening with a damper and hearth. More complex designs feature two, three, four, or more openings. Because fireplaces are difficult to construct, many are not well made and function poorly. One common problem is due to the downdraft, whereby smoke is blown into the building when there is wind outside. This happens frequently if the chimney does not extend at least 2 feet above any part of the roof within 10 feet of the chimney.

Many prefabricated fireplaces and flues are sold and often are installed in buildings that did not previously have fireplaces. Unless they are Underwriter Laboratory-approved and installed according to the manufacturer's instructions, they can be a potential fire hazard. To be safe, a fireplace should be supported with noncombustible material and should have a noncombustible hearth that extends at least 16 inches in front of the opening and at least 8 inches on each side. A wall-to-wall carpet or a rug that comes within a few inches of the front of a fireplace is a definite fire hazard.

Termite Protection

The termite, a destructive insect that once caused problems only in the southern part of the United States, is now causing problems in nearly every part of the country. Many older buildings were constructed without adequate termite protection and are now being attacked by the insects. An appraiser needs to know the adequate termite protection in an area. Whenever appraisers suspect termite damage, they recommend a termite inspection by a qualified inspector.

Miscellaneous and Special Features

Many industrial and commercial buildings have special features. Such industrial buildings include steel mills, oil refineries, chemical plants, concrete factories, and mines. Such commercial buildings include uniquely designed roadside restaurants. Amusement parks; sports complexes; wharfs and docks; terminals; TV and radio transmission towers; studios; and theaters are a few examples of the many special purpose improvements an appraiser describes and appraises. Photographs are especially helpful for conveying information about a building's special features. These buildings also present unique appraisal problems. An appraiser decides what, if any, contribution to value a special feature makes and keeps in mind that the contribution to value may be different for market value than it is for other value estimates (e.g., insurable value or use value).

Equipment and Mechanical Systems

Most buildings cannot perform the functions for which they were designed and constructed unless their equipment and mechanical systems are in good working order. Each item of equipment and each mechanical system is inspected and described by an appraiser.

In this chapter, the major equipment and mechanical systems are divided into two broad categories. They are those that consume significant energy and those that do not. A plumbing system is basically not an energy consumer, even though it may have pumps that require some electricity and even though the production of hot water consumes energy. Systems that consume energy are the hot water system, the heating system, the air-conditioning and ventilation system, and the electrical system. Certain buildings have other mechanical systems and equipment. Most of these systems use some electricity, but they are not major energy consumers.

Plumbing System

A plumbing system is an integral part of most buildings. It consists of piping, which is mostly covered or hidden except in industrial buildings, and fixtures or equipment, which are visible.

Piping

Often much of the cost of a plumbing system is due to the piping. It consists of pipes that carry water (and occasionally other fluids) under pressure and waste pipes that depend on the flow of gravity. The quality of the materials used for the pipes, the way in which they are installed, and how easily they can be serviced are significant when considering how long the pipes will last and how much they will cost to maintain. Worn galvanized steel, lead, or brass water pipes may need to be replaced. Copper is an excellent pipe material and has a long life, as does cast iron for below-grade waste lines. In many areas and types of buildings, a high-quality piping system can last throughout a building's economic life. However, many buildings have pipes that do not last. An appraiser describes the conditions of these pipes and notes approximately when they will need to be replaced.

Plastic pipes are widely used for waste and vent lines and water lines. Their durability and serviceability have yet to be ascertained. Water pipes must be strong enough to withstand the pressure necessary for water to flow through them. Because there is no pressure in a waste drain line, the pipes must be slanted so that the waste will flow from each fixture through the main line into the sewer or sewage disposal system.

Fixtures

Plumbing fixtures that are used in bathrooms include lavatories (washbasins), bathtubs, showers, toilets (known as water closets in the building trades), bidets, and urinals. Good-quality fixtures are made of cast iron, which is covered with acid-resistant vitreous enamel; however, fiberglass and other materials are also used.

Bathroom fixture design has undergone a substantial change, which may cause old fixtures to become obsolete during a building's economic life. An appraiser reports any modernization the bathroom may require. However, old fixtures of good quality, such as porcelain pedestal bases and legged tubs, are often rehabilitated.

Kitchen plumbing fixtures include single or double sinks, the better grades of which are installed in countertops and are made of Monel metal, stainless steel, enameled steel, and cast iron that is covered with acid-resistant enamel. Garbage disposal units, dishwashers, and instant hot water units are other kitchen fixtures. Some homes have specialized plumbing fixtures, such as laundry tubs, wet bars, and all the equipment that makes up a swimming pool or sauna.

Fittings are important parts of plumbing fixtures. Fittings include faucets, spigots, drains, shower heads, spray tubes, and so forth. Water in many areas contains minerals, such as calcium, magnesium, sulfates, bicarbonates, iron, and sulphur, that react unfavorably with soap and form a curdlike substance that is difficult to rinse from clothing, hair, and skin. This condition is known as hard water. Hard water cannot be used unless it is first treated. The type of equipment needed to treat it ranges from the simple to that of automatic, complex, and multistage treatment systems.

Commercial and industrial buildings have many of the same types of fixtures that are found in homes. In addition, they have drinking fountains, janitor sinks, handwashing and eyewashing fountains, floor drains, and a variety of other special purpose fixtures. An appraiser decides which fixtures in the buildings are part of the real estate and which are personal property. Only those that are part of the real estate are included in the building's value.

Energy Systems

An appraiser also describes the systems that consume energy. These are the hot water system, the heating system, the air-conditioning and ventilation system, and the electrical system. In addition, the appraiser describes the type of fuel used in the heating system.

Hot Water System

An adequate supply of hot water is required in all homes and in many commercial and industrial buildings. A typical hot water system in a residence receives its heat from a furnace or a self-standing water heater, which is powered by electricity, gas, or oil. Houses with inadequate hot water systems suffer from functional obsolescence. For residences, the size of the hot water tank needed is determined by the number of inhabitants and their water-using habits together with the recovery rate of the unit. Commercial and industrial buildings often require substantially more hot water than residences and thus have large cast iron or steel boilers and large tanks for storage.

Heating Systems

The most common types of heating systems are based on warm or hot air, hot water, steam, or electricity. The amount of heat a system can produce is rated in Btus. (The Btu requirement for heating-plant capacity relates to the cubic content, exposure, design, and insulation level of the structure to be heated.) An appraiser describes the heating system and analyzes whether it is appropriate to the local market area.

Warm or hot air heating systems.

Heating systems that are based on warm or hot air use either the natural force of gravity or some type of pressure blower to push heated air through the ducts. Air is heated in a furnace that is fired by gas, oil, electricity, or coal and is then distributed through one or more registers directly from the furnace or through ducts connected to registers throughout the building. Air circulation is maintained by means of a fan and a return duct system. Thermostats, filters, humidifiers, air cleaners, and air purification devices may be included.

The central air-conditioning equipment of certain systems uses the same ducts as the heating system. This is not always possible, however. Air-conditioning requires ducts that are of a different size from those in some heating systems. Generally, heating registers should be placed low on the walls, while air-conditioning registers should be placed high or should be put in the ceiling.

In the past, certain heating systems relied on gravity flow and involved the use of larger ducts with simpler distribution patterns for circulation. Warm air systems are used in new apartment construction, especially in garden apartments or townhouse developments. When gas is used, the warm air system may function through unit heaters, radiant gas heaters, wall or floor furnaces, or individual gas furnaces. Gas-fired heating units require adequate ventilation. All open-flame heating sources must have a supply of air that is sufficient enough to support complete combustion.

Hot water systems.

Heating systems based on hot water are also known as hydronic systems. In them, water is heated in a cast iron or steel boiler. Then the water moves due to gravity, which characterizes older systems, or due to its being pumped by a circulator, which is found in modern systems, through pipes and radiators where heat is transferred by convection and radiation to the areas being heated. The colder water then returns to the boiler where it is again heated, and the process is repeated over and over.

Radiant heating is a type of hot water heating. In such a system, hot water is circulated by a pump, called a circulator, through small diameter pipes that are embedded in floors, walls, and ceilings. The system depends primarily on heat being transferred to an area by radiation rather than by convection, which characterizes a conventional system. In a conventional system, air is warmed as it passes over the heated metal of the radiator and is then circulated in the area of colder air. Radiant heat can also be produced by electric heating elements that are buried in floors, walls, and ceilings.

Steam heating systems.   These systems use steam that is made in a boiler and fueled by gas, oil, coal, or electricity. Steam is delivered from the boiler by a piping system. In the simple one-pipe gravity system, which is usually used in small installations, radiators are served by a single riser from the main pipe. The condensate returns to the boiler through the same riser and is used again. The more complex and expensive two-pipe system is found in larger and higher-quality installations.

At one time, a vertical section cast iron boiler was used in larger installations. These units were more efficient and were covered with an insulated metal casing or jacket. Steel boilers were usually of a low-pressure fire-tube type, in which combustion gases passed through tubes that were inserted into a cylindrical drum that contained water. There were several types of either two-pass or three-pass construction, designed for better efficiency. Small, efficient "package boilers" recently have become popular for heating and process-steam generating.

A steam system also uses radiators to transfer heat by radiation and convection. The common cast iron radiator successfully accomplishes the dual process of transferring heat. Improvements in steam heating are still being developed to operate more efficiently. Zone control is now widely used to stabilize the effects of various heating needs in different parts of a building. The amount of heat available for distribution is controlled by separate temperature controls.

In many states, licenses are required for certain classes of steam boilers. Appraisers must be familiar with boiler license laws in their areas and must decide whether boilers have current, valid licenses.

Electrical heating systems.   The equipment used in electrical heating systems includes heat pumps, wall heaters, baseboard units, duct heating units, and heating units that are installed in air-conditioning ducts. Such equipment provides electrical heating systems with both heating and cooling capacity. Radiant floors, walls, and ceilings that use panels or cables under the surface; infrared units; and electric furnaces that use forced warm air or hot water can also be part of electrical heating systems. An electrical resistance system produces heat in the immediate area or room that is to be heated. It is the least expensive system to install because it requires no furnace, furnace room, ducts, flue, or plumbing. However, it does require a much larger electrical service than would otherwise be needed and a great deal of wiring to each unit in the building.

Heat pumps are increasing in popularity and combine heating and cooling functions. A heat pump is actually a reverse refrigeration unit. In the winter, the pump takes heat from the outside air or ground or from well water and distributes it in the house. The efficiency of the unit decreases when the weather is very cold and thus must be supplemented with resistance heating. In the summer, the pump cools by extracting heat from the inside of the house, as does a typical air-conditioning unit.

Finned heating elements that are designed for installation in baseboards or are concealed in walls or cabinets are called convectors. The type that is combined with a fan is called a unit or room heater. Unit heaters are found in commercial and industrial buildings where large spaces must be heated, such as stores, warehouses, and garages. The heaters are usually placed near the ceiling in the interior space that is to be heated.

The automatic regulation of a heating system helps it to operate efficiently. A multiple zone system with separate thermostats is more efficient than a single zone system with a single thermostat. Highly complex systems provide individual temperature controls for each room. The efficiency of certain systems can be further increased by putting a thermostat on the outside of a building. This helps to anticipate how much heat a system will need to produce.

Heating System Fuels

The type of fuel that is used in a building's heating system should be explained in a building description. In some areas and for some types of buildings, one type of fuel is more desirable than another. However, many buildings do not have heating systems that use the most economical fuel. For example, during the natural gas shortage in the middle to late 1970s, a moratorium was declared on the construction of new buildings using gas. Therefore, in certain areas, buildings have heating systems that use other fuels even though gas is now more economical. In any area, for a specific use, different fuels have significant advantages and disadvantages that change occasionally.

Coal. For much of our country's history, coal was the most popular fuel. Today it is still used to generate power for selected industrial and commercial uses. It is also used in residences for generating power to stoves and fireplaces.

Fuel oil. In spite of its increasing cost, fuel oil is still the least expensive fuel in parts of the northeast and northwest United States and is competitively priced in other areas of the country. Fuel oil is easy to transport and store. On-site tanks range from the common 275-gallon tank, which is used in millions of houses, to tanks that hold thousands of gallons, which are buried in industrial and commercial sites.

Natural gas.   This type of fuel offers the convenience of continuous delivery via pipelines without the necessity of storage tanks. In many areas of the country, gas has been the most economical fuel. However, deregulation of gas prices may change this status. Liquid petroleum gas, such as butane and propane, is used in many rural areas. It requires on-site storage tanks and is usually more expensive than natural pipeline gas, but in other respects it is similar to natural gas.

Electricity.   Electricity can be used to produce heat in a furnace or to heat water in a boiler in the same way as oil, gas, or coal is used. Electrical heating costs remain high except in a few lower-cost power areas. Good insulation and ease of control help to cut waste.

Fuel considerations.   An appraiser cannot assume that an existing heating system contributes maximum value to a property. The type of heating system that was installed when a building was constructed is often not acceptable to current potential buyers. Industrial users who formerly depended on gas alone now often install alternate facilities (such as oil or electricity) to provide heat during periods when gas supply is curtailed. Electric heat has become so costly in certain areas that buildings using it sell for substantially less than similar properties using other types of fuel.

Buyers are sensitive to energy costs. Apartments in which the owner supplies heat and hot water often sell for less than similar properties in which tenants pay for utilities. Buildings with high ceilings, many openings, poor insulation, and so forth, may be at a disadvantage in the market.

Solar heating systems and solar domestic hot water systems attract much publicity and interest. A variety of solar systems are on the market. Appraisers should stay current on solar development and its use in particular areas. A building's solar heating system should be carefully described and an estimate made of how much it contributes to the property's value. Residential appraisals done on FHLMC-FNMA forms require that solar and other special energy systems be described and valued separately.

Air-Conditioning and Ventilation System

Prior to World War II, ducts, fans, and open windows were usually used to reduce heat and to provide fresh air in most buildings. Ducts and fans are still used to provide fresh air to many buildings. In certain areas of the western United States, where the humidity is low even in periods of high heat, a simple system that blows air across wet excelsior or some other water-absorbing material cools the air substantially. Package units that use this process are still manufactured for home and commercial use. They use less power and are less expensive than conventional air-conditioning.

The most common type of air-conditioning system consists of an electric-powered compressor that compresses Freon from gas into liquid outside the area being cooled. During this process, heat is released, which is either blown away or carried away by water. The compressed Freon is then directed into thin tubes in the area being cooled, where it expands and absorbs heat from the air that is directed over the tubes by one or more fans. A variation is run by gas rather than electricity; ammonia, rather than Freon, is the refrigerant. House-sized air-conditioners range from small, portable 4,000-to-5,000 Btu units to units that provide many tons of cooling capacity. The capacity of air-conditioning units is rated in Btus and tons (12,000 Btus).

Commercial and industrial air-conditioning and ventilation is more complex. Certain systems simply bring in fresh air from the outside and distribute it throughout the building. Other systems merely remove foul air. Still other systems combine these two functions but do not have any cooling or heating capacity. More complex systems wash, filter, and add or remove humidity. The most complex systems perform all of the above functions and also heat and cool the air through a complex system of ducts and fans. In larger systems that use less electricity, water cools the pipes in which the gas has been compressed. The water can then be conserved through towers that cool the water and thus can be reused in the system.

An appraiser should describe the air-conditioning and ventilation systems in a building. The appraiser decides whether a system is appropriate to the geographic area and may have to investigate whether the building's systems meet current standards. If the appraiser decides that the building has either too much or too little air-conditioning, the report should contain the data upon which the decision is based.

Electrical System

A well-designed electrical system consists of an electrical service large enough to provide sufficient power for all electrical uses in the building. Certain single electrical services serve more than one building.

The power in an electrical system is distributed from the electrical service by wires, known as branch circuits and located throughout the building, to electrical outlets. Each branch circuit starts at a distribution box, where it is separated from the main service by a protection device such as a fuse or circuit breaker. When a short circuit or overload occurs on the branch circuit, the fuse or circuit breaker disconnects the branch circuit from the power supply and thus prevents a fire from starting.

The wiring between the distribution boxes and the outlets may be through a rigid or flexible conduit. In commercial and industrial buildings, such wiring is common. The most widely used type of wire in houses is the BX, or armored, cable. Plastic-coated wire is also used in certain areas. The old type of knob-and-tube wiring is still used in rural areas and is found in older buildings, although it is considered obsolete.

Most electrical wire is copper. After World War II, aluminum wire rapidly started to gain in popularity as the price of copper escalated, but its resistance to fire has been seriously questioned. In addition, the decreasing price of copper has prevented aluminum wire from being used as a substitute.

A typical residential system is a single-phase, three-wire system that provides a minimum of 100 amperes of electricity. The old 30-ampere systems are certainly obsolete. Residences that have 60 amperes of service now sell for less than those with larger services. Ampere services of 150, 200, 300, and 400 are needed when there is electrical heating and air-conditioning. Most of these services can provide up to 220 volts by connecting three wires to the outlet.

Power wiring is used in commercial and industrial buildings to operate utility systems, appliances, and machinery. The electrical power is generally carried at higher voltages (240, 480, 600, or more volts) and is usually three-phase or three-phase-four wire, which allows both lighting and three-phase power loads to be delivered by the same supply.

Power wiring is carried in conduit or by means of plug-in bus ducts. Overhead bus ducts are frequently encountered in manufacturing plants where flexibility of service is desired. Large-capacity power wiring may contribute to the value of an industrial improvement; however, if it is not a commonly used type and it adds to a building's operating costs or will be expensive to remove, it may result in functional obsolescence. Similarly, any building with insufficient electrical service or wiring suffers from functional obsolescence.

Switches and lighting fixtures are also part of the electrical system. Because lighting fixtures are stylized, and because styles change, they are often obsolete before they wear out. Fluorescent lighting (suspended, surface-mounted, or recessed) is used extensively in commercial and industrial buildings. Often, a design calls for continuous rows in large spaces. Incandescent fixtures may be used for smaller rooms, or for accents or other special purposes.

In newer lighting design, the intensity and quality of light over working and display surfaces are important considerations. Suitable degrees of intensity vary with the types of use. Certain installations are designed so that air moves past the lighting fixtures to augment the heating system.

Sound planning usually results in extensive use of floor outlets or floor duct systems in commercial or office buildings. These systems provide convenient electrical outlets for office machines and telephone outlets at desks and use with a minimum number of cords. Some houses and commercial buildings are controlled by a low-voltage switching system, in which many outlets and lights can be controlled from one place.

Miscellaneous Equipment

An appraiser also considers certain miscellaneous equipment, which is delineated below.

Fire Protection

Equipment for fire protection includes fire escapes, standpipes and hose cabinets, an alarm service, and automatic sprinklers. A wet sprinkler system requires adequate water pressure to ensure that pipes are always filled. A dry system contains air in pipes that are under pressure. When a sprinkler head opens, the pressure is relieved and water enters. This dry system is used where there is a danger of freezing, on loading docks or in unheated buildings, for example.

Elevators, Escalators, and Speed Ramps

Escalators are usually classified as passenger or freight and are either electric or hydraulic. Hydraulic elevators are suitable for low-speed, low-rise operations. Because attended passenger elevators require full-time operators, the high cost of operation has made them practically obsolete. The type, speed, and capacity of the elevator, as well as the number of floors served, are all related to the type of property and its utility. Most modern elevators are high-speed and completely automatic. Control systems collect signals and distribute service among all elevators in a system. Certain elevators have auxiliary controls that allow them to be manually operated if necessary.

The movement of large numbers of people up or down, or along horizontal or gradual slopes, can be accomplished with escalators and speed ramps. They must be adequate enough to accommodate the number of persons who use the building.

Signal, Alarm, and Call Systems

Signals, alarms, call systems, and similar devices should not be overlooked by an appraiser. Smoke detectors, increasingly common in residential and multifamily structures, are required by law in many areas. Many types of security alarm systems provide warnings of forced entry, fire, or both and are available for residential, commercial, and industrial use. Because of changes in fire and safety regulations, systems that were adequate when installed may later be substandard.

Among other items noted by an appraiser are clocks, pneumatic tube systems, mail chutes, incinerators, and telephone wiring. In smaller buildings, the telephone company supplies the wiring and equipment. Larger buildings may have extensive systems of cabinets, conduits, and floor ducts built in for telephone service. Telephone service in a building may be suitable for the current occupant but unsuitable for a potential buyer.

Unloading Facilities

Facilities for loading and unloading trucks and freight cars may be important in commercial and industrial buildings. Off-street loading docks are usually required by most zoning ordinances. Many older buildings have only loading doors or substandard loading facilities. These docks may be open or covered. In many cases the floor of an efficient one-story industrial building may be above grade at freight car or truck-bed level. In some cases the docks may be enclosed in the building for trucks and freight cars. Leveling devices may be provided to assist in loading or unloading. Proper industrial design provides adequate space in front of truck docks for vehicle movement.

Quality and Condition Survey

In the quality and condition survey of a building description, appraisers analyze and explain the quality and condition of the items being described. The character, quality, and appearance of the construction are reflected in each of the three appraisal approaches to a value estimate. They have a major influence on the cost estimate, the accrued depreciation estimate, the ability of the property to produce rental income, and comparability with other properties in the sales comparison approach. An analysis of the quality of construction methods and materials is an important complement to an appraiser's consideration of the quality of structural design and architectural planning.

A structure may have a good functional layout and attractive design but be built with inferior materials and reflect poor workmanship. These conditions increase maintenance and utility costs and adversely affect the marketability of a property. Conversely, a building can be built too well or at a cost beyond that justified by its utility. A purchaser will not pay for the excess cost. The loss may be recaptured only in part by the original owner through reduced future maintenance expense.

Economy of construction at a practical or reasonable level results in an improvement that will produce a rental income commensurate with its cost during its economic life. Maintenance and operation expenses may be slightly more than minimum, but the net result is more satisfactory than if the building were of superior construction, calling for a higher level of taxes, interest, and amortization charges.

To achieve this desired level of construction cost requires a proper choice and use of building materials and construction methods. Upon inspection, an appraiser recognizes the appropriate combination that results in a building adequate to serve its intended purpose.

On the date of the appraisal, an appraiser usually finds some items that need repair, even though certain buildings may be in an excellent state of maintenance. The quality of most buildings can be classified in terms of "average," "good," or "superior." Generally, when repairs that are considered normal maintenance are made, they should add more value to the property than the cost to make them. These items are classified as *curable physical deterioration* in the cost approach.

Immediate Repair Items

A list of items that may require immediate repair usually includes an appraiser's observations of any conditions that constitute a fire or safety hazard. The following is a list of items commonly found in need of immediate attention:

1. Touch-up on interior and exterior paints and removal of graffiti

2. Minor carpentry repairs

3. Leaky and noisy plumbing

4. Stuck doors and windows

5. Broken glass and torn screens

6. Loose and damaged gutters and leaders

7. Roof leaks and missing shingles, tiles, and slates

8. Cracked sidewalks, driveways, and parking areas

9. Infestation by vermin

10. Cracked and loose tiles in bathrooms and kitchens

11. Septic system

12. Safety hazards

13. Fire hazards

Deteriorated Items

During the inspection of a building, an appraiser discovers many items that show signs of wear and tear. However, it is not economical to repair or replace most of the items on the date of the appraisal. The appraiser must decide whether an item needs immediate repair or replacement or whether it can be repaired later.[6] If the cost of the repairs adds nothing to the value of the property, the maintenance can be delayed. For example, a building that has a 10-year-old roof without leaks may hold up well for at least 5 years. Although the roof has suffered some depreciation, replacing it probably would not add any value to the property over the cost of a new roof.

The final step in a quality and condition survey is to report on the condition of those items that should last for the remaining estimated economic life of the building, assuming they are not subject to abnormal wear and tear or that they are not accidentally damaged. Again, the emphasis is on items that are not in the same condition as most of the building. An appraiser describes all major building components, including what they are made of, their condition, and their design. The appraiser may decide that the building needs rehabilitation, modernization, or remodeling. These are subjects that are discussed in Chapter 25. The information of a building description helps an appraiser to proceed through the valuation process.

Summary

The building description is an important step in an appraisal. A complete description includes all details of the exterior, interior, and mechanical systems of the building, as well as the condition of each.

Size, one of the most noticeable features of a building, can be measured in a number of ways according to standards developed by the FHA, the VA, the FNMA, and the FHLMC. Single family residences are described in terms of gross living area, multifamily dwellings in terms of gross building area, and shopping centers in terms of gross leaseable area. Office building measurements are not so standardized, although the trend is away from net rentable area measurement (the area actually occupied by a tenant) and toward total area measurement.

In describing a property's exterior, an appraiser examines all details of a building's substructure and superstructure. Because the substructure or foundation is rarely visible, an appraiser relies on original building plans, information from construction professionals, or obvious warning signs, such as settling and cracking, to determine if footings and foundations are solid. A building's superstructure includes everything from its structural framing, insulation, and ventilation to its exterior walls, doors, and windows.

---

[6]How to consider deteriorated items is discussed in Chapter 20.

Turning to the interior of the property, an appraiser provides all information about the interior walls and the spaces between them, including how the space is divided and finished. In addition, a building's interior supports, amount of termite protection, and miscellaneous and special features are described.

Most properties with basements are too large to be supported only by foundation walls, so bearing beams are used to provide additional support. Cracks or sagging in these beams should be regarded as potential problems. Along these same lines, the subflooring system has to be sturdy enough to provide safe support of floor loads and adequate underlayment for finish materials. The floorings themselves should be examined for durability and conformity to building design or usage.

Walls, ceilings, staircases, elevators, escalators, fireplaces, and storage space are other pertinent features to consider in describing a property's interior. Some properties, especially industrial buildings such as steel mills and oil refineries, have unusual special purpose improvements. An appraiser suggests how much these contribute to the value of the property. However, their contribution may be different for market value than it is for other value estimates.

Mechanical systems are the heart of any property, residential or commercial. The major systems are divided into two broad categories—those that consume energy, as do heating and hot water systems, and those that do not, such as a plumbing system.

The plumbing system consists of piping that is hidden and fixtures that are visible. The quality of the materials used, the way the pipes are installed, and their accessibility for servicing affect the efficiency and durability of a plumbing system. For commercial or industrial properties, an appraiser decides which plumbing fixtures are part of the real estate and which are personal property. Only those that are part of the real estate are included in the building value.

Hot water, heating, air-conditioning and ventilating, and electrical systems are major energy systems. The most common types of heating systems are based on warm or hot air, hot water, steam, or electricity. Automatic regulation of a heating system increases its operating efficiency, and a multiple-zone system with separate thermostats is more efficient than a single-zone with one thermostat. The type of fuel used is also significant because buyers today are sensitive to the cost and availability of natural gas and other fuel supplies. Solar heating is becoming a more popular alternative to conventional heating systems, so the appraiser describes these systems and estimates how much they contribute to a property's value.

As machinery and appliances become more complex, greater attention is given to the amount of electrical service that comes into a building. A typical residential system is a single-phase, three-wire system that provides a minimum of 100 amperes of electricity. The power in commercial and industrial buildings is generally carried in three-phase, four-wire systems that provide higher voltages.

Although not so critical as plumbing, heating, and power systems, such miscellaneous items as fire protection equipment, alarms, call systems, pneumatic tube systems, telephone wiring, and loading facilities must be noted in a thorough building description. These features assume varying degrees of importance, depending on the type of property under consideration.

An appraiser considers the quality and condition of the items described. If a worn or defective item does not constitute a fire or safety hazard and if the cost of the repair adds nothing to the value of the property, an appraiser may recommend that maintenance be delayed.

A careful and thorough description of a building's exterior, interior, and mechanical systems gives an appraiser a reliable basis for a value estimate.

Chapter 10

Analysis of Building Style and Function

Architectural style and functional utility are interrelated; together they affect property value and must be analyzed by an appraiser. *Architectural style is the character of a building's form and ornamentation,* whereas *functional utility is the efficiency of a building's use.* Both architectural style and functional utility affect human lives by providing or withholding beauty, comfort, security, convenience, light, air, pride of ownership, reasonable maintenance expenditure, the preservation of tradition, and the need for change.

A building may have functional utility but a poor architectural style, or it may have an admired style but little utility. Form and function should work together, as is seen in the best architecture. Functional utility is not necessarily exemplified by the most minimal space or form; people's needs for comfort and pleasure must also be provided for in the designs of offices, stores, hospitals, and houses. An appraiser must recognize and rank the full range of market preferences regarding style and functional utility and relate these preferences to market value.

Considerations of style and functional utility are integral to an appraisal. They are noted, along with other physical characteristics, during inspection of a property. Moreover, through the use of comparable data, an appraiser analyzes the influences that style and function have on a property's market value. Style and functional utility are examined in relation to the function or use of each property—the use for which it was designed, its actual or contemplated use, and its most economic use. These three may be the same, or any two or all may differ.

Architectural Style

Architecture is the science and art of building. It requires the formal organization of three-dimensional elements on a large scale to serve many human needs. In its interpretation of this charge, architecture is a fundamental reflection of civilization. An architectural style is more specific; it is the manner of architectural expression of a particular society, region, area, or time. Technically, an architectural style is comprised of building characteristics that are categorized in terms of structure, space, decoration, and function.

Architectural style is influenced by market standards and tastes. Market standards are accepted norms, which are reflected in customary or typical architectural styles. Market standards can also be defined more negatively. According to this definition, market standards are existing and established forms and methods of construction that have not yet been surpassed by advances in technology or deemed to be lacking appropriate aesthetic qualities.

Market tastes are preferences, which are standard or nonstandard. Standard tastes characterize the major portion of the market for real estate, whereas nonstandard tastes characterize the minor portion. In a free economy, tastes shift either in reaction to or in accordance with market standards.

Market tastes and standards are partly influenced by the desire to preserve tradition and the desires for change, variety, and often efficiency. Architectural trends are a response to the market's desire to preserve tradition by including elements of architectural styles from the past; the market's desire for change provides impetus for development in the elements of architectural design.

Changes in architectural trends are precipitated by the market's tolerance of current styles. When a style has been taken to an extreme, a swing back to elements of past styles occurs. Thus, extreme ornateness is replaced by forms that are spare; however, when spareness reaches an extreme level, an architectural swing back to some form of ornateness occurs. A reactive swing, then, provides contrast to the preceding dominant architectural style. In addition, a reactive swing produces avant-garde or experimental building styles, which are tested in the market. Any experimental style eventually either is discarded or becomes an accepted standard. However, the design elements that are discarded in a reactive swing are not lost; old forms may disappear from dominance for a time, but reappear in some modification as a new reactive swing occurs.

Architectural swings are most evident in formalized, architecturally designed buildings. However, there is a different type of architecture that historically has been subject not so much to architectural swings as to available materials and local customs. This type of architecture, often known as vernacular architecture, is found in the more ordinary structures.

These structures were not professionally designed and were built one at a time, according to local custom. Before the age of mass production, vernacular structures usually looked quite different from those that were professionally designed. The log cabin, which was popular by the mid-eighteenth century in the wilderness and on the frontier, was introduced by early Swedish immigrants in the 1630s. It is an example of a modest vernacular style. The vernacular architecture of the present time is perhaps the subdivision house, which is mass-produced and homogenized in style.

Reactive swings in architecture can also be generated by external forces. The economic concern with energy costs and supplies and the resulting structural designs that must incorporate these concerns is an example of a reactive swing.

Architectural styles are modified over periods loosely related to the economic life cycles of buildings; a proliferation of new construction usually contrasts in style with buildings of the previous period. Major revisions of architectural styles typically occur only after an entire building life cycle, which is 30 to 50 years.

Newly constructed buildings of all architectural styles, whether professionally designed or not, tend to have maximum appeal to the market. However, when a building is no longer new, it is judged competitively with other buildings in terms of the quality and usefulness of its architectural style. A building's form and structure, which are the most basic components of its architectural style, limit and define possible uses and changes and become more value-influencing as the building ages. The maintenance of tradition may be more acceptable than change to the real estate market. The preservation of tradition as a goal can refer to continuing the architectural styles of the immediate past or earlier times.

During most of the period that modern architecture has dominated the market, which has spanned much of this century, earlier styles were appreciated by only a small segment of buyers and sellers in the market. The revived interest in historically and architecturally significant (and subsequently in the merely old and interesting) buildings that predate the 1930s has become widespread throughout the United States, particularly since the American bicentennial of 1976.

Because the quality of architecture and architectural style can affect market value, an appraiser should be familiar with the various styles of American architecture. The following is a brief history of that architecture.[1]

History of American Architectural Styles

Traditional building designs that are acceptable to the market vary regionally. Much of the reason for this variation has historical roots.

When the United States, or the New World, was settled in the 1660s, each group of settlers brought the architectural styles and techniques of its home country, partly to transplant traditional culture in the New World and partly because indigenous American Indian architectural styles were considered unsuitable, except in the Southwest. But in each region of the New World, the styles and techniques were modified because of the differences in climate between the region and the home country, the unavailability of traditional materials upon which the architecture of the home country was based, the lack of trained architects and craftspeople, and the general poverty of the settlers. As time went on, different styles developed in the various areas to reflect the lifestyles, economic status, and occupations of the inhabitants and the climate of the region.

Because of the abundance of wood, most early colonial structures were made of wood frames, although in Virginia bricks were made from mortar and clay. The houses of English settlements along the eastern seaboard were modeled after English medieval vernacular houses, which were modified to suit the conditions of the New World and the sometimes harsh climate. Most early houses were simple one- or two-room, single-story, half-timber structures with sloped roofs. The climate forced settlers eventually to cover their half-timber houses, to lower roof slopes, and to simplify the plans of English vernacular houses. Houses had simple facades, asymmetrical floor plans, exterior shapes, and elevations. They were hand-hewn and had windows with small frames. The interiors had wood partitioning, some plastering,

---

[1]For a thorough discussion of the history of American architectural styles, see Judith Reynolds, *Historic Properties: Preservation and the Valuation Process* (Chicago: American Institute of Real Estate Appraisers, 1982), pp. 9-28.

simple paneling, and low ceilings. There was some baroque trim. Large fireplaces and exposed timber ceilings were common.

These structures reflected the small-scale individual activities in farming, fishing, commerce, and lumbering that were pursued in the northern colonies. A distinctive type of colonial New England single family house emerged. It was compact, with small windows and low ceilings, and was suitable for the region's long, hard winters and moderate summers.

By the mid-seventeenth century, structures in the southern colonies looked quite different from those in the North. Southern buildings were somewhat more symmetrical and had high ceilings, large windows, arches, and porticoes, which were designed for the hot southern climate. Large mansion houses and plantations reflected the large-scale agricultural economy of the South and symbolized the region's center of economic and political control. In addition, the mansions were based on the growing formality and classicism of English architecture in the mid-seventeenth century.

In the Southwest, which was settled by Spanish settlers, houses were a combination of Spanish and Indian architectural techniques. Indigenous Indian techniques of working with adobe and small stone masonry were perfectly suited to the environment of the Southwest. Structures in the Southwest had flat roofs, thick walls, center courtyards, and broad plaster expanses. There were few windows in the outer facades and larger windows in the shaded patio. This type of design was suited to the dry heat of the Southwest.

In the wilderness and in areas west of the seaboard settlements, the log cabin was the common structure for homes.

In the eighteenth century, America's growing prosperity and commerce attracted many well-trained craftspeople from Europe. They and native craftspeople and designers skillfully adapted European styles to American conditions. In New Orleans, French-trained architects and engineers produced an architecture of great sophistication. The Louisiana French pavilion house appeared, which had galleries and balconies that shaded the house from the heat of the area and had floor-to-ceiling windows, high ceilings, and central halls, all of which helped to combat the area's great humidity.

But the prevailing architecture of the eighteenth century was English and the forms popular in England at the time were classical, renaissance, and baroque. They all emphasized regularity, horizontal line, and classical proportions. They came together in a style known as Georgian.

Georgian buildings typically had pitched roofs, a center entrance, and a balanced plan and elevations. Early Georgians had complex embellishments in the baroque manner. Georgians that were built later acquired a classic balance and simplicity. Interior structural elements were no longer exposed but were covered with paneling or plaster. Georgian balance repudiated the medieval symmetry of early colonial structures. Georgian houses are among the most common type of single family residences to this day.

The Georgian style was perfected and simplified by the emergence of the federal style. The federal style was influenced by the direct studies of Roman and Greek structures that were being undertaken in Europe toward the end of the American colonial period. The style was well suited to the architecture that would reflect the aims of the American republic. Characteristics of the federal style include purity of line, restrained ornamentation, nearly flat roofs, balustrades, and porticoes with columns. Structures had long facades and tall, narrow windows and chimneys. Interiors were often finished with delicate plaster work and had oval, circular, and hexagonal spaces that were copied from Roman palaces. The federal style pervaded the eastern seaboard, particularly the port cities, and imposed a uniformity of style in public buildings and in many houses of the wealthy mercantile class. However, regional styles in the various areas persisted in many cases despite the pressure for uniformity.

After the War of 1812, the neoclassicism of the federal period was further simplified in the structures of the Greek revival. Architects of the Greek revival emphasized pediments and columns, white-painted exteriors, and strong, simple moldings. Chimneys became smaller. The long facades of the Georgian style gave way to gable ends, which were frequently designed with column-supported entabulatures. In addition to the Georgian style, the Greek revival style is a very common architectural style for single family residences.

The extreme simplicity of the federal and the Greek revival styles was countered by a number of picturesque styles in the nineteenth century, beginning with the gothic revival. The gothic revival signaled the beginning of a chaotic and eclectic period in American architecture, in which Americans eagerly desired European styles of the day for their structures. The form and function of the structures they built or commissioned to be built were often at odds. A number of the styles, particularly the gothic, fall under the general category of the Victorian style. Many residential and commercial buildings in the older sections of U.S. towns and cities are of the Victorian style. Since the 1970s, there has been a widespread attempt to renovate them.

The gothic revival was already evident in a number of churches and public buildings that were constructed at the end of the colonial period. The style became popular in American houses in the 1830s. Structures of the gothic revival had upward thrusting spires and pointed arches and were quite ornate. The gothic revival was an attempt to return to the building styles of the Middle Ages and structures thus had a medieval symmetry. However, the symmetry was somewhat offset by classical balance. Thus, the gothic revival merged the proportions of the English gothic style and those of the Greek revival.

The Italian style emerged in the 1830s and 1840s and rivaled the gothic revival structures in popularity in these decades. The Italian style was marked by the asymmetrical arrangement of square shapes, arched windows, towers, and cupolas. One aspect of the Italian style, the Italiante, had flat roofs with projecting cornices, arches and columns framing the windows, and the use of cast iron for the facade. The cast iron fronts of such buildings provided structural support and decorative, wide window openings. This type of architecture has survived in many urban areas in rows of commercial buildings.

The Queen Anne style, which emerged in the latter nineteenth century, harked back to the life of the English countryside due to the extensive use of wood, informal trim, and its boxlike form. It was characterized by turrets, varied textures, very large chimneys, oriel windows with many panes, spindel work, terra-cotta ornamentation, porches, shingles, and horizontal banding. Interiors pointed to the beginning of the development of the open plan.

In the middle to latter part of the century, the second empire style emerged. In contrast to the Queen Anne style, the second empire style was marked by refined elegance. Structures had mansard roofs, dormer windows, and sculptural detailing. The style was strongly vertical and stone was used predominantly.

These latter century styles were adopted largely because Americans began traveling to Europe in great numbers, especially after the Civil War, which reinforced their desire for European architectural styles. But within the architectural eclecticism and rage for borrowed styles, existing local architecture persisted. Sometimes several picturesque styles were combined together or with older styles in odd ways. The unity of purpose between form and function that older architecture reflected broke down.

The nineteenth century, especially as it progressed, signaled growing urbanization and industrialization. The development of steam power, which produced standardized sawn and milled lumber, and the mass production of nails, which made balloon framing possible, changed the faces of structures and architectural styles. Building techniques changed greatly. Besides cast iron, steel and reinforced concrete began to be used in innovative ways. Increasingly large factory buildings needed stronger supports than simple wood framing.

After the Civil War, a hiatus in building construction occurred. Growing urbanization and westward expansion forced rapid and often crude construction. But the construction of buildings increasingly became an industry in itself. Construction became more organized so that projects of nearly any size could be swiftly and economically built.

Certain architects became concerned with planning interior space to be efficient again and began to stress the function rather than the beauty of a building, which was the major purpose of picturesque styles. The renewed concern with functionality as a basis for house design generated much experimentation with forms.

Thus emerged the Romanesque revival. The rounded arches, the heavy, rough stone texture, and the short, strong columns caused the structures of the revival to look rugged and massive. At the same time, the elements provided order and clarity of organization due to the arches and the incorporation of a single tower as the focal point. The Romanesque revival was based on load-bearing masonry construction. The style bridges the classicism of the Greek revival and the exuberance and originality of the Chicago style.

The desire for greater functionality reached the century's extreme expression in the structures of the Chicago style. The tenets of the style are best seen in surviving commercial buildings, which are unique in their power and originality. In fact, the Chicago style was the first truly original form of American architecture.

The Chicago style combined powerful modern technology with late-nineteenth century ornamentation so that multistory office buildings and steel-framed skyscrapers could be beautifully ornamented. For the first time, walls and floors were supported by steel frames. Most buildings were gray or brown terra-cotta and had detailed ornamentation. The bands of windows were indented and the projecting cornices were elaborate.

The Chicago style was one of a number of styles that flourished during the late nineteenth and early twentieth centuries and added to another period of architectural eclecticism. Included were picturesque styles, such as the Queen Anne and gothic, as well as new styles. Much of the functional *originality* of the Chicago school was ignored in all the styles except the Prairie school, which in some ways was the direct descendant of the Chicago school.

The Prairie school is known largely for the unique houses of Frank Lloyd Wright. However, the office buildings and residential structures that were designed by architects of the Prairie school were equally cohesive and unique. Ornamental excesses were rejected and buildings were well integrated with their sites. Concrete was used in innovative ways in blocks and great slabs, which were reinforced with steel rods and were fashioned in continuous, curvilinear forms. Basements and other features considered extraneous were eliminated. Furniture and fixtures were designed as integral components of the structures.

There was also a return to classicism in the period, but this type of classicism strongly stressed functionality, although it was not original in the sense that marked the Chicago style. The Columbian Exposition of 1893 in Chicago signaled the return to Greek and Roman forms. The Beaux Arts school in Paris, which was founded as a direct result of the Exposition, taught that the true principles of architecture were found in classical architecture. Structures that were built had large-scale elements in a formalized, functional manner. Columns were often used in pairs to indicate their load-bearing function. In the buildings of this style that remain, many have large flights of stairs and classical sculpture. The central portion dominates the structure. Less important details are indicated as such by their small size. Interior spaces are intricate but highly ordered.

This eclectic period also saw the emergence of the art nouveau style, which developed from the art moderne movement that began in Brussels in the 1880s. Art nouveau replaced Greek and Roman elements, such as columns and pediments, with curved, zigzagged, or geometric shapes and fanciful ornamentation. Art nouveau includes elements of technology, symbolism, functionalism, and naturalism. During the inception of art nouveau, structures had curvilinear forms that were decorated with vegetational shapes. By about 1910 the style became more rectilinear and naturalistic and abandoned the vegetational shapes. After 1918 art nouveau emphasized cubic geometry.

Art nouveau attempted a return to the craftsmanship of the preindustrial era. The number of buildings constructed in the art nouveau style is small; the style was more widely expressed in arts and crafts and interior design, known as art deco, which is sometimes simplistic in line or ornamentation and at other times is fairly intricate and includes geometric shapes and curvilinear forms. There has been a revival of interest in art nouveau and widespread restoration of such structures in major cities. Art nouveau bridged Victorian eclectic styles and the Bauhaus, or functionalist, movement.

The Bauhaus movement, which produced what is known as the international style of architecture, attempted to reintroduce much of the functional originality of the Chicago school, but without the ornamentation. The international style thus contrasted sharply with art nouveau as architects dispensed with ornateness and insisted on spare forms. Originally, in the middle to late 1920s, the German Bauhaus school of design planned structures to house German urban workers. However, architects in the United States later took the Bauhaus designs and applied them to nearly all types of structures.

The international style dispensed with the cornices and terra-cotta exterior of the Chicago school and provided skyscrapers with a streamlined appearance. Windows were set flush to emphasize the desired streamlined effect.

Structures designed by architects of the international style have lightweight frames and curtain walls, open room arrangements, openings that are linearly geometric, and flat roofs; they are made with industrial materials. The international style is the most recent traditional style in the United States and comprises much of the built environment. The style reached its height in the 1950s and 1960s. In the 1970s, however, the market turned away from the severe forms of the international style and desired more traditional forms, which were incorporated into the structures of postmodern styles.

Postmodern styles, which succeeded the international style, are still not definitive in terms of style and vary in form and ornamentation. Some postmodern structures include classical elements such as columns or pediments; other structures have geometric variations on the rectangular glass box of the international style; still others have softened lines and rounded forms, which are characteristic of art nouveau. Thus postmodern structures have a sculptured, rather than a streamlined, appearance.

Postmodern styles tend to reemphasize expanses of solid wall rather than glass. Thus, the texture and substance of exterior walls are again emphasized, rather than the international style's metal skeleton and minimal metal and glass sheathing. This change in architectural direction appropriately emerged at approximately the same time as the preservation and adaptive-use movement, which supports the recycling of older buildings that were constructed in prefunctionalist periods.

Before concluding the history of American architectural styles, a short history of the major single family architectural styles of the twentieth century must be given. In the early part of the century, bungalows became popular. From the 1920s to the 1950s, Cape Cods became the most popular. In addition, subdivision houses became popular after World War II. Ranch and split-level designs developed in the 1950s and 1960s. Townhouses that were based on Georgian rowhouse design emerged in the late 1960s and 1970s. Georgian, Dutch colonial, and Greek revival structures also have been popular throughout the decades.

Thus, architectural styles in the market have changed in response to the market's desire to preserve tradition or the desire for change, the changes in technology, and the tastes of a particular group at a particular time. Styles also change in response to construction and maintenance costs. In addition, styles vary regionally and according to a building's use. Architectural style as a consideration of market value is fundamentally measured by the prices buyers are willing to pay. Appraisers ascertain the degree of that willingness with regard to various styles.

Materials, Structure, Equipment, and Siting

Architectural style partly depends on a number of components for its expression, including materials, structure, equipment, and siting.

These components shape and change building style. The availability of natural materials, such as wood, stone, and clay and lime for making brick, was primarily responsible for the architectural styles that emerged and prevailed in the various areas. When post-and-beam construction was developed, greater spaces could be spanned. This type of construction made possible the large fabricating mills of the Industrial Revolution. The evolution of lightweight balloon framing and mass-produced, machine-made nails changed the form of buildings in the nineteenth century. Balloon framing also permitted buildings to be constructed much more rapidly because it used precut components.

The development of the Franklin stove and of central heating revised the shape and number of rooms in all structures because fireplaces were no longer relied on to provide heat. The production of domestic equipment in the early twentieth century eliminated the need for root cellars, pantries, and large laundry rooms, which thus decreased the size and changed room arrangements of dwellings.

The prevalent use of central air-conditioning and heating in the mid-twentieth century, made possible by modern technology being applied to residential, commercial, and industrial building equipment, resulted in a standardization of architectural styles throughout the country, particularly in houses. This standardization nearly obliterated the different regional building styles that had logically developed because of variations in climate. For example, the thick mud masonry walls and small windows of the Southwest had been well suited to the hot, dry weather of the region. Overhanging roofs of the rainy northwest coast had allowed windows to be open for ventilation without admitting the rain. The saltboxes of New England had provided protection against the harsh northern wind by turning the windowless, steeped-roof side of the house to the north. In the mid-1970s, such structural defenses against climate began to be reincorporated into new construction. Thus, because of an energy-conscious market, climate-compatible design has again emerged. Whether a building has such a design is important in estimating market value because consumers increasingly desire energy-saving features.

The use of steel for framing and the invention of the elevator made taller buildings possible. Curtain walls of glass and metal and the boxy forms of the international style were well suited to one another. Curtain-wall construction separated the functions of support and enclosure that had been welded in heavy masonry multistory buildings. Curtain walls can be of metal, masonry, precast concrete, or glass.

Bar joists have twice the load-bearing capacity of solid joists; they permit greater spans and allow pipes, ducts, and conduit to be threaded through open webbing. Lightweight structural support systems and the lamination and plastic glues that were developed in the aircraft industry have generated departures in form, such as butterfly and arcaded roofs.

The technology of concrete that has developed since the 1940s has permitted new building shapes because concrete can be used in large slabs, building blocks, or beams. Reinforced concrete elevator-building construction competes with steel framing. It offers an alternative that is less vulnerable to the twisting or torque that steel undergoes in a fire. Whereas building a structure with poured concrete is slow and must stop in cold weather, precast concrete assembly proceeds nearly as quickly as steel construction. Post-tensioning, a method whereby reinforcing rods are tightened while concrete hardens, provides additional strength. The bundled tube form of office tower construction permits reinforced concrete buildings to be built to a height equal to steel-framed towers.

As materials, structural components, and equipment become more refined through technological advances, architectural styles change accordingly. Technological advances are integrated in evolving architectural styles and sometimes produce modifications of architectural trends.

Architectural design is also influenced by the possibilities for placing a building on its site. Every building has a physical setting that includes the space that surrounds it. In cities where buildings directly abut one another, there is little choice about placement. However, in places where there is more flexibility, a building's design, placement, and landscaping can provide defense against the climate. High energy costs underscore siting as an element of compatibility, but appropriate placement on a site also serves to enhance architectural design.

Architectural design can be adjusted to the climate and an individual site. Trees can act as shade, windbreaks, sound barriers, and air filters. They can add moisture to the air. Deciduous trees are better placed on the western area of a property, where they can provide shade from a hot afternoon sun in summer, but allow the sun's warmth to shine through in winter. Conifers can be planted on the northern part to act as windbreaks. Shade and sunlight can also be controlled by the angle and direction of overhanging roofs. The roofs permit the sun's high-angle rays in summer to be deflected and the low-angle rays in winter to be admitted by windows.

Because increasing fuel costs have created the need for alternate energy sources, active and passive solar features have been introduced, although to a limited extent. Mechanical solar collectors are generally more cumbersome, unattractive, and expensive to install than are justified by the results. Passive solar techniques include strategically placed windows or glass walls, insulation, heat-retaining walls and floors, and careful siting. Rooms, roofs, and windows can be arranged so that warm air flows freely throughout the structure. The same kind of design and room arrangement can provide maximum ventilation and air cooling. Certain active solar heating systems use glass roof panels; others use glass attached to one side of a house. Warm air is stored in some medium, such as water, or pumped directly into the house.

A house that is underground takes advantage of below-grade temperatures that are in the moderate range year-round. Heating and cooling equipment can thus operate with less power, thereby significantly reducing energy costs. Underground housing in the United States is found primarily in the Central Plains region, where storm protection and energy cost reduction are primary concerns. Earth-covered dwellings are built of poured concrete and concrete block. They are usually located on grade and bermed, that is, set into a site that is partly or completely excavated. Berming overcomes the constraints of high water tables, expansive clay soils, rock strata, or flat rural sites. The most common siting involves partial excavation into a hillside. A sod-covered roof provides additional insulation.

Underground construction, solar heating techniques, climate-specific siting, and other energy-related building style adaptations should be considered in an appraisal with regard to their market acceptability and their influence on sale prices, rents, and other market value indicators.

Functional Utility

For something to be functional, it must work; it must be useful. However, the definition of functional utility is subject to changing expectations and standards. Optimum functional utility implies the maximum that design and engineering can produce in terms of perceived needs at any given time.

Functional inutility is defined as impairment of functional capacity or efficiency. It becomes equivalent to functional obsolescence because ongoing change, which is caused by technological advances and economic and aesthetic trends, renders layouts and features obsolete. However, functional inutility must be judged in the context of market standards of acceptability, specifically in the context of buyers who make up the market for a particular type of building.

As objectives of building design, functional utility and aesthetics are sometimes in conflict; market standards generally reflect a compromise between the two. The extremes of utilitarianism in housing design that omitted basements, entrance halls, and dining rooms were eventually rejected by much of the market and were replaced by more flexible designs. Similarly, the trend toward ultimate efficiency in the interiors of office buildings at one time produced "standard" space that had low ceilings, plain walls, and vinyl asbestos floors. Thereafter, such interior finish was considered substandard.

Thus, functional utility embraces more than the simple idea of practical utilitarianism. Yet overimprovement—that is, superadequate structural components or space—are also items of functional obsolescence because their cost exceeds their value. When an expensively finished retail space with high ceilings is included in an office building that is located where there is no market for retailing, the building incorporates functional obsolescence in the form of superadequacy.

Standards of functional utility vary with the type of property and its use. Considerations for different properties are discussed in the remainder of this chapter. However, some general standards of functional utility that should be considered by appraisers include

1. Suitability or appropriateness

2. Comfort

3. Efficiency

4. Safety

5. Security

6. Accessibility

7. Ease and cost of maintenance

8. Market standards

9. Attractiveness

There is an additional standard that must be given special treatment. In determining functional utility and appropriateness of architectural style, an appraiser must also consider compatibility.

Compatibility

Compatibility means that a building is in harmony with its use or uses and its environment. The harmony should extend to form, materials, and scale. Styles of different periods frequently clash; a cubistic dwelling is seldom in harmony with eighteenth-century colonial buildings that surround it. A monumental or ostentatious building often is quite incongruous in a modest setting. Two-story structures tend to be overwhelmed in a row of skyscrapers. Thus, market value is frequently diminished by incompatibility of design. There are various types of incompatibility. A structure can be incompatible with its function; a structure's various elements can be incompatible with one another; or the structure can be incompatible with its site or its location in the neighborhood.

Compatibility is influenced by zoning, historical districts, construction and maintenance costs, land value, physical features, architectural trends, and technology. Sometimes these influences impose conformity. *Conformity means that the form, manner, and character of structures correspond to one another.* Conformity, a narrow definition of compatibility, can thus result in unvarying dullness. The broader definition of compatibility does not preclude variation within a harmonious framework.

Usually, the predominant uses and building styles in a location are readily observable. However, the trend of development may be more difficult to observe; the architectural style that appears atypical may conform to the direction of the trend.

Because a building design that is typical of an area has less influence on value than a design that is atypical, the impact of the nonconformity should be considered carefully by an appraiser. A somewhat unusual design that is attractive and generally in harmony with other buildings that are typical could command a higher price than that of its more typical neighbors. An incongruous design, however, will probably sell below general market level price; if it does not, there may be offsetting qualities.

Isolated cases of nonconforming design may require an unsupported but reasoned appraisal judgment. However, if, for example, international style office buildings in a particular location sell regularly at lower prices per square foot than do buildings of a less simple style, the penalty can be determined from market data. Sometimes there is sufficient demand for a detached dwelling in a row-house neighborhood or for an art nouveau movie theater in a retail shopping district dominated by nineteenth-century buildings to support a market value equal to or greater than that for a more typical structure. Functional utility may override design as a primary market requirement; if the general proportions and scale of the atypical building are in harmony with the surroundings and the functional utility demands are met, any design penalty may be negated.

Materials should be in harmony with one another and with a building's architectural style. A building that is designed to be constructed of a particular material is not necessarily effective when constructed of another. Building materials should not be excessive in variety nor should an architectural design have too many distracting features. Architectural design and building materials should be well integrated and be in harmony with the site. A frame building in a wooded, hilly area will probably be more in harmony with its setting than is a brick building; however, wood may be inappropriate for the structure's particular function. A frame building in a masonry-dominated urban area usually suffers a market value penalty. An office building with a metal alloy facade may be penalized if stone facades are typical of the area.

Design and Functional Utility in Different Building Categories

Marketability is the ultimate test of functional utility. Generally, a building is functional if it successfully serves the purpose for which it was designed or adapted. Specific design considerations that affect functional utility in residential, commercial, industrial, agricultural, and special purpose buildings are discussed below.

Residential

Trends in single family houses and apartments alternate between inclusion and noninclusion of such items as porches, balconies, fireplaces, dining rooms, large kitchens, entry halls, and family rooms. Standards for dwellings vary widely in different income levels and regions. When judging functional utility in residential buildings, appraisers should be concerned with standard expectations of the market. However, the functional utility of single and multifamily dwellings results from the proper planning of layout, accommodation of specific activities, adequacy, and ease and cost of maintenance.

Layout

A layout develops from considering the traffic patterns in an apartment or a house—where kitchens and bathrooms should be located for convenience, and how private and public areas should be separated.

A layout has functional inutility if it causes awkward traffic patterns. For instance, inutility may result if people have to traverse the living room to get to a bedroom, if the dining space is not adjacent to the kitchen, or if groceries have to be brought through the living room to the kitchen.

Complete bathrooms, including facilities for bathing, are more convenient, accessible, and private when they are part of the bedroom grouping. They should be directly accessible or accessible through a hall, not a second bedroom. Powder rooms are best located off a hall and near, but not so near, to the living or the dining room. Poor floor plans are easily recognized by those who make up the market for apartments and houses, although standards often vary according to region and fad.

The location of various rooms in relation to the site can increase or diminish privacy, comfort, and serenity. Master bedrooms and living rooms, particularly in urban areas, are increasingly found in the rear of the residence. Often they have access to and views of a garden. This relatively new location is a reversal of what was formerly desired: that the living room and best bedroom should be at the front of the house and oriented to the street. Kitchens, which once were relegated to the rear, are now just as likely to be on one side of a hall and in the middle or at the front of a residence.

Layout is extremely important in a "shared" dwelling, which has two equal bedrooms and is purchased jointly by unrelated persons. Layout is also important in row housing, which is becoming increasingly popular again after being nearly disregarded from 1950 to 1970.

The emergence of condominiums as a major form of dwelling ownership has produced versatility in apartment design. Clustered, duplex, and townhouse units are designed in interesting configurations that maximize market appeal. Structures that were designed for other uses are often being converted to apartments. Silos, breweries, warehouses, and schools have been successfully converted to multiunit projects. Duplexes often have a strong market appeal and maximize salable square footage because vertical access is included in the unit rather than in the public space. Multiunit housing is also built in stacked configurations with access provided at more than one level so that stair climbing is minimized. The versatility of design permitted for these types of low-rise multiple housing projects is almost unlimited. Elevator apartment buildings tend to have more standardized and predictable floor plans that are geared to maximum use of space within the simple rectangular configuration.

Accommodation of Specific Activities

The accommodation of specific activities is accomplished by providing separate areas for food preparation, eating, conversation, sleeping, hygiene, hobbies, and relaxation. For most American housing, the trend throughout much of this century has been toward combining the functions of many rooms into fewer rooms. The living-dining room and the family room are examples of the trend. At one time, many houses did not have entrance halls. But for the most part, such extremes have been modified in the market.

Adequacy

Adequacy is a primary consideration when one appraises or plans for functional utility. Adequacy of size, windows, doors, rooms, ceiling height, closets, security, privacy, and comfort are considered in the planning and appraisal of dwellings.

Standards of adequacy vary. The one-bathroom dwelling unit or house has largely become anachronistic. Kitchens and baths are becoming larger, better equipped, and more expensively finished, thereby overshadowing the small utilitarian kitchens and baths of the immediate past. Dishwashers, garbage disposals, and wall ovens are usually standard in new construction; their absence may create a value penalty.

Ceramic tile in baths and more elegant fixtures are becoming more typical. The master bedroom frequently has its own compartmental bath and separate dressing area. Closets tend to be abundant throughout apartments and houses. Many ceiling heights have increased despite energy costs, especially in living rooms.

In general, more people have better housing than once was the case. An increasing number of amenities are now considered necessities and are thus taken for granted. Even in periods when average houses are smaller because of high construction and financing costs, the tendency is to retain extra bathrooms, labor-saving devices, and fireplaces.

Although it is a dwelling unit within a larger structure, an apartment must be seen as an integral part of the whole. Security, convenience, and ease of maintenance are primary considerations for apartments whether they are rental units or are owned as cooperatives or condominiums. It is generally more important for apartments to be easily accessible to places of employment and entertainment than it is for houses. Amenities tend to be more important than space; apartment buyers and sellers often prefer a fireplace or an extra bathroom to an additional 200 square feet. Because most apartments do not have gardens or yards, they should provide light, air, and an interesting view. Amenities such as convenient parking, swimming pools, tennis courts, and exercise facilities are important to apartment projects located where these features are not available nearby.

Smaller kitchens and bathrooms tend to be more acceptable to the market for apartments than houses. A dining area that is an ell or is one end of the living room is generally acceptable. A room too small to be an attractive bedroom can be used as a den or an extra bedroom. Living rooms need to be spacious to offset the relative smallness of other rooms. Closet space should be plentiful.

Kitchen and bath finishes and equipment that are designed according to fads can quickly render an apartment less than optimally desirable to the market. Examples are pastel ceramic tile in bathrooms and dark-colored kitchen equipment where all white or neutral color schemes are preferred. Dishwashers, garbage disposals, and central air-conditioning have become standard for apartments. Laundry equipment is becoming standard in more expensive units.

The mix of units in the project should meet market demands; deficiencies in the unit mix represent functional inutility.

Ease and Cost of Maintenance

The ease and cost of maintenance are increasingly crucial to the marketability of a single family dwelling or a condominium unit. More family members have become wage earners and there is less time for home maintenance. Interior and exterior finishes that require extensive maintenance have become noncompetitive.

The efficiency of energy use is a primary consideration in the dwelling market due to the high costs of heating, cooling, lighting, and cooking fuels. In seeking alternatives to electricity, natural gas, and oil, buyers have turned to insulation, fireplaces, wood stoves, ventilating fans, and passive solar techniques. In most markets, a house that wastes fuel and electricity suffers major functional obsolescence.

A free-standing building provides the maximum outside window-wall area, making the layout potentially more flexible and providing more windows in each unit. Windows, however, are primary sources of heat loss. Energy-conserving features are particularly important for multifamily dwellings and often mean the difference between a profitable and a nonprofitable operation. A large portion of the energy used in buildings is required to offset heat losses through cracks and openings and through the building envelope. Insulation, tightly installed windows with double- or triple-glazing, caulking and weatherstripping, and protection from solar gain in the summer, such as deciduous tree shading, blinds, or solar screens, all help to reduce energy loss. In addition, energy-efficient equipment and controls are necessary to meet new standards of functional utility in multifamily buildings.

Commercial

Commercial buildings are used for offices, stores, banks, restaurants, and service outlets. Commercial hotels constitute an important subcategory. Frequently, two or more uses are combined in a single building.

Structural and design features of commercial buildings constantly undergo change. The desire to have the most competitive building possible, within the cost constraints imposed by economic pressures, causes developers to incorporate changes in technology to meet demand for innovation whenever possible.

The efficiency of commerical construction is much greater than it was formerly. This is true for both the portion of the total area enclosed by the structure, which can produce direct income in the form of rent, and for the structural facilitation that has evolved out of new materials and construction methods. No method of commercial building construction predominates. Methods vie with one another; one surpasses others in given areas at particular times. Steel and reinforced concrete are commonly used structural alternatives.

An appraiser examines a number of specific elements of functional utility in commercial buildings. An additional concern—safety and security features—may be affected by the treatment of any of the specific elements, which are

1. Column spacing

2. Bay depth

3. Live-load floor capacity

4. Ceiling height

5. Module width

6. Elevator facilities

7. The work letter

8. HVAC adequacy

9. Energy efficiency

10. Public amenities

11. Parking ratios

Column Spacing

Column placement is related to a building's total height; greater spans
are more expensive to construct. Closely spaced columns limit the possibilities of interior partitioning. Column placement of 20 to 22 feet on
center is typical in some areas but is far more limiting than column
placement of 28 to 30 feet on center. A tenant usually prefers the
wider spacing, but the cost to construct it might prove prohibitive.

Bay Depth

Bay depth is the distance from the tenant side of the corridor wall to
the exterior wall. Bay depth controls the layout of interior space and is
dictated by the depth and width of the site, which prescribes a building's configuration. The boxy configurations of contemporary office
buildings are cost efficient; the ratio of perimeter wall to enclosed area
is optimized. A long thin building is more expensive to construct than
a square one that has the same area. The shallower bay depths of older
buildings are more adaptable to the needs of smaller tenancies,
whereas greater bay depths are more profitable to build if they do not
exceed market demand. Tenants are often guided more by the configuration of the space, relative to its ability to house staff and equipment,
than by square foot area per se.

Live-Load Floor Capacity

Floor loading capacity is measured in live-load pounds per square foot.
Inadequate floor loading capacity is a type of functional obsolescence
that often prohibits marketability and is expensive to cure. Live-load
includes everything that can be moved, excluding parts of the structure. A floor load capacity of 100 pounds (up from 70 pounds a gen-
eration ago) has generally been adequate for commercial buildings. Mi-
crofilm and microfiche record storage, as well as small-frame computer

equipment, have reversed the trend from ever-increasing live-load floor capacity.

Ceiling Height

New commercial buildings usually have finished ceiling heights. Finished ceiling heights depend on the building heights that are permitted by zoning and by market standards and preferences. Medical office buildings, for instance, may have lower ceiling heights because of ducting requirements. The higher end of a limited range is preferable for other types of office space.

Module Width

The basic building module is based on the distance between window mullions, which determines the size of the partitioned offices in a building. Ceiling tiles and other components of modern office finish also determine the dimensions of contemporary office space modules.

When older commercial buildings have considerable architectural charm or otherwise acceptable structural qualities, it can be cost effective to retrofit them with modern lighting, ventilation, and elevators even if their design does not conform to contemporary building module dimensions. High ceilings, narrow bay depths, wide public corridors, tall doors, and elaborate woodwork may be successfully preserved to meet the demand of certain markets for less streamlined space.

Elevator Facilities

Elevators in multilevel office buildings should be adequate in their speed, load capacity, safety, and number. They should be able to meet peak period demands adequately. Appraisers judge the adequacy of elevators by certain standards. A building should have one elevator for every 25,000 to 40,000 square feet of rentable area. In addition, elevators should be able to transport between 10% and 30% of the building's occupants within five minutes. Elevator speeds should be between 300 and 350 feet per minute. The standards vary according to a building's tenants. For example, a single organization may require more elevator service because of interfloor traffic. Many building codes require that elevators accommodate handicapped patrons; elevators should provide accessible control panels and interiors and doors that are wide enough for wheelchairs.

Elevator capacity is expressed in weight and in numbers of people. Electric elevators are faster than hydraulic ones and thus serve multistory buildings better. Hydraulic elevators are sometimes used to connect two or more floors.

An appraiser's assessment of functional utility in elevator service should be made in view of the number of tenants, the number of floors, and the total building area served by the elevators, as well as the service provided in competing buildings.

The Work Letter

An office building's standard level of lighting, partitioning, door allowances, and electrical capacity is called the work letter. The quality and dollar value of these standard installations vary. A typical work letter may include the following:

1. One lineal foot of partitioning per 12-15 square feet of office space

2. One suite entrance door per 5,000 square feet of office space and one interior door for every 200-300 square feet

3. One 2-by-4-foot lighting fixture for every 80 square feet

4. One light switch per room

5. One duplex receptacle per each 125 square feet

6. One telephone outlet per each 150 square feet of space

7. One lineal foot of closet door per each 800 square feet and one bifold closet door for every 5,000 square feet

Inadequacies or superadequacies in the work letter levels can result in market value penalties; such variations often result in a tenant payment or credit, or in a rental addition or concession.

HVAC Adequacy

In determining a building's functional utility, an appraiser considers whether the heating, ventilating, and air-conditioning systems are adequate. A particular consideration is the match between a building's principal use and its mechanical equipment. For example, medical office buildings contain substantially more plumbing lines and connections, ventilating diffusers, electrical wiring, and partitioning than do typical office structures.

Energy Efficiency

Energy consumption standards are becoming increasingly necessary for commercial buildings. To remain competitive, office buildings must incorporate up-to-date technological advances, such as controls programmed by computers, zoned heating and cooling, and highly efficient mechanical equipment. Public pressure in regard to economizing on energy consumption has been building due to rising energy costs, peak load pricing policies, and the threat of energy allocations.

Expenditures of British thermal units per square foot per year have ranged between 125,000 and 150,000 in nonenergy-efficient commercial buildings. In building areas that house computers, the figures are significantly higher. With improved building design, the amount of Btus that are consumed on a per-square-foot basis has been lowered to between 60,000 and 80,000 per year. However, experimental buildings can operate on less than 50,000 Btus per square foot per year.

Whereas most newer commercial buildings in cities have been constructed with fixed sash fenestration, certain ones are now being built with windows, which admit fresh air and regulate temperatures. If energy source allocation occurs, thereby making certain energy fuels unavailable at times, fixed sash windows could become functionally obsolete.

Public Amenities

Building amenities can contribute to functional utility. Such amenities include appealing public areas and grounds and adequate and well-located restroom facilities. For example, because of its function, a retail center must have good delivery access, suitable traffic patterns for shoppers, high lighting levels, adequate column spacing, and a sufficient number of escalators. Surface and finish elements should be durable and easily maintained. In addition, a retail center must have places for shoppers and workers to rest, ample restroom facilities, and attractive and coordinated signs.

A specialty shopping center, the newest type of retail grouping, has a number of retailing uses, most of which offer nonessential goods and services. In addition, such a center usually has no anchor tenants. Thus, a specialty shopping center needs to project a certain amount of magnetism through a central feature, integrated design elements, and attractive landscaping. In addition, restaurants and entertainment centers, such as movie theaters, should be included.

Thus, the quality and distribution of public amenities in shopping centers are important appraisal concerns. The need for adequate distribution of amenities affects the designs of shopping centers, which are as competitive in the market as are the designs for office buildings. But the configuration of the typical shopping center has tended to change even more drastically than that of the typical office building. Trends in shopping centers change rapidly enough so that many structures become functionally obsolete before they deteriorate physically. However, such retail space is relatively easy to renovate, and many centers can be streamlined and modernized when they lose their market appeal. Shopping centers have evolved from small strip centers, which were developed after World War II, to huge regional and superregional centers, which occupy up to 100 acres of land and include over one million square feet of building. In spite of the traditional trend toward greater size, however, most existing and newly built shopping centers are smaller than 200,000 square feet, with more than half being smaller than 100,000 square feet.

Supermarkets and drugstores that were traditional anchor stores of large suburban shopping centers now tend to be free-standing structures near but not a part of shopping centers. The major reason for this phenomenon is the increased merchandising competition between supermarkets, department stores, drugstores, and smaller mall stores. Larger suburban shopping centers are frequently town centers, where people go to shop, to socialize, to be entertained, and to attend political meetings.

Parking Ratios

Crucial to the success of retail centers, except those in dense urban areas, is the parking ratio. The emergence of multiuse shopping centers, as well as the trend to smaller automobiles, has increased the square footage of gross leaseable store area to parking spaces. A parking space for every 180 square feet of gross leaseable store area is not usually excessive. Orientation to the means of access is crucial for all commercial buildings.

There is a tendency for commercial uses to occupy separate structures in areas of low density of development. In such cases, the major access to buildings is usually by automobile so that sufficient adjacent parking is required. Pedestrian access from buildings to parking areas may still be required and should be accommodated. Pedestrian access to both public transportation and automobile parking are important to commercial buildings in densely developed urban areas.

Security and convenience govern the placement of parking facilities; access between a commercial facility and parking must be direct and visible. The quantity of parking must be determined in view of the availability of alternative sources of access, such as subway and bus systems, their proximity, and how much parking is provided by similar buildings. Certain commercial buildings in urban areas do not include on-site parking because other forms of transportation are considered convenient enough or adequate parking facilities are closeby.

An efficient parking garage design provides for a column placement of 28 feet, which permits three cars to be parked between columns. The increasing number of small cars has provided outdoor parking lots with greater capacity, which has been accomplished through restriping. However, parking garage design has not fundamentally changed due to the need for columns. When possible, drive aisles have been reduced in width, from 26 feet to 25 feet. Standard parking space has been reduced from 9 by 18 feet to 8¾ by 17½ feet. Compact size is about 8¼ by 16½ feet. A self-park garage averages from 300 to 350 gross rentable feet per car, which includes aisles and ramps. Garages with attendant parking average substantially less than 300 square feet per car.

The most efficient configuration is 90-degree-angle parking. A typical parking ratio in the absence of good public transit is five spaces per 1,000 square feet of rentable office area.

Hotels

Hotels range from tiny inns, with fewer than a dozen rooms, to huge convention hotels, which have more than a thousand rooms.[2] All hotels and motels formerly were measured against standard, up-to-date designs, and this tendency continues, particularly for medium-priced hotels. However, for many older hotels and luxury hotels, the trend is toward variety in architectural styles and interior finish.

Many older hotels and apartment buildings that have a classical or baroque architectural style and a quality of luxury difficult to replicate in a newer structure have been rehabilitated as hotels. The desire to rehabilitate older buildings has spread to picturesque country areas that have small inns.

The major categories of lodging facilities are (1) vacation or resort hotels, (2) convention hotels, (3) center city business and tourist hotels, (4) suburban hotels, (5) highway motor hotels, (6) airport hotels, (7) apartment hotels, and (8) country inns. Convention hotels are frequently large and centrally located. In urban areas, they cater to business persons and tourists, and to vacationers in country settings.

All lodging facilities benefit from suitable fireproofing, soundproofing, and systems that provide security and safety. Beyond these basic considerations, a hotel or motel's physical configuration is determined by the types of patrons it serves. A motor hotel must be oriented to the needs of automobile drivers who wish to spend only a minimum amount of time on the premises, whereas a resort hotel must provide a variety of forms of entertainment facilities. Although accommodations for automobiles are necessary, they are better situated away from direct view.

Functional inutility in hotel structures, as for other types of structures, can be categorized in terms of overimprovements, inadequacies, poor layout, inappropriate structural qualities or finishes, and inefficient equipment.

The amount of a structure's space that is used for guest rooms varies. A hotel that is used as a major meeting and entertainment center has a much lower proportion of guest rooms than an apartment hotel that provides residential comfort. Many apartment hotels are suc-

---

[2]For a thorough discussion of hotels, see Stephen Rushmore, *Hotels, Motels, and Restaurants: Valuation and Market Studies* (Chicago: American Institute of Real Estate Appraisers, forthcoming).

cessful transient operations that consist entirely of suites with small, equipped kitchens, living rooms, and separate bedrooms. The hotels have small lobbies and restaurants.

Guest rooms also vary according to the clientele. Larger rooms, dressing areas, and large closets are necessary when most guests usually stay more than one or two nights. Room size is geared to the necessary pieces of furniture; the room should provide ample space around and between them. Business travelers need desks; those on vacation usually do not. The trend toward larger beds requires larger rooms, but rooms that provide too much extra space are not an efficient use of space.

Support space for guest rooms includes hotel office and operations space, restaurants, lounges, public meeting rooms, and frequently athletic facilities.

Industrial Properties

More than most properties, one that houses industrial manufacturing requires that its site, buildings, and building equipment function together as an operating unit. Inutility should be measured against the standard of optimum efficiency in the market for similar properties.

Industrial properties are frequently designed and equipped to meet the needs of a specific occupant and thus have a limited appeal to other users. This is particularly true of buildings used for industries that involve bulky or volatile materials and products and that require specialized equipment and building designs. Buildings for research and development and for light fabricating or processing are less limited in their general appeal.

The measurement for all industrial buildings is in terms of gross building area. The GBA can be divided into finished and unfinished categories for comparison purposes and for measurement in terms of market standards. The greatest flexibility in industrial buildings, which can be translated into appeal on the open market, is embodied in a one-story square or nearly square structure that completely complies with local building codes.

Industrial buildings can be composed of many types of construction materials, but concrete and steel are used most often. Tilt-up construction, which incorporates concrete walls that have been cast horizontally and then put in place vertically, is common. The walls are often load-bearing. Flat roofs that are supported by steel bar joists are also common. Prefabricated steel buildings are cheaper and their appearances are currently considered more acceptable than they were in the past. Plastic skylights can be installed for natural light in lieu of expensive monitor and sawtooth roofs.

One predominant requirement for industrial properties is a land-to-building ratio that permits plenty of parking, truck maneuvering space, yard storage space, and often room for expansion. In addition to access, locational considerations include reasonable real estate taxes, labor pools, adequate utility services, beneficial zoning, and proximity to supply sources and customers.

Industrial parks are groups of industrial buildings that combine similar uses. They use landscaping, setbacks, building and lot size minimums, and professional architectural, engineering, and management services to create an industrial environment that occupants and government land-planning groups find acceptable.

The combination of old and new industrial space has substantial functional obsolescence when the new construction contributes less than its cost to the value of the whole. The operating layout should provide for maximum efficiency. To provide the best efficiency, receiving functions may need to be performed on one side of the building and shipping functions on the other. In addition, such special features as sprinkler systems, scales, loading dock levelers, refrigeration, conveyor belts, compressed air supply, power wiring, and locker and lunchroom areas must be included for maximum efficiency.

Storage Buildings

Storage structures range from the simplicity of cubicles, known as mini-warehouses, to huge, one million-square-foot regional warehouses with internal rail systems. Functional utility and location primarily affect the market value of storage buildings; obsolescence usually occurs sooner than physical deterioration. The functions of warehouses are to

1. Store materials in a protected environment

2. Organize materials in such a way so that they can be easily inventoried and removed

3. Provide facilities for efficient delivery

4. Provide facilities for efficient access and shipping

To provide optimum functional utility, warehouses should have adequate access, open spans, ceiling height, floor load capacity (often 300 or more pounds for heavy-duty industrial and storage buildings), humidity and temperature controls, shipping and receiving facilities, and substantial protection from the elements and from fire.

The primary consideration of warehouse location is to provide good access. Trucking is the major means of transporting goods that are stored; certain warehousing operations also require rail and water transportation. Operations that primarily depend on trucks to transport goods should be immediately near an arterial highway. A highway's access street or frontage road and the truck maneuvering area at a warehouse loading dock must be adequate to provide efficient use of loading facilities at all times. A site that slopes downward from a frontage road enables the loading dock to be constructed at truck bed level. For rail access, one portion of a site that is long and level is required.

Forklifts, conveyor belts, and railed conveyor systems move materials in warehouses. Truck docks need to be wide enough to accommodate truck widths and the interior servomechanism that moves goods and materials. If electric trucks are used, a battery-charging area must be included. Most storage operations are palletized. Ceiling height must accommodate the ideal multiple of a pallet's height. Wide spans provide more flexibility; a square configuration generally has the greatest flexibility and is the most cost effective.

Office space in warehouses often constitutes as little as 1%, but generally approximates 5% of the total gross building area. In distribution facilities, office space may comprise 35% to 50% of the total gross building area. An office space is well heated, cooled, and lighted and its finish is generally utilitarian.

In warehouses where flammable goods are stored, sprinkler systems are necessary. The nature of the merchandise determines whether a system should use water or chemicals.

Miniwarehouses are usually combined in one- or two-story rectangular structures. They are located near persons who use them and where they provide easy visibility and access. They must be surrounded by enough land for parking and maneuvering. The sizes of individual units vary and usually include small storage units, which have only passage doors, and larger units, which have roll-up truck doors.

Buildings on Agricultural Properties

Although the trend in most of the United States is toward larger and fewer farms, the contribution of farm buildings to the total value of farm real estate has been steadily decreasing. Figures from the U.S. Department of Agriculture indicate that buildings contribute less than 20% of the total farm property value. The number of farm buildings per acre of farmland has also decreased.

Farming is done by families and by large, specialized business operations. The equipment and management needed to run the operations have become increasingly specialized.

The operations are carried out in fewer types of farm buildings because each operation is usually responsible for fewer functions. Farm buildings must accommodate the appropriate machinery and equipment. A greater number of large machine sheds are required to house tractors, combines, disc plows, harrows, cultivators, pickers, sprayers, planter/fertilizers, bailers, and trucks. Pipeline milking machines and overhead feed bins dictate the requirements of the milking parlor, or shed, and the loafing shed. Poultry feeding and care practices have substantially modified poultry farm buildings.

The development of the United States has depended on certain types of buildings. Barns have been second only to houses in influence. Barns have successfully combined functional utility with picturesque design. Form, function, and materials have been combined in such a unique way as to render the barn the most successful type of vernacular building. Certain barns traditionally have been multifunctional; they have provided animal shelter, grain storage, and a threshing floor. However, other barns, such as tobacco barns as well as modern farm buildings, have fulfilled a single, specialized function.

The typical American barn has traditionally been 60 feet long and 30 feet wide, with two gable ends, a loft, and two double doors in the wide sides. It was built mostly of wood, but sometimes of stone, logs, or brick. Such a barn is still suitable for the general purpose farm, providing it is sufficiently adaptable. The use of baled rather than loose hay and the increased use of ensilage have lessened the need for barn storage. Silos, however, are larger and more prevalent.

Animal shelters need to be dry and clean, must provide protection from wind and sun, and must adapt to equipment. To be efficient, each farm building must contribute to the operating efficiency of the entire farm. Each building's usefulness is related to a farm's type and size. In addition, having too many farm buildings when fewer would be more efficient results in functional inutility.

Special Purpose Buildings

The architecture of special purpose buildings tends to limit them to a single use. Although almost any type of building can be converted to other uses, the conversion of special purpose buildings generally requires extra expense and design expertise. Special purpose structures include churches, synagogues, theaters, sports arenas, and other types of auditoriums. Automobile sales buildings and gasoline service stations have greater conversion flexibility than other special purpose structures.

The functional utility of a special purpose building depends on whether there is a continued demand for the use for which the building was designed, and, if there is such a demand, whether the building conforms to competitive standards. For example, there is a continued demand for movie theaters but their design has changed due to high maintenance and utility costs. The design of the traditional, ornate movie theater has been replaced by that of the simple, unembellished structure. However, there is a demand to convert the older movie theaters into concert halls and legitimate theaters.

The design and materials of newly built synagogues and churches are also simple for the same reasons. The functional utility of these structures and of sports and concert arenas is primarily related to seating capacity. However, the structure's various support facilities and its general attractiveness and appeal also must be considered.

The adaptive use movement has generated an awareness of the conversion potential inherent in special purpose buildings. Buildings usually outlive their functions. Energy shortages, the decline of modernism, and disproportionate construction costs have contributed to the movement. Railroad stations, schools, firehouses, and grist mills are popular structures for conversion. The functional utility of these buildings is related to their deviations from building codes and to any cost of rehabilitation that exceeds the amount that provides an economic return. One typical example of functional inutility in adaptive use projects is an insufficient number of staircases to meet building codes. By contrast, a high ceiling in a specialty property is not functional inutility if it is one of the unusual qualities that produces entire net income.

Mixed-Use Buildings

Many buildings successfully combine more than one use. In such buildings, each type of use creates a number of criteria, each of which requires separate analysis. In addition, the entire structure should be evaluated to assess its ability to combine the uses.

Combined uses should be compatible. Minor incompatibilities are often made more congruous by providing for separate entrances, elevators, and equipment. Without separate entrances and elevators, residential units in upper floors and office units on the lower levels would both suffer. A rather large building is required to justify the extra expense of such features. A hotel that is located in an office building should have its own entrance and elevators. Security and privacy should mark a building's residential portion; an appearance of professionalism and prestige should emanate from the office portion.

Mixed-use buildings are an architectural challenge; traditionally, the appearance of residential and commercial buildings has been sufficiently different to distinguish them from one another. These differences have been diminished, however, by the eclecticism of postmodern architecture.

Summary

Architectural style and functional utility are interrelated; together they affect property value and must be analyzed by an appraiser. Architectural style is the character of a building's form and ornamentation. An architectural style is more specific; it is the manner of architectural expression of a particular society, region, area, or time. Technically, an architectural style is comprised of building characteristics that are categorized in terms of structure, space, decoration, and function.

An appraiser studies architectural styles in two ways. First, the appraiser judges how well the style conforms to current market standards and tastes. Market standards are accepted norms, which are reflected in customary or typical architectural styles. Market tastes are preferences, which may be standard or nonstandard. Standard tastes characterize the major portion of the market, whereas nonstandard tastes characterize the minor portion.

Architectural trends in the market respond to the market's desire to preserve tradition by including elements of architectural styles from the past. The market's desire for change, on the other hand, provides impetus for changes in the elements of architectural design. Thus, an appraiser must be able to recognize all architectural styles and their status in particular markets. Architectural styles also change or are maintained in response to the state of technology and construction and maintenance costs. A style partly depends on materials, structure, siting, and equipment for its expression.

The second way an appraiser views architectural style is in terms of how well it provides functional utility. Functional utility is the efficient use of a building. Optimal functional utility implies the maximum that design and engineering can produce in terms of perceived needs at any given time. Functional inutility is an impairment of functional capacity or efficiency. An appraiser judges both functional utility and inutility within the context of market standards of acceptability.

Considerations pertinent to functional utility differ for different types of buildings. For example, in a residential building, the layout, accommodation of specific activities, adequacy, and ease and cost of maintenance are specific considerations that affect functional utility. Industrial properties, more than most, require the site, the building, and the building equipment to function together as an operating unit. Commercial buildings, hotels, storage buildings, agricultural buildings, special purpose buildings, and mixed-use buildings are judged in relation to specific functional utility criteria.

In determining functional utility, an appraiser must consider the compatibility of a building with its use or uses and its environment. Compatibility includes the form, materials, and scale of a building. Market value is frequently diminished by incompatibility of design; incompatibility of a structure with its function; incompatibility of elements of the structure as they relate to each other; or incompatibility of the structure in relation to its site or location within a neighborhood. Nonconforming designs may be compatible with their environments, but market data will reveal if a particular style usually sells for less in a certain location.

In addition to compatibility, an appraiser considers suitability or appropriateness, comfort, efficiency, safety, security, accessibility, ease and cost of maintenance, market standards, and attractiveness. Marketability is the ultimate test of a building's functional utility. A building is generally functional if it serves well the purpose for which it was designed or adapted.

Part III
Highest and Best Use

Chapter 11

Highest and Best Use

The market is the final arbiter of market value. One crucial determinant of value in the market is highest and best use. The market values of land or a site and of an improved property are both estimated under the assumption that potential purchasers will pay prices that reflect their analyses of the most profitable use of the land or the property as improved. The most profitable use assumption tends to produce the highest offering prices.

The highest and best uses of land or sites and improved properties are selected from various alternative uses. The highest and best use conclusions provide the bases for an appraiser's market value analysis. Thus, the remainder of the valuation process is conducted in relation to these conclusions. Consequently, it is essential that highest and best use conclusions relate to the motivations of the market for the subject property.

When an appraiser is asked to make an evaluation based on the needs of a particular client, the appraiser's advice as to future use may not necessarily be based on the market value concept of highest and best use due to the client's specific requirements. Highest and best use considerations in evaluations are discussed in Chapter 24. This chapter presents a discussion of highest and best use as it pertains to market value conclusions.

Definitions

Highest and best use is defined as

The reasonable and probable use that supports the highest present value, as defined, as of the date of the appraisal.

Alternatively, highest and best use is

The use, from among reasonably probable and legal alternative uses, found to be physically possible, appropriately supported, financially feasible, and that results in the highest present land value.

The second definition applies specifically to the highest and best use of land or sites as though vacant. When a site contains improvements, the highest and best use may be determined to be different from the existing use. The existing use will continue unless and until land value in its highest and best use exceeds the sum of the value of the entire property in its existing use and the cost to remove the improvements.

Implied in these definitions is that the determination of highest and best use takes into account the contribution of a specific use to the community and community development goals as well as the benefits of that use to individual property owners. An additional implication is that the determination of highest and best use results from the appraiser's judgment and analytical skill—that is, that the use determined from analysis represents an opinion, not a fact to be found. In appraisal practice, the concept of highest and best use represents the premise upon which value is based. In the context of *most probable selling price* (market value), another appropriate term to reflect highest and best use would be *most probable use*. In the context of investment value, an alternative term would be *most profitable use*.

The definitions of highest and best use indicate that there are two types of highest and best use. The first type is highest and best use of land or a site as though vacant. The second is highest and best use of a property as improved. Each type requires a separate analysis. Moreover, in each case, the existing use may or may not be different from the site's highest and best use.

Any determination of highest and best use includes identifying the motivations of probable purchasers. The motivations are based on perceptions of benefits that accrue to property ownership. Different motivations influence highest and best use and are significant to an appraiser's conclusions about the highest and best uses of any parcel of real estate.

When potential buyers contemplate purchasing real estate for personal use or occupancy, their principal motivations are such user benefits as enjoyment, prestige, or security. Such motivations are particularly evident in the purchase of residential properties. User benefits also apply to commercial and industrial property ownership. Benefits to the owner-occupant include assured occupancy, low management costs, control, and potential enhancement.

The benefits of investment properties that are not owner-occupied relate to net income potential and to eventual resale or refinancing. The highest and best use decision for investment property is often influenced by the income tax and inflation hedge aspects of the existing or proposed improvements. Determination of the type and intensity of the improvements to be placed on investor's land often requires an after-tax return analysis of various alternatives.

Land or improved property that has resale profit as its principal potential benefit is purely speculative land. The price such land commands in the market reflects the real motivation of the purchaser— speculation.

Highest and Best Use of Land or a Site as Though Vacant

The first type of highest and best use—highest and best use of land or a site as though vacant—assumes that a parcel of land is vacant or that it can be made vacant through the demolition of any improvements. The question to be answered in the analysis of this type of highest and best use is, If the land is (or were) vacant, what use should be made of it? That is, what type of building or other improvement (if any) should be constructed on the land?

When a property's highest and best use can reasonably be forecast to change in the near future, the prevailing highest and best use is considered an interim use. For instance, the highest and best use of a farm in the path of urban growth would be interim use as a farm, with its future highest and best use as a potential residential subdivision. If the farm is ready for development at the time of the appraisal, there is no interim use. Further, if the farm has no proximate subdivision potential, its highest and best use is as a farm with no interim use. In certain cases, an appraiser's conclusion is that the highest and best use of a parcel of land is to be held vacant until price appreciates. For most parcels of urban land, however, highest and best use requires some improvement. The highest and best use of the land as though vacant may include its subdivision into smaller parcels or its assemblage with other land.

If an improvement is required for highest and best use of the land, an appraiser must conclude which type of improvement, with which characteristics, should be constructed. For example, should highest and best use for a parcel of land be an office building, a retail building, or perhaps a hotel? If it should be an office building, how many stories should it have? How many offices? Which size offices? Which features? Which rental should be charged, and which level of operating expenses will be incurred? About how much will such a building cost? In other words, the conclusion about highest and best use of a parcel of land should be specific. General categories, such as an office building, a commercial building, or a single family residence, are inadequate for the purpose.

Even when a site is not vacant, it is often analyzed as though it were. For such properties, an appraiser first determines whether the existing improvement is the site's highest and best use. The appraiser considers whether, if the site were vacant, a building having the same use, size, quality, and function as the existing building would be constructed on the site. For this similar improvement to be the highest and best use of the land as though vacant, physical deterioration and functional obsolescence presumably would be eliminated in the new building. An appraiser also considers external obsolescence.

The prevailing use on the site may not be the highest and best use. The land may be suitable for a much higher (more intense) use than the existing use. For instance, the highest and best use of the land as though vacant may be a 10-story office building, whereas the current office building contains only three stories.

Highest and Best Use of Property as Improved

The second type of highest and best use—highest and best use of a property as improved—pertains to the use that should be made of the property as it exits. Should a 30-year-old hotel building be maintained as it is, renovated, expanded, partly demolished, or any combination of these? Or should it be replaced with a use different in type or intensity?

The use that maximizes the investment property's net operating income (NOI) on a long-term basis is its highest and best use. For uses that require no capital expenditures for remodeling, the NOIs estimated for various uses can be compared directly. However, for uses that would require capital expenditures to convert the structure from its existing use to another use, a rate of return must be calculated for the total investment in the property, including capital expenditures.

This rate of return can then be compared with rates of return for uses that do not require capital expenditures.

An appraiser's conclusions regarding the maximum highest and best use for owner-occupied properties also reflect the consideration of the rehabilitation or modernization that is consistent with owner-occupant motivations. For example, highest and best use conclusions for a luxury residence would reflect the amount of rehabilitation required for maximum enjoyment of the property.

Purpose of Highest and Best Use Analysis

The purpose of highest and best use analysis is different for each type of highest and best use. An appraiser should clearly separate the two types in the appraisal analysis. An appraiser's report should clearly identify, explain, and justify the purpose and conclusion for each type.

Highest and Best Use of Land as Though Vacant

The value of land is always estimated as though vacant.[1] For land that is, in fact, vacant, the reasoning is obvious: An appraiser values the land as it exists. For land that is not vacant, land value is dependent on the uses to which it can be put. Therefore, highest and best use of land as though vacant must be considered in relation to a variety of uses, including its existing and all potential uses.

As an example of land value being determined by potential rather than actual use, consider a valuable commercial site in an excellent location that currently has a service station or another retail use. A purchaser may pay a price for the property for elevator office use that includes no value (or even negative value) for the existing improvements. The potential use—not existing use—usually governs the price that will be paid.

Or, consider a valuable site in the downtown section of a large city, upon which is situated a 10-story, 20-year-old office building. Although the structure contributes $1 million to the property value, the property is purchased by a large national industrial firm for $10 million. The building is razed, and a new, 60-story headquarters building for the firm is constructed. The property's value, derived from its

[1]One exception to this rule concerns legally nonconforming improvements, which are discussed later in this chapter.

potential use, was contained in the site. This demolition would happen, however, only if an equally desirable vacant site were not available. Such a vacant site, if available, could presumably be obtained for less than the $10 million price of the developed site plus demolition costs.

Finally, consider the case of a five-year-old, 120-unit apartment building that is purchased and demolished to make way for a university expansion program. Highest and best use for the site changed rapidly after the university expansion was planned and put into effect.

The point is that any existing building can be demolished. The fact that most buildings are not demolished does not negate the possibility. The possibility is the premise for the concept of highest and best use of land as though vacant. Land values are never penalized because of deficiencies in existing buildings. Buildings can be changed; the basic characteristics of sites cannot.

A trend away from demolition and toward preservation of existing structures became clearly evident in the 1980s. The effect of the trend has been to decrease significantly the number of instances in which the highest and best use of a site is the demolition of its building or buildings. Historic district zoning controls that make demolition permits difficult or impossible to obtain have resulted from the preservationist trend. In addition, the special tax incentives available to older buildings can substantially enhance their value and thus alter highest and best uses in many cases.

The purpose of estimating the highest and best use for land or a site is to identify the use that causes the land to have value. Several appraisal techniques require a separate estimate of land value; therefore, the identification of the land's highest and best use is necessary for estimating the land's value. The highest and best use of comparable properties should be the same as or similar to that of the subject property. Thus, there are two reasons for identifying the highest and best use of land as though vacant in an appraisal. First, the identification is required in certain appraisal techniques that require a separate land value. Second, the identification helps to identify comparable properties.

Highest and Best Use of Property as Improved

There also are two reasons for analyzing the highest and best use of a property as improved. The first is to identify the use of the property that is expected to produce the highest overall return per dollar of invested capital. If the property is currently being used as rental apartments, will that use continue to provide the maximum level of benefits? Or would the rate of return be increased by converting the property to an apartment hotel? The value of the property would be different under those two use assumptions, and the use providing the highest present value would reflect the highest and best use.

The second reason is to help in identifying comparable properties. Just as the highest and best use of land as though vacant of the comparable properties should be the same as that of the subject property's, the reverse is true. For example, using a comparable property that has a highest and best use as offices in appraising a subject property that has a highest and best use as a hotel would be an inappropriate appraisal technique.

Relation to Economic Theory

Although modern economists have rejected the idea that land or real estate is less entitled to a return than other agents in production, the residual analysis implied by classical economic theory still prevails in highest and best use analysis. Although land may be as equally entitled to a return as the other agents in production, the fact that buildings can be changed while the essential characteristics of sites cannot leaves the income to any particular site dependent on the use decision. From an overall, or economic, point of view, the fact that one site can be substituted for another means that their returns are established in the general market for sites. For a particular site, however, land value is a function of the income that remains after improvement costs are compensated.

Highest and best use of land as though vacant is an old concept that is derived from classical economic theory. Highest and best use of a property as improved is a much newer concept. It has evolved since the 1960s to answer two important questions that the older concept does not address. How should the property as improved be used? Should the existing improvement be continued in use, or should it be demolished and a new improvement constructed? The older concept of highest and best use of land as though vacant addresses only the question of how the land should be used if it were vacant; it is primarily a tool for land valuation.

Elements in Highest and Best Use Analysis

For highest and best use of both land as though vacant and property as improved, a use must meet four criteria. The criteria are that the highest and best use must be (1) physically possible, (2) legally permissible, (3) financially feasible, and (4) maximally productive. These criteria should usually be considered sequentially; it makes no difference that a use is financially feasible if it is physically impossible to construct an improvement or if such a use is not legally permitted. Only when there is a reasonable possibility that one of the prior unacceptable conditions can be changed is it appropriate to proceed with the analysis. For example, if current zoning does not accommodate a likely candidate for highest and best use, but there is a possibility that the zoning can be changed, the proposed use could be considered on that basis. Each of the criteria is discussed in the following sections.

Physically Possible
Size, shape, area, and terrain affect the uses to which land may be developed. The utility of a parcel may depend on its frontage and depth. Irregularly shaped parcels may cost more to develop and, when developed, may have less utility than a regularly shaped parcel of the same area.

Because of limited size, certain parcels can reach their highest and best use only as part of an assemblage of a number of parcels. In such a case, an appraiser must either determine the feasibility and probability of assembly or make the highest and best use (and appraisal) decisions conditioned upon such assembly. For example, large petro-chemical plants on the Mississippi River below Baton Rouge may be constructed on the assembly of smaller acreage tracts. Individual small tracts do not have utility for industrial use and thus have a much lower unit value.

An appraiser also considers capacity and availability of public utilities. If a sewer main that is in front of a property cannot be tapped because of lack of capacity at the disposal plant, the property effectively does not have access to the public sewerage disposal system.

When a site's topography or subsoil conditions make utilization restrictive or costly, the site's potential future use is adversely affected. All sites available for a particular use compete with one another. If the cost for grading or filling or the cost to construct a foundation is higher for the site being appraised than for typical sites in the area, the site being appraised may be unusable at the time of highest and best use determination.

Highest and best use of a property as improved also depends on physical considerations. Whether the property is in good repair and can continue to accommodate the current use may be relevant. If the property should be converted to another use, the cost of conversion must be analyzed relative to the returns to be generated by the converted use. Obviously, the costs of conversion depend on the property's existing physical status.

Legally Permissible
Except for a legally nonconforming property, the first area of inquiry in questionable cases is to determine what is legally permissible. Private restriction, zoning, building codes, historic district controls, and envi-

ronmental regulations are considered because they may preclude many possible highest and best uses.

A long-term lease can influence a property's highest and best use by limiting the use for the remaining term of the lease to that which is permitted in the lease. In addition, time limitations might make a current highest and best use of the property unfeasible. With 12 years remaining in the lease, it is not possible to construct a new building with a 40-year remaining economic life. The highest and best use section of the appraisal report should state that the highest and best use determination is based on the lease.

Private or deed restrictions relate to the convenants under which the property was acquired. These might disallow certain uses or even specify building setbacks, height, types of materials, and so forth. If deed restrictions conflict with zoning laws or building codes, whichever is most restrictive prevails.

In the absence of private restriction, uses allowed under zoning typically constitute the available choices in most highest and best use determinations. However, a possible change of zoning should not be precluded from the appraiser's consideration of what is legally permissible.

If the highest present utilization of the site or property is not allowed under the current zoning, due to shifting economic and social patterns, and if there is a reasonable probability that a change in zoning is obtainable, these conditions can be considered in the highest and best use determination. However, the appraiser is obligated to disclose fully all pertinent factors relating thereto, including the time and expenses involved in the change and the risk that the zoning change may not be granted.

Building codes can prevent land from being developed to its highest and best use by imposing burdensome restrictions that increase the cost of construction. This is particularly true in metropolitan areas that include municipalities or jurisdictions with different building codes. Trends in residential development in metropolitan areas have been greatly influenced by different off-site requirements in building codes. A less restrictive code typically results in the least development cost per front foot and attracts developers, while the more restrictive tends to discourage development. Some areas restrict growth by using building codes to retard new construction.

Increasing concern over the effects of land use has made consistency with environmental regulations an additional consideration in highest and best use analysis. An appraiser must be concerned with certain regulations, such as those pertaining to clean air, clean water, and wetlands, in addition to public reactions to proposed projects. Adverse reactions by local residents and by the general public have stopped many real estate developments.

Financially Feasible

After determining the uses that are physically possible and legally permissible, an appraiser need not consider the uses that do not meet the criteria. The uses that do meet them are analyzed further to determine those that are likely to produce some income, or return, greater than the combined income needed to satisfy operating expenses, financial expenses, and capital amortization. All uses that are expected to produce a positive return are regarded as financially feasible.

In analyzing financial feasibility, appraisers estimate future gross income that can be expected from each potential highest and best use. Vacancy and collection losses and operating expenses are subtracted from the gross income to obtain the likely net income from each use. A rate of return on the invested capital can then be calculated. The calculation could also be made after financing expense if a given level of financing is considered typical and normal for the type of property being analyzed. Any positive net income or rate of return would indicate that a use is financially feasible.

Maximally Productive

Among financially feasible uses, the use that provides the highest rate of return, or value (given a constant rate of return), is the highest and best use. For determining highest and best use of land as though vacant, the same rate of return is often used to capitalize income streams from different uses into values. This procedure is correct if all competing uses have similar risk characteristics. The highest land value produced in the procedure reflects highest and best use.

The land income that is capitalized into value is the residual income remaining after the other agents in production (labor, capital, and coordination) are allocated a market-determined portion of the property's income. The allocation is calculated by multiplying the value of the improvements by a market-determined capitalization rate. The income allocated to the improvements is then subtracted from the total income produced by the property, and the remaining income is allocated to the land. This procedure is illustrated in the following section.

Potential highest and best uses of land are *usually* long-term land uses, or uses that are expected to remain on the site for the normal economic (useful) life of the improvements.[2] Depending on type, quality of construction, and so forth, most buildings are expected to last at least 25 years and may last more than 100. Therefore, the stream of benefits, or income, produced by the buildings reflects a carefully considered and usually highly specified land use program.

---

[2]Shorter-term, or interim, uses are discussed later in this chapter.

The capital investment required to convert the property to alternative uses may vary or be the same. When invested capital remains constant among alternative uses, total NOIs produced by the various uses can be compared directly, with the use producing the highest NOI being designated highest and best use. When invested capital varies among alternative uses, the income from each use must be related to its invested capital base by calculating the rate of return. The use producing the highest rate of return is the highest and best use of the property as improved.

Testing Highest and Best Use

To test highest and best use for the land as though vacant or for a property as improved, an appraiser analyzes all logical, feasible alternatives. Usually, the appraiser can reduce the number of such alternatives to three or four uses. Alternative uses must first meet the tests for physical possibility and legal permissibility. The number of uses meeting the first two tests can then be analyzed logically to limit the number of financially feasible alternatives that must be analyzed. For example, a market analysis might indicate need for a large office building in a community. However, if the site being analyzed is surrounded by modern single family residential developments, a large multistory office building probably would not be logical even if legally permitted. Similarly, development of housing for the elderly might be permissible for a site, but if most residents of the area are under 40 years old, such development might not be logical and probably would not satisfy the criterion of financial feasibility.

Highest and Best Use of Land as Though Vacant

The following examples illustrate the testing of highest and best use for land as though vacant.

Example 1: Single Family Residence

First, consider a site zoned to accommodate detached single family residences. A builder or an owner narrows the logical alternatives to two types of houses—one slightly larger and having better quality than the other. The larger house (with lot) would have an estimated market value of $125,000; the smaller house (with lot) would be worth about $100,000. Similar sites in the area have sold for about $30,000. The estimated reported costs of constructing the two houses are used with these figures to select the highest and best use of the appraised land. These calculations are shown below.

	Use	
	A	B
Market value	$100,000	$125,000
Cost to construct new	−75,000	−80,000
Land value	−30,000	−30,000
Anticipated profit (loss)	($5,000)	$ 15,000

The larger house (B) is the highest and best use among all alternatives considered. (Other alternatives would have been eliminated by prior criteria.) The builder or owner would incur a financial loss by constructing the smaller house (A). Further, a builder would invest time and effort in construction coordination, be exposed to entrepreneurial risks, and invest funds or personal time in marketing the property, which all would cause the loss from use A to be even greater. Obviously, no knowledgeable builder or owner would construct A over B.

This analysis assumes that site value is known or can be estimated—a typical situation for single family residential sites. The issue in these situations is how to use the land to realize the site's full market value. That is, the overall profit realized on the total property price must equal a market overall profit after allocating the full market value to the land. If the overall profit on the total property is less than a market overall profit, the use is not highest and best. In the example above, the overall profit on gross sale price on property B of 12% ($15,000/$125,000) must be competitive with profits on similar properties that have newly constructed improvements.

Example 2: Income-Producing Use

In estimating highest and best use among various income-producing uses, land value is not usually known. Indeed, as pointed out earlier in this chapter, the purpose for conducting a highest and best use analysis is to estimate land value. Thus, competing income-producing uses must be compared on the basis of residual income after deducting allocated income to improvments from total NOI under each use.

For example, consider a 100-by-200-foot site that, according to zoning, can contain apartments, retail stores, and offices. If an appraiser has limited the logical alternatives to an apartment building, an office building, and a retail building, the appraiser assembles data on construction costs, market rates of return, and income that can be expected for each alternative use. These costs and incomes are shown below, along with the market capitalization rate for the improvements.[3]

	Use		
	Apartment Building	Office Building	Commercial Building
Cost to construct	$1,200,000	$950,000	800,000
Net operating income	162,000	135,000	110,000
Return to improvement (12%)	−144,000	114,000	−96,000
Return to land	18,000	21,000	14,000
Indicated land value (at 10%)	$180,000	210,000	$140,000

According to this analysis, the site's highest and best use would be the office building. It produces the greatest residual income and the highest capitalized value. For the calculated value to be a reliable and accurate estimate of the land's market value, the analysis of costs, incomes, and capitalization rates must accurately reflect the market.

In addition, the calculations indicate that highest and best use is not determined by any single item, such as cost, size, total income, or rate of return. Highest and best use is the relationship among these items that determines the income remaining to the land after the other agents in production contained in the building are allocated their market-determined value. These items are compensated before land, and it is only in the case of a new or nearly new building that the residual income to land would be maximized. The tendency is for rents to be lower and expenses to be higher in an older building than in a new building. Thus, the older building would not be replicated on the site if it were vacant.

Highest and Best Use of a Property as Improved

An analysis of highest and best use of a property as improved can result in a determination that little or no capital expenditure is required, or that significant expenditures are required to convert the property to a different use or to rehabilitate or remodel the existing use.

---

[3]Market-derived land and building capitalization rates are discussed in depth in Chapters 14 and 16.

Example 1: No Capital Expenditures

Consider a single family residence that could be used for a combination apartment and rooming house or for single family occupancy. The combination house use would require no capital expenditures. The downstairs could be occupied by the owners or rented to another family. Three upstairs bedrooms, with no structural modifications, could be rented to college students.

Assume that for single family occupancy the property could be rented for $600 per month net; that is, the renters would pay all property-related expenses (including property taxes and insurance). Some vacancy or collection loss must be anticipated. Under the alternate use, the downstairs could be rented for $500 per month and each of the three upstairs rooms could be rented for $100. The downstairs rental would be net to the owners, but they would have to pay approximately $2,000 per year in expenses for the upstairs portion of the property (heat, power, repairs and maintenance, real estate tax, and insurance). In addition, some vacancy or collection loss must be anticipated in both the downstairs and upstairs rentals.

	Use	
	Single Family Occupancy	**Combination Apartment-Rooming House**
Capital invested	$60,000	$60,000
Gross income	7,200	9,600
Vacancy or collection losses (5%)	−360	−480
Effective gross income	6,840	9,120
Expenses	0	2,000
Net operating income	$ 6,840	$ 7,120
Return on investment	11.4%	11.9%

Thus, it appears from the calculation that the highest and best use of the property as improved would be as a combination apartment-rooming house.

Example 2: Capital Expenditure Required

A warehouse property can be rented for warehouse purposes for $75,000 completely net to the owners, who are considering adding office space in the warehouse to increase the rent. The addition would cost approximately $100,000 and would likely add to the market value of the property, which is currently $600,000 without the office space. An appraiser estimates that the annual rent could be increased to $85,000 with the office space even though the amount of warehouse space would be reduced. The highest and best use calculation would be:

	Use	
	Warehouse Only	**With Office**
Capital invested	$600,000	$700,000
Net operating income	75,000	85,000
Overall return	12.5%	12.14%

Thus, the calculation indicates that the warehouse without offices is the highest and best use of the property as improved. This calculation assumes that the income streams from both uses will be equal in length and that the market value estimate reflects the price for which the property could be sold in the market with and without the office construction.

Typical Highest and Best Use Statements

All appraisal reports should contain summary statements that describe the analyses and conclusions for highest and best use of land or a site as though vacant, or of a property as improved, or both if a separate land valuation is included. When the highest and best use conclusion is the primary objective of an evaluation report, the income and return calculations and reasoning should be included. If the conclusion of the highest and best use of an improved property is different from the existing use, similar justification should be included in the market value appraisal report. Whenever the highest and best use conclusions are based on application of techniques to discover the highest and best use among two or more potential uses, the full analysis is included.

In appraisals in which land value is estimated separately, it is appropriate to discuss in the report the highest and best use of the land as though vacant as well as the highest and best use of the property as improved. When land value is not estimated separately and a condition of the appraisal is continued use of the property as improved, the appraiser typically discusses only the highest and best use of the property as improved.

Each parcel of real estate may have one highest and best use of the land or site as through vacant and a different highest and best use of the property as improved. In cases in which an appraiser comments on both highest and best use of the land as though vacant and the property as improved, each highest and best use must be identified separately in the highest and best use section of the appraisal report. First, highest and best use of the land or site is given, along with a statement that the determination was made under the theoretical presumption that the land is vacant and available for development. Second, the highest and best use of the property as improved is given, along with a statement that the determination was made according to the future potential of the land and improvements as existing.

If the land is already improved to its highest and best use, the two statements may be combined. But the report should state specifically that the determination is the same for both the land as though vacant and the property as improved, or that the land is improved to its highest and best use.

The report also should identify the highest and best uses, both vacant and improved, of the comparable sales. If the improved comparables have different highest and best uses of the land if theoretically vacant and of the improved property as existing, this must also be explained. The difference could affect value, especially in the sales comparison approach.

The following examples, two for a single family residence and two for an income-producing property, illustrate highest and best use statements. Obviously, the actual statements for any particular appraisal would be tailored to the situation.

Example 1: Single Family Residence—Highest and Best Use of Land as Though Vacant

This type of highest and best use is employed to estimate the value of land separately from improvements. It recognizes that any significant elements of accrued depreciation would not be replicated if the land were vacant and a new building were constructed on the site. It is also helpful in identifying comparable properties, which is why it is used in this appraisal.

The existing structure is not the highest and best use of the land as though vacant. The house was constructed approximately 10 years ago and contains measurable elements of physical deterioration and functional obsolescence, as do most structures after they are two or three years old. If the site were vacant, a new single family residence would be its highest and best use. The new house would be more architecturally compatible with other houses in the neighborhood. It would contain approximately 2,000 square feet and would include three bedrooms and two baths. The living room would be larger. The house would have more electrical outlets. All elements of physical deterioration would be eliminated.

Example 2: Single Family Residence—Highest and Best Use of Property as Improved

This type of highest and best use recognizes that existing improvements should be continued in use until it becomes financially advantageous to demolish the structure and build a new one or to remodel the existing one. The existing use of the property as a single family residence is its highest and best use of the property as improved. No other use of the property would be so beneficial or profitable. The existing structure is well maintained and is in good repair. It has an effective age of about 8 years and a remaining economic life of approximately 50. The structure fits well into the neighborhood, which is zoned for single family residential occupancy only. The structure was designed as a single family residence, and no other use would be legally or financially feasible.

Example 3: Income-Producing Property—Highest and Best Use of Land as Though Vacant

The existing structure is not the highest and best use of the land as though vacant. This type of highest and best use recognizes that any significant elements of accrued depreciation would not be replicated if the site were vacant and a new building were constructed. The income allocated to the land under highest and best use is capitalized to estimate the value of the land separately from the improvements. [At this point, an appraiser might state: This valuation procedure is shown in the section entitled *Land Valuation*.]

If the site were vacant, a new commercial building would be its highest and best use. It would contain 16 store units (the maximum number permitted by zoning for this site), each having about 2,000 square feet. The building would be concrete block construction with poured concrete floor, flat, built-up roof, and attractive facade. It would be set back on the site to allow parking for approximately 40 cars in front. All physical deterioration would be eliminated in a new building, and its functional layout and design would be consistent with modern buildings of this type.

Example 4: Income-Producing Property—Highest and Best Use of Property as Improved

The existing use of the property as offices should be converted to commercial space to maximize the property's productivity and value. The property currently contains 12 office units that have had high vacancy rates during the past two years. The units require renovation and remodeling to remain competitive in the local office market. However, the surrounding area is in transition from residential and office uses to commercial and light industrial uses. Because substantial expenditures will be required to retain the present use or to convert to another use, it is recommended that conversion to commercial use be accomplished as soon as possible.

The following calculations show the existing capital investment and additional capital investment required for the existing use and for conversion to commercial use, and the returns estimated for both uses.

	Use	
	Offices	Commercial Space
Present capital investment	$250,000	$250,000
Additional capital investment	50,000	100,000
Total capital investment	$300,000	$350,000
Net operating income	30,000	50,000
Overall return	10%	14.3%

Thus, the figures indicate that conversion would be profitable at this time. Conversion would provide a substantially higher return on both the currently invested and new capital funds. Moreover, the income produced by commercial use would probably be less risky and would last longer. Vacancy rates would probably be lower than those that have characterized the current use.

Special Situations in Highest and Best Use Analysis

The basic premises of highest and best use analysis that have been discussed in the preceding pages are fundamental to all studies of the uses to which vacant land and sites or improved properties may be put. However, unique considerations in identifying and testing highest and best uses are necessitated by single use properties, interim uses, legally nonconforming uses, nonhighest and best uses, multiple uses, special purpose uses, speculative uses, and excess land. The special requirements for highest and best use analysis in each of these situations are discussed in the following sections.

Single Use Situations

The highest and best uses of land or sites as though vacant and properties as improved are generally consistent with and similar to surrounding uses. For example, single family residential use is usually not appropriate in an industrial neighborhood. Nevertheless, highest and best use may be an unusual or even a unique use. For example, demand may be adequate to support one large multistory office building in a community but inadequate to support more than one. A special purpose property, such as a museum, may be unique and highly beneficial to the site but not justifiable from surrounding land uses or comparable properties. The land value will be based on its highest and best use notwithstanding its most likely use.

Interim Uses

There are many instances in which highest and best use probably will change in the foreseeable future. For example, a tract of land at the edge of a city may not be ready for development now, but current growth trends of the city may suggest that the land will be ready in a few years. Or, there may be insufficient demand for office space to justify the construction of a multistory office building on a downtown site at the present time, but demand for such construction may be expected within five years. Current development of such sites and improved properties to their future highest and best uses is usually financially unfeasible.

The uses to which sites and improved properties are put until they are ready for their future highest and best uses are called interim uses. Interim uses are thus current highest and best uses that are anticipated to change in a relatively short, foreseeable time. Examples of these interim uses include farms, parking lots, old buildings, and temporary buildings.

Interim uses may or may not contribute to the value of a site or an improved property. Agricultural use of vacant land does not contribute to the site's value unless the income exceeds a typical return for vacant land that is not used for agricultural purposes. In addition, old buildings (or other uses) for which potential gross revenues are less than or no more than equal to reasonable operating expenses do not contribute to the property's value. If the net return is less than could be earned by the vacant land, the buildings do not have contributory value. Indeed, the value of such improved properties may be less than the value of the site as though vacant because of demolition costs. The values of these sites are based entirely on potential highest and best uses.

However, other interim uses, such as farming operations and parking lots, may be contributory uses. In comparing other properties with a subject property, differences in interim uses must be taken into account even though their future highest and best uses are identical. For example, assume that two sites are expected to be economically ready for high-rise office building construction in about five years, but one property has a commercial interim use that produces $40,000 more NOI per year than the other property, which has a parking lot as its interim use. The site with the commercial interim use might be worth $150,000 more than the other site ($40,000 for 5 years discounted at 10.5%; the factor is 3.743).

If the demolition costs of the two present uses were different, they would also have to be taken into account by making an adjustment. If the present value of the future demolition costs of the commercial building were $50,000, and the parking lot entailed no demolition costs, the difference in values would be only $100,000. Thus, appraisers need to identify interim uses of both the property being appraised and each of the comparables. Differences in prices paid may be caused by different return requirements and different anticipated demolition costs.

Legally Nonconforming Uses

Occasionally, parcels of land have been developed to an intensity that is higher than would be allowed under current zoning. For example, an apartment project might have more units per acre than allowed under a new land use plan and zoning regulations. If 25% more land would be needed to accommodate the same number of apartments, the land under existing improvements use may be worth more than if it were vacant. This type of situation is the one exception to the rule that land must be considered as vacant when estimating its highest and best use and value.

When valuing land under a legally nonconforming use, an appraiser recognizes that land under the current use may be producing more income (and thus value) than could the land if it were vacant. It could also produce more income and have a higher value than comparable vacant sites subject to the same zoning. Thus, in estimating the value of such a site by comparison with similar, competitive sites in the sales comparison approach, an appraiser would need to make an adjustment to reflect the higher intensity of use allowed for the subject site.

The remaining economic lives of most nonconforming uses are shorter than the economic lives of new improvements. Therefore, appraisers must capitalize the higher benefits over a shorter time period than the period over which benefits from a new improvement would be capitalized. The shorter capitalization period could offset the higher annual income from the nonconforming use, which would result in a conclusion that a new, less intensive use would be the site's highest and best use. Therefore, the question of whether an existing, legally nonconforming use is a site's highest and best use can be answered only by careful analysis of the residual income produced by the nonconforming use and alternative uses to which the land could be put if it were vacant.

Uses that Are Not Highest and Best

Most existing buildings and other improvements are not the highest and best use of their sites as though vacant. Nevertheless, the general category of the existing use remains the general category of highest and best use. For example, the highest and best use of a site with a 10-year-old apartment building may be a new and more functional apartment building. Or, the highest and best use of a single family residential site that contains a 20-year-old house may be a new and more modern single family residence. In such cases, the value of the improvement does not suffer from external obsolescence and need not be discounted for inappropriate use of the site.

For certain sites the general category of highest and best use has changed—for example, from apartments to industrial, or from single family residential to commercial. The improvements on these sites suffer from external obsolescence, and their values are less than the values of the same improvements on appropriate sites. Thus, it would be incorrect to value such an improvement as though it were on an appropriate site. The improvement must be valued on a consistent basis with the site's highest and best use. This procedure is in accord with the concept of consistent use.

As an example of consistent use, consider an apartment building on a site that has a highest and best use as industrial use. The site is now worth about $1 million—considerably higher than its value would be if its highest and best use were for apartments. The building would be worth $2 million if it were on a site appropriate for apartments. On the existing site, however, the building is worth only $1.5 million. Thus, the value of the property is $2.5 million, not $3 million. When valued separately, an improvement and a site must be appraised under a consistent highest and best use for the site.

Multiple Uses

Highest and best use often includes more than one use for a parcel of land or for a building. A large tract of land may be suitable for a planned unit development, with a shopping center in front, condominium units around a golf course, and single family residential sites on the remaining portions of the land. Industrial parks often have sites for retail stores in front and warehouse and light manufacturing structures in the rear. Farms often have family homes, storage areas for crops and equipment, and facilities for raising animals and crops.

Moreover, the same land may serve multiple functions. Lands for timber or pasture may also provide space for hunting, recreation, and mineral exploration. Land that serves as a right-of-way for power lines can double as an open space or a park. Public streets with railroad siding also are in this category.

Buildings can have multiple uses. A hotel may contain a restaurant, a bar, and retail shops, as well as guest rooms. A multistory building may contain offices, apartments, and retail stores. An office building may contain retail stores and a restaurant, as well as offices, and a single family, owner-occupied home may contain an apartment upstairs.

An appraiser can often estimate the contributory value of each use on a multiple use site or in a multiple use building. For example, if the market value of a timber tract that can be leased for hunting is compared on a unit basis with another timber tract that cannot, the difference should be the value of the hunting rights. In oil-producing areas, a common problem for appraisers is to segregate the value of mineral rights from the value of other uses of the land. Certain properties may have mineral rights value; others may not. In all such appraisals, an appraiser must make sure that the sum of the values of the separate uses does not exceed the value of the total property.

Special Purpose Uses

Special purpose properties are appropriate for one use or a very limited number of uses. Thus, an appraiser may encounter practical problems of specifying the highest and best uses of such properties. The highest and best use of a special purpose property as improved is probably its current use. For example, the highest and best use of a plant currently used for heavy manufacturing is usually to continue in heavy manufacturing. The highest and best use of a grain elevator probably is to continue as a grain elevator.

In certain cases, if the existing uses of special purpose properties are physically or functionally obsolete and no alternative uses are feasible, the highest and best use of the property as improved may be scrap or salvage.

Sometimes an appraiser needs to make two appraisals of the same special purpose property—one on the basis that a purchaser could be found who would use the property for its existing use, and one on the basis that a purchaser would use the property for an alternate purpose. This type of analysis may be required because the owner of a large, special purpose property decides to abandon the property to consolidate its operations. In such cases, it is usually not possible to determine in advance whether a purchaser can be found who has a need for the special purpose features of the improvements.

Speculative Uses

Land that is held primarily for future sale may be regarded as speculative land. The purchaser or owner may believe that the value of the
land will appreciate, but there may be considerable risk that the expected appreciation will not occur within the time the speculator in-
tends to hold the land. Nevertheless, the current value of the land is a
function of its *future* highest and best use. In such cases, an appraiser
should discuss potential, future highest and best use. The exact future
highest and best use may not be predictable, but often the future *type*
of highest and best use (such as a shopping center or industrial park)
is known or predictable because of zoning or surrounding land use
patterns. In addition, there may be several types of potential highest
and best uses, such as single family or multifamily residential developments. Appraisers usually cannot identify future highest and best uses
with much specificity, but they can discuss logical alternatives and general levels of the ensuing incomes and expenses.

As noted previously, interim uses may be the current highest and
best uses of properties for which highest and best uses are expected to
change in the foreseeable future. Such properties may derive the greatest value contribution from the future highest and best use. Nevertheless, the interim use may also contribute to present value.

Excess Land

Many parcels of land are too large for their principal highest and best
uses. Land in addition to that which is necessary to accommodate a
site's highest and best use is called excess land. Such parcels may have,
in effect, two highest and best uses—the primary highest and best use
and the highest and best use for the remaining, or excess, land. In
many cases, the highest and best use of excess land is for open space,
or nondevelopment. In other cases, the highest and best use may be
for some less intensive use. In any event, an appraiser should treat
parcels having excess land as two separate parcels. The land that supports the site's primary highest and best use usually has a higher unit
value than the excess land, which is valued separately.

Land that is required to support the primary use, such as a parking lot for an office building or a playground for a school, is not excess
land. Only land beyond the normal needs of a particular use, as determined in the market, can be considered excess land. Some atypically
large sites cannot be considered as having excess land because the
acreage that is beyond the normal needs of the particular use cannot
be separately used. For instance, the overly large lot in an area that is
100% built up, or a site that cannot be divided because of the location

of its buildings, are not considered to have excess land. An appraiser should clearly identify any land that is considered excess and indicate a separate unit value. The appraiser should then add the value of the excess land to the value of the primary parcel to obtain the value of the entire parcel.

Summary

Highest and best use analysis is basic in an appraisal. It reflects an assumption about market behavior—that sellers will pay prices for properties that are derived from conclusions about the most profitable use of a site or a property. Thus, sites and improved properties tend to be put to their highest and best uses.

Two types of highest and best use are relevant—highest and best use of land or sites as though vacant and highest and best use of properties as improved. Improvements can be changed; therefore, land is valued under its highest and best use as though vacant, whether or not an existing improvement is a site's highest and best use. Improvements that evidence any significant depreciation are precluded from being highest and best use of land as though vacant. In other words, such structures would not be replicated in their existing condition on the land if it were vacant, although the general use category often remains the same.

The second type of highest and best use recognizes that most improvements should not be demolished and replaced, even though they may not be highest and best use of their sites as though vacant. Until the return from a new improvement will more than offset the return obtainable from the existing improvement, costs of demolition, and costs of constructing a new improvement, the existing improvement should be continued in service. As long as an existing improvement is retained, the highest and best use question is, How should the entire property be used to maximize its benefits or the income it produces? The answer to this question is termed the highest and best use of the property as improved.

Highest and best use of land as though vacant is estimated as a step in the separate valuation of land in the cost approach and in some techniques of the income capitalization approach. It is also an aid in identifying comparable properties. Highest and best use of a property as improved is estimated as a basis for determining the type and quantity of income or other benefits that can be expected from a property. It, too, is an aid in identifying comparable properties.

Highest and best use is a residual concept, derived from classical economic theory, in which land income is regarded as an unearned, surplus increment. Land is entitled to a return only after the other agents in production are paid. Although this theory has been generally replaced as an explanation of modern market behavior for determining land values, highest and best use analysis has been retained as a governing concept in appraisal analysis.

Highest and best use may be tested quantitatively. The income and expenses produced under various use alternatives may be estimated, and the net income may be used to calculate returns on invested capital. Qualitatively, however, highest and best use is the product of four elements. It must be physically possible, legally permissible, financially feasible, and maximally productive. Statements of highest and best use conclusions should be included in every appraisal report and should contain the appropriate detail for the given situation.

Finally, several special situations may necessitate unique considerations in identifying and testing highest and best use. Such situations are single use situations, interim uses, legally nonconforming uses, uses that are not highest and best, multiple uses, special purpose uses, speculative uses, and excess land. In all special situations, the concepts of highest and best use are applicable; only the specific requirements of each situation differ.

Part IV
Valuation

Chapter 12

Collection and Analysis of Specific Data

Specific data are details about a property being appraised, comparable sales and rental properties, and relevant local market characteristics. Specific data about a subject property are provided by its land and building descriptions. These data help an appraiser to select comparable specific data pertinent to sales, rentals, and other local market characteristics. This chapter delineates the sources of secondary data and the methods for extracting pertinent data from the market and for organizing them to analyze specific value-producing elements.

In an analysis of general data, trends in value on national, regional, and local levels are emphasized; in an analysis of specific data, the set of properties most relevant to the property being appraised is studied. The analysis of relevant properties helps an appraiser to extract specific sale prices, rental terms, incomes and expenses, rates of return on investment, construction costs, expected economic life of improvements, and rates of depreciation. The figures are then used in the calculations that provide the indications of value for a subject property on the date of the appraisal.

An appraiser needs comparable specific data when applying any of the three approaches to value. The appraiser uses the data to generate adjustments for value-influencing elements, to isolate meaningful units of comparison, to analyze capitalization rates, and to refine measures of accrued depreciation, among other reasons. Essentially, the data provide the figures that are used in applying the valuation techniques. The process of extracting relevant data from the vast array of available market data helps an appraiser to develop a perception of the market. The perception is essential in applying appraisal judgment throughout the valuation process and in the final reconciliation of value indications. Therefore, the validity of a final estimate of market value largely depends on the extent to which it can be supported by market data.

Specific data are analyzed through a process of comparison. The key to the comparison is to locate in the data items that provide the information needed to apply the techniques in each of the approaches. A number of different data sets may be needed to extract all information pertinent to the appraisal problem. For example, if the subject property is an apartment building of three-bedroom units, the appraiser may be able to base adjustments for time of sale, location, and physical characteristics on information from comparable sales of similar apartment buildings. However, it may be necessary to analyze data on competitive properties that have not sold recently to obtain adequate rental rates and expenses for apartment buildings in the area.

An appraiser's analysis of highest and best use for both the land as though vacant and the property as improved determines the focus of comparable specific data collection and analysis. The nature and extent of the research appropriate to a specific assignment depends on the type of property and the purpose of the appraisal. When the purpose is to estimate market value, the appraiser researches market perceptions, opinions, and attitudes, particularly as they are revealed in recent sales, leases, or other types of direct market transactions. An appraiser attempts to gather all available data that may be pertinent to the assignment, to organize them, and to perform a preliminary analysis of them before applying any of the three approaches.

Investigation of Market Transactions

The detailed description and classification of the subject property's characteristics and components that are found in its land and building analyses help an appraiser to select the sales data used in the sales comparison, income capitalization, and cost approaches. Sales that are used for comparison should be those in the data that are most similar to the subject property. To use sales as a valid basis for further analysis, an appraiser must complete a full inventory of the characteristics and components of any property chosen as a comparable. The techniques used for investigating the subject property, which were presented in Chapters 8, 9, and 10, must also be applied in the investigation of comparable sales.

To select comparable sale properties, an appraiser uses information from public records, published sources, and office files, and from buyers, sellers, and other knowledgeable persons. Interviews with property owners may reveal relevant sales that have not been recorded. To some extent, the selection of comparables is directed by the availability and scope of the data. The investigation of an active market usually reveals an adequate and representative number of transactions within a restricted time and area.

An appraiser must ascertain a market's geographical dimensions. The area from which comparable sales can be selected depends on the property type. For certain types of retail property, only main street frontage may be pertinent. For large industrial properties and investment properties in general, the entire community should usually be studied. For the larger of such properties, the nationwide market may be relevant. For a residential appraisal, there may occasionally be adequate data within a block of the subject. Even in such cases, however, an appraiser should consider the broader market to place the subject property and the comparables in the proper perspective in relation to general market trends.

In selecting market transactions for analysis, an appraiser eliminates transactions that are not pertinent to the specific market for the subject property. For example, when an appraiser considers a 10-year-old single family residence that has three bedrooms, two baths, and 1,800 square feet of livable area, he or she usually eliminates two- and four-bedroom houses immediately if there is sufficient data concerning three-bedroom house sales. The appraiser would also probably ignore the sales of 25- or 30-year-old houses, and possibly the sales of new houses. If sufficient sales remained, sales of houses smaller than 1,600 square feet or larger than 2,000 square feet might be rejected. The first determinant, therefore, of the data that are ultimately used is the quantity of data that are available.

When comparable sale data in the subject property's area are limited, an appraiser may have to extend the data search to adjacent neighborhoods and communities that are similar to that of the subject property. When the selection of data is still limited to an unacceptably narrow sample of current market activity, the appraiser may decide to use sales that are less current and to interview brokers, buyers, sellers, owners, and tenants of similar properties in the area to discover evidence of potential market activity—that is, listings of offers to sell and offers to purchase. These may also be used as comparables if the proper adjustments are made.

An appraiser learns broad information about the market from the pattern of sales. Important information can be revealed by the

1. Number of sales

2. Period of time covered by the sales

3. Availability of property for sale

4. Rate of absorption

5. Rate of turnover (volume of sales, level of activity)

6. Characteristics and motivations of buyers and sellers

7. Terms and conditions of sale

8. Use of property prior and subsequent to the sale

9. Other significant characteristics

In analyzing available data for the selection of comparable sales, an appraiser begins to form certain conclusions about the general market, the subject property, and the possible relationships between the data and the subject property. The appraiser begins to ascertain market strengths and weaknesses; the probable supply of, demand for, and marketability of properties most similar to the property being appraised; and the variations and characteristics that are likely to have the greatest impact on the value of properties in the market. Thus, an appraiser does not analyze market data in a vacuum. He or she analyzes data against a background of information about the specific area and the specific type of property.

Locating Sales Data

The many sources of sales data include public records; lease records; published news; classified ads and listings; Realtors®, lenders, appraisers, and property managers; direct interviews; published and computerized sales and listings; and other local sources.

Public records.   An appraiser searches public records to acquire a copy of the property deed. Deeds provide important information about the property and the sales transaction. The full names of parties to a transaction and the transaction date are cited on the deed. A legal description of the property transferred is provided, and the property rights included in the transaction, as well as any outstanding liens on the title, are shown.

Occasionally, full names give clues as to unusual motivations for the sale. For example, a sale from John Smith to Mary S. Jones may be a transfer to a daughter, or a sale from John Smith, William Jones, and Harold Long to the SJL Corporation may not be an arm's-length transaction.

Statutes in some states require that the consideration paid upon transfer of title be shown on the deed. However, it is not always dependable as a reflection of the sale price because some purchasers deduct the estimated value of personal property (e.g., in motels or apartments) from the true consideration in order to reduce transfer taxes. These personal property values are sometimes inflated, making the recorded consideration for the real property less than the true consideration. Occasionally, too, the indicated consideration will be overstated in order to obtain a loan higher than actually justifiable, or understated in order to justify a low property tax assessment. Although some states require that the true and actual consideration be reported on the deed, other states allow the consideration to be reported as "$1.00 and other valuable consideration."

Records of the local tax assessor may include property cards for both the subject property and comparables, with land and building sketches, areas, sale prices, and so forth. In some localities, legal or private publishing services issue information about revenue stamps and other pertinent facts about current transfers.

Published news.   The newspapers of most cities feature real estate news. Some of the news is incomplete or inaccurate. However, an appraiser is able to confirm details because the names of the negotiating brokers and the parties involved are usually published.

Realtors®, appraisers, managers, and bankers.   These professionals often provide information about real estate transactions and may give valuable leads to important facts. Of course, all data gathered in interviews should be verified.

Multiple listing books.   These are published in many communities. Books of multiple listings include the properties listed for sale during a calendar year or a quarter and their listing prices. The books give fairly complete information about the property, including a photograph, a description, and the broker's name. However, certain details, such as the square footage, the amount of basement, or the exact age, may be inaccurate or excluded. In certain areas, multiple listing books can be purchased.

Listings and offers.   Whenever possible, an appraiser should accumulate information on listings of other properties offered for sale. The appraiser can request that his or her name be added to the mailing lists of banks, brokers, and others offering properties for sale. Classified ads also provide information on properties being offered for sale. In addition to providing asking prices, the ads give some measure of the strength or weakness of the local market for a particular type of property or the trend of activity in a particular area. Offers to purchase are also useful information, which may be obtained from brokers or managers. Listings are generally higher than the eventual transaction prices; offers are generally somewhat lower.

Filing Sales Data

The most efficient procedure for data collection and analysis is to maintain regular, ongoing data files. The first item of such a file is usually a published listing of daily transfers, which gives deed volume and page, the names of the seller and the purchaser, a partial legal description, the deed tax, and sometimes the sale price. From this information, an appraiser verifies the sale; determines land dimensions, building size and age, and other pertinent sales data; classifies the property by type; and files the sale for possible future use as a comparable. Many appraisers also inspect and photograph the property, which eliminates errors and the possible confusion about additions or improvements that are made after the sale date.

Office file storage system.   Data should be classified by property categories. One such classification is as follows:

Residential	Industrial
Single family residences	Factories and plants
Condominiums	Warehouses
Mobile homes	Loft buildings
Apartments	

Commercial	Agricultural
Retail stores	Farms
Office buildings	Ranches
Hotels/motels	Dairies
Service buildings	Orchards

	Special purpose
	Service stations
	Hospitals
	Nursing/retirement homes
	Institutional structures

It may be necessary to divide the categories into submarket preferences. For example, an appraiser can divide the apartment category into elevator, garden, walk-up, and conversion classes, and further divide the garden and walk-up classes into those that have 7 units and under, 8 to 24 units, 25 to 99 units, 100 to 199 units, and over 200 units.

An appraiser keeps the specific market data pertaining to location and type of property readily available by maintaining separate alphabetical address and area files and class-of-property files and by cross-indexing the information in them. The market data master sheet or card for each sale may be supplemented by an attached photograph or, for larger properties, a copy of the printed brochure that was prepared when the property was offered for sale.

Market transaction data may be put on index cards or in a computer, categorized by property type, location, age, or price. Computers are often advisable and are increasingly being used for data storage and analysis. Whether to use a computer depends on the size of the appraisal operation, the amount of information to be stored, and the practicalities of keeping the file updated. The system an operation should use largely depends on cost, convenience, and the types of property that are usually appraised.

Investigation of Additional Market Data

The investigation of the market extends beyond the determination of available comparable sale properties. Useful specific data are obtained by investigating properties that are similar to and competitive with the subject property, even though such properties have not sold recently. Information used in applying the cost and income capitalization approaches often must be sought from market sources in addition to sales. Such information may also be useful in refining adjustments made in the sales comparison approach. In the investigation of general and neighborhood data, an appraiser learns significant information on trends in such items as construction costs, lease terms, typical expenses, and vacancy rates. Investigation of these trends in the market where the subject property is located provides additional specific data that are needed to derive value indications through the three approaches.

Improvement Cost Data

Useful information about construction costs may be obtained from many sources. Contractors and suppliers of construction materials provide cost information pertaining to recent construction of buildings that are similar to those of the subject property. Cost estimators may also be consulted for costs involved in the construction of building improvements. Published cost estimates may or may not include soft, or indirect, costs such as loan interest during the period of construction.

In an active area, cost information is available through interviews with local property owners who have recently added building or land improvements similar to those found on the subject property. When available, work contracts and accounting records of recently improved properties can also provide details of significant cost information.

Cost estimates are made by assembling, analyzing, and cataloging data on actual building costs. These detailed costs should be classified by general categories, such as residential construction or commercial building costs, with separate figures for special finish or equipment. Costs for individual components of structures should also be ascertained and filed.

Several cost-estimating services publish cost manuals that provide costs by square-foot and cubic-foot. These unit costs for building types usually start with a building of a certain size (that is, a base area or volume) that serves as a benchmark to which additions or deductions can be made according to the actual number of square feet or cubic feet contained in the property for which cost estimates are being made. Data provided by cost-estimating reporting services are useful for confirming estimates developed from local cost data.

Cost manuals are updated periodically by the inclusion of cost index tables that reflect changes in cost of construction over a period of years. Cost indexes translate a known cost as of some past date to a current cost estimate. However, there is a practical limitation in the application of this procedure because increasing the time span tends to reduce the reliability of the current cost indication derived in this manner. Cost index tables sometimes may be used to adjust costs between different geographical locations.

Another difficulty in using cost index tables is that it may be difficult to ascertain the components that are included and those that are omitted in the reported original cost. Further, capital expenditures for improvements that are added subsequent to original construction must also be considered. Added improvements may affect the estimates of cost and accrued depreciation.

Certain appraisers rely almost entirely on published cost manuals; others keep files of specific cost comparables similar to their files of sale comparables. Such files may be based initially on the information furnished by contract reporting services. Certain of these give the building areas; others supply a general building description, the low bids, and the contract award. The appraiser may then obtain any missing information, such as areas, breakdowns of office and warehouse space, and so forth, and classify the building type for filing. When carefully developed, such a file can supply authentic square foot costs on specific buildings of all types that can be used as needed for particular appraisals.

Income and Expense Data

In deriving pertinent income and expense data, an appraiser investigates comparable sales and rentals, as well as information on competitive income-producing properties in the same market. Current gross income estimates should be reviewed in light of average rent levels for several successive years. Vacancy and collection losses and operating expenses typical for the property type help an appraiser to refine the forecasts of income and expenses for an income-producing property.

The published information on property values for several consecutive years suggests the rate of appreciation or depreciation that is evident for various property types. Interviews with owners and tenants in the area can provide lease and expense data. Lenders are a source of information on current terms of available financing.

An appraiser attempts to obtain all income and expense data for income property comparables. These figures should be derived and tabulated in reconstructed operating statement format (see Chapter 15), and filed by property type.

Rental information is probably the most difficult of all data to obtain except for expense data. Therefore, an appraiser should take every opportunity to add rents to the data plant. Long-term leases are usually on public record. A separate county index of leases may be available, which lists the parties to recorded leases and refers to the volume and page of the recorded lease. Sometimes this information is listed among the deeds and mortgages, but it is normally coded so that a lease may be spotted fairly easily. In certain cities, abstracts of recorded leases are printed by a private publishing service. Classified ads are also a source of rental information. Many appraisers regularly check for advertised rentals and post them to rent comparable cards for a particular property type or area. The final actual rental is usually much closer to the asking rental than is the case for asking prices. Rental data should be filed by property type and area according to the same classifications used for sale data.

The income and expense comparables should be filed chronologically and by property type. They can thus be retrieved easily to help estimate the expenses for a similar type of property. Income and expenses should be converted to units for comparison and analysis. Income may be reported in terms of rent per apartment unit, per room, per hospital bed, per square foot, and so forth. Expenses, such as insurance, taxes, painting, decorating, and other maintenance charges, can be expressed in any of the units of comparison used for income, but they may also be expressed as a percent of the effective gross rent. Any unit of comparison must be used consistently throughout the analysis.

The data for a rented property may show the experienced vacancy rate and operating expenses as a percentage of the effective gross rent. These data are essential in the valuation of income-producing properties. Other important information includes the age and type of construction and any utilities that are provided by the owner.

Capitalization Rates

Market capitalization rates are also an essential type of market data.[1] When income, expense, and mortgage data are available for sale properties, these indications may be used to calculate the overall capitalization rate and the equity dividend rate associated with the sale. Whenever possible, an appraiser should derive the overall and equity dividend rates of return, which are indicated by sales of comparable properties, and file the information for future reference. In the comparison, these rates would be analyzed according to the similarity of the comparable sale property's characteristics to those of the subject property.

Overall and equity dividend capitalization rates derived from sales may also be used as bases from which other rates used for capitalization could be derived. Therefore, it is important that appraisers consider these rate indications when information in sales is adequate for derivation.

Organization of Data

Before undertaking any analysis, an appraiser organizes all specific data that were accumulated during the market investigation. A spreadsheet that is carefully constructed provides a tabular representation of market data that are organized into useful and ultimately measurable categories. Depending on the complexity of the information that must be analyzed, an appraiser may have to design several spreadsheets to isolate and study specific data. On the initial spreadsheet, the appraiser lists each characteristic of the subject and comparable properties that can be isolated at that time.

The spreadsheet should include the total property sale price for each comparable and the date of each sale, which can be expressed in

---

[1]For a full discussion of market derivation of capitalization rates, see Chapter 16.

relation to the date of valuation of the subject property (for example, one month or 16 months ago). The spreadsheet also includes information about financial arrangements and any unusual motivation that resulted in a negotiating advantage for either the buyer or the seller, such as the desire to liquidate for inheritance tax or the desire to acquire a particular property for expansion. Financial arrangements and unusual motivations can significantly influence a property's sale price and thus must be carefully examined.

The spreadsheet often also contains other market data that may be significant to the appraisal assignment. Examples of such data are reproduction costs for building and land improvements, development costs, amount of accrued depreciation, indicated economic life attributed to improvements similar to those on the subject property, rates of return, percent of land value appreciation evident in the area, and average value of commodities produced on or services rendered by properties similar to the one being appraised.

The initial spreadsheet can include all characteristics of the subject and comparable properties, sales transactions, and pertinent market data from sources other than sales. However, an appraiser may decide to use one spreadsheet for comparable sales information and others for information derived from sources other than sales. This tabulation of data allows the appraiser to isolate aspects of both individual sales and the total market that may be significant in the valuation problem. The isolation of specifics provides an initial indication of the information an appraiser will be able to derive from the collected data, and it identifies variations among properties that may be significant to their value.

An analysis of the initial spreadsheet may indicate that certain data are not pertinent and thus will not be useful in the application of the approaches. An appraiser may also find that additional data are required. The analysis may point to the need to create other spreadsheets to include additional information or to isolate data required for specific approaches. Appraisers should view the analysis of data as a developing process and the spreadsheet as a tool that facilitates and helps advance that process to valid indications of a property's value through the approaches.

Data Analysis—Sales Comparison Approach

In the sales comparison approach to value, an appraiser primarily analyzes the data gathered from comparable sales. The goal of the analysis in this approach is to identify variations between the subject property and the comparable sales so that the value of the variations may be measured later in the application of the approach. The analysis of sales data shows what the market perceives to be valuable and indicates the mathematical computations that can be applied to the known values of the comparables to arrive at the unknown whole or per-unit value of the subject property.

The initial step in this analysis is to determine an appropriate unit of comparison. In appraising single family residential properties, adjustments are typically made to the total property sale price; hence the unit of comparison is the total property. However, use of the total property unit is rarely meaningful, or even possible, in appraising other types of property, principally because of size differences.

To adjust for size differences, the common practice is to reduce the total property to a unit that is representative of the whole. For example, knowledge that Warehouse A sold in the current market for $300,000 and Warehouse B sold for $400,000 does not provide the basis for a meaningful comparison with a property being appraised. However, if Warehouse A provides 20,000 square feet and Warehouse B provides 32,000 square feet, it is apparent that Warehouse A sold for $15 per square foot and that Warehouse B sold for $12.50 per square foot. By reducing these sales to a unit of comparison in terms of dollars per square foot of gross area, an appraiser can make meaningful comparisons.

Units of comparison are used in data analysis in all three approaches. In the sales comparison approach, the sale price may be divided by the unit of comparison. In the cost approach, the total cost to construct and the total accrued depreciation are divided by the unit of comparison. In the income capitalization approach, the income and expense items and the net operating income may be similarly divided by the chosen unit of comparison. In all approaches, several different units of comparison may be used, depending on the information the appraiser needs and the focus of the analysis. However, the same unit must be applied to both the subject property and all comparable sales in any single analysis.

Different units of comparison are typically used with different property types. Comparisons can be made on the basis of the price, cost, income, and expenses per unit, depending on the approach in which the comparable property is being analyzed. The following list shows common property types and the typical units of comparison that are used in appraising them:

Single family residences

1. Entire property

2. Square foot

3. Room

4. Potential or effective gross rent multiplier

Vacant land
1. Entire property

2. Square foot

3. Front foot

4. Potential subdivided lot

5. Building units per acre

Agricultural properties
1. Acre

2. Animal unit (AU)

3. Hundred weight (cwt), tons, or bushel per acre

4. Thousand board feet (Mbf)

Apartments
1. Square foot of livable area

2. Apartment

3. Room

4. Potential or effective gross rent multiplier

Warehouses
1. Square foot

2. Cubic foot

3. Loading dock/door

4. Potential or effective gross rent multiplier

Factories
1. Square foot

2. Cubic foot

3. Machine unit

4. Potential or effective gross rent multiplier

Offices
1. Square foot

2. Office

3. Room

4. Desk

5. Potential or effective gross rent multiplier

Hospitals
1. Square foot

2. Bed

Theaters
1. Square foot

2. Seat

After determining the appropriate unit of comparison, an appraiser reviews the data to ascertain the characteristics of the properties and sales transactions to use in the sales comparison analysis. The dates of sales show which properties provide the best initial indication of change in value over time. To derive the indication, an appraiser ideally would have records of a sale and later resale of a property with no substantial changes to the property between sales.

Further analysis helps an appraiser to decide where to begin to solve for the value contributed by individual property characteristics. Because properties usually have many separate value components, the appraiser attempts to find a single component for which a value can be derived. For instance, if the spreadsheet shows that two properties vary only in that one is fully landscaped and the other is not, the appraiser can estimate the contributory value of the landscaping by comparing the two sales and by solving for the value contribution of the landscaping. Another market variable may be isolated in other sales for a second calculation.

Thus, the analysis of sales is progressive. An appraiser isolates and solves for one variable at a time by comparing known indications against unknown characteristics. For example, in residential properties, value differences that result from such items as swimming pools or garages may have to be found.

This kind of analysis gives the appraiser an indication of the most useful data for the application of the sales comparison approach and suggests the pattern of calculations necessary to derive a value indication. Moreover, a careful review of market data may indicate that additional data are needed to substantiate a value indication reached through the sales comparison approach, or that relatively more weight should be attributed to value indications derived from application of the cost or income capitalization approaches.

Data Analysis—Income Capitalization Approach

Data from comparable sales, leases, and income and expense statements provide a variety of information that is useful in applying income capitalization approach techniques. Much of the data for the approach is derived from interviews with individuals who are familiar with the subject property or comparable sale properties. An appraiser also interviews owners and managers of similar properties for information on typical rent and other lease terms, vacancy rates, management fees, and other operating expenses.

If all necessary data are not reflected in comparable sales, an appraiser can use data gathered from other market sources. In the income capitalization approach, an appraiser should particularly have market indications of average income and expense trends on a unit basis, as well as indications of the various types of relationships between income and value. These trends provide support for the net income and rates that are projected for the subject property.

When the data provide an appraiser with adequate knowledge of the income, expenses, and mortgage associated with each sale, he or she can derive an estimate of the net operating income and equity dividend for each sale property. The overall capitalization rate and equity dividend rate that are reflected in each sale can then be determined by dividing the net operating income by the sale price for the overall capitalization rate and dividing the equity dividend by the equity investment for the equity dividend rate. This data analysis technique provides meaningful information only if an appraiser uses the same income and expense categories to derive net operating incomes from comparable sales and to project the net operating income for the subject property. For example, if an allowance for replacement is made in the expense statement for one comparable property and not in the others, the rate derived by dividing that property's net operating income by its sale price would not be comparable to those derived from other properties.

Analyzing the market-derived overall capitalization rate and equity dividend rate that are indicated in each comparable sale can help an appraiser develop the appropriate rate or rates to use in estimating the subject property's value by income capitalization approach techniques.

In many cases, however, adequate market data are not available to rely on this type of income capitalization analysis. The appraiser may need to use yield capitalization techniques to provide more refined indications of the possible relationships between income and value. Nonetheless, market-derived overall rates may serve as a point of departure for further analysis, and results obtained in all forms of income analysis should be explained in terms of observable market phenomena.

Data Analysis—Cost Approach

To apply the cost approach, an appraiser must often use both sales data and other cost and depreciation information from the market. Both sources of cost information may contribute significantly to the approach, and each may serve as a check on the other. An analysis of sales data can supplement cost and depreciation data from other sources. Sales analysis can provide direct indications of accrued depreciation, profit margin, and the value contributed by buildings or land improvements. The cost of a recently added improvement on a sale property may indicate current construction costs.

In developing cost estimates by analyzing data obtained through observation and interviews, an appraiser must ascertain precisely what the reported expenditure represents in relation to the total actual cost of property changes. Quoted costs for improvements may not reflect the owner's related risk, labor and equipment costs, financial charges, costs of land preparation, engineering costs, or other indirect expenses.

The appraiser must also be aware that cost estimates for reproduction or replacement of improvements as of the appraisal date, which are developed in this type of investigation, may not reflect any profit realized by the current owner because of a change in the property. Of course, final cost estimates should take such profit into consideration if it is evident in the market.

However, if the appraiser isolates and abstracts costs from direct sales analysis, this cost information includes any profit realized from the addition of the building or land improvement. For example, assume that a new office facility has been added to a warehouse and that the entire property sold for $1 million. The analysis of market data indicates that similar properties without office facilities have sold for $750,000. The analysis of these data indicates that office facilities added $250,000 to the sale price of the property, including the cost and any profit realized from the added improvement. This figure may then exceed actual cost data from other sources.

The analysis of sales may also provide a direct measure of accrued depreciation by comparing improvement contributions in a sale with current construction costs. Now assume that the office facilities in the previous example had been in existence for some time and that the sale price was $900,000. The following calculation provides a measure of the current value of the older improvements.

Value of property with improvements	$900,000
Value of property without improvements	−750,000
Current value of improvements	$150,000

By subtracting the current value from the cost new value, an indication of the total accrued depreciation can be obtained as shown below.

Cost new of improvements	(100%)	$250,000
Current value of improvements	(60%)	−150,000
Total accrued depreciation	(40%)	$100,000

This information can be used to measure the amount of depreciation for improvements on a property having facilities similar to those found in a sale.

Analysis Techniques

Specific market data are gathered from all available sources to provide insights into market indications of value. By investigating the various types of specific data, an appraiser can select appropriate information and analyze it for use in the valuation of a subject property. The remainder of this chapter illustrates three important techniques for analyzing specific data. The techniques are paired data set analysis, regression analysis, and graphic analysis.

Paired Data Sets

In comparison of data, sales may be paired to identify the effect of specific differences on market price. If two sale properties are closely comparable except in one respect, an analysis may indicate a reasonable adjustment for the specific difference. If a property was sold and was later resold with no significant changes in the property during the interim, comparison of the two sale prices can be used to derive the rate of change in property value due to changes in market conditions be-tween the time of the first and second sales.

Application of this technique is complicated by the fact that the comparable properties used for sales comparison analysis usually have different elements—that is, there may be differences in conditions of sale, financing terms, market conditions, location, physical characteristics, and income characteristics. Any of these elements may significantly influence a property's sale price and thus may affect the subject property's market value.

When paired data set analysis allows an appraiser to discover the market-perceived value of one of the elements, the value may then be used as the known in another matched pair. When successive pairings can each isolate a single element for which the value is unknown, a series of suggested values for the individual elements contained in the comparable sales data can be developed. The applicable, suggested values can then be used in deriving a value indication for the subject property.

Sales

Paired data set analysis can be applied to sales that are collected for a residential appraisal. For example, an appraiser is asked to consider a property that contains 1,500 square feet of livable area, is five years old, and has a full basement. The appraiser has concluded that the major causes of varying prices in the neighborhood are (1) time of sale, (2) size, (3) age, and (4) basement. The appraiser has located the following comparable sales:

1. Sale price $60,000, sale current, 1,500 sq. ft., 5 yrs. old, no basement

2. Sale price $66,000, sale current, 1,500 sq. ft., 5 yrs. old, full basement

3. Sale price $74,000, sale current, 1,700 sq. ft., 5 yrs. old, full basement

4. Sale price $63,000, sale current, 1,500 sq. ft., new, no basement

5. Sale price $70,500, sale 6 mos. prior to date of appraisal, 1,700 sq. ft., 5 yrs. old, full basement

6. Sale price $74,000, sale 6 mos. prior to date of appraisal, 1,700 sq. ft., new, full basement

Next, the appraiser organizes the sales data to analyze them.

Table 12.1   Data Summary—Residential Sales

	Subject	Sale 1	Sale 2	Sale 3	Sale 4	Sale 5	Sale 6
Price		$60,000	$66,000	$74,000	$63,000	$70,500	$74,000
Date	Current	Current	Current	Current	Current	6 mos.	6 mos.
Size (sq. ft)	1,500	1,500	1,500	1,700	1,500	1,700	1,700
Age	5	5	5	5	New	5	New
Basement	Yes	No	Yes	Yes	No	Yes	Yes

Next, the appraiser ascertains variances in market price by "pairing" sales.

	Date	
Sale 3	Current	$74,000
Sale 5	6 mos.	−70,500
		$ 3,500

$3,500 ÷ $70,500 = approx. 5%

	Size	
Sale 3	1,700 sq. ft.	$74,000
Sale 2	−1,500 sq. ft.	−66,000
	200 sq. ft.	$ 8,000

$8,000 ÷ 200 sq. ft. = $40 per sq. ft.

	Age	
Sale 4	New	$63,000
Sale 1	5 yrs.	−60,000
		$ 3,000

$3,000 ÷ $63,000 = 5%, or 1% per year

	Basement	
Sale 2	Yes	$66,000
Sale 1	No	−60,000
		$ 6,000

$6,000 ÷ 1,500 sq. ft. = $4 per sq. ft.

The appraiser can now create a sales adjustment chart.[2]

Table 12.2   Adjustment Chart—Residential

Sale	Sale 1	Sale 2	Sale 3	Sale 4	Sale 5	Sale 6
Price	$60,000	$66,000	$74,000	$63,000	$70,500	$74,000
Date					+3,500	+3,700
Size			−8,000		−8,000	−8,000
Age				−3,000		−3,700
Basement	+6,000			+6,000		
Adjusted sale price	$66,000	$66,000	$66,000	$66,000	$66,000	$66,000
Value indication for subject						$66,000

In the preceding example, the differentials are kept precise to ensure that the methodology is clear. The marketplace, of course, will probably not supply a set of sales for each appraisal with neat pairings of properties that are identical except for one element. However, the example illustrates the technique of analyzing paired data sets in the comparison of sale data. And, as sufficient quantities of data are gathered, increasingly clearer indicators of this type will emerge. However, an adjustment derived from a single pair of sales would have little validity in a statistical sense and should be considered only as a general guide, which is tempered by the appraiser's judgment and experience with previous data analysis.

Rents

The analysis of paired data sets is also used for rental comparisons. The following example shows how paired data set analysis can be applied to an appraisal concerned with office building rentals in a small city.

In making such an appraisal, the appraiser might conclude that the primary elements accounting for the varying rentals are (1) date of lease, (2) location rating, (3) quality of space, and (4) whether the space is serviced (utilities and cleaning furnished).

The appraiser locates the following rent comparables:

1. Current lease, location average, quality average, serviced, rent $8.50/ sq. ft.

---

[2]Adjustment charts are explained in Chapter 13.

2. Current lease, location good, quality average, unserviced, rent $6.75/ sq. ft.

3. Current lease, location good, quality good, unserviced, rent $7.25/ sq. ft.

4. Lease 3 mos. old, location average, quality average, serviced, rent $8.25/sq. ft.

5. Current lease, location good, quality average, serviced, rent $8.75/ sq. ft.

6. Lease 3 mos. old, location average, quality good, serviced, rent $8.75/ sq. ft.

Next, the appraiser organizes data for analysis as follows:

Table 12.3   Data Summary—Office Rentals

Comparable	Rent per sq. ft.	Lease Date	Location	Quality	Serviced
1	$8.50	Current	Av.	Av.	Y
2	6.75	Current	Good	Av.	N
3	7.25	Current	Good	Good	N
4	8.25	3 mos.	Av.	Av.	Y
5	8.75	Current	Good	Av.	Y
6	8.75	3 mos.	Av.	Good	Y
Subject		Current	Av.	Good	Y

Next, the appraiser derives rental variances by pairing the comparables.

	Age of Lease	
Comp. 1	Current	$8.50 per sq. ft.
Comp. 4	3 mos.	−8.25 per sq. ft.
		$ .25 per sq. ft.

	Location	
Comp. 5	Good	$8.75 per sq. ft.
Comp. 1	Av.	−8.50 per sq. ft.
		$ .25 per sq. ft.

Quality		
Comp. 3	Good	$7.25 per sq. ft.
Comp. 2	Av.	− 6.75 per sq. ft.
		$ .50 per sq. ft.

Serviced		
Comp. 5	Yes	$8.75 per sq. ft.
Comp. 2	No	− 6.75 per sq. ft.
		$2.00 per sq. ft.

Next, the appraiser can prepare an adjustment chart.

Table 12.4 Adjustment Chart—Office Rentals

Comparable	Rent	Lease Date	Location	Quality	Service	Adjusted Rent Indication
1	$8.50			+$.50		$9.00
2	6.75		− $.25	+ .50	+$2.00	9.00
3	7.25		− .25		+ 2.00	9.00
4	8.25	+$.25		+ .50		9.00
5	8.75		− .25	+ .50		9.00
6	8.75	+ .25				9.00
		Indicated rental for subject				$9.00 per sq. ft.

Again, the precise balancing figures do not imply that market data will often be so clear-cut. They have been used here to show how adjustments can be made when the values of the elements that make up the comparable sales are suggested by an analysis of paired data sets.

Operating Expenses

In addition to providing information regarding the sale, transaction data can also be used as guidelines to estimate operating expenses. Thus, the data provide important information for the income capitalization approach. When operating expense data are available, the data should be reduced to units of comparison for analysis and later for application in further comparisons. For example, it is wise to reduce operating statements on office buildings or shopping centers to a square-foot basis and then to tabulate individual expenses.

The operating statement for a nursing home normally covers at least five or six pages. The following extract from a summary and analysis of operating experience for 12 nursing homes gives an indication of the general procedure. Although the figures for only 3 nursing homes are included here, the average is based on all 12.

	Comparable			
	1	2	3	Av.
Salaries	$ .63	$ .27	$ .36	$ .29
Payroll, taxes	.05	.27	.03	.02
Supplies	.06	.02	.07	.05
Utilities	1.16	1.49	1.51	1.45
Other	.18	.20	.28	.25
Total	$2.08	$2.00	$2.25	$2.06

The tabulation is based on expense per patient per day. Each of the expense categories for all 12 facilities was analyzed in the same manner, along with, of course, similar analyses of the income items, total income, and total expenses. The expenses in the operating statements were also analyzed on the bases of cost per square foot and cost as a percentage of effective gross income. The tabulation provides an appraiser with guidelines as to the proper expense projections for the facilities being appraised. Each item can be analyzed in relation to the differences as to age, condition, occupancy, and the like, of the subject property.

Regression Analysis

Regression analysis is another technique used by appraisers in market data analysis. It is useful for both value estimation and for isolating and testing the significance of specific value determinants.

Simple Linear Regression

Simple linear regression analysis uses only one independent variable, or property characteristic ("simple"), to reflect a relationship that changes in a straight line ("linear")—that is, a change in the independent variable is reflected in exactly the same proportion in the dependent variable, or the unknown. The basic regression equation is expressed in the form

$$Y_C = a + bX,$$

where Y_C is the predicted value of the dependent variable; a is a constant; b is the coefficient, or multiplier, for the independent variable; and X is the value of the variable. For example, if the independent variable is the square foot area of a building, and the dependent variable is sale price, then the simple linear regression equation $Y_C = 10,000 + 45X$ means that the sale price of a building is predicted to be $10,000 plus $45 times its square foot area.

The constant, a, may be pictured by drawing a graph of the data for this regression. Increasing square foot areas are marked along the horizontal line, and increasing sale prices are marked along the vertical line. If a number of sales are posted in this manner, a line can be drawn that most evenly divides the dots representing sale data. This is the *regression line*, and its slope is the b coefficient. The point on the vertical line of the graph at which the regression begins is the *intercept*, or the constant, symbolized as a. In other words, this is a base value, representing all positive and negative factors *not* explained by the equation and to which the coefficients, or adjustment factors, are added.

The most important other statistic that results from a simple linear regression is the coefficient of determination, or r^2. The statistic represents, approximately, the amount in percentage terms of the variation in the dependent variable, which is explained by the equation and is one of the measures of efficacy of the regression. When a regression is performed on an electronic, hand-held calculator, the coefficient of determination given is unadjusted for *degrees of freedom* (number of observations minus number of variables). This adjustment should be applied to the resulting coefficient of determination:

$$r^2 = 1 - (1 - r^2)(n - 1/n - 2)$$

The standard error of estimate is another measure of the regression's goodness of fit. This is symbolized as S_{yx} and represents the remaining dispersion in the data after application of the regression equation. The b coefficient will also have a t value. This statistic is the coefficient expressed as a ratio to its standard deviation and is a measure of the significance of the coefficient. The precise degree of significance represented by a particular t value depends on several factors and must be calculated. As a general rule, however, coefficients with t values higher than 2 are usually significant at a reasonably high confidence level.

Simple regression analysis is particularly useful in valuation when one element is overwhelmingly important in determining a property's

Table 12.5   Lot Sales for Simple Linear Regression

Sale	Month	Price/sq. ft.
1	Jan.	$2.00
2	Mar.	2.10
3	July	2.18
4	Mar.	2.07
5	Sept.	2.20
6	Oct.	2.25
7	Apr.	2.12
8	June	2.15
9	Dec.	2.32

sale price. Perhaps more important, however, is the ability to analyze the relationships between, and the significance of the various components of, real estate values. Suppose, for example, that in the valuation of a commercial lot all but one of the elements that determine the value are fairly evident and noncontroversial; the adjustment for time of sale is the only value determinant at issue. The following sales are adjusted for all elements except time.

The data for a regression can be entered on a hand-held calculator, keying price per square foot as Y and the number of the month as X. The following results are obtained: $a = \$2.00$; $b = \$0.026$; $r^2 = .964$; adjusted $r^2 = .959$; predicted price for December $= \$2.31$. Therefore, the increase for one year is $\$0.31$. The element of time explains 96% of the remaining variation in prices, and a time adjustment at an annual rate of 15% is clearly supported.

One should note that in a regression all data must be entered as numbers. For yes or no items (fireplace or no fireplace), 1 or 0 should be entered, and for qualitative ratings, percentage factors (good = .85) should be used. Factors that express the relationship of size, age, or any other property attribute to price may likewise be used. Other relationships may also be analyzed with simple regression, such as population/number of motel units, traffic counts/gasoline sales, employment/housing starts, population/restaurant sales, and so on.

Multiple Regression Analysis

In multiple regression analysis, the basic methods of simple linear regression are used, but the analysis is expanded to include more than one independent variable. Certain hand-held calculators are preprogrammed or can be programmed for regressions using two or three independent variables, but multiple regressions are generally performed on a computer. An advance over the standard regression procedure is the stepwise regression, in which variables are added or removed according to their degree of explanatory power in the regression equation. This type of regression yields an optimum combination of variables by retaining only the most significant variables.

The following extract from an appraisal illustrates a common use of regression analysis. The appraisal was done for the acquisition of a group of 11 houses in an area of moderately priced homes; regression analysis was used as the sole technique in deriving a value indication. The following elements were selected as being the most useful in predicting sale prices in the neighborhood:

Size: square feet of livable area

Age: actual age, with the following adjustments—for fair condition, add 5 years; for poor condition, add 10 years

Percentage of brick veneer

Percentage of basement

Number of spaces of car storage

Forced-air heating as compared with floor furnace: forced air = 1; floor furnace = 0

Central air-conditioning: Yes = 1; No = 0

House recently redecorated: Yes = 1; No = 0

FHA or VA sale: Yes = 1; No = 0

Time of sale: number of months from earliest sale

Extras: range/oven = 1; window unit = 1; fence = 1; carpet = 3; drapes = 3

Forty-five sales were included in the regression, which resulted in the following price-estimating equation. Estimated sale price is $7,133.76 (this is a constant); plus $21.02 per square foot of livable area; minus $232.54 per year of age; plus $6,782.34 times percentage of brick veneer; plus $2,570.30 times percentage of basement; plus $1,254.44 times number of spaces of car storage; plus $926.48 if the house has forced-air heating; plus $1,996.26 if air-conditioned; plus $944.48 if recently redecorated; plus $1,266.50 if VA or FHA sale; plus $231.36 times the number of months from the date of Sale 1; plus $392.38 times the number of "extras" as defined above.

The following is the application of the equation to one of the subject properties:

Constant	$ 7,133.76
Size: 1,092 × $21.02	22,953.84
Age: 5 × −$232.54	−1,162.70
Brick veneer: .20 × $6,782.34	1,356.47
Basement: 1 × $2,570.30	2,570.30
Car spaces: 1 × $1,254.44	1,254.44
Forced-air heating: 1 × $926.48	926.48
Air-conditioning: 0 × $1,996.26	0
Redecorated: 1 × $944.48	944.48
FHA or VA sale: 0 × $1,266.50	0
No. mos. from Sale 1: 15 × $231.36	3,470.40
No. extras: 5 (window unit 1, carpet 3, fence 1) × $392.38	1,961.90
Value indication:	−41,409.37
Rounded:	$41,500.00

Although this regression was run primarily for valuation of 11 specific properties, it also indicated adjustment factors for use in standard appraisals of other houses of the same general type. The regression had an adjusted coefficient of determination of 93% and a standard error of $981.61. The t values for the variables were rather high (size = 6.22; age = −2.30; percentage of brick veneer = 3.86; time = 5.81, and so forth), which indicated the significance of the coefficients at a high level of confidence.

Because of the many statistical subtleties involved, adjustments should not be based solely on the strength of one regression run. However, a series of regressions that yield reasonably consistent coefficients provide a sound basis for guidelines to adjustment factors, which can then be applied in standard appraisal procedures.

In another instance, which involved the valuation of a large tract of commercial land, the principal adjustment factors were derived by running a stepwise regression on 47 comparable sales. Here the regression used the selling price per acre after adjustment for size as the dependent variable, and the time of sale and a location rating as independent variables. Although the location rating was a qualitative judgment factor, the ratings were tested in the regression and found to have a t value of 7.9. This, along with the t value of 3.2 for the time of sale factor, indicated that intuitive judgment and objective mathematical tools can work harmoniously to produce supportable value conclusions.

Regressions can also be used for the numerous insights they give an appraiser, even when they are not specifically used as a valuation technique. For example, in performing a group of rental appraisals in an unfamiliar city, appraisers were concerned about the relative amounts of adjustments for location and for condition and appearance. A series of regressions were run, using percentage ratings on both the variables, along with nine others. The regressions were not considered to have sufficient statistical validity to give reliable rental estimates, but the proportions of the two problem variables remained consistent from one run to another. For example, three regressions provided the following figures, which are expressed in rounded figures: location, $73, condition and appearance, $65; location, $76, condition and appearance, $48; location, $82, condition and appearance, $51; and so on. Although the individual figures in the regressions were not used in the appraisals, the regression analyses confirmed the suspicion that the particular area differed from the appraiser's usual working territory. Therefore, different proportionate weights would have to be applied to these two important adjustment factors, which would result in a substantial difference in the final rental estimates.

Nonlinear Regression Analysis

Although the preponderance of appraisal data does not assume straight-line relationships, the appraiser often deals with a segment of a curve that is short enough to permit the use of such tools as linear regression and correlation. However, inferences are sometimes distorted by assumptions of linearity in data that are clearly nonlinear. Fortunately, many such sets of curvilinear data can be transformed rather easily to be processed as if they were linear.

For example, the following is a portion of a tabulation that compares retail sales per capita of a county with those of its state and of the entire country:

Table 12.6   Retail Sales per Capita—Metropolitan County

Year	Sales
1979	$4,470
1978	$4,784
1977	$4,301
1976	$3,912
1975	$3,395
1974	$3,059
1973	$2,635
1972	$2,254

Source: *Sales and Marketing Management, Survey of Buying Power* (calculated from population and retail sales data in Section C), various issues from 1973 to 1980.

The problem was to predict retail sales per capita for 1980 prior to the availability of published data for the year. An easy calculation indicates that the simple linear average growth rate is 14% per year. Projecting this average would give 1980 sales of $5,098. However, this type of figure, like the Consumer Price Index, has a relation to its immediately preceding value rather than to its beginning value, and is therefore nonlinear.

Several types of curves can be fitted by using a hand-held calculator. First, the estimate can be improved somewhat by the use of linear regression because it at least separates the slope and intercept figures. In addition, an appraiser is not working with an extremely long-term trend. A simple linear regression gives these results: $a = -23,812.4$; $b = 363.095$; $r^2 = .942$; $S_{yx} = 219.07$; predicted Y (retail sales per capita for 1980) $= 5,235$.

The exponential curve is symbolized as

$$Y = ae^{bx}$$

It reflects a positive or negative compounding over time. It is transformed to linear format by substituting the natural logarithms of the Ys (dependent variables) and entering the Xs in their original form. This converts the equation to

$$ln\ Y = bX + ln\ a$$

Fitting the data to this type of curve gives the following results: $a = 1.13776$; $b = .106353$; $r^2 = .939$; $S_{yx} = .07143$; predicted $Y = \$5,638$.

Another curve that may fit when exploring nonlinear regressions on data is the logarithmic curve. The equation for this curve is

$$Y = a + b(ln\ X)$$

This means that the Xs, or independent variables, are not transformed. The natural logs of Xs (independent variables — 1972 to 1979) are used. With this nonlinear approach, the results are: $a = -115,052.34$; $b = 27,442.8$; $r^2 = .9538$ unadjusted, .9472 adjusted; predicted $Y = \$5,203$.

Next, the power, or geometric, curve can be used. This curve is symbolized as

$$Y = ax^b$$

which is transformed to

$$ln\ Y = ln\ a + b(ln\ x)$$

This equation indicates that the natural logs of both independent and dependent variables are entered, and these data points are then regressed as if they were linear. The results of this curve are

$$Y = 2.63162E - 12 \times X^{8.05383}$$

The b figure may well get lost in a small calculator because it has 11 zeroes in front of the first digit. Further, adjusted r^2 = .968; standard error = .06823; predicted Y = \$5,590.

This nonlinear relationship may be explored in a slightly more complex form with a polynomial regression. In addition to the original Xs, this type of regression uses the specified powers of the Xs. This results in an equation in the form of

$$Y = a + b_1X + b_2X^2 + b_3X^3 . . . b_nX^n$$

The highest power used in the regression is called the *order*, or *degree*, of the equation. Using a second-order equation, the results are: constant = 137089.9847499; first-degree coefficient = 3902.4547389; second-degree coefficient = 28.2440798; coefficient of determination = .929; standard error = 288.118; predicted Y = \$5,656.

Adding the cube of the Xs to the equation for a third-order polynomial regression gives: constant = -37241.803694; first-degree coefficient = 376.947096; second-degree coefficient = 6.434948; third-degree coefficient = $-.056301$; R^2 = .984; standard error = 160.889; predicted Y = \$5,271.

With fourth-order polynomial regression, the coefficient of determination has declined to .979 and the standard error has increased to 203.955. Although there is some difficulty in conceptualizing exactly what the standard error measures in a fourth-order polynomial, it does indicate that complicating the regression equation has resulted in passing the point of diminishing returns.

One variation on polynomial regressions may be noted. Using the Cramer's Rule algorithm, a parabolic regression program seems to give better results over the long term than the standard second-degree polynomial. In the present example, it gives: constant = -163746.7262; first-degree coefficient = 4073.3810; second-degree coefficient = -24.5714; coefficient of determination = .968; standard error = 163.227; predicted Y = \$4,867. It is of interest that the 1980 per capita retail sales figure was \$4,843. Not all regression-based predictions will be this close. However, by testing the variety of techniques available, the validity of the work product can always be enhanced.

Graphic Analysis

The understanding of a large body of data may be facilitated by the graphic presentation of the data in a condensed form. For example, an appraiser collected data concerning residential sales in a particular area. The mean sale price per square foot was tabulated for each quarter to establish a guideline for adjustments for time of sale. The reason the appraiser reduced the sales to price per square foot was to eliminate differentials caused by size. The average prices per square foot for each of eight quarters are as follows:

1980		1981	
1st Q.	$43	1st Q.	$52
2nd Q.	$45	2nd Q.	$54
3rd Q.	$52	3rd Q.	$54
4th Q.	$47	4th Q.	$56

The data are illustrated in graphic form in Figure 12.1.

Figure 12.1   Graph for Time Adjustments—Residential

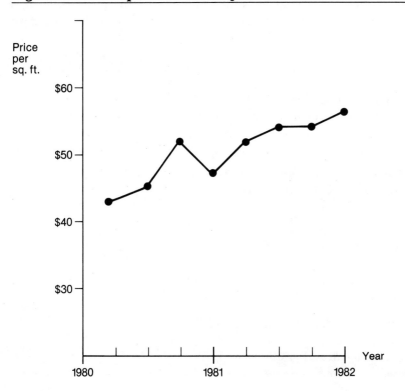

Figure 12.2   Distribution of Acreage Sales between $1186 and $1814 per Acre

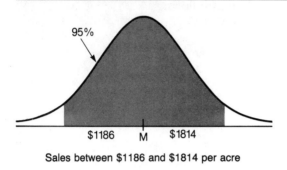

Sales between $1186 and $1814 per acre

Thus, the trend of prices in the area can be visualized. If an appraisal were being made in the second quarter of 1981, a sale in the fourth quarter of 1980 would be adjusted upward 15%. A sale in the first quarter of 1981 would be adjusted upward 8% to comparability with a property being appraised in the fourth quarter of 1981.

In another example, an appraiser collected 35 acreage sales in a rural county, with a mean price of $1,500 per acre and a standard deviation of $160. Again, the distribution of the data that shows the probabilities of various price levels can be illustrated graphically. Figure 12.2 shows the distribution of sales between $1,186 and $1,814 per acre, or plus and minus 1.96 standard deviations from the mean, which reflects a 95% confidence level.

Figure 12.3 shows another way of looking at the same distribution

Figure 12.3   Distribution of Acreage Sales Higher than $1800 per Acre

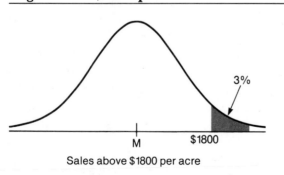

Sales above $1800 per acre

of sales. In this presentation, the proportion of sales that should lie above $1,800 per acre is calculated: $(1,800 \div 1,500)160 =$ a Z value of 1.88 (representing 1.88 standard deviations). The Z tables reveal a probability of .4699 for sales between $1,500 and $1,800. Because .50 represents the area to the right of the mean, subtracting .4699 from .50 indicates the probability of 3% of the sales lying above $1,800 per acre.

Figure 12.4 demonstrates graphically the distribution of 173 observations on the ratio of sale price to assessment in a county. The study was made to test whether a valid total value estimate could be

Figure 12.4   Distribution of Ratios of Sale Prices to Assessments—Metropolitan County

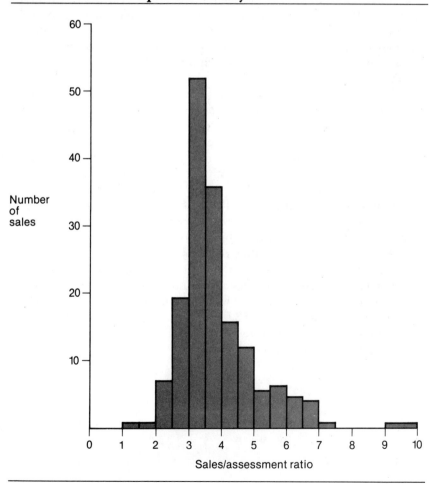

placed within a limited time on a holding of more than 200 properties in one county. The sample had a mean price/assessment ratio of 3.93, with a standard deviation of 1.39 and a standard error of the mean of 0.11. The extreme kurtosis of the distribution, 7.62, reflects a strong clustering around the mean. The small standard error enabled the appraiser to conclude that by placing a value on the total group of properties of 3.93 times their assessments, there was a 95% probability that the total valuation lay within plus or minus 5% of the probable total sale prices.

Cash Equivalence

Standard definitions of market value posit payment in "cash or its equivalent." The equivalent includes financing terms generally available in the market because the seller still receives cash under such typical terms. In many cases, however, comparable sales carry atypical financing terms that are adjusted to cash equivalence if sufficient supportive information can be obtained. However, if this information is not available, the sale should be eliminated from consideration as a market value indicator.

One financing term that is not consistent with accepted market value definitions is the payment of *points* by the seller rather than the purchaser. Points are a percentage reduction in the mortgage that are paid back to the lender at the time of the transaction. The normal market value assumption is that points are a cost of obtaining financing, which are incurred by the purchaser. When points are paid by the seller, as is common with FHA and VA transactions, an appraiser should simply deduct the full dollar amount of such points as an adjustment to the selling price. However, points should never be added to the value indication for the subject property.

Another arrangement that requires adjustment to the sale price of the comparable is financing by the seller at a below-market interest rate. For example, an appraiser might find a comparable sale of a single family residence at $114,700 with a down payment of $25,000 and a seller-financed mortgage of $89,700 for a 20-year term at 12% interest. If the current market rate is 15%, one approach to adjusting the sale to cash equivalence is as follows:

1. Mortgage $89,700, 20 years, 12%, monthly payment = $987.67
2. Present value of $987.67 for 20 years @ market rate of 15% =
   75.942278 × $987.67 = $75,006[3]

Market value of mortgage (R)	$75,000
Plus down payment	25,000
Sale price adjusted for financing	$100,000

A second approach to the calculation of cash equivalence under the financial arrangement cited above takes into account the average current actual life of a mortgage. Averages for different types of property can be obtained from lenders who use them in calculating yields. Assume that the current average life of residential mortgages to prepayment is 12 years. This factor is incorporated into the adjustment process as follows:

1. As above, monthly payment = $987.67
2. Present value of $987.67 for 12 years @ 15% = 66.627722 ×
   $987.67 = $ 65,806
3. Mortgage balance in 12 years (the 8 years' remaining term) =
   PV of $987.67 for 8 years @ 12% = 61.527703 × $987.67 =
   $60,769
   PV of One factor for 12 years @ 15% = .167153 × $60,769 =
   PV of future mortgage balance = $ 10,158

PV of mortgage	$ 75,964
Plus down payment	25,000
Adjusted sale price	$100,964
Rounded:	$101,000

Although this approach requires more calculation, it is preferable because it more accurately reflects the discounting procedure used by lending institutions.

At times, this type of adjustment will convert a puzzlingly inconsistent comparable sale into a usable comparable. Such was the case with a shopping center sale at $2,580,000. Routine investigation of the

---

[3]An alternative method of calculation of present worth of the mortgage is: constant (contract)/constant (market) x mortgage. In this case: .011011/.013168 = .836190 x $89,700 = $75,006.

sale indicated that the 10-year-old shopping center had a gross leaseable area of 60,110 square feet, gross rents of $238,259, and a net rental of $202,222. The sale, then, appeared to reflect a price of $42.92 per square foot, a gross rent multiplier of 10.83, and an overall rate of 7.84%. Because these pricing units were inconsistent with the local market, the appraiser was tempted to discard the sale.

Further inquiry, however, revealed that the seller financed the transaction on a 39.5-year mortgage at a 6% interest rate. The current market interest rate for this type of property was 12%, and typical mortgage life to prepayment was 15 years. Applying the adjustment technique illustrated above gave the following adjusted selling price:

---

1. Mortgage payments 39.5 years @ 6% = payment of
   $14,238.95. Present value of payments for 15 years @ 12% =
   83.321664 × 14,238.95 = $1,186,413
2. Mortgage balance in 15 years = PV of $14,238.95 for 294
   months @ 6% = $2,190,608
   PV of One factor 15 years @ 12% = .166783
   .166783 × $2,190,608 = PV of future
   mortgage balance =   365,356
   Adjusted sale price $1,551,769

                                                        Rounded: $1,552,000

After adjusting for financing, the pricing units were: price per square foot, $25.82; gross rent multiplier, 6.51; overall rate, 13%. Since these criteria were reasonably consistent with other local market data, the appraiser could include the sale in the data file.

Other types of atypical mortgage terms occur, such as payments of interest for a given period only, followed by payments that include even principal repayments. This type of mortgage can also be adjusted to its cash equivalent value by applying the illustrated adjustment technique to derive present value of the payments at the market rate, year by year, using present value of one factors. Assumptions of existing mortgages may also be adjusted to cash equivalence in the same manner as that for seller-financed transactions. However, an appraiser should be certain the existing loan was assumed and not nullified by a due on sale clause. When balloon mortgages are involved, present value factors may be applied to separate the contributory market value of the mortgage portion of the property.

An alternative approach to estimating cash equivalence involves seeking direct market evidence of the appropriate adjustments. In this approach, the appraiser attempts to locate sales both with and without unorthodox financing, adjust for other items, and attribute the remaining differential to the financing terms. This method can yield guidelines for the appraiser if substantial quantities of transactions in both categories are available.

Summary

The investigation, organization, and analysis of specific market data are central to appraisal. The validity of a final estimate of property value generally depends on reliable market data. Before applying the three approaches, an appraiser gathers all available pertinent data, organizes them, and performs a preliminary analysis. It is important to realize that all three approaches are based on data gathered in the market and that the market provides the final test of the validity.

An appraiser investigates market transactions through recent sales information that is obtained from office files and from interviews with buyers, sellers, and real estate professionals. The following information may be particularly useful: number of sales, period of time covered by sales, availability of property for sale, rate of absorption, rate of turnover, characteristics and motivations of buyers and sellers, terms and conditions of sale, and use of property before and after sale. An appraiser also needs information on improvement costs and depreciation. Information about building costs are usually available from contractors and construction material suppliers in the area. Information about specialized improvements can be obtained from the appropriate contractors or suppliers of equipment. Interviews with local property owners who have added improvements recently can be helpful. Various cost-reporting services are useful for checking estimates that are developed from local cost data.

To organize collected data, an appraiser often uses a spreadsheet. A spreadsheet includes information about the subject and comparable properties, such as sale price and date, financial arrangements, any unusual motivation of the buyer or the seller, location, physical characteristics, income amounts and sources, expenses, vacancy rates, reserves, rates of return, costs, and depreciation rates.

An appraiser uses appropriate data in each of the approaches. In the sales comparison approach, the goal of analysis is to identify variations between the subject property and the comparable sales to measure the value of the variations. The analysis of sales data shows significant elements of the sales and indicates the computations that can be applied to arrive at the whole or per-unit value of the subject property. In the cost approach, an appraiser uses both cost and depreciation data based on sales analysis and data obtained from other sources. Both types can be useful, and each can serve as a check on the other. For the income capitalization approach, an appraiser seeks information about income, vacancy rates, expenses, reserves, market-indicated capitalization rates, and sale prices. These market indications help an appraiser to develop appropriate income and expense estimates and capitalization rates for analysis by income capitalization approach techniques.

Three important techniques for analyzing the specific data needed for the application of all three approaches to value are paired data set analysis, regression analysis, and graphic analysis.

Paired data set analysis can be applied in the adjustment process for sales comparison and rental comparisons, and for guidelines as to operating expenses. Sales are paired to identify the effect of specific differences on probable price in the market. If two sale properties are closely comparable in all but one respect, the relative sale prices may indicate reasonable adjustment for the specific difference. When successive pairings can be reduced to single unadjusted elements, a series of adjustments for individual differences can be developed.

Regression analysis is useful for both value estimation and for isolating and testing the significance of specific value determinants. This procedure can be a simple linear regression analysis, a multiple regression analysis, or a nonlinear regression analysis.

A graphic presentation of specific data in condensed form can help an appraiser to understand the significance of a large body of data. For example, a graphic analysis can depict a trend of prices in an area.

Cash equivalence is a technique in which atypical financing terms for comparable sales must be adjusted to a cash equivalence if sufficient information can be obtained. If not, the sale should not be used for comparison. Atypical financing terms can include the payment of points by the seller rather than the buyer.

Chapter 13

The Sales Comparison Approach

The sales comparison approach is a method of estimating market value whereby a subject property is compared with comparable properties that have sold recently. Preferably, all properties are in the same area. One premise of the sales comparison approach is that the market will determine a price for the property being appraised in the same manner that it determines the prices of comparable, competitive properties. Essentially, the sales comparison approach is a systematic procedure for carrying out comparative shopping. As applied to real estate, the comparison is applied to the unique characteristics of the economic good that cause real estate prices to vary.

Relationship to Appraisal Principles

In applying the sales comparison approach, an appraiser employs appraisal principles. The appraiser is guided by the principles to ensure that all relevant issues have been considered in solving the appraisal problem. The delineation of the specific relationships between the approach and the principles follows.

Supply and Demand

Prices of properties are determined in the market. Prices result from negotiations among buyers and sellers in the market—buyers constituting the demand side and sellers the supply side. If the demand for a particular type of property is high, prices tend to increase; if demand is low, prices tend to decline. Shifts in the supply of real estate tend to lag behind shifts in demand. Thus, the emphasis in the analysis of real estate markets *at a particular point in time* tends to be on the demand side. In other words, supply is often treated as being constant over a short-term period of analysis, and attention is focused on demand. However, supply should not be overlooked because the relationship between supply and demand affects prices. Thus, the prospect of new properties being constructed or certain properties being demolished should be considered in assessing market conditions. On the demand side, the number of potential users of a particular property type, their financial capacity, and their tastes and preferences should be considered. Shifts in any of these elements may cause prices to vary between a property being appraised and a comparable property.

Balance

Supply and demand forces tend to produce an equilibrium (or balance) in the market; however, a point of static (unchanging) equilibrium is almost never attained. Forces of supply and demand change continually. Shifts in population, financial capacity, and consumer tastes and preferences cause demand to vary greatly over time. Similarly, the construction of new units and the demolition of certain existing units cause supply to vary, particularly over relatively long periods. Variations among properties must also be recognized as unbalancing forces. For example, how much does a two-car garage add to the value of a house when this type of house usually has a one-car garage? In other words, does a two-car garage create an imbalance for the size and character of the house? If an imbalance is created, the value added tends to be less than the cost of the item. Appraisers must watch for imbalances in the market and imbalances in properties, which cause the market to impute different prices to otherwise comparable properties.

Substitution

The principle of substitution as applied in the sales comparison approach holds that the value of a property that is replaceable in the market tends to be set by the cost of acquiring an equally desirable substitute property. The principle also suggests that when substitute properties are not available in the market, the reliability of the sales comparison approach may be less than that of other approaches to value.

Externalities

External forces, both positive and negative, impinge on all property types, but their impact is greatest on residential properties. Residents are particularly sensitive to potential negative influences—a new road or certain power lines through a neighborhood, for example.

One major reason an appraiser analyzes a subject property's neighborhood is to help identify all significant external influences. Examples of potential positive influences are attractive and clean streets and surrounding properties, parks and other types of recreational areas, desirable views, and proximity to shopping, schools, churches, and work places. Examples of potential negative influences are run-down and dirty streets and surrounding properties, adjacent industrial areas, pollution, noise, litter, and a substantial crime rate. The most well-maintained and attractive property suffers from such negative influences. Thus, a property's value is partly determined by environment.

Applicability and Limitations

The sales comparison approach is applicable to all property types for which there is a sufficient number of recent, reliable transactions to create value patterns in a market. For property types that are bought and sold regularly, the sales comparison approach often provides the most reliable indication of market value. It is considered reliable in such situations because it is direct and systematic.

When the market contains an insufficient number of transactions to create value patterns, the application of the approach may be limited or inappropriate. Large, special purpose properties are often insufficiently similar to other properties that have sold recently to allow an appraiser to impute value from them. For such properties, using one or both of the other appraisal approaches usually proves more reliable.

Rapidly changing economic conditions may also limit the usefulness of the sales comparison approach. Changes in government laws and regulations (such as those involving income taxes or zoning), in the availability and cost of financing, and in the supply of similar properties (such as the announcement of a large, new project) may cause the sale prices of comparable properties to be unreliable indicators of a subject property's value. There may be no market basis for making adjustments for such changes. Rapid rates of inflation or deflation may also subject an appraiser to hazardous adjustments, thus limiting the usefulness of the sales comparison approach.

The sales comparison approach is generally the most useful approach for single family residential properties. Such properties are relatively amenable to direct, comparative analysis because they are dealt with extensively in the market. Single family houses do not usually produce income and thus are not generally suited to the income capitalization approach. In addition, older properties may have relatively large amounts of accrued depreciation that make the cost approach less reliable.

Required Data and Sources

The sales comparison approach requires that an appraiser consider certain data. Such data include sale and listing prices of each property considered competitive with and comparable to the subject property; the date of sale of each transaction; financing terms; conditions of sale (motivations of buyer and seller); and each property's locational, physical, and income characteristics. For income-producing properties, additional data should be obtained. Such data include the property's potential or effective gross income, the number of square feet of total building area and net rentable area, and the size of the site. When using the sales comparison approach in appraising income-producing properties, an appraiser generally uses a potential gross income or rent multiplier (PGIM or PGRM) as a unit of comparison. Alternatively, an appraiser may use an effective gross income multiplier (EGIM). However, an appraiser may need to use other units of comparison when appraising properties with more specialized functions. Examples of such properties are golf courses, price per hole; theaters, price per seat; hotels and motels, price per room; restaurants, price per seat; mobile home parks, price per pad; truckstops and service stations, price per gallon; repair facilities, price per bay; farms, price per acre; ranchland, price per animal unit; tennis and racquetball facilities, price per court; and railroads, price per mile of track.

Generally, the most important source of required data is verification of sales with buyers and sellers. Often, an appraiser files information verified in the market so that it may be used in other appraisal assignments. Other sources of data are brokers who are involved in the sales of properties similar to the property being appraised, sales data services (such as multiple listing services), courthouse records, property managers, and lending institutions. In many cases, an appraiser needs to contact several sources and more than one party to a transaction to obtain and verify information and to learn the motivations behind a transaction. Certain motivations could be sufficient enough that an appraiser might disregard a sale not meeting the specifications of an arm's-length market transaction. Of course, transactions would never occur if buyers and sellers were not under some motivation to act. Only when the motivation causes the transaction to occur at a price or on terms substantially different from those that would have occurred without the motivation should the sale be disregarded as a market value indicator.

The ideal means of sale verification is the confirmation of statements of fact by one or both of the principals to a transaction. Alternatively, confirmation may be sought through the brokers, closing agencies, and lenders. Sometimes, owners and tenants of neighboring properties can provide leads to factual information.

The geographic limits of an appraiser's research depend on the nature and type of real estate being valued. If the type being valued is commonly bought and sold in the same neighborhood as the subject property, the limits probably will be in the neighborhood. If this is not the case, the appraiser must extend the limits to similar neighborhoods in other areas. In addition, certain types of properties have regional, national, and even international markets. The data search for the appraisal of such properties may extend over a substantial geographic area. Examples of such properties are large shopping centers, office buildings, hotels, multiuse complexes, and industrial buildings.

Procedure

In applying the sales comparison approach, an appraiser follows a systematic procedure. The appraiser must always compare like with like. That is, the appraiser must adjust each comparable to the subject property to impute an indicated value to the subject property. The steps of the procedure are as follows:

1. Research the market to obtain information about transactions, listings, and other offerings of properties similar to the subject property.

2. Verify the information by considering whether the
   a. Data obtained are factually accurate
   b. Transactions reflect arm's-length market considerations
   An appraiser verifies information by consulting a knowledgeable source, usually one of the participants in the transaction.

3. Determine relevant units of comparison (e.g., acre, square foot, multiplier), and develop a comparative analysis for each unit.

4. Compare the subject and comparable sales according to the elements of comparison and adjust the sale price of each comparable as appropriate *or* eliminate the property as a comparable.

5. Reconcile the multiple value indications that result from the comparables into a single value indication.

Units of Comparison

Units of comparison are components into which a property may be divided for comparison purposes. Typical units of comparison are square foot, front foot, cubic foot, room, bed, seat, and apartment unit. When an entire property is compared with other entire properties, the unit of comparison is the entire property. The function of using a unit of comparison is to adjust for size differences among properties. For example, even though two apartment buildings have similar apartment units, one is twice as large as the other. Thus, the entire property cannot be used as a unit of comparison, but comparisons could be made according to price per apartment or, perhaps, price per square foot.

A unit of comparison is selected in terms of its relevance to the appraisal problem. When appraising single family residences, an appraiser most often uses the total property unit as the unit of comparison. That is, adjustments for differences between the comparable sales and the subject property are made to the total property price. Cubic feet may be an important consideration that varies among warehouses, even among those having the same number of square feet. Comparison by cubic foot is necessary when storage capacity rather than floor area is the main consideration. However, for other types of properties, height (and thus volume) does not vary significantly by square footage.

A multiplier is usually employed as a unit of comparison in applying the sales comparison approach in the valuation of income-producing properties. Because multipliers tend to remain fairly constant over a period of time and are used only for properties exhibiting a high degree of uniformity, they can be derived from market data without adjustments. However, an analysis of property differences can be very helpful in revealing price patterns and in explaining any variance in multipliers. Recent multipliers are usually the most reliable.

Elements of Comparison

Elements of comparison are the characteristics of properties and transactions that cause prices to vary. Certain elements should be considered and compared, if necessary. Adjustments for them should be made to the price of each comparable property. The elements of comparison are (1) financing terms, (2) conditions of sale, (3) market conditions (time), (4) location, (5) physical characteristics, and (6) income characteristics.

Financing Terms

The transaction price of one property may differ from that of an identical property because financing arrangements vary. If the purchasers of a comparable property had assumed an existing mortgage at a favorable (below current market) interest rate, they may have paid a higher price than purchasers of the subject property can be expected to pay under current market financing terms. The financing arrangements for each comparable property should be considered, and the necessary adjustments should be made to reflect the financing terms under which the subject property is expected to sell. The methods of making such adjustments are presented in Chapter 12.

Conditions of Sale

When the conditions of sale are atypical, the result may be a price that is higher or lower than that of a normal market transaction. One member of a family may sell property to another at a reduced price. Or someone may pay a higher-than-market price for a property because it was constructed or owned by the buyer's grandparents. Special income tax situations could also cause the price to differ from the price that would be paid by other, more typical buyers.

When nonmarket conditions of sale are detected in a transaction, the sale should be related to the subject property only with great care. Market-based adjustments are more difficult to make for such situations. If possible, the sale should not be used in an appraisal. Occasionally, such a transaction may have to be used because of a lack of other comparables, but an adjustment should be made only after careful research into the nonmarket motivations of buyers and sellers and the probable amount of premium or penalty paid for the property because of the motivation.

Market Conditions (Time)

Market conditions may change between the time of sale of a comparable property and the date of the appraisal of the subject property. Under such circumstances, the price of the comparable property would be different at the later time (the date of the appraisal), and an adjustment would have to be made to the actual transaction price if the sale were used as a comparable. Changed market conditions often result from various causes, such as inflation, deflation, changing demand, and changing supply. For example, the economy might suffer a general recession that would tend to deflate all real estate prices. Or an owner of a factory might expand operations, thus leading to an increase in the number of employees and in the general population in the community. The increased population, with no increase in housing units, would tend to push prices higher.

It should be emphasized that the cause of the adjustment is not time itself. Market conditions may shift over time, but the cause of the adjustment is not time. Indeed, if market conditions do not change, no adjustment is required even though considerable time may have elapsed.

Changes in market conditions are usually measured on a percentage basis, relative to previous prices. An appraiser might compare prices of properties that sell several times over a given time period and compute the monthly average or compound rate of change. This rate could then be applied to similar properties in the same neighborhood or comparable neighborhoods.

Location

An adjustment for location may be required if the locational characteristics of a comparable property are significantly different from those of the subject property. Usually, most properties in a neighborhood have similar locational characteristics. Thus, locational adjustments are not generally needed for comparables that are in the same neighborhood as the subject property.

A property's location is analyzed in terms of the relative time-distance relationship between it and all likely destinations and origins. The relationship is relative because the location of a property can be judged only in relation to that of others. An appraiser can say only that one location is equal to, or better or worse than, another location. No location is absolutely desirable or undesirable.

To judge the desirability of one location relative to others, appraisers may analyze sales of physically similar houses that sell in different neighborhoods. If houses in one neighborhood consistently sell for more or less than similar houses in another neighborhood, an appraiser is justified in making an adjustment to a property located in one neighborhood and used as a comparable for a property being appraised in the other. However, sale prices of properties in different neighborhoods might be the same, but homes in one neighborhood might sell after a 30- to 60-day exposure, and homes in another neighborhood might remain on the market for six months. Location adjustments are usually made in percentage terms, which reflect the extent to which houses in one neighborhood sell for more or less than those in another. For example, an adjustment of 10% might be added to a comparable to reflect the tendency in the subject property's neighborhood for houses to sell for about 10% more than houses in the comparable's neighborhood.

Physical Characteristics

Physical characteristics may differ between a comparable property and a subject property. The differences might require a number of comparisons and adjustments to the comparable. For residential properties, such differences often include building or room size, quality of construction, age, condition, architectural style, the number of bathrooms or bedrooms, site size, desirability of site or view, considerations pertaining to the kitchen, dining room, garage, swimming pool, and appliances, and any other potential physical difference.

An appraiser may be required to judge the amount of value that is added by a bathroom, bedroom, two-car garage, spectacular view, swimming pool, or landscaping. The value added or lost by the existence or lack of a physical item in a comparable property does not usually equal the cost of installing or removing the item. Most existing properties are not new, and a new item added to an older property is usually not worth as much as the same item included in a new property. Therefore, appraisers may analyze prices of sale properties that have an item relative to similar sale properties without the item. For example, the value of a swimming pool should be judged by the greater amount for which properties with swimming pools sell than similar properties without pools.

Income Characteristics

When appraisers analyze income-producing properties by the sales comparison approach, they make comparisons and adjustments on the basis of the property's income characteristics, which can affect desirability and sale prices. In the sales comparison approach, an appraiser makes adjustments for income differences by using the potential or effective gross income multiplier or by using a rent multiplier.

Types of Adjustments

Essentially, adjustments can be applied to a comparable property in two ways: in percentages and in dollars. Any percentage can be converted to dollars and then simply be added to or subtracted from the comparable's price. The type of adjustment is determined by the way in which the adjustment is derived.

Percentage Adjustments

Adjustments for market conditions and location are usually derived in percentage terms. For example, appraisers might conclude that market conditions have increased by, say, 5% during the past year or that prices are increasing 0.5% per month. Similarly, appraisers often conclude that properties in one location bring prices approximately 10% higher than similar properties in another location. Such percentages are converted to dollars by multiplying them by relevant price figures that may have been adjusted for differences in financing terms, market conditions, and physical characteristics. The dollar amounts can then be added to or subtracted from the relevant price of the comparable.

Cumulative percentage adjustments are sometimes used. Such an adjustment is obtained by multiplying all the percentage adjustments, based on the subject property's equaling 100%, and applying the resulting percentage to the comparable property's sale price. For example, if a subject property had three characteristics that differed from the comparable property, with the first being 10% better, the second equal to the subject, the third 10% inferior, the adjustment would be

$$1.10 \times 1.00 \times .90 = .99$$

The comparable would be considered 99% as valuable as the subject property, and the indicated value of the subject would be derived by dividing the known sale price of the comparable by .99. Further, if the comparable sold for $100,000, the indicated value of the subject property would be

$$\$100,000 \div .99 = \$101,010, \text{ rounded to } \$101,000$$

This method is applicable only in a few situations because it assumes that the adjustments are causally interrelated. For example, the method would assume that a swimming pool adjustment is partly caused by a size adjustment, and that both are partly caused by an adjustment for quality of construction. It also ignores the sequence of adjustments that is recommended in the following section.

Dollar Adjustments

Adjustments for differences in financing terms and physical characteristics are typically derived in dollars. For instance, an appraiser may conclude that favorable financing terms for a comparable resulted in a $5,000 premium paid by the buyer. Percentages are often not appropriate because each financing package would require a dollar calculation as to its value. Thus, the dollar premium (or penalty) would be subtracted from or added to the comparable's sale price.

Similarly, the values of many physical characteristics are estimated in dollar amounts and are added to or subtracted from the comparable's sale price. For example, the value of a bedroom might be estimated as $5,000, or the value of a two-car garage over a one-car garage as $2,000.

Sequence of Adjustments

A sequence for making adjustments[1] is required whenever percentage adjustments are used either solely or in combination with dollar adjustments. An appraiser obtains intermediate price figures and applies suc-

[1]This sequence was first presented in Halbert C. Smith, *Real Estate Appraisal* (Columbus, Ohio: Grid, Inc., 1976).

ceeding adjustments to each prior adjusted price. The sequence, which includes *all* percentage adjustments, appears below.

Transaction price	$100,000
Financing terms	−5%
Conditions of sale	+10%
Normal sale price	$105,000
Market conditions	+10%
Time-adjusted normal price	115,500
Location	+5%
Physical characteristics	−20%
Adjusted sale price	$ 98,175

The first adjustment is for financing terms, which is applied to the transaction price. The adjustment reduces the price for which the property would have sold under normal market financing. In addition, any adjustment for conditions of sale would be made at this stage. Unless the required adjustment can be ascertained from the market, any sale that requires the adjustment should not be included. However, an adjustment is included here for illustrative purposes. Conditions of sale should always be considered. If no adjustment is needed, a 0 should be entered. The resulting price figure at this stage in the sequence reflects the amount for which the property would have sold under normal financing and sale conditions.

Next, an appraiser adjusts for market conditions. Presumably, the market conditions adjustment has been derived from properties that sold under normal financing and conditions of sale. The adjustment would be distorted if applied to an actual transaction price that includes nonmarket considerations. The adjustment for market conditions results in a figure that represents what the comparable would sell for at the appraisal date under normal financing and conditions of sale.

Next, an appraiser applies adjustments for location and physical characteristics to the time-adjusted normal price. These adjustments account for the differences between the comparable and the subject properties. They are applied to the price of the comparable that would pertain at the date of the appraisal under normal financing terms and sale conditions. After all adjustments are made for locational and physical characteristics, the resulting figure is called the adjusted sale price. It is the price that as realistically and accurately as possible reflects the price for which the comparable property would sell on the date of the appraisal if it were exactly like the subject property. It is thus a value indication for the subject property.

Note in the above example that if the percentage adjustments were added and the resulting percentage was applied to the transaction price, the adjusted sale price would be $100,000; that is, +25% − 25% = 0%. This procedure would result in an error of almost $2,000, or almost 2%. Obviously, errors could be larger or smaller in situations in which a sequence is not used.

Although a sequence is not required when only dollar adjustments are made, its use is recommended in all applications of the sales comparison approach. In most appraisals, some percentage adjustments are made, and the format helps a reader of an appraisal report to follow the rationale of the adjustments.

In deriving and applying adjustments, appraisers should always state the percentage relationship of the subject to the comparable. For example, the appraiser should state that the subject property's location is 10% better than that of the comparable or that the quality of construction of the subject is 5% inferior to that of the comparable. The price of the comparable is known; the price or value of the subject property is not. It is incorrect to state a percentage relationship in terms of the unknown, such as the location of the comparable is 10% inferior to that of the subject.

Application of the Sales Comparison Approach

The following examples illustrate the application of the sales comparison approach to a single family residence, an apartment building, a retail property, an industrial property, and an office property.

Single Family Residence

Assume that the house being appraised is a 1,200-square-foot, ranch-style, frame structure with a finished basement. It has six rooms, three bedrooms, 1½ baths, and no garage. It is in average condition and is located in the same neighborhood as all the comparables. The comparables are described as follows:

Comparable A is a 1,200-square-foot frame ranch with unfinished basement. It has six rooms, three bedrooms, 1½ baths, and an attached two-car garage. It sold in the current year for $62,000.

Comparable B is a 1,450-square-foot frame ranch with unfinished basement. It has seven rooms, three bedrooms, 1½ baths, and an attached two-car garage. It sold in the current year for $70,000.

Comparable C is a 1,200-square-foot frame ranch with unfinished basement. It has six rooms, three bedrooms, 1½ baths, and an attached two-car garage. It sold one year prior to the date of the appraisal for $56,500.

Comparable D is a 1,450-square-foot frame ranch with finished basement. It has seven rooms, three bedrooms, 1½ baths, and an attached two-car garage. It sold one year prior to the date of the appraisal for $70,000.

Comparable E is a 1,200-square-foot frame ranch with unfinished basement. It has six rooms, three bedrooms, 1½ baths, and no garage. It sold one year prior to the date of the appraisal for $53,500.

The use of a final spreadsheet, or summary grid, facilitates a comparative analysis of the comparables with the subject property. The summary grid is shown in Table 13.1.

As can be seen, the comparables vary from the subject property in terms of date of sale, size (number of rooms), garage, and finished basement. To derive adjustments for these elements, the paired sales technique is used. This technique involves the matching of properties that are closely similar except for one important element. Due to isolation in paired sets, the price difference can be attributed to this element.

A comparison of Comparables A and C indicates an adjustment for market conditions of 9.7% for the year preceding the date of the appraisal ([[($62,000 − $56,500) ÷ $56,500]). The adjustment is rounded to 10%.

A comparison of Comparables A and B indicates an adjustment for size and an additional room of $8,000 ($70,000 − $62,000 = $8,000).

A comparison of Comparables C and E indicates an adjustment for the lack of a garage one year prior to the date of the appraisal of $3,000 ($56,500 − 53,500 = $3,000). This adjustment should be updated by the market conditions adjustment 10%, or to $3,300.

The adjustment for a finished basement can be obtained by a comparison of Comparables B and D after adjusting D for market conditions ($77,000 − $70,000 = $7,000).

These adjustments are then made in the proper sequence to each comparable's transaction price, as shown in the following adjustment grid, Table 13.2.

If each comparable is an equally good indicator of value, an appraiser might reconcile the adjusted sale prices by calculating the mean

Table 13.1 Summary Grid—Single Family Residence Appraisal

		Comparables				Subject
	A	B	C	D	E	
Price	$62,000	$70,000	$56,500	$70,000	$53,500	NA
Financing terms	Market	Market	Market	Market	Market	
Conditions of sale	Arm's length	Arm's length	Arm's length	Arm's length	Arm's length	
Date of sale	Current	Current	1 yr. ago	1 yr. ago	1 yr. ago	
Location	Same	Same	Same	Same	Same	1327 N.E. 12th St.
Physical characteristics						
Size	1,200 sq. ft.	1,450 sq. ft.	1,200 sq. ft.	1,450 sq. ft.	1,200 sq. ft.	1,200 sq. ft.
Rooms	6	7	6	7	6	6
Bedrooms	3	3	3	3	3	3
Baths	1½	1½	1½	1½	1½	1½
Garage	2-car	2-car	2-car	2-car	None	None
Finished basement	No	No	No	Yes	No	Yes

Table 13.2   Adjustment Grid—Single Family Residence Appraisal

| | Comparables | | | | | |
	A	B	C	D	E	Subject
Transaction price	$62,000	$70,000	$56,500	$70,000	$53,500	
Financing terms	Normal	Normal	Normal	Normal	Normal	Normal
Conditions of sale	Normal	Normal	Normal	Normal	Normal	Normal
Normal sale price	$62,000	$70,000	$56,500	$70,000	$53,500	
Market conditions	Equal	Equal	+10%	+10%	+10%	
Time-adjusted sale price	$62,000	$70,000	$62,150	$77,000	$58,850	
Location	Equal	Equal	Equal	Equal	Equal	1327 N.E. 12th Street
Physical characteristics						
Size (extra room)	Equal	−8,000	Equal	−8,000	Equal	1,200 sq. ft. 6 rooms
2-car garage	−3,300	−3,300	−3,300	−3,300	Equal	None
Finished basement	+7,000	+7,000	+7,000	Yes	+7,000	Yes
Adjusted sale price	$65,700	$65,700	$65,850	$65,700	$65,850	

x = $65,760; range = $65,850 − $65,700 = $150

and then by rounding the answer probably to the nearest $100. If certain comparables were considered better indicators than others, they would be given more weight in the reconciliation procedure. In the above example, the range of adjusted sale prices is quite narrow, which allows the value indication from the sales comparison approach to be rounded to the nearest $100. If the value range were greater, rounding would be commensurately greater—to the nearest $500 or $1,000. Because all comparables in the example are considered equally good indicators of value, the mean of $65,760 was rounded to $65,800 as the indicated subject property value.

Apartment Building

Because it is unusual to find an adequate number of sales of apartment buildings that are similar in number and size of units, an appraiser often analyzes comparable transactions by using units of comparison other than total property. Relevant units of comparison for apartment buildings are living unit, room, square foot, or multiplier. When an appraiser uses price per room, he or she adopts a standardized system of room counting. If an income multiplier is used, either potential gross income or effective gross income[2] may be used. However, the multiplier must be applied to the income for the subject property in the

[2]See Chapter 15 for an explanation of these terms.

Table 13.3   Summary Grid—Apartment Appraisal

	Comparables				
	A	B	C	D	Subject
Transaction price	$7,000,000	$2,050,000	$2,590,000	$5,600,000	
Time of sale	1 yr. ago	1 yr. ago	Current	1 yr. ago	Current
Units	400	90	114	384	117
Rooms	1,724	455	678	1,536	880
Rooms per unit	4.31	5.06	5.94	4.00	
Potential gross income	$1,070,650	$305,900	$435,625	$800,000	$574,000
Rent/room/mo.	$51.75	$56.03	$53.54	$43.40	$54.36
Price per room	$4,060	$4,505	$3,820	$3,646	
Price per unit	$17,500	$22,780	$22,719	$14,585	
GRM	6.54	6.70	5.95	7.00	

same manner as was used in its derivation. In addition, an appraiser makes certain crucial assumptions when using a GIM or GRM. One of the most important assumptions is that only multipliers from properties having operating ratios similar to the subject property's operating ratio should be used.

The summary grid in Table 13.3 shows a subject apartment property and four comparables. Three units of comparison are employed to adjust for size: room, unit, and GRM. In this example, financing terms, conditions of sale, and location were all normal or equal.

A study of the sales shows that Comparable B has the same average number of rooms per unit as the subject. This fact might indicate that the price per unit from this sale is the best comparison. Sale D has a significantly lower rent per room, which would be a reason to analyze this sale further. It also has the highest GRM, which might indicate that the purchasers felt they could raise rents significantly after purchase. These elements suggest that Comparable D may not be in the same market as the other properties. Disregarding this sale gives the following ranges from the units of comparison:

Unit	Indicated Range for Subject
Price per room	$3,361,600 to $3,964,400
Price per unit	$3,097,500 to $4,032,060
GRM	$3,415,300 to $3,845,800

Sale B, which is most comparable in terms of rooms per unit, gives the highest indication in all of the comparisons. Because this project rents for more per room than the subject, it is logical that some indicated value below the upper limit would be estimated. Again, disregarding Sale D, the average GRM is 6.40, which gives an indicated value of about $3,672,000. The average price per unit is about $21,000, giving an indicated value of $3,717,000, and the average price per room is about $4,128, giving an indicated value of about $3,633,000. A final indicated value of about $3,700,000 would appear to be justified.

Retail Property

The units of comparison used in the appraisal of retail properties are multiplier, price per square foot (gross or net rentable area), and price per front foot. The summary grid in Table 13.4 contains data pertaining to a retail property and four comparables.

The grid shows the abstraction of the GRM and the price per square foot units of comparison from sales of comparable retail properties. A GRM is usually not subject to adjustment because relative desirability in the market is presumably reflected in both the rental the properties can command and the prices for which they sell.

Property A has the closest ratio of parking area to rental area to

Table 13.4   Summary Grid—Retail Property Appraisal

| | Comparables | | | | |
	A	B	C	D	Subject
Construction	Brick/steel	Brick/steel	Brick/steel	Brick/steel	Brick/steel
Age	5	3	12	8	10
Number of stores	3	5	5	3	4
Rental area, sq. ft.	6,000	8,000	6,000	5,400	6,000
On-site parking, sq. ft.	3,000	5,000	1,000	6,000	3,500
Rent-to-parking ratio	2:1	1·6:1	6:1	.9:1	
Gross rent (at sale)	$18,000	$27,200	$15,000	$16,200	$18,600
Tenant credit	A	C	C	A	B
Average rent/sq. ft.	$3.00	$3.40	$2.50	$3.00	$3.10
Years since sale	½	1	2	1	
Sale price	$165,500	$217,500	$124,500	$146,000	
GRM	9.2	8.0	8.3	9.0	
Price/sq. ft., gross bldg. area	$27.58	$27.19	$20.75	$27.04	

that of the subject property. Property C has very little parking, which may be causing lower rent. Property B, which has the highest rents, has the lowest GRM. Properties A and D are the most comparable in terms of time of sale and rental rate. These properties are both occupied by tenants with higher credit ratings than the tenants in the subject property, which might indicate higher GRMs due to less risk.

These data appear to indicate GRMs between 8.5 and 9.0, with price per square foot between $27.00 and $27.50. These numbers give ranges in value as follows:

GRM	$158,100 to $167,400
Price per sq. ft.	$162,000 to $165,000

Industrial Property

Light industrial properties generally include warehouse properties that are used primarily for storage and distribution. Other types of industrial properties are generally more specialized and may require the use of special units of comparison that have been adopted in specific industries.

In the appraisal of light industrial properties, the units of comparison most often used are a multiplier, price per square foot of building, and price per square foot of building exclusive of the land. The GRM is a reliable unit of comparison when the properties are leased and the owner pays only such expenses as taxes, insurance, and exterior maintenance. This limited expense requirement provides fairly consistent expense ratios. Most properties in this category contain some office space, which may require separate analysis. Other considerations are clear ceiling height for palletized storage, column spacing, load capacity of flooring, and docks or loading facilities.

In the appraisal of a small, light industrial building built five years prior to the date of the appraisal, the appraiser has found two sales of similarly located properties. The summary grid in Table 13.5 shows data pertaining to a light industrial property and two comparables. The building being appraised is 56 x 90 feet on a site 70 x 198 feet. The office space is 56 x 25, of average quality, with paneled walls, asphalt tile floor, acoustical ceiling, and air-conditioning. Office space of this type is estimated to command a sale price premium of $10 per square

Table 13.5   Summary Adjustment Grid—Industrial Building Appraisal

	Comparables		Subject
	A	B	
Sale price	$120,000	$210,000	NA
Financing terms	Normal	Normal	Normal
Conditions of sale	Normal	Normal	Normal
Normal sale price	$120,000	$210,000	NA
Date of sale	2 yrs. ago	Current	Current
Market conditions	+10%	0	
Time-adjusted normal sale price	$132,000	$200,000	
Location	Equal	Inferior	Good
Land value/sq. ft.	$2.50	$2.00	$2.50
Land area	11,600	18,000	13,860
Land value	$29,000	$36,000	$34,650
Building allocation	$103,000	$174,000	
Office premium/sq. ft.	$15.00	$10.00	$10.00
Office space area	1,250	2,500	1,400
Office space premium	$18,750	$25,000	$14,000
Net to basic building	$84,250	$149,000	
Building area	4,800	8,500	5,040
Indicated price/sq. ft. of basic building	$17.55	$17.53	

These sales would indicate a value for subject property from the analysis as follows:

Building gross area
56 x 90 ft. =   5,040 sq. ft.   5,040 x $17.55 = $ 88,452

Office premium
56 x 25 ft. =   1,400 sq. ft.   1,400 x $10.00 = $ 14,000

Land value
70 x 198 ft. = 13,860 sq. ft.   13,860 x $2.50 = $ 34,650

Total $137,102

                                      Rounded: $137,000

foot more than the rate for warehouse space in the same building. The value of the site is estimated to be $2.50 per square foot. Sale A has a similar land value but the office quality is superior. Sale B is inferior in land value, due to poor access, but has similar quality.

Other types of industrial properties might be compared by using other units of comparison. Truck terminals are compared on the basis of price per door, and grain elevators are compared on price per bushel of storage capacity. Processing facilities are compared on the basis of the quantity of goods that can be processed in a day or another period of time.

As the methods of storing and moving products and inventory have changed, the design of industrial buildings has changed, which has resulted in functional obsolescence. Therefore, an appraiser should become familiar with modern facilities to compare existing buildings that have different amounts of functional obsolescence. The appraisal of large industrial properties is often difficult. In many instances, sales of similar properties are not available for comparison or have occurred in a different market.

Office Buildings

When appraising office buildings, an appraiser can use several units of comparison. A multiplier proves helpful if expense ratios are closely similar. Price per square foot of gross area and price per square foot of rentable area are also generally reliable. Price per square foot of net rentable area is especially useful because the percentage of rentable area often varies considerably among competitive and otherwise comparable properties.

Table 13.6 summarizes the data and comparison procedure for a two-story office building. Four comparables were found that are somewhat physically different from the subject property but are competitive with it.

Sales B and C are probably the best comparables because they are two-story buildings. Sale D is a four-story elevator building. It illustrates how the higher expense ratio that is typical of an elevator building lowers the GRM. Sale C is currently renting for $9.32 per square foot on the average, while the property being appraised is renting for $8.50 per square foot. Sale B was renting for $7.50 per square foot two years prior to the date of the appraisal. If rents have gone up at the same rate as prices, the current rent for Sale B would be $9.00 per square foot. If Sale D is disregarded, the range is as shown on page 330.

Table 13.6 Summary Adjustment Grid—Office Building Appraisal

	Comparables				Subject
	A	B	C	D	
Transaction price	$750,000	$900,000	$1,200,000	$2,400,000	
Financing terms	Normal	−50,000	Normal	Normal	Normal
Conditions of sale	Arm's length	Arm's length	Arm's length	Arm's length	Arm's length
Normal sale price	$750,000	$850,000	$1,200,000	$2,400,000	
Market conditions	+10%	+20%	0	+10%	
Time-adjusted normal price	$825,000	$1,020,000	$1,200,000	$2,640,000	
Location	Equal	Equal	Equal	Equal	Good
Gross area, sq. ft.	15,000	20,000	24,000	60,000	25,000
Net rentable area	13,000	16,000	18,500	40,000	20,000
Number of stories	1	2	2	4	2
Potential gross income	$104,000	$120,000	$172,500	$450,000	$170,000
GRM	7.21	7.5	6.96	5.33	
Time adjusted normal price/sq. ft. gross	$55.00	$51.00	$50.00	$44.00	
Time adjusted normal price/sq. ft. net	$63.46	$63.75	$64.86	$66.00	

GRM	$1,183,200 to $1,250,000
Price per sq. ft.—gross	$1,250,000 to $1,375,000
Price per sq. ft.—net	$1,269,200 to $1,297,200

The data show a range of indicated values of $1,183,200 to 1,375,000, with the midpoint being $1,279,100. Comparable C was considered most similar to the subject in terms of both number of stories and time of sale (current). The values indicated by C's GRM, time-adjusted normal price per gross square foot, and time-adjusted normal price per net square foot are $1,183,200, $1,250,000, and $1,297,200, respectively. Thus, the reconciliation process indicates a final value indication of approximately $1,280,000.

Reconciliation in the Sales Comparison Approach

At the conclusion of the sales comparison approach, an appraiser often derives a single indication of value, or reconciles the data. The appraiser thus reviews the data that were used in the approach and examines them in terms of their reliability, degree of similarity, and adequacy. Generally, the appraiser gives the greatest consideration to the sales that have occurred most recently and have the greatest degree of comparability. Thus, sales that require large adjustments are generally given less consideration. In realizing that the market is not perfect, many appraisers use the sales comparison approach to indicate a range of value for the property being appraised and arrive at a single value estimate only after completing all three approaches. The appraisal gains credibility if the indications of value from the other approaches fall in the range that is indicated by the sales comparison approach.

Summary

The sales comparison approach involves the comparison of a subject property and several comparable properties that have sold recently. Characteristics of the transactions (financing terms, conditions of sale, and market conditions), location, physical characteristics, and income characteristics for the comparables should be as similar as possible to the subject property. Appraisers make adjustments to the price of each comparable to reflect value differences between it and the subject property.

For properties that vary significantly in size, appraisers may make comparisons according to units of comparison. Typical units of comparison in the sales comparison approach are multipliers, price per square foot, front foot, cubic foot, room, apartment, bed, seat, bushel of storage capacity, and so forth. When properties are compared on a unit basis, the unit of comparison is considered to be the entire property.

Appraisers compare properties and make adjustments for six general areas in which properties can vary. These areas are called elements of comparison and include conditions of sale, financing terms, market conditions (time), location, physical characteristics, and income characteristics. An appraiser follows a sequence when making the adjustments to develop intermediate prices. The appraiser then applies subsequent percentage adjustments to the prices. The appraiser first adjusts for financing terms and conditions of sale to obtain a normal sale price for the comparable property. Then the appraiser adjusts for market conditions to obtain the time-adjusted normal sale price. Next, the appraiser makes adjustments to the time-adjusted normal price for location and all physical and income characteristics. The subsequent final figure is called an adjusted sale price.

The two basic types of adjustments that appraisers make are in dollars and in percentages. The type of adjustment depends on how the adjustment is derived from the market, in lump-sum dollar amounts or in percentages. An appraiser must carefully follow the sequence for percentage adjustments.

The sales comparison approach is particularly useful for most single family residential property appraisals. However, the approach can also be used for other property types for which there are active, viable markets. The unit of comparison for single family residences is usually the entire property, while for income-producing properties a multiplier and other units of comparison are usually required. When adequate data are available, the sales comparison approach is usually considered the most accurate and reliable appraisal approach.

Chapter 14

The Income Capitalization Approach

Income-producing property is typically purchased for investment purposes, and from the investor's point of view, earning power is the critical element that affects the property's value. One essential investment premise is that the higher the earnings, the higher the value. An investor who purchases income-producing real estate is essentially trading a sum of present dollars for the right to receive future dollars. The income capitalization approach to value consists of methods, techniques, and mathematical procedures that an appraiser uses when analyzing a property's capacity to generate monetary benefits and when converting the benefits into an indication of present value.

The income capitalization approach is one of the three traditional approaches an appraiser may use in the valuation process. However, it is not an independent system of valuation unrelated to the other approaches. The valuation process considered as a whole is comprised of integrated, interrelated, and inseparable techniques and procedures that have the common objective of a convincing and reliable estimate of value, usually market value. The analysis of cost and sales data is often an integral part of a comprehensive income capitalization approach; similarly, capitalization techniques are frequently employed in the cost and sales comparison approaches. For example, in the sales comparison approach, capitalization techniques are commonly used in the analysis and adjustment of sales data; and in the cost approach, obsolescence is often measured by capitalizing an estimated rental loss. The income capitalization approach is described here as part of the systematic valuation process, but the various methods, techniques, and procedures used in the approach are general-purpose analytical tools that are applicable in the valuation and evaluation of income-producing properties.

This chapter provides a broad overview of the income capitalization approach, including discussions of rationale, methodology, and historical background. Chapters 15, 16, and 17 amplify the discussions with more detailed explanations of specific methods, techniques, and procedures for projecting and capitalizing future benefits.

Relationship to Value Influences and Appraisal Principles

The application of the income capitalization approach is based on and is consistent with the operation of value influences and appraisal principles.

Anticipation and Change

The relevance of anticipation to the approach cannot be overstated. Value is created by the expectation of benefits to be derived in the future, and value may be defined as the present worth of all rights to future benefits. All income capitalization methods, techniques, and procedures represent attempts to quantify expected future benefits.

The influence of change on the value of income-producing properties is a major focus of the approach. Investors' expectations of changes in income levels, expenses necessary to ensure income, and probable increases or decreases in property value must be accurately addressed and measured to provide sound indications of value. As stated by the late L. W. Ellwood, "The professional appraiser. . . is profoundly concerned with community, neighborhood, and economic trends as indicators of future changes in value."[1]

---

[1]L. W. Ellwood, *Ellwood Tables for Real Estate Appraising and Financing*, 4th ed. (Chicago: American Institute of Real Estate Appraisers, 1977), p. 55.

Supply and Demand

The principle of supply and demand and the related concept of competition are particularly relevant when an appraiser projects future benefits and estimates rates of return as required in the approach. Both income streams and rates of return are determined in the market. The rents charged by the owner of a motel, a shopping center, an office building, an apartment building, or any income-producing property usually should not vary greatly from those charged by owners of competing properties that offer the same quality of service. If the demand for a particular type of space is great, owners may be able to charge high rents that yield high rates of return. Therefore, in estimating rates of return and in forecasting future benefits, appraisers consider the demand for the particular type of property and the impact of demand on supply.

Substitution

The limits of prices, rents, and rates tend to be set by the prevailing prices, rents, and rates for equally desirable substitutes. The principle of substitution is market oriented and provides an appraiser with the basis for crucial tests to use when estimating market value. Although anticipation may provide the basic premise of value in the income capitalization approach, the principle of substitution may be applied to test the validity of the approach and the reliability of the assumptions and data used in applying it.

Balance

The principle of balance and all related concepts are especially significant in the application of the approach. A reasonable balance between the types and locations of income-producing properties creates and sustains value; any imbalance in efficient land use may result in a decline in value. The efficiency of land use is assisted by good planning and zoning laws.

The related concept of contribution suggests that a reasonable balance of the agents in production in any income-producing property is essential to create and sustain maximum profit. For example, if a property is over- or underimproved, its rate of profit may be adversely affected.

Externalities

External forces, both positive and negative, affect the value of income-producing properties. Apartments and office buildings are subject to the same types of external forces (e.g., the availability and quality of public transportation and shopping facilities) as are single family residences. Similarly, commercial establishments are enhanced by attractive, uncluttered, accessible surrounding areas and are damaged by unattractive, poorly maintained, dirty surroundings. The negative externalities imposed by high crime rates have affected all types of income-producing properties in recent years. Further, such external conditions as pollution, unattractive surrounding areas, and high crime rate can affect even heavy industrial factories.

Interests to Be Valued

The rights of ownership in income-producing property are not always held in fee simple. Income-producing property is likely to be leased, thereby creating a lessor's interest (the leased fee, which is often referred to as the lessor's marketable interest) and a lessee's interest (the leasehold estate). Appraisers typically estimate the value of the lessor's marketable interest. The value of this interest may differ from the value of all rights in the property considered as a whole, or as if unleased. Thus, an appraiser of income-producing property must identify and carefully define the rights to be appraised.

Although typical appraisal assignments call for the valuation of a lessor's marketable interest in real property, an appraiser may be asked to appraise a marketable leasehold interest or to allocate total market value to the various lease interests. Valuations of partial interests in real property are discussed in Chapter 23.

Market Value and Investment Value

The income capitalization approach is typically used in market value appraisals of income-producing properties. The approach may also be used to estimate investment value, or the subjective value of a property to a particular investor. Market value and investment value may coincide when a client's investment criteria are consistent with those that are typical in the market. In this case, the two value estimates may be numerically the same, but the two types of value are not interchangeable. Market value is objective, impersonal, and detached; investment value is subjective and personal. In estimating market value, an appraiser must be satisfied that all data and assumptions used in the income capitalization approach are market oriented.

Future Benefits

The benefits of owning fee simple or partial interests in income-producing real estate include the right to receive all profits accruing to the real property interest during the holding period (the term of ownership) plus the proceeds from the resale of the property or the reversion of the property interest at the termination of the investment. Various measures of future benefits are used in applying the income capitalization approach. Commonly used measures include potential gross income, effective gross income, net operating income, equity dividend, and reversionary benefits.

Potential gross income is the total potential income attributable to the property under full occupancy. Gross income may refer to the level of rental income prevailing on the date of the appraisal or expected during the first full month or year of operation, or the periodic income during a holding period.

Effective gross income is the anticipated income from all operations of the real property after allowances are made for vacancies, credit losses, or fluctuations.

Net operating income is the anticipated net income remaining after deducting all operating expenses from effective gross income but before deducting mortgage debt service. Net operating income is customarily expressed as an annual amount. In certain income capitalization techniques, a single year's net operating income may represent a steady stream of fixed income that is expected to continue for a period of years. In other techniques, the income may be the starting level for a stream of income that is expected to change over the years according to a prescribed pattern. Still other techniques may require successive measurements of net operating income, one for each year of an analysis.

Equity dividend is the portion of net operating income remaining after payment of mortgage debt service. A single year's equity dividend, like the net operating income, may represent a steady stream of fixed income, a starting level of income, or the equity income for a particular year of an analysis. Equity dividend is also referred to as pre-tax cash flow.

Reversionary benefits are a lump sum an investor receives at the termination of an investment. Such benefits differ according to the interest being valued. For instance, reversionary benefits for the fee simple estate are the expected proceeds from resale at the termination of an investment. For the mortgagor, benefits consist of the balance of a mortgage when it is paid off. Reversionary benefits are measured as a predicted dollar amount or as a relative change in value over the presumed holding period. Reversionary benefits may or may not require separate measurement, depending on the purpose of the analysis and the method of capitalization employed.

Rates of Return

When using the income capitalization approach, an appraiser assumes that an investor's objective is an eventual total return that exceeds the amount invested. The investor's total expected return, therefore, consists of (1) full recovery of the amount invested, or the return *of* capital, and (2) a profit, reward, or return *on* capital. Numerous rates, or measures of return, are used in capitalization. Commonly used rates include the interest rate, discount rate, internal rate of return, equity yield rate, overall capitalization rate, and equity dividend rate.

The rates of return can be categorized as either *yield rates* or *income rates*. The interest rate, discount rate, internal rate of return, and equity yield rate are yield rates. The overall capitalization rate and equity dividend rate are income rates.

Under certain conditions, the yield rate for a particular property might be numerically equal to the corresponding income rate, but the rates are never the same conceptually. An income rate is always the ratio of one year's income amount to value, while a yield rate is applied to a series of incomes to discount each to present value.

In the income capitalization approach, both income rates and yield rates can be derived for and applied to either the total investment or any of its components. For instance, an appraiser may need to analyze the total property income in terms of income to land and income to building or income to the mortgage and equity components. Similarly, an appraiser may seek the total investment yield or may need to analyze the separate yields to land and building or to mortgage and equity. Practical examples of these symbols, formulas, and procedures are presented in Chapters 16 and 17.

An interest rate is a rate of return on capital; it is usually expressed as an annual percentage of the amount loaned or invested. An interest rate does not provide for the recovery or payment *of* capital. The term *interest rate* is usually used in reference to debt capital, not to equity capital.

A discount rate is a rate of return on capital used to discount future payments or receipts to present value. The discount rate used in any instance corresponds mathematically to the interest rate, the internal rate of return, and the yield rate used in the same instance.

An internal rate of return is a rate of return on capital generated or capable of being generated in an investment or portfolio during the holding period. Like an interest rate, an internal rate of return usually is expressed as an annual percentage of the amount invested. The internal rate of return for a specific investment also may be defined as a yield rate that is used to discount the value of the future benefits to the present value of the cumulative investment capital. The internal rate of return applies to all expected benefits, including the proceeds from resale at the termination of the investment. It is used to measure the return on any capital investment before or after income taxes.

An equity yield rate is a rate of return on equity capital, as distinguished from debt capital. The equity yield rate is the equity investor's internal rate of return.

A capitalization rate is any rate used to capitalize income. It reflects the relationship between one year's income and its corresponding capital value. Overall capitalization rates and equity dividend rates are specific capitalization rates.

An overall capitalization rate is an income rate for a total property that reflects the relationship between one year's net operating income and total price or value. An overall capitalization rate is not a rate of return on capital or a full measure of performance. It may be more or less than the eventual equity yield on invested capital, depending on future changes in income and value.

An equity dividend rate is an income rate that reflects the relationship between one year's equity income and equity capital. When applied in capitalizing the subject property's equity income into value, the equity dividend rate is referred to as the equity capitalization rate, or the "cash on cash" rate. Like the overall capitalization rate, the equity dividend rate is not a rate of return on capital and may be more or less than the eventual equity yield rate, depending on future changes in income and value.

Return of Capital

In real estate investments, capital may be recaptured gradually as part of regular income, or it may be recaptured, all or in part, through resale of the property at the termination of the investment. When capital is recovered gradually through income, the difference between the rate reflecting the interest being appraised and the required internal rate of return on the capital invested in that interest is commonly referred to as the *recapture rate.* A recapture rate is usually used to provide for a loss in capital value; however, the rate may be positive or negative. When the proceeds from resale at the termination of the investment exceed the total amount invested, the yield rate exceeds the income rate, and the recapture rate may be said to be negative. A capitalization rate may therefore be envisioned as the sum of (1) a rate of return *on* capital and (2) a rate of return *of* capital.

Rate Selection

For appraisal purposes, the rate of return used to convert income to property value, whether a yield rate or an income rate, should represent the annual rate of return necessary to attract investment capital. Such a rate is influenced by many considerations, including the degree of apparent risk, market attitudes with respect to future inflation, the prospective rates of return for alternative investment opportunities, historical rates of return earned by comparable properties, supply of and demand for mortgage funds, and the availability of tax shelter. Because the rates of return used in the income capitalization approach represent *prospective* rates, as distinguished from historical rates, special consideration is given to market perceptions of risk and changes in purchasing power.

Although it is not possible to prove conclusively the suitability of a particular rate of return on the basis of market evidence, the chosen rate should be consistent with the available evidence. Rate selection requires appraisal judgment and knowledge concerning prevailing market attitudes and economic indicators.

Risk

The appraiser considers the element of risk throughout the application of the income capitalization approach. The anticipation of receiving future benefits creates value, but the possibility of losing future benefits detracts from value. The belief that higher rewards are gained in return for higher risk is fundamental in the valuation of income-producing properties. It is generally accepted that all investments are predicated on the expectation of receiving a return on capital that represents the time value of money, adjusted upward for perceived risk. This minimum rate of return for invested capital is sometimes referred to as the safe rate, or the "riskless" rate. In theory, the difference between the total rate of return on capital and the safe rate may be viewed as a premium to compensate for risk, inflation, burden of management, and lack of liquidity.

To a real estate investor, risk is the chance of financial loss and the uncertainty of realizing projected future benefits. Most investors are risk averters. They prefer certainty to uncertainty and expect a reward in return for assuming a risk. An appraiser recognizes such tendencies when analyzing market evidence, when projecting future benefits, and when applying capitalization procedures. The appraiser must be satisfied that the income rate or yield rate used in capitalization is consistent with market evidence and properly reflects the level of risk associated with receiving the benefits as projected.

Inflation and Deflation

The outlook for inflation or deflation necessarily affects the projection of future benefits and the selection of an appropriate income rate or yield rate. The anticipation of inflation, or the erosion of currency, tends to increase the desired real rate of return (the rate of return unadjusted for inflation) on invested capital by an increment sufficient to compensate for the loss of purchasing power. It is the real rate of return which investors try to protect over time. In theory, the total desired rate of return on capital includes the expected inflation rate, if any. Therefore, the anticipated yield rate generally varies directly with the expected inflation rate.

Because the inflation rate and the yield rate tend to fluctuate together, there can be no proof that a particular combination of rates provides the best reflection of current market attitudes. The chosen combination of inflation rate and yield rate must, however, be in line with general market expectations, and the relationship or difference between the two rates must be plausible and supportable. For appraisal purposes, the objective is to simulate the expectations of the typical investor, not necessarily to make the most reliable prediction of the yield and inflation rates.

Although inflation does not create true value, certain properties are unquestionably better hedges against inflation than others. Moreover, the outlook for inflation may indeed affect value. An appraiser can consider the effects of inflation in capitalization by expressing the future benefits in terms of constant dollars (adjusted to reflect constant purchasing power) and by expressing the discount rate as a real or uninflated rate of return on capital. Usually, however, appraisers project income and expenses in terms of unadjusted (inflated) dollars and express the discount rate as a nominal or apparent rate of return on capital. It is convenient and customary to project income and expenses exactly as they are expected to occur, with no attempt to convert the amounts to constant dollar equivalents. The use of a corresponding, unadjusted discount rate, as distinguished from a real or adjusted rate of return, permits comparison with other rates that are customarily quoted in the open market, such as mortgage interest rates and bond yield rates.

Income Capitalization Approach Methods

The following discussion describes two capitalization methods: direct capitalization and yield capitalization. These methods are based on different measures of expected earnings and different assumptions concerning the relationship between the expected earnings and value.

Direct Capitalization

Direct capitalization is used to convert an estimate of a single year's income expectancy into an indication of value in one direct step. The income is divided by an appropriate rate or multiplied by an appropriate factor. The chosen rate or factor represents the relationship between income and value as observed in the market. The rate is revealed in comparable sales analysis by dividing income, usually annual net operating income, by sale price. The factor or multiplier is revealed by dividing sale price by either potential or effective gross annual income.

Direct capitalization is market oriented and stresses the analysis of market evidence and valuation by inferring the assumptions of investors. Because of the emphasis on market rates and factors, direct capitalization is sometimes called market capitalization.

Direct capitalization does not provide for allocation between return on and return of capital because investors' assumptions are not specified. However, it is implicit that the selected multiplier or rate will satisfy a typical investor and that the prospects for future monetary benefits, over and above the amount originally invested, are sufficient.

Direct capitalization may be based on gross potential income, effective gross income, net operating income, or equity dividend. The selection of the income to be capitalized is determined by the purpose of the analysis and data availability.

Yield Capitalization

Yield capitalization uses the discounting procedure to convert future benefits to present value on the premise of a required level of profit or rate of return on invested capital. The method is profit or yield oriented; it simulates the typical investor's investment assumptions by formulas that calculate the present value of expected benefits according to a presumed requirement for profit or yield.

The conversion of future benefits at the specified yield rate is called discounting, and the required rate of return is called the discount rate when used in this analytical procedure. The discounting procedure presumes that the investor will receive a satisfactory rate of return on the investment plus a complete recovery of the capital investment. Yield capitalization is sometimes referred to as annuity capitalization, but because the requirement for a particular level of profit or *yield* is critical, *yield capitalization* is the preferred term.

The term *annuity* literally means an annual income, but it has come to mean a program or contract of regular payments of stipulated amounts. Payments can be made more often than annually, but the time interval must be regular. An annuity can be level, increasing, or decreasing, but the amounts must be scheduled and predictable. Income that has the characteristics of an annuity is income that is expected at regular intervals in predictable amounts. Obviously, real estate income or rental income may have the characteristics of an annuity.

Certain appraisers distinguish between assured income and unassured income when making the comparison to annuity income, particularly when the unassured income is considered speculative and subject to fluctuation. In contemporary usage, however, yield capitalization is not restricted to assured income, and it is recognized that unassured income may be subject to increase as well as decline. In yield capitalization, the expected earnings may be expressed as a stable stream of income, a stream of income changing according to a prescribed pattern, one or more lump sum payments, or any combination of these.

In yield capitalization, a number of analytical techniques and procedures are available for the valuation of an entire property, specific benefits, or a partial interest in property. Present value may be calculated with or without considering the impact of financing and with or without considering the impact of income taxes. The selection of the techniques and procedures is determined by the purpose of the analysis and the availability of data and might also be influenced by the availability of suitable computer hardware and software.

Because yield capitalization always involves the analysis and discounting of incomes, the term *discounted cash flow analysis* may apply literally to any yield capitalization technique. In common usage, however, the term refers to a specific procedure whereby all future benefits are itemized, scheduled with respect to time, and converted to present value. Discounted cash flow analysis did not become a practical appraisal tool in the income capitalization approach until modern computer technology automated the procedure and removed the drudgery of repetitive calculations. The various discouting procedures, including contemporary discounted cash flow analysis, are discussed in Chapter 17.

Direct Capitalization and Discounting

Direct capitalization is simple and thus easily understood. The capitalization rate or factor can be derived directly from market facts. Direct capitalization does not specify a distinction between return on and return of capital, nor does it explain value in terms of specific assumptions made by investors.

Yield capitalization tends to be complex: it often requires the use of special tables, calculators, or computer programs. Selecting a market-oriented discount rate requires interpreting market attitudes and expectations. In yield capitalization, investment goals pertaining to the return on and of invested capital are specified and simulated by means of formulas and numerical multipliers (factors), designed to reflect various investment expectations. These formulas and factors facilitate the conversion of the various income stream patterns and reversions into present value by applying the investor's anticipated yield rate in the discounting procedure. Formulas and factors are available from financial tables. Further, they can be calculated and used on hand-held financial calculators or programmed for computer calculations.

The income capitalization approach need not be limited to a single capitalization method. Properly used, both methods should point to the same value indication. Using standard discounting procedures, an appraiser can test the results of direct capitalization for profitability and market appeal from a typical investor's point of view. Similarly, the results of discounting can be tested using direct capitalization techniques to ascertain whether the indicated value is reasonable in terms of market evidence.

Residual Techniques

Residual techniques may be employed in the income capitalization approach to permit the separate consideration of such property components as land and building or mortgage and equity. The residual techniques presume that the value of a component or portion of the property is known or can be estimated. The income attributable to the known portion is then deducted from total income to reveal the residual income, which is then capitalized to indicate the value of the unknown portion of the property. Residual techniques are used in both direct and yield capitalization.

A Short History of the Income Capitalization Approach

To understand fully the development of the various methods, techniques, and procedures used in the income capitalization approach, one should place them in an historical framework. The following discussion is divided into two time periods. Those periods are the early years, when the primary works that formed the theoretical bases for the direct and yield methods of capitalization were written, and the modern era, which is divided into three subperiods: pre-1959, 1959 to the mid-1970s, and the mid-1970s to the present.[2]

Early Writings

The mathematical foundations of discounting can be traced to John Newton, who was among the first to provide theories of compound

---

[2]See James H. Burton, *The Evolution of the Income Approach* (Chicago: American Institute of Real Estate Appraisers, 1982).

interest, and Edmund Halley, who was the notable astronomer and published the first present value tables in 1693. John Smart is credited with publishing the first comprehensive set of tables and the first partial payment table in 1726. His work *Tables of Interest and Annuities* is identical to the present value and compound interest tables in most modern appraisal books.

In 1811, William Inwood published tables that had originally appeared in the works of others, including those of John Smart. Of particular significance to appraisers was Inwood's use of real estate valuation examples to illustrate the use of Smart's tables. Included in Inwood's book was a present value of an income in perpetuity table, which seems to be the first example of an author converting an interest rate into a coefficient. Inwood multiplied the coefficient by the investment's annual income, which was assumed to be in perpetuity, to calculate the current value of the investment. The so-called Inwood Premise has been used by real estate appraisers ever since.

In 1890, Alfred Marshall became the first economist to give significant attention to valuation techniques. He pointed out that the interest rate is the link between income and value and thus arrived at the formula

$$\text{Value} = \frac{\text{Income}}{\text{Interest rate}}$$

which, with variations, is a basic formula used in the direct capitalization method. In the early 1900s, Irving Fisher also contributed to capitalization theory. He is best remembered for his analysis of the proposition that value is the present worth of future benefits. The proposition is fundamental in modern appraisal theory and is recognized directly in discounted cash flow analysis. Thus, by the early 1900s, the mathematical and conceptual foundations of both direct and yield capitalization methods had been established. In the periods that followed, the concepts were applied in a manner consistent with prevailing investor thinking and behavior.

Modern Era: Pre-1959

Two characteristics tend to separate appraisal practice in the period prior to 1959 from the periods that followed. First, prior to 1959, there was an emphasis on the division of property into its land and improvement components. The dominant techniques used during this period were the land and building residual techniques. Their use reflected the concern with physical components and the necessity of recapturing the cost of depreciating improvements.

Second, in the pre-1959 period, value was estimated without explicit consideration of financing. Thus, while band-of-investment techniques for synthesizing the overall capitalization rate (by weighting the required returns to the debt and equity investors) were available, capitalization methods were dominated by physical residual techniques.

The concern with the productive (economic) life of the improvements and the lack of explicit concern with investment attributes, such as financing, were consistent with the prevailing investment environment. Prices were relatively stable, and the effects of physical deterioration were not obscured by inflation. For much the same reason, capital gains were not perceived to be a significant source of equity return. Both loan-to-value ratios and interest rates were at relatively low levels; and creative financing, variable interest rates, and lender participation were rarely used. Because of the predictable regularity of financing, its effect on value did not concern investors to the extent it does today.

Modern Era: 1959 to the Mid-1970s

The year 1959 is important for appraisal theory and practice and is a natural dividing point in appraisal history. The publication of *The Ellwood Tables* by L. W. Ellwood signaled the shift in dominance from the physical residual techniques to the techniques based on the investment components of debt and equity.

Ellwood's contribution to the income capitalization approach was monumental because his system accommodated the capitalization of a stream of cash flows and provided a basis for the analysis of specific investment assumptions in the valuation process. Ellwood popularized the idea that financing affects value, and he included financing in his formula. He recognized that a potentially important benefit of real property investment is property appreciation or depreciation reflected in the proceeds of resale (reversion). His formula explicitly recognized those proceeds, including the effects of mortgage amortization. Ellwood also recognized that a finite, relatively short holding period was the proper framework for valuation. Finally, Ellwood simplified the discounting procedure by publishing tables of precalculated rates that could be combined into a recognizable overall capitalization rate. These tables were especially useful prior to the availability of electronic calculators.

Many appraisers began to popularize the investment component (band-of-investment) techniques of synthesizing the overall capitalization rate. The use of the specific variation of the band-of-investment technique that employed the loan constant and the equity dividend rate as the appropriate returns to the lender and to the equity investor became widespread. This technique was similar to that introduced by S. Edwin Kazdin in 1944. It has been especially significant in the income capitalization approach during the past two decades.

Ellwood's techniques and the band-of-investment techniques began to dominate the income capitalization approach for several reasons. First, stable income streams were seen less frequently as inflation, and real increases in property values began to swamp the effects of physical depreciation. For the same reason, capital gains became more significant. Second, investors were becoming increasingly sophisticated and began to think more in terms of tax shelters, leveraging opportunities, and (partly because of IRS regulations) shorter holding periods and less in terms of the economic lives of properties, recapture rates, and long-term holding periods. In addition, during this period major appraisal organizations first recognized financing effects in the accepted definition of market value.

Modern Era: Mid-1970s to the Present

From the mid-1970s on, capitalization theory and practice have been affected by inflation and recurring national recessions. The real estate market has experienced (1) the marketing of partial interests, such as limited partnerships and joint ventures, (2) rapid increases in market rent levels, (3) the use of complex participating mortgages, (4) high mortgage interest rates, which at times have resulted in a preponderance of all cash transactions, (5) the inflow of foreign investment in U.S. real estate, and (6) cycles of overbuilding, underbuilding, excessive demand, and lack of sufficient demand. In current times, appraisers have focused on the reaction of market participants to the dynamics of the market and the capitalization methods, techniques, and procedures that can properly simulate investor decision making.

The income capitalization methods found to be the most useful during this period include direct methods that emphasize equity dividend rates derived from comparable sales and yield capitalization that employs discounted cash flow analysis. In many instances, these methods were found to best reflect the behavior of market participants. The role of computer-assisted analysis has also been a major development affecting investment analysis and valuation. Computers process data quickly and are useful for storage of comparable data, statistical analysis, discounted cash flow analysis, and business accounting.

Not all appraisers agree on the appropriate income valuation techniques to be applied today, and there is ongoing debate concerning the relevance of traditional capitalization techniques and the validity of discounted cash flow analysis.

Summary

Because income-producing properties are usually purchased as investments, their earning power is of critical concern to investors and appraisers. Appraisers use the income capitalization approach when appraising such properties because it measures the present value of the expected future benefits of ownership. The approach is based on anticipation and change and the principles of supply and demand, substitution, balance, and externalities.

The value of any interest in real property that has an income can be estimated by the income capitalization approach. The approach may be used to estimate market value, which is objective, or investment value to a particular investor, which is subjective. Because most income-producing properties are leased, it is typical to estimate the market value of the lessor's interest in real property.

The future benefits of investment consist of the income received during the holding period and the proceeds of resale of the property or reversion of the property interest at the end of the holding period. The incomes commonly measured are potential gross income, effective gross income, net operating income, equity dividend, and reversionary benefits.

The investor receives both a return *of* capital and a return *on* capital, or a profit. Many different rates are used to measure return in capitalization. The interest rate, discount rate, internal rate of return, and equity yield rate are yield rates, which are applied to a series of incomes to discount them to present values. The overall capitalization rate and the equity dividend rate are income rates, which reflect a ratio of one year's income to value. Both yield and income rates can be applied to a total investment, to partial interests, or to separate property components. The rate of return of capital can be provided for in a recapture rate, which may be either positive or negative.

The capitalization rate is the annual return necessary to attract capital to the investment. The selection of a capitalization rate is influenced greatly by risks and the market's perception of inflation, and to a lesser extent by historical rates for comparable properties, the supply of and demand for mortgage funds, and tax shelter considerations.

The two main capitalization methods are direct capitalization and yield capitalization. Direct capitalization, sometimes called market capitalization, is market oriented and relatively simple. Value is estimated by dividing one year's income by an appropriate rate derived from the market or multiplying one year's income by an appropriate factor. Unlike direct capitalization, yield capitalization simulates investor assumptions with mathematical formulas that discount future benefits to present values. This profit-oriented method measures the present value of expected earnings. Residual techniques may be used in both direct and yield capitalization to value property components separately.

The history of the income approach began in the seventeenth century with the theories of interest developed by John Newton. Later, John Smart and William Inwood published interest and annuity tables. In the late nineteenth century, Alfred Marshall developed the basic valuation formula

$$\text{Value} = \frac{\text{Income}}{\text{Interest rate}}$$

In the early 1900s, Irving Fisher defined value as the present worth of future benefits.

Before 1959, physical residual valuation techniques were commonly used, and the influence of financing was largely ignored. This was appropriate for the stable economic conditions that characterized the real estate market at the time. In 1959, however, L. W. Ellwood revolutionized appraisal theory and practice by dividing real estate investments into debt and equity components. New emphasis was placed on financing terms, appreciation and depreciation, amortization, and shorter holding periods. Ellwood simplified discounting by developing precalculated factors for computing capitalization rates. Band-of-investment techniques also gained acceptance. These new techniques came to dominate appraisal thinking because they reflected prevailing economic realities.

Capitalization theory and practice are strongly influenced by inflation and recession. When these conditions exist, appraisers use direct methods that emphasize equity dividend rates derived from comparable sales and yield capitalization that employs discounted cash flow analysis. Currently, emphasis is placed on market interpretation and simulation of typical investment expectations.

Chapter 15

Income Estimates

An appraiser's first step in determining a property's earning power is performing an analysis of net operating income expectancy. The appraiser begins such an analysis by estimating income and expenses after researching and analyzing the (1) subject property's history of income and expenses, (2) histories of competitive properties, (3) recently signed leases, proposed leases, and asking rents for the subject and competitive properties, (4) actual vacancy levels for the subject and competitive properties, (5) management's expense budget for the subject and competitive properties, (6) published operating data, and (7) tax assessment policies and utility company projections of rate changes.

An appraiser often presents all such information in tabular form to assist the reader of the report. Income and expenses are generally analyzed on the basis of annual or monthly dollar amounts and in terms of total dollar amount, dollars/cents per rentable area, or dollars/cents per other unit of comparison.

Depending on the data available and the capitalization method that will be used, an appraiser can estimate net operating income for a single year or series of years. The analysis can be based on the actual level of income at the time of the appraisal, a forecast of the first year's income, a forecast of income over a specified holding period, or a stabilized (average) annual income over a holding period. For a market value estimate, the income forecast should reflect the expectations of market participants. In investment value assignments, the appraiser often forecasts income expectancy based on the specific requirements of an investor.

In the valuation of partial interests, such as an equity interest in the fee simple or leased fee estate, the equity dividend is usually capitalized. Therefore, it is often necessary for an appraiser to deduct mortgage debt service from net operating income to calculate an equity dividend. In certain cases, the debt service is based on an existing mortgage in which the debt service amount is specified. In other cases, the debt service estimate may be based on typical mortgage terms indicated by current mortgage activity in the market.

Rent

Income for investment properties consists primarily of rent. Four different types of rent affect the quality of income studied in the income capitalization approach to value. These are contract rent, market rent, excess rent, and overage rent.

Contract rent is the actual rental income accruing to a property under the terms of a lease (a contract). It is the agreed rent between the landlord and the tenant. Contract rent paid can be the same as or higher or lower than market rent.

Market rent is the rental income that a property would most probably command in the open market as indicated by current rents being paid and asked for comparable space as of the date of the appraisal. Market rent is sometimes referred to as economic rent and fair rent.

Excess rent is the amount by which contract rent exceeds market rent at the time of the appraisal. Excess rent is created by a favorable lease and might reflect a locational advantage, unusual management, or lease execution in a previously stronger rental market. It may be expected to continue for the remaining term of the lease creating it. However, because of the higher risk inherent in the receipt of excess rent, it may be calculated separately and capitalized at an appropriately higher rate.

Overage rent is percentage rent paid over and above the level of a guaranteed minimum rent. This type of rent is not to be confused with excess rent. Overage rent is a contract rent and may be market rent, part market and part excess rent, or only excess rent.

Lease Analysis

An appraiser begins an income and expense analysis by studying all existing and proposed leases for the subject property. These leases provide information on rent and other income and on the division of expenses between landlord and tenant.

When leases exist and the income estimate is based on the continued existence of the lease income, an appraiser obtains information about the lease provisions that affect the quantity, quality, and durability of the stipulated income. To accomplish this task, the appraiser may read the leases or rely on the full disclosure of all pertinent provisions by the client or another authorized party.

Lease Types

Although a lease may be drawn to fit any situation, most leases fall into one of several classifications. Leases can be broadly classified as flat rental, graduated rental, revaluation, index, and percentage. Within such classifications, a lease may be on either a *gross rental basis,* with the lessor paying all operating expenses for the real estate, or a *net rental basis,* with the tenant paying all such expenses. A lease frequently reflects terms that fall between these extremes, with a specified division of expenses.

Leases can also be categorized by term of occupancy, such as month to month, short-term (5 years or less), and long-term (more than 5 years).

Flat Rental

Flat rental implies a specific level of rent that continues throughout the lease term, or duration of the lease. In a stable economy, this type of lease is typical and acceptable. However, in a changing economy, it usually is superseded by leases that are more responsive to fluctuating market conditions. When flat rental leases are used in periods of inflation, they tend to be short-term.

Graduated Rental

Graduated rental leases provide for specified changes in the rent at one or more points during the lease term. A step-up lease allows smaller rent payments in the lease's early years. Such leases can be advantageous to tenants establishing new businesses, perhaps in pioneering locations. Such a lease can also be used to recognize tenant expenditures on a property that are effectively amortized during the lease's early years. In long-term ground leases, such provisions for increasing rent reflect an expectation of future increases in real estate value. Because property value is expected to increase, tenants are expected to pay commensurately increasing rents. Step-down leases are less common than step-up leases and generally reflect some unusual circumstances particular to a property, such as the likelihood of its having reduced tenant appeal in the future or the recognition of capital recapture during the early years of a long-term lease.

Revaluation

Revaluation leases provide for rent adjustments at periodic intervals based on a revaluation of the real estate under market rental conditions at that time. Although revaluation leases tend to be long-term, they sometimes are short-term, with renewal option rents based on a revaluation at the time the option is exercised. When the parties to a lease cannot agree on what the revaluation should be, appraisal revaluation or arbitration is often provided for under the lease's terms.

Index

Index leases are generally long-term, with a provision for periodic rent adjustment based on the change in some specific index, such as a nationally published index relating to changes in the cost of living.

Percentage

In percentage leases, the rent, or some portion of it, represents a specified percentage of the volume of business, of productivity, or use achieved by the tenant. Percentage leases may be short- or long-term. They are used most frequently for retail properties. A straight percentage lease that requires no minimum rent may be used. However, it is customary to include a guaranteed minimum rent with the percentage rent (sometimes a graduated percentage) payable on sales above a specified level.

Lease Data

Typical data contained in a lease include

1. Date of the lease

2. Reference information (if lease is recorded)

3. Legal description or other identification of leased premises

4. Lessor's name (owner or landlord)

5. Lessee's name (tenant)

6. Lease term

7. Occupancy date

8. Commencement date for rent payment

9. Rent amount: percentage clause, if any; graduation, if any; escalation provisions, if any; payment terms

10. Landlord's covenants: items for which owner or landlord is responsible, such as taxes, insurance, and maintenance

11. Tenant's covenants: items for which tenant is responsible, such as taxes, insurance, maintenance, utilities, and cleaning

12. Right of assignment or right to sublet: whether leasehold (tenant's interest) may be assigned or sublet and, if so, under what conditions; whether assignment relieves initial tenant from future liability

13. Option to renew: date of required notice, term of renewal, rent, and any other renewal provisions

14. Options to purchase

15. Security: advance rent, bond or expenditures by tenant for leasehold improvements, and so forth

16. Casualty loss: whether lease continues in the event of fire or other disaster and, if so, on what basis

17. Lessee's improvements: whether they can be removed at time of lease expiration or to whom they then belong

18. Condemnation: respective rights of lessor and lessee in the event that all or any part of property is appropriated by a public agency

19. Revaluation clauses

20. Special provisions

Certain standard lease data merit special attention in a lease analysis. These include rent, lessor/lessee division of expenses, renewal options, escalation clauses, purchase options, escape clauses, and tenant improvements.

Rent
The quantity of income is basic lease data. An appraiser considers rent from all sources, which may include base (or minimum) contract rent, percentage rent, and escalation rent. The source of rent should be clearly identified.

Lessor/Lessee Division of Expenses
Most leases delineate the obligations of lessor and lessee for the payment of taxes, utilities, heat, repairs, and other expenses of maintain-

ing and operating the leased property. An appraiser should identify the division of such expenses for each lease in the analysis and compare rentals or estimate rental value in relation to a known lease of comparable space.

Renewal Options

Renewal options are frequently included in both short- and long-term leases. They allow a tenant to extend the lease term for one or more prescribed periods of time. A renewal option typically requires advance notice of the tenant's election to exercise the option, identifies the length of the renewal period or periods, and specifies the rent(s) or method of determining rent(s) to be paid. The option rent may be the same as that during the original lease period or at a level determined when the lease was negotiated. Alternately, a provision may be made to arrive at the rent through some established procedure or formula at the time the option is exercised. Renewal options are binding on the lessor but permit the tenant to reach a decision in light of the circumstances at the time of renewal. Thus, they are generally considered favorable to the tenant rather than the lessor.

Escalation Clauses

As the economy became increasingly inflationary in the 1970s, one practice that became common was to add tax-stop clauses to traditional gross or flat rental leases. Such clauses provide that any increase in taxes over a specified level are passed on to the tenant. As inflation continued, the practice was extended to include other operating expenses.

As operating expenses increase, escalation clauses provide that all increases become additional obligations of the lessee. For multi-tenant properties, whether retail or office buildings, the increased expenses are prorated among the tenants in proportion to the area each occupies or on some other equitable basis, and the prorated share is added to their rent. Expenses allocated to vacant space normally remain the responsibility of the owner. In certain areas, the escalation payment is based on the change in a local wage rate. In New York City, for example, the porter wage escalation formula typically provides for approximately a one-cent increase in charges per square foot for every cent increase in the porter wage rate. Escalation clauses may be drawn so broadly that the lease approaches a net rental basis.

Purchase Options

Certain leases include a clause granting the lessee an option to purchase the leased property. The exercise of this option may be limited to the lease termination date or some point or points during the lease term, or it may be available at any time. The option price can be fixed or change periodically, perhaps related to an empirical formula or a depreciated book value. The option can provide only that the lessee has a prior right to purchase the property ahead of any offer to purchase by a third party. This provision is referred to as a *right of first refusal.*

In each case, an option acts to restrict marketability and, unless the property is being appraised as if unencumbered by the lease, an exercisable option price represents a limit on the market value of the leased fee estate.

Escape Clauses

Escape clauses are provisions that permit tenant cancellation of a lease under circumstances that would not ordinarily be considered justification for lease cancellation. For example, a typical condemnation or casualty clause might permit cancellation if the extent of a condemnation or casualty loss creates a serious obstacle to continued tenant operations. In the case of a casualty loss, a reasonable time might be permitted for necessary repairs by the lessor with an appropriate abatement of rent during the interim period. Or, a landlord might require a demolition clause to preserve sale or redevelopment prospects. This type of escape clause might affect rent levels and market value.

Tenant Improvements

Extensive tenant improvements can influence the lease rent. When capital expenditures are made by the lessor, reimbursement may be provided by rent increases that amortize the lessor's expenditures over the lease period or over some portion of the period. When capital expenditures are made by the tenant, the lessor may lower the tenant's rent to less-than-market level for all or some portion of the lease term.

Rent Analysis

To a certain extent, the interest being appraised determines how rents are analyzed and estimated. The valuation of fee simple interests in real estate is based on the market rent the property is capable of achieving. Typical situations include proposed projects (without actual leases), properties leased at market rent, and owner-occupied properties. In such instances, only market rent estimates are used in the income capitalization approach.

The valuation of a lessor's marketable interest (leased fee) in real estate generally requires considering both existing contract rent (which may or may not be at market rent) for leased space and market rent for vacant and owner-occupied space. In addition, when discounted cash flow analysis is contemplated, future market rent estimates are required. Appraisers generally estimate the value of the lessor's marketable interest in either of the following ways:

1. The appraiser values the property (fee simple) at market rent and deducts the present value of the rent loss (market rent less contract rent). In using this technique, the appraiser extracts capitalization rates or factors from comparable sales of fee simple real property interests. Such transactions are rare for multi-tenanted buildings. Consequently, this technique is rarely applicable.

2. The appraiser values the property (leased fee estate) subject to existing contract rent for leased space and market rent for vacant and owner-occupied space. Because most real estate transactions reflect such income characteristics, market-derived capitalization rates and factors may be adequate to reflect reasonable value estimates of lessors' marketable interests. If adequate comparability exists, a rent loss analysis is unnecessary.

Rent analysis, then, begins with a study of the present rent schedule for the subject property. Reference to audits and leases, and interviews with selected tenants during the property inspection, can verify the schedule. Further verification may be necessary if there is any doubt concerning an owner's or a manager's representation of the schedule.

The sum of the scheduled current rents may be compared with the totals for previous accounting periods. Operating statements for the past several years facilitate this procedure. Individual statements of the rents paid, including those under a percentage lease or escalation clause, should be examined for each tenant on the premises.

After analyzing the existing rent schedule for the subject property, the appraiser reduces all rents to a unit basis for comparison in the property. All differences are described and explained. The appraiser then assembles rent data for comparable space in the market. The market rents are adjusted as necessary to an equivalent rent basis and reduced to a unit of comparison.[1]

Before computing any unit of comparison, an appraiser should identify the division of operating expenses between the lessee and the lessor. Any lessee obligation for operating expenses effectively increases the rent payment, and any lessor obligation for operating expenses effectively reduces the rent received.

When a market rent estimate is required, the appraiser gathers, compares, and adjusts the data to make a sound conclusion of market rent for the subject property. The appraiser should identify the parties to a lease to assure that the party reported as being responsible for rent payments is actually a party to the lease or, by endorsement, in the

---

[1]Typical units of comparison for rental properties are discussed in Chapter 12.

position of guarantor. It is also important to assure that the lease represents a freely negotiated arm's-length transaction. Leases that fail to meet these criteria cannot be trusted to provide indications of rental terms typical in the market.

Rents from comparable properties can provide the basis for estimating the market rent for a subject property. Only when an appraiser has reduced the basis of rent payment for comparable rentals to a unit basis equivalent to the unit used for the subject can the appraiser make a meaningful comparison. Moreover, tha appraiser might need to adjust comparable rents, just as the appraiser might need to adjust transaction prices of comparable properties in the sales comparison approach. The elements of comparison are conditions of rental (arm's-length lease terms), market conditions (time), location, and physical and income characteristics as provided in the lease. Rents for comparable properties can be analyzed and adjusted for differences in these categories to develop a market rent estimate for the subject property.

The extent of data required to support an estimate of market rent for a subject property depends on the complexity of the problem, the availability of closely comparable rentals, and the extent to which the pattern of adjusted rent indications derived from the comparables varies.

When closely comparable rental data are unavailable in sufficient quantity, an appraiser should include data that require adjustment. First, legal rights and other conditions of rental must be analyzed. Certain rentals may not reflect arm's-length bargaining and might have to be eliminated as comparables. The appraiser analyzes each rental individually for a possible adjustment in market conditions.

Economic conditions change, and leases negotiated earlier than the date of the appraisal might not reflect prevailing rents. The stability or trend of the location might also affect rent income potential and require adjustment. Physical differences are then analyzed and adjustments are made for these differences. Finally, income characteristics pertaining to the responsibilities of the landlord and tenant for the payment of operating expenses are analyzed and adjustments are made to reflect any differences. A reasonably clear pattern of market rent should develop if an appraiser uses proper judgment when making the adjustments.

Developing an Income Estimate

After completing a thorough analysis of property and lease data for the subject and comparable properties, an appraiser develops a net operating income estimate for the subject property. When the appraiser is to focus on the benefits accruing to the equity interest, he or she also estimates the equity dividend. A complete outline for net operating income and equity dividend estimates is presented in Table 15.1.

Potential Gross Income

Potential gross income is the total income attributable to a real property at 100% occupancy before deduction for operating expenses. An appraiser usually analyzes the potential gross income on an annual basis. Potential gross income is comprised of rents for all spaces in the property, rent from escalation clauses, and all other income to the real estate.

Scheduled Rent

Scheduled rent is the portion of the potential gross income that is derived from the rent levels contained in leases in effect on the date of the appraisal. Certain appraisers refer to this income as existing lease or contract income (rent). Scheduled rent may or may not coincide with rent levels currently obtainable in the local market if the space were vacant and available for leasing.

Table 15.1 Income Estimate

Potential gross income		
Scheduled rent[a]	$xxxx	
Escalation income	xxxx	
Market rent[b]	xxxx	
Other income	xxx	
Total potential gross income		$xxxx
Vacancy and collection loss		− xx
Effective gross income		$xxxx
Operating expenses		
Fixed	$ xx	
Variable	xx	
Replacement allowance	xx	
Total operating expenses		− xxx
Net operating income		$ xxx
Total mortgage debt service		− xxx
Equity dividend (pre-tax cash flow)		$ xx

[a]Rent from existing leases.
[b]Rent attributed to vacant and owner-occupied space, or, in the case of fee simple valuation, rent attributable to the whole property.

Escalation Income

Escalation income is derived from the implementation of lease escalation clauses. Escalation income reflects additional charges to tenants for a portion or all of the increases in operating expenses or the exercise of a specific escalation formula as provided in existing leases.

Market Rent

Rent for vacant or owner-occupied space is usually estimated at market rent levels and is distinguished from scheduled rent in the income estimate. In fee simple valuations, all leaseable space is assumed to be at market rent. Therefore, no scheduled rent would be included in the income estimate. In developing market rent estimates, an appraiser assumes that property management is competent.

Other Income

All income generated by the operation of the real property but not derived directly from space rentals is other income. This category includes income from services supplied to the tenants, such as switchboard service, antenna connections, and garage space. Income from coin-operated equipment or parking fees is also included.

Vacancy and Collection Loss

Vacancy and collection loss is an allowance for reductions in potential rental income because space is not leased or rents that are due cannot be collected.

Annual rent collections are typically less than the potential annual gross income; therefore, an allowance for vacancy and collection loss is typically included in an appraisal of income-producing property. The allowance is usually estimated as a percentage of potential gross income. The percentage varies according to the type and characteristics of the physical property, the quality of tenancy, current and projected supply and demand relationships, and general and local economic conditions.

Published surveys of similar properties under similar conditions may provide indications of an appropriate percentage for vacancy and collection loss. An appraiser surveys the local market to support an appropriate current vacancy estimate. The appraiser's conclusion, however, may differ from the current level indicated by primary or secondary research to reflect a typical expectancy over the holding period assumed or projected in the income capitalization approach.

Effective Gross Income

Effective gross income is the anticipated income from all operations of the real property after allowance for vacancy and collection losses.

Operating Expenses

Whether the value indication from the income capitalization approach is derived by using the net operating income or the equity dividend estimate, a comprehensive analysis of the annual expenses of operation is essential. *Operating expenses are the periodic expenditures necessary to maintain the real property and to continue the production of the effective gross income.*

For appraisal purposes, an operating statement that conforms to the above definition of operating expenses may differ from statements prepared for an equity owner or for accounting purposes. Actual current or historical operating statements for a property being appraised are either on a cash or accrual basis, and it is important for an appraiser to know the accounting basis of operating statements. These statements may be valuable sources of factual data, and they are useful in identifying individual operating expense trends.

Expense records may be maintained according to categories selected by an owner, or they may follow a standard system of accounting established by an association of owners or by accounting firms that specialize in serving a particular segment of the management market. However, an appraiser generally analyzes and reconstructs such statements to develop a typical expense expectancy on an annual accrual basis.

The items included in an operating expense estimate are

1. Fixed expenses

2. Variable expenses

3. Replacement allowance

Fixed Expenses

Fixed expenses are the operating expenses that generally do not vary with occupancy and that have to be paid whether the property is occupied or vacant. Real estate taxes and building insurance costs are typically included as fixed expenses. Although these expenses rarely remain constant, they generally do not fluctuate widely from year to year. Moreover, these expense items do not vary in response to changing levels of occupancy and are not subject to budget control by management. Therefore, an appraiser usually can identify a trend from which he or she can construct a legitimate charge for the items.

Tax information may be found in public records, and the assessor's office may provide information concerning projected changes in assessments or rates and their probable effect on future tax anticipations. If a property is found to be unfairly assessed, an adjustment in the operating expense may be necessary for the reconstructed operating statement used in the appraisal. In cases of high or low assessment or apparent exceptions to the standard pattern of the jurisdiction, a thorough analysis of the most probable amount and trend of taxes may be made. Records of changes that have been made in the assessment of the subject property should be studied. If the assessment is low, the assessor may raise it sooner or later; but if the figure is high, a reduction may not be easily obtained. In a real estate tax projection, an appraiser attempts to reflect a reasonable anticipation of tax assessments based on past tax trends, present levy, and future revenue expenditures of the municipality.

For properties that are not yet constructed or are not currently assessed, an appraiser can develop operating statement projections without including real estate taxes. The resulting net operating income estimate is actually net operating income before, instead of after, real estate taxes. A provision for real estate taxes is included as an addition to the capitalization rate used for converting the net income into a property value estimate. For example, if real estate taxes normally approximate 2% of market value, and net operating income after real estate taxes (NOI) would be capitalized at 11% to derive a market value estimate for the property, the estimated net operating income before real estate taxes could be capitalized at 13% (11% + 2%) to derive the same property value indication. Alternatively, the real estate taxes for a proposed project may be estimated based on building cost or a comparative analysis of taxes paid by recently constructed competitive properties.

An owner's operating expense statement may reflect insurance premium payments on a cash basis. If the premiums are paid other than annually, an appraiser adjusts them to an annual accrual basis for inclusion in the reconstructed statement. Fire and extended coverage and owner's liability insurance are typical insurance items. Depending on property type, however, elevator, boiler, plate glass, or other coverage may be included. The appraiser also confirms the amount of insurance and, if necessary, adjusts the annual cost to indicate appropriate coverage for the property.

Insurance on business inventory or other personal property contents is an occupant's obligation and therefore is not chargeable to the operation of the real estate. When questions arise concerning co-insurance or other terms of coverage, an appraiser might need to seek professional insurance counsel.

Variable Expenses
Variable expenses are all operating expenses that generally vary with the level of occupancy or intensity of property operation. Individual variable expense items may vary substantially from year to year, although for specific types of property the total might reflect a reasonably consistent pattern in relation to gross income. Because fewer services are provided to the

tenants of retail or industrial properties, such properties usually have a much lower ratio of expense to gross income than apartments or office buildings.

The ratio of total operating expense to the effective gross income is the *operating expense ratio*. The complement of this ratio is the *net income ratio* (net operating income to effective gross income). These ratios tend to fall within limited ranges for different property categories. The appraiser recognizes approximately correct ratios, which immediately helps to identify statements that deviate from typical patterns and hence require further analysis.

Nationwide studies of apartment and office building properties by the Institute of Real Estate Management (IREM) and by the Building Owners and Managers Association (BOMA) can often suggest a general guide for which operating expense ratio to use. Sometimes local BOMA or IREM chapters, or real estate appraisal organizations or their group chapters, conduct and publish studies of operating expenses that can be used as market indicators. These published studies, however, cannot serve as a replacement for the appraiser's development of operating expense ratios from comparable properties in the subject property's market or verification of the applicability of published ratios in that market.

Operating statements for large properties frequently list many types of variable expenses, but the typical broad categories include

1. Management charges

2. Leasing fees

3. Utilities
    a. Electricity
    b. Gas
    c. Water
    d. Sewerage charges

4. Heat

5. Air-conditioning

6. General payroll

7. Cleaning

8. Maintenance and repair

9. Decorating

10. Grounds and parking area maintenance

11. Miscellaneous
    a. Security
    b. Supplies

   c. Rubbish removal

   d. Exterminating or other items

Management charges.   Management charges are proper expenses of operation, whether management services are contracted or management is provided by an owner. The expense of management is usually expressed as a percentage of effective gross income and reflects the local pattern for such charges.

   Multi-tenancy properties require a considerable amount of time for supervision, accounting, and other duties. Larger properties may have on-site offices or apartments for resident personnel and attendant expenses for maintaining and operating the offices and/or apartments. Other management expenses may include telephone, clerical help, legal or accounting fees, printing and postage, advertising, and so forth.

Leasing fees.   Leasing fees are the commissions paid to an agent for negotiating and securing a property lease. When these fees are spread over the life of a lease or a lease renewal, they are included in the operating statement. However, initial leasing fees, which may be extensive in a new shopping center or another large development, are usually treated as part of the capital expenditure for developing the finished project. In such cases, the actual initial leasing fees are not included as periodic expenses. When a net income or equity dividend forecast over a period of time is contemplated, leasing fees, when appropriate, can be deducted in the year payable or expensed over the lease term, depending on the local custom.

Utilities.   Utility expenses for an existing property are usually projected from a familiarity with past charges and current trends. Comparison of the subject property's utility requirements with known unit utility expenses for similar properties provides a basis for projecting probable utility expenses. Hours of tenant operation may prove significant in the analysis. Shopping center policy, with regard to the number of nights per week the center will be open and the hours of after-dark operation, will be directly reflected in the consumption of electricity, and perhaps indirectly reflected in other expenses, such as those for maintenance and garbage removal. An appraiser recognizes local circumstances and the increasing costs of all energy types in an analysis of utility expenses.

   Although the charge for *electricity* is frequently a tenant expense, and therefore not included in the operating expense statement, the owner still can be responsible for the lighting in public areas and for the power needed to run elevators or other owner-operated equipment.

   Gas is a major expense item when used for heating, air-conditioning, or manufacturing. In such cases, the expense is frequently paid by the tenant or reflected in the rent. *Water* is generally not a major consideration except for laundries, restaurants, taverns, hotels, or similar operations. In such cases, the lease may provide for the tenant to incur this expense. Only when the owner typically pays for gas and water are they included in the expense statement.

In municipalities that contain citywide *sewerage* systems, a separate charge may be levied on real estate for the use of the system. This expense may be paid by the tenant or the owner.

When the owner is responsible for all utility charges, the total may be substantial. This is particularly true for hotels, motels, recreation properties, and certain apartments and office buildings.

Heat.   The charge for heat is generally a tenant expense in single occupancy properties, in industrial or retail properties, and in many apartment projects with individual heating units. It is an essential item in the owner's operating statement for office buildings and many apartment properties. The fuel may be coal, oil, gas, electricity, public steam, or perhaps a combination. Heating supplies, maintenance, and applicable wages are included in this expense category under certain accounting methods. Public steam suppliers and gas companies maintain records of the degree days from year to year. Reference to these records and fuel costs makes it practical to compare the expense for the most recent year or years with the typical expense. Prospective changes in the cost of the fuel used are reflected in the appraiser's projection.

Air-conditioning.   Air-conditioning expenses may be segregated and charged under the individual headings of electricity, water, payroll, or repairs, or both heating and air-conditioning may be combined under heating, ventilating, and air-conditioning (HVAC). The charge for air-conditioning varies substantially according to local climatic conditions and installation type. Typical unit charges for a community and property type provide a basis for projection. Most office buildings and many apartment buildings have central HVAC systems for which operating expenses are included in the annual statement. Most commercial properties and many apartment projects have individual heating and air-conditioning units operated by the tenants. However, in such cases, maintenance and repair, particularly for apartments, may continue to be obligations of the property owner.

General payroll.   General payroll includes payments to all employees who are essential to the property's operation and management, but whose salaries are not included in other specific expense categories. In certain areas, the charge for custodial or janitorial service is based on union schedules; in others, the charge is left to bargaining, which is governed by local custom and practice. If a custodian or manager occupies an apartment as partial payment of services, the apartment's rental value may be included as income with an identical amount deducted as expense. In certain properties, there are additional expenses, such as those of employing watchmen, doormen, porters, or elevator starters. Unemployment and social security taxes for employees may be included under general payroll or may be carried in a separate expense category.

Cleaning. In office buildings, cleaning is a major expense. The expense is usually estimated in terms of cents per square foot of the rentable area, whether the work is done by payroll personnel or by a contract cleaning firm. Its equivalent in hotels and furnished apartments is maid service or housekeeping. For hotels or motels, such expenses, attributable to the Rooms Department, may be based on a percentage of department gross that reflects previous experience and industry standards. Whether cleaning is an owner or tenant expense depends on property type and lease provisions.

Maintenance and repair. Maintenance and repair expenses may include roof repair, window caulking, tuckpointing, exterior painting, heating, lighting, and plumbing equipment repairs. There may be a contract for elevator maintenance and repair. Because such contracts vary, it is important that an appraiser learn the probable extent of additional operating expenses not covered by a maintenance contract. A similar contract covering air-conditioning equipment would probably be included under the air-conditioning expense category.

Alterations may be considered capital expenditures and are therefore not included as a periodic expense under repair and maintenance. The lessor may perform certain alterations in the rented space, the expense of which may or may not be amortized by additional rental. Alternately, the tenant may pay for alterations.

The extent of the total maintenance and repair expense is affected by the extent to which building component and equipment replacements are covered in the replacement allowance. If extensive replacement allowances are included in a reconstructed operating statement, the effect is to reduce the annual maintenance and repair expenses. However, maintenance and repair of the main portion of the building should always remain in the maintenance and repair category.

Decorating. Decorating expenses may include interior painting, papering, or wall cleaning in tenant or public areas. Lease provisions may relieve ownership of responsibility for interior tenant space decorating except for the preparation of vacant space to attract new tenants. The extent of such expenditures can vary with local practice and with supply and demand for the type of space.

Grounds and parking area maintenance. The expenses for maintaining grounds and parking areas vary widely, depending on property type and total area. The maintenance of a hard-surfaced public parking area with drains, lights, and marked car spaces, which is subject to intensive use and wear, may be substantial. Such expenses may be compensated for, entirely or in part, by an increment added to the rent of tenants served by the facility. In this case, both the added income and the added expenses are included in an appraiser's reconstructed operating expense statement.

Miscellaneous.   Expenses for miscellaneous items vary according to the property. However, if this expense category includes more than a minor percentage of the effective gross income, it may be analyzed and individual expense items may be reallocated to specific categories or clearly explained.

Certain types of buildings in some areas require *security* provisions, which vary in cost according to the number of employees needed to control entries and exits and to circulate throughout the property. Moreover, maintenance and power expenses are incurred when provisions for security include electric alarm systems, closed circuit television, and flood lighting.

Supplies include the cost of cleaning materials and miscellaneous small items not covered elsewhere. *Rubbish removal* and *exterminating* expenses are usually contracted services and are included in the expense statement. Expenditures for *snow removal* are frequently substantial in northern states, particularly in properties with outdoor parking in addition to typical walks and drives.

Replacement Allowance

A replacement allowance provides for the periodic replacement of building components that wear out more rapidly than the building itself and must be replaced periodically during the building's economic life. These components may include

1. Roof covering

2. Carpeting

3. Kitchen, bath, or laundry equipment

4. Compressors, elevators, and boilers

5. Specific items of the structure or equipment that have a limited economic life expectancy

6. Interior improvements to tenant space made periodically, usually at lease renewal and at the landlord's expense

7. Sidewalks

8. Driveways

9. Parking lots

10. Exterior painting

The annual allowance for each such item is usually the anticipated cost of replacement prorated over the anticipated remaining economic life of that item provided it does not exceed the remaining economic life of the structure. Proration may be based on a simple average or provided for by the use of a sinking fund. New elevators or other replacements that can be expected to have a life equal to or exceeding the remaining economic life of the structure do not require an allowance for replacement.

When an appraiser uses a short-term projection period in the income capitalization approach, items that will not require replacement prior to the end of the projection period need not be handled by a replacement allowance. Rather, their impact may be reflected in the anticipated resale price. However, when a long-term projection is being considered, the appraiser might need to recognize identifiable future expenditures for replacements. In either situation, an appraiser attempts to reflect market evidence in the use of a replacement allowance.

The scope of items to be covered by the replacement allowance is a matter of appraisal judgment based on market evidence, but the extent of a replacement allowance is judged in relation to the annual repair and maintenance expense to avoid duplication. Historical operating statements on a cash basis may include periodic replacement expenses under repair and maintenance. Extensive provision for replacement in a reconstructed statement may duplicate these charges unless the annual maintenance expense estimate is reduced.

In certain real estate markets, space is rented to a new tenant at lease expiration only after substantial interior improvements are made. In markets in which this work is performed at the landlord's expense and is required to achieve a market rent rate, the expense of such interior improvements should be included in the reconstructed operating statement as part of the replacement allowance.

A total expense estimate, including a provision for all items of repair and replacement, may exceed the actual expenditures shown on the owner's operating statements for the most recent or prior years. This is particularly true when the building is reasonably new and when the owner does not set up a replacement allowance. In preparing a reconstructed operating statement for a typical year, an appraiser recognizes that replacements must eventually be made and that replacement costs affect operating expense, which can be reflected in increased annual maintenance or recognized on an accrual basis as an annual replacement allowance.

Understanding whether a replacement allowance is included in an operating statement may also be important in deriving a capitalization rate from the market for use in the income capitalization approach. A capitalization rate derived from a comparable sale property is valid only when applied on the same basis to the subject property. Consequently, a rate derived from a market sale with an expense estimate that does not provide for a replacement allowance is not applicable to an income estimate for the subject property that includes such an allowance.

Total Operating Expenses

Total operating expenses are the sum of the fixed and variable expenses and the replacement allowance cited in an appraiser's operating expense estimate.

Net Operating Income

Net operating income is the anticipated net income remaining after the deduction of all operating expenses from effective gross income but before the deduction of mortgage debt service.

Total Mortgage Debt Service

Total mortgage debt service is the periodic payment for interest on and retirement of the mortgage loan (principal). An appraiser deducts the mortgage debt service from the net operating income to derive the equity dividend, which the appraiser uses in certain capitalization procedures. If the definition of value for the appraisal assumes existing financing, the mortgage debt service to be deducted from the net operating income is specified in the existing mortgage. If the definition of value assumes financing at market terms, the mortgage debt service to be deducted would be based on such terms.

Equity Dividend

Equity dividend is the income that remains after an appraiser deducts the total mortgage debt service from the net operating income.

Exclusions from Appraiser's Reconstructed Operating Statement

Operating statements prepared for owners of real estate typically reflect all expenditures made during a specific year. They may include items that are nonrecurring and hence should not be included in an expense estimate intended to reflect typical annual expense anticipation. They may also include items that reflect specific circumstances of ownership.

Items frequently included in operating statements prepared for property owners but that are omitted in the preparation of a reconstructed operating statement used for appraisal purposes include book depreciation, income tax, special corporation costs, and additions to capital.

Book Depreciation

Book depreciation for improvements on a parcel of real estate is based on an historical cost or another previously established figure that might not have a relation to current market value. Moreover, computation of book depreciation may be based on a formula designed for tax purposes. A provision for the recapture of invested capital is inherent in the selected capitalization method and procedure, and including depreciation in the operating expense statement would be redundant.

Income Tax

The amount of income tax varies with the type of property ownership, which may be a corporation, a partnership, a public utility, or an individual. The income tax obligation of the owner is not an operating expense.

Special Corporation Costs

Expenses attributable to corporate operation also pertain to the type of ownership. Purely corporate expenses are not part of a reconstructed operating statement for appraisal purposes.

Additions to Capital

Expenditures for capital improvements do not recur annually and therefore are not properly part of an estimate reflecting typical annual expenses of operation. The capital improvements may enhance value because either the annual net operating income or the economic life of the property is increased. However, the capital expenditure itself is not treated as a periodic operating expense.

Example of a One-Year Net Operating Income Forecast

The property being appraised is a 55-unit apartment project with a potential annual rent of $147,600 per year at 100% occupancy. Open parking is included in the rent. Additional income from coin-operated equipment averages about $1,150 per year. Total potential gross income at 100% occupancy is $148,750. Annual vacancy and collection loss is estimated at 4%. Local management services are available at 5% of collections. In addition, a superintendent receives an annual salary (including fringe benefits) of $4,200.

Last year's tax bill was $16,250. Taxes are expected to approach $17,000 by the end of the current year. The owner carries $1 million in fire and extended coverage insurance, for which the three-year premium is $4,300. The appraiser believes that this coverage should be increased to $1,200,000. An additional expense, other insurance totals $700 per year.

Payroll covering site maintenance and snow removal averages $5,400 per year. Trash removal costs $40 per month. Miscellaneous supplies are estimated at $300 per year. Pest control costs are $60 per month. Other miscellaneous expenditures are projected at $300 per year.

Tenants pay their own utilities, including gas and electricity for individual apartment heating and air-conditioning units. Electricity for public space, based on experience and anticipated rate changes, is expected to total $2,000 in the coming year. Other utility expenses, including water, are consistently adding about $900 each year.

The repair and maintenance expense has been between $12,000 and $13,000 per year, with replacement expenditures included. The appraiser anticipates that replacement expenses will increase, and a reconstructed statement should include a replacement allowance separate from normal repair and maintenance expenses. Exterior painting, which is estimated to cost $4,200 in the present market, is scheduled for every three years.

Most of the apartments are on three-year leases, with a typical redecorating cost of $200 per apartment at lease renewal. Public space is nominal, and redecorating the space adds about $240 every third year. There are 55 stoves, refrigerators, dishwashers, disposals, and exhaust fans that require a replacement allowance of $1,300 per apartment. The economic life of these items varies, but it is estimated to average 10 years. Carpeting replacement by the owner averages about $900 per unit, and the average economic life of carpeting is 6 years. Roofing is considered to have a 20-year life and a replacement cost of $18,000.

The operating statement in Table 15.2 has been prepared to reflect these data. The precision of each entry reflects the appraiser's decision, but normally the closest $5 to $10 is well within the estimating accuracy of any entry.

Table 15.2 ABC Apartments: Reconstructed Operating Statement

Potential gross annual income

Rents	11 units @ $2,400/yr.	$ 26,400	
	12 units @ $2,580/yr.	30,960	
	16 units @ $2,760/yr.	44,160	
	16 units @ $2,880/yr.	46,080	
		$147,600	
Other income		1,150	
Total potential gross income @ 100% occupancy		$148,750	
Less vacancy and collection loss @ 4%		− 5,950	
Effective gross income			$142,800

Operating expenses

Fixed

Real estate taxes	$17,000	
Insurance F&EC $\dfrac{4,300 \times 1.2}{3}$	1,720	
Other	700	
Subtotal	$ 19,420	

Variable

Management, $142,800 × 5%	$ 7,140
Superintendent	4,200
Payroll	5,400
Electricity	2,000
Other utilities	900
Repair and maintenance	6,500
Exterior paint, $\dfrac{\$4,200}{3}$	1,400
Interior decorating	3,750[a]

Miscellaneous

Trash removal	480
Pest control	720
Supplies	300
Other	300
Subtotal	$ 33,090

Replacement allowance

Kitchen and bath equipment

$\dfrac{\$1,300 \times 55}{10}$	$ 7,150

Carpeting

$\dfrac{\$900 \times 55}{6}$	8,250

Table 15.2   (Continued)

Roof		
$18,000		
20 yrs.	900	
Subtotal	$16,300	
Total operating expenses		−68,810
Operating expense ratio:		

$$\frac{\$\ 68,810}{\$142,800} = 48.2\%$$

Net operating income		$73,990
(Net operating income ratio:		

$$\frac{\$\ 73,990}{\$142,800} = 51.8\%)$$

[a]55 units × $200 = $11,000; $11,000 + $240 = $11,240; $11,240 ÷ 3 = $3,750. This entry could be included under *replacement allowance*.

Example of a Multiyear Net Operating Income and Equity Dividend Forecast

In certain appraisals, such as those in which discounted cash flow analysis is used, an appraiser forecasts expected future monetary benefits over a total projected holding period. The expected benefits may include the net operating income and the equity dividend for each year of the expected holding period plus the reversion (resale price after deduction of the expenses of sale and the mortgage balance, if appropriate). In the following example of a 10-year forecast of future benefits for an office building, both net operating income and equity dividend estimates are illustrated for each year. In addition, the proceeds from the property's resale at the end of the tenth year are estimated.[2]

All the techniques discussed in this chapter are used to arrive at a net operating and equity dividend estimate for the first year of the forecast. Estimates for the other years are based on existing lease provisions and assumptions regarding lease renewals and growth rates applied to other income and operating expenses.

[2]Adapted from Peter F. Korpacz and Mark I. Roth, "Changing Emphasis in Appraisal Techniques: The Transition to Discounted Cash Flow," *The Appraisal Journal*, January 1983.

Property Analysis

The subject property is a 50,000-square-foot site improved with a 50-year-old, 25-story office building in a secondary location north of the downtown commercial district. Rentable area totals 951,049 square feet of office and retail space. The retail space is small; it includes five leases with 13,293 square feet of space. The building is fully occupied by 19 tenants under 21 leases. Many of the leases are old and will expire soon. Leases representing approximately 58.4% of the building's rentable area will expire and be available for renewal or re-leasing in 1984 and 1985. The last existing lease will expire in 2003. Hence, 100% of the leases will not roll over[3] until 22 years from the current date. The lease expiration profile is summarized in Table 15.3.

The current average gross rent per square foot of rentable area is $8.57. The appraisers estimated current average market rent at $18 per square foot for office space and $25 per square foot for retail space. The weighted average market rent is estimated to be $18.10 per square foot. Hence, the market differential[4] ($18.10 − $8.57) initially

Table 15.3   Lease Expiration Profile

Year	No. of Expiring Leases	Rentable Area (Sq. Ft.)	Percent of Total Area (Cumulative)
1982	0	0	
1983	0	0	
1984	7	268,458	28.2
1985	6	286,706	58.4
1986	2	51,302	63.8
1987	2	22,730	66.2
1988	1	7,930	67.0
1989	1	46,979	71.8
1990-1991	0	0	71.8
1992	1	924	71.9
1993-2002	0	0	71.9
2003	1	267,020	100.0
Total	21	951,049	

[3]The occurrence of lease expiration and subsequent re-leasing is referred to as a lease rollover.

[4]Market differential is defined as the difference between potential gross income (market rent) and existing contract rent.

is $9.53 per square foot, and the total actual rent is 47.35% of market rent. The market for office space is in balance, and there is above-average demand for space in this building. Although the building is old, it was recently remodeled with extensive capital expenditures to improve its mechanical systems and to maintain its competitive position. It is well located (although in a secondary area) and is ideally suited to back office operations (computer, bookkeeping, storage, and so forth) that require large, contiguous space.

Rationale Regarding the Forecast

The appraiser determines that investors in office buildings similar to the subject property typically forecast net operating incomes or equity dividends over a projected holding period (usually 10 years) and then determine a purchase price that will justify the degree of risk inherent in the proposed investment by discounting the forecast net operating incomes or equity dividends and the reversion at an appropriate yield rate.

To simulate typical investors' analysis, an appraiser

1. Analyzes current income, establishes a market rent level for each tenant space, and forecasts future income each year for a 10-year period based on existing leases, probable renewals at market rentals, and expected vacancy experience

2. Forecasts other income, including income from escalation clauses in existing leases and assumed escalation provisions in new leases

3. Forecasts future property expenses based on an analysis of historical operating expenses, the experience at competitive properties, and the current budget for the property

4. Forecasts mortgage debt service based on the terms of existing or proposed financing

5. Calculates the net operating incomes or equity dividends to be generated by the property for each year of the forecast holding period

6. Estimates the reversionary benefits to be received at the end of the forecast holding period

For a market value appraisal, it is essential that the application of these steps reflect the thinking of participants in the market. For the case illustrated, the appraiser assembles pertinent information regarding recent sales of office buildings in the subject property's market. As part of verifying the sales, the appraiser reviews with the participants, usually the buyer, the net operating income or equity dividend forecast assumptions used in connection with each sale. An example of the detailed information ascertained for each comparable sale is shown in Table 15.4, which indicates information gathered for Comparable Sale l.

Assumptions for the Subject Property

Based on the results of gathering and analyzing data pertaining to local market conditions and income and expense expectations of comparable properties, the appraiser develops assumptions about the subject property.

Forecast Period
The forecasts are prepared on the assumption of a 10-year holding period commencing on the date of valuation. A 10-year forecast period is typical in this market. This forecast allows for the effects of re-leasing 71.8% of the entire building space. A lease representing one major space user (28.1%) does not expire until the year 2003.

Existing Rents
Contract rents and rent adjustments are forecast in accordance with the existing leases, including escalation provisions.

Escalation Income
Escalation income is computed in accordance with the specific terms of existing leases. With respect to expected new leases, escalation income is based on a pro rata share of operating expense and real estate tax increases plus an annual increase in base contract rent equal to 25% of the increase in the Consumer Price Index multiplied by the initial rent. According to local custom, escalation income is assumed to be collected in the year after it accrues.

Although specific escalation provisions vary, the analysis reveals that prospective investors use a combination of escalation provisions that, when taken together, increase total tenant collections annually so that total collections in any given year do not lag far behind market rent rates.

Renewal Options
Renewal options contained in existing leases, which specify new contract rentals or escalation provisions, are assumed to be exercised, and the resulting rent income specified under these renewals is incorporated into the forecast. One lease provides for a seven-year renewal option, beginning in 1983 at specified annual rent, which will be less than the expected market rent in 1983 ($19.80 market compared with $13.00 contract). The renewal options that do not specify either contract rent or escalation provisions are also assumed to be exercised; however, market rental rates and new escalation provisions are applied.

Table 15.4   Sale 1 Data

Sale No.	1
Address	110 Main St.
	Subject city, subject state
Date of sale	June 1981
Sale price	$60 million
Seller	ABC Investment Co.
Purchaser	110 Main Street Co.
Description	A 32-story multi-tenanted office building that was built in 1960 and contains 748,701 sq. ft. on floors that range from 8,100 sq. ft. to 30,600 sq. ft., situated on a 32,609-sq.-ft. plot
Comments	The property was sold on an all-cash basis; the buyer expects above-average growth in net income.
Sale price	
per sq. ft.	$80.14
Average scheduled rent	
per sq. ft.	
at sale date	$12.44

Anticipated first-year financial information (buyer's estimate)

Average market rent per sq. ft.	$27.50
Average scheduled rent per sq. ft.	$12.44
Fixed expenses per sq. ft.	$ 2.67
Variable expenses per sq. ft.	$ 4.79
Replacement allowance	$ 0.00
Net operating income per sq. ft.	$ 4.98
Overall capitalization rate	6.2%
Equity dividend rate	6.2%
Anticipated 10-year yield (IRR)	18.5%

When a property is not mortgaged, the equity dividend rate is the same as the overall capitalization rate.

Purchaser's assumptions

Market rent rate	Average of $27.50 per sq. ft. in Yr. 1, growing at 10% per year for 2 yrs. and 8% per yr. thereafter
Escalation income	Typical, resulting in total rent closely approximating market rent rates
Expense growth	Fixed expenses, assumed to grow at 6% per yr.; energy expenses, assumed to grow at 10% per yr.; other operating expenses, assumed to grow at 8% per yr.
Re-leasing	All space assumed to be re-leased for successive 5-yr. terms
Vacancy	75% of space being re-leased assumed to be vacant for 3 mos.

Leasing fees	Standard commission schedule payable in first yr. of lease
Interior improvements to tenant space	None; space assumed to rent in "as is" condition
Resale	Computed by application of a 10% overall capitalization rate to the 10th yr. net operating income after deducting 2.5% for selling expenses

Tenant Turnover

Approximately 35% of the space in the building (occupied by three major corporations) is assumed to be re-leased to the existing tenants. An additional 50% of the building is assumed to be re-leased to existing tenants, and 15% is assumed to be leased to new tenants. These assumptions are consistent with those revealed in the comparable sales data, given the character of the property and its tenancy.

New Lease Terms

Upon expiration of the existing leases and any renewal options, all space is assumed to be re-leased for successive 10-year terms. In this market, 10-year leases are prevalent for such space.

Market Rental Rates

The market rental rates applied to leasing activity are

| Office space: | For the year beginning January 1, 1982, an average of $18 per square foot; market rate assumed to grow 10% per year for two years and 8% thereafter. |
| Retail space: | For the year beginning January 1, 1982, an average of $25 per square foot; market rate assumed to grow 8% per year. |

The office rental rate assumptions are supported by an analysis of actual leases of office space in competitive buildings. Conversation with local rental agents, building managers, and owners reveals that (1) vacant space is rapidly renting due to the shortage of available space; (2) rent levels are rising quickly; and (3) large blocks of contiguous space are almost nonexistent. Growth rate assumptions are based on an analysis of the assumptions made by buyers of all but one of the comparable sales (see Table 15.5).

Vacancy and Collection Loss

Space being leased to new tenants (15%) is assumed to remain vacant for an average of four months. The balance of space (85% re-leased to

Table 15.5   Analysis of Growth Ratio Assumptions
Derived from Office Building Sales

| | | Market Rent Growth Rates | | | | | Expense Growth Rates | | |
| | | 1st Period | | 2nd Period | | | | | Real Estate |
Sale No.	Date	%	No. of Years	%	No. of Years	Thereafter	Variable Operating	Electric	Taxes and Insurance
1	9/81	8.0	—	—	—	8.0%	10.0%	12.0%	6.0%
2	9/81	10.0	—	—	—	10.0	10.0	10.0	10.0
3	6/81	10.0	2	—	—	8.0	8.0	8.0	10.0
4	7/80	10.0	3	—	—	7.0	9.0	11.0	5.0
5	3/81	12.0	2	9.0	2	6.0	8.0	8.0	5.0
6	3/81	12.0	2	9.0	2	6.0	8.0	8.0	5.0
7	4/80	7.0	—	—	—	7.0	9.0	10.0	5.0
8	4/80	7.0	—	—	—	7.0	9.0	10.0	5.0
9	7/80	6.0	—	—	—	6.0	10.0	10.0	6.0
10	10/80	12.0	3	10.0	3	7.0	8.0	10.0	5.0
11	8/81	10.0	2	8.0	2	6.0	8.0	8.0	7.0

existing tenants) is assumed to suffer no vacancy. The rent loss associated with these vacancies is reflected by not accruing contract rent or escalation income for the space for a four-month period beginning at expiration of each lease. Furthermore, an additional allowance for the underlying level of vacancy and collection loss inherent in any multi-tenanted office building is provided at 0.5% of total gross revenue.

Real Estate Taxes and Insurance
Real estate taxes and insurance are estimated at $998,000, or $1.03 per square foot of rentable area, for the year ending December 1982. The combined real estate tax and insurance expense is assumed to grow at 25% for 1983 and at 5% per year thereafter. The 25% increase for 1983, which relates primarily to the real estate taxes, is based on a recently announced reassessment that resulted from a recent sale of the property.

Management
Management fees are estimated to be $75,000 for 1982 and to grow at 8% per year thereafter. Although the building is large, the small number of tenants and the significant leasing activity scheduled for the near term are an adequate inducement to attract competent management at this rate.

Leasing Fees
Leasing fees are estimated by applying a weighted-average leasing commission rate of 17.15% of the first year's base rent to all re-leasing ac-

tivities. This reflects 35% of space being re-leased to the three major corporations at a commission rate of 14% of first year's contract rent, 50% of space re-leased to existing tenants at a commission rate of 14% of first year's contract rent, and 15% of space leased to new tenants at a commission rate of 35% of the first year's contract rent. Commissions are assumed to be paid in full upon occupancy and are deducted from income. This commission schedule is consistent with the typical rates of local real estate brokers.

Variable Operating Expenses

Variable operating expenses (excluding leasing fees and management, which are treated separately in this case) are estimated to be $2,161,000 in 1982, or $2.23 per square foot of rentable area (see Table 15.6). The expense estimates are supported by an analysis of recent actual operating histories of competitive buildings. The HVAC estimate decreased from 1982 to 1983 to reflect the savings of converting from steam to oil. Expenses for energy-related items are estimated to grow at 10% per year, and other expenses are estimated to grow at 8% per year. The growth rate assumptions are based on the expense growth rate assumptions indicated by the comparable sales. Expenses for tenant electricity and cleaning of tenant space are omitted from the operating expense estimate because existing tenants pay their own cleaning and electricity. This is not unusual in this type of back office space. The

Table 15.6   Estimate of Variable Operating Expenses for Subject Property[a]

	1981 Budget	1982 Estimate
HVAC	$ 500,000	$ 400,000[b]
Payroll	154,000	175,000
Repairs and maintenance	385,000	440,000
Building electricity	600,000	660,000
Security	175,000	200,000
Cleaning (public areas)	25,000	30,000
Garbage collection	5,000	6,000
Administrative and general	185,000	200,000
Water and sewer	44,000	50,000
Total	$2,073,000	$2,161,000
Total per rentable sq. ft.	$2.14	$2.23

[a]Excluding management expenses and leasing fees, which are estimated separately.
[b]Reflects conversion to oil heat for part of the year.

market rent estimate of $18 per square foot assumes that future tenants will continue this practice.

Replacement Allowance (Interior Improvements to Tenant Space)
All space being re-leased to existing tenants or leased to new tenants until 1987 is assumed to be leased on an "as-is" basis, with any space preparation costs at the tenant's expense. This practice is common in a tight office market, particularly for long-term bulk space users. Beginning in 1987, interior space preparation costs are assumed to be necessary and absorbed by the owner. The cost per square foot is calculated by applying an 8% annual growth rate to a 1987 cost estimate of $7 per square foot. No space preparation cost is charged for the retail space.

Mortgage Debt Service
One existing mortgage is included in the forecast. The principal amount at the beginning of the forecast is $28,500,000; the interest rate is 12%; and annual debt service is $3,654,475 based on monthly payments. The loan is self-amortizing over a remaining term of 23 years.

Reversion
The resale price is forecast by applying a 10% overall capitalization rate to the net operating income in the last year of the projection period. Sales expenses of 2.5% are deducted to arrive at net resale price. The balance of the mortgage is deducted to derive the owner's net sale proceeds, or equity reversion.

There are several alternative ways of estimating a resale price, including the application of a market-derived capitalization rate to the appropriate income in the last year of the forecast or the year following the end of the forecast.

Forecast Results

The mathematical calculations based on the assumptions result in the forecast shown in Table 15.7. The appraiser then converts the future benefits into value using the appropriate capitalization procedure.

This example demonstrates one way of forecasting future benefits and is not intended to represent the only accepted forecasting procedure. Rent levels, growth rates, expense levels, and all other economic and financial information are particular to the specific property and real estate market used in the example. In market value appraising, forecasting of future benefits should be based on market-derived information. In investment value assignments, the appraiser has more latitude to reflect market interpretations and specific investor preferences.

	1982	1983	1984	1985	1986	1987	1988	1989	1990	1991
Income										
Contract and market rents[a]	$8,149,802	$8,149,802	$9,459,569	$13,310,714	$16,043,837	$16,879,699	$17,352,971	$18,350,177	$20,513,347	$21,359,450
Escalation income	0	283,867	360,523	528,617	625,906	772,808	1,074,136	1,455,791	1,816,841	2,061,857
Vacancy and collection loss	−40,749	−42,168	−49,100	−69,197	−83,349	−88,263	−92,136	−99,030	−111,651	−117,107
Effective gross income	$8,109,053	$8,391,500	$9,770,991	$13,770,135	$16,586,394	$17,564,244	$18,334,971	$19,706,938	$22,218,537	$23,304,200
Operating expenses										
Fixed expenses										
Real estate taxes and insurance	$ 998,000	$1,247,500	$1,309,875	$ 1,375,369	$ 1,444,137	$ 1,516,344	$ 1,592,161	$ 1,671,769	$ 1,755,358	$ 1,843,126
Variable expenses										
HVAC	$ 400,000	$ 400,000	$ 440,000	$ 484,000	$ 532,400	$ 585,640	$ 644,204	$ 708,624	$ 779,487	$ 857,436
Payroll	175,000	189,000	204,120	220,450	238,086	257,132	277,703	299,919	323,913	349,826
Repair and maintenance	440,000	475,200	513,216	554,273	598,615	646,504	698,225	754,083	814,409	879,562
Electricity	660,000	726,000	798,600	878,460	966,306	1,062,937	1,169,230	1,286,153	1,414,769	1,556,245
Security	200,000	216,000	233,280	251,000	272,098	293,866	317,375	342,765	370,186	399,801
Cleaning	30,000	32,400	34,992	37,791	40,815	44,080	47,606	51,415	55,528	59,970
Garbage	6,000	6,480	6,998	7,558	8,163	8,816	9,521	10,283	11,106	11,994
Administrative and general	200,000	216,000	233,280	251,942	272,098	293,866	317,375	342,765	370,186	399,801
Water and sewer	50,000	54,000	58,320	62,986	68,024	73,466	79,344	85,691	92,547	99,950
Management	75,000	81,000	87,480	94,478	102,037	110,200	119,016	128,537	138,820	149,925
Leasing fees	0	0	1,010,580	716,834	223,514	106,953	40,299	252,348	660,461	0
Replacement Allowance	0	100,000	108,000	116,640	125,971	136,049	40,299	252,348	660,461	0
Total operating expenses	$3,234,000	$3,743,580	$5,038,741	$ 5,052,723	$ 4,892,264	$−5,135,853	$−5,458,992	$−6,093,039	$−6,958,152	$−6,792,729
Net operating income	$4,875,053	$4,647,920	$4,732,250	$ 8,717,412	$ 11,694,130	$ 12,428,391	$ 12,875,979	$ 13,613,899	$ 15,260,385	$ 16,511,471
Mortgage debt service	−3,654,475	−3,654,475	−3,654,475	−3,654,475	−3,654,475	−3,654,475	−3,654,475	−3,654,475	−3,654,475	−3,654,475
Equity dividend	$1,220,578	$ 993,445	$1,077,775	$ 5,062,937	$ 8,039,655	$ 8,773,916	$ 9,221,504	$ 9,959,424	$ 11,605,910	$ 12,856,996
Resale price	(Property reversion)				$165,114,710					
Less sale expenses					−4,127,868					
Net resale price					$160,986,842					
Less mortgage balance					−24,005,550					
Equity reversion					$136,931,292					

[a]Also reflects added vacancy associated with lease rollovers, as discussed earlier under vacancy and collection loss.

Summary

The valuation of income-producing property is based on an analysis of the property's earning power. Data from the subject and comparable properties concerning historical income and expenses, leases, rent rates, vacancy levels, tax assessment, insurance expenses, management budget, leasing fees, and other operating expenses are used to develop a reconstructed operating statement. The property's net operating income or net income after debt service (equity dividend) may be estimated for one year, a series of years, or over the entire holding period depending on the data available and whether direct or yield capitalization is used. As with all appraisal estimates, the income forecast should reflect the thinking and behavior of investors in the real estate market.

Income forecasting begins with lease analysis. Gross leases stipulate that the lessor pays the expenses of the property's operation; net leases provide that the lessee pays operating costs. To reduce lessor risk, new leases increasingly contain escalation or percentage rent clauses, or they may call for graduated rents, periodic reevaluation, or the indexing of rents. The rent data used in the income projection may be contract rent (including rent from escalation clauses), market rent, or a combination. The division of expenses between the lessor and the lessee is also identified in the lease.

To compare the rent rate of the subject property with the rates of comparable properties, rents must be reduced to a common unit of comparison. Data must reflect equivalent terms of lessor/lessee obligation. Conditions of rent, time, location, and physical and income characteristics must be as similar as possible, or adjustments must be made for any dissimilarities.

The valuation of fee simple interests of owner-occupied property is based on market rent. However, most income-producing properties are leased, so it is the lessor's marketable interest that is appraised. In valuing the lessor's interest, contract rent from existing leases, as well as market rent from vacant and owner-occupied space, must be considered. Future rents must also be estimated when discounted cash flow analysis is used.

The income and expense items estimated include potential gross income, vacancy and collection loss, fixed and variable operating expenses, replacement allowance, net operating income, mortgage debt service, and equity dividend. Typical operating expense ratios or net income ratios for a particular type of property provide a guide against which to judge the subject operation's performance. Although published data on operating expense ratios are available, an appraiser develops ratios that reflect the specific market.

To complete appraisal assignments using discounted cash flow analysis, the future benefits to the investor over the holding period are forecast. Estimating equity dividends follows the rationale of investors who risk capital to reap future rewards. The discounted future net operating income, or equity dividend, plus the reversion of the real property interest being appraised is capitalized to indicate the value of the investment.

Chapter 16

Direct Capitalization

Direct capitalization is a method used to convert a single year's estimate of income into a value indication in the income capitalization approach. An appraiser accomplishes this conversion in one step by either dividing the income estimate by an appropriate income rate or by multiplying the income estimate by an appropriate income factor. The income rates and factors express the relationship of income and value and are derived from market data. It is essential that the market comparables reflect risk, income, expenses, and physical and locational characteristics similar to those of the property being appraised.

In direct capitalization, a precise allocation between return on and return of capital is not made because investor assumptions or forecasts concerning the holding period, pattern of income, or changes in value of the original investment are not simulated in the method. However, a satisfactory rate of return for the investor and the return of the capital invested is implicit in the rates or factors used in direct capitalization because they are derived from similar investment properties.

Direct capitalization may be based on potential gross income, effective gross income, net operating income, equity income, mortgage income, land income, or building income. Thus, the income rates used in direct capitalization include the overall (property) capitalization rate (R_O), the mortgage capitalization rate (R_M), the equity capitalization rate (R_E), the land capitalization rate (R_L), and the building capitalization rate (R_B). The income factors include the potential gross income multiplier $(PGIM)$, the gross rent multiplier (GRM), and the effective gross income multiplier $(EGIM)$.

In addition to direct capitalization procedures based on direct application of a rate or factor to the income estimate, procedures based on physical, financial, economic, and legal residual techniques may also be used.

Derivation of Overall Capitalization Rates

Although any interest in real estate with an income stream can be valued by direct capitalization, the most common interest appraised is the fee simple estate, or all the property rights in the entire real estate. The direct capitalization formula applicable to this type of valuation is

$$\text{Value} = \frac{\text{Net operating income}}{\text{Overall capitalization rate}}$$

An appraiser can estimate an overall capitalization rate by using various techniques. The techniques the appraiser uses depend on the quantity and quality of data. The accepted techniques include (1) derivation from comparable sales, (2) derivation from effective gross income multipliers, (3) band of investment—mortgage and equity components, (4) band of investment—land and building components, and (5) the debt service coverage formula.

Derivation from Comparable Sales

This technique is preferred when sufficient data are available for transactions of similar, competitive properties. Data concerning sale price, income, expenses, financing terms, and market conditions at the time of sale must be available for each transaction. Appraisers must be confident that the net operating income from each comparable is calculated and estimated in the same way as that for the subject property and that neither nonmarket financing terms nor different market conditions have affected the transaction prices of the comparables. When these requirements are met, the appraiser estimates the overall rate by dividing each property's net operating income by its sale price. This procedure is illustrated in Table 16.1 for four comparable sales that meet the data requirements.

If all four transactions are equally reliable and comparable, the appraiser might conclude that the overall rate to apply to the subject property is in the range of .1320 to .1378. The final selection in the range would depend on the appraiser's judgment of the comparability of each sale to the subject property.

If there are differences between the comparable sale and the subject property that could affect the overall capitalization rate chosen for the subject, the appraiser must account for those differences. In such cases, the appraiser makes a judgment as to whether the rate for the subject property should be higher or lower than the rate in a specific sale. Judgment is also required in determining whether the rate chosen for the subject should fall within the range established by the sales or, in certain cases, should be above or below the range.

When using rates derived from comparable sales, an appraiser applies the overall capitalization rate to the subject property in a manner consistent with that used for rate derivation. Hence, if the market-derived capitalization rates are based on net operating income expectancy for the first year, the capitalization rate for the subject property is applied to its expected first year's net operating income.

Further, the net income to capitalize may be estimated before or after the appraiser considers the annual allowance for replacements. Again, it is essential that the appraiser analyze comparable sales and derive capitalization rates in the same manner that is used to analyze the subject property and to capitalize its income.

The following examples illustrate the importance of deriving and applying rates consistently. The replacement allowance for the property is estimated to be $2,500. In analyzing comparable sales in which a replacement allowance was not deducted as an operating expense, the indicated overall rate was .0850. Alternatively, if the replacement allowance was deducted as an operating expense, the indicated overall rate was .0825. In the first example, the allowance has not been included as an expense item to be deducted from effective gross income. Therefore, the net operating income is $2,500 more than in the second example. In each case, the valuation conclusion is identical.

Table 16.1   Estimate of Overall Capitalization Rates from Comparable Sales

	Comparables			
	A	**B**	**C**	**D**
Price	$368,500	$425,000	$310,000	$500,000
Net operating income	50,000	56,100	42,718	68,600
Indicated R_0	.1357	.1320	.1378	.1372

Before Deducting Allowance for Replacements

Net operating income $85,000
Overall rate   .0850
Capitalization: $85,000 ÷ .0850 = $1,000,000

After Deducting Allowance for Replacements

Net operating income $82,500
Overall rate   .0825
Capitalization: $82,500 ÷ .0825 = $1,000,000

When income and expenses are estimated on the same basis for the subject property and all comparables; when market expectations about resale prices, tax benefits, and holding periods are similar for all the properties; and when financing terms and market conditions that affect the comparables are similar to those affecting the subject property (or an adjustment can be made for them), this technique of estimating overall capitalization rates is preferred and will provide a reliable indication of value by the income capitalization approach.

Derivation from Effective Gross Income Multipliers

Sometimes the direct derivation of an overall capitalization rate is impossible because the stringent data requirements cannot be met; however, reliable sales transaction and *gross* income data can be obtained from several comparable sales transactions. In such cases, the effective gross income multiplier can be derived and used in conjunction with the operating expense ratio (*OER*) to derive an overall capitalization rate.[1]

The operating expense ratio is the ratio of operating expenses to effective gross income. Although effective gross income multipliers can be based on annual or monthly income, annual income is used unless otherwise specified. Monthly income is the base used primarily for small single or multifamily residential properties. Frequently, it is pos-

[1]The derivation of income multipliers is discussed later in this chapter.

sible to obtain marketwide averages of operating expense ratios as well as indicated effective gross income multipliers from several sales.

The formula for deriving an overall rate from the effective gross income multiplier and operating expense ratio is calculated as follows:

$$R_O = \frac{1 - OER}{EGIM}$$

As shown in Table 16.1, Comparable A was sold recently for $368,500. Potential gross income is $85,106, effective gross income is $80,000, and operating expenses are $30,000. Thus, the effective gross income multiplier is 4.6063 ($368,500 ÷ $80,000), and the operating expense ratio is .3750 ($30,000 ÷ $80,000). Therefore, the overall capitalization rate extracted from the effective gross income multiplier of Comparable A is

$$R_O = \frac{1 - .3750}{4.6063}$$
$$= \frac{.6250}{4.6063}$$
$$= .1357$$

This calculation would be performed for all comparables, and an estimate of the overall capitalization rate would be reconciled from the derived overall capitalization rate indications. For the effective gross income multiplier to be supportable, the same property comparability requirements that apply to the direct derivation of the overall rate must be met.

Band of Investment—Mortgage and Equity Components

Because most properties are purchased with debt and equity capital, the return on investment component of the overall capitalization rate must satisfy the market return requirements of each investment position. Lenders must anticipate receiving a competitive interest rate commensurate with the perceived risk or they will not make funds available. Similarly, equity investors must anticipate receiving a competitive equity yield commensurate with the perceived risk or they will divert their investment funds elsewhere.

The capitalization rate for debt is called the mortgage constant (R_M). It is the ratio of the annual debt service to the principal amount of the mortgage loan. If the loan is amortized (paid off) more frequently than annually (e.g., monthly), the mortgage constant is obtained by multiplying each period's payment by the frequency and then by dividing this amount by the amount of the loan. For example, the annual constant for a monthly payment loan is obtained by multiplying the monthly payment by 12 and dividing the result by the amount of the loan. Of course, the same result is obtained by multiplying the ratio of monthly payments to mortgage amount (monthly constant) by 12.

The mortgage constant is a function of the interest rate, the frequency of amortization, and the term of the loan. It is the sum of the interest rate and sinking fund factor and, given the loan terms, can be found in financial tables.[2] Care must be taken to use a table that corresponds to the frequency of amortization (e.g., monthly, quarterly, annually, and the like).

The equity investor also seeks a return *on* and *of* the equity investment. The rate used to capitalize equity income is called the equity dividend rate (R_E). The equity dividend rate is the ratio of equity dividend to the amount of equity. For appraisal purposes, the equity capitalization rate for the subject property is the anticipated return to the investor usually for the first year of the holding period.

The overall rate must satisfy both the mortgage constant requirement of the lender(s) and the equity dividend requirement of the equity investor. It is a composite rate, weighted by the proportions of total property investment represented by the debt and the equity. The loan-to-value ratio (M) represents the loan or debt portion of the property investment; the equity ratio is indicated by $(1 - M)$. Mortgage terms and conditions may be derived by surveying active lenders in the market area. Equity dividend rates are derived from comparable sales by dividing the equity dividend by the equity investment. The final conclusion of an appropriate equity dividend rate for use in capitalizing equity income depends on the appraiser's judgment.

The band of investment or weighted average formula for deriving an overall rate when the mortgage constant and equity dividend rates are known is

$$R_O = M \times R_M + (1 - M) \times R_E$$

To illustrate the calculation of the overall rate by this band of

[2]See Appendix C.

investment technique, assume that the following characteristics are appropriate for the subject property:

Available loan   75% ratio, 13.5% interest, 25-year amortization period, .1399 constant (R_M)

Equity dividend rate   12.0% (derived from comparable sales)

Therefore, the overall rate would be calculated as follows:

$$R_O = (.75 \times .1399) + (1 - .75)(.1200)$$
$$= (.75 \times .1399) + (.25 \times .1200)$$
$$= .1049 + .0300$$
$$= .1349$$

Although this technique is used frequently to derive an overall capitalization rate, an appraiser should be careful when using it for this purpose. This technique is particularly useful in real estate markets where sufficient market data are available and where it can be demonstrated that the equity dividend rate is the primary investment criteria used by buyers and sellers. A capitalization rate for estimating market value should be justified and supported by market data. Such data are often not available for deriving information for mortgage-equity analysis. Rather, survey and opinion data about equity dividend rates, available loan terms, and loan-to-value ratios are often substituted for market-derived data. When survey and opinion data or any other data that are not derived from market transactions are used, mortgage-equity techniques are more appropriately used to test market-derived capitalization rates.

Band of Investment—Land and Building Components

A band of investment formula can also be applied to the physical components of a property—land or site and buildings. Just as weighted rates are developed for mortgage and equity in mortgage-equity analysis, weighted rates for land and buildings can be developed if the rates for these components can be estimated independently with confidence, and the proportion of total property value that each component represents can be identified. The formula is

$$R_O = L \times R_L + B \times R_B$$

where L = land percentage of total property value; R_L = land capitalization rate; B = building percentage of total property value; and R_B = building capitalization rate.

Assume that the land represents 45% of the property and the building represents 55%. Land and building capitalization rates derived from comparable sales data are R_L = .1025, and R_B = .1600. Therefore, the indicated R_O is calculated as follows:

$$R_O = (.45 \times .1025) + (.55 \times .1600)$$
$$= .0461 + .0880$$
$$= .1341$$

Debt Service Coverage Formula

In addition to the traditional terms of lending (interest rate, loan-to-value ratio, amortization term, maturity, and payment period), real estate lenders have used another constraining factor, the debt service coverage ratio (DCR). This is the ratio of net operating income to annual debt service.

This measure of constraint is used particularly by institutional lenders, who generally are fiduciaries. They handle and lend the money of others, including depositors and policyholders. Because of their fiduciary position, institutional lenders are particularly sensitive to the safety of loan investments, especially that of principal. For safety and profit reasons, they are anxious to avoid default and possible foreclosure. Accordingly, in underwriting income property loans, institutional lenders attempt to provide a "cushion," which, in the event of a decline in building income, will enable the borrower to meet the debt service obligations on the loan.

One procedure by which the debt service coverage ratio can be used to estimate the overall rate is by multiplying the debt service coverage ratio by the mortgage constant and the loan-to-value ratio.[3] Thus, the formula is

$$R_O = DCR \times R_M \times M$$

Assume that net operating income is $50,000 and the annual debt service is $43,264. This gives a debt service coverage ratio of 1.1557.

$$DCR = \frac{\$50,000}{\$43,264}$$
$$= 1.1557$$

[3]See Ronald E. Gettel, "Good Grief, Another Method of Selecting Capitalization Rates," *The Appraisal Journal*, January 1978.

Moreover, the R_M equals .1565, and M is .75. Thus, R_O is estimated as

$$R_O = 1.1557 \times .1565 \times .75$$
$$= .1357$$

Residual Techniques

Residual techniques allow for the capitalization of income allocated to an investment component of unknown value after all investment components with known values have been satisfied. The physical (land and building) residual techniques and the financial (mortgage and equity) residual techniques are the primary residual techniques used in direct capitalization.

Regardless of which known and residual (unknown) components of the property are being analyzed, the appraiser starts with the value of the known item(s) and the net operating income. Then the appraiser

1. Applies the appropriate capitalization rate to the value of the known component to derive the annual income necessary to support the investment in that component

2. Deducts the annual income necessary to support the investment in the known component from the net operating income to derive the residual income available to support the investment in the unknown, or residual, component

3. Capitalizes the residual income at the capitalization rate appropriate to the investment in the residual component to derive the present value of the residual component

4. Adds the values of the known component and the residual component to derive a value indication for the entire property

Building Residual Technique

When using this technique, an appraiser assumes that land or site value can be estimated independently. Starting with the known land value, the appraiser applies the land capitalization rate to the land value to obtain the amount of annual net income necessary to support land value. The appraiser then deducts this amount from the net operating income to derive the residual income available to support the investment in the building(s). The appraiser capitalizes this residual income at the building capitalization rate to derive an indication of the building(s)'s present value. Finally, the appraiser adds the land value to the building value to derive an indication of property value. The appraiser applies the land and building capitalization rates derived from the market to the subject property as shown below.

Estimated land value		$200,000
Net operating income	$85,500	
Land value $\times R_L$ ($200,000 $\times$ .09)	$-18,000$	
Residual income to building	$67,500	
Building value (capitalization: $67,500 $\div$ .15)		$+450,000$
Indicated property value		$650,000

The building residual technique requires information about present land value, current net operating income, and the land and building capitalization rates. If such information is unavailable or not reliably supported, the technique should not be employed.

When the required information is available, the building residual technique can help an appraiser value improved properties when the improvements have suffered substantial accrued depreciation. Indeed, the current reproduction or replacement cost less the present value of the improvements provides an estimate of total accrued depreciation. In addition, by directly measuring the contribution of the improvements to total property value, the building residual technique can help an appraiser determine when demolition or major renovation is economically feasible.

Land Residual Technique

This technique assumes that the value of the building can be estimated separately. When the land residual technique is used, building value is usually the current cost to construct a new building that represents the highest and best use of the land or site. An appraiser applies the building capitalization rate to the building value to obtain the amount of annual net income necessary to support the value of the building. This amount is then deducted from net operating income, indicating the residual income available to support the investment in the land. The residual income is capitalized at the land capitalization rate to derive an indication of the value of the land. Then building value is added to the land value to derive an indication of the total property value. As in the building residual technique, the land and building capitalization rates derived from the market are applied to the subject property as shown below.

Estimated building value		$450,000
Net operating income	$85,500	
Building value $\times R_B$ ($450,000 $\times$ .15)	−67,500	
Residual income to land	$18,000	
Land value (capitalization: $18,000 $\div$ .09)		+200,000
Indicated property value		$650,000

The land residual technique helps an appraiser estimate land values when recent land sales data are unavailable. The technique can be applied to both proposed construction (to test the highest and best use of the land or site) or to new structures that do not suffer from accrued depreciation. However, it is not applicable when the cost to produce a new building is inconsistent with the market contribution of such a new building to property value. The building cannot suffer from physical deterioration or functional or external obsolescence.

Equity Residual Technique

In using this technique, an appraiser deducts annual debt service from net operating income to obtain the residual income for the equity interest. The appraiser assumes that mortgage loan terms can be obtained from the market and that the dollar amount of the debt can be estimated. The residual equity income is then capitalized into value using a market-derived equity capitalization rate as shown below. This

Mortgage amount		$375,000
R_M	12.0%	
Mortgage term (for amortization)	25 yrs.	
Net operating income	$60,000	
Mortgage $\times R_M$ ($375,000 $\times$ .12639)	−47,400	
Residual income to equity	$12,600	
Equity value (capitalization: $12,600 $\div$ .09)		+140,000
Indicated property value		$515,000

technique is especially useful in appraising the fee simple interest in a newly constructed property or the equity interest in a property subject to a specific mortgage.

Mortgage Residual Technique

In this technique, the available equity amount is the known component, and the mortgage amount or value is unknown. The income necessary to satisfy the equity component at the equity capitalization rate is deducted from net operating income to obtain the residual income for the mortgage component. The residual mortgage income is then capitalized into value at the mortgage capitalization rate as shown below.

Available equity		$140,000
Net operating income	$60,000	
Equity $\times R_E$ ($140,000 $\times$ .09)	$-12,600$	
Residual income to mortgage	$47,400	
Mortgage value (capitalization: $47,400 $\div$ .1264)		$+375,000$
Indicated property value		$515,000

Gross Income Multipliers

Gross income multipliers are used to compare the income characteristics of properties in the sales comparison approach. Nevertheless, converting a potential or effective gross income stream into a lump-sum capital value through the application of a gross income multiplier is also capitalization. Thus, the derivation and use of multipliers are discussed in direct capitalization.

For a gross income multiplier to be derived from market data, there must be sales of properties that are rented at the time of sale or are anticipated to be rented within a short time. The ratio of sale price to annual gross income *at the time of sale* or projected over the first year of ownership is the gross income multiplier.

In attempting to derive and apply gross income multipliers for valuation purposes, an appraiser must be careful for several reasons. First, the properties must be comparable with both the subject property and one another in physical, locational, and investment characteristics. Properties with similar or even identical multipliers may have very different operating expense ratios, and thus may not be effectively comparable for valuation purposes.

Second, the term *gross income multiplier* is sometimes used because a part of the gross income from a property (or type of property) comes from nonrental sources. The *gross rent multiplier* applies to rental income only.

Third, an appraiser must use similar income data in deriving the multiplier for each transaction. Sale price can be divided by either potential gross income or effective gross income. The data and measure must be consistent throughout any given analysis; otherwise the results will be inconsistent. Different income measures may be used in different valuation studies and appraisals, however. The choice of the appropriate measure is dictated by the availability of market data and the purpose of the analysis.

To illustrate the difference between different gross income multipliers, Comparable A in Table 16.1 is used to derive the following data.

Potential gross income:

$$\text{Potential gross income multiplier} = \frac{\text{sale price}}{\text{potential gross income}}$$

$$= \frac{\$368,500}{\$\ 85,106} = 4.3299^{a}$$

Effective gross income:

$$\text{Effective gross income multiplier} = \frac{\text{sale price}}{\text{effective gross income}}$$

$$= \frac{\$368,500}{\$\ 80,000} = 4.6063^{a}$$

[a]In practice, multipliers are typically rounded to two decimal places (e.g., 4.33 and 4.61).

After the gross income multiplier is derived from comparable market transaction data, it must be applied to the *same* base from which it was derived. In other words, an income multiplier based on effective gross income must be applied to only the effective gross income of the subject property; an income multiplier based on potential gross income must be applied only to the potential gross income of the subject property. It is also essential that the timing of income to which the multiplier is applied be comparable. If sales are analyzed by using the next year's income expectation, the derived multiplier must be applied to the subject property's next year's income expectation.

Summary

Direct capitalization converts one year's income into a value indication either by dividing the income by an income rate or multiplying it by an income factor derived from the market. A number of income rates can be applied: the overall capitalization rate, the mortgage capitalization rate, the equity capitalization rate, the land capitalization rate, or the building capitalization rate. Factors for capitalizing income into value include the potential gross income multiplier, the gross rent multiplier, and the effective gross income multiplier.

The return on and of capital is implicit in this method because the rates and multipliers are derived from comparable sales. The direct capitalization method can also be applied with physical and financial residual techniques.

A variety of techniques can be employed to derive the overall capitalization rate to apply in the valuation of a fee simple estate. Rates can be derived from comparable sales or effective gross income multipliers; calculated with band-of-investment techniques applied to land and building components or to mortgage and equity components; or computed using the debt service coverage ratio.

Derivation from comparable sales is the preferred technique, but its application requires highly comparable data. Derivation from gross income multipliers and operating expense ratios is also reliable and uses gross income data, which often are more available. The band-of-investment technique applied to mortgage and equity components uses the mortgage constant, the ratio of annual debt service to the total amount of the loan, and the equity dividend rate, the ratio of equity dividend to the total equity. The band-of-investment technique uses a weighted average formula that calculates the overall rate when the mortgage constant and the equity dividend rate are known. Another band-of-investment technique can be applied to the investment's physical components—the land and building(s). The debt service coverage factor is used by institutional lenders acting as fiduciaries who are sensitive to the safety of capital. The overall capitalization rate is calculated by multiplying the debt service coverage ratio by the mortgage constant and the loan-to-value ratio.

Residual techniques capitalize income to one property component when other income values are known. Residual techniques are applied to physical (land and buildings) and financial (debt and equity) property components. Both the building residual technique and the land residual technique are based on the assumption that land and buildings can be valued separately and, if one value is known, the other can be estimated. Ultimately, a value indication is reached by capitalizing the incomes of each component. The building residual technique is most applicable to buildings that have suffered substantial accrued depreciation; the land residual technique is helpful in estimating land value when comparable data are available, and can also be used to value proposed or new construction that has no depreciation. In the equity residual technique and the mortgage residual technique, an appraiser calculates the property value using the capitalized incomes of each component. The equity residual technique is especially useful in valuing new property or property interests subject to a set mortgage.

Gross income multipliers are used to compare the income characteristics of properties in the sales comparison approach. They are capitalization tools that convert potential or effective gross income into value. To derive multipliers from the market, highly comparable property rental data must be available. Gross income multipliers must be used cautiously. It is essential that the properties used as comparables be similar to the subject in terms of physical, locational, and investment characteristics.

Chapter 17
Yield Capitalization

Yield capitalization is the method an appraiser uses to convert future benefits to present value by applying an appropriate yield rate. For market value appraisals, the appropriate yield rate is selected by analyzing market evidence pertaining to the yield anticipated by typical investors. When investment value is sought, the yield rate used reflects an individual investor's requirements, which may differ from requirements typical in the market. In yield capitalization, an appraiser (1) selects a holding period, (2) identifies all future cash flows or patterns and relationships between present and future cash flows, (3) selects the appropriate yield (discount) rate, and (4) converts the future benefits to value by discounting each annual future benefit or by developing an overall rate that reflects the income pattern, value change, and the yield rate. Yield capitalization procedures consist of the application of capitalization rates that reflect an appropriate yield rate, the use of present value factors, and discounted cash flow analysis. Mortgage-equity formulas and yield rate/value change formulas may be used to derive overall capitalization rates. As in direct capitalization, residual techniques also may be used.

Discounted Cash Flow Analysis

Discounted cash flow (DCF) analysis specifies the quantity, variability, timing, and duration of cash flows.[1] First, each cash flow is discounted to present value, and then all present values are totaled to obtain the total value of the income to the real property interest being appraised. The future value of that interest, which is forecast at the end of the projection period (holding period or remaining economic life) is also discounted as a cash flow. The cash flows that are discounted by means of a DCF formula may be net operating income for the entire property or the flows to specific interests, such as equity dividend or after-tax cash flow for the equity interest and debt service for the mortgage interest.

The DCF formula is a yield formula. It is expressed as

$$PV = \frac{CF_1}{(1 + Y)^1} + \frac{CF_2}{(1 + Y)^2} + \frac{CF_3}{(1 + Y)^3} + \cdots + \frac{CF_n}{(1 + Y)^n}$$

where

PV = present value
CF = the cash flow for the period specified
Y = the appropriate yield, or discount, rate
n = the number of periods in the projection

The DCF formula allows an appraiser to discount each payment of income separately and to add all present values to obtain the present value of the property interest being appraised. The formula treats the reversion as a cash flow that can be valued separately from the income stream. The formula can be used to estimate total property value (V_O), loan value (V_M), equity value (V_E), leased fee value (V_{LF}), leasehold value (V_{LH}), or any other interest in real property by calculating the cash flows to the interest being appraised.

When a series of periodic incomes varies irregularly, the basic discounted cash flow formula is used in its analysis and valuation. However, any series of periodic incomes, with or without a reversion, can be valued by this basic formula. Formulas for valuing various patterns (such as level annuities, increasing and decreasing annuities, deferred annuities, and step-up or step-down annuities) are merely shortcuts for use in those special situations.

---

[1]The terms *cash flow* and *income flow* are commonly used synonymously. In this chapter, *cash flow* is the term used to refer to the periodic income attributable to the interests in real property.

Selection of the Yield Rate Used to Discount

The selection of the yield rate is critical in discounted cash flow analysis. Rate selection requires that an appraiser verify and interpret the attitude and expectations of market participants (buyers, sellers, advisers, and brokers, among others). Although *actual* yield on an investment cannot be calculated until the investment is sold, an investor may consider a target yield for the investment prior to or during ownership. Historical yield rates derived from comparable sales are noteworthy but, because they reflect past, not future, benefits in the mind of the investor, they are not reliable current yield indicators. Therefore, in selecting yield rates at which cash flows are to be discounted, the appraiser should emphasize the prospective or forecast yield rates anticipated by typical buyers and sellers. This can be done directly, by verifying the assumptions with parties to comparable sales transactions, or indirectly, by estimating income expectancy and likely reversion for a comparable property to derive a prospective yield rate.

By comparing the physical, economic, and financial characteristics of the comparable properties and the property being appraised, the appraiser attempts to narrow the range of indicated yield rates to select an appropriate rate. In certain situations, there are reasons to select a yield rate above or below the range. The final selection of a yield rate involves judgment by the appraiser. This is analogous to the judgment used in the selection of an overall rate or equity dividend rate from a range indicated by comparable sales. The appraiser's challenge in selecting the yield rate is to stay current and to reflect the actions and perceptions of real estate investors.

Different Rates

Yield rates are partly a function of perceived risks. Different portions of forecast future income may have different levels of risk. Thus, they can have different yield rates. For example, in lease valuation, one rate may be used to discount the series of net rental incomes under a lease, and a different rate may be used to discount the reversion. One rate reflects the benefits, constraints, and limits of a contract, while the other is subject to free, open-market conditions. An appraiser's decision to use a single yield rate to apply to all benefits, or different rates to apply to different benefits, should be based on investors' actions in the market.

Compounding and Discounting

An appraiser converts periodic income and reversions into present value by the general procedure called *discounting*, which is based on the assumption that benefits received in the future are worth less than the same benefits received in the present. The device that compensates all types of investors for foregoing present benefits (immediate use of capital) in favor of accepting future benefits is the payment of *a return on the investment*. This payment is also called *interest* (usually for lenders) and *yield* (usually for equity investors). An inherent assumption in the discounting procedure is that the return of capital will be accomplished through the periodic income, the reversion, or a combination of both.

Problems involving the valuation of investments that offer profit in the form of periodic interest or yield generally belong to either of two broad classifications:

1. The future value of money at interest—the amount to which deposits of money will grow in a given length of time when invested or deposited at a given rate of interest

2. The present value of future receipts—the present value of money to be received at a specific future time when discounted from that time to the present at a given rate of interest

The amount deposited or received can be in the form of a single lump sum or a series of periodic installments, such as rent. Often, there is a combination of both.

When amounts are compounded or discounted, the rate used is the *effective interest rate* which, on an annual basis, is identical to the *nominal interest rate*. When amounts are compounded or discounted less often than annually (e.g., semiannually or monthly), the effective interest rate is derived by dividing the nominal interest rate by the number of compounding or discounting periods. For example, a nominal rate of 12% is a 6% effective rate for semiannual conversion periods, or a 1% effective rate for monthly conversions. The use of standard tables of factors or preprogrammed financial calculators facilitates the application of factors, but the user is cautioned to select the appropriate conversion frequency (monthly, quarterly, or annually).

Implicit in each precomputed factor and yield capitalization formula are specific built-in investment assumptions that are automatically effected when the table is employed or the factor is calculated. Therefore, an appraiser first identifies the assumptions applicable to the subject property and then uses the factor table and capitalization formula that correspond to the assumptions. Thus, an appraiser's starting point when compounding or discounting is learning the basic formulas, how the various factors relate to one another, and how they may be used or combined to simplify income capitalization.[2]

The tables and factors provide means for solving many arithmetic

[2]See Appendix C for a discussion of financial tables.

problems that are fundamental in the valuation process, thus aiding the appraiser in applying capitalization techniques. However, in the final analysis, a value estimate reflects appraisal judgment based on appropriate research and market-developed data. Mathematical tables and formulas provide the appraiser with the tools necessary to help develop a sound value estimate.

Income Stream Patterns

After an appraiser has specified the amount, timing, and duration of the cash flows to the property interest being appraised, he or she specifies the income stream pattern that is expected to occur during the projection period. These patterns may be grouped into three basic categories. They are variable annuity, level annuity, and increasing or decreasing annuity, with subcategories under the latter two categories.

Variable Annuity: Nonsystematic Change

A variable annuity is a determinable income stream in which amounts vary per period. To value a variable annuity, an appraiser calculates the value of each income payment separately and totals all present values to obtain the present value of the entire income stream. This procedure is discounted cash flow analysis.

Any income stream can be valued as if it were a variable annuity. Level and systematically changing annuities are special cases that can be handled by special formulas that reflect the systematic pattern of the income stream. These formulas are shortcuts, which save time and effort in certain cases. However, using a hand-held calculator to value an income stream as a variable annuity may be just as quick and simple as using a shortcut formula.

Level Annuity

A level annuity is an income stream in which the amount of each payment is the same as the amount of every other payment; it is a level, unchanging flow over time. In addition, the payments are equally spaced; there are no irregularities in timing. There are two types of level annuities. They are ordinary annuity and annuity payable in advance.

Ordinary Annuity
An ordinary annuity is probably the most common type of level annuity. Its distinguishing feature is that the income payments are received at the *end* of each period. Instruments that fit the pattern of the ordi-

nary annuity are standard fixed-payment mortgage loans, many corporate and government bonds, endowment policies, and certain lease arrangements.

Annuity Payable in Advance

An annuity payable in advance is similar to an ordinary annuity except that the payments are received at the *beginning* of each period. A lease that requires payments at the beginning of each month fits the pattern of the annuity payable in advance.

Increasing or Decreasing Annuity

An income stream that is expected to change in a systematic pattern is either an increasing or a decreasing annuity. There are three basic patterns of systematic change. They are step-up and step-down annuities, constant dollar change per period, and constant ratio change per period.

Step-Up and Step-Down Annuities

A step-up or step-down annuity is usually created by a lease contract that calls for a succession of level annuities at different levels over different portions of a lease term. For example, a lease might require monthly payments of $500 for the first three years, $750 for the next four years, and $1,200 for the next six years. Over the 13-year term of the lease, there would be three different level annuities—for three years, four years, and six years in succession.

Constant Dollar Change per Period

An income stream that increases or decreases by a fixed dollar amount each period fits this pattern. Such income streams are also called straight-line increasing or decreasing annuities. For example, a property estimated to have a first-year net operating income of $100,000 is forecast to increase $7,000 per year. Thus, the second year's net operating income would be $107,000, the third year's net operating income would be $114,000, and so forth. Similarly, a straight-line decreasing annuity means that the income stream is expected to decrease by a constant dollar amount each period.

Constant Ratio Change per Period

Also referred to as an exponential annuity, this type of income stream either increases or decreases at a constant ratio, and as a result, the

increases or decreases are compounded. For example, a property estimated to have first-year equity dividend income of $100,000, which is
forecast to increase 7% per year over each preceding year's equity dividend income, would have an equity dividend income for the second
year of $107,000 ($100,000 × 1.07). However, the third year's equity
dividend income would be $114,490 ($107,000 × 1.07). The fourth
year's equity dividend income would be $122,504 ($114,490 × 1.07).

Reversion

As noted previously, income-producing properties typically provide
two types of financial benefits. They are periodic income and the future value obtained from sale of property at the end of the holding
period. This future cash flow is called a reversion because it is identified with return of capital upon conclusion of the investment. For any

**Table 17.1   Summary of Incomes and Reversions Associated
with Various Real Property Interests in an Income-Producing
Property**

Real Property Interest	Income	Reversion
Property: fee simple	Net operating income	Proceeds of resale
Lender (mortgagee)	Mortgage debt service	Balance if paid prior to maturity
Equity	Equity dividend	Equity proceeds of resale
Leased fee	Net operating income based on contract rent	Property reversion or proceeds of resale of leased fee position
Leasehold	Rental advantage when contract rent is below market rent	None if held to end of lease or proceeds of resale of leasehold position

Note: Incomes and reversions may be calculated before or after income taxes.

single property, there can be one or several property interests that have their own streams of periodic benefits and reversions. For example, a property may have an equity interest with equity dividend as the periodic benefit and the equity reversion (property reversion less mortgage balance at loan maturity or property resale) as the reversionary benefit. The same property would have a mortgage with debt service as the periodic benefit and the mortgage balance as the reversionary interest. Table 17.1 summarizes the possible investment positions in an income-producing property and shows the income streams and reversions associated with each interest.

The reversion is often a major portion of the total benefits to be received from an income-producing property. If the investor's capital is not returned, the effective rate of return *on* investment will usually be negative. For certain investments, *all* capital recapture will occur through the reversion, although for other investment properties, part of the recapture will be provided by the reversion and part will be provided by the income stream.

In judging the portion of the return of the investment to be provided by the reversion, an appraiser should realize that there are three general situations that may occur relative to the original investment. First, the property may increase in value over the holding period. Second, the property may not change in value. That is, the value of the property at the end of the holding period or remaining economic life may be equal to the value of the property at the beginning of the period. Third, the value of the property may decline over the period being analyzed. Therefore, because these possibilities affect potential yield and acceptable amounts of income, the appraiser must judge the change, if any, there will be in the original investment or property value over the holding period. For example, is the property expected to increase in value by 10%, or decline by 20%?

When a property is expected to be sold, an appraiser projects the reversion to the property, that is, the proceeds of resale. The term *proceeds of resale* means the net difference between transaction price and selling expenses. Typical selling expenses include brokerage commissions, legal fees, fix-up costs, and possibly penalties for prepayment of debt.

An appraiser's judgment of the likely value of the reversion is guided by the expectations of investors in the market for the type of property being appraised. The relevant questions for an appraiser are, Do investors expect a change in the values of the type of property being appraised in the given locale? By how much? In which direction? The appraiser thus analyzes and interprets the market and bases a judgment of the value of the future reversion on the amount or percentage of reversion that investors expect.

Mortgages

Debt secured with real estate as collateral is frequently used in the purchase and ownership of real properties. Certain mortgage information—both in dollar amounts and as rates or factors, depending on the data that are available—can assist an appraiser in the valuation of income-producing properties. Such information includes the monthly or periodic payments and annual debt service on a level-payment, fully amortized loan, together with their accompanying partial payment factors and annual constants (R_M). This information also includes the balance outstanding (B) on any amortized loan at any time prior to full amortization, whether as a dollar amount or as a percentage of the original loan amount. In addition, the percentage or proportion of any principal amount paid off prior to full amortization (P) needs to be calculated, especially for use in mortgage-equity/Ellwood analysis.

Periodic (Monthly) Payment

The monthly payment factor for a fully amortized, monthly payment loan with equal payments is the direct reduction loan factor (monthly constant) for the given loan interest rate and amortization term. Thus, for a 30-year, fully amortized, level monthly payment loan at 15.5% interest, the monthly payment factor is .013045. The number is found by consulting a direct reduction loan table or by solving for the monthly payment (PMT) on a preprogrammed financial calculator, given the number of periods (n), interest (i), and the present value (PV).

Suppose the loan identified above had an initial principal amount of $160,000. The monthly payment to amortize the principal over 30 years and to provide interest at the nominal rate of 15.5% on the outstanding balance each month would be

$$\$160,000 \times .013045 = \$2,087.20$$

Annual Debt Service and Loan Constant

Because cash flows are typically converted to an annual basis for real property valuation purposes, it is useful to have an annual debt service figure as well as monthly payments. In the case of the 30-year, 15.5%, fully amortized, level monthly payment loan of $160,000, the annual debt service is

$$\$2,087.20 \times 12 = \$25,046.40$$

The annual loan constant (also widely called the mortgage constant) is simply the *ratio* of annual debt service to the loan principal. The annual loan constant is given the symbol R_M to signify that it is a capitalization rate for the loan or debt portion of the real estate investment.

$$R_M = \frac{\text{Annual debt service}}{\text{Loan principal}}$$
$$= \frac{\$25,046.40}{\$160,000.00}$$
$$= .156540$$

An R_M can also be obtained when the dollar amount of the loan principal is known. The monthly payment factor is simply multiplied by 12.

$$R_M = \text{monthly payment factor} \times 12$$
$$= .013045 \times 12$$
$$= .156540$$

Although these figures are rounded to the nearest cent, in actual practice loan constants are rounded up to make sure that the loan is repaid during the stated amortization period.

Outstanding Balance

Properties are frequently sold, or loans are refinanced, before the loan on the property is fully amortized. Moreover, loan contracts often call for maturity dates prior to the completion of loan amortization. In all such cases, there is a balance outstanding on the note. From the point of view of the lender, this is the loan or debt reversion.

The balance outstanding (B) on any level-payment amortized loan is the present value of the debt service over the *remaining* amortization period. Thus, the balance at the end of 10 years, for the 30-year note in the preceding illustrations, is the present value of 20 years of remaining payments. It is calculated as the monthly payment times the present value of one per period factor (monthly) for 20 years.

$$B = \$2,087.20 \times 73.861752$$
$$= \$154,164.25$$

Similarly, the balance outstanding at the end of 18 years is equal to the monthly payment times the present value of one per period factor (monthly) for 12 years.

$$B = \$2,087.20 \times 65.222881$$
$$= \$136,133.20$$

The balance outstanding can also be expressed as a *percentage* of the original principal. This is often useful, and sometimes necessary, when dollar amounts are not given or not available.

For a 10-year projection, 20 years remaining,

$$B = \frac{\$154,164.25}{\$160,000.00}$$
$$= .963527$$

For an 18-year projection, 12 years remaining,

$$B = \frac{\$136,133.20}{\$160,000.00}$$
$$= .850833$$

This percentage balance can also be calculated as the *ratio* of the present value of one per period factor for the remaining term of the loan, divided by the present value of one per period factor for the full term of the loan. This is represented as

$$B = \frac{PV\ 1/P\ \text{remaining term}}{PV\ 1/P\ \text{full term}}$$

In the case of the 30-year, 15.5% loan, this would be calculated as follows:

For a 10-year projection, 20 years remaining,

$$B = \frac{73.861752}{76.656729}$$
$$= .963539$$

For an 18-year projection, 12 years remaining,

$$B = \frac{65.222881}{76.656729}$$
$$= .850844$$

These results are similar to those that are obtained by using dollar amounts.

Percentage of Loan Paid Off

Especially in mortgage-equity/Ellwood analysis (but not only in that context), it is often necessary to calculate the percentage of loan paid off prior to full amortization over the projection period. This is given the symbol P. It is also most readily calculated as the complement of B:

$$P = 1 - B$$

For the 30-year note example used throughout this section,

$$P_{10} = 1 - .963539$$
$$= .036461$$
$$P_{18} = 1 - .850844$$
$$= .149156$$

The percentage of loan paid off prior to full amortization over the projection period (P) can also be calculated directly. There are many different procedures for doing so, and not all are presented here. The simplest and most direct procedure is to calculate P as the *ratio* of the sinking fund factor for the full term (monthly), divided by the sinking fund factor for the projection period (monthly):

$$P = \frac{1/S_{\overline{n}|}}{1/S_{\overline{n}|}P}$$

In the example used above, with a 30-year monthly payment note at 15.5%,

$$P_{10} = \frac{.000129}{.003524}$$
$$= .036606$$
$$P_{18} = \frac{.000129}{.000862}$$
$$= .149652$$

The differences are the result of rounding.

Applications of the Discounting Procedure

The discounting procedure is appropriate to each income stream pattern explained in the preceding section. The following discussion shows particular applications of discounting.

Variable Annuity plus Reversion

The following example illustrates the use of the basic DCF formula in valuing a stream of net operating incomes plus the reversion through sale of the property at the end of the projection period. The same procedure would be used (with the appropriate discount rate) to value a stream of incomes relating to any real property interest in real estate.

DCF Example

Assume that an office property (ABC Office Building) has a forecast schedule of income and expenses as shown in Table 17.2. This schedule represents a projection of rents based on leases, some of which expire during the 10-year projection period. All the leases have three-year terms, which begin at different times. As the leases mature, rents are renegotiated or the office space is put on the market. A 4% annual vacancy and collection loss allowance is anticipated to be adequate to cover vacancies that might occur between the occupancy terms of different tenants. Operating expenses are projected as shown in Table 17.2.

In addition to the annual net operating income, the property is expected to produce another benefit for the owner-investor: reversion at the end of the projection period. This amount was estimated by capitalizing the tenth year's net operating income by direct capitalization using an overall rate of 15% and deducting transaction costs of 5%. The result was $372,115. Alternatively, the projected net operating income in the year after the forecast (Year 11 in this example) may be capitalized to arrive at a reversion estimate.

The present value of the forecast net operating income stream and reversion at a 14% discount rate would be $390,605, calculated as shown in Table 17.3.

As shown in Table 17.2, the property's income and expenses are estimated individually over the 10-year projection period. This is because both income and expenses vary nonsystematically. One year's income and expenses are not related systematically to those of previous years. Within a year's projection, however, certain categories are related to others. For example, the vacancy and collection loss is estimated as a percentage of potential gross income, and management is consistently 3.8% of effective gross income. Utilities are estimated to grow at 10% per year, and all other operating expenses are estimated to grow nonsystematically.

Each year's net operating income and the reversion are discounted to present value by multiplying each year's income forecast by the present value discount factor at 14%. Although the reversion is discounted separately in this example, it could have been added to the tenth year's net operating income and discounted with it as long as the same yield rate is considered appropriate. When a financial calculator is used, the present value of each year's net operating income and the reversion are calculated, held in the calculator, and totaled with the other present values. Alternatively, all the assumptions could be put

Table 17.2 ABC Office Building Income and Expenses—10-Year Projection

	Year 1	Year 2	Year 3	Year 4	Year 5	Year 6	Year 7	Year 8	Year 9	Year 10
Potential gross income										
Rents	$93,000	$94,500	$98,200	$100,000	$110,300	$114,400	$112,200	$120,800	$125,000	$130,000
Other income	1,200	1,800	1,500	2,000	1,800	2,200	2,300	2,500	2,600	2,700
Total potential gross income	$94,200	$96,300	$99,700	$102,800	$112,100	$116,600	$114,500	$123,300	$127,600	$132,700
Vacancy and collection losses (4% of rentals)	−3,720	−3,780	−3,928	−4,032	−4,412	−4,576	−4,488	−4,832	−5,000	−5,200
Effective gross income	$90,480	$92,520	$95,772	$98,768	$107,688	$112,024	$110,012	$118,468	$122,600	$127,500
Operating expenses										
Property tax	$14,000	$14,600	$16,800	$17,400	$17,600	$19,000	$19,000	$21,000	$22,000	$25,000
Management	3,438	3,516	3,639	3,753	4,092	4,257	4,180	4,502	4,659	4,845
Utilities, HVAC	12,500	13,750	15,125	16,638	18,300	20,130	22,145	24,359	26,795	28,500
All others	7,000	7,200	7,800	8,000	8,300	8,500	9,000	9,300	9,800	10,400
Total operating expenses	$36,938	$39,066	$43,364	$45,791	$48,292	$51,887	$54,325	$59,161	$63,254	$68,745
Net operating income	$53,542	$53,454	$52,408	$52,977	$59,396	$60,137	$55,687	$59,307	$59,346	$58,755
Expected resale price, end of Year 10		$391,700								
Transaction costs		−19,585								
Proceeds of resale (property reversion)		$372,115								

Table 17.3   Present Value Calculations

Year	NOI (Reversion)	Present Value Discount Factor @14%	Present Value[a]
1	$ 53,542	0.877193	$ 46,967
2	53,454	0.769468	41,131
3	52,408	0.674972	35,374
4	52,977	0.592080	31,367
5	59,396	0.519369	30,848
6	60,137	0.455587	27,398
7	55,687	0.399637	22,255
8	59,307	0.350559	20,791
9	59,346	0.307508	18,249
10	58,755	0.269744	15,849
10	372,115	0.269744	100,376
Total present value			$390,605

[a]Rounded to the nearest $1.00

into a computer program for faster calculations; easy sensitivity analyses using different assumptions could also be accomplished quickly and effectively.

Level Annuity

A level annuity is an income stream with the very special and specific characteristics of equal and equally spaced payments.

Ordinary Level Annuity

An ordinary level annuity is valued by multiplying the payment amount by the discount factor for one per period at the appropriate yield rate over the estimated projection period. For example, consider a 5-year income stream of $10,000 per year, discounted at 12%. The 5-year present value of one per period discount factor at 12%, with annual discounting, is 3.604776.

Thus, the present value of this income stream is

$$3.604776 \times \$10,000 = \$36,047.76$$

This calculation is quick, direct, and easy; its applicability is limited, however, to income streams with characteristics of an ordinary annuity.

Annuity Payable in Advance

The present value of an annuity payable in advance may be calculated when appropriate adjustments are made via the base.[3] The present value of a 5-year, $10,000 annuity payable in advance, with annual payments discounted at 12%, is

$$3.604776 \times 1.12^a = 4.037349$$
$$4.037349 \times \$10,000 = \$40,373.49$$

or

$$3.604776 \times \$10,000 = \$36,047.76$$
$$\$36,047.76 \times 1.12^a = \$40,373.49$$

[a]The base is $(1 + i) = (1 + .12) = 1.12$.

Level Annuity plus Reversion

A 10-year level net operating income of $10,000 per year plus a $75,000 reversion, discounted at 15%, is

PV NOI: $10,000 × 5.018769[a]	= $50,187.69
PV Reversion: $75,000 × 0.247185[b]	= 18,538.88
Total present value	$68,726.57

[a]*PV 1P@* 15%, 10 years.
[b]*PV @* 15%, 10 years.

Increasing and Decreasing Annuities

In increasing or decreasing annuities, the periodic payments are evenly spaced and ordinarily received at the end of the periods. The common patterns of changes may be either on a straight-line basis or a constant ratio (exponential-curve) basis.

Straight-Line Changes

The formula for a straight-line decreasing (or increasing) annuity is

$$PV = (d + hn)a_{\overline{n}|} - \frac{h(n - a_{\overline{n}|})}{i}$$

where

d = first year's income
h = dollar amount of periodic income change after first period (plus or minus)

[3]The base is the sum of 1 plus the effective interest rate per period.

n = projection period

$a_{\overline{n}|}$ = present value factor for ordinary level annuity at yield rate for the projection period

i = yield rate

Thus, if a property is expected to produce a first-year net operating income of \$10,000, and the net operating income is expected to decline by \$600 each year for 10 years, the present value (discounted at 14%) would be

$$PV = [\$10,000 + (-\$600 \times 10)] \, (5.216116) - \left[\frac{-\$600 \, (10 - 5.216116)}{.14} \right]$$

$$= (\$10,000 - \$6,000) \, (5.216116) - \left[\frac{-\$600 \, (4.783884)}{.14} \right]$$

$$= (\$4,000) \, (5.216116) - \left[\frac{-\$2,870.33}{.14} \right]$$

$$= \$20,864.46 + \$20,502.36$$

$$= \$41,366.82$$

Constant Ratio (Exponential-Curve) Changes

The valuation formula for a constant percentage decreasing (or increasing) annuity is

$$PV = \frac{1 - [(1 + x)^n \div (1 + i)^n]}{i - x} \times d$$

where PV = present value

x = constant ratio change in income (plus or minus)

d = first year's income

i = yield rate

n = projection period

Thus, if a property is expected to produce a first-year net operating income of \$10,000, and the net operating income is expected to decline at a compound rate of 6% per year over a 10-year period, the present value (discounted at 14%) would be

$$PV = \frac{1 - \{[1 + (-.06)]^{10} \div (1 + .14)^{10}\}}{.14 + (-.06)} \times \$10,000$$

$$= \frac{1 - (.538615 \div 3.707221)}{.14 + .06} \times \$10,000$$

$$= \frac{1 - .145288}{.20} \times \$10,000$$

$$+ \frac{.854712}{.20} \times \$10,000$$

$$= 4.273560 \times \$10,000$$
$$= \$42,735.60$$

Increasing (or Decreasing) Annuity plus Reversion

If a property has a 10-year net operating income stream, starting at $10,000 in the first year and decreasing thereafter at 6% per year on a compound basis, and a reversion of $75,000, all discounted at 14%, its total present value is

PV income flow	$42,735.60
PV reversion	
$75,000 × .269744	20,230.80
Total present value	$ 62,966.40

Step-Up Lease plus Reversion

The present value of a step-up or step-down lease's income stream can be calculated through the use of deferred factors, illustrated in deferred annuity examples. Suppose that a lease calls for net rent at $1,000 per month for three years, $1,300 per month for the next three years, and $1,750 per month for the next four years. At the end of 10 years, the reversion is forecast to be $150,000. The rate of discount is indicated to be 14.25%.

The present value of this property is then calculated as

PV Yrs. 1-3: $1,000 × 29.155218[a]	=	$ 29,155.22
PV Yrs. 4-6: $1,300 × 19.061157[b]	=	24,779.50
PV Yrs. 7-10: $1,750 × 15.570081[c]	=	27,247.64
PV Yrs. 10 reversion: $150,000 × 0.263899[d]	=	39,584.85
Total present value		$120,767.21

[a]*PV* 1/*P*, 36 months @ 14.25% monthly.
[b]Deferred factor, *PV* 1/*P*, months 37-72 @ 14.25%.
[c]Deferred factor, *PV* 1/*P*, months 73-120 @ 14.25%.
[d]*PV* 1 @ 14.25%, 10 years, annual.

The reversion in this example is discounted at an *annual* rate. Depending on the analysis, it could alternately be discounted on the same basis as the income flows (monthly).

Deferred Annuity

A deferred annuity is an income stream that begins at some time in the future. In determining its present value, an appraiser performs a two-stage calculation. First, the appraiser calculates the present value of the income stream as of the time it begins. Second, the appraiser discounts the future value to a present value.

For example, suppose that a lease calls for annual payments at the end of periods (an ordinary annuity) as follows:

Yrs. 1-3 $ 8,000 per yr.
Yrs. 4-7 $ 9,000 per yr.
Yrs. 8-11 $11,000 per yr.

This income stream actually consists of three separate ordinary annuities: $8,000 per year for 3 years; $9,000 per year for 4 years, but deferred 3 years; and $11,000 per year for 4 years, but deferred 7 years. Assuming that the appropriate rate of discount is 15%, the problem of identifying the present value of this income stream could be solved as follows:

1. Present value of $8,000 per year for 3 years, discounted at 15%:

PV 1/P for 3 yrs. at 15% = 2.283225
2.283225 × $8,000 = $18,265.80

2. Present value of $9,000 per year for 4 years, deferred 3 years, discounted at 15%:

PV 1/P for 4 yrs. at 15% = 2.854978
PV 1, 3 yrs. hence, at 15% = 0.657516
2.854978 × $9,000 = $25,694.80

However, this is what the 4-year income stream will be worth in 3 years:

0.657516 × $25,694.80 = $16,894.74

(or, alternatively:
1.877194[a] × $9,000 = $16,894.74)

3. Present value of $11,000 per year for 4 years, deferred 7 years, discounted at 15%:

PV 1/P for 4 yrs. at 15% = 2.854978
PV 1, over 7 yrs. hence, at 15% = 0.375937
2.854978 × $11,000 = $31,404.76

However, this is what the 4-year income stream will be worth in 7 years:

0.375937 × $31,404.76 = $11,806.21

(or alternatively:
1.073292[b] × $11,000 = $11,806.21)

4. Total present value of income stream $46,966.75

^aDeferred factor = 2.854978 × 0.657516 = 1.877194
^bDeferred factor = 2.854978 × 0.375937 = 1.073292

An alternative procedure is to subtract present value of one per period (ordinary level annuity table) factors for the successive ending years of the step-up lease: 3 years, 7 years, and 11 years. The rationale for this can be seen from one illustration, for Years 4 through 7.

The second portion of the income stream might be depicted and valued as follows:

Year	Income	Discount Factor at 15%	Present Value
4	$9,000	0.571753	$ 5,145.78
5	9,000	0.497177	4,474.59
6	9,000	0.432328	3,890.95
7	9,000	0.375937	3,383.43
		1.877195	$16,894.75

The 1.877195 discount factor for Years 4 through 7 at 15% is, therefore, the *sum* of the present value of one factors for Years 4 through 7 at 15%. It is also the *difference* between the 7-year present value of one per period factor at 15% and the 3-year present value of one per period factor at 15%:

PV 1/P, 7 yrs. @ 15%:	4.160420
PV 1/P, 3 yrs. @ 15%:	− 2.283225
Discount factor, Years 4-7:	1.877195

Similarly, the discount factor for Years 8 through 11 is

PV 1/P, 11 yrs. @ 15%:	5.233712
PV 1/P, 7 yrs. @ 15%:	− 4.160420
Discount factor, Years 8-11	1.073292

Thus, the present value of the income stream under the 11-year step-up lease, discounted at 15%, is calculated as

PV yrs. 1-3: $ 8,000 × 2.283225 = $18,265.80
PV yrs. 4-7: $ 9,000 × 1.877195 = 16,894.76
PV yrs. 8-11: $11,000 × 1.073292 = 11,806.21
Total present value of income stream = $46,966.77

This is essentially the same result as that produced in the previous example. The procedure works whether the successive income receipts (lease payments) are increasing or decreasing (or both) in successive time periods.

The calculated present value of income flows is based on end-of-period payments. To convert to the present value of beginning-of-period payments, the end-of-period present value is simply multiplied by the base $(1 + i)$. The reversion is always received at the *end* of the holding period. When there is a lease, the reversion is received only when the lease expires, which is at the *end* of the contract period, no matter when the rent payments are received.

Overall Capitalization Rates in Yield Capitalization

A further possibility in yield capitalization is the use of overall rates. This technique permits the conversion of a single year's income into value by applying the formula

$$\text{Value} = \frac{\text{Net operating income}}{\text{Overall capitalization rate}}$$

Depending on the procedure used, either the first year's projected income or the average income projected for the holding period is capitalized. In certain cases, notably in using the Ellwood *J*-Factor, the previous year's income is used.

Overall rates are used in lieu of discounting when the pattern of the income flows is systematic and when the reversion is specified as a percentage change from the original investment, rather than estimated as a specific income amount.

The formula used to convert income to value in this yield capitalization procedure is identical to the one used in direct capitalization. However, the major difference between yield capitalization and direct capitalization is still operative in this procedure. Overall rates used in yield capitalization are based on the inclusion of all investor assumptions about income flows and reversion value. Moreover, the specification of the yield rate is the key ingredient in the development of an overall rate in yield capitalization. The overall rate must reflect specific indications of investor expectations for return on investment (yield) and income pattern and allow for future change in value of the original investment.

In yield capitalization, an overall capitalization rate may be derived by several procedures. The best procedure in any appraisal assignment depends on the quantity and quality of data and the appraiser's assumptions about time frame, income patterns, and the change in value of the original investment. Among the available procedures for derivation of overall rates in yield capitalization are the application of yield and change formulas and mortgage-equity procedures.

Yield and Change Formulas

In yield capitalization, an overall capitalization rate is the sum of specified investor expectations pertaining to the annual rate of return on the investment (yield rate) and an annualized component that allows for return of capital. The formula for developing this rate[4] is

$$R_O = Y_O - \Delta a$$

where

R_O	=	the overall capitalization rate
Y	=	the yield (discount) rate
Δ	=	delta, the expected percentage change in the value of the total property over the projection period
a	=	the annualizer, which converts the total change in capital value over the projection period to an annual percentage

In the formula, the annualizer would be specified by a straight-line rate if the appraiser believed that the income stream pattern would be that of a constant dollar increasing or decreasing annuity. For example, if a property generating income that decreases at a constant dollar amount is expected to decline 20% in value over a 10-year projection period, the annualizer would be .02 (20% decline ÷ 10 years).

If the yield rate is 12%, the capitalization rate for the property would be

---

[4]Although illustrated here as a formula for developing an overall rate, this formula can be used to derive a capitalization rate for any interest in real property, as long as the patterns of change and income/value relationships are consistent with the formula.

$$R_O = Y_O - \Delta\, a$$
$$= .12 - (-.20 \div 10)$$
$$= .12 - (-.02)$$
$$= .14$$

If the income stream to a property interest is expected to be that of an ordinary level annuity, the annualizer is specified as the sinking fund factor at the yield rate for the projection period. For example, assume the same property as in the previous example except that income is expected to be level. The capitalization rate would be

$$R_O = .12 - (-.20 \times .056984)$$
$$= .12 + .011397$$
$$= .131397$$

A capitalization rate can also be obtained by adding to the yield rate a sinking fund factor at a rate other than the yield rate. The relevance of such a rate depends on the actual establishment of a sinking fund. For example, if the sinking fund factor were obtained using a yield rate of 8%, the capitalization rate in the prior example would be changed to

$$R_O = .12 - (-.20 \times .069029)$$
$$= .12 + .013806$$
$$= .133806$$

In this case, the application of a sinking fund factor at a different rate than the yield rate produces a higher capitalization rate and lower value. This reflects the reduced capacity of the sinking fund to accumulate the value loss.

If the income stream to a property is not expected to change over the holding period, Δa is zero, and the capitalization rate equals the yield rate. For example, if a property being appraised is expected not to lose or gain value in the foreseeable future, Δ equals zero, and zero times any annualizer equals zero:

$$R_O = .12 - (0 \times a)$$
$$= .12 - 0$$
$$= .12$$

Level annuities and increasing and decreasing annuities can be capitalized by rates that contain assumptions about the relevant income pattern.

The overall capitalization rate can also be derived by weighting the land and building capitalization rates. Assume that the land represents 15% of total value and will grow by 15% over a 5-year period, the building represents 85% of total value and will grow by 10% over a 5-year period, and equity yield will remain at 12%. Also assume that the income and value will change on a related straight-line basis.

The land capitalization rate is

$$R_L = Y_O - \Delta_L \frac{1}{n}$$
$$= .12 - .15 \times \frac{1}{5}$$
$$= .12 - .03$$
$$= .09$$

The building capitalization rate is

$$R_B = Y_O - \Delta_B \frac{1}{n}$$
$$= .12 - .10 \times \frac{1}{5}$$
$$= .12 - .02$$
$$= .10$$

The weighted overall rate is

Component	Ratio ×	Capitalization Rate =	Weighted Rate
Land	.15 ×	.09 =	.0135
Building	.85 ×	.10 =	.0850
Property(R_O)	1.00		.0985

Mortgage-Equity: Ellwood Formula

L. W. Ellwood, author of the *Ellwood Tables*, was the first to organize, develop to a practical conclusion, and promulgate the concepts of mortgage-equity analysis within the area of real property valuation.[5] The original Ellwood equation for the overall rate is

[5]L. W. Ellwood, *Ellwood Tables for Real Estate Appraising and Financing*, 4th ed. (Chicago: American Institute of Real Estate Appraisers, 1977).

$$R_O = Y - MC \begin{smallmatrix} +\,dep \\ -\,app \end{smallmatrix} 1/S_{\overline{n}|}$$

where

Y = equity yield rate
M = ratio of mortgage to value
C = mortgage coefficient[6]
$1/S_{\overline{n}|}$ = sinking fund factor at equity yield rate for the ownership projection period
dep = depreciation in property value for the projection period
app = appreciation in property value for the projection period

Although the *Ellwood Tables* provided precalculated mortgage coefficients (C) for many combinations of equity yield rates (Y_E) and various mortgage terms, the mortgage coefficients are no longer required or particularly useful since the advent of hand-held calculators.

The Ellwood formula assumes a level income flow; overall property value may be assumed to increase, decrease, or remain stable. If the income flow is not level, the formula *must* be modified to reflect the effect of changing income streams. This is accomplished by using the J-Factor. When it is assumed that there is level income and no change in value, the derived rate is known as the *basic capitalization rate* (r). This rate reflects the effect of financing and is developed as follows:

$$R_O = Y_E - MC$$
$$R_O = r$$
$$r = Y_E - MC$$

Thus, the basic capitalization rate is a building block to develop overall capitalization rates with additional assumptions. For example, when there is a change in value, the formula is

$$R_O = r - \Delta_O\ 1/S_{\overline{n}|}$$

Using current symbols, the equation is restated as

$$R_O = Y_E - M(Y_E + P\ 1/S_{\overline{n}|} - R_M) - \Delta_O 1/S_{\overline{n}|}$$

where

R_O = overall capitalization rate
Y_E = equity yield rate

---

[6]The mortgage coefficient may be computed by the formula $C = Y + P\ 1/S_{\overline{n}|} - R_M$.

M = mortgage
P = ratio paid off (mortgage)[7]
Δ_O = change (in total property value)
$1/S_{\overline{n}|}$ = sinking fund factor at the equity yield rate
R_M = mortgage capitalization rate (mortgage constant)

The following is an example of the application of the Ellwood formula to a level annuity:

Net operating income	$ 50,000
Loan terms	
Interest rate	9%
Amortization term (monthly payments)	25 yrs.
Ratio of loan to value	75%
Property value change	10% loss
Holding period	10 yrs.
Yield	15%

The formula used to develop the overall rate is

$$R_O = Y_E - M(Y_E + P1/S_{\overline{n}|} - R_M) - \Delta_O\, 1/S_{\overline{n}|}$$
$$= .15 - .75\,(.15 + .172608 \times .049252 - .100704) -$$
$$(-.10 \times .049252)$$
$$= .15 - .75\,(.15 + .008501 - .100704) - (-.004925)$$
$$= .15 - .75\,(.057797) + .004925$$
$$= .15 - .043348 + .004925$$
$$= .111577$$

Capitalization: $\$50,000 \div .111577 = \$448,121$

Mortgage-Equity: Akerson Format

In the mortgage-equity procedure originated by Charles B. Akerson,[8] an arithmetic format is substituted for the algebraic equation in the Ellwood formula. This format is applicable only to level income situations. It can also be modified with the J-Factor to apply to changing income situations.

---

[7]The ratio of mortgage paid off may be computed using the formula $P = (R_M - i) \div (R_{MP} - i)$ where R_M = the mortgage capitalization rate for the full amortization term, and R_{MP} = the mortgage capitalization rate for the projection period.

[8]Originally cited in Charles B. Akerson, "Ellwood without Algebra," *The Appraisal Journal,* July 1970.

The Akerson format is

1. Loan ratio × annual constant   = _____
2. Equity ratio × equity yield rate   = + _____
3. Loan ratio × part paid off × $1/S_{\overline{n}}$ = − _____
   Basic rate (r)   = _____
4. + dep *or* − app × $1S_{\overline{n}}$ = ± _____
   Overall capitalization rate   = _____

$1/S_{\overline{n}}$ is the sinking fund factor at the equity yield rate for the projection period. Dep/app is the change in value from depreciation/appreciation during the projection period.

Given the same assumptions as those used in the Ellwood formula example, the same answer is derived by applying the Akerson format and overall capitalization as follows:

1. .75 × .100704   =   .075528
2. .25 × .15   = + .037500
3. − .75 × .172608 × .049252   = − .006376
   Basic rate (r)   =   .106652
4. .10 × .049252   = + .004925

R_O =   .111577

Capitalization: \$50,000 ÷ .111577   =   \$448,121

Use of *J*-Factors

The use of the *J*-Factor (either straight-line or Ellwood) allows an appraiser to handle changing annuities as stabilized or level annuities. The *J*-Factor is an income adjustment or income stabilization factor that is used to convert a changing stream of income to its level equivalent. The factor may be obtained from precomputed tables or through the use of the *J*-Factor formula.[9] To handle changing annuities, the Ellwood formula is modified to

$$R_O = \frac{Y_E - M(Y_E + P1/S_{\overline{n}} - R_M) - \Delta_O\, 1/S_{\overline{n}}}{1 + \Delta_I\, J}$$

where

Δ_I = total ratio change in income

J = *J*-Factor

[9]James J. Mason, ed., comp., *American Institute of Real Estate Appraisers Financial Tables*, rev. ed. (Chicago: American Institute of Real Estate Appraisers, with tables computed by Financial Publishing Company, 1982).

Assume the facts given in the example of the Ellwood formula for a level annuity, but instead of a 10% property loss and level income, assume that there is a 20% property gain in value and a 20% change in income. The application of the straight-line J-Factor is based on income for the first year of the holding period. The application of the Ellwood J-Factor is based on income in the year prior to the first year of the holding period.

Example of straight-line *J*-Factor:

$$R_O = \frac{.15 - .75(.15 + .172608 \times .049252 - .100704) - (.20 \times .049252)}{1 + .20 \times .3383}$$

$$= \frac{.15 - .043348 - .009850}{1 + .067660}$$

$$= \frac{.096802}{1.067660}$$

$$= .090667$$

Capitalization: $50,000 ÷ .090667 = $551,469

Example of Ellwood *J*-Factor (Curvilinear):

$$R_O = \frac{.15 - .75(.15 + .172608 \times .049252 - .100704) - (.20 \times .049252)}{1 + .20 \times .3259}$$

$$= \frac{.15 - .043348 - .009850}{1. + .065160}$$

$$= \frac{.096802}{1.065160}$$

$$= .090880$$

Capitalization: $50,000 ÷ .090880 = $550,176

Testing Overall Rate Conclusions

Because growth or decline in the value of the equity position contributes to the equity yield rate, the analysis of value change is important in determining the reasonableness of an overall capitalization rate conclusion and the prospect for achieving a specific yield. The mortgage component of value represents a current commitment and can be projected from current mortgage market research. Assuming that there is a supportable net income projection, changes in income and value are the variables affecting the prospects for equity yield.

Mortgage-equity analysis provides an appraiser and an investor with an effective tool for gauging the prospects for yield within a range of possible resale prices. Assume that an appraiser has derived capitalization rates from the best available market data and developed a market value estimate for the subject property through an appropriate capitalization method. Assuming purchase on this basis, with currently available financing, a reasonable range of equity yields can be related to the property value changes that must occur to produce the yields. If it is reasonable to expect that the subject property can be resold for a price that would produce a yield within the established range, this is supportive evidence of probable investment appeal at the appraised value.

The formula for change in value, based on the previously developed equation, $R = Y - \Delta a$, is

$$R_O = r - \Delta_O 1/S_{\overline{n}|}$$

This may be expressed as

$$\Delta_O = \frac{r - R_O}{1/S_{\overline{n}|}}$$

If the result is a negative number, depreciation in overall property value is indicated. If the result is positive number, appreciation in overall property value is indicated.

If the overall rate has not been part of the capitalization procedures used, it can be computed for use in the formula from the net income projection and the market value estimate. Assume that a property with a $36,000 per year level net operating income projection was valued at $400,000. The overall rate is 9.0%. Assume that typical financing is available at 75% of value at 8.5% on a 25-year monthly payment amortization schedule. Tables 17.4 and 17.5 show the computations to derive the changes in property value corresponding to a selected range of equity yield rates, assuming resale after a 5- or 10-year period of ownership.

The changes in property value corresponding to each yield rate may then be plotted on a graph as shown in Figure 17.1.

The appraisal at $400,000 is presumably based on current attitudes of buyers and sellers in the current market. However, even the most probable investment objectives are not always achieved. Accord-

Table 17.4   Five-Year Projection

Yield rate	$(r - R_O)$	÷	$1/S_{\overline{n}|}$	=	Δ_O
.09	(.085928 − .09)	÷	.167092	=	−.024370
.12	(.093956 − .09)	÷	.157409	=	.025132
.15	(.101952 − .09)	÷	.148315	=	.080585

The basic rate (r) can be calculated by formula or found in the *Ellwood Tables, op. cit.*

Table 17.5   Ten-Year Projection

Yield rate	$(r - R_O) \div$	$1/S_{\overline{n}}$	$= \Delta_O$
.09	$(.085969 - .09) \div .065820 =$		$-.061243$
.12	$(.094686 - .09) \div .056984 =$		$.082234$
.15	$(.103252 - .09) \div .049252 =$		$.269065$

The basic rate (r) can be calculated by formula or found in the *Ellwood Tables, op. cit.*

ingly, it helps an appraiser to have a graphic representation of the relationship between possible changes in property value during a probable period of ownership and the corresponding effect on equity yield prospects.

Figure 17.1 indicates that even if the property declines 6.1% in value over the next 10 years, equity yield will not fall below 9%. However, inflationary trends in dollar values and other real estate market conditions may result in resale at essentially the present price (equity

Figure 17.1   Graphic Analysis of 9% Overall Capitalization Rate

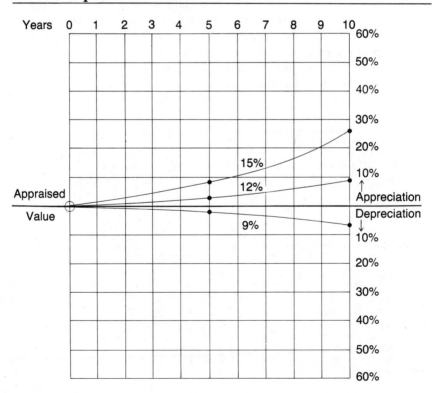

yield would be 10%±), or if the price is 27% higher, the equity yield would approximate 15%.

Such considerations, indicated trends, and the character of the property itself are studied by an informed investor in income-producing property equities. In providing consulting services or in confirming a market value estimate, an appraiser is similarly thorough in developing a comprehensive analysis.

Computation of the Equity Yield Rate

The equity yield rate (internal rate of return) includes both components of equity return--income and reversion--expressed as an annual rate. Because the amount of the reversionary component cannot be identified until the investment is liquidated, only prospects for an equity yield rate can be estimated at the moment of investment.

Assume that a property can be purchased for $100,000. It is leased for 10 years at an annual rent of $8,400. The property value is expected to remain stable over the next 10 years. Mortgage financing is available at a 75% loan-to-value ratio, and monthly payments are at 8.75% interest, with an amortization term of 25 years. The investment forecast can be set out as follows:

Purchase		Holding Period		Resale after 10 Years	
Purchase	$100,000	NOI	$8,400	Sale	$100,000
Mortgage	75,000	Debt service	7,399[a]	Mortgage balance	61,695[b]
Equity	$ 25,000	Equity dividend	$1,001	Equity reversion	$ 38,305
				Original equity	25,000
				Equity growth	$ 13,305

[a]$75,000 × .098657 mortgage constant.
[b]Unamortized portion of $75,000 mortgage at end of 10-year projection period.

$$R_E \text{ (equity dividend rate)} = \frac{\$1,001}{\$25,000} = .040040$$

$$\Delta_E \text{ (equity growth)} = \frac{\$13,305}{\$25,000} = .532200$$

The equity yield rate may now be computed through iteration (successive approximations) or by formula and interpolation. In iteration, the definition of Y_E is

$$Y_E = R_E + \Delta_E 1/S_{\overline{n}|}$$

Because the sinking fund factor for 10 years at the Y_E rate cannot be identified without knowing Y_E, a trial-and-error procedure can be used to develop Y_E. Without discounting, the 53.2% equity growth during the 10-year holding period would add 5.32% annually to the equity dividend rate of 4%. Consequently, Y_E will exceed 4.00% and be less than 9.32% (4.00% + 5.32%).

An initial computation may be made, assuming that Y_E = 6%. When the correct equity yield rate is used, the equation will balance.

Estimated Y_E	R_E	+	Δ_E	×	$1/S_{\overline{n}}$	=	Indicated Y_E
.0600	.04	+	.532	×	.075868	=	.0804
.0775	.04	+	.532	×	.069853	=	.0772
.0750	.04	+	.532	×	.070686	=	.0776

Y_E Conclusion = .0772 or 7.72%[a]

[a]The calculated yield of .0772 is closer to the assumed yield of .0775 than is the calculated yield of .0776 to the assumed yield of .0750.

The proof of this procedure for computing Y_E is based on the definition that Y_E is the rate that makes the present value of the future equity benefits equal the original equity. The future benefits in this situation are $1,001 per year for 10 years plus a reversion of $38,305 at the end of the 10-year period.

The present value of the two benefits at a Y_E of 7.72% may be computed as follows:

$$\begin{array}{rcl} \$ 1{,}001 \times 6.795658 &=& \$ 6{,}802 \\ \$38{,}305 \times .475375 &=& \underline{18{,}209} \\ && \$25{,}011 \end{array}$$

Thus, the equity yield rate has been confirmed at 7.7%. Precision to 0.1% represents a level of accuracy within the normal requirements of the computation and current practice.

The previous example was based on level income. The same procedure may be applied to changing income streams by using the J-Factor in the formula.

An investor may have completed negotiations for the purchase of investment real estate, including the terms of financing. The income stream projection might be reliable, perhaps based on a long-term net lease, and the investor might want to know what equity yield can be anticipated, assuming some specific range of changes in market value over a projected period of ownership. Use of the above procedures enables an appraiser to provide the requested information.

The potential uses of mortgage-equity procedures in valuation analysis and investment counseling are extensive. The appraiser is able to analyze the relative impacts of equity dividend rates and the potential for capital gain or loss. Overall capitalization rates derived from market evidence may be analyzed and explained in terms of equity investor motivation and the impact of financing. Because market value is a reflection of the mortgage market and equity investor thinking, the mortgage-equity procedures are realistic and provide an appraiser with valuable analytical tools.

Residual Techniques

Land and building residual techniques similar to those used in direct capitalization may be used in yield capitalization. Capitalization rates for these residual techniques come from yield and change formulas and mortgage-equity formulas. In the development of building and land capitalization rates, the appropriate annualizer must be used to reflect the income change assumption. The following examples assume level annuity income flows.

Yield and Change Formulas

Assume that the first year's net operating income for a property is estimated at $50,000, that the initial land value is estimated at $175,000 and is forecast to increase 150% in 10 years, and that building value is forecast to decline 20% over the next 10 years. Thus,

$$\Delta_L = +1.50$$
$$\Delta_B = -.20$$

and

$$n = 10$$

The yield rate (Y_O) is 16%.
The land capitalization rate is

$$R_L = Y_O - \Delta_L a$$
$$= .16 - (1.50 \times .046901)$$
$$= .16 - .070352$$
$$= .089648$$

The building capitalization rate is

$$R_B = Y_O - \Delta_B a$$
$$= .16 - (-.20 \times .046901)$$
$$= .16 + .009380$$
$$= .169380$$

Building Residual Example

Net operating income	$ 50,000
Land income	
$(V_L \times R_L) = \$175,000 \times .089648$	− 15,688
Residual income to building	$34,312
Present value of building	
$(I_B \div R_B) = \$34,312 \div .169380$	$202,574
Land value	+ 175,000
Indicated property value	$377,574

Land Residual Example

Given the information of the preceding example, assume that a new building representing the highest and best use of the land would cost $203,000. In addition, the net operating income is $50,000, the R_L is .089648, and the R_B is .169380.

Net operating income	$50,000
Building income	
$(V_B \times R_B) = \$203,000 \times .169380$	− 34,384
Residual income to land	$15,616
Present value of land	
$(I_L \div R_L) = \$15,616 \div .089648$	$174,192
Building value	+ 203,000
Indicated property value	$377,192

Mortgage-Equity Formulas

The land and building residual techniques may be used with land and building capitalization rates based on mortgage-equity procedures. Either the Ellwood formula or the Akerson format can be used to derive the basic rate, which is then used to develop the land and building capitalization rates.

For example, assume that a property is expected to produce level annual income of $15,000 per year over a 10-year term. Mortgage financing is available at a 75% loan-to-value ratio, and monthly payments are at 11% interest, with an amortization term of 25 years. The land is currently valued at $65,000; it will have a value of $78,000 (20% growth) at the end of the projection period. The building is expected to be of no value at the end of the projection period. The equity yield rate is 15%. The first step is to derive the basic rate (r).

The Ellwood formula for deriving the basic rate is

$$r = Y_E - M (Y_E + P1/S_{\overline{n}|} - R_M)$$
$$= .15 - .75 (.15 + .137678 \times .049252 - .117614)$$
$$= .15 - .029375$$
$$= .120625$$

The Akerson format for deriving the basic rate is

1.	.75 × .117614 =	.088211
2.	.25 × .15 =	.037500
3.	.75 × .137678 × .049252 =	−.005086
	Basic capitalization rate (r) =	.120625

The next step is to derive the capitalization land and building rates. The formula used to derive the land capitalization rate (R_L) is

$$R_L = r - \Delta_L 1/S_{\overline{n}|}$$
$$= .120625 - (.20 \times .049252)$$
$$= .120625 - .009850$$
$$= .110775$$

The formula used to derive the building capitalization rate (R_B) is

$$R_B = r - \Delta_B 1/S_{\overline{n}|}$$
$$= .120625 - (-1.0 \times .049252)$$
$$= .120625 + .049252$$
$$= .169877$$

Building Residual Example

Net operating income	$15,000
Land income	
$(V_L \times R_L)$ = $65,000 × .110775	−7,200
Residual income to building	$ 7,800
Present value of building	
$(I_B \div R_B)$ = $7,800 ÷ .169877	$ 45,916
Land value	+ 65,000
Indicated property value	$110,916

Land Residual Example

Net operating income	$15,000
Building income	
$(V_B \times R_B) = \$46,000 \times .169877$	−7,814
Residual income to land	$ 7,186
Present value of land	
$(I_L \div R_L) = \$7,186 \div .110775$	$ 54,870
Building value	+46,000
Indicated property value	$110,870

Summary

In yield capitalization, future benefits to investors are identified and then simulated by applying an appropriate anticipated yield rate to future benefits. Yield capitalization can be accomplished by selecting a holding period, identifying future cash flows, selecting a yield rate, using present value factors, and performing discounted cash flow analysis. Overall capitalization rates can also be derived for use in yield capitalization by applying mortgage-equity or yield rate-value change formulas. Residual techniques may also be used.

The appraiser using discounted cash flow analysis applies a formula to discount each period's income to present value. These values are first totaled and then added to the present value of the reversion. The procedure can be used to discount any variable annuity; there are also shortcut procedures that can be employed to estimate the present value of income from level, increasing or decreasing, and deferred annuities. Selecting the proper yield rate is essential. The appraiser must consider the target yield sought by investors and historical and prospective yields derived from comparable sales. According to local custom, various portions of an investment may be discounted with different yield rates because they carry different risks. Present value factors are useful appraisal tools found in published financial tables or computed with preprogrammed financial calculators.

An investment's income stream may vary systematically or nonsystematically. Because a variable annuity follows no systematic pattern, each year's income must be estimated and discounted separately. The basic discounted cash flow formula is used to value variable annuities. Level annuities, both ordinary (end-of-the-month payment) and payment in advance, can be valued with a simpler formula. Decreasing and increasing annuities may change in a step-up or step-down manner, in constant dollars, or by a certain ratio. Formulas can also be applied to these income patterns.

Every property interest has unique income benefits over the projection period and reversionary benefits that are realized at the end of the projection period. Specific incomes and reversions are associated with particular investment positions. For example, net operating incomes or equity dividends and the proceeds of resale are associated with fee simple property interests. When estimating reversion, an appraiser seeks to simulate investor expectations concerning the probable future direction and amount of property value change (appreciation or depreciation).

Mortgage information is critical to investment analysis. Monthly payment factors for standard loan terms are published and can be computed with the aid of a calculator. Annual debt service and mortgage constants can be developed from market information. When the investment term is shorter than the loan contract, the outstanding balance, expressed as a dollar amount or as a percentage or ratio, is sought. The percentage of the loan paid off is used in Ellwood mortgage-equity analysis and can be calculated by several procedures.

Capitalization rates may also be developed and applied in yield capitalization. The overall capitalization rate is developed in a manner that reflects investor motivations and expectations about income flows, reversion values, and yield. It is applied, as in direct capitalization, to convert one year's income into value. In yield capitalization, overall capitalization rates are used when a systematic pattern is assumed for the income flows, and when the reversion is specified as a percentage change from the original investment.

Procedures for overall rate derivation include application of yield and change formulas and mortgage-equity formulas. Rates derived by these procedures may be tested for reliability in terms of investor motivations. In addition, the equity yield rate may be calculated by applying formulas that are part of the yield capitalization method. Land and building residual techniques similar to those used in direct capitalization may also be used in yield capitalization.

Chapter 18

The Cost Approach

The cost approach to value, like the sales comparison and income approaches, is based on comparison. In the cost approach, the cost to construct a building and the value of an existing building are compared. The cost approach to value reflects market thinking in the recognition that market participants relate value to cost. Buyers tend to judge the value of an existing structure by comparing it to the value of a newly constructed building with optimal functional utility. Moreover, buyers adjust the prices they are willing to pay by estimating the costs to bring an existing structure to desired levels of functional utility.

Thus, by applying the cost approach, an appraiser attempts to estimate the difference in worth to a buyer between the property being appraised and a newly constructed building with optimal utility. An appraiser makes a sound value estimate by estimating the cost to construct a reproduction of or replacement for the existing structure and then deducts all evidence of accrued depreciation in the property being appraised from the cost of the reproduction or replacement structure. The resulting figure, plus the value of the land, plus any entrepreneurial profit provides a value indication through the application of the cost approach.

Data used in the sales comparison approach often reflect the result of market reaction to all items of accrued depreciation. The total amount of accrued depreciation in the comparables can be estimated by allocating the sale price between land and improvements and by then deducting the contribution of the improvement from the estimated reproduction or replacement cost. In all cases in which the price allocation is less than current reproduction or replacement cost, there is accrued depreciation, the causes of which can be identified. The cost approach attempts to identify and quantify these causes and to relate them to the subject property.

Relation to Appraisal Principles

Substitution

The principle of substitution is basic to the cost approach. The principle affirms that no prudent investor would pay more for a property than the amount for which the site can be acquired and for which improvements that have equal desirability and utility can be constructed without undue delay. Older properties can also be substituted for properties being appraised, and their value is relative to the value of the new, optimal property. Consequently, the reproduction cost on the date of the appraisal plus the site value provides a measure against which prices for already improved properties may be judged.

Supply and Demand

Although markets tend toward equilibrium, market forces change. As the forces change, different points of equilibrium (or price) result. Shifts in supply and demand cause prices to increase or decrease. Thus, different values for the same property may result over time. If costs do not shift proportionately to price changes, the construction of buildings will be more or less profitable, and the value of existing buildings will increase or decrease commensurately.

Balance

The principle of balance affirms that the proper apportionment among the agents in production is essential if optimum value is to result or be sustained. Improper economic balance may be reflected in an under- or an overimprovement. An underimprovement results from too little investment in the improvements relative to the land. An overimprovement results from the opposite condition.

A loss in value results from any excess or deficiency in the proportionate contributions of the land and the improvements. A loss in value also results from an imbalance in the various components of the improvements. Excess or deficiency are measured in the cost approach by deducting depreciation from the estimate of the reproduction or replacement cost of the improvement on the date of the appraisal.

Externalities

When supply and demand are in balance and credit is available, the cost of new improvements plus the value of the land tends to equal market value. However, properties can gain or lose value because of external conditions or events. Gains or losses in value from such causes may accrue to both land and buildings. Construction costs can significantly affect the market value of new construction. In turn, market value for older but substitutable properties can be affected by rising construction costs.

In the cost approach, losses to a building's value that result from external causes are due to external obsolescence, one of the three main types of accrued depreciation. For example, the ban on urea-formaldehyde foam insulation has affected the value of buildings in which it was installed. External conditions can also cause the value of a newly constructed building to be worth more or less than cost. When there exists a scarcity of certain types of properties or a difficulty in constructing new competitive properties, the value of a newly constructed building might be higher than reproduction or replacement cost. On the other hand, the external condition of a recession might cause an oversupply of industrial warehouse space, which would result in the value of a new warehouse being less than reproduction or replacement cost. Externalities also affect older properties.

Highest and Best Use

Fundamental to real property value is the concept of highest and best use. In one application of the concept, land is valued as if vacant and available for its highest and best use; in the other, highest and best use of the property as improved is estimated. Thus, a site may have one highest and best use as if vacant, and the existing combination of site and improvements may have another highest and best use. Existing improvements have value in an amount equal to their contribution to the site or are a penalty on value by an amount equal to the cost to remove them from the site.

Existing improvements that do not develop the land to its highest and best use usually are worth less than reproduction or replacement cost. A new building that is badly designed can be worth less than cost because of the functional obsolescence of design. Thus, the highest and best use improvement is the one that adds the greatest value to the site.

Applicability and Limitations

Because cost and market value are closely related when properties are new, the cost approach is an important approach used to derive a market value indication for new or relatively new construction. The approach is especially persuasive when the improvements are new or suffer only minor physical deterioration, functional obsolescence, or external obsolescence, and therefore represent a use that either is or is close to the highest and best use of the land as though vacant.

The approach is also widely used in estimating the market value of special use properties and other properties that are not frequently exchanged in the market. Buyers of such properties measure the price they will pay for an existing building by the cost to build a replacement, less accrued depreciation, or to purchase an existing structure and make any necessary modifications. Because comparable sales are not always available for analyzing the market value of such properties, the currently accepted market indications of depreciated cost, or the costs for acquiring and refurbishing an existing building, provide the best reflections of market thinking and thus of market value.

When improvements are older and do not represent the highest and best use of the land as though vacant, the physical deterioration, functional obsolescence, and external obsolescence that have accrued to the structure are more difficult to estimate. This fact tends to make the cost approach a less effective tool for estimating market value in these cases, and thus the other approaches may be relied on more heavily.

However, in a single market, any building can be related to the cost to create a reproduction of or replacement for the building. This is especially important when the lack of market activity limits the use of the sales comparison approach. To estimate market value, an appraiser can identify the cost of the replacement or reproduced building and then deduct for the depreciation in the existing improvement.

Furthermore, when considerable physical differences exist in comparable properties, the relative values sometimes can be identified more precisely by the cost approach than by sales comparisons alone. Because the cost approach starts with the cost to construct an optimal substitute property, it can aid an appraiser to determine accurate adjustments for physical differences in comparable sale properties. For example, an appraiser must make an adjustment for inadequate elevators in a comparable property. By estimating the cost to cure the deficiency, the appraiser can be provided with a basis for the adjustment that should be made.

Because the cost approach requires separate valuation of land and improvements, it is also useful in special situations, such as for

1. Insurance purposes

2. Tax purposes, when ad valorem tax laws require separation

3. Accounting purposes, when depreciation must be estimated for income taxes

Procedure

After an appraiser has inspected the neighborhood, the site, and the improvements, and has gathered all available relevant data, he or she follows certain steps to derive a value indication by the cost approach. The appraiser

1. Estimates the value of the land as though vacant and available to be developed to its highest and best use.

2. Estimates the reproduction or replacement cost of the structure on the effective appraisal date.

3. Estimates the amount of accrued depreciation in the structure, categorized by three major types:
   a. physical deterioration
   b. functional obsolescence
   c. external obsolescence

4. Deducts the appropriate estimated depreciation from the reproduction or replacement cost of the structure to derive an estimate of the structure's contribution to total value.

5. Estimates reproduction or replacement cost and depreciation for any accessory buildings and for site improvements, and then deducts estimated depreciation from the reproduction or replacement cost of these improvements. Site improvements and minor buildings are commonly appraised at their net value—that is, directly on a depreciated cost basis.

6. Adds the depreciated reproduction or replacement cost of the structure, accessory buildings, and site improvements to obtain an estimated total present value of all improvements.

7. Adds the estimated total present value of all improvements to land value to obtain an indication of value for the subject property.

Land Value

In the cost approach, the estimated market value of the land is added to the depreciated cost of the improvements. The value of land is determined by its potential highest and best use and can be estimated by the use of several procedures: (1) the sales comparison approach, (2) allocation, (3) extraction, (4) the capitalization of ground rental, and (5) the land residual technique of the income capitalization approach.

Sales Comparison Approach

Of the various procedures available for estimating land value, none is more helpful or persuasive than the sales comparison approach. In this approach, sales of similar unimproved sites are analyzed, compared, and adjusted to derive an indication of value for the site being appraised. In employing the approach, appraisers typically use paired data sets or patterned analyses. In paired data set analysis, an appraiser looks for comparable site sales that are similar (or to which adjustments have been made to make them similar) in every respect except for one feature. In this manner, the adjustment is found for one particular element of comparison from an analysis of the two comparable sale sites.

An example of patterned analysis is shown in estimating an adjustment for market conditions (time). The adjustment can be made by analyzing several comparable sales and by recognizing trends in sale prices due to time of sale. This type of analysis can also be made for locational and physical characteristics.

When sufficient comparative data are not available, or when the sales comparison indication is inconclusive, the site value may be estimated by other methods, which include the allocation method, the extraction method, the capitalization of ground rental, and the land residual technique.

Allocation Method

The allocation method involves an analysis of sales of improved properties to establish a typical ratio of site value to total value, which may be applicable to a property being appraised.

Extraction Method

The extraction method also involves an analysis of improved properties. The contribution of the improvements is estimated and deducted
from the total sale price to arrive at a sale price for the land. This
technique works best when the contribution of the improvements to the
total sale price is small.

Capitalization of Ground Rental

The ground rental attributable to a property can be capitalized into an
indication of the value of a site. This procedure is useful when comparable rents, rates, and factors can be developed from an analysis of
sales of leased land.

Land Residual Technique

In the land residual technique, the site is assumed to be improved to
its highest and best use, and the net operating income attributable to
the site is capitalized by the land capitalization rate into an indication
of land value.

Reproduction or Replacement Cost of the Improvements

The cost of constructing an improvement on the date of the appraisal
may be developed as the cost to reproduce the improvement or the
cost to replace it. The theoretical base for the cost approach is reproduction cost, but replacement cost may also be used. There is an important distinction between the terms.

*Reproduction cost is the cost of construction at current prices of an exact dupli-
cate, or replica, using the same materials, construction standards, design,
layout, and quality of workmanship, and embodying all the deficiencies, superadequacies, and obsolescence of the subject building.*

*Replacement cost is the cost of construction at current prices of a building hav-
ing utility equivalent to the building being appraised but built with modern
materials and according to current standards, design, and layout.*

The use of replacement cost eliminates the need to estimate some
forms of functional obsolescence, but does not affect the necessity to
measure other forms of functional obsolescence, or physical deterioration and external obsolescence.

Although reproduction cost is sometimes difficult to estimate because identical materials are not available, or construction standards
have changed, the use of the procedure generally provides a basis from
which depreciation from all causes can be measured.

Even well-built, sound improvements with considerable remaining economic life may evidence significant functional obsolescence. The replacement cost estimate automatically eliminates some functional obsolescence, but if it is used, an appraiser must consider the added costs of removal of the functional curable items (those that can be economically corrected at a cost not in excess of their contribution) and any excess carrying costs of superadequate construction. By estimating replacement cost, however, the procedure for measuring accrued depreciation is simplified in those instances of excessive or superadequate construction.

The decision of whether to use replacement or reproduction cost is often related to the purpose of the appraisal. Because courts of law have generally held that reproduction is the more applicable cost estimate, litigation appraisals most often use reproduction cost estimates. For most other types of appraisal assignments, replacement cost estimates are usually adequate. However, when using replacement cost, an appraiser should indicate that the estimate is based on substitute materials because they are as functional for the purpose, and the structure's value would not be diminished by their use. If reproduction cost is used, the excess reproduction cost of superadequacies, such as excess thickness of brick walls, would be an item of functional obsolescence.

Types of Costs

In providing complete building cost estimates, an appraiser must consider direct (hard) costs, and indirect (soft) costs. Both types of costs are essential for a reliable reproduction or replacement cost estimate. In addition, any entrepreneurial profit likely to be realized from the building project must be estimated.

Direct construction costs include the cost of labor and materials necessary to construct the improvement new at the time of the appraisal. Costs not included in the direct construction of improvements, such as professional fees, financing costs, and taxes during construction, are indirect costs. There are three techniques for estimating structural costs—the quantity survey method, the unit-in-place method, and the comparative unit cost method. These are discussed fully in Chapter 19.

Anticipation of profit may provide a primary motivation for properties to be developed. The total cost of the project should be less than the market value upon completion to reward the investors for taking this risk. The difference between the cost of development and the value of the property after completion is the entrepreneurial profit (or loss). Whether a profit is actually realized depends on how well the job is done in selecting the site, constructing the improvements, obtaining the proper tenant mix, providing the leases, and so forth, and in analyzing the market demand for the property.

Accrued Depreciation

Accrued depreciation is the difference between the reproduction or replacement cost of the improvements on the effective date of the appraisal and the market value of the improvements on the same date. Depreciation is caused by deterioration or obsolescence. Deterioration is evidenced by wear and tear to the structure. Functional obsolescence is also caused by internal property characteristics, such as poor floor plan, inadequate mechanical equipment, or functional inadequacy or overadequacy due to size or other characteristics. External obsolescence is caused by conditions external to the property, such as a lack of economic demand or changing property uses in an area, or sometimes by national economic conditions. The various types of depreciation may interact with one another, and the analysis of depreciation from all causes is cumulative.

Several methods may be used to estimate accrued depreciation. They are the economic age-life method, the modified economic age-life method, the breakdown method, sales comparison techniques, and income capitalization techniques. These procedures are discussed and illustrated in Chapter 20.

Final Value Indication

To complete the final steps in the cost approach, an appraiser uses the techniques discussed above to make current depreciated cost estimates for all the improvements, including site improvements and accessory buildings. Then the appraiser adds together the depreciated reproduction or replacement costs of all improvements, including any entrepreneurial profit, to estimate the total present value of all improvements. The appraiser then adds the land value to the total present value of all the improvements to obtain an indication of the total value of the subject property. Finally, to avoid a false implication of precision, the appraiser rounds the amount.

Summary

The cost approach is one of the three approaches used in the valuation process. Underlying the theory of the cost approach is the principle of substitution, which suggests that no prudent person will pay more for a property than the amount for which he or she can obtain, by purchase of a site and construction of a building without undue delay, a property of equal desirability and utility. Consequently, current reproduction cost, prior to any deduction for accrued depreciation, plus land value, plus entrepreneurial profit, provide a measure against which prices for already improved properties may be judged. For the cost approach to produce a valid indication of market value, it is necessary to consider the accrued depreciation evident in the property being appraised due to all causes—physical, functional, and external.

When it is properly applied, the cost approach to value helps an appraiser gain significant insights about a property's value and the reasons that an existing structure is less valuable than the optimal new structure against which it is measured. The approach is particularly significant in deriving market value indications for properties that are new or nearly new and for properties for which comparable sales and income information are not readily available. Cost approach techniques can also help an appraiser to recognize the effect of depreciation on the components of a property, and therefore help in developing more precise measures of value adjustments for physical property features. The cost approach, because it requires a separate estimation of land and building value, is used for appraising certain insurance, tax, and accounting functions.

In applying the cost approach, land value is estimated by one of several alternate procedures—the sales comparison approach, allocation, extraction, capitalization of ground rental, or the land residual technique of the income capitalization approach. The reproduction or replacement cost of the structure on the effective date of the appraisal is then estimated. Cost estimates must include all direct and indirect costs. All depreciation in the structure caused by physical deterioration, functional obsolescence, and external obsolescence is then subtracted from the reproduction or replacement cost estimate. The value of the land plus any entrepreneurial profit are then added to the current depreciated value of all improvements to derive an indication of the value of a property by applying the cost approach.

Chapter 19
Building Cost Estimates

To derive an indication of property value through the cost approach, an appraiser adds the depreciated cost of the improvements to the value of the site as though vacant and available for its most profitable use. The appraiser derives the depreciated cost of improvements by deducting any accrued depreciation from the estimated reproduction cost or replacement cost of the improvements on the date of the appraisal. Methods for estimating accrued depreciation are discussed in Chapter 20. This chapter presents the methods an appraiser uses in estimating reproduction and replacement costs. The accepted cost-estimating methods—the comparative-unit method, the unit-in-place method, and the quantity survey method—may be used whether reproduction or replacement costs are being estimated.

To apply any of these methods competently, an appraiser must understand construction plans, specifications, and building techniques. In addition, an appraiser performs a careful inspection, and gives a complete description, of the improvements. When an appraisal assignment involves proposed improvements, the appraiser may rely on descriptions from the plans and specifications to estimate costs.

Reproduction and Replacement Cost Estimates

Cost estimates can vary significantly depending on whether reproduction cost or replacement cost is used as the base for deriving the cost estimate. Thus, an appraiser must use one base consistently when developing cost estimates for the subject property and comparable properties.

When a reproduction cost estimate is to be made, an appraiser must ascertain the cost to construct a replica of the existing building using the same or similar materials at their current prices. Even when the improvement contains superadequate features, such as excessively high ceilings, the cost to reproduce them is included in the reproduction cost estimate.

When a replacement cost estimate is to be made, an appraiser estimates the cost to construct an equally desirable substitute improvement, not necessarily constructed with similar materials or to the same specifications. Because improved or more readily available materials would probably be substituted for the outdated or more costly materials used in the existing structure, the appraiser estimates the cost of the substitute materials. Further, if the present structure contains superadequacies, such as high ceilings, the costs involved in producing the extra space in the existing building, and all other costs resulting directly from the superadequate ceiling height, would be eliminated in the replacement cost estimate.

Costs

Any method used for estimating reproduction or replacement cost requires the calculation of direct (hard) and indirect (soft) costs. Both types of costs are equally necessary for construction and must be measured accurately to ensure a reliable value indication by the cost approach.

Indirect Costs

Indirect costs are expenditures other than material and labor costs, such as administrative costs; professional fees; financing costs; taxes, interest, and insurance during construction; and lease-up costs. Indirect costs are usually calculated separately from direct costs. Frequently, indirect costs are figured as a lump-sum percentage of direct costs. The percentage is converted to a dollar amount and is added to the direct costs of material, labor, and contractors. However, certain indirect costs are not related to the size and direct cost of the improvements. Such costs are added as a lump-sum dollar figure. Indirect costs include

1. Demolition and removal costs

2. Architectural and engineering fees, including plans, plan checks, surveys to establish building lines and grades, and environmental and building permits

3. Appraisal, consulting, and legal fees

4. Permanent financing fees, as well as interest on construction loans, interest on land costs, and processing fees or service charges

5. Insurance and ad valorem taxes during construction

6. Lease-up costs

7. Administrative expenses of the owner

8. Title changes

9. Survey or feasibility studies

Direct Costs

Direct costs are expenditures for labor and materials used in the construction of the improvement(s). A contractor's overhead and profit are generally treated as direct costs; a building contractor usually includes them in the construction contract. Depending on the source of the cost data, the direct costs reported may or may not include the subcontractors' profit and overhead. Direct costs generally include

1. Labor used to construct buildings

2. Materials, products, and equipment

3. Contractor's profit and overhead, including job supervision, workers' compensation, fire and liability insurance, and unemployment insurance

4. Performance bonds, surveys, and permits

5. Use of equipment

6. Watchmen

7. Contractor's shack and temporary fencing

8. Materials storage facilities

9. Power-line installation and utility costs

An appraiser should know the cost that is being estimated and the appropriate date. The same building can cost substantially more if such items as thicker slabs with better floor loads and insulated walls and windows are used. The quality of materials and labor greatly influences costs. An appraiser must be familiar with current costs for materials that are used in the subject property.

Entrepreneurial Profit

For the cost approach to provide a sound indication of value, an appraiser must add to the direct and indirect costs a figure for the entrepreneurial profit that is reflected in the market. Essentially, entrepreneurial profit should be a market-derived figure that the entrepreneur, who may also be the developer, expects to receive in addition to costs. The profit may be a percentage of the total direct and indirect costs. For a structure that will cost $2 million to build (in both direct and indirect costs), an appraiser may add a 10%, or $200,000, profit expectation to derive the total indication of value. The appraiser can derive the figure for profit expectation from market analysis. Properties that have sold recently in the same market show entrepreneurial profit as the difference between the sale price and the sum of the direct costs, the indirect costs, and the current market land value.

For example, a cost approach analysis of a comparable sale might indicate the following:

Improvements	
Direct cost	$300,000
Indirect cost	50,000
Total improvement costs	
(entrepreneur's profit is not included)	$350,000
Land value	100,000
Total	$450,000

If this property's sale price was $500,000, the difference of $50,000 represents the entrepreneur's profit—roughly 14.25% of the total direct and indirect costs.

Because the extent of entrepreneurial profit varies with economic conditions, a typical relationship between it and other costs is difficult to establish; however, entrepreneurial profit should not be omitted from the cost approach. Entrepreneurial profit is a necessary element in the motivation to construct improvements. Part or all of the profit may be deducted (as with direct and indirect costs) as functional or external obsolescence if the market indicates that the improvements have a market value less than the current reproduction or replacement cost less physical deterioration.

Although prices of materials and wage scales for labor usually can be determined for any date, the resulting cost of combining them in a completed building cannot be predicted with certainty. The profit incentive (or lack of it) can raise or lower the cost estimate. This phenomenon is illustrated by competitive contractor bids. Building cost estimates based on the same set of specifications frequently vary substantially. A contractor who is working at capacity is inclined to make a high bid, but one who is not so busy may submit a lower figure.

Cost Data Sources

Construction contracts for buildings similar to that being appraised are primary sources of comparable cost data. Building contractors and professional cost estimators in the subject area are reliable sources in estimating construction costs. An appraiser may also maintain a comprehensive file on current cost data. Such a file could include current costs for completed structures, such as residences, apartments, hotels, office buildings, other commercial buildings, and industrial buildings. The costs can provide the basis for computations used in deriving the cost of construction of an existing or proposed building.

Many cost-estimating services publish data for estimating current cost of improvements. A few of the services are Marshall and Swift Publication Company; Boeckh Publications, a division of American Appraisal Associates; and F. W. Dodge Corporation. Computer-assisted, cost-estimating services also provide necessary data.

The cost manuals published by the cost-estimating services usually include direct and unit costs. The appraiser must research to find the costs most applicable to the appraisal. Depending on the source of the cost data, the quoted construction costs may not include certain necessary items. Cost manuals often do not include indirect costs, such as escrow fees, legal fees, interest on construction loans, financing fees, property taxes, demolition, storm drains, rough grading, or other land improvement costs, such as soil compaction. In addition, discounts or bonuses paid for financing may not be included. Often, site costs, such as roads, utilities, and jurisdictional utility hookup fees and assessments, are not included in the costs furnished by national cost services.

The appraiser estimates such costs separately and includes them in the total reproduction or replacement cost estimate.

Cost-Index Trending

Cost services often include cost-index trending information. Cost indexes are used to translate a known historical cost to a current cost estimate. In cost manuals, time adjustments are made on a national level. In using cost-index trending, an appraiser studies the cost of a building similar to the one being appraised, such as an office building constructed and completed in January 1979. At that time, $500,000 was the cost to construct the building. The appraiser would then look at the index for January 1983, which lists 1004.3, while the index for January 1979 was 753.9. To bring the known historical cost up to date, the appraiser divides the current cost index by the historical cost index for the period of construction, and multiplies the result by the historical cost:

$$\frac{1004.3}{753.9} = 1.33 \times \$500,000 = \$665,000$$

Thus, the current cost is estimated at $665,000.

Certain problems arise when using such data to help estimate current reproduction or replacement cost. The problems are that the national figures must apply to the local area; that the accuracy of the figures cannot always be ascertained, especially when no indication is given of which components are used in each figure (i.e., only direct costs, or direct and some indirect costs); that historical costs may not be typical or normal for the time period; and that construction methods used at the time of the historical cost may differ from those in use at the time of the appraisal. Even though cost-index trending helps an appraiser to confirm a cost estimate, it is not necessarily an accurate substitute for the three methods of estimating building costs.

Cost-Estimating Methods

To perform a comprehensive reproduction or replacement cost estimate, an appraiser would prepare a detailed inventory of the materials and equipment that comprise the improvements and then adjust these figures to the current prices of similar materials, equipment, labor, overhead, and fees necessary to reproduce or replace the property on the date of the appraisal. Such a cost estimate would be accomplished by the quantity survey method. In practice, cost estimates are more often derived by the comparative-unit method or the unit-in-place

Figure 19.1   Plan of a Warehouse Property

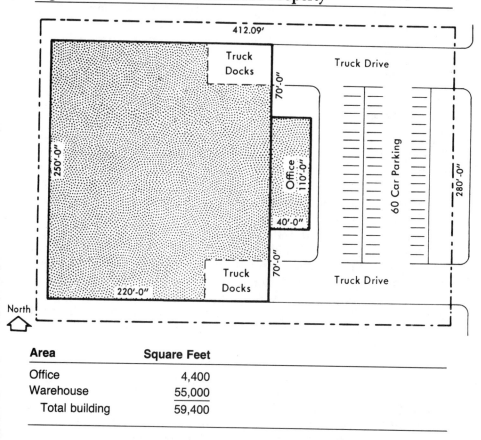

Area	Square Feet
Office	4,400
Warehouse	55,000
Total building	59,400

method. Although these methods are less detailed, they are generally adequate for appraisal purposes.

The three methods of estimating costs are shown in Figure 19.1, which illustrates a warehouse structure. The details of the warehouse are as follows:

Office area.   Heated, with air-conditioning equipment rated at 15 tons; ceiling height, 9 feet; flooring, asphalt tile over concrete slab; illumination, 60-foot, candle-intensity fluorescent lighting; ceiling, acoustic tile; partitions; stud and drywall; two washrooms that contain six fixtures.

Warehouse area.   Heating to 65° at −10° outside temperature; clear ceiling height, 18 feet; bays, 41 ½ x 36 ½ feet; structural steel framing; insulated roof deck and slab over steel bar joists; 6-inch concrete floor slab at grade, waterproofed; electric service, 600 amperes, 120/240 volt. Four overhead wood truck doors; one washroom that contains three fixtures.

Exterior walls, block and brick facade; structural steel columns, steel deck; rigid insulation; built-up tar and gravel roofing. Structure has full sprinkler system. Other details are typical.

Measurement

Buildings can be measured in several ways. Appraisers usually measure buildings in the way that is customary in the subject area. To use a cost service effectively, an appraiser must understand the measurement technique used by the service.

An appraiser uses outside measurement to compute a building's total square feet. The building is squared (front equals back, and left side equals right), and the width is multiplied by the depth. Measurements of projections are added, and those of inserts are subtracted. The gross building area is the sum of the areas of all floor levels. However, in certain locations, dwellings are measured in terms of square footage of ground floor coverage. In others, the area is the gross square feet of living space; for example, a two-story house, 24 by 24 feet, with unfinished basement and attic, has an area of 1,152 square feet (24 x 24 x 2).

To estimate the cubic feet of space in a building, an appraiser multiplies the width by the depth and the mean height, using outside measurements. The mean height is measured from 6 inches below the basement floor surface to the roof's mean height. Thus, the mean height of a gable roof is one-half the distance from the top of the ceiling joists to the ridge; the mean height of a hip roof, one-third the distance. If the subject building does not have a basement, the method of cubing is the same, except that the height is figured from 1 foot below the surface of the first floor or from grade, whichever is lower.

An appraiser must judge the advantages or disadvantages of square-foot and cubic-foot measurements in terms of local tradition, custom, and personal choice. Appraisers sometimes prefer the square-foot unit, particularly for single-story structures. Generally, the unit is less flexible, although not necessarily less accurate, because costs are substantially affected by ceiling heights, roof pitches, and similar elements. Although such elements are difficult to incorporate when using square-foot measurement, the measurement is nevertheless widely used and is applicable to warehouses, loft buildings, store buildings, and similar structures. Cubic-foot measurement may be applied to apartments and office buildings—structures that have considerable interior finish and partitioning—although square-foot measurement is also widely used. Cubic-foot measurement is particularly relevant in places of worship because of substantial variations in ceiling heights.

Comparative-Unit Method

The comparative-unit method is used to derive a cost estimate in terms of dollars per square foot or per cubic foot, based on known costs of similar structures and adjusted for time and physical differences. Indirect costs may be included in the unit cost or computed separately. If the properties used as comparables and the property being appraised are in different construction markets, an appraiser may need to make an adjustment for location.

Unit costs vary according to size: If a similar cost is spread over a larger area or cubic content, the unit cost is less. It reflects the fact that plumbing, heating units, elevators, doors, windows, and similar items do not necessarily cost proportionately more in a larger building than in a smaller one.

The comparative-unit method represents a relatively uncomplicated, practical approach to a cost estimate and is widely used. The unit-cost figures are expressed in terms of gross building dimensions. An appraiser estimates total cost by comparing the subject building with similar buildings, recently constructed, for which cost data are available either in the appraiser's files or through current research. In the comparative-unit method, an appraiser divides the actual costs of similar buildings by the number of cubic feet or number of square feet of floor or ground area. The result is the unit cost per cubic foot or square foot.

Alternately, a unit-cost figure may be developed by using a recognized cost service. A unit cost computed in this manner provides a confirmation of figures an appraiser develops from using specific examples in the local market.

Unit costs for benchmark buildings found in cost-estimating manuals usually start with a base building of a certain size (that is, a base area or volume), with additions or deductions according to the actual number of square or cubic feet involved. If a building is larger than the benchmark building, the unit cost is smaller. A building smaller than the benchmark building tends to cost more on a unit basis.

Because few buildings are exactly similar in terms of size, design, and grade of construction, the benchmark building rarely is identical to that being estimated. Variations of roof design and irregularity of perimeter and of building shape affect the comparative unit cost, sometimes substantially. For example, the cost of walls alone, per square foot of ground area enclosed, may vary substantially from a building 100 x 100 feet to one that is 40 x 250 feet, although each contains the same area. The example is illustrated in Table 19.1.

Table 19.1   Effect of Shape (Wall Ratio) on Cost

	Building A	Building B
Building size	100 × 100 ft.	40 × 250 ft.
Area enclosed	10,000 sq. ft.	10,000 sq. ft.
Linear feet of wall	400	580
Wall ratio[a]	25/1	17.24/1
Cost of wall		
Per linear foot[b]	$50	$50
Total cost	$20,000	$29,000
Per square foot of		
enclosed area	$2	$2.90

[a]Ratio of the number of square feet of area enclosed to each linear foot of enclosing wall.
[b]Assumed.

To develop a reliable conclusion through the comparative-unit method, an appraiser should calculate the unit cost from closely similar improvements, or adjust it to reflect such variables as size, shape, finish, and equipment.[1] The unit cost should also reflect cost level changes occurring between the date of the benchmark unit cost and the date of valuation.

In using square-foot or cubic-foot cost estimates, an appraiser assembles, analyzes, and catalogs data on actual building costs. Such costs should be classified in general construction categories, such as warehouses or office buildings, with separate figures for special finish or equipment—sprinkler systems, for example. An overall square-foot or cubic-foot unit cost can then be broken down into its components. This, in turn, helps an appraiser adjust a known cost for presence or absence of items in later comparisons.

The apparent simplicity of the comparative-unit method can be misleading. To develop dependable unit-cost figures, an appraier must exercise care and judgment when comparing the subject building with similar or standard structures for which actual cost is known. Inaccuracies may result if an appraiser selects a unit cost that is not comparable to the building being appraised. However, the correct application of the method provides an appraiser with reasonably accurate reproduction or replacement cost estimates.

[1]The ratio of equipment to the basic building shell cost has been consistently increasing through the years. Equipment tends to increase unit building costs and to depreciate more rapidly.

This example illustrates application of the comparative-unit method on a square-foot basis to the warehouse illustrated in Figure 19.1.[2] The procedure may be used to confirm a cost indication derived from available data in the same construction market as the property being appraised. It may also be used independently when no local cost data are available.

In Table 19.2, an adjustment was made for a complete sprinkler system by using a square-foot unit cost. Similar adjustments for items such as the extent of office areas, construction features, or equipment may be necessary.

Actual cost data for similar structures from a local market constitute a base to which an appraiser may make adjustments to derive a cost indication for the subject property. Such adjustments are made for

Table 19.2   Warehouse Property—Comparative-Unit Method

Estimated costs[a]		
Comparative cost per sq. ft.	$	12.98
Add for sprinkler system	+	.71
	$	13.69
Adjustment for 18′ ceiling height	×	1.086
	$	14.87
Adjustment for area/perimeter	×	.895
	$	13.31
Current cost multiplier (adjust benchmark cost to date of valuation)	×	1.11
	$	14.77
Local cost multiplier (adjust standard manual cost to specific city)	×	0.96
Cost per sq. ft.	$	14.18
Total cost: 59,400 sq. ft. @ $14.18		$842,292.00
Rounded:		$842,000.00

[a]Contractor's overhead and profit are included in these base costs.

Source: *Marshall Valuation Service* (Los Angeles: Marshall and Swift Publication Co.), Section 14, August 1976, p. 13; Section 44, January 1978, p. 3; Section 99, January 1978, p. 2.

[2]The structure of this building is estimated to be Class C, midway between average and good, steel framed with space heaters.

observed physical differences, using unit-in-place costs applied to the differences.

For example, a two-story brick residence cost $46,320 to build three years prior to the date of the appraisal, exclusive of detached garage or other site improvements.[3] The quality of construction is roughly comparable to that of an average mass-produced home with asphalt shingle roofing, ½-inch drywall, good average finish and equipment, with combination forced-air heat and air-conditioning, plus a dishwasher, disposal, and fireplace. Included are 3 bedrooms, 2 ½ baths, and a full basement. Ground floor measurements are 22 x 34 feet. The residence contains 22,440 cubic feet, or 1,496 square feet, costing approximately $2.06 per cubic foot, or $30.96 per square foot of gross area.[4]

In preparing a cost estimate for a house that is roughly comparable to the house just described, an appraiser makes adjustments for several differences. The house being appraised contains 24,700 cubic feet and a gross area of 1,648 square feet. It has a concrete block foundation rather than poured concrete, no fireplace, and a good grade of wood siding instead of brick exterior walls. The downward adjustments to be made include $300 for the block foundation, $1,800 for no fireplace, and $2,800 for wood siding. The result is unit costs of $1.85 per cubic foot, or $27.69 per square foot. If the contractor's overhead and profit are not included in the unit-cost adjustments, the totals may be increased by an additional 15% to 20% or whatever is typical in the market.

Assume that the cost of construction has risen 12% in the past three years. An appraiser includes this by increasing the $1.85 unit cost by 12% to $2.07 per cubic foot. The $27.69 per square foot becomes $31.01.

The application of the derived current cubic- or square-foot unit costs to the house being appraised results in current cost estimates of $51,129 and $51,104, respectively, which would usually be rounded to $51,100. The minor difference is probably due to a small variation in size, ceiling height, roof pitch, or roof design, which slightly altered the average height. It should be noted that cubic-foot and square-foot mea-

---

[3]In using or comparing building reproduction or replacement cost on a unit basis—dollars per square foot of gross area, for example—an appraiser should eliminate land improvements. Because such improvements vary widely, their inclusion distorts the overall unit cost and makes comparison difficult. Individual estimates are needed for auxiliary building improvements, such as garages and various outbuildings, or for land improvements, such as drives and paving, pools, underground drainage, rail sidings, fences, or landscaping. These may be individually estimated from applicable unit prices on a square-foot, square-yard, or linear-foot basis. Such comparative-unit costs may be developed to be applicable to any situation.

[4]The appraiser may compute the basement area separately at an appropriate square-foot unit cost.

Table 19.3   Comparison and Time Adjustment

	Cost of Comparable House 3 Years Prior to Appraisal Date	Estimated Current Cost of Comparable House
Cost	$46,320.00	$46,320.00
Adjustments		
Wood siding		− 2,800.00
Block foundation		− 300.00
Fireplace		− 1,800.00
Estimated reproduction cost (as of 3 yrs. previous to appraisal date)		$41,420.00
Area sq. ft.	1,496.00	1,648.00
Volume, cu. ft.	22,440.00	24,700.00
Per sq. ft.	30.96	$ 27.69[a]
Per cu. ft.	2.06	$ 1.85
Time adjustment to present		+ 12%
Estimated present reproduction cost		
Per sq. ft.		$ 31.01
Per cu. ft.		$ 2.07
Total		$51,104.00[b]
Rounded:		$51,100.00

[a]$41,420/1,496 sq. ft.
[b]24,700 × $2.07 = $51,129; 1,648 × $31.01 = $51,104.

surements do not always produce identical estimates. Table 19.3 summarizes the procedure of comparison and time adjustment.

The application of the comparative-unit method to a residence in the example above is no different in principle than its application to any other type of improvement. However, the discrepancy may be substantial between a one-story warehouse with a 14-foot ceiling height and one with a 20-foot height. Thus, in the use of cubic- or square-foot unit costs, it is essential that their application be to very similar structures.

Unit-in-Place Method

The unit-in-place, or segregated-cost, method employs unit costs for the various building components as installed and uses square foot, linear foot, or other appropriate units of measurement.

An appraiser may compute a unit cost on the basis of the actual quantity of brick and other materials plus the labor of assembly required per square foot of wall. The cost may be applied on the basis of square or linear feet of wall of a certain height. The same procedure is followed for other structural components.

Unit-in-place cost estimates are made in terms of standardized costs for structural components as installed. Excavating costs are typically expressed in dollars per cubic yard. Foundation costs may be expressed in dollars per linear feet or cubic yards of concrete. Floor construction may be reduced to dollars per square foot. The basic unit for roofing is a square (100 square feet). Interior partitions may be reduced to dollar per linear foot. The unit in place on which the cost is based may be one used in a particular trade, such as cost per ton of air-conditioning, or it may be any selected basic unit of measurement. The assembled total of all constituent unit costs provides an estimated direct cost for the entire improvement. Contractor's overhead and profit may be included in unit cost figures (as in some cost services) or may be computed separately. In using any unit price, an appraiser must ascertain exactly what is included. Indirect costs are typically computed separately.

A cost estimate for a brick veneer wall can illustrate this method. Assume that the exterior walls above the foundation are 4-inch face brick tied to impregnated 4 x 8-foot, $\frac{1}{2}$-inch sheathing on 2 x 4-inch studs, 16 inches on center, with insulation between. The stud wall has $\frac{1}{2}$-inch drywall on the inside with two coats of paint. The wall is 17 feet high to the cornice line; for each square foot of wall surface, $7\frac{1}{2}$ bricks are required. The following unit prices are developed for the wall (such figures vary according to time and location):

Face brick, installed; common bond, $\frac{1}{2}$ in. struck joints, mortar, scaffolding, and cleaning included	$460.00 per 1,000 bricks
Dimension lumber in 2 × 4 in. wood stud framing, erected	360.00 per 1,000 board ft.
Sheathing, erected	.42 per sq. ft.
Insulation, installed, 2 $\frac{1}{2}$ in. foil backing, one side	.22 per sq. ft.
$\frac{1}{2}$-in. drywall with finished joints	.30 per sq. ft.
Painting, primer and one coat flat paint	.25 per sq. ft.

Thus, an estimate of the cost per square foot of wall might be:

7.5 bricks	$3.45
⅔ foot board measure wood studding	.24
1 ft. sheathing	.42
1 ft. insulation	.22
1 ft. drywall	.30
1 ft. painting	.25
Total per sq. ft.	$4.88

Therefore, the estimate for a wall 17 feet high would be $83 per linear foot. The cost is estimated, without detailed quantities, for an above-ground exterior wall, including the interior finish. The base unit figure covers the greater percentage of the cost of the total wall.

In actual practice an estimator may refine the procedure by adding for waste and extra framing and by recognizing the existence of windows and doors (that require wall openings, lintels, facing corners, and so forth) with a resulting increase or decrease in the basic unit cost. After establishing the basic unit figures, an appraiser can estimate the cost of an entire building.

The unit-in-place method breaks down the cost of a building into figures for component parts. Such a cost estimate is adapted to an appraiser's various needs, such as recording the condition of components or computing the cost of replacement. However, to assemble the basic costs of equipment, material, and labor and to combine them into a final unit-in-place cost may require specialized knowledge. When completely developed, the method substitutes for a complete quantity survey. The method should produce an accurate reproduction or replacement cost estimate with considerably less effort.

The application of the unit-in-place method is not limited to cubic, linear, or area units and may be applied by using the cost in place of complete components, such as the cost of a roof truss fabricated off-site, delivered, and erected.

Unit-in-place cost estimates may be based on an appraiser's compiled data and are also available through certain cost-estimating sources that provide updated monthly figures.

Using the unit-in-place method, an estimated reproduction cost of the warehouse illustrated in Figure 19.1 might be calculated as in Table 19.4.

The estimated cost of $859,635 must be adjusted to bring the figure to current cost from the date on which the unit-in-place costs were estimated. The cost must also be adjusted for the effect of location

Table 19.4 Warehouse Property—Unit-in-Place Application

Excavation	
59,400 cu. ft. @ $.11	$ 6,535[a]
Site	
115,385 sq. ft. @ $.07	8,075
Foundation	
59,400 sq. ft. @ (70% × $.69) = $.48	28,510
Framing	
59,400 sq. ft. @ ($2.42 × 1.2) = 2.90	172,260
Floor—concrete	
59,400 sq. ft. @ ($1.22 + $.20) = $1.42	84,350
Floor—asphalt tile	
4,400 sq. ft. @ $.54	2,375
Ceiling—acoustical tile, suspended	
4,400 sq. ft. @ $1.45	6,380
Plumbing (3 washrooms)	
9 fixtures @ $1,050	9,450
Drains @ $155 × 2	310
Sprinklers	
59,400 sq. ft. @ $.71	42,175
Heating, cooling, and ventilating	
55,000 sq. ft. @ ($.49 × 1.12) = $.55	30,250
4,400 sq. ft. @ $2.19	9,635
Electricity and lighting	
59,400 sq. ft. @ $.83	49,300
Exterior wall—8″ concrete block, brick facade	
15,180 sq. ft. @ $5.36	81,365
5,060 sq. ft. @ $6.77	34,255
Partitions—2 × 4 wood studs, 16 in. o.c., drywall, painted	
8,650 sq. ft. @ $1.45	12,540
10 doors @ $61.50	615
Overhead doors (4)	
10 ft. × 12 ft. × 4 = 480 sq. ft. @ $8	3,840
Roof joists and deck	
59,400 sq. ft. @ $3.44	204,335
Roof cover and insulation	
59,400 sq. ft. @ $.93	55,240
Miscellaneous specified items	17,840
Total[b]	$859,635

Source: *Marshall Valuation Service* (Los Angeles: Marshall and Swift Publication Co.), Segregated Cost Method, Sections 44, 52, and 99, January 1978.

[a]Figures are rounded.

[b]Contractor's overhead and profit, insurance, taxes, and permits are included. Architect's fees and indirect costs are not included.

(city, community, or area) on the estimated unit prices. Such adjustments would be calculated or derived from the cost service being used. Consider factors of 1.00 and 0.96, respectively, in the following illustration:

Total (from estimated costs)	$859,635
Current cost multiplier	× 1.00
	$859,635
Local cost multiplier	× 0.96
Indicated reproduction cost	$825,250
Rounded:	$825,000

Quantity Survey Method

The most comprehensive and accurate method of cost estimating is the quantity survey method. In its strictest application, it is a repetition of the contractor's original method of developing a bid figure. A quantity survey is a computation of the quantity and quality of all materials used and of all categories of labor hours required, to which unit cost figures are applied to arrive at a total cost estimate for materials and labor. To this estimate an appraiser adds estimates for other contractor costs, such as permits, insurance, equipment rental, field office, supervision, and other overhead, plus a margin for profit.

A summary of a contractor's cost breakdown for the building illustrated in Figure 19.1 is shown in Table 19.5. The summary is based on a breakdown of labor and material, which is not included here.

Based on the summary, an appraiser may estimate current reproduction cost at $841,000. This example is not in itself a complete quantity survey breakdown. It represents a recapitulation of the contractor and subcontractor's quantity survey analyses. Items above, not subcontracted, are computed by the contractor on the basis of estimated labor hours at prevailing wage levels plus material quantities at current delivered cost to the contractor.

In recent years, the percentage of a general contract that consists of subcontract work has increased. Subcontractors have become more efficient in their specialties; subcontract unit-in-place cost compares favorably with the cost at which the work could be accomplished with the general contractor's own employees. Each contractor and subcontractor has a breakdown of material, labor, indirect costs, overhead, and profit items, which are part of the total estimated cost.

Overhead and profit are variables depending on, among other things, the volume of work the contractor may also have in prospect.

Table 19.5   Contractor's Breakdown of Labor and Material

General conditions of contract	$ 4,415
Excavating and grading	13,930
Concrete	102,335
Carpentry	14,320
Masonry	109,180
Structural steel	157,585
Joists, deck, and deck slab	185,400
Roofing	32,320
Insulation	18,200
Sash	2,955
Glazing	6,368
Painting	4,278
Acoustical material	3,262
Flooring	1,875
Electric	42,346
Heating, ventilating, air-conditioning	36,290
Piping	3,630
Plumbing and sprinkler system	43,542
Overhead and profit	59,030
Total	$841,261
Rounded:	$841,000

Contingencies represent another category, particulary if renovation is involved. A contractor may also allocate the anticipated profit among the various components of cost, rather than as a separate item, in a cost breakdown available to an appraiser.

The quantity survey method leading to a complete cost breakdown is time consuming and costly. Its preparation usually requires the services of an experienced cost estimator. An appraiser, however, may accumulate available quantity survey cost summaries for various types of improvements. With suitable adjustment for physical differences or for time, such summaries provide an appraiser with a sound basis for estimating the reproduction or replacement cost of reasonably similar improvements through direct comparison.

The cost estimate for the warehouse (Figure 19.1) constitutes the basis for a general contract bid. All indirect costs must be included in the final cost estimate. Land improvements—parking facilities, landscaping, and signs, for example—may or may not be included in the general contract. The costs for items not included are estimated separately and are then added to the general contract figure to derive a direct cost estimate for all improvements.

Summary

An accurate indication of value in the cost approach partly depends on an accurate estimate of reproduction or replacement cost of the improvements on the date of the appraisal. Three methods used for such estimates are the comparative-unit method, the unit-in-place method, and the quantity survey method. The choice of a method for estimating reproduction or replacement costs depends on the type of property under consideration and the demands of the particular situation. For all methods, an appraiser calculates direct and indirect costs, as well as market-indicated entrepreneurial profit.

The comparative-unit method is widely used in appraisal. It derives a reproduction or replacement cost by comparing unit costs of similar structures in terms of dollars per square or cubic foot. An appraiser can often refer to a cost-index manual to update known costs and to verify estimates. By maintaining an accurate record of actual building costs, which are properly classified and broken down into square- or cubic-foot units, an appraiser can make reasonably reliable comparative cost estimates.

In comparing unit figures, an appraiser must adjust for cost differentials caused by variations in building perimeters, number of exterior corners, total linear feet of interior partitions, and extent and quality of mechanical equipment. The accuracy of the comparative-unit method rests on the estimator's skill in identifying and adjusting for these differences.

The unit-in-place, or segregated-cost, method of estimating reproduction or replacement costs breaks down the overall cost of a structure into costs for individual components as installed, such as roofing, flooring, and foundations. The total of such constituent unit costs reflects direct costs for the entire improvement. Unit-in-place cost estimates are also available through published cost-estimating manuals that provide updated monthly figures.

The quantity survey method examines the quantity and quality of each type of material, the categories of labor required for construction, and the contractor's margin of profit and insurance costs. Strictly speaking, it is a re-creation of the contractor's initial method of developing a bid. The quantity survey method is the most comprehensive and precise approach to estimating reproduction or replacement costs, but it is also the most costly and time consuming. It is usually not necessary for routine appraisal assignments.

Chapter 20

Accrued Depreciation

Accrued depreciation is a loss in value from the reproduction cost or replacement cost of improvements from any cause, as of the date of an appraisal. A loss to structures or other improvements emanates from one or more of three sources. The sources are physical deterioration, functional obsolescence, or external obsolescence. After identifying and measuring the separate elements of the accrued depreciation, an appraiser deducts the dollar amounts of the applicable types of depreciation from the reproduction or replacement cost of the improvements. The resulting difference is the estimated present value of the improvements.

Theoretically, depreciation can begin to accrue from the moment construction is completed, even in a building that is functionally the highest and best use of a site. Although physical deterioration can be corrected or at least stabilized for a time, it nevertheless tends to persist. As time progresses, functional obsolescence also tends to occur. In addition, even certain new buildings contain various forms of functional obsolescence, such as those attributable to poor design.

In the cost approach, depreciation from all causes should be subtracted from current cost new. However, depreciation is a penalty only to the extent that it is recognized as a loss in value by the market. In older buildings, the loss in value may be offset by a temporary undersupply relative to demand or by a building's historical significance or architectural excellence.

An appraiser's use of replacement cost rather than reproduction cost to derive the current cost estimate may affect the estimate of accrued depreciation. The calculation of most functional obsolescence is eliminated at the outset by the use of replacement cost. However, because of the extent of subjective determinations required in replacement cost estimates, reproduction cost estimates are frequently preferred, particularly in litigation appraising.

Definitions

An appraiser who performs an analysis of accrued depreciation should understand several terms. The terms are depreciation, accrued depreciation, book depreciation, economic life, remaining economic life, effective age, and actual age.

Depreciation is a loss in value from any cause. Deterioration, or physical depreciation, is evidenced by wear and tear, decay, dry rot, cracks, encrustations, or structural defects. Other types of depreciation are caused by obsolescence, either functional or external. Functional obsolescence may be caused by such items as inadequacy or superadequacy in size, style, or mechanical equipment. Physical deterioration and functional obsolescence are evident in the improvement. External obsolescence is caused by changes external to a subject property, such as changes in demand, changes in general property uses in the subject property's area, and changes in zoning, financing, and national regulations.

Accrued depreciation is the difference between an improvement's reproduction or replacement cost and its present value as of the date of the appraisal. In measuring accrued depreciation, an appraiser identifies and measures the loss in value experienced by the subject structure in its present condition, as compared with the value it would have as a new improvement. Accrued depreciation is sometimes referred to as diminished utility.

An accounting term, *book depreciation is the amount of capital recapture charged off on an owner's books.* Generally, the term refers to the amount allowed under the tax laws to a particular owner to provide for the retirement or replacement of an asset. Accountants generally have based depreciation on book value or original cost.

Economic life is the period over which improvements to real estate contribute to property value. Economic life and physical life can differ widely. For example, improvements that have varying degrees of physical integrity are ordinarily replaced with new structures. A property's economic life cannot exceed its physical life; typically it is shorter.

Remaining economic life is the estimated period over which improvements continue to contribute to property value. An appraiser's determination of remaining economic life partly derives from interpreting the attitudes and reactions of typical buyers of competitive properties.

Actual age, sometimes called historical or chronological age, *is the number of years that have elapsed since an original structure was built.*

Effective age is the age indicated by the condition and utility of a structure. If a building has had better-than-average maintenance, or is of better quality or design, or if there is an undersupply of such buildings, its effective age may be less than its actual age. For example, a 40-year-old building may have an effective age of 20 years due to rehabilitation or modernization. However, if the building has been inadequately maintained, its effective age may be greater than its actual age.

Methods of Estimating Accrued Depreciation

An appraiser identifies depreciation due to physical deterioration, functional obsolescence, and external obsolescence by analyzing improvements and the market's reaction to their observed condition. The measure of depreciation that can be charged as a deduction from an improvement's current reproduction or replacement cost is typically indicated by the difference between the contribution of the improvement to current market value and the market-value contribution of a similar improvement constructed new on the date of the appraisal.

An appraiser can use any of several methods to estimate accrued depreciation; each is acceptable provided that the appraiser applies it consistently and logically and that it reflects the manner in which an informed, prudent buyer would react to the conditions encountered in the structure being appraised. The key to an accurate and supportable estimate of accrued depreciation, irrespective of the method used, is that the appraiser considers all property elements that may cause a diminution in value and, in addition, that the appraiser considers each element only once. The methods for estimating accrued depreciation are the economic age-life method, the modified economic age-life method, the breakdown method, sales comparison techniques, and income capitalization techniques. An additional method for estimating physical deterioration *only* is the physical age-life method.

Economic Age-Life Method

In the economic age-life method, the ratio of effective age to total economic life is applied to the current cost of the improvements to obtain a lump sum deduction for accrued depreciation.

$$\frac{\text{Effective age}}{\text{Total economic life}} \times \text{reproduction or replacement cost} = \text{accrued depreciation}$$

The simplicity of this method is deceptive; too many items of accrued depreciation are obscured by being lumped together. Thus, one major weakness is that curable items are not treated separately. Also there is no recognition that short-lived items may have a shorter remaining economic life than the total structure.

Modified Economic Age-Life Method

The effect of curable items of accrued depreciation is recognized in the modified economic age-life method. According to the method, an appraiser first estimates the cost to cure all curable items of physical deterioration and functional obsolescence (deferred maintenance). The appraiser then deducts the sum from the current cost of the improvements. Finally, to arrive at a percentage lump-sum deduction that covers all incurable elements, the appraiser applies to the current cost of improvements less the curable physical and functional items the ratio of effective age to total economic life (see Table 20.2).

Although immediately curable items are recognized in this

Table 20.1   Estimating Accrued Depreciation by the Economic Age-Life Method

	Replacement Cost	Reproduction Cost
Current cost	$213,560	$222,725
Total economic life	50 yrs.	50 yrs.
Remaining economic life	34 yrs.	32.5 yrs.
Effective age	16 yrs.	17.5 yrs.
Ratio applied to current cost	16 ÷ 50 = 32%	17.5 ÷ 50 = 35%
Less total accrued depreciation	68,339	77,954
Depreciated value of improvements	$145,221	$144,771
Plus land value	60,000	60,000
Indicated value by the cost approach	$205,221	$204,771
Rounded:	$205,000	$205,000

Table 20.2 Estimating Accrued Depreciation by the Modified Economic Age-Life Method

	Replacement Cost			Reproduction Cost		
Current cost			$213,560			$222,725
Less physical and functional curable items			1,975			2,250
			$211,585			$220,475
Total economic life	50 yrs.			50 yrs.		
Remaining economic life[a]	35 yrs.			33.5 yrs.		
Effective age[a]	15 yrs.			16.5 yrs.		
Ratio applied to cost less physical and functional curable items	15 ÷ 50 = 30%			16.5 ÷ 50 = 33%		
Less incurable items	$211,585 × .30 =		63,475	$220,475 × .33 =		72,757
Total depreciated value of improvements			$148,110			$147,718
Plus land value			60,000			60,000
Indicated value by the cost approach			$208,110			$207,717
Rounded:			$208,000			$208,000

[a]After curable physical deterioration and curable functional obsolescence have been accounted for, the remaining economic life would be increased and the effective age lessened, depending on the magnitude of the changes.

method, it still does not always allow for individual differences in remaining economic life among a structure's components, particularly
among short-lived items. The method is instead predicated on the assumption that one age-life ratio is applicable to the entire structure.

The modified economic age-life method is based on the assumption that utility is reduced on a straight-line basis. It therefore has the
advantage of being simple. However, the method may be most appropriate when applied to situations in which there is no external obsolescence or in which a structure is relatively new.

Breakdown Method

To apply the breakdown method of estimating accrued depreciation,
an appraiser estimates the total loss in value due to accrued depreciation by analyzing each cause of depreciation separately and measuring
the amount of each. The appraiser then totals the estimates to derive a
lump-sum deduction from the estimated reproduction or replacement
cost. When using replacement cost, the appraiser should not include
deductions for certain types of functional obsolescence in the estimate
of accrued depreciation.

The five basic elements of accrued depreciation in structures are

1. Curable physical deterioration

2. Incurable physical deterioration

3. Curable functional obsolescence

4. Incurable functional obsolescence

5. External obsolescence

To facilitate an understanding of these separate items, the order
in which they are discussed in this chapter follows the sequence in
which they are traditionally treated in appraisal reports. However, an
appraiser typically measures all curable items (physical and functional)
first and then analyzes physical, functional, and external incurable
items. This procedure is necessary because incurable items cannot be
measured properly until all curable items have been measured.

In typical appraisal practice, especially in the valuation of single
family properties, the nature of the appraisal problem does not require
the detailed method shown in Table 20.2. However, the simple cost per
square foot derived from a national cost service and the lump-sum accrued depreciation estimate from the age-life methods are distillations
of the methods illustrated in the pages that follow. Appraisers should
be familiar with the more exacting and detailed methods to apply the
simpler ones accurately.

The following tables illustrate applications of the breakdown method. In the tables, site value is presumed to be supported by market analysis. The tables are based on a two-story office building that has 4,667 square feet of gross building area and 3,770 square feet of net rentable area and that is on a 2,372-square-foot site. The building contains most forms of accrued depreciation. Both reproduction and replacement costs are used for current cost estimates.

A summary of the reproduction and replacement cost estimates is included in Table 20.3 so that one can easily follow the calculations of accrued depreciation. Subsequent tables illustrate the estimations of each category of depreciation in relation to both reproduction and replacement cost estimates.

Curable Physical Deterioration

Curable physical deterioration refers to items of deferred maintenance; the estimate of curable physical deterioration is applicable only to the items subject to current repair. Thus, the measure of this element of accrued depreciation is the cost of restoring an item to new or reasonably new condition (that is, the cost to cure)—the cost of exterior painting, roof repair, or tuckpointing, for example. Tables 20.4 and 20.5 show the calculations for physically curable items.

The cost to cure is not the measure of any difference in value unless an appraiser can demonstrate that the condition of depreciation is curable at the time of the appraisal. The test of the curability of any observed condition in improvements to be appraised is whether the cost of fixing or curing the condition would result in an equal or greater value increase. Nearly every structural defect, deficiency, or superadequacy can be corrected in terms of construction technology. However, the crucial consideration is economic. Will curing restore function? Is it prudent to cure at this time?

Appraisers differ on how to categorize an otherwise curable item that is only partly worn. For example, a five-year-old roof of the type that might be expected to have a total physical life of 25 years obviously contributes less than if it were new. Some appraisers argue that the 20% loss cannot economically be cured as of the date of the appraisal; others argue that deteriorated roofs are indeed curable. The pro-rata loss of such an item must be deducted in one or the other category; an appraiser's decision as to which category is immaterial to his or her opinion of market value.

Incurable Physical Deterioration

Incurable physical deterioration involves an estimate of deterioration that is not practical or currently feasible to correct. It pertains to all structural elements that were not listed in the physically curable cate-

Table 20.3   Difference between Reproduction and Replacement Cost by the Quantity Survey Method

	Reproduction Cost	Replacement Cost
Direct costs (includes labor, materials, equipment, and subcontractor's fees)		
Excavation and site preparation	$ 395	$ 395
Foundation	4,685	4,685
Exterior walls	53,275	53,275
Roof structure	9,720	9,720
Roof cover	2,505	2,505
Frame[a]	19,590	12,690
Floor structure	12,925	12,925
Floor cover (carpet)	5,995	5,995
Ceiling	5,505	5,505
Interior partitions	33,300	33,300
Painting (exterior and interior)	1,250	1,250
Plumbing system	5,675	5,675
Plumbing fixtures[b]	2,685	2,135
Electrical system	6,560	6,560
Electrical fixtures	3,415	3,415
HVAC	13,580	13,580
Total direct costs	$181,060	$173,610
Indirect costs and entrepreneurial profit (including builder's overhead and profit, architect's fees, survey, legal fees, permits and licenses, insurance, taxes, financing charges, selling expenses, leasing expenses, and holding expenses)[c]	41,665	39,950
Total reproduction cost	$222,725	
Total replacement cost		$213,560
Per sq. ft. of gross building area	$ 47.72	$ 45.76

[a]The building was designed and built to accommodate three stories, not two. The difference is the additional frame cost.

[b]A special medical sink was installed for one office unit. There is no market demand for medical office space in this location, and typical lessees would not want the sink.

[c]Part of the indirect costs is based on a percentage of direct costs, which would account for the slight difference in indirect costs.

Table 20.4   Reproduction Cost
Curable Physical Deterioration (Deferred Maintenance)

	Reproduction Cost	Cost to Cure	Remainder
Roof cover (repair)	$2,505	$ 250[a]	$2,255
Painting	1,250	1,350[b]	0
Total curable physical deterioration		$1,600	

[a]A new roof is not necessary on the date of the appraisal; however, the roof requires some repair.

[b]Cost to cure exceeds current cost due to additional labor and preparation work not involved in new construction.

Table 20.5   Replacement Cost
Curable Physical Deterioration (Deferred Maintenance)

	Replacement Cost	Cost to Cure	Remainder
Roof cover (repair)	$2,505	$ 250[a]	$2,255
Painting	1,250	1,350[b]	0
Total curable physical deterioration		$1,600	

[a]A new roof is not necessary on the date of the appraisal; however, the roof requires some repair.

[b]Cost to cure exceeds current cost due to additional labor and preparation work not involved in new construction.

gory. In addition, it applies to the current reproduction or replacement cost of the entire structure *less* the components treated as curable.

For purposes of analysis, items that evidence incurable physical deterioration are classified as long-lived and short-lived. A long-lived item is a component that is expected to have a remaining economic life that is the same as that of the entire structure. A short-lived item is a component that is expected to have a remaining economic life that is shorter than the remaining economic life of the entire structure.

Whether items of physical deterioration (other than items of deferred maintenance) are classified as curable or incurable, deterioration in short-lived items must be measured consistently. Moreover, each element of the structure must be measured only once. Tables 20.6 to 20.9 show the calculations for estimating the physical deterioration evident in both short- and long-lived items.

In the following tables, incurable physical deterioration is estimated by using the economic age-life method. An alternative method
of estimating such deterioration is based on physical age-life, which is
particularly appropriate when the market does not provide reliable
data from which to measure economic life.

When applying the physical age-life method to an entire structure, an appraiser assumes that deterioration occurs at a constant average annual rate over the estimated life of the improvements. If, for
example, the appraiser assumes that a building's physical life is 100
years, the appraiser assumes that physical deterioration will accrue at
the rate of 1% per year ($\frac{1}{100}$ = 1%). The appraiser then deducts this
percentage from the current reproduction cost less physical curable deterioration to arrive at a cost estimate that reflects physical deterioration.

The physical age-life method can also be applied to a structure's

Table 20.6 Reproduction Cost
Incurable Physical Deterioration
Short-Lived Components

	Reproduction Cost Remaining	Effective Age	Useful Life	Depreciation in Percent	Depreciation in Dollars
Roof cover	$ 2,255[a]	10 yrs.	15 yrs.	67%	$ 1,511
Floor cover	5,995	7 yrs.	10 yrs.	70	4,197
Ceiling	5,505	5 yrs.	15 yrs.	33	1,817
Painting	0	New	5 yrs.	0	0
Plumbing fixtures	2,685	10 yrs.	20 yrs.	50	1,343
Electrical fixtures	3,415	8 yrs.	10 yrs.	80	2,732
HVAC	4,750[b]	10 yrs.	15 yrs.	67	3,183
	$24,605				
Total incurable physical deterioration, short-lived components					$14,783
Rounded:					$14,785

[a]$250 of the current reproduction cost of $2,505 was "cured" in physical curable, leaving a
remainder of $2,255.

[b]$4,750 of the current reproduction cost of $13,580 for the entire HVAC system is considered short-lived (i.e., items such as fans, controls, or other mechanical components will
need repair or replacement before the estimated end of the structure's economic life).

Table 20.7 Reproduction Cost
Incurable Physical Deterioration
Long-Lived Components

Reproduction cost		$222,725
Less reproduction cost of		
Curable physical	$ 1,600	
Incurable physical	24,605	
(short-lived)		
		− 26,205
Total long-lived		$196,520
Effective age—5 yrs.		
Economic life (new)—50 yrs.		
$\dfrac{\text{Effective age}}{\text{Economic life}} = \dfrac{5}{50}$		× .10
Total incurable physical deterioration, long-lived components		$19,652
Rounded:		$19,650

Table 20.8 Replacement Cost
Incurable Physical Deterioration
Short-Lived Components

	Replacement Cost Remaining	Effective Age	Useful Life	Depreciation in Percent	Depreciation in Dollars
Roof cover	$ 2,255[a]	10 yrs.	15 yrs.	67%	$ 1,511
Floor cover	5,995	7 yrs.	10 yrs.	70	4,197
Ceiling	5,505	5 yrs.	15 yrs.	33	1,817
Painting	0	New	5 yrs.	0	0
Plumbing fixtures	2,135	10 yrs.	20 yrs.	50	1,068
Electrical fixtures	3,415	8 yrs.	10 yrs.	80	2,732
HVAC	4,750[b]	10 yrs.	15 yrs.	67	3,183
	$24,055				
Total incurable physical deterioration, short-lived components					$14,508
Rounded:					$14,510

[a]$250 of the current replacement cost of $2,505 was "cured" in curable physical deterioration, leaving a remainder of $2,255.

[b]$4,750 of the current replacement cost of $13,580 for the entire HVAC system is considered short-lived (i.e., will need replacement before the estimated end of the structure's economic life) for such items as fans and mechanical parts. The $8,830 remaining is included in the long-lived category.

**Table 20.9   Replacement Cost
Incurable Physical Deterioration
Long-Lived Components**

Replacement cost		$213,560
Less replacement cost of		
Curable physical, short-lived	$ 1,600	
Incurable physical, short-lived	24,055	
		−25,655
Total short-lived		$187,905
Effective age—5 yrs.		
Economic life (new)—50 yrs.		
$\dfrac{\text{Effective age}}{\text{Economic life}} = \dfrac{5}{50}$		× .10
Total incurable physical deterioration, long-lived components		$18,790.50
Rounded:		$18,800

components, such as its foundation; walls; floors; plumbing; electrical, heating, and air-conditioning systems; elevators; and other mechanical equipment. When using this application, an appraiser estimates the expected physical life of each component.

Curable Functional Obsolescence

Functional obsolescence is the adverse effect on value resulting from defects in design. It can also be caused by changes that, over time, have made some aspect of a structure, material, or design obsolete by current standards. The defect may be curable or incurable. To be curable, the cost of replacing the outmoded or unacceptable aspect must be at least offset by the anticipated increase in value. The measure of curable functional obsolescence is the cost to effect the cure. Curable functional obsolescence may be subclassified into

1. *Deficiency requiring additions,* which is measured by the excess of the cost of the addition over the cost if installed new during construction

2. *Deficiency requiring substitution or modernization,* which is measured by the cost of installing the modern fixture less the depreciated value, if any, of the existing fixture or component

3. *Superadequacy,* which is measured by the current reproduction cost of the item plus any physical deterioration already charged less the cost to install a normally adequate or standard item. Superadequacy is cur-

able only if curing it on the date of the appraisal is economically feasible; otherwise, it is considered incurable.

Tables 20.10, 20.11, and 20.12 show the calculations for curable and incurable functional obsolescence with respect to reproduction estimates.

Functional Obsolescence in Replacement Cost Estimates

If current cost is based on a replacement instead of a reproduction, the cost of excess or superadequate items is not included; thus, no deduction to eliminate them is necessary. However, the cost to cure (for example, removing an existing unwanted medical sink) would still constitute a charge, and $75.00 represents the extent of curable functional obsolescence due to the superadequacy. Tables 20.13, 20.14, and 20.15 illustrate the appropriate calculations that are used when an appraiser is involved in replacement cost estimating.

Table 20.10   Reproduction Cost
Curable Functional Obsolescence
Deficiency Requiring Additions

Measured by the excess of the cost of an addition if added on the date of the appraisal over the cost if installed as part of new construction on the date of the appraisal.
    There is no lavatory facility for the offices on the second floor, which has caused difficulty in renting space. There is adequate space available for the addition.

Cost to install in the existing structure	$1,200
Cost to install in the existing structure as if the structure were being built new on the date of the appraisal	−900
Loss in value	$ 300

Table 20.11   Reproduction Cost
Curable Functional Obsolescence
Deficiency Substitutions or Requiring Modernization

Measured by cost to cure after deducting the contributory value, if any, of the deteriorated items.
No loss in value was observed.[a]

[a]Outdated light fixtures may be considered an item of curable functional obsolescence. If the cost of replacing the outdated fixtures with modern ones is $1,000, the $1,000 *minus* the depreciated cost, if any, of the existing fixtures is the measure of the curable functional obsolescence.

Table 20.12 Reproduction Cost
Curable Functional Obsolescence
Superadequacy

Measured by the current reproduction cost of the item less physical deterioration already charged plus cost to install a normally adequate item. This item is curable only if it is economically feasible to cure it on the date of the appraisal. Otherwise, it is incurable.

Current reproduction cost of the item[a]	$550
Less physical deterioration already charged	−275
Plus cost to remove the functionally adequate component and cost to refinish	+ 75
Loss in value	$350

[a]One office was originally occupied by a doctor, and a special medical sink is in place. Rental of this space to another doctor is highly unlikely, and the special sink is not desired by typical tenants.

Table 20.13 Replacement Cost
Curable Functional Obsolescence
Deficiency Requiring Additions

Measured by the excess of the cost of the addition if added on the date of the appraisal over the cost if installed as part of new construction on the date of the appraisal.

There is no lavatory facility for offices on the second floor, which has caused difficulty in renting space. There is adequate space available for this addition. Although space allocation would be included in a replacement cost estimate, fixtures would not be. The logic of the calculation is that it would be improper to take a component from cost that was not included in cost.

Cost to install in the existing structure	$1,200
Cost to install in the existing structure if the structure were built new on the date of the appraisal	− 900
Loss in value	$ 300

Table 20.14 Replacement Cost
Curable Functional Obsolescence
Deficiency Requiring Substitutions and Modernization

No loss in value was observed for curable functional obsolescence due to a deficiency that would need to be corrected by either substitution or modernization. The use of replacement cost would eliminate obsolete components. However, if a structure did contain an obsolete component, there would still be a loss in value equivalent to the cost of removal of the obsolete component plus any repairs. Current replacement cost includes the functionally adequate component.

Table 20.15   Replacement Cost
Curable Functional Obsolescence
Superadequacy

One office contains a special medical sink used by a former tenant who was a doctor. The rental of the office to another doctor is highly unlikely, and the special facility is not desired by typical tenants.

Cost to remove the sink plus repair and refinishing of the space less $75[a]
   salvage value

---

[a]This would be the only charge because the special sink was not included in the current replacement cost estimate.

Incurable Functional Obsolescence

Incurable functional obsolescence may be caused by a deficiency or by a superadequacy. A deficiency is measured by the net income loss attributable to the deficiency by comparison with otherwise competitive properties. The net income loss is divided by the building capitalization rate, as developed in the income capitalization approach. The net income loss may also be measured by the sales comparison approach. There are instances in which this form of obsolescence may be measured by applying the gross rent multiplier to the rent loss.

The sales comparison approach is effective in measuring incurable functional obsolescence from a deficiency if sufficient sales data are available. Such sales must have the same deficiency as the subject property. However, even if such sales are used, an additional problem is how to properly account for other types of depreciation found in the comparable properties. The choice of which method to use for measuring incurable functional obsolescence from a deficiency depends on the adequacy of available data.

Incurable functional obsolescence caused by a superadequacy is measured by capitalizing the net income loss due to the superadequacy. Net income loss is based on the added cost of ownership, such as increased taxes and extra heating or other maintenance costs attributable to the superadequacy. The excess current reproduction cost of the item over and above the cost that may be supported by an increase in market rental as a result of the superadequacy is added to the capitalized net income loss.

A superadequacy that is incurable may occasionally create a rental value that is higher than that of an otherwise equivalent property, but the rent may still not be high enough to meet capital requirements of the item's cost. In such a case, the measure of the incurable functional obsolescence due to the superadequacy is the difference between the

Table 20.16   Reproduction and Replacement Cost
Incurable Functional Obsolescence
Deficiency

Measured by capitalizing the rent loss due to the deficiency. The net income loss (or the gross income loss if the gross income multiplier is used) is capitalized by the rate or multiplier developed in the income capitalization approach. A gross income multiplier may be used if data are adequate. For income-producing properties, capitalizing the net income loss is preferable.
   The property lacks parking facilities for the tenants. Street parking is not available.

Estimated net operating income loss due to the deficiency	$ 1,274[a]
Building capitalization rate applicable to subject property as developed in the income capitalization approach to value	10.5%
Net operating income loss of $1,274 divided by the building capitalization rate of .105	$12,133
Estimated functional incurable loss in value due to deficiency (rounded)	$12,135

[a]Market analysis indicates a differential of 75¢ per square foot of net rentable area between office buildings with adequate parking and those without it. As applied to the subject property, this would indicate an annual gross income loss of $2,830 less vacancy and expenses of $1,556, or a net operating income loss of $1,274 per year. In many cases, net income loss as a percentage of gross income loss attributable to functional obsolescence differs from the general income and expense ratio for the property because certain expenses, such as utilities and insurance, are not affected by the deficiency, while other expenses, such as taxes and management, may be affected.

Table 20.17   Reproduction Cost
Incurable Functional Obsolescence
Superadequacy

Measured by the current reproduction cost of the component less physical deterioration already charged plus the present value of the added cost of ownership, if any, due to the condition. This added cost might include taxes, insurance, and maintenance that are attributable to the superadequacy.

Current reproduction cost of the excess component	$6,900[a]
Less physical deterioration already charged	690[b]
Plus present value of added cost of ownership	0[c]
Estimated incurable functional obsolescence due to superadequacy	$6,210

[a]The building was designed and built to accommodate a three-story structure; however, only two stories were constructed. It would not be economically feasible to add the additional floor.

3-story cost new	$19,590
2-story cost new	12,690
Difference	$ 6,900

[b]In incurable physical deterioration, long-lived, a 10% charge was made.

[c]No ownership expenses occur for this type of superadequacy.

Table 20.18   Replacement Cost
Incurable Functional Obsolescence
Superadequacy

This building was designed and constructed to accommodate a three-story structure instead of the existing two-story building. It would not be economically feasible to add the additional floor. Therefore, the building suffers incurable functional obsolescence due to the superadequacy.

If replacement cost is used as the measure of current cost, it does not include the cost of the superadequacy and, therefore, no loss in value is considered except a charge for the burden of ownership due to the superadequacy. This charge includes such items as additional taxes, insurance, and utility charges. The capitalized value of these additional expenses would be the extent of the loss in value. The particular superadequacy found in the subject property would not call for any of these additional expenses. Therefore, in this case there is no loss in value due to the superadequacy.

capitalized rent added by the obsolete item and the item's current cost (less physical deterioration), to which has been added the present value of the added cost of ownership. Methods for calculating incurable functional obsolescence are illustrated in Tables 20.16, 20.17, and 20.18.

External Obsolescence

External influences can cause a loss in value to any property. In the cost approach, the total loss in value due to such influences is allocated between the land and the improvements. Only the portion of the loss that is applicable to the improvements is deducted from the current reproduction or replacement cost as external obsolescence. The effect of external influences on land value is calculated in land valuation.

External obsolescence, which is the result of the diminished utility of a structure due to negative influences from outside the site, is always incurable. The estimate of external obsolescence is based on a thorough neighborhood or district analysis. Its justification must be stated clearly in the neighborhood data section of the appraisal report.

An appraiser can use either of two methods to measure external obsolescence. The appraiser uses the method that is supported by the best market evidence. The two methods are (1) capitalizing the rent loss attributable to the negative influence, or (2) comparing sales of similar properties, some of which are subject to the negative influence and some that are not. If pertinent sales data are abundant, the second method is preferable to the first.

After an appraiser estimates the loss to the entire property that is attributable to external forces, if appropriate, he or she then allocates the loss between land and improvements. The basis for the allocation

Table 20.19   Reproduction or Replacement Cost External Obsolescence

Measured by capitalizing the portion of the net income loss due to the deficiency that is attributable to the building. The net income loss (or the gross income loss if the gross income multiplier is used) is capitalized by the overall rate developed in the income capitalization approach. An alternative method divides the loss in income due to the deficiency between land and building and capitalizes the building portion at the building capitalization rate. Either method should give the same results. A gross income multiplier may be used if adequate data are available. For income-producing properties, capitalizing the net income loss is preferable.

Estimated annual net operating income if not subject to external obsolescence after curing physical and functional sources of accrued depreciation	$10,180[a]
Subject's current net operating income after curing physical and functional sources of accrued depreciation	−7,635
Estimated annual net operating income loss due to external influences	$ 2,545
Overall rate from the income capitalization approach to value	10.0%
Capitalized net income loss $\dfrac{\$2,545}{.10}$	$25,450
Loss to the entire property	$25,450
Proportion of overall rate attributable to the building	73.5%
Amount of external obsolescence applicable to the building	$18,705

is the ratio of the value of the improvements to total property value. For example, if improvements are estimated to constitute about 80% of total property value, the proportion of total external obsolescence allocated to the improvements is 80%. The ratio of the value of the improvements to total property value is based on the ratio for similar properties in the area. Table 20.19 illustrates the estimate of external obsolescence.

The subject property is adjacent to older apartments that are generally in poor condition. Office buildings competitive with the subject and in the same market area and not subject to this detrimental influence are renting for $1.50 more per square foot of net rentable area than the property being appraised. Therefore, the estimated annual net operating income is calculated as follows:

3,770 square feet × $6	$22,620
Less vacancy and expenses	−12,441
NOI	$10,179
Rounded:	$10,180

3,770 square feet × $4.50	$16,965
Less vacancy and expenses	−9,331
NOI	$ 7,634
Rounded:	$ 7,635

Net operating income loss
$10,180 − $7,635 = $2,545

Total Estimates of Accrued Depreciation

After accurately estimating each element of depreciation, an appraiser summarizes the results of the analysis, as illustrated in Tables 20.20 and 20.21.

Table 20.20   Reproduction Cost
Total Estimate of Accrued Depreciation
by the Breakdown Method

Physical deterioration		
Physical curable, deferred maintenance	$ 1,600	
Physical incurable, short-lived items	14,785	
Physical incurable, long-lived items	19,650	
Total		$36,035
Functional obsolescence		
Functional curable	$ 650	
Functional incurable	18,345	
Total		$18,995
External obsolescence		18,705
Total accrued depreciation		$73,735

**Table 20.21　Replacement Cost
Total Estimate of Accrued Depreciation
by the Breakdown Method**

Physical deterioration		
Physical curable, deferred maintenance	$ 1,600	
Physical incurable, short-lived items	14,510	
Physical incurable, long-lived items	18,800	
Total		$34,910
Functional obsolescence		
Functional curable	$ 375	
Functional incurable	12,135	
Total		$12,510
External obsolescence		$18,705
Total accrued depreciation		$66,125

Final Value Indication

When an appraiser measures accrued depreciation by the breakdown method, the appraiser derives the final value indication in the cost approach first by deducting the estimate of accrued depreciation from the reproduction or replacement cost of the improvements on the date of the appraisal and then by adding the figure to the market value of the land on the same date. These final calculations are shown in Tables 20.22 and 20.23. Table 20.24 provides a comparison of value indications derived by the use of the replacement and reproduction cost estimates.

**Table 20.22　Reproduction Cost
Summation and Final Value Indication
by the Cost Approach**

Estimated current reproduction cost	$222,725
Estimated accrued depreciation	− 73,735
Estimated reproduction cost less accrued depreciation	$148,990
Estimated depreciated value of site improvements	0
Estimated land value	60,000
Value indicated by the cost approach	$208,990
Rounded:	$209,000

Table 20.23 Replacement Cost Summation and Final Value Indication by the Cost Approach

Estimated replacement cost	$213,560
Estimated accrued depreciation	−66,125
Estimated replacement cost less accrued depreciation	$147,435
Estimated depreciated value of site improvements	0
Estimated land value	$ 60,000
Value indicated by the cost approach	$207,435
Rounded:	$207,400

Table 20.24 Comparison of Cost Approach Value Indications by Use of Replacement and Reproduction Costs

	Reproduction Cost	Difference in Dollars	Replacement Cost
Direct	$181,060	(7,450)	$173,610
Indirect	41,665	(1,715)	39,950
Total	$222,725	(9,165)	$213,560
Accrued depreciation			
Curable physical	$ 1,600	(0)	$ 1,600
Incurable physical, short-lived	14,785	(275)	14,510
Incurable physical, long-lived	18,650	(850)	18,800
Subtotal	$ 36,035	(1,125)	$ 34,910
Curable functional, deficiency	0	(0)	0
Curable functional, deficiency	300	(0)	300
Curable functional, superadequacy	350	(275)	75
Subtotal	$ 650	(275)	$ 375
Incurable functional, deficiency	$ 12,135	(0)	$ 12,135
Incurable functional, superadequacy	6,210	(6,210)	0
Subtotal	$ 18,345	(6,210)	$ 12,135
External obsolescence	$ 18,705	(0)	$ 18,705
Total accrued depreciation	$ 73,735 (33.1%)	(7,610)	$ 66,125 (31.0%)
Depreciated value of improvements	$148,990	(1,555)	$147,435
Land value	$ 60,000		$ 60,000
Value indication	$208,990	(1,555)	$207,435
Rounded:	$209,000		$207,400

Table 20.25   Indirect (or Market Abstraction) Method of Estimating Accrued Depreciation

	Sale 1	Sale 2	Sale 3
Sale price	$215,000	$165,000	$365,000
Estimated land value	−60,000	−40,000	−127,750
Present value of improvements	$155,000	$125,000	$237,250
Estimated replacement cost of comparable sale on date of sale	$230,000	$195,000	$375,000
Less present allocated value of improvements	−155,000	−125,000	−237,250
Indicated total accrued depreciation in dollars	$ 75,000	$ 70,000	$137,750
Indicated total accrued depreciation as % of current replacement cost (rounded)	33%	36%	37%

Estimating Accrued Depreciation by Sales Comparison and Income Capitalization Approaches

An appraiser can measure accrued depreciation by applying the techniques of the sales comparison and income capitalization approaches. The applicable rule is that reproduction or replacement cost on the date of the appraisal minus the value contribution of the improvements on the same date equals total accrued depreciation.

Although this is a reliable method for measuring accrued depreciation, its accuracy depends on the existence of truly comparable sales of both improved properties and vacant sites. For an example, see Table 20.25, which indicates a total depreciation of between 33% and 37%.

The above sales are current and their physical, functional, and external elements of accrued depreciation are similar to those of the subject property. Adjustments should be made for any dissimilarities. The above sales indicate a close range of between 33% and 37%, as compared with the total percentage of depreciation estimated by the other methods, which were as follows:

	Replacement Cost	Reproduction Cost
Economic age-life	32%	35%
Modified economic age-life	30%	33%
Breakdown	31%	33%

In this method of estimating depreciation, whether the total depreciation is physical, functional, or external, is immaterial. If the sale is an open-market transaction, if the site value is market-supported, and if the estimate of current replacement or reproduction cost is accurate, the total represents a reliable indication of accrued depreciation.

However, this method of measuring accrued depreciation has certain limitations, which are that

1. An adequate quantity of comparable sales data of high quality is needed. Truly comparable sales are not always available. In addition, certain special purpose properties are not frequently bought and sold in the open market. In such cases, the method would be of little use.

2. The method essentially is another way of applying the sales comparison approach. It is not a check on the other approaches to value because it uses their conclusions to develop its own.

3. The allocation of sale price between site value and present improvement value for comparable sale properties is usually very difficult to justify.

Summary

In the cost approach to value, an appraiser must estimate all depreciation that has accrued to property improvements. Accrued depreciation is the loss in value from the reproduction or replacement cost of improvements from any cause, as of the date of an appraisal. Depreciation can begin the moment construction of an improvement is completed and is sometimes referred to as diminished utility.

There are three sources of accrued depreciation. They are physical deterioration, functional obsolescence, and external obsolescence. Physical deterioration and functional obsolescence can be curable or incurable. Curable physical deterioration is represented by items in need of immediate repair. Items that incur incurable physical deterioration are short- and long-lived. A short-lived item is a component that is expected to have a remaining economic life that is shorter than that of the entire structure; a long-lived item is a component that is expected to have a remaining economic life the same as that of the entire structure. Functional obsolescence can be caused by defects in design or by changed standards that cause design features or existing materials to be outdated. Functional obsolescence can be curable or incurable. External obsolescence, however, is always incurable; it is a loss in value that results from negative influences outside a site's boundaries.

In estimating depreciation, an appraiser must often calculate the cost to cure some aspect of the depreciation that is evident in the structure. The cost to cure an improvement is a measure of a difference in value only if an appraiser demonstrates that the condition of depreciation is curable at the time of the appraisal. If the cost of fixing or curing such an observed condition would result in an equal or greater value increase, it is worth being cured. In effect, the test of curability is not based on the technological capability to cure the defect (or deficiency, etc.), but is a market test of feasibility. The existence of depreciation from physical deterioration, functional obsolescence, and external obsolescence is identified through an analysis of the improvements and the market's reaction to the observed condition of the improvements.

There are several methods of estimating accrued depreciation. Appraisers most often use economic age-life, the modified economic age-life, and the breakdown methods. Appraisers also use techniques of the sales comparison and income capitalization approaches. Physical deterioration can also be measured by the physical age-life method.

Regardless of the method used, an appraiser must make certain that any property element that may cause a diminution in value is considered, and that each is considered only once. Moreover, in deducting the measure of depreciation from the current reproduction or replacement cost, an appraiser must carefully choose which type of cost to use because the estimate of accrued depreciation will not necessarily be the same for both.

In the economic age-life method, a figure for the entire deduction for accrued depreciation is arrived at by using the following calculation:

$$\frac{\text{Effective age}}{\text{Total economic life}} \times \text{Reproduction or replacement cost} = \text{accrued depreciation}$$

Although this method is concise, it has several disadvantages, the most important being that curable items and items that may have an economic life of shorter duration than the total structure are not recognized separately.

The modified economic age-life method is based on the assumption that utility is reduced on a straight-line basis. In this method, the cost to cure all curable items is estimated first, and the sum is deducted from the current cost of the improvements. A lump sum deduction for all incurable elements is obtained by using the same formula employed in the economic age-life method *after* the curable physical and functional items are deducted.

In the breakdown method, an appraiser estimates the loss in value of all elements of depreciation separately and measures the amount of each. The appraiser considers all the curable physical and functional items first and then analyzes the physical, functional, and external incurable items. The appraiser then totals the estimates to derive the lump-sum deduction from the estimated reproduction or replacement cost.

If accrued depreciation is to be measured by applying sales comparison or income capitalization techniques, the appraiser subtracts the market-derived contribution of the improvements to current market value from the reproduction or replacement cost on the date of the appraisal. The accuracy of this method depends on the existence of truly comparable sales of both improved properties and vacant sites.

Chapter 21

Reconciliation of Value Indications

An appraisal is performed because a client has a question about real estate. For example, a prospective buyer may want to know the market value of the fee simple estate in a property. To answer this question, an appraiser follows the valuation process. According to the process, an appraiser identifies, gathers, and analyzes general and property-specific data; determines highest and best use; and applies the sales comparison, income capitalization, and/or cost approaches as warranted by the question and pointed to by the available data.

When more than one approach is used, each results in a separate, usually different, indication of value. Thus, if two or three approaches are used, an appraiser will have derived at least two or three value indications. Furthermore, several value indications may be included in a single approach. In the sales comparison approach, each comparable produces an adjusted sale price, which is an indication of value. In the income capitalization approach, different indications of value may result from direct capitalization, yield capitalization, and gross income multiplier analysis.

When multiple value indications are derived in any single approach, an appraiser often resolves the discrepancies in the indications as part of the application of the approach. In certain cases, however, it may be advantageous for the appraiser to perform the procedure after reviewing the entire appraisal so that the appraiser can apply all pertinent information to derive a single value indication from each approach. Resolution of the differences among the various value indications is called reconciliation. *Reconciliation is the analysis of alternative conclusions to arrive at a final value estimate.*

Review

To prepare for reconciliation, an appraiser may review the entire appraisal to make certain that the data used and the analytical techniques and the logic followed are valid, realistic, and consistent. Data may be checked for authenticity and representation of pertinent market activity. In addition, an appraiser should be certain that all meaningful market evidence has been considered.

The methods and techniques of analysis may be reviewed. Have all relevant approaches been used? Have any irrelevant approaches, methods, or techniques been used? Have the methods been correctly employed? Have the data and analyses been applied in such a manner as to ensure consistency? For example, is the property's effective age that is used in the cost approach consistent with the stated condition for which adjustments may have been made in the sales comparison approach? Have the same highest and best use conclusions of both the land as though vacant and the property as improved been the bases for all approaches? Do the results of the three approaches confirm the selection of highest and best uses?

When checking for internal consistency, an appraiser would realize that there is not necessarily a direct relationship between the dollar adjustments in the sales comparison approach, the expenses in the income capitalization approach, and the elements of accrued depreciation in the cost approach. The bases are different. For example, an adjustment in the sales comparison approach for physical condition would represent the value difference between the subject and the comparable properties. A deduction for physical deterioration in the cost approach would represent the part of the value difference between a hypothetical new property and the existing property, which is the result of physical wear and tear. Further, in the income capitalization approach, an allowance for replacement may be included in the expense estimate, or recapture of capital, when applicable, may be provided for by the capitalization rate. The assessment of the property's existing condition should be consistent throughout the appraisal.

Finally, in the review, an appraiser may rethink the logic employed in the valuation process. Do the approaches and methods most efficiently and realistically lead to meaningful conclusions related to the purpose and use of the appraisal? Will the final result lead to a solution of the client's problem? For example, if the client's problem is to establish a basis for depreciation deductions for federal income tax computation, does the appraisal separate the values of improvements and land? If the client's problem is to establish a basis for insurance coverage, does the appraisal contain a well-supported estimate of reproduction or replacement cost of the insured improvement? Or, if the client's problem is to decide which use should be made of a parcel of land, have all reasonable and realistic potential highest and best uses been examined?

Mathematical calculations should be checked, preferably by someone other than the person who originally made them. Errors in arithmetic can lead to errors in value indications and destroy the credibility of the entire appraisal. It is easy for the person who makes calculations to overlook errors when attempting to check them. Therefore, an independent check of numerical calculations is an important part of the review.

Reconciliation Criteria

Although a review of an appraisal substantiates the accuracy, consistency, and logic leading to value indications, an appraiser's professional experience, expertise, and judgment are exercised in reconciliation more than in any other part of the valuation process.

Reconciliation is the step in the valuation process in which an appraiser considers and selects from alternate value indications to arrive at a final value estimate. The appraiser weighs the relative significance, applicability, and defensibility of each value indication and relies most heavily on that which is most appropriate to the appraisal's purpose. All the assignment's influences are brought into focus in relation to the client's question, which guides the appraiser's deliberations in reconciliation.

Although reconciliation necessarily involves judgment, the appraiser's judgment results from a careful, logical analysis of the procedures leading to each indication of value. The analysis is based on several criteria that enable an appraiser to form a meaningful, defensible conclusion about the final value estimate. These criteria are appropriateness, accuracy, and quantity of evidence. The criteria are equally important in analyzing multiple value indications within each approach and in reconciling the indications into a final estimate of the defined value. The applications of the criteria to both situations are discussed below.

Appropriateness

An appraiser uses the criterion of appropriateness to judge each approach's pertinence to the purpose and use of the appraisal. The appropriateness of an approach is usually most directly related to property type and market viability. For example, the appraisal to estimate the market value of a 20-year-old, single family residence would ordinarily employ the sales comparison approach. The cost approach would be much less appropriate, and income multiplier analysis would be appropriate only if the property or comparable properties were typically rented. Thus, sales comparison might be the only approach used; even if other approaches were used, sales comparison normally would receive the greatest weight.

If the subject property were income-producing, the income capitalization approach would probably be considered more appropriate than the sales comparison or cost approaches. However, if the property were relatively small, and there were an active, viable market for highly similar properties, the sales comparison approach might be considered equally appropriate. Moreover, if the property were fairly new and evidenced little accrued depreciation, the cost approach might also be considered appropriate.

Although the final value estimate is based on the approach that is most applicable, the final value estimate may be different from the value indication from the most applicable approach. If two approaches are significant in the valuation, the final estimate of value may be closer to the value indication from one than the other. For example, assume that the indication of value derived from the income capitalization approach is lower than that derived from the sales comparison approach. If the market is being influenced heavily by income-earning potential, the final estimate may be closer to the value indication from the income capitalization approach than that derived from the sales comparison approach.

The criterion of appropriateness is also applied in judging the relevance of each comparable property and each significant adjustment in an approach. Is a comparable property a valid and reliable indicator of the subject property's value? Is it physically and locationally similar? Is it bought and sold in the same market? Were the characteristics of the transaction the same as those expected for the subject property? If the subject property produces income, are the income and expenses of a comparable property sound indicators of similar items for the subject property? Are cost data appropriate, and are estimates of accrued depreciation justified by market analysis?

Accuracy

The accuracy of an appraisal is measured by an appraiser's confidence in the correctness of the data, of the calculations in each approach, and of the adjustments to the sale price of each comparable property. For example, are cost data and estimates of accrued depreciation in the cost approach as accurate (correct) as adjustments in the sales comparison approach, or as income, expenses, and capitalization rates in the income capitalization approach? An appraiser may have more confidence in the accuracy of the data and calculations in one approach than in the others.

The number of comparable properties, the number of adjustments, the gross dollar amount of adjustments, and the net dollar amount of adjustments may be indicators of relative accuracy. The availability of a large number of comparable properties for one approach may suggest greater accuracy, and therefore an appraiser would rely on it more than the others. For example, if a number of properties competitive with the subject property are available from which an appraiser can extract income, expenses, and capitalization rates, the appraiser might attribute greater accuracy to the income capitalization and sales comparison approaches than to the cost approach.

If, within an approach, fewer total adjustments must be made to one or two comparable properties than to other comparables, an appraiser might attribute greater accuracy to the value indications obtained with fewer adjustments. Such a conclusion, however, would normally depend on the relative equality of the size of adjustments. If the number of adjustments is similar among comparable properties, the gross or net dollar size of total adjustments might vary considerably. For example, the number of adjustments for five comparable properties in the sales comparison approach might be nine each. However, for one comparable property, the gross dollar amount of adjustments might total 15% of the sale price, while the gross dollar amount of the remaining four properties might be less than 5% of each sale price. Other considerations remaining similar, less accuracy would probably be attributed to the comparable property requiring the largest percentage of dollar adjustments.

In certain cases, however, the gross size of dollar adjustments may not be a good indicator of accuracy, particularly if fewer total adjustments are required. A single large adjustment may be more accurate and defensible from market evidence than many smaller adjustments. For example, there may be abundant market evidence in a community to indicate the value added by a swimming pool, a garage, or an extra bedroom. Although an adjustment for the presence or absence of such a large item, as compared with the subject property, might result in a larger gross adjustment than for other comparables, greater accuracy might be attributed to it because of the availability of reliable market evidence as to its value contribution.

Usually, a less reliable indicator of accuracy is the net dollar amount of adjustments, which is obtained by adding the positive and negative adjustments and then subtracting the smaller amount from the larger amount. One cannot assume that inaccuracies in positive and negative adjustments will cancel out each other. Several adjustments that are all positive (or negative) may be more accurate and may produce a smaller total gross adjustment than a combination of positive and negative adjustments.

Furthermore, inaccuracies may compound each other. For example, if too small a percentage adjustment for a poor location is applied to a sale price to which the adjustment for market conditions was too large, the final adjusted sale price will be understated by more than the sum of the two individual adjustments. Thus, this measure should not be regarded as an indicator of accuracy unless an appraiser is confident of every adjustment.

Quantity of Evidence

Appropriateness and accuracy deal with quality—how relevant and correct the value indication produced by a comparable or an approach might be. Although such criteria are separate considerations in reconciliation, both must also be considered in relation to the quantity of evidence provided by a particular comparable or approach. Even when the data meet the criteria of appropriateness and accuracy, they can be weakened by lack of sufficient evidence.

As an example of the importance of the quantity of evidence, consider the extraction of an overall capitalization rate from three comparable properties. Each property is considered appropriate in terms of the similarity of the transactions and the physical and locational characteristics. The available data for each are verified and considered reliable. Each comparable would produce an accurate indication of value. Nevertheless, the available data for one comparable delineate the income and expense forecast for a 10-year holding period, while data for the other comparables are less detailed. Nevertheless, the available data for one comparable delineate the income and expense forecast for a 10-year holding period, while data for the other comparables are less detailed. In one case, no income and expense data could be obtained; in the other, only income and expense data for the first year of the holding period could be obtained. The greater quantity of data for the first comparable would give the appraiser greater confidence in the value indication obtained from it than in those obtained from the other comparables. In statistical terms, the confidence interval in which the true value lies would be narrowed by additional data. They would add precision to accuracy.

Final Value Estimate

The final value estimate may be stated in an appraisal report as a single figure or as a range. Or, an appraiser may show the range and cite the value as a single figure in the range. The traditional way of reporting a value estimate is by stating a single dollar amount—called a point estimate—such as $83,500; $120,000; or $1,300,000. Such an estimate is an appraiser's best dollar estimate of the property's value. A point estimate is required for many purposes, such as real estate taxation, calculation of depreciation deductions for federal income tax, other tax matters, compensation in condemnation cases, determination of lease terms that are based on value, and perhaps certain property transfer decisions. Moreover, because a single figure has typically been used by appraisers in reporting value estimates, many clients have come to expect a single point estimate of value.

Although a point estimate of value may be rounded to reflect a lack of precision in the value estimate, even a rounded number may imply greater precision than is warranted. As an estimate, an appraised value implies a range in which the property's value may lie. For example, a value estimate of $100,000 may mean that an appraiser regards the value as probably between $95,000 and $102,000. The value estimate, $100,000, is the most probable value, or, in statistical terms, the mean of the probability distribution. The appraiser may conclude from the valuation process that he or she is highly confident (80 or 90%) that the value lies in the $7,000 range between $95,000 and $102,000. The range is therefore called a confidence interval.

Although perhaps less satisfying to certain clients than a point estimate, a value estimate stated as a confidence interval has some advantages. First, it provides explicit warning to clients and other readers of an appraisal report that the value estimate is not a precise number. Second, it provides more information to a client by stating the range in which an appraiser believes the value lies and the degree of confidence attributed to the range. Third, such a method of reporting may allow the appraiser to attach probability estimates to values in the range. For example, the appraiser might conclude there is a 50% probability that the property's value is as high as $100,000, a 30% probability that the value may be $97,500 or lower, a 10% probability that it may be $95,000 or lower, and a 10% probability that it could be $102,000 or higher.

The different advantages of a point estimate and a range of value are obtained by reporting both. The point estimate of value might be $100,000, and the relevant range around this value might be $95,000 to $102,000. Probability estimates of points can be included, as noted above. The client is warned that the value estimate is not a precise number. The added information may enable clients to establish limits for asking or bid prices. However, if a single number is needed for a particular purpose, the point estimate can be used.

Rounding

Because a final value estimate is not a precise number, it may be rounded. The general rule for rounding is that answers should be rounded to reflect the input numbers that have the least degree of precision. For example, if the number 15.54 is multiplied by 10 (15.54 x 10), the calculated answer is 155.40, which should be rounded to 155. Such rounding recognizes that the number 10 is not as precise as the number 15.54. Ten could be any number between 9.50 and 10.49, which means the true answers to the multiplication problem could range between 147.63 and 163.01.[1]

Similarly, appraisers should attempt to identify and measure the least precise inputs to the valuation process and use that degree of precision as a guide to rounding. For example, is the value of a swimming pool accurate within $500? $100? If an adjustment for a swimming pool is regarded as accurate only within $500, and it is considered the least accurate (and precise) adjustment, the final value estimate from the approach should be rounded to the nearest $500.

Generally, the more valuable the property being appraised, the less accurate in dollar amount may be the value estimate, and the less precise should be a point estimate of value. The value of properties selling under $50,000 or $75,000 might be estimated to the nearest $500, while the value of properties in the $75,000 to $250,000 range might be estimated to the nearest $1,000 or $5,000. The value of properties selling above $1 million might be estimated to the nearest $10,000 or $50,000.

Summary

Reconciliation is the step in the valuation process in which an appraiser analyzes alternative conclusions and selects a final value estimate from

---

[1]The number 10.00 would be as precise as the number 15.54. The number of significant digits determines the degree of precision.

among two or more indications of value. A thorough review of the entire valuation process may precede this step.

Reconciliation is the part of the valuation process in which the appraiser most directly draws upon his or her experience, expertise, and professional judgment to resolve differences among the value indications derived from the application of the approaches. The appraiser weighs the relative significance, applicability, and defensibility of each value indication and relies most heavily on the one that is most appropriate to the purpose of the appraisal. The conclusion drawn in the reconciliation is based on the appropriateness, the accuracy, and the quantity of the evidence in the entire appraisal.

Appropriateness concerns the relevance of each comparable property and of the approach and techniques used in the valuation process. Accuracy pertains to the capability and reliability of the comparable properties or the approach and techniques to provide a sound indication or final value estimate. The amount of evidence serves to indicate the degree of confidence the appraiser has in a value indication. Much evidence provides more confidence (a more narrow confidence interval), while less causes the appraiser to have less confidence (a wider confidence interval) in the value estimate.

A final value estimate can be stated as a single figure, a range, or a combination of both. The combination of point estimate and range of value provides the most information to a client and thus often increases the usefulness of an appraisal to a client.

A final value estimate may be rounded. The extent of rounding usually increases as the magnitude of value of the subject property increases.

Chapter 22

The Appraisal Report

The function of an appraisal report is to lead a reader from the definition of an appraisal problem to a specific conclusion through reasoning and relevant descriptive data. Thus an appraiser's facts, reasoning, and conclusions must be presented clearly and succinctly. The length, type, and content of appraisal reports are dictated by client requirements, property type, and the nature of the problem.[1]

An appraisal report is either oral or written. Written reports are letter, form, or narrative reports. Usually, an appraiser presents a report in the manner that is requested by the client. However, even if a client requests only the appraiser's opinion without detailed documentation, an appraiser must still perform the detailed requirements of a complete appraisal. All material, data, and working papers used in the preparation of a report are kept in a permanent file. Although an appraiser may never be asked to submit a written substantiation of an

[1]For a thorough discussion of appraisal reports, see Robert L. Foreman, *Communicating the Appraisal: A Guide to Report Writing* (Chicago: American Institute of Real Estate Appraisers, 1982).

opinion that is submitted in abbreviated form, he or she may have to explain or defend the opinion at some time.

Regardless of the type of report, the analysis, opinion, or conclusion that results from an appraisal must be imparted in a manner that is meaningful to a client and will not be misleading in the market. To assure the quality of any type of report, professional appraisal organizations have set requirements for the minimum content of facts, descriptions, and statements of work and purpose in all types of appraisal reports. The requirements adopted by the American Institute of Real Estate Appraisers for oral and written appraisal reports[2] include

1. A clear and reasonably complete description of the real estate (or an interest in the real estate) that is the subject of the appraisal

2. An explanation of the assumptions and limiting conditions on which the appraisal is based

3. All significant facts on which the appraisal is based

4. A reasonably complete summary of the work done and of the appraiser's reasoning

5. The date of valuation and the date of the appraisal report

6. A statement of the interest(s) appraised; if the appraisal is of a fractional interest, a clear statement to that effect and a statement that the value of all other fractional interests may or may not equal the value of the entire fee simple estate considered as a whole

7. If a small part of a large property is being appraised, a clear statement that the appraisal is of the smaller parcel and that the value reported may or may not equal the value of the entire parcel considered as a whole

8. A statement that the appraiser has no direct or indirect current or prospective personal interest in the property being appraised and that the appraiser has no personal bias with respect to the parties involved in the appraisal

In addition to the requirements for all types of reports, written reports should also contain

1. An acknowledgment of all significant appraisal assistance to the appraiser

2. A certified statement that the appraiser has or has not inspected the subject property; that to the best of the appraiser's knowledge and be-

---

[2]See Regulation 10 of the American Institute of Real Estate Appraisers for greater detail and the official language concerning specific requirements for all appraisal reports signed by members or candidates.

lief, the statements of fact in the report are true and correct; that the report sets forth all the assumptions and limiting conditions affecting the analysis, opinions, and conclusions in the report [3]

3. A statement regarding the distribution and use of the report

Oral Reports

An appraiser may make an oral report when circumstances or the needs of a client do not permit or warrant a written report. In an oral report, an appraiser provides a property description and the facts, assumptions, conditions, and reasoning on which the conclusion is based. After making an oral report, an appraiser keeps all notes and data, together with a complete memorandum of the analysis, conclusion, and opinion.

Letter Reports

Sometimes, by prior agreement with a client, an appraiser submits the results of an appraisal in a letter report. A letter report generally sets forth only the conclusions of the appraiser's investigations and analyses. Although much data and reasoning are omitted from the letter, certain items must be included to make the report meaningful. These items include the certificate, an adequate identification of the property, the date of valuation, all limiting conditions, an acknowledgment of the contributions of others, and a statement of nonbias. Although the use of a letter report is limited, a client may desire and specifically request the appraiser's opinion in a letter without detailed documentation.

Form Reports

Form reports often best meet the needs of financial institutions, insurance companies, and government agencies. Because these clients use many appraisals during a year, a standard report form may be more efficient and convenient for their purposes. Such a form enables those responsible for reviewing the appraisal to know exactly where to find any particular category or item of data in the report. By completing the form, an appraiser ensures that no item required by the reviewer is overlooked. Figure 22.1 is a completed form report for a small residential income property.

If a report form seems too rigid, with no provision for certain data the appraiser believes to be pertinent, the relevant information and comments are added as a supplement.

[3]Members of the American Institute of Real Estate Appraisers must also include a statement regarding their status in the Institute's voluntary program of continuing education.

Figure 22.1 Appraisal Report—Small Residential Income Property

APPRAISAL REPORT—SMALL RESIDENTIAL INCOME PROPERTY

File No.

Borrower	
Property Address Any Street	
City Anywhere	County Any	State	Census Tract	Map Reference	Zip Code

Legal Description Lot 13 McMasters Subdivision

Sale Price $ 18,500 Date of Sale 2/4/82 Loan Term 20 yrs. Property Rights Appraised: ☒ Fee ☐ Leasehold ☐ Other

Actual Real Estate Taxes $ 382.85 (yr) Loan charges to be paid by seller $ None Other sales concessions None

Lender/Client Banking and Loan Association Address

Occupant Appraiser Instructions to Appraiser Find and report market value

NEIGHBORHOOD

Location	☒ Urban	☐ Suburban	☐ Rural
Built-up	☒ Over 75%	☐ 25% to 75%	☐ Under 25%
Present land use	____% Condominiums	60% 1-Family	30 % 2-4 Family
	____% Apartments	____% Commercial	____% Vacant	10 % School
Change in present land use	☒ Not likely	☐ Likely (*)	☐ Taking Place(*)
	(*) From		To

Property values	☐ Increasing	☒ Stable	☐ Declining
Housing demand/supply	☒ In balance	☐ Shortage	☐ Oversupply
Predominant occupancy	☒ Owner	☐ Tenant	____% Vacant
Single Family: Price range $ 25,000 to $ 35,000 Predominant $ 30,000

| Age | 70 yrs. to 90 yrs. Predominant 80 yrs |
| Typical multifamily bldg. Type Detached No. Stories 2 No. Units 2-3 |
| Age 80 yrs. Condition Fair-good |
| Typical rents $ 175 to $ 225 ☒ Increasing ☐ Stable ☐ Declining |
| Est. neighborhood apt. vacancy 2% ☐ Decreasing ☒ Stable ☐ Increasing |
| Rent controls ☒ No ☐ Yes ☒ Not likely ☐ Likely |

OVERALL RATING	Good	Avg.	Fair	Poor
Adequacy of Shopping		X		
Adequacy of Utilities		X		
Employment Opportunities	X			
Police and Fire Protection		X		
Recreational Facilities	X			
Property Compatibility		X		
Protection from Detrimental Conditions		X		
General Appearance of Properties		X		
Appeal to Market		X		

| | Distance | Access or Convenience |
		Good	Avg	Fair	Poor
Public Transportation	1 block		X		
Employment Centers	½ mile	X			
Shopping Facilities	1 mile		X		
Grammar Schools	1 mile		X		
Freeway Access	1½ mile		X		

Note: FHLMC/FNMA do not consider race or the racial composition of the neighborhood to be reliable appraisal factors.

Describe those factors, favorable or unfavorable, affecting marketability (incl. mkt. area population size & financial ability). Neighborhood is located on northern side of City of Anywhere near a large corporate office. Grade, high school and parochial schools are located nearby as well as neighborhood park and recreation center.

SITE

Dimensions 50⁺' x 60⁺' = 3,000± Sq. Ft. or Acres ☒ Corner Lot

Zoning classification Low-medium density residential Present improvements ☒ do ☐ do not conform to zoning regulations

Highest and best use: ☒ Present use ☐ Other (specify) Substandard lot - legal - built prior to zoning ordinance

OFF-SITE IMPROVEMENTS	Topo Level
Street Access: ☒ Public ☐ Private	Size Slightly smaller than average
Surface Blacktop	Shape Rectangular
Maintenance ☐ Public ☐ Private	View Average
☐ Storm Sewer ☐ Curb/Gutter	Drainage Adequate
☐ Sidewalk ☐ Street Lights	Is the property located in a HUD Identified Special Flood Hazard Area? ☒ No ☐ Yes

	Public	Other (Describe)
Elec.	☒	
Gas	☒	
Water	☒	
San. Sewer	☒	
	☐ Underground Elec. & Tel.	

Comments (favorable or unfavorable conditions including any apparent adverse easements or encroachments) No known easements or encroachments which would adversely affect marketability. Lot adjoins alley.

To be completed by Lender

☐ Existing ☐ Proposed ☐ Under Construction Type: ☐ Elevator ☐ Walk-up ☐ Det. ☐ Semi-Det. ☐ Row No. Stories 2

No. Bldgs. 1 No. Units 2 No. Rooms 9 No. Baths 2 Parking Spaces: No. 1 Type Off street No. Stories 2

Basic Structural System Frame Exterior Walls Asphalt shingle Roof Covering Asphalt shingle

Foundation Walls Field stone Basement 100% Finished 0 % Describe use Utilities and storage only

Interior Walls Lath and plaster Floors Hardwood – W/W/C Bath Floor and Walls VAT-plaster

Insulation Unknown Adequacy ___ Adequacy of Soundproofing Average

Heating: ☐ Central ☒ Individual Type ___ Fuel Gas Adequacy & Condition Average

Air Conditioning: ☐ Central ☐ Individual Fuel ___ Make ___ Adequacy & Condition ___

Kitchen Cabinets, Drawers and Counter space ☒ Adequate ☐ Inadequate

Total No. Appliances: ___ Range/Oven ___ Fan/Hood ___ Dishwasher ___

Disposal ___ Refrigerator ___ Washer ___ Dryer ___ Compactor ___

Water Heater(s) (make, capacity, fuel) A.O. Smith–40 gal. gas

Plumbing Fixtures (make) Standard

Electrical Service (amps per unit) 120/240 V – 125 amps (2)

Security Features None

Special Features (including energy efficient items) ___

OVERALL PROPERTY RATING	Good	Avg.	Fair	Poor
Quality of construction (materials and finish)		X		
Condition of improvements		X		
Room sizes and layout		X		
Closets and storage		X		
Plumbing–adequacy and condition		X		
Electrical–adequacy and condition		X		
Kitchen equipment–adequacy and condition		X		
Amenities and parking facilities		X		
Overall livability		X		
Appeal to market		X		

Age: Actual 102 yrs. Effective 35 yrs. to 40 yrs. Est. Remaining Economic Life 25 yrs. to 30 yrs. Est. Explain if less than Loan Term

COMMENTS: (including functional or physical inadequacies, repairs needed, modernization, etc.) Lower unit in very good condition with modern kitchen and bath. Upper unit bath, semi-modern kitchen. All updated electrical, plumbing and heating.

ESTIMATED REPRODUCTION COST NEW

x 1st floor - irregular sq. ft. x 964 (Stories) = 1 sq. ft. x $ 30.00	$ 28,920
x 2nd floor - irregular sq. ft. x 695 (Stories) = 1 sq. ft. x $ 30.00	$ 20,850
x ___ sq. ft. x ___ (Stories) = ___ sq. ft. x $ ___	

OTHER IMPROVEMENTS (including special energy efficient items) ___

SITE IMPROVEMENTS: 500

TOTAL ESTIMATED COST NEW OF IMPROVEMENTS $ 50,270

LESS DEPRECIATION: Physical $ 15,000 Functional $ 20,000 Economic $ ___ 35,000

DEPRECIATED VALUE OF IMPROVEMENTS $ 15,270

ADD-ESTIMATED LAND VALUE (If leasehold, show only leasehold value – attach calculations) $ 3,000

INDICATED VALUE BY THE COST APPROACH ☒ FEE SIMPLE ☐ LEASEHOLD $ 18,270

ATTACH LAYOUT SKETCHES SHOWING UNIT ENTRIES, LOCATION MAP AND DESCRIPTIVE PHOTOGRAPHS OF SUBJECT PROPERTY AND STREET SCENE

Figure 22.1 continued

COMPARABLE RENTAL DATA

ITEM	COMPARABLE No. 1	COMPARABLE No. 2	COMPARABLE No. 3
Address	94-96 Parkway	77 Warren	320 Ravine
Proximity to subject	1 mile	1 mile	1 mile
Rent survey date	2/17/81	9/10/81	3/23/81
Description of property and conditions	No. Units 2 No. Vac. 0 Yr. Blt.: 19.14 Boston-style double, good condition	No. Units 2 No. Vac. 0 Yr. Blt.: 19.00 Boston-style double, good condition	No. Units 2 No. Vac. 0 Yr. Blt.: 19. Very similar Boston-style double

Individual unit breakdown:

COMPARABLE No. 1

Rm.Count Tot BR b	Size Sq. Ft.	Monthly Rent $	⊄	Rm
5 2 1	1,112	175	.11	35
4 2 1	1,000	150	.15	37.5

COMPARABLE No. 2

Rm.Count Tot BR b	Size Sq. Ft.	Monthly Rent $	⊄	Rm
4 1 1	908	200	.22	50
4 1 1	908	190	.21	47.5

COMPARABLE No. 3

Rm.Count Tot BR b	Size Sq. Ft.	Monthly Rent $	⊄	Rm
4 2 1	851	170	.20	40
4 2 1	851	170	.20	40

	COMPARABLE No. 1	COMPARABLE No. 2	COMPARABLE No. 3
Utilities, furniture and amenities incl. in rent	Water included, all other utilities paid by tenant	Rent includes hot water, tenants share cost of heating	Water included, all other utilities paid by tenant
Compare comps to subj.	Similar Boston double	Similar Boston double	Very similar double
Utilities included in actual rents:	☒ Water ☐ Gas ☒ Heat ☐ Electric ☐ Air Conditioning	☐ Water ☐ Gas ☐ Heat ☐ Electric ☐ Air Conditioning	☐
Utilities included in forecasted rents:	☒ Water ☐ Gas ☒ Heat ☐ Electric ☐ Air Conditioning		☐

RENT SCHEDULE

ACTUAL RENTS

No. of Units	Individual Unit Rm Count Tot. BR b	Total Rooms	Sq. Ft. Area Per Unit	No. Units Vacant	Per Unit Unfurnished	Per Unit Furnished	Total Rents
1	5 2 1	6	964	0	$ 180	$	$ 180
1	4 2 1	5	695		135		135
TOTAL							$

FORECASTED RENTS

Per Unit Unfurnished	Per Unit Furnished	Per Sq. Ft. or Room	Total Rents
$ 195	$	.20 $ 39	$ 195
140		.20 35	140
			$ 330

Other Monthly Income (Itemize): None

Vacancy: Actual last yr. 0 % Prev. yr. 0 % Forecasted: 0 % $ _____ Total Gross Monthly Forecasted Rent $ 330

Discuss rental concessions, forecasted rents: Existing rental somewhat low and should be raised slightly.

ITEM	SUBJECT	COMPARABLE No. 1	COMPARABLE No. 2	COMPARABLE No. 3
Address	Any Street	Park	Varney	Arthur
Proximity to subject				
Price	$18,500 ☒ Unf. ☐ F.	$19,000 ☒ Unf. ☐ F.	$19,500 ☒ Unf. ☐ F.	$18,500 ☒ Unf. ☐ F.
Date of sale	2/4/82	4/30/81	9/28/81	3/25/81
	Yr. Blt: 19 80 No. Vac.: 0	Yr. Blt: 19 14 No. Vac: 0	Yr. Blt: 19 00 No. Vac: 0	Yr. Blt: 19 80 No. Vac: 0

Individual unit breakdown:

	SUBJECT No. of Units	Tot.	BR	b	COMP 1 No. of Units	Tot.	BR	b	COMP 2 No. of Units	Tot.	BR	b	COMP 3 No. of Units	Tot.	BR	b
	1	5	2	1	1	5	2	1	1	4	1	1	1	4	2	1
	1	4	2	1	1	4	2	1	1	4	1	1	1	4	2	1

	SUBJECT	COMPARABLE No. 1	COMPARABLE No. 2	COMPARABLE No. 3
Compare to subject, including condition, terms of sale/financing		Boston-style double, slightly larger 2nd floor	Rents include heat and hot water	Similar Boston-style double
Gross Bldg. Area (GBA)	1,659± sq. ft.	2,112 sq. ft.	1,816 sq. ft.	1,702± sq. ft.
Gross Monthly Rent	$ 315	$ 325	$ 390	$ 340
Gross Mo. Rent Mult. (1)	58.73	58.46	50.00	54.41
Price Per Unit	$9,250	$9,500	$9,750	$9,250
Price Per Room	$2,055	$2,111	$2,438	$2,313
Price Per S.F. GBA	$ 11.15 /sq. ft. GBA	$ 9.00 /sq. ft. GBA	$ 10.74 /sq. ft. GBA	$ 10.87 /sq. ft. GBA

(1) Sale Price ÷ Gross Monthly Rent | Value Indication for Subject

Val. Per Unit $ 9,500 × 2 Units = $ 19,000 Val. Per S.F. G.B.A. $ 10.75 × 1,659 S.F. Bldg. Area = $ 17,834

Val. Per Rm $ 2,100 × 9 Rms = $18,900 G.R.M. 55 × 335 Total Monthly Rent = $ 18,425

Reconciliation: Due to the fact that this is a nonowner-occupied income property, the value as indicated by the gross rent multiplier is most appropriate.

INDICATED VALUE BY MARKET DATA APPROACH $18,500

ANNUAL EXPENSE SUMMARY - (If for FNMA - Lender must prepare operating data on sep. form for appraiser to review, comment on & attach to appraisal)

			ACTUAL	FORECAST	CALCULATIONS OR COMMENTS
1. Utilities: ☐ Heat $ NA ☐ Electric $ NA ☐ Gas $ NA ☐ Water & Sewer $ 125	Total: $125	$	$125	523	
2. Real Estate Taxes $ 382.85 3. Insurance $ 140	Total:				
4. Management $ NA Salaries $ NA	Total:		225		
5. Maint. & Decor.$ 100 Repairs $ 25 Reserves $ 25	Total:				
6. Other	Total:				

TOTAL EXPENSES & REPLACEMENT RESERVES $ 873 | $ Same

This appraisal is made ☒ "as is" ☐ subject to the repairs, alterations, or conditions listed below ☐ completion per plans and specifications.

Comments, Conditions and Final Reconciliation: Based on the quantity and quality of data available, greatest consideration is given the market data approach which indicates a value as shown below.

This appraisal is based upon the above requirements, the certification, contingent and limiting conditions, and Market Value definition that are stated in ☒ FHLMC Form 439 (Rev. 10/78)/FNMA Form 1004B (Rev. 10/78) filed with client November 22, 19 78 ☐ attached.

I ESTIMATE THE MARKET VALUE, AS DEFINED, OF SUBJECT PROPERTY AS OF February 15, 19 82 to be $ 18,500

Appraiser(s) _____ Review Appraiser (If applicable) _____ ☐ Did ☐ Did Not Physically Inspect Property

Narrative Reports

A narrative appraisal report affords an appraiser the opportunity to support and explain opinions and conclusions and to convince the reader of the soundness of the final value estimate. Because a narrative report is the most complete appraisal report, this chapter is focused primarily on it.

Each appraisal report is intended to answer a particular question and to provide the facts needed by a client. Examples of appraisal questions are: What is the market value of the property? What is the highest and best use of the land as though vacant or the property as improved? In condemnation, what is the value of the part taken? What is the damage to the remainder of the property as a result of the taking?

The objectives of a narrative appraisal report are to (1) set forth in writing the answers to the questions asked by a client, and (2) substantiate those answers with facts, reasoning, and conclusions. To achieve these objectives and to be of maximum service to a client, an appraisal report must present an appraiser's conclusions in a manner that guides a reader to reach similar conclusions through the adequacy and pertinence of supporting data and the logic of the analysis.

In a sense, a narrative report is a summary of the facts and of the appraisal methods and techniques an appraiser has applied to factual material, within the framework of the valuation process, to arrive at a value estimate. A narrative report reflects an appraiser's ability to interpret pertinent data and to select appropriate valuation methods and techniques to derive an estimate of a specifically defined value.

Narrative Report Format

Each narrative appraisal report that is made with the expectation that its conclusions will be accepted must be aimed at maximum communication with the reader, who may be the client or another person to whom the report may be submitted. Readers may scan rather than study a narrative report. Thus, a narrative report is best presented in a manner that readily discloses the property description, the essential analysis of the problem, and the value conclusion.

A well-prepared report goes beyond thorough research, logic of organization, and soundness of reasoning. These basic attributes are enhanced by good composition, excellence of style, and clarity of expression. Technical jargon is avoided, and the report is set forth as succinctly as possible to achieve effective, efficient communication with the reader.

Because an appraiser may not be present when a narrative report is reviewed or examined, the report becomes the appraiser's representative; it creates a favorable impression of professional competence. Certain considerations tend to improve the impression created by a report. They include the following:

1. A good grade of paper, cover, and binding should be used. The paper may show an appraiser's imprint mark.

2. The report may be typed or printed. In either case, type should be attactive, and the size and style chosen for easy readability. Graphic aids, such as photographs and charts, should be well prepared. The style of main and subheadings should be consistent with the subject matter.

3. A good report often has illustrative material on the pages facing the subject matter under discussion. For example, a photograph of the subject property could be placed on the page facing that which gives the verbal identification of the property. An area map could be used on the facing page to the regional and area data to show the location of the neighborhood. A neighborhood map could be a facing page to the neighborhood description to show the location of the subject property. Charts and graphs may be facing pages when they relate to the subject of the narrative discussion. Comparable sales may be facing pages to the narrative discussion of how the sale has been adjusted to reflect the value of the subject property. Illustrative material that is not directly relevant to the report may be placed in the addenda.

4. A report's contents should be presented in the appropriate sections, which are clearly identified in the table of contents.

Outline of a Narrative Report

Although narrative appraisal reports vary in content and arrangement, they all contain certain common elements. Essentially, a narrative report follows the order of the valuation process.

A report usually has three major divisions, the contents of which either are formally separated into sections with subheadings or are not formally separated so that the information flows continuously and provides for easier reading. However, each of the major divisions should have a heading and should be separated from the others. The major divisions are the introduction; the factual description (of the area, the neighborhood, the subject property); and the appraiser's analysis, conclusions, and opinions of value. In addition, a report often contains a fourth major division at the end, addenda, in which are included information and illustrative material that would interrupt the body of the text if included in it. Within the divisions, the organization of the report often varies. The following is a typical example of good organization.

Part One—Introduction

Title page

Letter of transmittal

Table of contents

Certification of value

Qualifying and limiting conditions, including general underlying
  assumptions

Summary of important conclusions

Purpose of the appraisal

Definition of value and date of value estimate

Property rights appraised

Part Two—Factual Descriptions

Identification of the property with photographs

Area, city, neighborhood, and location data

Zoning and taxes

Site data

Description of improvements

History

Part Three—Analysis of Data and Opinions of the Appraiser

Highest and best use of the land as though vacant

Highest and best use of the property as improved

Land value

The sales comparison approach

The income capitalization approach

The cost approach

Reconciliation of the value indications to a final value estimate

Addenda

Detailed legal description (if not included in Part Two)

Detailed statistical data

Leases or lease summaries

Qualifications of the appraiser

The arrangement of this outline is flexible and can be adapted to nearly all appraisal assignments and classifications of real property. In practice, an appraiser adapts the outline to the particular requirements of an assignment and to personal preference. Specific types of property may suggest unique treatment within or in addition to the above outline.

Part One—Introduction

Title page.   The title page introduces the property address, the date of valuation, and the name and address of the appraiser. It may also include the name of the client and the name and address of the person authorizing the report.

Letter of transmittal.   The letter of transmittal formally presents the appraisal report to the person for whom the appraisal was made and is drafted in compliance with approved practices of business correspondence. It is as brief as the character and nature of the assignment permit. A suitable letter of transmittal may include the following:

1. Date of letter and salutation

2. Street address of the property and a brief description, if necessary

3. Statement as to the interest in the property being appraised

4. Statement that inspection of the property and necessary investigation and analysis were made by the appraiser

5. Reference that the letter is accompanied by a complete appraisal report or supported by the appraiser's file

6. Effective date of the appraisal

7. Value estimate

8. Appraiser's signature

Table of contents.   The identification and sequence of components in the report are customarily listed in the table of contents. The headings of the three major divisions and the addenda, if included, should be listed, and subheadings, if used, should also appear.

Certification of value.   A certification of value may follow or may be combined with the final value estimate. The signature of the appraiser, the date, and (when appropriate) a seal are then added. The certification states that an appraiser personally conducted an appraisal in an objective manner. It includes statements that the appraiser

1. Did or did not inspect the property

2. Considered all available factors affecting value in forming an opinion of value

3. Has no present or contemplated interest in the property

4. Conducted the appraisal in conformity with the ethics of the appraisal profession, with reference to membership in any professional organization

5. Did not base the fee on the value reported

6. Attests that the data included in the report are correct to the best of the appraiser's knowledge

Whether included in the transmittal letter or in a separate, signed page, the certification is important because it permits a statement of the appraiser's position, thereby protecting both the appraiser's integrity and the validity of the appraisal.

A frequently used form of certification is the following:

I, the undersigned, do hereby certify that I have personally inspected the property located at:

Property address
County, City, State

To the best of my knowledge and belief the statements of fact contained in this report and upon which the opinions herein are based are true and correct, subject to the assumptions and limiting conditions explained in the report.

Employment in and compensation for making this appraisal are in no way contingent upon the value reported, and I certify that I have no interest, either present or contemplated, in the subject property. I have no personal interest or bias with respect to the subject matter of the appraisal report or the parties involved.

This appraisal report identifies all of the limiting conditions (imposed by the terms of my assignment or by the undersigned) affecting the analyses, opinions, and conclusions contained in this report.

No one other than the undersigned prepared the analysis, opinions, or conclusions concerning real estate that are set forth in this appraisal report.

In my opinion, the subject property has a value on [date] of:

[Dollar amount]

_____

[Signature]

Assumptions and limiting conditions.   Assumptions and limiting conditions, which may be stated in the letter of transmittal, are usually included as separate pages in the report. They are statements used for the appraiser's protection and for the information and protection of the client and others using the report. Appropriate standard conditions are an important part of a report and should be stated clearly. The following section includes examples of general assumptions and general limiting conditions. The section begins with a statement an appraiser can make about general assumptions.

This appraisal report has been made with the following general assumptions:

1. No responsibility is assumed for the legal description or for matters including legal or title considerations. Title to the property is assumed to be good and marketable unless otherwise stated.

2. The property is appraised free and clear of any or all liens or encumbrances unless otherwise stated.

3. Responsible ownership and competent property management are assumed.

4. The information furnished by others is believed to be reliable. However, no warranty is given for its accuracy.

5. All engineering is assumed to be correct. The plot plans and illustrative material in this report are included only to assist the reader in visualizing the property.

6. It is assumed that there are no hidden or unapparent conditions of the property, subsoil, or structures that render it more or less valuable. No responsibility is assumed for such conditions or for arranging for engineering studies that may be required to discover them.

7. It is assumed that there is full compliance with all applicable federal, state, and local environmental regulations and laws unless noncompliance is stated, defined, and considered in the appraisal report.

8. It is assumed that all applicable zoning and use regulations and restrictions have been complied with, unless a nonconformity has been stated, defined, and considered in the appraisal report.

9. It is assumed that all required licenses, certificates of occupancy, consents, or other legislative or administrative authority from any local, state, or national government or private entity or organization have been or can be obtained or renewed for any use on which the value estimate contained in this report is based.

10. It is assumed that the utilization of the land and improvements is within the boundaries or property lines of the property described and that there is no encroachment or trespass unless noted in the report.

This appraisal report has been made with the following general limiting conditions:

1. The distribution, if any, of the total valuation in this report between land and improvements applies only under the stated program of utilization. The separate allocations for land and buildings must not be used in conjunction with any other appraisal and are invalid if so used.

2. Possession of this report, or a copy thereof, does not carry with it the right of publication. It may not be used for any purpose by any person other than the party to whom it is addressed without the written consent of the appraiser, and in any event only with proper written qualification and only in its entirety.

3. The appraiser herein by reason of this appraisal is not required to give further consultation, testimony, or be in attendance in court with reference to the property in question unless arrangements have been previously made.

4. Neither all nor any part of the contents of this report (especially any conclusions as to value, the identity of the appraiser, or the firm with which the appraiser is connected) shall be disseminated to the public through advertising, public relations, news, sales, or other media without the prior written consent and approval of the appraiser.

Summary of important conclusions.   When an appraisal report is long and complicated, a statement of the major points and important conclusions in the report may be desirable. Such a statement provides a reader with a convenient summary and affords an appraiser an opportunity to stress points that have been considered in reaching the final estimate. The following is a list of the type of material that is frequently included. However, all of the items do not apply to all appraisal assignments.

1. Estimates of highest and best use of both land as though vacant and property as improved

2. Age of improvements

3. Estimate of land value

4. Value indication from the sales comparison approach

5. Value indication from the income capitalization approach

6. Value indication from the cost approach

7. The final estimate of defined value

8. The allocation of value between land and improvements or between the leased fee and leasehold estates

An appraiser may use a different summary for longer or more complex reports. A summary is omitted in many appraisal assignments, particularly if the letter of transmittal contains some brief discussion of conclusions concerning the more important items.

Purpose of the appraisal.   This section states the purpose of the report, that is, the question to which the client seeks an answer. It can easily be combined in the property identification section of the report. The appraiser may simply state that

The purpose of this report is to estimate market value on [a given date].

Definition of value and date of the value estimate.   An acceptable definition of the value that is the purpose of the appraisal is included in the report to eliminate any confusion in the mind of a client or another reader of the report. Acceptable definitions of the types of value are cited in Chapter 2.

An appraisal assignment may involve an estimate of current value or of value as of some past point in time. The date as of which a conclusion of value is applicable is integral to a report.

Property rights appraised.   In identifying a subject property, an appraiser must clearly define particular rights or interests. This is particularly important in assignments that involve a partial interest in a property, limited rights such as surface or mineral rights, the value of the fee subject to a long-term lease, or a leasehold interest. Any other encumbrances—easements, mortgages, or special occupancy or use, for example—are also identified and explained in relation to the defined value that is to be estimated.

Part Two—Factual Descriptions

Identification of the property. The subject property must be so identified that it cannot be confused with any other parcel of real estate. An appraiser can achieve this by giving the full legal description. When a copy of the official plat or an assessment map is used, the appraiser refers to it at this point and includes it on a facing or following page. In the absence of a plat, the appraiser describes the property by name, by the side of the street on which it fronts, by street number, and by a lot and block number. A photograph of the subject on a facing page may enhance this section of the report.

Area, city, neighborhood, and location data. All facts about a city and its surrounding territory that the appraiser has judged pertinent to the specific appraisal problem may be included in the area data. The types of data, their appropriate uses in relation to the various classifications of property and to specific types of problems, and their degrees of influence are discussed in Chapters 6 and 7. In an appraisal, an appraiser weighs and considers all pertinent factors but should confine the discussion to data found significant to the problem under consideration.

When an appraisal problem involves a considerable amount of supporting statistical data—such as population figures, cost-of-living indexes, or family income figures—an appraiser usually places such data on facing pages and refers to them in support of his or her conclusions. A separate section is not needed for area data in many reports; the data may be combined with neighborhood data.

The data that may be significant to an appraisal report include

1. Distance and direction from employment centers

2. Public transportation

3. Road pattern, layout, and width of streets

4. Adequacy of utilities and street improvements

5. Proximity to shopping

6. Proximity to schools

7. Proximity to parks and recreation

8. Proximity to nuisances

9. Police and fire protection; rubbish collection

10. Trends in the neighborhood or district

11. Population trends

12. Percentage of homeownership

13. Types of employment and wage levels

14. Conformity of development

15. Vacancy and rent levels

16. Restrictions and zoning

17. New construction activity

18. Percentage of vacant land

19. Changing land use

20. Level of taxes

21. Adequacy of street and off-street parking

22. Street traffic, type, and amount

23. Pedestrian traffic, type, and amount

24. Proximity to expressways, tollroads, and airports

25. Rail connections and service for freight

26. Concentration of advertising by retail merchants

As in other sections of the report, the extent of neighborhood and location data depends on certain circumstances. For example, when an appraiser does work for an out-of-town client who is unfamiliar with the property or even the community, an appraiser may find it desirable to include more community and neighborhood data than is necessary for a local client. When appraising an important business property for which income is derived from the purchasing power of the entire supporting area, an appraiser should have a detailed description of the neighborhood and of the influence of the population and its purchasing power on the value of the subject property.

An appraiser describes the presence of special amenities or detrimental conditions and includes the reasons or data that support any conclusion about such items. For example, when an appraiser states that an area is growing, he or she refers to actual growth figures or building projects. If a neighborhood is in decline, from abnormal deterioration or poor maintenance in an area, an appraiser refers to specific properties that exhibit these detrimental conditions. The appraiser can use photographs to illustrate neighborhood conditions.

Area and neighborhood data represent the background against which the property being appraised is considered. The data acquire significance in proportion to the extent that they affect property value. Hence, these sections of an appraisal are incomplete when they do not include some analysis of the trends that are indicated by the data.

Thus, an appraiser presents a conclusion that is the result of professional experience and judgment in interpreting the data in terms of their effect on the marketability of the subject property. Without this interpretation, city and neighborhood data lose significance in a report; proper use of these data may be critical in establishing the potential of the property being appraised.

Zoning and taxes.   Zoning data are included in the land description section of an appraisal report or are shown elsewhere as a separate section. When they are of significant importance, zoning and private restrictions are discussed in detail. The text of the specific zoning may be in the body of the report or reproduced in the addenda. If the specific zoning is not included, sufficient data are provided to help a reader identify the limitations zoning regulations place on the use or development of the site. When appraising vacant land, an appraiser discusses the possibility of zoning changes and points out existing public and private restrictions and their effect on the utility and the value of the property. In addition, an appraiser reports current assessed values and ad valorem tax rates, and also analyzes existing assessment trends or prospective changes in tax rates.

Site data.   Pertinent facts about a site belong in a report's site data section. Among such facts are descriptions of the frontage, depth, site area, shape, soil and subsoil conditions, utilities, and improvements that benefit a site.

Description of improvements.   In the description of improvements section, an appraiser includes and discusses all building and improvement data relevant to the appraisal problem. Although an appraiser considers and processes much data during an appraisal, the appraiser sets forth only the significant elements that influence conclusions. These elements include

1. Building age and size

2. Unit number and size

3. Structural and construction details

4. Mechanical equipment

5. Physical condition

6. Functional utility or inutility

An appraiser may support the presentation of this information by using drawings, photographs, floor plans, and elevations. If descriptions of structural and mechanical details are long, an appraiser needs only to present an outline in the body of the report, with an emphasis on the important items.

History.   The history section of a report may include original assemblage, acquisition, or construction cost information; capital additions or modernization expenditures; financial data or transfers of ownership; casualty loss experience; history and type of occupancy; reputation or prestige; and any other information that may pertain to or affect the computations, estimates, or conclusions of the report.

Part Three—Analysis of Data and Opinions of the Appraiser

Highest and best use of the land as though vacant.   If an appraiser's estimate of the value of the land as though vacant is based on a suggested program to achieve a particular highest and best use, the report must clearly state this fact. The report must also include a statement that the estimate of value does not apply unless the future use of the property will be in accordance with the program proposed. If for some reason the property cannot be thus adapted and used, the report indicates this fact and states the use that underlies the appraiser's value estimate. The character and amount of data presented and analyzed depend on the purpose of the appraisal.

Highest and best use of the property as improved.   The conclusion of highest and best use of the property as improved recognizes that removal and replacement of existing improvements are not economically warranted on the date of the appraisal. As long as an existing improvement is retained, the highest and best use conclusion is based on how the entire property should be used to maximize its benefits or the income it produces. An appraiser may make suggestions pertaining to such actions as rehabilitation, improved maintenance, or better property management.

Land value.   The land value section of a report includes the presentation of market data or other information pertaining to land value, together with an appraiser's analysis of the data and the reasoning leading to a value conclusion.

Approaches to value.   An appraiser develops the applicable approaches to achieve indications of value. In each approach used, an appraiser presents the factual data and the analysis and reasoning leading to each indication.

Because many clients may not be familiar with the mechanics of the three approaches, an appraiser may explain the procedures in the development of the data to the extent that appears appropriate to the circumstances of the appraisal. Simple statements that explain what is included in each of the three approaches help the reader to understand what is to follow. Examples of such statements are:

In the sales comparison approach, the subject property is compared to similar properties that have been sold recently or for which listing prices or offering figures are known. Data for generally comparable properties are used, and comparisons are made to demonstrate a probable price at which the subject property would sell if offered on the market.

In the income capitalization approach, the current rental income is shown with deductions for vacancy and collection loss and operating expenses. A conclusion about the prospective net operating income of the property is developed. In support of this net operating income estimate, operating statements for previous years may be reviewed, together with available operating-cost estimates. An applicable capitalization method and appropriate capitalization rates are developed for use in computations that lead to an indication of value by the income capitalization approach.

In the cost approach, an estimated reproduction or replacement cost of the building and land improvements as of the date of the appraisal is developed, together with an estimate of the losses in value that have taken place due to wear and tear, design and plan, or neighborhood influences. To the depreciated building cost estimate is added the estimated value of the land. The total represents the value indicated by the cost approach.

Rarely are the three approaches completely independent. An appraisal comprises a number of integrated, interrelated, and inseparable procedures that have the common objective of arriving at a convincing and reliable estimate of value. At times, the three approaches are so intertwined that some appraisers prefer a "one-approach" concept and do not subscribe to the custom of separate presentations.

Reconciliation of value indications. A sound rule that an appraiser should follow in the preparation of an appraisal report is to keep descriptions separate from analysis and interpretation. This implies that factual and descriptive data are limited to the sections of the report where they may logically be presented as such. Analysis and interpretation then include references to the facts and indicate their influence on the final value estimate. Repetition or unnecessary duplication is also undesirable in a report, and application of the above rule may depend on the character and length of a specific report.

Reconciliation of value indications should lead logically to an appraiser's statement of the final estimate of value. The concluding statement of the final estimate of the defined value may be presented in many ways. The following is a simple example:

As a result of my investigation and analysis, it is my opinion that the market value of the property, on July 20, 19___[4] is:

FOUR HUNDRED THOUSAND DOLLARS
($400,000)

When it is desirable to allocate the value conclusion, an appraiser may add (after the amount):

. . . that may be allocated as follows:

Land	$ 80,000
Improvements	320,000
Total	$400,000

An appraiser's qualifications. An appraiser's qualifications are usually included in an appraisal report as evidence of competence to make such an appraisal. These qualifications include facts concerning

1. Professional experience

2. Educational background and training

3. Business, professional, and academic affiliations and activities

4. Clients for whom the appraiser has rendered professional services, the types of properties appraised, and the nature of the appraisal assignment

The use of such statements is so widespread that many appraisers have found it expedient to prepare a printed statement of their qualifications for insertion in each appraisal report.

Addenda

Depending on the size and complexity of an appraisal assignment, addenda may be used to avoid interrupting the narrative portions of the report. If not presented as facing pages in the body of the report, data such as the following may be included:

Plot plan

Plans and elevations of buildings

Photographs of properties referred to in the report

[4]Date on which the value opinion applies may differ from that of the letter of transmittal.

City, neighborhood, and other maps

Charts and graphs

Abstracts of leases

Historical income and expense data

Specifications of buildings

Detailed estimates of reproduction or replacement costs of buildings

Sales and listing data

Tax and assessment data

Summary

An appraisal report is written to portray the property, the facts concerning the property, and the reasoning by which the estimate of defined value has been developed. The estimate is an opinion that reflects the consideration of all data in light of an appraiser's experience and judgment.

Because it states the answer to a client's question, each report presents the problem or a definition of the value that is the purpose of the appraisal and sets forth the facts considered. It clearly outlines the reasoning employed by an appraiser in developing the reported conclusions. Whether a report is brief or lengthy, the report states that the appraiser has made an appraisal, defines the purpose of the assignment, sets forth what was done, describes the property, presents the reasoning leading to the conclusion, and states the underlying assumptions and qualifying or limiting conditions. A report should be a systematic and orderly presentation that enables a reader to understand the conclusions and the reasoning of an appraiser.

Part V
Specialized Topics

Chapter 23

Valuation of Partial Interests

The bundle of rights theory holds that total real property ownership, or title in fee, includes several distinct rights, each of which can be separated from the bundle and conveyed by the fee owner to other parties in perpetuity or for limited time periods. When a right is separated from the bundle and transferred, a partial, or fractional, property interest is created.

Lease practice is one practical application of the bundle of rights theory. An owner of the total bundle (a lessor) may convey to a tenant (a lessee) rights to use and occupy a property for a fixed time period. In return, the tenant assumes an obligation to pay an agreed-upon periodic rent.

The division of property interests may be examined from physical, legal, economic, and financial viewpoints. In real estate appraisal, the cost approach to value, which is essentially a summation procedure, is frequently used to value a property's physical elements. An appraiser views a property as a group of physical components to which values are ascribed and added together to provide an indication of total property value. The simplest example of this procedure is the addition of land and building values. However, the building itself is a composite of many physical components, each of which can be examined and valued separately. The summation of the component values indicates the full value of improvements. Any component can be considered and valued separately.

From the legal viewpoint, property interests can be divided in various ways. For example, in a specific property, several parties may own undivided partial ownership rights through joint tenancies, tenancies in common, or tenancies by the entirety. In a land trust, another example of partial property interests, a group of property owners continues to operate and manage the property while conveying the title to a trustee. Other legal arrangements and title holding entities that divide property rights among groups of owners include corporations, partnerships, cooperative corporations, condominiums, and interval ownerships or timeshares. In such situations, property rights or interests are divided among several parties, and an appropriate legal entity is chosen to hold title.

In the economic division of property rights, the bundle of rights is divided into leased fee, leasehold, and often subleasehold interests through an established body of lease practices. The constitutional right of freedom of contract allows for flexibility in lease arrangements, and consequently a variety of lease contract clauses and provisions have been developed, used, and, in many cases, tested for meaning through litigation leading to judicial constructions. The flexibility has resulted in leasing practices that are responsive to changing economic and financial conditions.[1]

Financial divisions of property interests strongly influence real estate investment practices. The major financial division of property rights is into mortgage and equity components. Mortgage funds are secured debt positions; equity is a venture capital situation. Financial property divisions vary, including senior and subordinated debt, purchase-leaseback finance, and equity syndications.

Physical, legal, economic, and financial property interests are usually freely transferable and mortgageable. Thus, appraisals are needed for the valuation of partial interests.

Physical Division

Real property ownership usually implies control of a property's surface and subterranean area, as well as the space above to a reasonable ele-

---

[1]Lease terms and provisions are fully discussed in Chapter 15.

vation. All property rights are subject to the limitations of zoning, eminent domain, taxes, and other reasonable police power restraints. For example, air rights are subject to the requirements of normal aviation traffic. From the physical viewpoint, property ownership may be (and often is) fractionalized into surface, subterranean, and air rights; all of these rights can be dealt with separately in sales, leases, mortgaging, and other real estate transactions.

Horizontal Subdivision

The most common division of property rights is the subdivision of surface areas. It is the normal pattern of real estate development, by which an owner breaks a large plot into smaller parcels with the expectation of selling or leasing them. A subdivision is designed to create higher, better, and more intense property use than the original use. A subdivision plan does not automatically create improved use; it can do so only when zoning, availability of utilities, harmonious community conditions, access, and a host of other elements favorably combine. Traditionally, those involved in subdivision projects in the United States have divided large surface tracts into smaller plots and have created roads, drainage, public utilities, and other improvements as required by local law and zoning.

The approaches used most often to value subdivision partial interests are the sales comparison approach, which is preferred and used most extensively, and the development cost technique. After a subdivision development has been completed, with roads and utility hookups in place, the sales activities in the subdivision or in others with comparable facilities and locational qualities provide the most reliable indicators of value of partial interests or lots. When valuing an entire proposed subdivision, an appraiser must consider the rate of unit absorption because it indicates the time frame for total property disposition. When the time period is substantially long, expected sales proceeds must be discounted to account properly for the time value of capital employed.

Before the development of a subdivision begins, an appriaser can use a development cost technique to estimate the "as-is" value of proposed lots. The appraiser begins the procedure with a study of market transactions to estimate future sell-out prices for fully improved parcels. Then the appraiser makes a forecast of absorption rate, which indicates an expected sales time frame and related discounting requirements. The appraiser must reduce sell-out prices by the direct and indirect costs and the entrepreneurial profit necessary to bring the parcels to a marketable state. The product, or residual, is a fair expression of "as-is" value of the particular parcels.

Vertical Division

Although not so common as horizontal subdivision, vertical division is becoming more widespread. For many years, surface owners disposed of subterranean rights through sale or lease to permit extraction of minerals or to allow the creation of tunnels for railroads, motor vehicles, and public utilities. Because major urban centers have been developed with high-rise office buildings, the cost of buildable sites has risen astronomically. Thus, developers have had to investigate air rights over parcels in centrally located areas where present surface use is not highest and best use and is often devoted to railroad functions, such as freight or traffic-marshaling yards. For example, office buildings situated along Park Avenue in New York City are constructed on air rights over the surface facilities of the Penn Central Railroad.

Developers also use air rights to add to a proposed project's floor area ratio (FAR). By acquiring air rights over adjacent low-rise structures, the builder of a high-rise project is permitted in certain municipalities to build more floor area than could have been built without the rights. The feasibility of the project is determined by ascertaining whether the value of the additional office space exceeds the construction cost and the cost of the rights.

When a building is to be constructed in air space to which air rights apply, the site can be visualized as a platform constructed at some level above the surface, such as 30 or 40 feet. For support, the level area must have columns, which extend down to column lots and must rest on caisson foundations built on subsurface lots. Figures 23.1 and 23.2 illustrate typical construction in air space to which air rights apply.

To value air rights, an appraiser may use the sales comparison approach to establish the value of the platform area as if it were a normal land surface. From this value the appraiser subtracts (1) the loss in value resulting from any diminution of usability as compared with the surface, (2) any additional or extraordinary construction costs in creating the building platform, such as difficult column placement and construction costs, and (3) the cost of providing lighting or ventilation to the surface area. However, any savings that result from not having to construct a structure with a typical full basement should be added to the market value of the surface. The net result of all subtractions and additions is the value of the air rights. If an appraiser finds that the value of the rights is less than the cost of comparable surface sites, a developer may be interested in using the air rights. The remaining consideration is whether the building will produce sufficient earnings to justify the cost of the site and the improvements.

Figure 23.1   Three-Dimensional Division for Air or Tunnel Rights (schematic drawing)

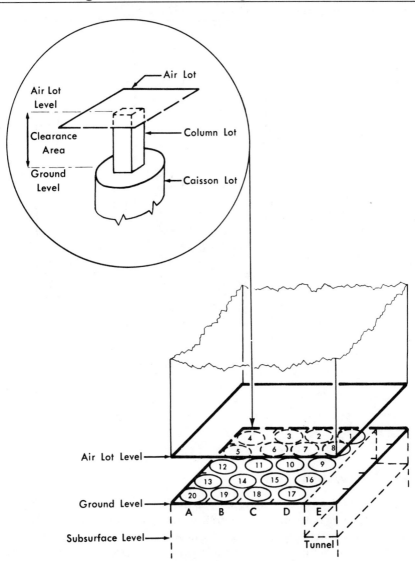

As an example, these may be identified as air rights above air lot level; column lots between air lot level and ground (1-20); caisson lots below ground level (1-20); tunnel rights between ground level and subsurface level (E).

**Figure 23.2   Three-Dimensional Division for Air
or Tunnel Rights (electrical transmission
lines right of way)**

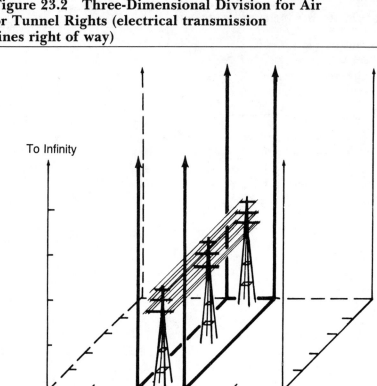

Legal Division

The law has always accorded special importance to the ownership of
real estate. Legal forms of ownership have been created to meet the
special requirements of many individuals by whom title to real estate is
held. To help achieve certain objectives of real property owners, certain legal procedures allow for the division of properties into partial
interests.

Easements

An easement is an arrangement whereby a property owner, while retaining full legal title, conveys a right to another party. The right permits the use of a specific portion of the property for access to an ad-

joining property or as a public right of way. Although surface easements are the most common, many subterranean and overhead easements are used for such purposes as public utilities, subways, bridges, and so forth.

Clearly, a property that acquires rights is a beneficiary, and one that is subjected to them is burdened. Easement rights can be conveyed in perpetuity or for limited time periods. The rights can be created contractually by private parties or can be arranged by states, municipalities, or public utilities through the exercise of eminent domain. In any case, a valuation is needed to estimate the price to be paid by the easement beneficiary to the burdened party.

As a result of an easement that affords ingress and egress, an otherwise landlocked parcel enjoys increased value. Easement rights to a development's recreational facilities normally enhance the value of plots that have such an advantage. Thus, the value of an easement is usually estimated as some part of the value increment to the property that benefits, although the burdened property's loss in value can also help indicate the value of the easement. In such a case, value reflects the basic economic concept of contribution: It makes no sense to pay more for an easement than the gain in value to the property that benefits. It also makes little sense to pay the exact amount or to break even. The benefit, then, is the gain that results from paying less than the added value.

When easements are acquired by public utility companies for such items as overhead power lines, valuation considerations become more complicated. Such a company acquires a benefit: the ability to bring its product to a broad market. Product users are benefited by their ability to purchase the service they need. The owners of the property over which utility lines must run are burdened, they lose part of their original bundle of rights, but they may gain access to the utilities involved. In all such cases, the easement is a partial interest in the burdened real property estate. The easement is created by deed and has measurable value.

Preservation easements are used to protect certain historic properties through the prohibition of certain physical changes, usually based on the condition at the time of the donation of the easement or immediately after a proposed restoration. Under federal legislation, the easement can be deeded to properly qualifying nonprofit organizations or government agencies. In such instances, the donor receives an income tax reduction that can be equal to but may not exceed the market value of the real property rights donated.

The underlying economic theory of the valuation of preservation easements is generally the same as that which governs eminent domain appraising, despite the fact that the acquirer receives rather than takes rights. Each easement document is an individual set of controls and restrictions. An appraiser must carefully analyze the deed of easement to determine its effects on the encumbered property. The level of controls of historic district or individual landmark designations, if any, should be related to the subject property and to the provisions of the easement.

Condominiums

A condominium unit is a separate ownership, with title in an individual owner. The unit may be leased, sold, mortgaged, or refinanced separately. A condominium owner has title to a partial interest in a total project, whether it be housing or commercial property. A condominium owner has ownership of a three-dimensional space within the outer walls, roof or ceiling, and floors. In addition, the owner, together with other owners, has an undivided interest in common areas, such as the land, the public portions of the building, the foundation, the outer walls, and in the spaces that provide for parking and recreation. In a condominium project, owners usually form an association to manage the real estate in accord with adopted bylaws. The expenses of management and maintenance are divided pro rata among the owners and are levied as a monthly fee.

An appraiser usually performs the valuation of individual condominium units by the sales comparison approach. Recent sales of units of comparable size, location, and quality are the best guides. For the valuation of entire condominium projects, whether new constructions or conversions, an appraiser often uses a discounted cash flow analysis. Such a procedure essentially consists of estimating the amount and timing of all capital outlays, as well as expected monetary receipts and returns, and the discounting of such amounts at a rate consistent with competitive investment yield. Key elements in the procedure are estimates of future sellout prices and timing of sales.

Undivided Partial Interests

Often, more than one party has ownership in a specific property. In many such cases, the partial interests are said to be undivided, that is, they cannot be dealt with freely by the separate parties. All interest owners must join to effect conveyances, leases, or mortgages. Among such types of ownership are tenancy in common, joint tenancy, and tenancy by the entirety.

In tenancy in common, title is held by more than one party. Each party has a partial share in ownership, and there are no rights of survivorship. When an owner dies, the partial share passes to the decedent's estate. Joint tenancy also involves undivided partial interests but includes survivorship rights. A surviving partial owner acquires title to the entire property. In certain jurisdictions, tenancy by the entirety is the vehicle for joint ownership by husband and wife. It has the same survivorship arrangements as a joint tenancy.

The valuation of undivided partial interests poses a difficult problem for appraisers. Because no party can exercise complete control, the interest of each is usually worth something less than the corresponding fraction of the market value of the whole property. Minority interests have little market appeal, so the appraiser's problem becomes how to judge the appropriate adjustment. Because each party can bring a legal action, known as partition, the cost of the proceeding is one measure of value diminution. However, because a sale in partition is a forced event, it does not reflect free market action. Thus, because of the lack of pertinent market transactions, valuations of undivided partial property interests often reflect significant subjectivity.

Land Trusts

Land trusts originated in the state of Illinois and are sometimes used as legal vehicles for partial ownership interests in real property. In land trusts, independently owned properties are conveyed to a trustee to effect a profitable assemblage. The trustee holds legal title in the property for a specified time and performs only the functions outlined in the trust indenture. The trustee usually does not actively manage the property or collect rent; such functions remain with the beneficiaries, the original owners. The trustee can convey or mortgage only upon direction of the beneficiaries. An important legal aspect of such an arrangement is that a judgment against a beneficiary is not a lien against the real estate, as would be the case with other property ownership arrangements. An appraiser begins the valuation of a beneficiary's partial interest by making a market value estimate of the total property involved. The appraiser then adjusts the estimate appropriately for any effect on value that results from the trust indenture provisions that identify the rights and obligations of beneficiaries. The beneficiary's minority position will call for significant adjustment.

General and Limited Partnerships

Partnerships are used extensively in real estate acquisition because they pool funds for property ownership and operation. In a general partnership, all partners share in business gains and each is fully responsible for all liabilities.

To value a partner's partial interest, an appraiser first makes an estimate of the market value of the partnership's total assets. The appraiser then adjusts the estimate to reflect the partner's percentage of ownership. An appraiser's additional adjustment should be assessed in light of the terms of the partnership agreement because the terms define the partners' rights and liabilities in sales and liquidations. One important aspect of a partnership is that it automatically terminates upon the death of a general partner. The provisions of partnership contracts that shape and limit ownership benefits influence an appraiser's valuation of the partial interests involved.

Limited partnerships have both general partners and limited partners. The general partners manage the business and assume full liability for partnership obligations. The liability of each limited partner is restricted to his or her respective partnership capital contribution. The investment value of limited partnership interests, or syndicate shares, is judged by assessing income tax shelter benefits. It is not unusual for such investments to offer small income returns, at least during the early years. Rather, the value of these investments is the perceived income tax benefits of building depreciation, mortgage interest, and other shelter benefits. Such items can be used as tax deductions against an investor's income from other sources. The resulting tax deferrals are deemed an earnings element of the partnership interest even though the dollars involved do not flow from partnership property. Frequent tax law changes alter the values of the various shelter benefits. In addition, early property disposition or foreclosure can damage the income tax recapture of shelter advantages. This should be weighed in rating the risk of the investment.

Corporate Ownership

A common form of partial ownership is an ordinary stock corporation. Such a corporation is organized to hold title to a single asset, often a parcel of real property, although it could have a portfolio of investments. Corporate ownership is broken into partial interests by the sale of shares to an investment group. Any specific stock holding represents a percentage of total corporate ownership. The percentage is derived from the ratio of the number of shares owned by the particular interest to the total number of shares issued by the corporation. The percentage is an ownership share in the corporation, and it has a book value that is usually found by multiplying the corporate net worth by the ownership percentage.

However, the market value of a share of stock in a corporation that has a parcel of real estate as its only asset may be higher or lower than its book value. The difference in the values exists because of the lack of investment control involved in minority interests, the limited marketability, the inability of shareholders to force liquidations to realize asset value gains, the unavailability of property tax shelter benefits to shareholders, and the double taxation that results from corporate payment of taxes along with shareholder tax payments on declared dividends.

Because stock market values often represent a discount from corporate net worth, the accounting profession and the Securities and Exchange Commission (SEC) permit publicly owned real estate corporations to prepare annual financial statements that display both customary book values and current valuation of assets. Such figures frequently reveal present values that greatly exceed book values (cost less accumulated depreciation), and hence a larger net worth than that indicated by the book figures. Such corporations seek the current valuations used in financial reports from professional appraisers. Certain corporations establish current values internally and employ appraisers to attest to the reasonableness of the valuations.

Cooperative Ownership

In certain areas, the cooperative ownership of apartments is popular and affords the selling owner/developer or converter an attractive price and gives purchasers control of their living accommodations. A "co-op" begins when a stock corporation is organized to have an authorized number of shares issuable at a specified par value. The corporation takes title to an apartment house and then prices the various apartments. The price per unit determines the number of shares an apartment occupant must purchase to acquire a proprietary lease. The lease obliges the occupant to pay a monthly maintenance fee, which may be adjusted at various times by the corporation's board of directors. The fee covers the expenses of management, operations, maintenance of public areas, and the like. In addition, the fee includes debt service on any mortgage the cooperative has on the property. Shareholders can vote their shares in the elections of directors, thereby exercising some degree of control over property conditions.

One important difference between cooperatives and condominiums has occurred recently in some areas. While condominium owners have always held individual mortgages on their units, cooperative corporations formerly arranged mortgages on entire apartment properties. The cooperative shareholder had to be able to fund 100% equity or to borrow short term from a commercial bank on a personal note. Now, for example, a corporation can arrange a mortgage on the total property, and individual apartment shareholders can mortgage their equities up to 75% of value. Such mortgage arrangements have contributed greatly to cooperative apartment marketability.

If the market for cooperative apartments is active, an appraiser can value an apartment by the sales comparison approach. When adequate comparable sales are available, an appraiser frequently uses the price per room as a unit of comparison. However, the appraiser must remember that prices are influenced by the amount and terms of the mortgage financing the corporation has placed on the building. In recent years, corporate mortgages have ranged between 25% and 50% of total value, with the balance financed by individual apartment shareholders, either as pure equity or with a cooperative apartment mortgage. Corporate bylaws often impose limitations on marketability that affect the validity of comparable data.

Transferable Development Right

During the 1970s, transferable development rights (TDRs) emerged in the real estate industry. TDRs are used to preserve certain property uses, such as use for agricultural production, open green space, or historic buildings. Through a TDR, a preservation district and a development district are identified. Landowners in the preservation district are then assigned development rights. However, they cannot use the rights to develop the land, but can sell them to landowners in the development district, who can then use the rights to build at higher densities than zoning laws in the development district usually permit. TDRs have been explained as a means of "reducing or eliminating the public costs of acquiring development rights by shifting the responsibility for purchasing them from the government to private developers."[2]

An appraiser can value TDRs through ordinary sales comparison techniques, provided a sufficient number of transactions are available to constitute a market. When the market is inadequate, an appraiser can use the income capitalization approach. In such cases, the economic concept of contribution should provide a foundation. The value increment to a property through the acquisition of a TDR is adjusted for the administrative, legal, and other costs incurred. Finally, some, though not all, of the net value increase is the TDR value because no one is likely to undertake such a complicated procedure without the prospect of a reasonable profit.

Timesharing

In recent years, a new real estate partial interest has been marketed extensively, with reasonable success. It is called timesharing, or interval ownership, and is a variation of the condominium. Timesharing is the sale of limited ownership interests in residential apartments or hotel rooms. The ownership is described as limited because a purchaser receives a deed conveying title to the unit for a specific part of a year.

[2]Dale J. Price, "An Economic Model for the Valuation of Farmland TDRs," *The Appraisal Journal* (Chicago: American Institute of Real Estate Appraisers, October 1981).

For example, a person might purchase the first two weeks in July or the last two weeks in December.

Certain timeshare projects are marketed on the basis of the *right to use* a specific unit for a particular time interval. This form of time-share equates to a long-term lease on, for example, Unit 3-A for the last two weeks in December for a period of 20 years. The purchaser does not have an equity interest in the property, but, in effect, has a leasehold interest for a specified time. Other characteristics are similar to interval ownership timeshares. It is imperative that the appraiser distinguish between interval ownership and right to use when apprais-ing timeshare projects or analyzing timeshare comparables.

Timeshare owners receive a title in fee that covers exclusive use of a specific apartment for the agreed-upon interval, along with rights to use public spaces and common areas. The title is recordable and the interest is mortgageable. Interval owners pay their expenses, including a proportionate share of taxes, insurance, and the like. They also pay a fee for common area maintenance and management. In many proj-ects, 50 weekly intervals per year are created, and the remaining 2 are reserved for performance of major repairs and maintenance.

The valuation of such partial interests is accomplished through sales comparison. Because the practice of timesharing is relatively new, an appraiser may not find many comparable sales in certain areas. However, comparables are abundant in resort and vacation areas. An appraiser must give appropriate weight to (1) the time required for sellout; (2) seasonal variations that affect sales; (3) true costs, both di-rect and indirect, necessary to create a facility that will command the price envisioned; and, most important, (4) the element of competition.

Life Estates

Another partial interest in real estate is a life estate. A life estate con-sists of total rights of use, occupancy, and control, but is limited to the lifetime of a designated party, who is often called the life tenant. The estate can be created by a deed of conveyance or may arise by the pro-visions of a last will and testament. The instrument that creates the life estate provides that, upon its termination, the property will either re-vert to an original owner or pass to a designated remainder person.

An appraiser may value such interests by the sales comparison approach (provided market data are adequate) or by the income capi-talization approach. The difference between the property's earning ca-pacity and its cost of operation and maintenance may be regarded as the monetary benefits of ownership. To estimate the probable duration of the income, an appraiser must rely on actuarial studies. If benefits and duration are established, an appropriate discounting rate can be selected and applied.

Economic Division

The most prevalent economic division of property interests is that into leased fee and leasehold estates. A lease contract effects a division of the property interests that constitute the total bundle of rights. It creates rights and privileges for its parties and imposes obligations and burdens. It also establishes the parties' claim priorities to the leased property's earnings.

An appraiser must know what is expected of the lessor and the lessee in terms of fulfilling the obligations delineated by the terms of a lease. Lease terms are intended to shape the quantity and quality of future benefits likely to flow to interests created by the contract. Thus, the agreement provides that, during the term of the lease, the lessor will receive specified rental, money, or services, and on termination will receive a reversion of the tenant's rights of use and occupancy. The lease contract endows the tenant with exclusive rights of use and occupancy during its term, subject to rental or service obligations. Many other divisions of rights are common, such as subleasing by an original tenant and mortgaging both the leased fee and leasehold positions. Types of leases, lease provisions, the analysis of income and expenses, and valuation procedures for valuation of leased-fee estates are discussed in Chapters 14 through 17, which deal with the valuation of income-producing properties.

A lease sets rental terms and presumably indicates gross income to the leased fee. However, in a market value estimate, an appraiser must judge the probability that lease provisions will be honored. For example, in a single-tenant building a lease may oblige the tenant to pay rent in excess of market levels. If the tenant has an insubstantial credit rating, an appraiser could not accord great weight to the lease arrangement. Consequently, the market value estimate for this property would probably be based on current market rents rather than contract rent. If the same lease provisions are assumed, but the tenant is a major business entity that is AAA rated, the appraiser would accord significant weight to the lease terms. The outlook for future income benefits is much clearer in such a situation, and the value of the leased fee may exceed the property's market value unencumbered by the lease.

Lease terms sometimes create advantages for the leasehold position to the detriment of the leased fee position. Thus, an appraiser may be asked to estimate the value of the leasehold, often to determine the penalty the value places on the market value of the property held in leased fee.

The following section presents valuation procedures for various types of lease appraisal problems.

Leasehold

A leasehold interest is held by a lessee, or tenant, who acquires rights to the use and occupancy of a property subject to various obligations, chief among which is the payment of rent. Contract rent is the periodic rent paid by the tenant to the lessor; it is specified in the lease as to both amount and timing. A leasehold interest is said to have value when contract rent is less than market rent, which is the amount a property could earn in a competitive real estate market. Market rent is not profit from a business operated on the premises. It is the rent the real estate can command in the market. In a perfectly negotiated lease, contract rent would probably not differ from market rent.

When market rent exceeds contract rent, the leasehold interest acquires value. When contract rent exceeds market level, there is no leasehold value.

The following example illustrates the valuation of a leasehold interest with a long-term lease.

Assume that:

Rents paid at year's end

Contract rent	$8,000 per yr.
Market rent	$9,000 per yr.
Lease term	25 yrs.
Discount rate for leasehold interest	14% annual

Procedure:

Value of leasehold interest = (market rent − contract rent) × PV of $1 per period for 25 yrs. @ 14% annual

Value = ($9,000 − $8,000) × 6.8729 = $1,000 × 6.8729 = $6,873

Sandwich Lease

Under normal lease terms, a tenant is free to sublease all or part of a property. Many leases require that the lessor's consent be obtained for a sublet, but usually provide that consent "will not unreasonably be withheld." Over the years, court decisions have made clear that subleasing is relatively free. To deny permission, lessors usually must show that the security of their position would be impaired.

In a sublease, a tenant is "sandwiched" between a lessor and a subtenant. The tenant's interest then acquires value when the contract rent is less than the rent collected from the subtenant. Again, valuation is simply the arithmetic of compound interest discount, as the following computation shows.

Assume:
Rents paid at year's end
    Lease contract rent $ 8,000 per yr.
    Sublease rent $ 9,000 per yr.
    Market rent $10,000 per yr.
Lease term   25 yrs.
Discount rate   12% annual
Procedure:
    Value of sandwich position = (sublease rent − lease rent) × PV of $1 per
        period @ 12% for 25 yrs.
    Value = ($9,000 − $8,000) × 7.8431 = $1,000 × 7.8431 = $7,843

The following example illustrates the valuation of a sublessee position.

Assume:
Rents paid at year's end
    Sublease rent $ 9,000 per yr.
    Market rent $10,000 per yr.
Lease term   25 yrs.
Discount rate   16% annual
Procedure:
    Value of sublessee position = (economic rent − sublease rent) × PV of $1
        per period @ 16% for 25 yrs.
    Value = ($10,000 − $9,000) × 6.0971 = $1,000 × 6.0971 = $6,097

Different discount rates are employed in different lease interest valuations because their selection involves risk rating. Under normal circumstances, a lessor's interest, or leased fee, entails less risk than a lessee's interest, or leasehold. The lessee has less risk than the sublessee, whose position is exposed to the greatest risk.

A lease contract may contain a provision that expressly forbids any subletting. Without a right to sublet, a leasehold position could not be conveyed and would have no market value. However, it would have a use value to the lessee involved.

Leasehold Mortgaging

In recent years, leasehold mortgaging, which affords excellent financing and an optimum tax shelter, has been frequently used. To be secure, a leasehold mortgagee who finances building improvements should be certain that the ground rent is not above the level representing a competitively attractive yield on the land value. The mortgagee should also be certain that lease terms afford the right to cure any tenant default. When these precautions are taken, if the leasehold mortgagee must foreclose, he or she can take possession of the property subject to the terms of the lease, and thus be obliged to pay only the required ground rent.

In current investment practice, maximum financing is sought for favorable leveraging and for the best tax shelter. Leases, the mortgaging of lease interests, and subordinations provide the necessary tools. In major investment projects, a property may be divided into a leased fee and a leasehold interest, and then a mortgage may be arranged on the leased fee, and, finally, a leasehold mortgage may be arranged to construct improvements. The leasehold mortgagee may require that the fee mortgage be subordinated to the lease. Hence, if a default occurs on the fee mortgage, and foreclosure ensues, the fee mortgagee will acquire the property subject to the lease. Then, if ground rent is paid either by the leasehold tenant or the leasehold mortgagee, the positions will not be damaged by fee mortgage foreclosure. It is possible for one party, using different legal entities, to hold both the fee position and the leasehold position; however, expert legal advice and draftsmanship is required to assure that documentation adequately supports the separation of the various interests and does not effect a merger of these interests.

Valuation of Mortgaged Lease Interests

Valuation of mortgaged lease interests consists of two mortgage-equity analyses. There is a leased fee equity and leased fee mortgage. Ground rent is paid to the lessor, who allocates the required amount to fee mortgage debt service, and the balance is the lessor's cash flow. In addition, the leased fee enjoys reversion of all property rights at the end of the lease term. Hence, leased fee value subject to the mortgage can be estimated by adding the amount of the leased fee mortgage, the present discounted value of the leased fee cash flow, and the present discounted value of the reversion.

An appraiser begins a leasehold valuation by forecasting the property's gross income earnings, from which operating expenses, ground rent, and leasehold debt service are subtracted. The remaining income is leasehold cash flow. The value of the leasehold subject to the mortgage can be estimated by adding the amount of the leasehold mortgage and the present discounted value of anticipated leasehold cash flow and reversion if appropriate. When leases are used as financing vehicles, ground rent is the equivalent of first mortgage debt service, and leasehold mortgage charges are the equivalent of second mortgage debt service.

When appraising leasehold mortgages, an appraiser can run into difficulties because rent provisions of the ground lease may be variable, perhaps tied to the Consumer Price Index (CPI); debt service on the fee mortgage may be variable; and debt service on the leasehold mortgage could be variable or could contain equity kicker arrangements.

Financial Division

Traditionally, real estate investments have been structured with a substantial amount of debt capital (mortgage money) and less venture capital (equity money). In any situation, the relative proportions of the two types of capital may vary, depending on monetary conditions and investor objectives. For many years, the United States was a capital surplus country; inexpensive, long-term, and fixed-rate debt capital was readily available. The implicit leveraging advantages fostered the typical mortgage-equity combination of real estate. When mortgage funds are less costly than a real estate investment's overall earnings rate, the equity investor, referred to as the property owner, is motivated to leverage the earnings rate by borrowing as much debt capital as possible. Investment structure is a clear example of the financial division of real estate interests.

Possessory Interests

A possessory interest is the right to the occupancy and the use of any benefit in the transferred property, granted under any lease, permit, license, concession, or other type of contract. In a typical lease, such an interest represents a substantial portion of the rights conveyed to a tenant. The interest is not necessarily all tenant rights because the lessee may also enjoy a leasehold advantage measured by the difference between market rent and the contract rent being paid. Although a possessory interest is a tenant right, its value inures to the lessor.

The value of a possessory interest is measured by discounting tenant rental for the lease period at a rate judged appropriate, considering risk and investment competition. For example, a property is net leased to a tenant for 20 years at $8,000 per year, payable at the end of each year. The property's market rental value is estimated to be $10,000 per year, also payable at the end of each year. The value of the possessory interest is $8,000 per year, discounted at an appropriate rate (12% per annum) or $8,000 x 7.4694 = 59,755. (7,4694 is PV of $1 per period @ 12% for 20 yrs.) The leasehold value is the present value of the difference between market rent and contract rent, discounted for the time period at an appropriate rate, say 14%. Value is $10,000 − $8,000 = $2,000 x 6.623 = $13,246. (6.623 is PV of $1 per period @ 14% for 20 yrs.)

The above example clearly differentiates the value of the possessory interest from the leasehold value. Again, the value of the possessory interest inures to the lessor, while the value of the leasehold benefits the lessee.

Because monetary conditions change frequently, and often sharply, the financial division of a typical investment will vary to achieve optimum investment performance. Monetary conditions often change abruptly, and capital availability can be restricted to top credits for short periods. During times of high inflation and high interest rates, long-term debt capital can be relatively unavailable for real estate projects, and the maintenance of market activity would depend on more extensive equity contributions.

Equity contribution is capital invested for a yield consisting of future cash flow dividends. These dividends, and therefore the investment yield, can be augmented by investment growth or diminished by depreciation. This yield, expressed as a compound annual rate, must be competitive with other investment opportunities, such as stock or other securities, or this venture capital will not be available. Equity investors have no contractual right to a specific earnings rate, and they must shoulder most risks of the venture. An equity investor makes modest cash flow demands during early developing investment years but looks for attractive and growing future benefits. Traditionally, equity capital has been less available than debt, or mortgage, funds. Hence, current emphasis on the need for equity has created a new financial atmosphere. Unless venture funds are reasonably available, market activity and velocity may experience a downtrend.

Money managers have developed a method to maintain a mortgage-equity financial division of real estate investments, yet give it a heavier equity emphasis. This is accomplished by creating mortgage investments that can be characterized as quasi-equity. One version is a mortgage with kicker. It provides the mortgagee with a reasonable guaranteed interest return plus a share of either gross or net property income earnings. The ability to negotiate these terms indicates a lender's market. The mortgagee is assured of decent interest earnings, a secured real estate lien position, and a share in increased earnings produced by inflation or other economic forces.

Other methods that permit a mortgagee to share equity benefits have been designed. For example, a mortgage can provide the mortgagee with rights to convert the debt position to equity. Such an arrangement usually involves reasonable mortgage interest earnings during early contract years plus a privilege to change at specified times all, or part, of the mortgage position to an ownership interest. These contracts are attractive to a mortgagee, who can follow a real estate investment's progress from a secured mortgage position. If the investment shows attractive growth, the mortgagee can convert to equity and enjoy the benefits. If it does not, the mortgagee can retain protection of the lien. The ability to negotiate such a contract also indicates a lender's market.

Partnership Interest

In partnerships, the major money delineation is between debt and equity. Partnerships, often called syndications, are an effective means of raising equity capital. This is particularly important in times of high interest rates when debt funds, or mortgage money, may be more expensive and less readily available. Real estate investment earnings abilities cannot cope with unlimited mortgage interest rate demands. Therefore, investors who believe in the future growth of real estate values may be willing to take equity positions. Instead of contractual earnings rates, they will opt for future benefits flowing from income enhancement and value increases.

For such an investor, syndications are attractive because they offer the possibility of investment income and value growth, along with a pass through of tax shelter. It is not unusual, therefore, for realty investments to be structured with whatever debt capital can be acquired at feasible rates, and the balance financed with equity obtained through partnership vehicles. These situations are, on occasions, called joint ventures. A joint venture is a contract that spells out the relationships between co-venturers, covering respective duties, obligations, and the sharing of income and expenses. Clearly, partnership arrangements represent useful, workable arrangements for dividing a real estate investment's financial participations.

Summary

Each individual right that makes up the bundle of rights inherent in real property ownership can be conveyed to other parties. Any such conveyance creates partial ownership rights in real property. Certain appraisal assignments involve the valuation of such rights. Physical, legal, economic, and financial property divisions create partial ownership interests.

The physical components of a property, particularly the land and the buildings, are often valued separately. Further, a building itself is a composite of many physical components that can also be examined and valued separately. Usually, all separate values are added to arrive at an indication of the total property value.

Property ownership can be divided into surface, subterranean, and air rights, all of which can be dealt with separately in sales, leases, mortgaging, and other realty transactions. The most common division of property rights is the subdivision of surface areas, or what is known as horizontal subdivision. Valuation techniques for horizontal subdivisions include the sales comparison approach and the development cost technique.

Vertical division, which includes subterranean and air rights, is less common than horizontal subdivision. To value air rights, an appraiser estimates the value of a platform area, as if it were a normal land surface, through the sales comparison approach.

The legal division of real estate creates forms of partial ownership interests. A common legal division of property is the easement, an arrangement whereby a property owner, while retaining full legal title, conveys to another party a right to use a specific portion of the property.

Other legal partial interests that are valued by an appraiser include condominiums, undivided fractional interests, land trusts, general and limited partnerships, corporate ownership, cooperative ownership, transferable development rights, timeshares, and life estates.

The division of property into leased fee, leasehold, and subleasehold estates is the most common economic division. An appraiser must be familiar with the lease terms for both the lessor and lessee because the terms shape the quality and quantity of future benefits that may be gained by the interests created by the contract. When lease terms create advantages for the leasehold position, to the detriment of the leased fee position, an appraiser may be asked to estimate the value of the leasehold. The leasehold interest usually has value when contract rent, the periodic rent paid by tenant to lessor, is less than market rent. This situation can occur with a long-term lease and can affect those involved in a sublease, whereby the tenant is "sandwiched" between a lessor and a subtenant.

Another form of an economic partial interest can arise through leasehold mortgaging. Valuation of such lease interests consists of two mortgage-equity analyses. Although such analyses employ ordinary mortgage-equity procedures, an appraiser must also be aware of any difficulties that may arise in the appraisal of leasehold mortgages because of the variability of rent provisions and debt service on the leased fee mortgage and possibly on the leasehold mortgage.

Possessory interests and partnership interests, through various forms or arrangements, divide the property—a financial division—into mortgage and equity components. The value of a possessory interest is measured by discounting tenant rental for the lease period at a rate appropriate in light of rate ruling and investment competition.

Monetary conditions are subject to frequent and sometimes rapid changes. In response to such changes, a typical investment will vary to achieve the optimum investment performance. Thus, methods that permit the mortgagee to share equity benefits have provided a way to maintain the mortgage-equity financial division of real estate while giving it equity emphasis. Partnerships, or syndications, which are employed to raise equity capital, are attractive to investors because they offer the possibility of investment income and value growth and tax advantages.

Chapter 24

Evaluation

Evaluation encompasses a wide variety of client-specific services that an appraiser may perform. Real estate transactions, however simple they may appear on the surface, are quite complex, and any of the involved parties may call on an appraiser for services beyond a value estimate. Buyers, sellers, lenders, lessors, lessees, and developers must consider a host of matters related to the transaction if they are to behave rationally. Each party must decide on the merits of a transaction opportunity in terms of individual judgments about importance. The needs, goals, resources, limitations, and desires of the parties, as well as other investment alternatives open to them, determine the positions they take in the negotiation and the decisions they eventually make.

Appraisers also perform real estate services that are not specifically transaction-related. Members of a local community, for example, may want to know how they can more effectively encourage the revitalization of their downtown business section; whether the condition of their housing stock is satisfactory; which policies might be adopted to encourage landmark preservation without impairing property values; what the impact of a given project is likely to be.

Relationship of Evaluation to Valuation

Valuation can be an important part of evaluation. In a transaction, each party generally wants to know the market value of the property and may also be interested in other types of value, such as book value, insurable value, investment value, or use value. These values may be relevant in analyzing the income tax implications of the transaction, judging the adequacy of insurance coverage, weighing risk, or measuring the economic contribution of a specific group of assets. But valuation is not the primary purpose of *evaluation,* which is aimed at providing answers to real estate questions other than questions pertaining to value.

The judgments of individual market participants and regulators collectively determine value. Together they provoke and delimit the play of market activity. Policy decisions and actions taken by government bodies, lending institutions, labor unions, and others have an obvious bearing on the use and value of real estate. These decisions and actions—zoning decisions, planning decisions, and construction wage settlements, for example—result from individual assessments of a real estate market or situation.

In reaching decisions, each participant must deal on his or her own terms with many questions in addition to questions about value. Certain questions, such as those relating to individual legal problems and income tax needs ordinarily require the services of attorneys, accountants, and other specialized advisers. However, both client and advisers will have evaluation questions that the qualified real estate appraiser may answer. Such questions relate to the acquisition or disposition of a property, its financial structuring, its probable performance, the risks accompanying it, and how it can be used to enhance the client's well-being. The answers to such questions can be framed in terms of the client's situation and in terms of other available choices, whether the client is an individual, a corporation, or a public body. The answers result from evaluation.

Market Value and Investment Value

Estimates of market value and of investment value may be significant aspects of an evaluation assignment. Sometimes, market value is considered in arriving at investment value conclusions. However, an investor might not consider market value when a property's price is consistent with predetermined investment goals.

Value to the client may be different from value in the market. In any transaction, the parties approach the property from different starting points, seeking to reach agreement on the transaction's essential elements through give and take. They may well be able to agree on price while still holding very different ideas about what the property is actually worth.

Implicit in the usual definition of market value is that both seller and buyer can assume there are enough active buyers and sellers in the market at any given time to assure at least some degree of competition. This definition reflects the assumption that market behavior does not depend on any one participant's characteristics and takes into account market influences that may or may not affect the property's investment value.

Investment value, however, is linked to the characteristics and requirements of a specific individual or class of individuals whose behavior may or may not resemble that of other market participants. An institutional investor, for example, may use criteria substantially different from those of the typical purchaser in evaluating a small commercial property; therefore, the institutional investor might not be interested in such a property even if it were offered at a bargain price.

If the property is clearly an investment property—that is, if it is of a type usually bought and sold purely for its value as an investment and not for use—investment value may tend to equal market value. Market value in such cases reflects a synthesis of the property's investment values to its most likely sellers and purchasers, each of whom computes investment value according to his or her own rules. These rules reflect an investor's needs, goals, resources, limitations, psychology, and thinking; the rules take into account both investment strategy and income tax consequences.

By contrast, market value, as typically defined for valuation, reflects a synthesis of the ideas about the value of a property likely to be held by its typical sellers and purchasers, a synthesis that partly depends on an appraiser's ability to understand the motivations of those sellers and purchasers. The motivations may be purely investment oriented or not, as in the case of properties that sell more for the prestige associated with their ownership than for their economic productivity in the narrow sense. To the extent that an appraisal is concerned solely with investment requirements, that appraisal may be said to aim at estimating *investment value* rather than *market value*.

The remainder of this chapter explores the techniques used by investors, lenders, developers, and real estate professionals in estimating investment value and in evaluation, and emphasizes the aspects of evaluation that relate to specific transaction opportunities. Its purpose is to show how the parties to a transaction analyze a problem and reach decisions. The chapter discusses the various measures of investment performance; the techniques used in investment analysis and risk analysis; and the place of the techniques in development and redevelopment studies, including feasibility, market, marketability, and highest and best use studies. The chapter also summarizes income tax considerations.

Measures of Investment Performance

Investors apply a number of different tests when assessing the economic productivity of a given property. Such tests vary tremendously in their assumptions, logic, and degree of sophistication. Perhaps the most familiar test is the overall rate of return, which is the R in the familiar appraisal formula

$$R = \frac{I}{V}$$

where I is the projected annual net operating income and V is value. This rate can also be applied to the valuation of equity investments by translating it into cash-on-cash terms, using I to mean the net cash flow (equity dividend) after debt service and V to mean the cash investment required.

The overall rate incorporates many assumptions about inflation, depreciation, financing, income taxes, variability of returns, resale potential, and other matters. It can serve as a reasonable substitute for more sophisticated measures of investment performance in many common situations; it is widely used in evaluating small or simple investment properties. However, I and R may vary from one period to the next, especially during inflationary times; other conditions affecting the property can also change. Therefore, the overall rate may be a misleading measure of investment performance.

Pay-Back Period

The *pay-back period* is a simple and commonly used measure of investment performance. It is defined as *the length of time required for the stream of cash flows produced by the investment to equal the original cash outlay.* The investor simply wants to know how long it will take to recover the initial outlay, hoping to minimize the period during which his or her funds are at risk and to rule out purchases with low rates of return or returns deferred too far into the future.

When before-tax cash flows are constant, the pay-back period is simply the reciprocal of the overall rate as applied to cash flows and equity contributions—that is,

$$PB = \frac{\text{Cash outlays}}{\text{Annual net cash flow}}$$

When anticipated cash flows are not constant, the pay-back period must be determined by adding up the expected cash flows for successive years until the total equals the original investment.

Although pay-back periods are commonly used to compare investments, they can be misleading. Consider, for example, two investments that each require $100,000 in cash. Investment A returns net cash proceeds of $100,000 at the end of Year 1 and nothing thereafter; Investment B returns $100,000 at the end of Year 1 and $12,000 per year thereafter. Both investments have the same pay-back period, but Investment B is obviously more desirable.

Similarly, consider two $100,000 investments. Investment C returns $75,000 the first year, $25,000 the second, and $12,000 annually thereafter; Investment D returns $25,000 the first year, $75,000 the second, and $12,000 annually thereafter. Obviously, although both have the same pay-back period, Investment C is more desirable because it returns the investment earlier.

Using the same examples, if Investment D were to produce not $12,000, but $15,000 annually after the second year, one might not be able to judge which investment is the more desirable by comparing only the pay-back periods. Investment C returns a major share of the cash outlay more rapidly than Investment D, and both return the entire investment over two years; however, Investment D will produce more net cash flow thereafter. For a sound decision, a more refined measure of investment performance is obviously necessary.

Therefore, the pay-back period has two evident weaknesses. It fails to consider (1) cash flows received after the pay-back date and (2) differences in the timing of proceeds during the period. Although the technique is widely used, it is clearly inadequate for comparing or evaluating investments.

Proceeds per Dollar Invested

Investments are sometimes ranked according to anticipated total proceeds divided by the amount invested. Such a technique fails to take into account the timing of anticipated cash flows; $1 received in the second year is treated exactly the same as $1 received in the first year. The proceeds-per-dollar-invested technique is thus inferior to techniques that take timing into account.

Discounted Cash Flow

Discounted cash flow analysis permits an appraiser to consider the timing of individual cash outlays and inflows over the entire life of an investment.

Discounted cash flow analysis (DCF) is based on the compound interest theory—the fact that $1 received in the future is worth less than $1 in hand today—and it uses mathematical procedures to translate future dollars into present values. Individual cash outlays over a period of time, such as might be required in a land development program extending over several years, can be factored into the calculation as readily as anticipated net cash inflows, so that complex investment programs extending over long periods can be analyzed successfully. The formula is

$$PV = \frac{CF_1}{1 + Y} + \frac{CF_2}{(1 + Y)^2} + \cdots + \frac{CF_n}{(1 + Y)^n}$$

where Y is the discount rate used to reflect the time value of money and CF_n is the anticipated cash flow, whether positive or negative, for the period n.

The calculations can be performed either on a before- or after-tax basis, although investment analysis sometimes requires the use of after-tax cash flows. The procedures used provide for the return *on* and *of* an investor's outlays in the same manner the discount procedure is used in ordinary present value computation. Here, however, the procedures are applied to each individual cash flow, whether positive or negative. They resemble the calculations used to estimate stock and bond yields and values, making the results readily comparable to those derived from other forms of investment.

In using discounted cash flow analysis, an appraiser can consider the inflation expectations of investors usually by factoring a suitable inflation component into anticipated cash flows, including the eventual reversion upon a property's sale. The appraiser can also consider the element of risk, although much less easily. In current practice, anticipated cash flows are adjusted by an inflation factor, which is also applied to the eventual reversion. A reversion period of 10 or 15 years is commonly used.

DCF takes a number of forms but is most frequently encountered as internal rate of return (IRR) analysis or net present value (NPV) analysis.

Internal Rate of Return

In employing *internal rate of return* analysis, an appraiser begins with the anticipated net cash outlays and inflows associated with the investment and seeks to infer the rate of discount that will reconcile the flows. The idea is to find a rate of discount that will make the net present value of the cash inflows expected from an investment exactly equal to the present value of the anticipated cash outlays.

To find the rate, an appraiser uses trial and error. Calculations can be accomplished manually, using present value tables or a hand calculator, or with the help of an advanced calculator, designed for financial applications, or a computer. The appraiser selects a rate as a starting point and tests it against the schedule of anticipated outlays and inflows. If the resulting present value of the inflows is greater or less than the present value of the outlays, the rate is adjusted, and the appraiser tries again. The appraiser repeats this procedure until the correct rate is approximated. The formula is

$$O = CF_0 + \frac{CF_1}{1 + i} + \frac{CF_2}{(1 + i)^2} + \cdot \cdot \cdot \cdot + \frac{CF_n}{(1 + i)^n}$$

where i is the discount rate to be found and CF_n is the anticipated cash flow for period n.

The rate of return found by this procedure, also commonly known as the *yield* of the investment, is identical to that used in security markets to evaluate the yields of bonds and notes. It is widely used in corporate financial practice and in the valuation and evaluation of investment real estate, although other procedures might be more desirable because of this procedure's flaws.

Implicit in the IRR is the assumption that cash flows received are reinvested at the same rate. Because this assumption is not always realistic, financial analysts have sought to refine the formula to allow for the reinvestment of the portions of incoming cash flows considered to be recapture of the initial outlays at rates different from (and usually lower than) the yield rate applicable to the investment property. At the end of the holding period, these reinvested funds, which may be considered as having been deposited in a sinking fund at a "safe rate" (as used in the Hoskold formula), with interest, will suffice to replace the investment.

In many cases, the IRR analysis leads to the same decision indicated by NPV analysis. In other situations, however, IRR leads to different decisions. In such cases, NPV tends to give better results. The most serious problem associated with IRR is that it is susceptible to multiple solutions, a defect not shared by NPV.[1] The weaknesses of IRR are dealt with more or less adequately by related procedures, such as the financial management rate of return (FMRR), the modified IRR,

[1]See Harold Bierman, Jr., and Seymour Smidt, *The Capital Budgeting Decision,* 5th ed. (New York: Macmillan, 1980), *inter alia.*

and the geometric mean IRR, all of which give unique solutions. Although it may be convenient to use one of these rather than NPV, NPV is often preferred and gives satisfactory results.

Despite its defects, IRR can be used in valuing and evaluating investment real estate, particularly equity investments subject to existing debt. Buyers and sellers of such equities tend to analyze their worth in terms of net cash outlays and inflows using procedures essentially similar to IRR analysis. An equity that produces a yield (IRR) at least equal to the yields of other available properties and to the investor's target rate will signal, at acceptable risk, a purchase opportunity; the offered property's failure to meet these tests will lead to a rejection. The procedure offers a ready tool for making comparisons among investment opportunities and is widely used in the analysis of larger and more complex investments.

Net Present Value

The discounted cash flow technique known as *net present value* (NPV) is a direct application of the present-value concept. Unlike IRR, it does not start with the schedule of cash flows. Instead, it starts with the selection of an appropriate rate of discount. An appraiser makes the selection depending on circumstances, in terms of the investor's target rate and its cost of capital, or some other standard. Using this discount rate, an appraiser computes the present value of cash proceeds expected from the investment and the present value of the cash outlays required.

NPV may be defined as

$$NPV = CF_0 + \frac{CF_1}{1 + i} + \frac{CF_2}{(1 + i)^2} + \cdot \cdot \cdot \cdot + \frac{CF_n}{(1 + i)^n}$$

where i is the specified discount rate. Any excess of the present value of the proceeds over that of the outlays represents the net present value of the investment. In theory, at least, any investment with a present value greater than or equal to zero should be accepted, and any investment with a present value less than zero should be rejected.

One way to define NPV is *the maximum amount a firm or investor could pay for the investment without being financially damaged.*[2] The presumption is that the needed funds can be borrowed in the market at the discount rate used. The net present value of the investment thus becomes an unrealized capital gain over and above the minimum specified return on the investor's capital—a gain that will be realized if expected cash inflows materialize. Discount rates used by different inves-

[2]*Ibid.*

tors and analysts vary greatly and produce quite different results. Even such different rates, however, tend to rank investments in the same order of desirability, reinforcing the thesis that NPV is preferred over other procedures.

Although it takes full account of the timing and size of anticipated cash flows and can adjust for anticipated inflation, NPV by itself does not deal adequately with the problem of risk. As with other forms of simplified investment analysis, NPV merely attempts to reflect a judgment of risk in the discount rate, which is intended to cover both the time value of money and a component for risk. Better procedures to deal with this issue are discussed later in this chapter.

The "Correct" Measure

Generally speaking, the correct measure is the one that is appropriate to the problem. A pension fund manager who is contemplating the use of pension fund capital to purchase a major office building or shopping center would ordinarily use NPV as the primary test, while a corporate manager accustomed to using IRR in investment decisions might do well to use the same procedure for consistency. It should be remembered that none of the measures discussed in this section deals adequately with the many problems associated with risk analysis, portfolio design, or individual investment policy; any might force a decision quite different from that suggested by DCF.

It should also be remembered that fortunes have been made—and lost—by investors who were content to use the simplest available yardsticks. For many small investors, the overall rate is as good a test as any, and very likely the only one that will be sufficiently understood to be useful. Even the pay-back period can make sense to an investor who takes large risks in an environment of extreme uncertainty. Larger properties and complex situations, however, force the use of a more refined measure.

Risk Analysis

The measures of investment performance discussed in the previous section are point estimates, as are the measures of property value. Implicitly or explicitly, the measures just discussed reflect an appraiser's best judgment of each cash flow likely to be associated with an investment, the timing of the flows, and the rate or rates at which the flows should be discounted—all of which are stated in specific numbers, not as ranges or probabilities. Such point estimates offer a specious appearance of precision, and actual outcomes will almost certainly differ from the forecast. Investors usually want to know more about both the extent and characteristics of the range of possible outcomes associated with a given property investment than the simple point estimate can tell them.

Point estimates can be considered judgments about probability; typically, they represent the mean or mode of a range of possibilities that is not otherwise described. To measure the accuracy of such estimates requires more knowledge about the populations from which they are drawn. If the point estimate is the only possible value of the variable, as may be the case when dealing with ground rent receivable or payable under a long-term, fixed-rent net lease, the point estimate is entirely appropriate. The value selected is not only the mean of the population; it also represents the entire population, which has a standard deviation of zero. If, however, the value selected is merely the mean of a highly diverse population, greater knowledge about the population being represented is needed.

Modern risk analysis addresses this problem directly. Its common denominator is the direction and degree to which the possible values of each variable in the investment analysis vary around the expected value, which is ordinarily the mean value in a normal distribution. The probability of variation between the actual and the expected outcomes for each variable forms an operational definition of risk, which is the measurable likelihood of variance from the most probable outcome. When possible outcomes are arrayed against their associated probabilities, the result is a probability distribution that amounts to a risk profile of the specified events. When dealing with random variations of variables, such as individual rents and expense items, which tend to be distributed normally, a relatively simple statistical analysis of the resulting distributions provides a quantitative measure of risk.[3]

Utility/Probability Analysis

The likelihood of variance from the expected value defines risk in a technical sense but fails to recognize individual differences among investors and their situations. Certain investors will be totally unwilling to accept risks that would be taken in the ordinary course of business by others. The assessment of risk thus incorporates elements of personal psychology and decision-making philosophy, which can be translated into quantitative terms by using *utility functions*. Such a function assigns a number to each possible outcome of an uncertain event, based on the relative satisfaction the individual would expect to derive if the

[3]Cf., for example, Fadil H. Zuwaylif, *General Applied Statistics*, 2nd ed. (Reading, Mass.: Addison-Wesley, 1974).

outcome actually occurs. The investor will then make the choice that provides the highest expected utility.

To make this clear, assume that a person who wants to invest $10,000 has two options. The investor can keep his or her money in the form of holdings in a municipal bond fund yielding a tax-exempt 10% return, or can place the money in a real estate equity currently yielding 10% after taxes, which has a 30% chance of losing all its value and a 70% chance of doubling it.

The calculation below shows that for this investor, the expected utility of the real estate investment totals 170, as compared with 150 for the municipal bond fund. Therefore, the investor will prefer the real estate.[4]

	NPV of Possible Outcomes	Utility Function	Probability	Utility x Probability
Municipal bond fund	$ 0	150	1.0	150
Real estate investment				
Failure	(−10,000)	100	0.3	30
Success	20,000	200	0.7	140
Total				170

Risk Measurement Techniques

A number of risk measurements are now in use. Some depend on a computer-assisted analysis of significant variables; others are much simpler. Such measurements attempt to portray risk in intelligible terms by addressing the specific concerns of users, without resorting to detailed probability analysis.

Debt Coverage Ratio

The debt coverage ratio (DCR) is frequently used as a measure of risk by lenders wishing to measure their margin of safety and by purchasers analyzing leveraged property. The ratio commonly used is

$$\frac{\text{NOI}}{\text{Annual debt service}}$$

where both values are assumed to remain stable over time or to increase proportionally so that the ratio remains constant. It is possible, however, to calculate the DCR with other assumptions concerning the

[4]For further discussion of utility/probability analysis, see Bierman and Smidt, *op. cit.*

future. Lenders ordinarily require a debt coverage ratio greater than some specified minimum, often 1.2 to 1.5, before they will agree to make a mortgage loan. Developers who test feasibility also use the ratio to ascertain whether they will be able to meet the lender's tests and their own financial goals. Strictly speaking, the DCR is not a measure of risk. It is a measure of the cushion against adversity offered by the anticipated income stream.

Pay-Back Period

The pay-back period is often used as a measure of investment return, but it also serves as a measurement of risk in the minds of certain investors. Such investors assume that faster return of capital equals lower risk—an assumption that may be reasonable in a rapidly changing environment but is much less relevant in more stable environments.

Upside/Downside Potential

Often used by developers and investors in speculative situations, upside/downside potential attempts to quantify the outcome of the investment under the best and worst possible assumptions so that both the size of the hoped-for bonanza and the scope of the feared disaster can be considered in the investment decision. This method can be used with a discounted cash flow analysis by selecting for each variable in the analysis the highest plausible value on the income side and the lowest plausible value on the expense side. Often, intuitive measures of highest and lowest are used, although they might be quantified at specific percentiles for income values. This technique is simplistic and can be misleading, but it offers a distinct improvement over decision-making that depends solely on point estimates taken at the mean or the mode.

Weighted Probabilities

Weighted probability analysis carries the preceding best/worst-case method a step further. A probability is assigned to each of three possible outcomes of the investment in the following manner:

	Net Present Value Using Discounted Cash Flow Analysis	Assigned Probability	Weighted Net Present Value
Best case	$100,000	.30	$30,000
Worst case	$ 10,000	.30	$ 3,000
Most probable case	$ 50,000	.40	$20,000
		1.00	$53,000

The probability estimates used in this type of table may be based on standard deviations if the range of possible values follows the normal distribution. Another level of sophistication might be added by using intervals rather than point estimates for NPV or by injecting utility functions.

Subjective Risk Measurement

First proposed by Frederick Hillier, the subjective risk measurement is based on standard discounted cash flow procedures. It assigns subjectively estimated standard deviations to each cash flow and to the reversion, taking into account the appraiser's judgment as to the likelihood that the cash flow will actually correspond to its estimated value. The resulting Z value is used to estimate the probability that the net present value will be less than zero—that is, that the investment will not earn its target rate of return.[5]

Monte Carlo Simulation

When using the Monte Carlo simulation technique, the appraiser analyzes repeated estimates using randomly selected values within a specified range for each significant variable, sets down a probability distribution from the resulting estimates for a series of runs, and examines the probability distribution to ascertain the likelihood of various possible outcomes. A random-number generator is used to produce variations within the expected range of each significant variable, thus simulating reality at the operating level. Because the law of large numbers tends to reduce the distributions produced by this procedure to the form of normal distributions, its use may be an empty exercise. It is, however, flexible and precise within the limits of the judgment factors provided by the appraiser. A suitably programmed computer is required.[6]

Discount and Risk Rates

The risk-adjusted discount rate approach is flawed both theoretically and practically. Except in certain special cases, to include a risk factor in the time value discount rate does not effectively incorporate attitudes toward risk into the evaluation of an investment. It also does not reflect the information or the quality of the information that may be available about the correlation between the returns predicted from a

---

[5]See Michael S. Young, "Evaluating the Risk of Investment Real Estate," *The Real Estate Appraiser,* September-October 1977; Gaylon E. Greer, *The Real Estate Investment Decision* (Lexington, Mass.: D. C. Heath & Co., 1979); Bierman and Smidt, *op. cit.*

[6]See Jared Shlaes and Michael S. Young, "Evaluating Major Investment Properties," *The Appraisal Journal,* January 1978, pp. 101-11.

particular investment and the returns of other investments. In addition, it seriously distorts the discounting procedure as a means of accounting for the time value of money. For that reason alone, the appraiser is justified in rejecting this familiar technique in favor of a method that treats risk in another way.

Development and Redevelopment Studies

Real estate appraisers are often called on for assistance in connection with the development of real estate. This assistance is by no means confined to providing value estimates. Value concepts, however, are implicit in each discussion of development or redevelopment economics; the measure of feasibility is sometimes taken as the ability of a project to generate property values in excess of project costs.

This discussion uses feasibility analysis as the framework for considering other types of real estate studies relating to development. Graaskamp and others propose a cash concept of the real estate enterprise, which makes feasibility analysis central to the valuation process as well as to market and highest and best use studies. This concept employs a capital budgeting model that treats "the realities of business cash flows on an in-and-out basis, rather than accepting convenient assumptions necessary to the continued use of the income capitalization approach with a single capitalization rate."[7] The concept lends itself to a wide variety of land use and development studies and is consistent with the techniques of financial analysis used by securities analysts and corporate planners.

Feasibility Studies

For any project, the test of feasibility is the soundness of the required investment. The calculation of the amount and timing of the required investment, the anticipated recovery of and return on the investment, and the risks attached to the recovery and the returns is the core of feasibility analysis. Its derivation requires a full investigation of alternate uses; market characteristics; development costs; development constraints and risks; financing possibilities; selling prices; absorption rates; and, for income-producing properties, projected rents and other income, occupancy levels, and debt service requirements.

Such estimates and forecasts must reflect the anticipated chronol-

---

[7]James A. Graaskamp, "A Rational Approach to Feasibility Analysis," *The Appraisal Journal*, October 1972.

ogy of the development. They are not static, but unroll over a period of time that, in many cases, extends years into the future. Techniques of investment and risk analysis applicable to the purchase or sale of other real estate holdings are also appropriate to feasibility analysis, which ordinarily makes use of discounted cash flow procedures in assessing the soundness of an investment.

Critical to feasibility analysis is the assumption of a specific client, or at least a hypothetical range of clients with known characteristics sufficiently detailed to permit reasoned judgments about feasibility in terms of their needs, goals, resources, and limitations. A large corporation with ample cash reserves, a high marginal income tax rate, and a skilled real estate development staff will be in a far different position when evaluating the feasibility of a given project than a small individual developer with slim capital resources, little financial staying power, and a low marginal income tax rate resulting from other tax-sheltered investments. Thus, feasibility for one may not mean feasibility for another. Along the same line, of two financially competent and similarly motivated developers, one may be far more attracted to a project than the other by reason of local connections, prior experience, special market knowledge, personal motivation, or the availability of secondary profit centers. A feasibility study that does not address the client's specific needs is incomplete and will sooner or later have to be expanded or interpreted in terms of those needs before the client can make a rational decision.

Feasibility studies are conducted on both pre- and after-tax bases. Pre-tax studies may be useful for comparing one venture with another or for making preliminary feasibility judgments. The ultimate decision, however, can be made only after income tax effects are reviewed and after-tax feasibility is determined in light of the income tax position of the actual or supposed parties to the venture. Modern feasibility analysis thus takes into account after-tax results to the developer and may also consider the tax implications of the venture to other participants, including lenders and limited partners.

A critical concept is "satisficing." Although certain developers and investors seek to maximize their returns, many more operate on the belief that the information available to them is far too imperfect to permit optimization or maximization. They are satisfied if their investments can be expected to return a yield that will "satisfice" their own standard. The procedure is the same as that used in net present value analysis: The investor selects a target rate of return, and if the project can be expected to meet that rate, it is judged feasible.

To test the feasibility of a specific project, an appraiser develops a spreadsheet on which anticipated cash outlays and inflows are scheduled over the development period. This requires careful attention to the market from which the anticipated inflows must come and the project costs to which the outlays must be devoted. When only the first of these two aspects is considered, the study is a market study; when only the second is considered, the study is a cost analysis. Together they form the framework of the feasibility analysis that, in addition to these items, must also provide procedures for discounting to present value terms and of dealing with the risks attached to the development and the uncertainty of the projections themselves. Implicit or explicit in any such analysis are assumptions about the continuity or discontinuity of observed trends, including the degree of monetary inflation to be expected.

In conducting a feasibility study, an appraiser first carefully examines the project, noting any similarities to and any differences from existing competitive projects. Then the appraiser seeks additional information to help formulate the required demand projections. This may entail market research, including in-depth interviews and opinion sampling, or simply the observation of market reactions to other similar developments, with appropriate adjustments for comparability. In many cases, direct comparisons with competitive developments, coupled with close analysis of the elements involved in their degree of market acceptance, are an adequate guide; in cases in which comparable data are inadequate, however, the entire market available to the subject property must be defined and analyzed to ascertain the scope and character of probable effective demand.

From these market investigations, an appraiser should be able to derive both anticipated rent or price schedules over time and an anticipated rate of absorption for the finished product. This information permits the formulation of the cash inflow projection over the development period. The anticipated costs of development must be offset against this projection.

There is no substitute for detailed investigation of the ranges of actual revenues and costs most likely to be experienced at the subject location. Costs require particularly careful consideration. Even detailed drawings and cost estimates provided by the client must be carefully checked against other sources before they are accepted as sound. If such information is unavailable, the appraiser must seek out the best available data, whether from professional cost-estimating services or trade sources that are familiar with competing developments.

Essentially, the appraiser must prepare a replacement or reproduction cost estimate, using the best available sources and taking into account the effects of the passage of time on construction and development costs over the development period. Such costs include not only direct costs for land, buildings, and equipment, but also indirect costs such as interest and other carrying charges during the development period, points paid to construction lenders, housekeeping costs for completed but unsold units, marketing costs, selling costs, insurance, legal and accounting fees, and real estate commissions. These outlays are not made in a single lump sum but are spread out over time; their scheduling requires detailed knowledge of industry practices and will have a measurable effect on the calculated net present value or internal rate of return.

An essential element of feasibility analysis is the consideration of constraints affecting development. A project must be legally and technically feasible, as well as economically feasible in the narrow sense. Accordingly, an appraiser verifies the appropriateness of existing zoning or the likelihood of needed zoning adjustments and checks into the applicability of other land use and environmental controls that might impede the desired development. The appraiser also considers the availability of needed public services, including utilities, police and fire protection, and schools, as well as other amenities that may be relevant. Such amenities might include attractive and conveniently located shopping facilities, recreational resources, and job opportunities or, in the case of industrial parks, trucking and communications facilities and perhaps support services such as central accounting and computer service bureaus. The site itself must be checked for suitability in terms of contour, grading costs, absorptive and bearing capacity, drainage, access, and freedom from excessive encroachments. The community in which the property is located must be evaluated in terms of its appropriateness to the project and the trends likely to affect it over time.

Although formal critical path analysis of the development may not be necessary in an ordinary feasibility study, some degree of network analysis will usually be appropriate.[8] This entails identifying key events in the development and arranging them in an orderly and realistic sequence; it often involves ordering several chains of events that intersect from time to time. The preparation of a site for development, for example, may be carried out simultaneously with the detailed design of dwellings to be built on the site and the search for appropriate end-loan financing. The diagram that results from careful consideration of the development sequence will be of invaluable aid in scheduling related cash outlays and inflows. An appraiser will also make use of the diagram to identify risk points and make judgments about the likelihood of achieving—or failing to achieve—key project objectives. When appropriate, probability factors may be attached to specified outcomes, or risk analysis may be used to quantify risk judgments as part of a feasibility analysis.

The schedule of anticipated cash outlays and inflows prepared by an appraiser reflects the full extent of such investigations. It is dis-

---

[8]See, for example, Gene Dilmore, *Quantitative Techniques in Real-Estate Counseling* (Lexington Mass.: D. C. Heath & Company, 1981), Ch. 3.

counted to present value, using either a financial calculator or an appropriate computer program. An appraiser weighs pre- and after-tax results of such discounting against an investor's target returns, and judges whether it is feasible or infeasible. The quality of the judgment will be no better than the quality of the inputs, which will be carefully and responsibly monitored by the appraiser and the client.

As Graaskamp points out, factors extraneous to the narrow feasibility calculation may be very important to a specific developer. These include opportunities for cash profits in land write-ups, construction contracts, management contracts, insurance commissions, and captive markets among tenants and other users. In other words, "The feasibility analyst must consider the cash potential inherent in the business environment of the decision maker, before and after the commitment to the real estate."[9]

However, feasibility is not simply a matter of dollars and cents. Emotional reasons often predominate in deciding whether to proceed with a given project. A developer must be reasonably confident that a project will meet certain objectives within a reasonable time period, and that the risks of failure fall within acceptable limits. Without such confidence, no amount of quantitative analysis will convince a developer that the project is, in fact, "feasible."

Market and Marketability Studies

Market and marketability studies are merely aspects of a general feasibility study. The literature on the subject is vast and extends to fields other than real estate. Markets should be studied not only for their past performance, but also to aid in forming judgments about the possibilities of change. Because sudden shifts in market behavior have become the rule in many locations, it seems reasonable to anticipate that, in the future, change will be more common than stability. The past behavior of real estate users is thus less reliable as a predictor of future behavior than it may seem. Therefore, an appraiser should keep current even while considering evidence from the past.

Highest and Best Use Studies

Highest and best use studies usually concern the most profitable and appropriate use of vacant sites. They are intended to provide a property owner or planning agency with a guide to the future development of a parcel of land. As with market analyses, highest and best use stud-

[9]Graaskamp, *op. cit.*

ies may reasonably be considered part of a general feasibility study because a feasibility study is incomplete if the appraiser has not considered alternate development possibilities.

Studies of this type generally are systematic investigations of development options by category, by office, industrial, residential, and commercial, for example. Certain categories of potential use usually can be ruled out for zoning or environmental reasons; others will be clearly impractical in view of the level of property values or the character of neighboring improvements.

After narrowing the range of options as much as possible, an appraiser explores the remaining options in some depth, projecting anticipated costs and revenues in sufficient detail to permit intelligent comparisons. This may involve engineering, legal, marketing, and planning judgments, as well as real estate judgments, and may thus require the advice of experts in such fields.

As with feasibility analysis, the use of statistical probability techniques can be valuable in performing market studies. Risks as well as returns are appropriate considerations in the analysis of highest and best use and should be weighed quantitatively as much as possible. A prediction that depends on a specific future event, such as a favorable zoning determination, cannot be justified if the probability of that event has not been carefully considered and factored into the feasibility analysis.

Often, the use of land is decided by planners, architects, and engineers who are unfamiliar with market behavior and basic land economics. A real estate appraiser or analyst equipped to address land use questions, whether alone or as part of a professional group in the related disciplines, can significantly contribute to the proper use of a precious resource.

Income Tax Considerations

Federal and state income taxation is significant in investment decisions and has direct and indirect effects on real estate use, value, and ownership. Corporate and individual taxpayers include tax consequences in their decisions to buy, sell, lease, mortgage, develop, demolish, hold, or renovate real property. Such decisions, in turn, influence the physical forms and functioning of all developed areas in a market economy. Therefore, appraisers should understand the provisions and implications of the income tax provisions that bear on real estate.

Real estate has long enjoyed a favorable position in federal and state income tax laws. Interest paid on personal debt, including home mortgages, is deductible from income for tax purposes; so are property taxes. Depreciation deductions can be taken on property improvements used in a trade or business or held for investment, even though the improvements may actually be gaining in value. They are based on the entire value of the improvements even though the property may be heavily mortgaged and the owner's cash investment may be smaller than the depreciable basis in the property. Interest deductions may be taken even on debt that exceeds the owner's basis and does not carry personal liability, being secured only by the real estate.

These already substantial advantages were further enhanced by the Economic Recovery Tax Act of 1981 (ERTA), which reduced the marginal rate of tax on income, whether earned or unearned, to 50% for individual and 46% for corporations while reducing the maximum tax on capital gains to 20% for individuals. These reductions resulted in a significant increase in the net after-tax revenues associated with many forms of investment, of which real estate was only one. But the act also conferred on real estate a significant array of new provisions intended to support and encourage the ownership and rehabilitation of improved real estate, placing special emphasis on income property and certain types of rehabilitation. These benefits have a major bearing on both investment and feasibility decisions. Because they already have been changed, and further changes are to be expected, an appraiser should check the status of current literature and consult with qualified income tax advisers.

Depreciation

The former system of depreciating improvements over a building's useful life is replaced under the ERTA by a system (called the accelerated cost recovery system, or ACRS) that permits the recovery of capital costs, using straight-line or accelerated methods, over predetermined recovery periods much shorter than those previously allowed. For eligible real estate, the recovery period is 15 years, although taxpayers may elect a 35- or 45-year extended recovery period in conjunction with the straight-line method. These lives apply to both new and used properties, eliminating the long-standing bias in favor of new construction.

For all real property, except low-income rental housing, recovery deductions are calculated either by the straight-line method or in accordance with an IRS table that approximates the benefits of using the 175% declining-balance method for the early years and the straight-line method for later years with a crossover at the optimum point. For low-income rental housing, an appraiser can use the equivalent of a 200% declining-balance method with a switch to straight-line. All properties have the option of having the straight-line method used for them, which with a 15-year life produces an annual deduction of 6⅔% depreciable basis.

Nonresidential property is subject to full recapture of *all* recovery deductions upon disposition if the 175% declining-balance method is used. If, however, the optional straight-line system is used, all gain is capital gain and is taxed at the new favorable rates. For residential property, gain upon disposition is treated as ordinary income only insofar as the recovery deductions allowed under the new law exceed those permitted using the straight-line method with a 15-year life, so that if the straight-line method is used, all gain is treated as capital gain.

The new rules do not permit the use of component depreciation; deductions for an entire building must be computed using one recovery method and period. An exception is provided for a substantial improvement to the building, which is treated as a separate building.

Investment Tax Credits

Deductions permitted under the "accelerated cost recovery system" are supplemented by a system of investment tax credits (ITCs), which are directly deducted from income tax, not income, and are therefore of great interest to taxpayers. As a general rule, buildings do not qualify for the regular 10% investment tax credit but, under the Revenue Act of 1978, the ITC was extended to certain qualified rehabilitation expenditures. The 1981 act creates three levels of ITC for rehabilitation expenditures based on a building's age. For commercial and industrial structures at least 30 years old, the ITC is 15%; for structures at least 40 years old, it is 20%; and for certified historic structures, it is 25%. To qualify, a building must be "substantially rehabilitated" as defined in the act, must have been in use prior to beginning the rehabilitation, and must retain 75% of the existing external walls. To be certified as historic, a building must be listed in the National Register of Historic Places or located in a registered historic district and certified by the Secretary of the Interior as being of historic significance to the district. Rehabilitation work on historic properties must be certified as consistent with the character of the building or district to be eligible for the 25% ITC.

Unlike prior law, the depreciable basis of the property must be reduced by the amount of the tax credit unless the credit is for a certified historic rehabilitation, which under the provisions of the 1982 Tax Equity and Fiscal Responsibility Act (TEFRA) entails a reduction in depreciable basis equal to 50% of the amount of the credit taken. The resulting reductions in basis also reduce the deductions allowed by the ordinary cost recovery process. ITCs are available to residential structures only if the rehabilitation is a certified historic rehabilitation that meets the standards of the Internal Revenue Service and the Secretary of the Interior. Lessees may take the historic rehabilitation credit under certain conditions. Generally speaking, these provisions apply to expenditures incurred after December 31, 1981, and taxable years ending after that date, except that ITCs taken for historic rehabilitation are not deductible from basis if the property is placed in service during 1982.

The investment tax credit is subject to numerous restrictions and is particularly subject to a recapture tax imposed on a property's early disposition. One hundred percent of the credit is considered to be recaptured and taxable at ordinary rates if a property is not held at least one year; 80% is recaptured if it is not held at least two years; 60% if not held at least three years; 40% if not held at least four years, and 20% if not held at least five years. The amount of used property eligible for the investment tax credit is set at $125,000 for taxable years beginning 1981 through 1984 and $150,000 for subsequent years. Only straight-line depreciation may be used in conjunction with the ITC.

Under the 1982 TEFRA, accelerated recovery deductions on real property are subject to the alternate minimum tax (AMT) for noncorporate taxpayers. The preference amount is the excess of the recovery deduction over what it would have been on a straight-line allowance using a 15-year life. In addition to the burden created by the AMT, there are other limitations on the use of the ITC that should be discussed with competent tax advisers before the credit is claimed. Particularly important is a limitation on the amount of taxable income that may be offset by an ITC, which was reduced under the 1982 act from 90% to 85%, effective for taxable years beginning after December 31, 1982.

The 1981 act conferred on real estate builders or renovators certain advantages: accelerated depreciation and investment tax credits on personal property installed in conjunction with a project. The combined effect of these advantages and those applicable to real property can make eligible rehabilitation projects extremely attractive in after-tax terms, leading to a resurgence in the rehabilitation of eligible properties and in their value.

Certain "at-risk" rules limit the investment tax credit on new and used property and apply to all activities other than real estate. The act requires a separate at-risk computation and has its own rules that differ from the at-risk rules applicable to tax losses. The relevant provisions should be carefully reviewed and, if applicable, discussed with a qualified tax adviser.

Implications for Real Estate

Although a full discussion concerning the impact of recent income tax changes is beyond the scope of this text, it can be safely stated that for most taxpayers and commercial property, the straight-line method proves the most advantageous. Residential property owners may or may not prefer the 175% declining-balance method. Of particular interest are the provisions relating to historic buildings, which are eligible for a 25% ITC in connection with approved rehabilitation, whether they are nonresidential or residential buildings. This ITC is allowed only if there has been a substantial rehabilitation of the building, meaning that rehabilitation expenditures must exceed the greater of either the taxpayer's adjusted basis in the property (cost of the building plus capital improvements less depreciation) or $5,000 within a 24-month period, and that certain other tests must be met. An alternative 60-month period is allowed in the case of rehabilitation that may reasonably be expected to be completed in phases set forth in architectural plans completed before rehabilitation begins. Such rehabilitations allow depreciation on the full amount of the rehabilitation expenditure reduced only by 50% of the amount deducted for the ITC. This feature, coupled with the greater credit available to historic properties, creates a substantial after-tax advantage for the rehabilitator.

The 1981 act represents a revolution in the economics of U.S. real estate ownership. Traditionally, the after-tax rate of return associated with most forms of U.S. real estate has been lower than the before-tax return. This situation is reversed under the 1981 act, which makes available after-tax returns significantly higher than pre-tax returns for many properties and offers extraordinarily high after-tax returns to successful renovators of historic buildings. This change will certainly affect the relative values of various property categories dealt with under the act and will modify long-established investment strategies.

Two considerations are significant: Projections are seldom fulfilled in all details, and income tax laws are subject to change, as are personal circumstances. Any analysis that depends on anticipated future effective income tax rates will be misleading insofar as those rates are not actually realized. An investor is, thus well advised to consider the risk of change in income tax laws along with other risk factors in evaluating an investment.

Counseling

The American Society of Real Estate Counselors, an affiliate of the National Association of Realtors®, defines real estate counseling as

Providing competent, disinterested, and unbiased advice, professional guidance, and sound judgment on diversified problems in the broad field of real estate involving any or all segments of the business such as merchandising, leasing, management, planning, financing, appraising, court testimony, and other similar services. Counseling may involve the utilization of any or all of these functions.

Counseling is an advisery or supportive function that starts with, is done for, and is focused on the needs of a specific client, in contrast to appraising, which may be done for or at the request of a specific client but that is focused on the subject property and is intended or at least likely to be used by others as well. The client relationship constitutes the defining characteristic of counseling.

Much as a solicitor in the British legal system, a counselor sorts out a client's problems, offers advice, and, when necessary, procures outside assistance. Like the barrister, the counselor may also act as the client's advocate or representative.

Counseling is a professional activity compensated on a fee basis and not by means of commissions or trading profits. Professional counselors maintain high ethical standards and avoid defining the profession in profit terms. There is no direct physical product except, perhaps, a written report. Counseling is not limited to the estimation of value and related activities, but includes the entire array of real estate problems that confront present or prospective owners, lessees, users, sellers, lessors, lenders, managers, administrators, or other persons or organizations concerned with the use, value, operations, or impact of one or more properties or property interests.

The Counseling Procedure

Counseling may be seen as a systematic procedure with a number of steps, carried out for a specific purpose or purposes on behalf of a specific client, dealing with specific subject matter, using specific materials and skills, and couched in an appropriate form. When following the procedure, a counselor

   I. Defines the problem as to
   a. Client: nature, relationship to property, goals and priorities, needs, resources, constraints, attitudes, tax and investment position
   b. Subject matter: kind and type of real estate involved, special characteristics, if any
   c. Purpose: questions to be answered, problems to be solved, goals to be achieved
   d. Materials and skills required
   e. Form: type of report needed

   II. Establishes the counseling relationship: confirms the nature of the problem with client, defines the relationship, and enters into a contract

III. Plans the assignment
    a. Establishes deadlines
    b. Reviews contents of files and library for available data and methodologies
    c. Establishes time budgets
    d. Establishes expense budgets
    e. Allocates tasks and schedules work, with appropriate points for consultation and review

IV. Does the work
    a. Collects preliminary data
    b. Formulates hypothesis
    c. Tests hypothesis
    d. Reformulates hypothesis as necessary and follows with additional testing
    e. Considers and compares alternative hypotheses
    f. Formulates conclusions and recommendations

V. Prepares report: may be an oral presentation supported by a brief memorandum for record purposes or a formal report analogous to an appraisal report

VI. Reviews report, checks computations, tests assumptions when possible

VII. Presents report

Types of Counseling Assignments

In addition to market studies, feasibility studies, highest and best use studies, property evaluations, and general advice, a real estate counselor is often called on to provide opinions or reports on a variety of subjects. These may include community analyses, either for the benefit of property owners or on behalf of public bodies and civic groups concerned with observed trends; commercial and residential revitalization studies and programs; tax and school impact studies, often in connection with zoning or other land use decisions; zoning analyses and presentations; alternate use and rehabilitation studies, either for property owners or civic groups interested in landmark preservation; property analyses and property management reviews, usually commissioned by property owners interested in improving economic performance; investment analyses, ordinarily performed on behalf of prospective purchasers; and distressed property studies. Counselors may also be called on to develop detailed plans for a real estate development project, a marketing campaign, a distressed property work-out, or the liquidation of a portfolio of properties. The services may extend to actual project supervision, employee training, and the periodic evaluation of project results.

In addition, counselors may carry on direct or supervisory marketing functions on a fee basis, provide asset management services, or prepare portfolio designs. They are frequently called on to provide testimony in contested matters and also to provide situation analyses and assistance in the formulation of strategy. Cost-benefit analyses, often in the guise of impact studies or situation analyses, are fundamental to the counselor's art and are widely used in real estate matters. Other common assignments include various types of forecasting, market searches and acquisition programs, risk analyses, and site selection studies and estate planning.

The range of possible assignments is so broad that no summary can possibly touch on every type of counseling report or function. Whatever the assignment, counseling should be done on a professional basis and must be thorough and objective.[10]

Counseling Tools

A counselor uses all available analytical tools likely to prove useful in addressing the appraisal problem. Although judgment, experience, and common sense are essential in counseling, and may be sufficient in many cases, a counselor has a variety of tools to help solve specific problems. Such tools include the following.

Probability Analysis

The use of the normal distribution curve and basic concepts of probability are integral counseling tools. The curve enables a counselor to measure the confidence in an estimate within a specified range of error. Use of Z and t values helps to test hypotheses testing and the precise quantification of confidence.

Probability techniques are used to compute desirable sample sizes and to evaluate the information garnered from market and opinion research. They are useful in testing the accuracy of data provided by others and in statistical inference. The following publications offer further discussion on probability analysis:

Dilmore, Gene, *Quantitative Techniques in Real Estate Counseling* (Lexington, Mass.: D. C. Heath & Company, 1981).

Spurr, William A., and Charles P. Bonini, *Statistical Analysis for Business Decisions* (Homewood, Ill.: Richard D. Irwin, 1973).

Zuwaylif, Fadil H., *General Applied Statistics* (Reading, Mass.: Addison-Wesley, 2nd ed., 1974).

---

[10]The foregoing is adapted from Jared Shlaes, "The Counseling Process," *The Appraisal Journal,* January 1975. Reprinted in *Real Estate Counseling: A Professional Approach to Problem Solving,* the American Society of Real Estate Counselors, 1976.

Sensitivity Analysis

Sensitivity analysis is implicit in the term *ceteris paribus* (other things being equal). It holds all the variables $(a, b, c, . . .)$ in any function of the form $X = f(a, b, c, . . .)$ constant except for one, then changes that variable to see how the change affects the outcome (X). This procedure is used to test feasibility, run an investment analysis, design a portfolio, or plan a development.

A simple example can be found in the formula

$$V = \frac{I}{R}$$

Change I, and V changes. If

$$R = 10$$

and

$$I = \$100,$$

then

$$V = \$1,000$$
$$99, . . . = 990$$
$$98, . . . = 980$$

In other words, a $1 reduction (increase) in I produces a $10 reduction (increase) in V. The sensitivity of V to changes in I can be said to be

$$\frac{V}{I} = \frac{\$10}{\$1} = 10$$

Similarly, holding I constant and changing R, if

$$I = \$100$$

and

$$R = .10,$$

then

$$V = 1,000$$

.09 . . . =	1,111	(rounded to nearest dollar)
.08 . . . =	1,250	
.07 . . . =	1,429	
.06 . . . =	1,667	
.05 . . . =	2,000	

In this case,

$$\frac{V}{R}$$

is not a constant as in the previous case, but follows the curve

$$V = \frac{I}{R}$$

This analysis can also be used in much longer equations that involve many variables, such as in the DCF analysis of a major investment property or development project. An appraiser can change one or several assumptions about the amount and timing of individual cash flows to measure the effect of these changes on NPV, IRR, or feasibility. With the help of a computer, such analyses become relatively easy, so that the game of "What if . . .?" can be and is played regularly by investors and their real estate counselors.

Network Analysis
This technique, exemplified in the PERT format, allows for the systematic analysis of possible variations in a given sequence of events, discloses the possibility of shifting resources in dealing with the sequence, permits the coordination of the work of two or more people, indicates how to avoid backtracking, and clearly sets forth the events that must be completed before another event is possible. Use of the method forces an appraiser to think in an orderly fashion, serves as a method of communicating project plans, and provides a standard against which progress can be measured. Although the use of computers is not essential for networks of moderate size, microcomputers can be programmed to process virtually any network problem a real estate appraiser may encounter.[11]

Rating Grids
The use of rating grids allows an appraiser to make reasoned choices among several options in quantitative terms based on individual value judgments. The grid sets forth the factors upon which the choice is to be made and assigns a weight or rating to each factor to represent the degree of importance attached to that factor by the client.

In choosing from a group of available warehouses, for example, relevant factors might be chosen and weighted as follows on a scale of 1 to 10, 10 being the highest level of desirability.

---

[11]For a useful discussion of network analysis, see Dilmore, *op. cit.*

Factor		Weight
1	Rail service	1
2	Truck loading	10
3	Ceiling height	8
4	Column spacing	6
5	Sprinkler protection	10
6	ADT service	10
7	Physical condition	8
8	Appearance	4
9	Employee parking	3
10	Office areas	4
11	Bell system telephone service	2

The available warehouses would then be rated in terms of the same factors, using, for simplicity, the same scale:

Warehouse	Factors											Total Score
	1	2	3	4	5	6	7	8	9	10	11	
A	2	7	9	3	10	10	1	4	5	9	10	70
B	8	9	2	3	5	4	6	10	1	1	4	53
C	3	10	9	4	8	7	10	6	1	2	6	66
D	1	3	2	4	5	6	8	7	10	9	1	56

If all factors were equally weighted, Warehouse A, which scores highest, would be preferred. But if we multiply each factor by the appropriate weight, the result is as follows:

Warehouse	Factors											Total Score
	1	2	3	4	5	6	7	8	9	10	11	
A	2	70	72	18	100	100	8	16	15	36	20	457
B	8	90	16	18	50	40	48	40	3	4	8	325
C	3	100	72	24	80	70	80	24	3	8	12	476
D	1	30	16	24	50	60	64	28	30	36	2	344

Now Warehouse C would be preferred.

The use of such grids requires judgment. Certain factors may not be merely desirable, but essential, so that in the above illustration a warehouse lacking, say, top-rated truck loading might be rejected regardless of its total score. But the technique, appropriately used, can offer valuable guidance in selecting among available options.

Linear Programming

Linear programming can be used to determine the optimum allocation of limited resources by maximizing or minimizing a linear function. To be resolved by the linear programming approach, a problem must be one that can be quantified, i.e., stated in numerical terms. The linearity of relationships is assumed; when the relationship between variables is not substantially linear, the method does not work. There must be a choice among two or more alternative courses of action, and the problem must have constraints or restrictions on the variables that prevent maximizing the objective function by assigning an infinite value to a variable. Finally, the choice to be made must be not simply of a feasible course of action, but of the optimum course.

The use of a computer is ordinarily required for linear programming.[12]

Regression Analysis

Simple linear regression uses an equation in the form

$$Y_C = a + bX$$

where Y_c is the predicted value of the dependent variable, a is a constant, b is the coefficient or value of the independent variable, and X is the independent variable. The equation allows an appraiser to graph, based on limited observations, the Y intercept (a) and the slope of a line setting forth the linear relationship of the variables.

Multiple regression uses more than one independent variable. The equation is in the form

$$Y_C = a + b_1X_1 + b_2X_2 \ldots + b_nX_n$$

where Y_c is the predicted value of the dependent variable, a is the constant or intercept; b_1, $b_2 \ldots b_n$ are the coefficients or values of the independent variables; and X_1, $X_2 \ldots X_n$ are the independent variables.

Multiple regression is merely an extension of the basic principle of simple linear regression. Usually, a computer or programmable calculator is used. The most obvious application of the procedure is in value estimation and is widely employed in the valuation of residential

---

[12]Examples, further discussion, and a bibliography are to be found in Dilmore, *op. cit.*

properties by taxing authorities. For real estate counselors, however, such techniques are most useful in isolating specific value determinants and in testing their significance.[13]

Risk Analysis
This tool has been discussed under *Risk Measurement Techniques*, earlier in the chapter. An appraiser should consult Gaylon Greer's *The Real Estate Investment Decision* and Bierman and Smidt's *The Capital Budgeting Decision*.

Income Processing
Whether or not explicitly combined with risk analysis, income processing is the basic tool of a real estate counselor. Simple procedures of income processing, such as straight-line, sinking-fund, or annuity capitalization, have long been used in estimating property values and analyzing income-related counseling problems. In recent years, however, these procedures, along with the Ellwood and so-called mortgage-equity procedures, have been largely replaced by discounted cash flow (DCF) analysis that, among other advantages, can consider an analyst's expectations about monetary inflation and risk. DCF and the related NPV and IRR analysis are now widely considered to be the most suitable for use in real estate evaluation and counseling applications.

The Counseling Report

In many instances, an oral report will suffice; in other instances, a brief memorandum report may be necessary. In other instances, a complete counseling report is required.

Summary

In evaluation, an appraiser weighs the significance of financing, taxation, encumbrances, risk, and other elements involved in a real estate transaction. Because each transaction involves a new set of buyers and sellers, the importance of the elements varies from case to case. Thus, an appraiser must be sensitive to the goals of a particular transaction.

---

[13]The uses of simple linear regression and multiple regression are amply documented in the literature; see, in particular, N. R. Draper and H. Smith, *Applied Regression Analysis* (New York: John Wiley & Sons, 1966); Harry H. Harman, *Modern Factor Analysis* (Chicago: University of Chicago Press, 1976); R. J. Rummell, *Applied Factor Analysis* (Evanston, Ill.: Northwestern University Press, 1970); and Zuwaylif, *op. cit.*

Market value is one of the first concerns to arise in a real estate transaction. Its determination is based on a hypothetical market populated by "typical" buyers and sellers. A more meaningful measure is investment value, which is linked to the characteristics and needs of a specific investor or class of investors. An appraiser interested in a property's investment value relies on rate of return, pay-back period, proceeds per dollar invested, or discounted cash flow for measures of economic performance.

Discounted cash flow procedures are used for internal rate of return analysis or a net present value analysis. The former begins with a schedule of anticipated cash outlays and inflows and looks for a rate of discount that will reconcile the flows. The net present value procedure starts with the selection of an appropriate rate of discount. With this rate, an appraiser can compare the present value of cash proceeds expected from the investment and the present value of cash outlays, which enables an investor to determine how much he or she can afford to pay for the investment without being financially damaged. Generally, an investment with a present value greater than or equal to zero is acceptable.

Discounted cash flow and other measures of investment value are point estimates, stated in specific numbers rather than in ranges or possibilities. Risk analysis, on the other hand, avoids the often misleading illusion of precision. It seeks to determine the degree to which the possible values of each variable in the investment analysis vary around the expected value, which is ordinarily the mean in a normal distribution curve. Risk itself is defined as the measurable probability of variance from the expected outcome.

Real estate appraisers are often called on for an opinion regarding the feasibility of a project. Calculation of amount and timing of the required investment, anticipated return, and attendant risk are the core of feasibility analysis. A sound feasibility analysis is the result of market research, cost analysis, highest and best use analysis, and analysis of legal/technical restraints.

The 1981 Economic Recovery Tax Act contains provisions intended to encourage investment in improved real estate, and its benefits have had a major impact on investment and feasibility decisions. It reduces the marginal rate of tax income to 50% for individuals and 46% for corporations and permits recovery of capital costs in much shorter periods than those previously allowed. Recovery deductions can be calculated either by the straight-line or accelerated method. Deductions permitted under the accelerated system are supplemented by investment tax credits, which are deducted from income tax, not income. The act created three levels of investment tax credit based on the age of the building. On the whole, the act represents a revolution in the economics of real estate ownership. Traditionally, after-tax rate of return associated with real estate has been lower than before-tax returns; the situation is reversed under the new act. Among the provisions of the 1982 Equity and Fiscal Responsibility Act are those that affect investment tax credits.

The American Society of Real Estate Counselors has set forth precise definitions and standards for real estate counseling. Essentially, counseling is a sequence of steps carried out on behalf of a client. The client, the type of property involved, and the purpose of the transaction are analyzed; deadlines and budgets are established; data are assembled and hypotheses tested; and, finally, a report is prepared and presented.

Chapter 25

Renovation

The appraisal of an older structure or historic building is becoming one of the most challenging of appraisal assignments. Such an assignment often involves the analysis of possible renovation, its cost, and its economic feasibility. This type of analysis demands particular knowledge of the economic trends and societal attitudes that influence renovation, technical expertise in estimating renovation costs, and an awareness of laws that affect and may benefit properties that might be renovated.

The renewing of existing structures for new uses and new forms of old uses has become part of both commercial and residential construction. This activity has provided greater opportunities for developers, construction companies, architects, engineers, artisans, lawyers, accountants, and, consequently, appraisers.

Because construction costs have typically risen faster than general price levels, existing buildings may be converted to current uses at costs that are lower than those for new construction. Existing buildings often represent a reservoir of energy forces, the effect being that energy conservation policies favor reclamation by alteration rather than replacement through demolition. Because supplies of land, energy, and raw materials are limited, the move to reuse existing structures to conserve these resources has become widespread.

Although the preservation of our architectural heritage was recognized as part of national policy as early as the Antiquities Act of 1906, tax laws to encourage restoration and preservation were not suggested until 1964. They were finally passed in the Tax Reform Act of 1976. The most far-reaching regulations regarding renovation of buildings are found in the Economic Recovery Tax Act of 1981.[1]

In any appraisal of midlife or older buildings, an appraiser should consider that additional value might be created by a well-designed renovation program. Various types of renovation programs may create additional amenity value and additional net income, enhance aesthetic and historic significance, prolong economic life, and produce an economic margin of value above the cost of the work.

Depending on client motivation, such as personal or aesthetic concerns, increased market value, or increased income potential, renovation appraisals can take any of several forms. One type of assignment may require an appraiser to estimate the most probable market value of a dilapidated property that might be attractive to buyers who would carry out some type of renovation. Another type of assignment may call for an appraiser to estimate market values for the property before and after a specified renovation program so that the client may judge the relative increase in value achieved for certain selected expenditures. Still another type of appraisal assignment might require that an appraiser estimate the value of a preservation easement or any possible diminished economic potential of a property due to its designation as a national landmark.

When property owners or interested investors propose a renovation, the subsequent appraisal requires the application of many of the procedures discussed in this text. However, the application of the procedures is structured in relation to property type, the motivation for the renovation, and the purpose of the appraisal.

Types of Renovation

There are three major types of renovation. They are remodeling, restoration, and modernization.

---

[1]For a detailed discussion, see Judith Reynolds, *Historic Properties: Preservation and the Valuation Process* (Chicago: American Institute of Real Estate Appraisers, 1982).

Remodeling changes the use of a property by changing its design or plan.

Restoration returns a property to its original appearance and condition.

Modernization replaces worn or outdated elements with current versions of these elements.

Remodeling

Remodeling becomes a practical consideration when the present use or configuration of a structure is not consistent with its highest and best use, and a program involving extensive changes to achieve the most economic use becomes necessary. Functional and external obsolescence usually are the main causes of such a remodeling program. The effects of these causes are found in all cities where large, old buildings no longer serve the physical or economic purposes for which they were built, but through remodeling programs can retain their original use or attain a new highest and best use.

Sometimes, however, unnecessary or impractical remodeling is undertaken. To ensure against such actions, any remodeling program must be carefully analyzed to ascertain whether the results can be economically justified. For example, remodeling the attic space of a residence to provide an apartment may not increase the market value of the property by as much as the cost of the remodeling. If remodeling is done without complying with building codes, it may result in health or safety ordinance violations. Expenditures for such remodeling in any type of structure may not be reflected in increased market value.

Restoration

Restoration is the return of a property to its original condition and appearance with careful adherence to its architectural and historical elements. Unlike modernization or remodeling, which are primarily concerned with functional utility and current competitive market expectations, restoration places a premium on replication and compatibility with the detailed imagery and values of an earlier era. The project may require full conformity to existing building codes, particularly in regard to safety elements, even though great care is taken to conceal the mechanics of contemporary building code conformity. Complete restoration is the type of renovation that is the ideal for any building listed in the National Register of Historic Places or is deemed significant in a designated historical district, although this level is not always achieved.

National Register of Historic Places

The National Register of Historic Places is the official list of properties in the United States that are designated to be saved from destruction, damage, or decay. These properties receive protective and economic benefits, particularly tax incentives for restoration. Penalties are imposed for demolition. In addition to individual buildings, entire districts may be listed.

Estimates of the list place the number of buildings included between 700,000 and 1 million. Each year the number increases. In addition to nationally registered districts, registered historic districts include state or locally designated districts when the ordinance under which the district is designated has been certified and when the district itself has been certified by the Secretary of the Interior as substantially meeting national register criteria for evaluation.

A restoration of a certified historic structure may be controlled by a variety of local, state, and federal regulations. Certain types of historic designations affect only the demolition of structures, not renovation. The appraisal of such structures necessitates careful attention to existing regulations as well as familiarity with tax benefits and liabilities associated with renovation.[2]

Modernization

Modernization refers to the use of replacements that are specifically designed to offset the effect of obsolescence or physical deterioration, or of additions that are necessary to meet standards of current demand. The replacement of old heat radiators, lighting, or plumbing fixtures with new items of essentially the same type is improving the *condition* of the old installation; it is not modernization. The substitution of convectors for cast-iron radiators, of built-in bathtubs for tubs on legs, or of modern lighting fixtures for old-fashioned types frequently constitutes a functional improvement of the property. These expenditures offset obsolescence and may be classified as modernization. Modernization may or may not be economically justified when it offsets the obsolescence inherent in the older type of equipment.

Modernization and simple renewals differ in their effects on a value estimate. Although rehabilitation may result in sustaining or increasing tenancy and income and in reducing operating costs, the effects may be temporary. By contrast, modernization usually has the additional effect of extending a structure's economic life. Thus modernization can return a property to a competitive level closer to that which it held when it was practically new.

[2]For a full discussion of appraising historic properties, as well as an explanation of the application of the sales comparison, income capitalization, and cost approaches in the valuation of renovated properties, see Reynolds, *op. cit.*

The need for modernization is recognized when parts of a structure are subject to curable functional obsolescence. The necessary corrective action may involve additions to the structure or to the equipment, or it may take the form of changes to the existing structure or equipment.

Changes in layout that are made to obtain or satisfy tenants may be temporary or permanent. Temporary changes are usually referred to as alterations; longer-lasting changes, which involve a revised program of use and added value, constitute remodeling.

In this context, alterations add to value indirectly, through extending and preserving lease rents. In major properties, such changes are frequent, and office space that is subdivided one year may be re-joined again in two or three years. Such changes are not considered to affect the structure permanently.

To be justified, a modernization program must be economically feasible. It should be initiated only after a feasibility study, with the modernization program related to a soundly conceived plan of operation for the property.

Deferred Maintenance

Appraisers often find that expenditures are necessary to bring properties to a competitive level. Curable physical deterioration that should be corrected immediately is called deferred maintenance. When inspecting improvements, an appraiser examines whether there is a need for painting, tuckpointing, carpentry repairs, roof repairs, or decoration of rentable or public space. In addition, an appraiser checks the condition of fixtures, piping, and other equipment. In analyzing accrued depreciation, an appraiser allows for the cost of rehabilitating the property to a satisfactory condition. This competitive standard of condition for an old building could be at a level that is lower than that required for a new building. All curable deterioration would not necessarily be rehabilitated because all defects included in the curable physical depreciation category do not require immediate attention.

Table 25.1 presents a summary of the attributes of each type of appraisal problem with respect to aging structures and neighborhoods.

Special Considerations in Renovation Appraisal

All aspects of a building and a site must be described and analyzed in relation to their effect on total property value. The same rule applies to structures for which any kind of renovation is being considered. However, there are many special concerns in appraising properties for which renovation is planned.

Table 25.1 Attributes and Methodologies Appropriate to the Appraisal of Aging Structures and Neighborhoods

	Rehabilitation	Modernization	Remodeling	Restoration
1. Extent of corrective action	Deferred maintenance	Curable functional obsolescence	Incurable functional obsolescence	Return to previous condition and appearance for aesthetic as utilitarian objectives
2. Extending useful life	May	Yes—to a limited degree	Yes—to an extended degree	Yes—for a term beyond life cycle of utility function
3. Change in use	No	No	Probable change in use	Probable, but use is secondary to structural conservation
4. Impact on expenses	Minor, temporary	Significant temporary reduction in operating expenses	Long-term economies of operation for the building and for user operation	May increase expenses more than other types of renovation
5. Impact on real estate revenues	Protects existing rent levels	Often increases competative rent level	Redirects property toward higher rent, higher profit market segment	Redirects property toward higher rents but primary emphasis on aesthetic satisfaction and community benefit

6. Impact on market value	Reduces decline in value due to deferred maintenance	May improve market-ability if not value	Must improve market value to justify capital expense	Must consider social value as well as market value increase
7. Type of professional study	Life cycle casting structural survey	Before- and after-value estimates to justify cost of alternatives counseling	Alternative use study. Market and marketability study. Legal/political study. Appraisal value to equal cost plus entrepreneurial fee	Alternative use study market and marketability study. Alternative funding source supply
8. Federal income tax benefits	Minor—most outlays can be expensed	In addition to expenses, those outlays that extend to accelerated depreciation	In addition to expenses and accelerated depreciation, commercial buildings entitled to special federal investment tax credit; historic residential units may be provided with special investment tax credit for substantial rehabilitation in excess of $5,000	All of the previous plus special investment tax credits for buildings registered as federal and state landmarks

The appraiser must make a variety of judgments about the proposed renovation. What is the highest and best use of the older property? What are the possible alternative uses? Must the integrity of the structure be preserved to maintain the income-earning potential of the building? Does the proposed renovation plan provide the required utility at a reasonable cost?

Zoning regulations.   Renovation can proceed only where zoning regulations permit the new uses. Historic district zoning adds more constraints. Sometimes, however, zoning changes or exceptions are possible, and the design review process required in historic districts is not necessarily a deterrent to rehabilitation. Improved tax revenues, increased employment, and the elimination of dilapidated structures are attractive incentives to city governments to change zoning regulations that may otherwise be roadblocks to change.

Energy conservation.   Energy conservation has become a crucial component of the trend toward renovation. Every building in reasonable physical condition represents a stockpile of energy that can be conserved. Old masonry structures insulate against temperature changes; curtain wall construction makes much greater demands on heating and cooling systems. Window openings in older structures occupy a much smaller proportion of the exterior facades than do curtain wall buildings. Office buildings with windows that open provide insurance against temperature extremes when power shortages shut down mechanical cooling or ventilation.

Building codes.   Perhaps the most significant stumbling blocks to successful recycling of old buildings are building codes. Fortunately, certain cities have code provisions for historic structures; others have special appeal boards to settle the conflicts that arise between building codes and the needs and desires of those involved in renovation projects.

The fact remains that the rehabilitation of an existing structure provides fewer design options than does new construction, despite structural integrity, quality of materials, attractive architecture, and energy conservation. Bearing walls, columns, hallways, and stairwells are very expensive, and sometimes impossible, to alter. Stringent building codes may require additional stairwells and emergency exits. In areas where earthquakes occur, renovation may require expensive seismic-protective alterations that usually were not included in the original construction.

Generally, the less that is changed in a structure, the fewer code requirements have to be observed. According to most building codes, when a major portion of a building is to be changed, the renovation must conform to the building code in its entirety. Thus, building codes discourage changes of use.

It should be noted that modernization, remodeling, or restoration that affects more than 20% or 25% of a property's floor area or assessed value is likely to trigger the applicability of local ordinances that require nonconforming buildings to be brought up to present standards. Therefore, remodeling, restoration, and modernization involve a review of all nonconforming features. However, the retention of old walls and floor plans may permit much larger floor area ratios on the site than those permitted by existing zoning. In addition, certain income tax advantages may be possible for an owner if a building is remodeled rather than replaced. Thus, an appraiser must consider the interaction of zoning, building codes, and the degree of modernization and remodeling when estimating the after-renovation market value or the economic feasibility of any type of renovation. An appraiser must investigate and, as in all appraisal assignments, seek technical advice when needed.

When appraising an historic property, an appraiser must know how properties qualify as historic or architecturally significant and must understand the relationships between real estate and society. This includes knowledge of how architectural styles and construction techniques are related to history and a careful analysis of how the current market determines the value of such properties.

Appraisal Procedures

When the restoration of an older or historic structure is planned, several appraisal procedures in addition to estimating market value before and after renovation are warranted. For most renovation projects, an appraiser is asked to estimate the cost of the renovation itself. Many renovation appraisals also necessitate feasibility studies to determine whether the benefits accruing to the renovation provide an incentive in addition to the cost of the renovation. Feasibility studies include highest and best use analyses, cost estimates based on alternative uses, an analysis of tax incentives that accrue to renovation projects, and an estimate of the renovated property's earning potential.[3]

Feasibility Analysis

The test of feasibility for any project is the soundness of the investment required. The calculation of the amount and timing of the required investment, of the anticipated recovery of and return on the investment, and of the risks attached to the recovery and the returns is the

---

[3]For a detailed discussion of feasibility studies, see Chapter 24.

core of a feasibility analysis. Such an analysis requires a full investigation of alternate uses; market characteristics; development costs; development constraints and risks; financing possibilities; selling prices; absorption rates; and, in the case of income-producing properties, projected rents and other income, occupancy levels, and debt service requirements. Potential renovation, like new construction, must be evaluated in terms of an entire economic setting. Income, expenses, costs, flexibility, utility, manageability, tax advantages, and resale value all must be considered.

Highest and Best Use
The cost to put a property into proper condition for a potential use is sometimes the major determinant of the use's feasibility. In such matters, the crucial consideration is how the increase in a property's value relates to the cost to rehabilitate. The cost to create the desired quality and character in a new building may be economically prohibitive if the property's market value after rehabilitation has not increased at least commensurately with the rehabilitation costs.

The justification for any renovation program depends on the property's highest and best use. The criteria for ascertaining the highest and best use of a renovation project are similar to those for determining the highest and best use of a vacant site, except that the functional limitations of the existing building may be excessively costly to overcome. However, if the building is in sufficiently sound condition for remodeling, if the district standards and trends are materially higher than those reflected in the property's present condition, and if the prospective income improvement is substantial, a comprehensive program may be feasible.

The study that an appraiser employs to ascertain highest and best use includes the cost estimates necessary for a program to achieve highest and best use; the estimates provide the basis for a decision on the program's economic justification. A variety of potential programs may justify consideration, but the only satisfactory way to select a final plan is to explore the alternatives, to estimate the cost and potential income (value) benefits, and then be guided by the results of a comparison of the data thus developed.

The method of ranking the alternative possible uses for an older structure is similar to the analysis of new construction: costs must be related to benefits. Regarding renovation projects, certain available benefits may be added to income or resale potential, such as income tax credits, preservation grants, ad valorem tax abatement, and the potential for preservation easement credits.

Regardless of the degree of rehabilitation involved, the budget required for any program depends on the most probable highest and best use for the property and the value that results from that use. It is not a foregone conclusion that the current use of an older building is its highest and best use. An appraiser must first carefully identify all potential highest and best uses or reuses of the land as though vacant and the property as improved, select the use that has the highest probability of being legal, technically possible, effectively supported in the marketplace, and financially viable. Finally, an appraiser applies the techniques of the valuation process.

Costs

General standards of cost data for renovation are developed through experience and research. Current reproduction cost, which is frequently estimated by the unit-in-place method, represents basic cost, to which is added any additional cost for performing the work on an existing structure. Rehabilitation estimates may be based on actual recent costs for the same or equivalent work performed on the property or on similar properties. Management records may include bids for specific rehabilitation items that have not been performed, such as exterior painting, roof repair, or interior decorating.

The cost of certain rehabilitation work may approximate that for similar work in new construction. However, the cost of modernization or remodeling work is usually higher than for new construction for several reasons. Although the quantity of material may be the same as for new work, more labor is involved and the conditions are different. The alteration of a structure generally involves tearing out old work and performing small quantities of new work under conditions not conducive to the degree of efficiency attainable in new construction. If a contractor makes an estimate on a flat-fee basis, he or she may charge substantially more than the cost of identical work in new construction to ensure against complications that may develop as the remodeling progresses, such as the unforeseen placement of existing conduits, pipes, and structural load-bearing members.

Other costs to be considered are those that may be incurred by the owner rather than the contractor. These include items such as the architect's fee, the owner's cost of supervision, and the loss of rents due to vacancies while the work is being done. These costs are additional to the direct cost estimate.

When the actual reproduction of architectural components and original materials is required by historic district ordinances or by encumbering preservation easements, the cost of restoring or repairing a particular property may greatly exceed typical costs. Such a requirement might be special duplicate nonstandard-sized bricks or individually cast terra-cotta ornamentation. Appraisers need to ascertain whether such careful duplications are required and how much they will cost. Such extra cost constraints can significantly alter the economics of rehabilitating an historic property.

Table 25.2 Four Valuation Examples for an Older Eight-Flat Historic Building on a Site Zoned for Sixteen Units

	As Is	Correction of Deferred Maintenance	Partial Modernization	Conventional Remodeling	Historic Restoration
1. Prospective gross annual income					
As is: 8 units @ $96 x 12	$9,216				
Deferred maintenance: 8 units @ $100 x 12		$ 9,600			
Modernization: 8 units @ $110 x 12			$10,560		
Remodeling: 16 units @ $85 x 12				$16,320	
Restoration: 12 units @ $100 x 12					$14,400
2. Allowance for vacancy and collection loss					
As is: 10%	−922				
Deferred maintenance: 10%		−960			
Modernization: 8%			−845		
Remodeling: 7.5%				−1,224	
Restoration: 7.5%					−1,080
Effective gross annual income	$8,294	$8,640	$9,715	$15,096	$13,320
3. Expenses					
Fixed	$1,200	$1,200	$1,000	$1,200	$1,400
Variable	1,450	1,450	900	1,600	1,200
Repairs and replacements	900	900	450	700	900
Total expenses	−3,550	−3,550	−2,350	−3,500	−3,500
Net operating income	$ 4,744	$ 5,090	$ 7,365	$11,596	$ 9,820
4. Imputable to land, 12% of $16,000	−1,920	−1,920	−1,920	−1,920	−1,920
Net operating income imputable to building	$ 2,824	$ 3,170	$ 5,445	$ 9,676	$ 8,380[a]
5. Capitalized at					
As is: 17%	$16,612				
Deferred maintenance: 16%		$19,813			

Modernization: 14%			$38,893		
Remodeling: 12%				$80,633	
Restoration: 14%					$59,857
6. Add land value	16,000	16,000	16,000	16,000	12,000[a]
Total unadjusted indicated value	$32,612	$35,813	$54,893	$96,633	$71,857
Less allowance for deferred maintenance necessary to maintain present net income level	-1,212				
Total indicated value	$31,400	$35,813	$54,893	$96,633	$71,857
Total indicated value		$35,813	$54,893	$96,633	$71,857
As is value		-31,400	-31,400	-31,400	-31,400
Projected value increment		$4,413	$23,493	$65,233	$40,457
7. Cost of renovation program including contingencies		$2,213	$11,830	$33,600	$40,900
Estimated loss of rent during program implementation			2,800	3,100	3,100
Total renovation costs and estimated rent loss		-2,213	-14,630	-36,700	-44,000
Net incentive (in dollars)		$2,200	$8,863	$28,533	$(3,543)
Total investment		$33,613	$46,030	$68,100	$75,400
Net incentive as average percentage of investment		6.5%	19.3%	41.9%	-4.7%[b]

Net incentive before investment tax credit	$(3,543)
Investment tax credit .25 × $40,900 =	10,255
	$ 6,682
Total investment	$ 75,400
Net incentive as average percentage of investment after-tax credit	8.9%

[a] 12% of $12,000
[b] Although a negative incentive appears for historic restoration, with the 25% investment tax credit the results are as follows:

The use of renovation cost comparables provides a balance in analyzing renovation cost as a contribution to market value. For certain renovation projects, however, specific tax benefits or funds available for historic preservation are necessary to offset what would otherwise be noneconomic rehabilitation costs.

Frequently, significant variations exist between the actual costs of similar projects, depending on the skill and experience of construction management and capability. Appraisers must remain current on changing construction costs and technological advances that affect costs. Assembling cost data from more than one source ensures a greater degree of accuracy in cost estimating. National cost data services are very helpful, but information from these sources must be carefully weighed against the characteristics of the subject property and the actual project costs of similar properties.

The hard costs per square foot of rehabilitation may not be lower than new construction. However, the reduction in total time required for renovation, perhaps one year as contrasted with two years for new construction, is frequently adequate enough to justify a rehabilitation project as an alternative to new construction, considering the difference in carrying costs. In addition, recent tax benefits have been crucial in attracting capital to rehabilitation projects.

Economic Feasibility of Alternative Renovation Programs

A thorough review of a building's physical attributes suggests potential uses, which are screened to find a use compatible with legal and political realities of the property's neighborhood, zoning, position on the Register, and the submarket for space of various possible types of uses. In short, feasibility analysis implies a responsibility to find the use that best fits the limitations of the site; the structure to be altered; the neighborhood plan; the long-term well-being of the occupant; and possible implications arising from the National Register. Many alternative courses of action are financially viable but are incompatible with the rights, sensibilities, or values of an immediate community of interests. These elements must be considered when assessing the highest and best use or most probable use. However, given alternative uses that are legal and feasible, the use that is most viable in terms of finance or economics is the object of an appraiser's search.

Table 25.2 illustrates the method of feasibility analysis when the purpose of renovation is to arrive at the alternative legal and possible use that will produce the highest net income. At that point, the tests for economic feasibility that are suggested in the four comparative properties in the table become critical appraisal or investment decision tools.

Summary

Appraisers may be asked to appraise older commercial and residential structures. The renewal of existing structures is often undertaken to preserve historical sites or as a cost-effective measure. Such assignments may include an analysis of the possibility of building renovation, its cost, and its economic feasibility.

An appraiser who undertakes such an appraisal needs to consider the economic trends and societal attitudes that influence renovation, the technical expertise for estimating renovation cost, and the laws that affect and may benefit properties that could be renovated. Tax laws, in particular, affect building renovation.

There are several forms of renovation appraisals, all of which employ the appraisal procedures discussed in the text, but in relation to the type of property, the motivation for the renovation, and the purpose of the appraisal. In addition, an appraiser must consider that certain renovations may result in additional value accruing to a property.

There are three major types of renovation. They are remodeling, restoration, and modernization. The use of a property is changed, or remodeled, when its design or plan is changed. A property is returned to its original appearance and condition through restoration, and is modernized when worn or outdated elements are replaced with current versions. An appraiser should consider when it is practical to perform one of the three types of renovation, what kind of obsolescence or deterioration necessitates such a renovation, whether it is economically sound, and how it affects highest and best use and market value. Properties listed in the National Register of Historic Places receive protective and economic benefits, particularly tax incentives for restoration.

While inspecting improvements, an appraiser determines whether they have any curable physical deterioration that should be corrected immediately, or deferred maintenance items. Such items are painting and tuckpointing. Expenditures on these items may be necessary to bring properties to a competitive level. Deferred maintenance can be part of basic rehabilitation that may result in temporary positive effects on a property, or it can be part of a modernization renewal, which usually has the additional effect of extending the property's economic life.

In analyzing aging structures and neighborhoods for renovation appraisal, an appraiser considers several items. They include the corrective action needed; whether useful life will be extended; what the change in use will be; the impact on expenses; the impact on real estate revenues; the impact on market value; type of professional study necessary; and federal income tax benefits.

Special considerations in renovation appraisal include judgments concerning the highest and best use of the property and the preservation of its income-earning potential; ascertaining if zoning regulations permit the proposed new uses; the energy conservation potential of the building; and the effects of building codes. An appraiser must consider the interaction of zoning, building codes, and the degree of modernization and remodeling when estimating the after-renovation market value or the economic feasibility of any type of renovation.

In addition to estimating market value before and after renovation, an appraiser usually estimates the cost of renovation itself. Sometimes the appraiser performs a feasibility study to determine whether the benefits accruing to the renovation provide an incentive in addition to the cost. Feasibility studies include highest and best use analyses, cost estimates based on alternative uses, an analysis of tax incentives that accrue to renovation projects, and an estimate of the earning potential of the renovated property. When performing a feasibility analysis, an appraiser is responsible for finding the use of the property that best fits the limitations of the site; the structure to be altered; the neighborhood plan; the long-term well-being of the occupant; and possible implications arising from the National Register. An appraiser must consider these elements when determining highest and best or most probable use. However, given alternative uses that are legally feasible, the use that is most viable in terms of finance or economics is the object of an appraiser's search.

Chapter 26

Appraisal Specialties

Many appraisers are involved in a general practice and perform a variety of appraisal assignments; others concentrate on a particular aspect of appraisal. Certain appraisal specialties are discussed in this chapter because of public interest in them or because of the ramifications they produce.

Areas of specialty may be divided into two basic categories. They are those that deal with appraisal purpose and use, and those that are concerned with administrative matters.

Because the purpose and use of an appraisal may point to an area of specialty, appraisers may specialize in appraisals performed for

1. Mortgage loans

2. Casualty loss

3. Eminent domain, a particular acquisition situation

4. Business valuation

5. Real estate, or ad valorem, taxation

Mortgage loan appraisals are perhaps the most publicly recognized types of appraisals. When financing is the purpose of an appraisal, the property is appraised as if unaffected by the proposed mortgage loan or by any loans that would be junior to the proposed mortgage. The property is, however, considered subject to any senior loans, liens, or leases, but not to subordinated leases, loans, or liens.

Ordinarily, the defined value in a mortgage appraisal is market value, although many lenders specify use value for industrial or commercial properties. In certain instances, the client or employer may stipulate that the present value of the property be based on the discounted value of its future incomes under assumed future inflation rates.

Casualty loss appraisal is usually performed for income tax or insurance claim purposes. In a casualty loss appraisal, an appraiser estimates the decrease in property value due to fire, storm, or some other casualty. The loss is not valued as a separate entity. The appraiser usually must estimate the contribution that a damaged item made to the total value of the property before the casualty, without the advantage of having inspected the property before that time. More than one valuation may be required in insurance cases because the policy may give the carrier a choice by specifying that restitution be the lowest amount of (1) the limit of the policy, (2) the contributory market value, or (3) the cost to duplicate or restore. In certain casualty-loss cases, an evaluation of the highest and best use of the damaged property is requested. Such an evaluation may provide information on the economic feasibility of restoring the damaged property to precasualty condition.

Eminent domain is the power that enables government entities, quasi-government bureaus, or public utilities to acquire interests in real estate. In the United States, the owner of the taken property must receive just compensation for loss when property is acquired in this manner. Compensation is established through negotiation between the condemnor and the condemnee or, if the parties cannot reach agreement, through the operation of law. Establishing the amount of just compensation always requires at least one valuation; usually the defined value is market value.

Business valuation is requested in situations in which an appraisal is needed that includes value of the real estate considered as an entity with an established enterprise. This is different from valuation of real estate only, ready to operate but without a going business. The defined value in such an appraisal is going-concern value. It includes consideration of the efficiency of the facility, the expertise of management, and the sufficiency of capital. Going-concern value is an excess of value over cost that arises as a consequence of a complete and well-assembled operation; it is the value of an efficient layout and operational control system resulting in the most desirable synchronization of the merchandising, production, or distribution activities of the enterprise; it includes goodwill.

In *real estate taxation, or ad valorem, appraisal,* appraisers work for municipalities, counties, or states in carrying out the assessment function—that is, in ascertaining the value of real estate for taxation. Most properties in the nation, including many that are tax-exempt, are assessed and are therefore subject to some value opinion for real estate tax purposes.

There are two subspecialties within the ad valorem specialty. They are *mass appraisal,* in which an approximate property value estimate is the goal; and *reappraisal,* or assessment appeal appraisal, which is conducted when an assessment is appealed by a taxpayer and a more precise appraisal than a mass appraisal is required.

Certain appraisal specialties are derived from the particular responsibilities related to an appraiser's work. These appraisal practitioners can be divided into four categories. They are

1. Field appraisers

2. Managing appraisers

3. Review appraisers

4. Arbitrators

Of course, an appraiser can be involved in one or more of these areas.

Field appraisers are the majority of appraisal practitioners. Often the basis of specialty appraisal, a field appraiser's work consists of four functions. Field appraisers conduct primary and secondary research, analyze researched data, form data-supported opinions, and prepare written or oral appraisal reports. Although field appraisers may not perform all the functions in each appraisal, they must be competent in them all.

Managing appraisers supervise appraisal staffs. Their work often includes acquiring appraisal assignments; negotiating fees, devising completion schedules, and determining the type of report required by the client or employer; and delegating work to staff field or review appraisers. Managing appraisers often suggest data sources and collection methods, serve as technical advisers, ensure editorial consistency, maintain production schedules, administer personnel, provide training and educational opportunities, and manage office finances. They may also serve as field or review appraisers.

Review appraisers examine the reports of other appraisers to determine whether reported conclusions of the field appraiser are consistent with the reported data and with other generally known information.

Review appraisers usually do not inspect subject properties. Thus, they are not held responsible for the accuracy of an appraisal opinion based on another person's research and analysis.

The review function is not practiced throughout the appraisal field; many clients receive and act on a field appraiser's report without the advantage of a review appraiser's report. Certain such clients rely on the advice of lawyers, brokers, or other advocates. Although they are not always consulted by clients, impartial review appraisers represent a significant group in the total number of real estate appraisers.

Arbitrators are persons who are chosen to decide a dispute. They perform functions that are different from those of a mediator, who attempts to bring about a voluntary settlement of differences, and a conciliator, who espouses the interest of one party and attempts to win out over the other. An appraiser's role in arbitration is discussed in more detail later in this chapter.

Eminent Domain Appraisal

Appraisals are often required when private property is taken through the power of eminent domain.[1] Eminent domain gives the government the right to acquire interests in private property for public use without the consent of the owner.

Condemnation is the act or process of carrying out the right of eminent domain. The legal exercise of eminent domain requires that the government have a specific need to own the condemned rights and that the former owner be in the same pecuniary position after the taking as he or she was before. The offsetting payment is known as just compensation. Appraisers are asked by taking agencies, and sometimes by property owners, to estimate just compensation when the right of eminent domain is exercised.

In a typical condemnation case, an appraiser is called on to estimate the market value of the fee simple estate. However, there may be one or more space tenants, land tenants, or mortgagees who have a marketable interest in the real estate. Generally, the court awards just compensation to the fee simple estate and leaves it to the interested parties to agree on the apportionment of the award. Failing their

---

[1]The presentation of eminent domain appraisal here is confined to discussion of it as an appraisal specialty, concentrated on the reason for such appraisals and some of the special knowledge required to perform these appraisals. For a complete discussion of all aspects of eminent domain valuation, see James D. Eaton, *Real Estate Valuation in Litigation* (Chicago: American Institute of Real Estate Appraisers, 1982).

agreement, a separate trial may be held to divide the award.

The power of eminent domain is established in the Fifth and Fourteenth Amendments of the U.S. Constitution. The Fifth Amendment states: "No person shall be . . . deprived of life, liberty, or property, without due process of law; nor shall private property be taken for public use, without just compensation." Section 1 of the Fourteenth Amendment states: ". . . nor shall any state deprive any person of life, liberty, or property, without due process of law." Every state has similar versions of the Fifth Amendment; however, certain state constitutions include an additional provision that private property shall not be "taken or damaged for public use, without just compensation."

The federal government and all state governments can delegate the power of eminent domain to any branch of a government agency, quasi-government agency or corporation, public utility, or other private firm. Agencies at the same government level ordinarily pool resources for two reasons. First, it is generally more efficient to have one office of real estate experts to serve several agencies, such as the fire department, school board, and sewer district. Second, if each agency of the jurisdiction independently acquired property, the government would sometimes be competing with itself and, thereby, unnecessarily increasing the price it would pay.

Just Compensation

The U.S. Constitution does not define *just compensation*. Therefore, the courts have been compelled to interpret it. Just compensation has been held to be a matter solely for judicial inquiry; it is not prescribed by the legislature. The courts generally adhere to the belief that the best test of just compensation is the market value of the acquired interest in the real property taken. The Supreme Court has ruled that, for its purposes, *market value, fair value,* and *fair market value* are synonymous terms. Use of the market value concept in determining just compensation is based on the reasoning that neither the value to the condemnor nor the value to the condemnee would invariably reflect equity. Instead, value in the open market most closely approaches the constitutional ideal. In an eminent domain court case, market value is defined as the property's value not merely at its highest and best use, but its value for "all of the uses for which it may be adapted."

The court's determination of just compensation is invariably tied to evidence presented by expert witnesses. Experienced appraisers may qualify as experts regarding the market value of properties they have appraised.

The just compensation for the expropriated property may be less or greater than its market value in certain cases: when the property is a restricted market property, when the taking is a partial taking, when damages are noncompensable, and when evidence is not admissible.

Restricted market properties have very limited marketability. Because sales of similar properties are nonexistent, rare, or affected by duress or conditions other than open-market conditions, market value would be difficult to estimate. For example, an electric generating plant located where there is only one electric utility company is a restricted market property. In cases that involve restricted market properties, an appraiser is governed by legal instructions to seek the use value of the subject property.

Severance refers to a situation in which only part of a property is taken. The remainder may have a market value that is less than the value the remainder portion contributed to the whole property before the taking. This may result because the remainder property has an awkward configuration, is no longer accessible by public road, or is less than optimum size. When a partial taking causes a diminution in the value contribution made by the remaining property, the remainder is said to have been "damaged" by the taking. The payment of an amount equal to the market value of the part taken would not be just compensation; although it compensates for the property taken, it fails to compensate for the damage to the property not taken.

As a matter of law, some damages are *noncompensable*. When the inherent rights of real estate ownership—the right to view and be viewed, the right to ingress and egress, and the right to natural light and air—are completely taken, just compensation unquestionably follows. However, a government project may partly impede views from the remainder, add circuity to the remainder's egress, or cast a shadow over part of the remainder. Some such damages are classified as legally noncompensable.

An appraiser generally lists the various damages (and benefits) caused by the taking and allocates dollar amounts to each. This action is necessary when the legal compensability of some or all of the estimated damages is in doubt.

In controversial cases, legal advocates for the adversaries frequently give contradictory instructions to their respective appraisers. These instructions may, in turn, produce a disparity between the opinions of the appraisers retained by the condemnor and those by the condemnee. Neither side knows which position will be upheld until the court rules, and even then the ruling may be subject to appeal. Regardless of legal instructions, an appraiser understands that he or she serves as an impartial valuation expert and that the lawyer serves as the adversary's advocate. Even when eminent domain cases are settled out of court, the settlements reflect the legal positions that the parties would have taken if the issue were litigated. In either case, the appraisal advice is impartial.

Legal admissibility of evidence may influence the determination of just compensation in a taking. Although most courts accept the opinions of experienced appraisal experts as to appropriate valuation techniques, in certain instances the court instructs the witness that one or more facts, appraisal approaches, or analytic techniques must be excluded from the appraiser's consideration and testimony. Certain judges hold that the income capitalization approach or a discounting procedure is not admissible because it includes speculation on future happenings. Other judges object to the cost approach on the theory that its conclusion is the sum of the land value and the building contribution separately estimated, when land and building are not separable.

Occasionally, a judge requests the testimony of, or affidavits from, parties to unrecorded real estate transactions, such as leases, rather than relying solely on the evidence of the appraisal witness who allegedly has interviewed those parties. Often, transactions that are not arm's length are forbidden from consideration. These might include sales between related or friendly persons, sales where there is a perceived degree of undue market duress, sales in lieu of foreclosure, sales under the threat of eminent domain, or sales for which the title closing has not yet transpired or transpired subsequent to the date of taking. Offers to purchase or refusals of such offers, listings, mortgages, and options may also be forbidden from consideration. Sometimes a judge will rule that a sale or other comparable is not admissible into evidence because its location, date of sale, or physical characteristics are not sufficiently similar to the appraised property. Another court may admit such transactions as evidence, but might leave the weighing of the evidence to the discretion of the jury.

Courtroom Testimony

An appraiser engaged in eminent domain cases prepares both written and oral reports on each property valued. The nature of the written report is established by the client's attorney, who may specify that a lesser or greater degree of information be included or omitted, depending on the jurisdiction's rules of discovery and the relative strength of the opposition's case. Sometimes an appraiser who is retained by the condemnor is required to submit an appraisal report with much more detail than the condemnor's attorney chooses to divulge to opposing counsel.

The appraiser's testimony is the oral report. Whether by deposition or trial testimony, oral reporting in eminent domain cases consists of responding to questions posed by friendly counsel, opposing counsel, and, occasionally, the trier of law. In court, the oral report might typically consist of direct examination and cross-examination concerning the appraiser's professional background, with each side attempting to influence the jury as to the degree of ability and integrity of the witnesses. After the witness's credentials are established, questions concerning the valuation are posed. Usually there occurs a series of redirect and then re-cross questions before the court excuses the witness. Occasionally, the appraiser is recalled to the stand to rebut facts or theories presented by the opposing counsel's witness.

Special Training and Experience

Most properties acquired for public use are transferred to the condemning authority as part of a negotiated settlement. Therefore, the few cases that are litigated usually concern more significant properties or more difficult appraisal problems. When performing any appraisal that might result in public testimony, the appraiser should keep in mind that the following questions may be asked in court:

1. How (not *why*) are you qualified to give an opinion of value in this case?

2. What did you do in valuing this property?

3. What did you consider in arriving at your opinion?

4. What is your opinion of value?

5. How do you support that opinion?

Appraisers qualify as experts on the basis of education, training, experience, and reputation. Published writings, university appointments, lecturing assignments, a list of well-known clients, professional designations, and prior qualification as an expert in one or more courts all may lend stature to a witness.

Appraisers who choose to practice in the condemnation field must accept the evidence-admissibility rules that are expounded by the court. Other peculiarities of courtroom testimony include that the appraisal report is oral, that the appraiser must be able to explain why certain market transactions were rejected as indicative comparables, and that one or more officers of the court will be striving to discredit the appraiser on grounds of ignorance, dishonesty, or carelessness. The greatest advantage a condemnation appraiser can have during a trial is the awareness that he or she knows more about the property and the theory and practice of appraising than anyone else in the courtroom.

Business Valuation

A business is typically appraised to determine the present and future monetary rewards of complete or partial rights in its ownership. Procedures for business appraisals vary according to the type of business being appraised and the form of its ownership, and appraisers are guided by the procedures and methods that have been found appropriate to each situation.[2]

Among the most common reasons for business appraisals are sale or purchase of a business, allocation of purchase price, sale of a business asset, estate or inheritance taxes, gift tax, spinoff of part of a business, and liquidation of a business.

An appraisal assignment may be to estimate the market value of real estate on which a business is conducted. In such an assignment, the complication is that the income imputable to the real estate is combined with that of nonrealty assets, including intangibles such as goodwill. In other instances, an appraisal is required of the business entity. In such instances, the real estate appraiser may be the lead appraiser if the major assets of the firm are real estate.

More than one appraiser may be participating in appraising businesses, and the practitioner must exercise care that each element to be valued is included in the final appraisal, but that no element is included more than once. In addition, each element's contributory value to the whole, not its intrinsic value, is appraised. To value each element separately would violate the consistent-use theory.

For example, if a small manufacturing firm is being appraised for merger negotiations, use value is probably the defined value. In this case, the contributory value of the integral machinery and equipment to the factory buildings and, hence, to the land depends on an accurate analysis of their productivity that in turn depends on the effectiveness of the location of the property relative to raw materials, labor, and consumer markets. For these reasons, the same items of equipment may contribute a good deal more or less at competing factories. Certain items of equipment on the premises may be obsolete and may require replacement. The value of these noncontributing items is the price a buyer, who assumes the cost of dismantling and shipping them, will pay in competition with other potential buyers. This noncontributing market value is referred to by appraisers as salvage value if the item can be sold for off-site use at another location. If the item cannot be used in

---

[2]The presentation of business valuation here is confined to discussion of the topic as an appraisal specialty, concentrated on the reasons for such appraisals and some of the special knowledge required to appraise businesses. For a full discussion of business valuation, see Glenn M. Desmond and Richard E. Kelley, *Business Valuation Handbook* (Llano, Calif.: Valuation Press, Inc., 1977).

another location, except through a physical change or reconstitution, the market value is said to be scrap value.

Extent of Assignment

The needs of a client and the nature of an appraisal assignment determine the property assets to be valued. In all business valuation assignments, an appraiser must be aware of the business activity surrounding the property. For example, a client may specify that all "fixed assets and intangibles" be included in the appraised property, but that the "current assets and investments" be excluded. Therefore, the security for a mortgage loan would include land, building, fixtures, furniture, and goodwill, but not cash, inventories, and securities. In another instance the furniture or fixtures on the premises might be the subject of a separate chattel loan. In either case, a valuation of the excluded inventories is made as either an allocation of capitalized value or as a precapitalization income deduction. If the assignment excludes intangibles, a separate valuation of goodwill, going concern, or entrepreneurial return is required.

When estimating the value of shares of corporate stock or of single- or partner-proprietorship interests, the assistance of a real estate appraiser may be requested. Conversely, a real estate appraiser may seek professional advice from a business management analyst, industry representative, securities analyst, auditor, or commercial accountant.

Goodwill and Other Intangibles

A parcel of real estate that supports a business may have a value in excess of the contribution made by its tangible assets. This value, going-concern value, includes goodwill.

Goodwill can be defined as elements of a business that cause customers to return to the business and usually enable a firm to generate profit in excess of that required for a reasonable return on all of the other assets of the business, including a return on all other intangible assets that can be identified and separately valued. Goodwill always runs with the business and cannot be sold separately. Part or all of business goodwill can sometimes be sold separate from the owners and employees of the business, but it cannot be sold separate from the business. Similarly, personal goodwill can be sold in part or fully separate from a business but not separate from the individual.[3]

Four agents are involved in the production of income: labor, capital (tangibles affixed to the land), coordination, and land. If the use of

---

[3]*Ibid.*, p. 166.

land, building, and employees is efficient, goodwill or going-concern value is produced. This intangible has imputed income, although it ranks behind wages, rent, and entrepreneurial reward in the order of payment.

In valuing goodwill, an appraiser assumes that the goodwill will continue to benefit future operations. Goodwill, however, may have a different use value and market value. Other intangibles include trademarks, copyrights, patents, and leaseholds.

Special Training and Experience

In valuing business interests, an appraiser must have substantial knowledge of appraisal theory and practice to make sound judgments related to the valuation. The appraiser must also have the ability to report this knowledge orally and in writing. In addition, the appraiser must understand the workings of the business community, particularly the aspects of finance and marketing.

An appraiser must be able to perform or direct library research and must be familiar with various published business reports. Moreover, the appraiser must have knowledge of accounting procedures, which interpret, analyze, and summarize business transactions, so the appraiser can intelligently discuss the trends and tendencies of general business activity and the financial condition of a particular firm.

To reach a sound conclusion in a business valuation, an appraiser should become acquainted with the business that is the subject of the appraisal. By interviewing employees and managers and by inspecting the operations of the business, often accompanied by those who possess expertise in engineering, industry, and other matters, an appraiser should also gather and analyze all available information regarding the firm from public and private sources. When information is found contradictory, the appraiser attempts to reconcile the information. Information regarding product development, pending law suits, and contracts under negotiation is, of course, confidential; but the appraiser can presume such information has not been withheld. The appraiser must also ensure that the appraisal does not compromise the confidentiality of information given.

Ad Valorem Taxation

Local assessors usually employ staff appraisers. In certain jurisdictions, the assessed value of property is established annually; in others, the same assessment applies for several years unless the building has been physically changed by renovation, demolition, or casualty loss. Assessments may also be adjusted on an interim basis so that each property reflects its last sale; more often, however, all sales are used as a basis for all assessments. When a county or a municipality establishes assessments less often than annually, the value estimates are often made by a team of state employees or a private firm.

The real estate tax rate is determined by the amount of budgeted funds the elected officials approve relative to the sum of the assessment roll. Elected officials also decide such policy issues as whether the tax rate should be uniform or should differ for differing types of property, which properties should be entirely or partly exempt from taxation, and which properties should get an abatement. Thus, the tax rate is not established by assessment office appraisers.

In various states the value estimated for real estate taxation may be called *full, true, fair, reasonable, just, cash,* or *actual* value. The phrase *market value* is used in a few states, and the concept of a hypothetical sale or market premise is implicit in the rules of other states. In about half the states, assessments are established by law at a prescribed fraction of value. Even in states where assessments are pegged at 100% of value, the defined value is as of a date one year or more before the effective date of the assessment. The time lag provides a single valuation date for all properties in the jurisdiction, ample notice to the taxpayers, and a period for appeals prior to the effective taxation date.

Appraisal estimates for assessment purposes can be traced to market value. One or more of the three approaches may be applicable in specific cases. However, for common properties, multiple regression procedures are often employed. In some assessment offices, one team of appraisers estimates the land value of each property and subtracts the value from the total value estimate formulated by another assessor, thereby deriving the building's contribution to the total assessed value.

To avoid the criticism that an ad valorem tax punishes those who take good care of their buildings and rewards those who do the opposite, assessors may exempt maintenance from the assessed value and increase the assessment only when structural or mechanical improvements are made. An extension of this general idea (called SVT, or site value taxation) is a system wherein land is assessed, but buildings or other improvements to the land are not. This system is used in certain foreign countries, but it has not gained popularity in the United States.

In appeal cases, appraisers focus on value of the total property. In litigation involving improved properties, the portion of the total applicable to the land is often stipulated by the adversary parties so that it is removed from judicial determination.

The identification of the rights to be assessed is not well settled in the law; judicial interpretation varies in at least two areas—private encumbrances and agents in production. In cases in which private agreements have created a dominant easement tenement or a space rent leasehold, certain authorities suggest that the fee owner's interest should be assessed. Others argue that this would leave the leasehold interest illegally exempt from taxation and therefore believe that the fee simple estate should be the subject of the assessment.

Similarly, certain authorities argue that real estate assessments should be confined to the sum of the contribution made by land and capital; other authorities make no deduction for the contribution made by operating coordination. All authorities agree that the contribution made to a property by labor should be deducted because employees are not included in the price at which properties sell.

Appraisal Review

In virtually any livelihood, certain persons criticize, inspect, examine, judge, or comment on the work of others. In this context, the appraisal review procedure is the quality control function by which various appraisers in an office review the work of one another before it is submitted to staff managers or clients.

Typically, a formal review function exists in offices that receive a large volume of appraisal reports. Certain government offices fall into this category (e.g., taxation offices, eminent domain offices, and mortgage offices). Private lending organizations, including thrift institutions, insurance companies, pension funds, investment trusts, and commercial banks, employ review appraisers as staff members. Reviewers are also hired on a fee basis.

Before an appraisal is submitted to a review appraiser, a compliance review may be conducted by another staff member to determine if the field appraiser's report meets basic content specifications and if calculations are correct. If the compliance review reveals any errors or omission of items specified in the appraisal contract, the review appraiser judges the significance of the errors and decides if there is justification for the omissions.

The review appraiser conducts a complete technical review of the appraisal report and submits a written opinion of whether to accept, reject, or modify the opinions contained in the report. To produce this written opinion, the review appraiser accomplishes several different tasks.

A review appraiser first checks the appraisal file on the subject property or project. The file reveals the purpose of the appraisal and the requirements of the contract.

Many review appraisers then read the entire appraisal report quickly for an overall impression. This initial perusal may suggest certain intermediate actions, such as obtaining additional market data, requesting a corrected page as suggested by the compliance review, scheduling interviews with people familiar with the property (including the field appraiser), or seeking the assistance of authorities in other disciplines, such as timber cruising, building demolition, property management, or real estate law. If more than one field appraisal has been made and is to be reviewed, a comparison of the reports at this point may uncover inconsistencies.

A review appraiser then analyzes the appraisal report's contents. This analysis may be focused by posing questions such as

1. Are the field appraiser's data adequate in quantity and quality?

2. Are the limiting conditions imposed by the field appraiser necessary? (Too many limiting conditions may diminish the report's usefulness.)

3. If more than one field appraiser is working on the assignment, are the methodologies consistent?

4. If rehabilitation is the highest and best use, what is the level of rehabilitation being suggested?

5. If the purpose of the appraisal is for a mortgage loan, does the report satisfy the rquirements of the regulatory agency?

6. If the report is a matter of litigation, is the nature of the supporting evidence admissible in court?

If a field review is needed, an abbreviated appraisal may be performed by another appraiser or the review appraiser may conduct a more thorough field review. In some offices in which field appraisal reports are relatively routine, most reports are typically subject to a desk review, and a field review is required for only a few. A field review may be performed to augment the data reported by the field appraiser or to resolve a conflict between the facts reported by two field appraisers who have reported separate estimates of the market value of the same property.

Information can often be obtained or clarified by telephone or mail. Most offices do not routinely conduct field reviews; others do for each submitted appraisal report. The extent of review considered necessary is often determined by the relative importance of the investment decision contemplated by the client.

A review appraiser must determine whether the field appraiser's opinion or the report containing that opinion is being reviewed. The review appraiser is usually not called on to form a written opinion of the reasonableness of the field appraiser's value estimate. Instead, the review appraiser determines if the field appraiser's report justifies the opinion. In many instances, a review appraiser does not have the means to notice errors of omission committed by a field appraiser who neglected to ascertain or at least report some pertinent market transactions.

Review Report Format

There is no standard format for review reports. Obviously, each identifies the field appraiser; the property interests appraised; the appraisal purpose, the date, and the defined value; the qualifying conditions and appraisal assumptions; the conclusion(s); and the review appraiser's opinions, conclusions, and recommendations. The review must be dated, signed, and, in some cases, certified.

The reviewer is obligated to prepare the review report promptly and impartially and to maintain the confidentiality of the opinion of the value of the assets and the judgments of the field appraiser. Of course, review appraisers should operate according to the standards of professional practice.

Testimony

Appraisers in litigation situations may also perform a type of appraisal review. A lawyer may retain a fee appraiser or a staff appraiser as a technical adviser during a trial. Such an appraiser assists the attorney in preparing questions by which they attempt to discredit the witnesses of opposing counsel and to reflect credit on the witnesses of friendly counsel. There is no impropriety in an appraiser assisting an advocate in this manner because the appraiser is not being presented as impartial.

A review appraiser usually will not testify to the market value of a property expressed by another appraiser. Nevertheless, supervisory assessors sometimes appear before tax appeal boards to report the assessment office's position on a series of cases. In most jurisdictions, the burden of proof in an appeal rests with the taxpayer because the law presumes the assessment is accurate. This presumption has less weight in law courts.

Special Training and Experience

Most professional review appraisers have field appraisal experience, and many are equal in experience and competence to the field appraisers whose work they review. It is as appropriate for a field appraiser to inquire into the professional credentials of the review appraiser before accepting an assignment as it is for a client to approve the field appraiser's credentials before issuing an assignment.

Arbitration

An arbitrator is chosen to decide a dispute to avoid a court determination. Matters are arbitrated because the parties to a dispute agree to submit to the arbitration. For example, the parties to a construction contract may voluntarily agree that, should any dispute arise under the terms of the contract, the matter will be arbitrated. Although the premise of arbitration is voluntary, the results of the arbitration are compulsory.

Appraisers are not commonly called on to arbitrate disputes, principally because most government agencies will not submit to arbitration for eminent domain, ad valorem taxation, income tax, or zoning disputes. However, there are certain incidences of appraisal arbitration between private parties.

Arbitration may be formal or informal. In formal arbitration, a hearing is conducted, with relaxed rules of evidence, and the dispute is decided. Such a hearing may be conducted by an appraiser, a nonappraiser, or a panel including one or more appraisers. Informal arbitration is more common and may be used in cases such as a long-term land lease, under which the rental is reestablished periodically either by mutual consent or by the binding decision of one or more appraisers. Such leases are drafted by lawyers and typically contain similar provisions regarding appraisal arbitration. The leases generally specify that the landlord and the tenant each select an appraiser, and that the two appraisers attempt to agree. Failing that, the appraisers select a third appraiser, and the opinion of the appraiser, who is neither high nor low, is binding on the disputing parties. Of course, various leases contain modifications of this formula. Some leases require an averaging of the three opinions; others specify that the third appraiser's opinion is binding. Generally, these leases do not require an appraisal report, only a decision regarding the rent for the ensuing period. This is convenient for the arbitrators, each of whom may have arrived at a compromise opinion for arbitration purposes rather than an independent opinion for appraisal purposes.

It is possible that in a case such as this, both the landlord and the tenant might select the same appraiser. Provided both parties are informed of this fact, the arbitration process is as efficient as possible. One of the advantages of arbitration is that it is less time consuming and less expensive than litigation.

A more formal type of arbitration is supervised by the American Arbitration Association. In formal arbitration, an appraiser (a nonappraiser, or a panel including one or more appraisers) conducts a hearing, with relaxed rules of evidence, and decides the dispute. In formal arbitration, an appraiser may serve as a witness or an arbitrator.

Summary

Appraisers may perform a variety of appraisal functions, or they may limit their practice to a particular appraisal specialty. Areas of specialty may be divided into those that deal with the purpose of the appraisal and those that are concerned with administrative matters. An appraisal may be sought to secure a mortgage loan, to estimate a casualty loss, to determine just compensation in eminent domain proceedings, to value a business concern, or to estimate a value for real estate assessment, or ad valorem taxation. Appraisal specialists can be categorized as field appraisers, managing appraisers, review appraisers, and arbitrators. An appraisal specialist may interact with legal and business professionals in eminent domain litigation, business valuation, and appraisal review.

The U.S. government has the power to acquire private property rights for the public good provided the property owner is given just compensation. The taking of a property by eminent domain may require the services of an appraiser to determine the just compensation to be awarded. Because just compensation is not defined in the Constitution, it is interpreted differently in different states. Generally, market value is considered the basis for just compensation. In some cases, however, market value will not equal just compensation due to a restricted market for the property taken, severance, noncompensability, or legal admissibility. An appraiser must be familiar with the legal concept of just compensation in the jurisdiction in question to complete the written report properly and to appear competent during direct testimony and cross-examination in the courtroom.

An appraiser performing a business valuation tailors the report to the client's needs and the nature of the assignment. In addition to the land and buildings, goodwill and other intangibles are valued. A thorough understanding of the operation of the enterprise, general accounting procedures, and published sources of business information is essential. If the appraiser cannot acquire all the necessary expertise, the assistance of other experts must be obtained.

Many appraisers are employed by assessment offices to perform mass appraisals and reappraisals. Because the tax rate and other taxation policy issues are set by local officials, the value to be estimated may differ in different areas. Any or all of the three approaches to value may be employed, and multiple regression techniques are commonly used.

Appraisal review is the quality control of the appraisal profession. Large offices may require formal review of all reports; smaller operations may review only a sampling. A compliance review is undertaken to check the report for minimum content and mathematical accuracy; in a technical review, the reviewing appraiser determines if the information in the report justifies the preparer's value opinion. In some offices most reports are subject to desk review, and a few receive field reviews to augment data or to resolve a conflict. Appraisers may be retained to testify as expert witnesses in court. It is perfectly acceptable for an appraiser to refute the testimony of another appraiser so long as he or she performs ethically and renders an impartial opinion. Appraisers may occasionally be asked to act as arbitrators to settle a dispute out of court. A formal arbitration may involve a hearing supervised by the American Arbitration Association. A more common assignment is an informal arbitration in which an appraiser is retained by private parties to reestablish periodically the rental in a long-term property lease. In most cases the appraiser acting as an arbitrator is not required to submit an appraisal report; by mutual consent of the interested parties, the appraiser's decision is binding. Individuals may choose to settle claims by arbitration to avoid the time and expense of litigation.

Appendix A

Professional Practice

The body of knowledge that comprises the discipline of appraisal is the beginning of professional practice. However, in solving most appraisal problems, the final conclusion depends largely on the ability, judgment, and integrity of the individual appraiser. The soundness of the conclusion is contingent in part on the availability of relevant data and the appraiser's commitment to finding and analyzing the data; it also depends in part on the skill with which appraisal techniques are applied. But appraisal is an inexact science. Great responsibility is placed on the appraiser to reach his or her conclusion in an impartial, objective manner, free of bias or any desire to accommodate self-interests or the interests of the client. Commitment to acquiring the requisite knowledge and applying it capably and objectively mark the professional appraiser.

A profession, as distinct from a trade or service industry, is identified through a combination of the following factors:

1. High standards of competence in a specialized field

2. A distinct body of knowledge that is continually growing by the contributions of the members and can be imparted to future generations

3. A code of ethics or standards of practice and agreement by the members to be regulated by peer review

These were the precise criteria that guided the founders of the American Institute of Real Estate Appraisers in 1932. The nation was in the midst of a period of unparalleled economic chaos, caused to a substantial degree by the inadequacy of sound data concerning the value and utility of real estate. The Institute was formed for three primary purposes:

1. To establish criteria for the selection and recognition of persons with skills in real estate valuation who also were committed to competent and ethical practice

2. To develop a system of education to train new appraisers and sharpen the skills of practicing appraisers

3. To formulate a code of professional ethics and standards of professional conduct for the guidance of members of the Institute and as a model for all practitioners

The first act of the new organization was to publish a Code of Professional Ethics and Standards of Professional Practice, which would protect the public and the appraiser.

The heart of the document is the Eight Canons.

Canon 1

A Member or Candidate of the Institute must refrain from misconduct that is detrimental to the real estate appraisal profession.

Canon 2

A Member or Candidate of the Institute must assist the Institute in carrying out its responsibilities to the users of appraisal services and to the public.

Canon 3

When performing a real estate appraisal assignment, a Member or Candidate of the Institute must perform such appraisal assignments without advocacy for the client's interests or the accommodation of his or her own interests.

Canon 4

A Member or Candidate of the Institute must not violate the confidential nature of the appraiser-client relationship by improperly disclosing the confidential portions of a real estate appraisal report.

Canon 5

In securing real estate appraisal assignments and in promoting a real estate appraisal practice, a Member or Candidate of the Institute must refrain from conduct which is deceptive, misleading, or otherwise contrary to the public interest.

Canon 6

A Member or Candidate of the Institute who has specific knowledge of the requirements of the Institute's Standards of Professional Practice must not deliberately or recklessly fail to observe such requirements.

Canon 7

In arriving at an analysis, opinion, or conclusion concerning real estate, a Member or Candidate of the Institute must use his or her best efforts to act competently and comply with the Institute's Standards of Professional Practice relating to competency.

Canon 8

In communicating an analysis, opinion, or conclusion concerning real estate, a Member or Candidate of the Institute must comply with the Institute's Standards of Professional Practice relating to written and oral appraisal reports.

Appendix B
Mathematics in Appraising

Appraising requires the use of a wide variety of mathematical techniques ranging from simple arithmetic through algebraic formulas to the statistical techniques of multiple regression analysis. Adding, subtracting, multiplying, and dividing can be done with only a pencil and paper or a simple calculator. More sophisticated calculators are helpful for solving algebraic formulas and some linear regression analysis. Computers are required for almost all stepwise multiple regression analysis. Use of the more sophisticated techniques is increasing in appraisal procedures.

This section is a review of the mathematical procedures and language used by appraisers. Familiar processes and the rules that apply to each are shown.

Basic Arithmetic for Data Processing

Data collected in the market are analyzed in the valuation process to derive an estimate of value. Included are building dimensions, population figures, reproduction and replacement costs, rentals, and sales. The numbers that represent this data can be processed to produce other numbers leading to final conclusions or value estimates, which are also expressed in numbers. In addition to the fundamental operations of addition, subtraction, multiplication, and division, appraising involves the use of ratios, percentages, rates, and factors. Percentages, rates, and factors are usually expressed in decimals rather than as fractions.

Ratios

Ratios are the result of dividing one number by another number. A ratio may be expressed as a whole number (integer), decimal, or fraction.

Example: In a community school there is a ratio of 58 students to 2 teachers.

The ratio of 58 to 2 is $58 \div 2 = 29$, usually expressed as a ratio of 29 to 1.

The ratio of 2 to 58 is $2 \div 58 = .0345$ (rounded)

The ratio of 2 to 58 is $\dfrac{2}{58} = \dfrac{1}{29}$

Percentages

Percentages are ratios (decimal) multiplied by 100 (or expressed on a base of 100). When the numerator of a fraction is divided by the denominator, the ratio represented by the fraction becomes a decimal relationship to 1, the whole, which is 100%. Multiplication of the resulting figure by 100 translates this figure to a percentage relationship to 1.

Continuing the above example:

$$\frac{2}{58} = .0345$$

$.0345 \times 100 = 3.45\%$ of a teacher for each student

Rates

Rates are percentages expressed in terms of a time period. For example:

$8 interest per year on $100 principal $= 8\%$ interest per year
$.50 interest per month on $100 $= .005$ or $.5\%$ interest per month

A rate expresses the relationship of one quantity to another. In the above example, 8% relates the $8 of interest return to the $100 of principal invested. In appraising, rates may be used to find an unknown capital amount when only the rate and the quantity of the annual return are known.

Decimals

Figures expressed in decimals are added, subtracted, multiplied, and divided similar to whole numbers (integers) with some additional rules for placing the decimal point.

When decimal figures are added or subtracted, the number of places to the right of the decimal point is equal to the largest number of places in any of the numbers being added or subtracted.

Example

```
   242.071
+   63.12
+    4.2
+    2.7983
   312.1893
```

When decimals are multiplied, the number of places to the right of the decimal point is the total number of places to the right of the decimal point in all the numbers being multiplied.

Example

$$3.23 \times 7.459 = 24.09257$$
$$17.31 \times 6.9 \times 41.27 = 4929.24753$$

The number can be rounded for practicality and still maintain the degree of accuracy necessary for the valuation process.

When decimals are divided, the decimal points in the dividend (numerator) and divisor (denominator) are moved to the right to make the divisor a whole number (integer); the decimal point is moved the same number of places and in the same direction in both numbers.

Example

$$896.487 \div 57.31 =$$
$$57.31 \overline{\smash{)}896.487}$$

$$\overset{15.64 \text{ (rounded)}}{5731 \overline{\smash{)}89648.7}}$$

Significant Digits

The significance of a digit reflects its correctness to within one-half of its unit. A measurement of "100 feet" means between 99.5 and 100.5 feet. A measurement of "100.00 feet," however, means between 99.995 and 100.005 feet.

When numbers are multiplied or divided, the result can have only as many significant digits as the number with the least significant digits. For example: .75 × 102.525 = 76.89, not 76.89375; .6 × .7 = .4, not .42. The 76.89375 and the .42 would be expressing a spurious precision. Subtracting an exception of 1.1705 acres from a total known area of 10.8 acres gives 9.1 acres, not 9.0895 acres. This factor becomes particularly relevant when the appraiser is dealing with large numbers that are the products of rounded numbers, or with lengthy but meaningless decimal places produced by computers and electronic calculators.

Reciprocals

The reciprocal of a number is 1 (unity) divided by that number. For example, the reciprocal of 4 is 1/4, which may be expressed as 0.25.

When a reciprocal relationship exists between two numbers, 1 (unity) divided by either number equals the other number. This reciprocal relationship exists between certain of the financial table factors in Appendix C. For example, the present value of 1 per period factors and the partial payment factors are reciprocals. These annual factors in the 10% tables for 10 periods are, respectively, 6.144567 and 0.162745. Since they are reciprocals,

$$\frac{1}{6.144567} = 0.162745$$

$$\text{and}$$

$$\frac{1}{0.162745} = 6.144567$$

When this reciprocal relationship exists, multiplication by either number is equivalent to division by the other.

Factors

Factors are the reciprocals of rates and may be similarly used in appraising to express relationships between income and capital value. Using I, R, and V to represent income, rate, and value, with F to represent factor, the relationships may be expressed as:

$$I = V \times R \qquad\qquad I = \frac{V}{F}$$

$$R = \frac{I}{V} \qquad\qquad F = \frac{V}{I}$$

$$V = \frac{I}{R} \qquad\qquad V = I \times F$$

These relationships may be shown

and

Commonly referred to as *IRV* and *VIF*, the formula for any single component is represented by the horizontal or vertical relationship of the remaining two components as one multiplied by, or divided by, the other.

The financial tables of Appendix C are at various rates applicable for specified numbers of compounding (or discounting) periods.

Algebra

In algebra letters or symbols representing numerical quantities may be combined with numbers to state a mathematical relationship. These statements are expressed as equations. An equation is a statement that a number or group of quantities is equal to another quantity or group of quantities.

Example

$$6 + 10 = 16$$
$$12 - 8 = 3 + 1$$
$$44 + (5 + 4) = 53$$
$$15 + (6 \times 5) = 25 + (5 \times 4)$$
$$\frac{200}{20} = 10$$
$$\sqrt{36} = 3 \times 2$$
$$\left(\frac{12}{3} + 1\right)(11 - 1) = (7 \times 8) - 6$$

If one of the quantities is unknown, it may be represented by a letter or symbol in the equation. In solving equations every change in the statement of the equation must maintain the integrity or accuracy of the equation. One side of the equation must continue to equal the other side.

In the application of symbols:

1. The commutative laws state that, as with numbers in addition or multiplication, the sum or product is the same regardless of the sequence of the addition or multiplication.

Example

2 + 4 + 10 = 10 + 4 + 2
        16 = 16

or

$X + Y + Z = Z + Y + X$

and

8 × 12 × 5 = 12 × 5 × 8
      480 = 480

or

$X \times Y \times Z = Z \times Y \times X$

2. The associative laws state that when quantities are enclosed in brackets, the operations within the brackets are performed first. When two or more brackets are encountered, computation begins with the innermost bracket and continues successively outward.
Example

18 + [(5 × 9) − (18 − 3) + (4 × 5)] =
18 + [45 − 15 + 20]   =
18 + 50   = 68

3. The distributive law states that a number or symbol outside a bracket is multiplied by each number or symbol within the bracket.
Example

8(4 + 12) =

can be solved

        = 8(16)
        = 128

but according to the distributive law may also be solved

8(4 + 12) = 32 + 96 = 128

or using symbols

$X(Y + Z) = XY + XZ$

The commutative, associative, and distributive laws are used to simplify equations in the process of solving for an unknown quantity contained in the equation.

Example of simplification using the commutative law:

$10 + (2Y + 3Y + 6Y) = 10 + 11Y$

Example of simplifications using the associative law:

$(7 + 8X) + 3X = 7 + (3X + 8X)$

This same equation can be simplified using the distributive law:

$(7 + 8X) + 3X = 7 + (3 + 8)X$
$$= 7 + 11X$$

Equations are mathematical expressions that relate one group of numbers and symbols to another group of numbers and symbols.
For example

$X = 5Y$

If it is known that Y equals 4, the equation can be solved to find that X equals 20.

$X = 5Y$
$X = 5(4)$
$X = 20$

Algebraic equations consist of two groups of quantities, expressed in terms of numbers, constants, coefficients, or variables, that are equal to each other. This is shown by an equal sign. The following are examples of types of algebraic equations in which the variables are unknowns and are represented by letters of the alphabet.

Reflective equation: $X = Y$
Symmetric equation: if $X = Y$, then $Y = X$
Transitive equation: if $X = Y$ and $Y = b$, then $X = b$

In solving algebraic equations it is axiomatic that both sides will remain equal after equal quantities are added to, subtracted from, multiplied by, or divided into both sides of the equation.
The effect of adding or subtracting equal amounts on both sides of an equation is equivalent to transposing items from one side to the other. For example

$9X + 2 = 29$

Subtracting 2 from each side of the equation results in:

$9X + 2 - 2 = 29 - 2$

and now

$$9X = 27$$

In effect, the + 2 on the left side of the equation has been transposed to the right side with a change in sign from plus to minus. This procedure is applicable for addition, subtraction, multiplication, or division, provided the sign changes (+ to ÷, ÷ to +, × to ÷, or ÷ to ×). For example

$$3 (9X) = 81$$

To move the multiplier 3 to the other side divide each side by 3

$$\frac{3 (9X)}{3} = \frac{81}{3}$$
$$9X = 27$$

This brief review of basic algebra illustrates techniques useful for the solution of some equations encountered in appraisal procedures. The illustrated techniques may be used in the solution of an equation containing one unknown quantity, X, as follows:

$$13X - 6X + 12 = -6X + 3X + 32$$

Step 1: Collect like terms

$$7X + 12 = -3X + 32$$

Step 2: Clear the negative terms by adding equal amounts to both sides.

$$
\begin{array}{lll}
7X + 12 &=& -3X + 32 \\
+3X & & +3X \\
\hline
10X + 12 &=& 32
\end{array}
$$

Step 3: Clear the equation by adding or subtracting equal numbers to both sides.

$$
\begin{array}{lll}
10X + 12 &=& 32 \\
 12 & & -12 \\
\hline
10X & =& 20
\end{array}
$$

Step 4: Divide each side of the equation by equal numbers to find the value of the unknown letter (X)

$$10X = 20$$
$$\frac{10X}{10} = \frac{20}{10}$$
$$X = 2$$

Basic Statistics

Statistics can be an effective tool for the interpretation of available data and the support of a value conclusion. In the language of statistics, a *population* refers to all the items in a specific category. If the category is houses in Chicago, the population consists of all the houses in Chicago. However, data pertaining to an entire population is rarely available and conclusions often must be developed from incomplete data.

The use of statistical concepts permits the derivation and evaluation of conclusions about a population from sample data. A *sample* is part of a population; the quality of conclusions based on a sample will vary with the quality or extent of the sample.

One item in a population is a *variate.* For appraisal purposes, one function of statistics is to identify attributes of the typical variate in a population. When observations about a population can be measured, the analysis may be *quantitative.* Observations about a population that do not permit quantitative measurement are *qualitative,* referring to attributes of the population.

A variate is called *discrete* when it can assume only a limited number of values on a measuring scale and *continuous* when it can assume an infinite number of values. A typical population of attributes would be house types—for example, one-story houses, two-story houses, split levels. It is usually impractical to display or identify a population of variates because there are many.

One of the problems in statistics is to describe a population in universally understandable terms. For example, how does one describe all the houses in a community that have sold in the past year without an individual description of each sale?

One way is to use a single number to describe the whole population. This is called a *parameter.* One parameter that is used to describe a population is an *aggregate,* which is the sum of all the variates. All the house sales in a community in any given year can be described by the total dollar amount of all the sales. This is written in statistical language as

Σ = sigma = sum of
X = variate
ΣX = aggregate (summation of the variates)

Three commonly used measures are the mean, the median, and the mode. These are three measures of *central tendency.* They are used in an effort to identify the typical variate in a population or in a sample. Measures referring to a population are called parameters, and similar measures for a sample are called statistics.

The *mean* is commonly called the average. It is obtained by dividing the sum of all the variates in the population by the number of variates. The mean is by far the most commonly used parameter. In real estate appraising some common uses of the mean are average sale price, average number of days for sale, average apartment rent, and average cost per square foot.

The problem with the use of the mean to describe a population is that it can be distorted by extreme variates. A list of 36 house sales in a neighborhood follows.

$ 72,000
      74,600
      76,000
      77,200
      78,000
      79,000
      79,800
      79,800
      82,000
      82,000
      84,000
      85,600
      85,800
      86,000
      87,000
      87,200
      87,400
      87,800 ←——median (Md.) = $87,800
      87,800
      87,800
      88,000
      89,800
      90,000 ⎤
      90,000 ⎬ mode (Mo.) = $90,000
      90,000 ⎥
      90,000 ⎦
      90,600
      91,000
      91,000
      93,800
      93,800
      96,600
      97,000
      97,200
      97,200
      98,800
 $3,131,600

$$\text{Mean} = \overline{X} = \frac{\Sigma X}{N} = \frac{\$3,131,600}{36} = \$86,989$$

where ΣX = sum of the variates and N = number of variates

This same procedure can be performed with grouped data. This involves identifying the frequency with which a given sale price occurs and effectively weighting its contribution.

X	f	fX
$72,000	1	$72,000
74,600	1	74,600
76,000	1	76,000
77,200	1	77,200
78,000	1	78,000
79,000	1	79,500
79,800	2	159,600
82,000	2	164,000
84,000	1	84,000
85,600	1	85,600
85,800	1	85,800
86,000	1	86,000
87,000	1	87,000
87,200	1	87,200
87,400	1	87,400
87,800	3	263,400
88,000	1	88,000
89,800	1	89,800
90,000	4	360,000
90,600	1	90,600
91,000	2	182,000
93,800	2	187,600
96,600	1	96,600
97,000	1	97,500
97,200	2	194,400
98,800	1	98,800
	N = 36	ΣfX = $3,131,600

$$\text{Mean} = \overline{X} = \frac{\Sigma fX}{N} = \frac{\$3,131,600}{36} = \$86,989$$

The "average (or mean) price in this example—$86,989—might not give a fully accurate picture of the population of houses that have been sold at prices substantially outside the indicated range.

The *median* is also used to describe a population or sample or the average variate. The median divides the variates of a population or sample into equal halves. To compute the median the variates are arranged in numerical order (as are the 36 sale prices in the example). If the total number of variates is odd, the median is the middle variate. If the total number of variates is even (as it is in this example), the median is the arithmetic mean of the two middle variates.

In the example of 36 house sales the middle two variates are $87,800 and $87,800. The mean of these two variates is $87,800, which is the median of the 36 sales in the sample. As many sales occurred above this figure as below it.

Like the median and mean, the *mode* is another parameter that describes the typical variate of a population. The mode is the most frequently appearing variate or attribute in a population. Of the 36 house sales, four sold at $90,000. No other sale price occurs with this frequency, so the mode in this sample is $90,000. If two prices were to occur with equal frequency, both would be modes and the sample would be bi-modal.

Here is another example, showing a population of types of condominium apartments available in a nine-unit complex:

efficiency
efficiency
efficiency
town house ⎤
town house │
town house ⎬   mode (the most frequent attribute)
town house │
town house ⎦
multi-bedroom

One of the problems in using statistics is to select the appropriate measure of central tendency to describe a population. The following single numbers can be used to describe the 36 variates in the group of house sales:

$\bar{X}$ = $86,989 = the mean of all the sales
Md. = $87,800 = the median of the sales
Mo. = $90,000 = the mode of the sales

The mean is often selected to describe a sample or population because the mean is a more widely understood concept, and is also amenable to further statistical analysis.

Measures of Variation
The parameters mean, median, and mode are used to describe central tendencies of the population. Other sets of parameters are used to pro-

vide more information about the population being described. They measure the disparity among values of the various variates comprising the population. These parameters, called *measures of variation,* or *dispersion,* indicate the degree of uniformity among the variates and reflect the quality of the data as a basis for a conclusion.

One way to measure the disparity between the variates is known as the *range* (denoted by R). It is the difference between the highest and lowest variate.

R = maximum variate minus minimum variate

Using the figures in the example of 36 house sales

R = \$98,800 − \$72,000 = \$26,800

The range as a measure of variation is of limited usefulness since it considers only the highest and lowest values and neglects the variation in the remaining values. It also does not lend itself to further statistical treatment.

Average Deviation

Another parameter used to measure deviations between the variates is the *average deviation,* also known as the average absolute deviation because plus or minus signs are ignored. It is a measure of how much the actual values of the population or sample deviate from the mean (average). It is the mean of the sum of the absolute differences of each of the variates from the mean of the variates.

To demonstrate the average deviation the 36 sales are listed again on page 638.

This indicates that the average deviation of the individual values in the sample population from the mean is \$5,336, or about 6%. This is a relatively small variation and suggests that the mean is an acceptable representation of this sample.

Like the range, the average deviation does not lend itself to further statistical calculations.

Standard Deviation

The *standard deviation* provides a way of describing a sample or a population that lends itself to further mathematical treatment. It permits application of rules of probability to draw inferences from samples concerning attributes of the population. In this method the square of the difference between each observation and the mean of the observations is used in lieu of the absolute deviation. This serves to magnify the effects of extreme variance from the mean.

In the example the mean sale price is \$86,989; for an \$82,000 sale the measure of deviation is \$4,989 squared, or \$24,890,121.

Ungrouped Data

X Sale Price	$\|X - \bar{X}\|$ Absolute Deviation between Each Variate and the Mean Sale Price of $86,989
$ 72,000	$14,989
74,600	12,389
76,000	10,989
77,200	9,789
78,000	8,989
79,000	7,989
79,800	7,189
79,800	7,189
82,000	4,989
82,000	4,989
84,000	2,989
85,600	1,389
85,800	1,189
86,000	989
87,000	11
87,200	211
87,400	411
87,800	811
87,800	811
87,800	811
88,000	1,011
89,800	2,811
90,000	3,011
90,000	3,011
90,000	3,011
90,000	3,011
90,600	3,611
91,000	4,011
91,000	4,011
93,800	6,811
93,800	6,811
96,600	9,611
97,000	10,011
97,200	10,211
97,200	10,211
98,800	11,811
$3,131,600 Total of sale prices	$192,088 Total deviation from mean $\Sigma\|X - \bar{X}\|$

		Grouped Data	
X	X − X̄	f	f X − X̄
$72,000	$14,989	1	$ 14,989
74,600	12,389	1	12,389
76,000	10,989	1	10,989
77,200	9,789	1	9,789
78,000	8,989	1	8,989
79,000	7,989	1	7,989
79,800	7,189	2	14,378
82,000	4,989	2	9,978
84,000	2,989	1	4,989
85,600	1,389	1	1,389
85,800	1,189	1	1,189
86,000	989	1	989
87,000	11	1	11
87,200	211	1	211
87,400	411	1	411
87,800	811	3	2,433
88,000	1,011	1	1,011
89,800	2,811	1	2,811
90,000	3,011	4	12,044
90,600	3,611	1	3,611
91,000	4,011	2	8,022
93,800	6,811	2	13,622
96,600	9,611	1	9,611
97,000	10,011	1	10,011
97,200	10,211	2	20,422
98,800	11,811	1	11,811
		36	$192,088 Total deviation from the mean Σ f X − X̄

$$A.D. \text{ (ungrouped data)} = \frac{\Sigma|X - \overline{X}|}{n} = \frac{\$192,088}{36} = \$5,336$$

$$A.D. \text{ (grouped data)} = \frac{\Sigma f|X - \overline{X}|}{n} = \frac{\$192,088}{36} = \$5,336$$

A.D. = average deviation
Σ = sum of
f = frequency
X = observed value
|| = ignore the + or − signs
n = number of observations in sample (N = population)
X̄ = mean of sample (σ = population)

When the standard deviation of a *whole* population is being calculated, it is symbolized by sigma (σ). Expressed verbally, the formula is: *Standard deviation of a population is the square root of the sum of the squared differences between each observation and the mean of all the observations in the population, divided by the number of observations in the population.*

When the standard deviation of a sample of a population is being calculated, it is symbolized by the letter s. Expressed verbally, the formula is: *Standard deviation of a sample is the square root of the sum of the squared differences between each observation and the mean of all the observations in the sample, divided by the number of observations in the sample minus 1.*

The reason 1 is subtracted from the number of observations in a sample is to adjust for one degree of freedom that is lost when the mean is calculated. A set of data originally has as many degrees of freedom as there are observations. Every time a statistic is calculated directly from the data, a degree of freedom is lost.

Formulas for calculating the standard deviations follow.

For a population:

Ungrouped   **Grouped**

$$\sigma = \sqrt{\frac{\Sigma(X - \overline{X})^2}{N}} \qquad \sigma = \sqrt{\frac{\Sigma f(X - \overline{X})^2}{N}}$$

For a sample:

Ungrouped   **Grouped**

$$s = \sqrt{\frac{\Sigma(X - \overline{X})^2}{n - 1}} \qquad s = \sqrt{\frac{\Sigma f(X - \overline{X})^2}{n - 1}}$$

In real estate appraising samples are usually used, so the second formula is applicable, as in the example of 36 house sales for grouped data only (see Table B.1).

The standard deviation is an important way to describe the dispersion of a population or sample. It tells how representative of the whole sample or population the mean is by describing a standard measure of variation. It is a number that is used and understood in many disciplines. With the availability of electronic calculators, it now can be calculated easily. It undoubtedly will become more widely used by appraisers in the future.

When used for this purpose, the standard deviation can indicate what percent of the sample of the population may be expected to fall within selected ranges of *confidence intervals* (see page 646).

Approximately 68.26% of the sample or population will generally

Table B.1   Standard Deviation for 36 House Sales

X	f	(X − X̄)	(X − X̄)²	f(X − X̄)²
$72,000	1	$14,989	$224,670,000	$224,670,000
74,600	1	12,389	153,487,000	153,487,000
76,000	1	10,989	120,758,000	120,758,000
77,200	1	9,789	95,824,500	95,824,500
78,000	1	8,989	80,802,100	80,802,100
79,000	1	7,989	63,824,100	63,824,100
79,800	2	7,189	51,681,700	103,363,000
82,000	2	4,989	24,890,100	49,780,200
84,000	1	2,989	8,934,120	8,934,120
85,600	1	1,389	1,929,320	1,929,320
85,800	1	1,189	1,413,720	1,413,720
86,000	1	989	978,121	978,121
87,000	1	11	121	121
87,200	1	211	44,521	44,521
87,400	1	411	168,921	168,921
87,800	3	811	657,721	1,973,160
88,000	1	1,011	1,022,120	1,022,120
89,800	1	2,811	7,901,720	7,901,720
90,000	4	3,011	9,066,120	36,264,500
90,600	1	3,611	13,039,300	13,039,300
91,000	2	4,011	16,088,100	32,176,200
93,800	2	6,811	46,389,700	92,779,400
96,600	1	9,611	92,371,300	92,371,300
97,000	1	10,011	100,220,000	100,220,000
97,200	2	10,211	104,265,000	208,529,000
98,800	1	11,811	139,500,000	139,500,000
				$1,631,760,000

$$s = \sqrt{\frac{\Sigma f\,(X - \bar{X})^2}{n - 1}}$$ Mean: $86,989

$$s = \sqrt{\frac{\$1,631,760,000}{36 - 1}}$$

$$s = \sqrt{\$46,621,714}$$

$$s = \$6,828$$

fall within plus or minus one standard deviation from the mean, provided the data meet certain tests of normal distribution (as explained later). Many types of real estate data conform to the pattern of a normal distribution when developed through appropriate sampling techniques.

In the example, assuming normal distribution, 68.26% of the house sales in the population will be between $80,151 and $93,817 ($86,989 − $6,828 and $86,989 + $6,828). Approximately 95.44% of the sales should fall within two standard deviations and approximately 99.74% should fall within three standard deviations from the mean.

Because the standard deviation lends itself to further mathematical treatment, it can be used for analytical purposes in addition to its use to describe a population.

Statistical Inference

Statistical inference is based on the assumption that the past actions in the market are a valid basis for forecasting present or future market actions. In the example, past sale prices are used to estimate current sale prices. This technique can also be used to forecast rentals, costs, depreciation, and so on, using rules of probability.

The *normal curve* plots a normal distribution and is a technique to illustrate a distribution of data. Where original data may not be normally distributed, repeated random samples may be drawn with results that approximate a normal distribution. Sales are often treated as though they were normally distributed in competitive, open market situations. The normal curve is often graphed in a form known as a bell curve.

A major characteristic of a bell curve is that it is symmetrical. Both halves have the same shape and contain the same number of observations. The mean, median, and mode are the same value; and this value is the midpoint (apex) of the curve.

Figure B.1 is a bell curve and shows that 68.26% of the observations will fall within the range of the mean plus or minus one standard deviation, 95.44% within plus or minus two standard deviations, and 99.74% within plus or minus three standard deviations. It depicts an analysis of the probable population distribution for the 36 sales, assuming a normal distribution.

In this example, the ranges for one, two, and three standard deviations are shown. The percentage of the population that will fall within any given distance from the mean or within any specified range can be calculated. For example, the percentage of sales included within a range of $81,989 to $91,989 (the mean of $86,989 plus or minus $5,000) may be estimated by first calculating the Z value for this range (using the formula below) and then entering a table of areas under the curve of normal distribution with the calculated value of Z.

Figure B.1   Area under the Normal Curve

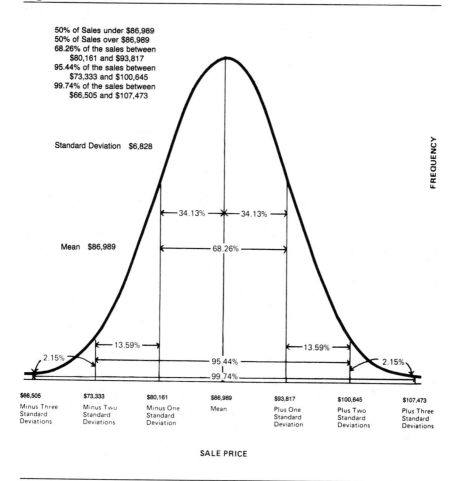

50% of Sales under $86,989
50% of Sales over $86,989
68.26% of the sales between
$80,161 and $93,817
95.44% of the sales between
$73,333 and $100,645
99.74% of the sales between
$66,505 and $107,473

Standard Deviation $6,828

FREQUENCY

←34.13%→✳←34.13%→

Mean $86,989

←———— 68.26% ————→

←13.59%→   ←13.59%→

2.15%   2.15%

←————— 95.44% —————→
—— 99.74% ——

$66,505	$73,333	$80,161	$86,989	$93,817	$100,645	$107,473
Minus Three Standard Deviations	Minus Two Standard Deviations	Minus One Standard Deviation	Mean	Plus One Standard Deviation	Plus Two Standard Deviations	Plus Three Standard Deviations

SALE PRICE

Z = the deviation of X from the mean measured in standard deviations

$$Z = \frac{X - \text{mean}}{\text{standard deviation}}$$

$$Z = \frac{\$91,989 - \$86,989}{\$6,828} = \frac{\$5,000}{\$6,828} = .73$$

This formula shows that $91,989 and $81,989 each deviate from the mean of $86,989 by .73 standard deviations.

The percentage of sales within this Z range of plus or minus .73

standard deviations can be developed from Table B.2 by first finding
0.7 under the Z column and then looking across the top of the page
for the next digit. Accordingly, 26.73% of the sales are shown to fall
between $86,989 and $91,989 or between $86,989 and $81,989; and
53.46% of the sales will be between $91,989 and $81,989.

Table B.2   Areas under the Normal Curve

Z	.00	.01	.02	.03	.04	.05	.06	.07	.08	.09
0.0	.0000	.0040	.0080	.0120	.0160	.0199	.0239	.0279	.0319	.0359
0.1	.0398	.0438	.0478	.0517	.0557	.0596	.0636	.0675	.0714	.0753
0.2	.0793	.0832	.0871	.0910	.0948	.0987	.1026	.1064	.1103	.1141
0.3	.1179	.1217	.1255	.1293	.1331	.1368	.1406	.1443	.1480	.1517
0.4	.1554	.1591	.1628	.1664	.1700	.1736	.1772	.1808	.1844	.1879
0.5	.1915	.1950	.1985	.2019	.2054	.2088	.2123	.2157	.2190	.2224
0.6	.2257	.2291	.2324	.2357	.2389	.2422	.2454	.2486	.2517	.2549
0.7	.2580	.2611	.2642	.2673	.2704	.2734	.2764	.2794	.2823	.2852
0.8	.2881	.2910	.2939	.2967	.2995	.3023	.3051	.3078	.3106	.3133
0.9	.3159	.3186	.3212	.3238	.3264	.3289	.3315	.3340	.3365	.3389
1.0	.3413	.3438	.3461	.3485	.3508	.3531	.3554	.3577	.3599	.3621
1.1	.3643	.3665	.3686	.3708	.3729	.3749	.3770	.3790	.3810	.3830
1.2	.3849	.3869	.3888	.3907	.3925	.3944	.3962	.3980	.3997	.4015
1.3	.4032	.4049	.4066	.4082	.4099	.4115	.4131	.4147	.4162	.4177
1.4	.4192	.4207	.4222	.4236	.4251	.4265	.4279	.4292	.4306	.4319
1.5	.4332	.4345	.4357	.4370	.4382	.4394	.4406	.4418	.4429	.4441
1.6	.4452	.4463	.4474	.4484	.4495	.4505	.4515	.4525	.4535	.4545
1.7	.4554	.4564	.4573	.4582	.4591	.4599	.4608	.4616	.4625	.4633
1.8	.4641	.4649	.4656	.4664	.4671	.4678	.4686	.4693	.4699	.4706
1.9	.4713	.4719	.4726	.4732	.4738	.4744	.4750	.4756	.4761	.4767
2.0	.4772	.4778	.4783	.4788	.4793	.4798	.4803	.4808	.4812	.4817
2.1	.4821	.4826	.4830	.4834	.4838	.4842	.4846	.4850	.4854	.4857
2.2	.4861	.4864	.4868	.4871	.4875	.4878	.4881	.4884	.4887	.4890
2.3	.4893	.4896	.4898	.4901	.4904	.4906	.4909	.4911	.4913	.4916
2.4	.4918	.4920	.4922	.4925	.4927	.4929	.4931	.4932	.4934	.4936
2.5	.4938	.4940	.4941	.4943	.4945	.4946	.4948	.4949	.4951	.4952
2.6	.4953	.4955	.4956	.4957	.4959	.4960	.4961	.4962	.4963	.4964
2.7	.4965	.4966	.4967	.4968	.4969	.4970	.4971	.4972	.4973	.4974
2.8	.4974	.4975	.4976	.4977	.4977	.4978	.4979	.4979	.4980	.4981
2.9	.4981	.4982	.4982	.4983	.4984	.4984	.4985	.4985	.4986	.4986
3.0	.4987	.4987	.4987	.4988	.4988	.4989	.4989	.4989	.4990	.4990

Another question that can be answered using the Z value is the probability of a randomly selected sale falling inside a given range.

Continuing to use the population based on the sample of 36 sales, which has a mean of $86,989 and a standard deviation of $6,828, the probability of a randomly selected sale falling in any selected range of values can be calculated.

For example, the probability of a randomly selected sale falling between $86,989 and $88,989 ($2,000 over the mean) is calculated as follows:

$$Z = \frac{X - \text{mean}}{\text{standard deviation}} = \frac{\$88,989 - \$86,989}{\$6,828} = \frac{\$2,000}{\$6,828} = .29$$

Looking at the table of areas under the normal curve, a Z value of .29 corresponds to .1141. This indicates an 11.41% chance the sale will fall within $2,000 above the mean. Since the curve of normal distribution is symmetrical about the mean, the same probability exists that a sale will fall within $2,000 below the mean.

Probability a sale will fall between $88,989 and $86,989	11.41%
Probability a sale will fall between $84,989 and $86,989	11.41%
Probability a sale will fall between $84,989 and $88,989	22.82%

If the range is expanded in the same example to $4,000 plus or minus the mean of $86,989, to $82,989 and $90,989, respectively, the probability of a randomly selected sale falling within this range would be increased.

$$Z = \frac{X - \text{mean}}{\text{standard deviation}} = \frac{\$90,989 - \$86,989}{\$6,828} = \frac{\$4,000}{\$6,828} = .59$$

Looking at the areas under the normal curve table .59 = .2224.

Probability a sale will fall between $90,989 and $86,989	22.24%
Probability a sale will fall between $82,989 and $86,989	22.24%
Probability a sale will fall between $82,989 and $90,989	44.48%

In the above examples, the range being tested is equally above and below the mean sale price. However, the probability of a randomly selected sale falling between any selected range in the population can also be tested, for example, between $80,000 and $100,000:

$$Z\ area^1 = \frac{X^1 - mean}{standard\ deviation} = \frac{\$\ 80,000 - \$86,989}{\$6,828} = \frac{\$\ 6,989}{\$\ 6,828} = 1.02$$

$$Z\ area^2 = \frac{X^2 - mean}{standard\ deviation} = \frac{\$100,000 - \$86,989}{\$6,828} = \frac{\$13,011}{\$\ 6,828} = 1.91$$

Looking at 1.02 in the table for areas under the normal curve tables gives	.3461
Looking at 1.91 in the table for area under the normal curve table gives	.4719
Probability	.8180

This indicates an 81.80% chance that a randomly selected sale in this sample will fall between $80,000 and $100,000.

Confidence Level

Using statistical inference and the laws of probability for a normal distribution, the previous examples have shown how *confidence intervals* may be constructed for a sample where there is an assumption (or approximation) of normally distributed data. These calculations may be valuable in a number of real estate decision-making situations, including loan administration, housing development, and appraising.

As seen in the previous examples, with 36 sales as a sample, an appraiser may say *with a 95% degree of confidence* that any sale randomly selected from the population will fall between $73,333 and $100,645. Similarly, there is a 68% level of confidence that the sample will fall between $80,161 and $93,817.

Such measures may be meaningful in connection with other statistical conclusions. However, because they are dependent on the accuracy of the estimated mean (as representative of the true population mean), some degree of confidence about the reliability of the mean must be established. Regardless of population size, there is a specific sample size that will permit a given level of confidence in the estimated mean.

In the continuing example of 36 sales, the standard deviation for price has been calculated as $6,828. The arithmetic mean is $86,989, or about $87,000. If an appraiser wants to be 95% certain that the true mean is within $1,000 of the estimated mean ($86,989), or between about $86,000 and $88,000, calculation of the necessary sample size is:

n = Sample size required
z = Z statistic at 95% confidence level
s = Standard deviation of the sample
e = Required maximum difference in the mean

$$n = \frac{z^2 s^2}{e^2}$$

$$n = \frac{(1.96)^2 \, (\$6,828)^2}{(\$1,000)^2} = 179 \text{ sales}$$

Thus, with 179 sales in a sample, the required standard of confidence could be met. Similarly, for a confidence interval of not more than $1,500, calculations would be

$$n = \frac{(1.96)^2 \, (\$6,828)^2}{(\$1,500)^2} = 80 \text{ sales}$$

In the original sample of 36 sales, an appraiser may ask, "At a 95% confidence, what are the limits between which the true population mean may fall?" By substitution

$$e^2 = \frac{z^2 s^2}{n}$$

and

$$e^2 = \frac{(1.96)^2 \, (\$6,828)^2}{36} = \$4,975,041$$

$$e = \sqrt{\$4,975,041} = \$2,230$$

Thus the appraiser in this case may be statistically 95% certain that the true population mean falls between $84,759 and $89,219.

Although such calculations may seem to have an obscure relationship to day-to-day appraising, professional appraisers have a continuing interest in the availability of adequate data and in knowledge and understanding of the markets in which they appraise. Calculations such as these assist in quantifying change or in performing the neighborhood analyses essential to value estimation. Many appraisers, for example, routinely analyze the inferences to be drawn from such measures as the standard deviations of raw and adjusted sale or rental data. Such calculations are also important for appraisal review, loan underwriting, and other analyses.

Regression Analysis

Simple Linear Regression Analysis

In estimating a probable sale price in the market, it is seldom sufficient to develop a sample of sales, calculate the standard deviation, and base an estimate on this evidence. The range of values is usually too great at the confidence level required to be useful. Appraisers recognize that the accuracy of the estimate can be substantially increased by considering one or more characteristics of each sale property, in addition to their sale prices.

Using the 36 sales in the earlier example, it may be demonstrated that there is an apparent relationship between sale price and the number of square feet of living area. The square footage of gross living area (GLA) for the 36 sales is exhibited in Table B.3. Typically, an appraiser might use only sales that have approximately the same square footage as the property being appraised and essentially ignore the others.

Note the appraiser's dilemma in appraising a 1,375 square foot dwelling. Sales 1, 2, and 3 are reported as $57.53, $64.14, and $55.95 per square foot, respectively. Other sales may give a clue to the "right answer," but Sales 5 and 6 do little to resolve the conflict. Adjustments will probably be made for other differences, but complications may develop when multiple adjustments involve overlapping effects.

Sales 1 through 3 indicate a range of $55.95 to $64.14 per square foot, or when applied to the appraised property's 1,375 square feet, an indicated value range of $76,931 to $88,192. (These would be rounded in a report.) However, the remaining market information cannot effectively be applied to the analysis in traditional appraising except generally to reinforce the appraiser's judgment.

Simple linear regression provides a technique in which more market data may be applied to this analysis. For application in the simple linear regression formula, $Y_c = a + bX$, the 36 sales were analyzed by calculator and produced

a = \$49,261
b = \$22.59
 r = .6599 (simple correlation coefficient)
r^2 = .4354 (adjusted coefficient of determination)

Thus, for the 1,375-square-foot property appraised

Y_c = \$49,261 + \$22.59 (1,375)
Y_c = \$80,322
        (or \$58.42 per square foot)

Table B.3   Comparable Sales Data Set for
Simple Regression Analysis

Sale	GLA in Square Feet	Sale Price	Price per Square Foot GLA
1	1,321	$76,000	$57.53
2	1,372	88,000	64.14
3	1,394	78,000	55.95
4	1,403	74,600	53.17
5	1,457	85,800	58.89
6	1,472	87,400	59.38
7	1,475	84,000	56.95
8	1,479	85,600	57.88
9	1,503	72,000	47.90
10	1,512	77,200	51.06
11	1,515	82,000	54.13
12	1,535	79,000	51.47
13	1,535	87,800	57.20
14	1,577	91,000	57.70
15	1,613	90.000	55.80
16	1,640	79,800	48.66
17	1,666	91,000	54.62
18	1,681	79,800	47.47
19	1,697	87,200	51.38
20	1,703	87,000	51.09
21	1,706	89,800	52.64
22	1,709	90,600	53.01
23	1,709	93,800	54.89
24	1,720	93,800	54.53
25	1,732	82,000	47.34
26	1,749	97,200	55.57
27	1,771	97,200	54.88
28	1,777	86,000	48.40
29	1,939	87,800	45.28
30	1,939	90,000	46.42
31	1,939	90,000	46.42
32	1,939	90,000	46.42
33	1,939	96,600	49.82
34	1,940	87,800	45.26
35	2,014	98,800	49.06
36	2,065	97,000	46.97

The calculated regression line and a plot of the 36 sales is shown in Figure B.2. Also shown is another statistical measure, the *standard error of the estimate*, which allows construction of confidence intervals about the regression line. Calculations in this example produce a standard error estimate of $5,205. When applied to the property being appraised, the appraiser may now state that the 36 sales in this market support an estimate of about $80,300 for the appraised property

Figure B.2   Plot of Sales, Regression Line and Standard Error for 36 Sales

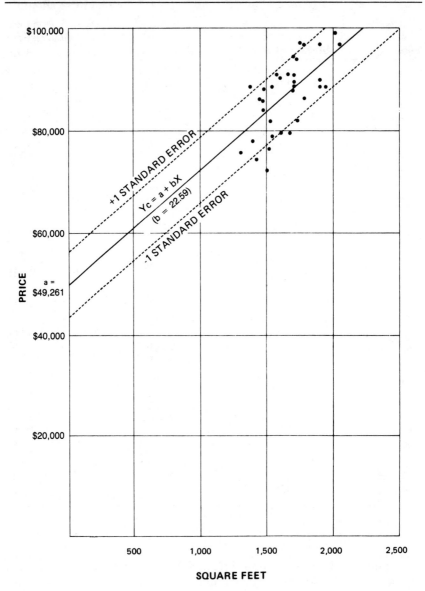

(based only on comparison of square footage). Further, at a 68% confidence level, the market price should lie between $80,300 ± $5,205 (or $75,095 to $85,505). At a 95% confidence level, the price should lie between $80,300 ± (2) ($5,205), or $69,890 to $90,710.

Although other statistical measures such as the *standard error of the forecast* may be used, this analysis is often considered sufficient and reasonably representative of most single family market situations. A more refined analysis of these data is possible, but this example illustrates simple application of a regression technique. The standard error of forecast for the appraised property would be calculated as follows:

$$Sf = Syx \sqrt{1 + \frac{1}{n}} = \frac{(X_K - \overline{X})^2}{(X - \overline{X})^2}$$

$$Sf = 5,205 \sqrt{1 + \frac{1}{36}} = + \frac{(1720 - 1670)^2}{1,469,045}$$

$$Sf = 5,281$$

Thus, applying this adjustment to the standard error made only a small change. This is attributable to the fact that the measure of value, square footage, of the subject was quite close to the mean square footage of the sample data. The more the appraised property differs from the mean of the sample in regard to any property attribute, the more this distortion affects the standard error as a measure of variation in the regression prediction.

Example of Stepwise Multiple Regression Analysis[1]

An appraiser is asked to appraise a residential property located on a lot containing 7,575 square feet, improved with a recently constructed residence. The residence contains 1,720 square feet of living area with three bedrooms and two full baths. There are no porches and no swimming pool, although some swimming pools are found in the neighborhood. The dwelling has central air-conditioning and physical characteristics that are similar to other properties in the neighborhood. There is an attached two-car garage.

After an inspection of the property and the collection and verification of comparable sales, a stepwise multiple regression analysis is selected for use in the market data approach to value.

---

[1]Figures B-3 through B-13 adapted by Realty Researchers (Birmingham, Alabama) from a model developed by Valuation Systems Company (Tulsa, Oklahoma). Used with permission.

Figure B.3 shows a computer printout of the 36 sales selected for initial analysis. These sales were randomly selected from the total file after the appraiser identified the independent variables involving the porch, number of bedrooms, lot size, garage size, living area, and any time parameters as the essential elements of the search. As shown in the last column, sale price was selected as the dependent variable for multiple regression analysis.

Figure B.4 is a summary of arithmetic means of each of the variables and their standard deviations. Also shown is a simple correlation matrix of the calculated interaction among each of the variables selected.

Each of the steps of multiple regression analysis applied to the comparable sales data set is summarized in Figure B.5. After the initial regression equation has been computer-calculated (as shown in Step 5 of Figure B.5), the computer uses the regression equation to calculate the expected prices of each of the 36 comparable sale properties. By comparing actual sale prices with estimated sale prices for each, differences are shown in Figure B.6 as the "residuals," along with calculated percentages of error in estimate and the magnitude of the error expressed in the number of standard deviations of the dependent variable. In this projection of actual comparable sales information, only two sales were found to have more than a 10% error, and the majority have less than 5%.

The percentage of error in the residuals is shown in Figure B.7, which is a dynamic plot of residual error with the lowest amount of error at the left side of the plot and the highest error at the right.

A second run of the regression equation is made, deleting observations (sales) that produced the highest amount of error or were indicated by further analysis to be nonarm's-length transactions or were found to involve nonconventional financing terms. Extreme caution must be taken in discarding any observation in a regression. Accounting for variations in price is the basic objective of regression analysis, and this objective can be thwarted by an overzealous effort to retain only closely comparable sales. The results of the second run are shown in Figures B.8 through B.12. With the deletion of the least comparable sales, this second run produces a maximum residual error of 3.44% of actual price.

Recognizing and accepting the validity and statistical reliability of the analysis, the computer now may be employed to produce a final indication of value using the stepwise multiple regression analysis procedure. Final results of the projection for the property being appraised are shown in Figure B.13. The final projection indicates an estimated price essentially equal to the actual price of the property in a recent sale and establishes, for a 95% confidence interval, a range of approximately ± $4,000 as the reasonable price of the property being appraised.

Figure B.3   Selected Sales—First Analysis

STEPWISE MULTIPLE REGRESSION ANALYSIS

OBSERVATIONS

OBS NUM ***	PROPERTY I.D. # *************	1 PORCH *****	INDEPENDENT VARIABLE 2 BDRMS *****	3 LT SZ *****	4 GAR A *****	5 LIV A *****	DEP VAR. PRICE *****
1	6358500000230	1	3	8100	468	1666	91000
2	6358500000290	1	3	8100	484	1457	85800
3	6358500000110	1	3	7575	520	1720	93800
4	6358500000270	3	3	9936	448	1749	97200
5	6358500000120	1	3	7568	459	1709	93800
6	6358500000150	3	4	10002	501	2014	98800
7	6358500000100	1	3	7560	459	1709	90600
8	6358500000070	1	3	10781	449	1771	97200
9	6358500000140	4	2	9033	421	1479	85600
10	6594300000220	1	3	7861	444	1939	87800
11	6594300000150	1	3	13040	444	1939	90000
12	6594300000300	1	3	7700	444	1940	87800
13	6594300000250	3	3	9800	444	1939	90000
14	6594300000010	1	3	8400	459	1706	89800
15	6594300000100	1	3	11085	444	1939	90000
16	6594300000110	3	3	11022	444	1939	96600
17	6594300000080	1	3	19300	479	1681	79800
18	6268800040010	1	3	9191	441	1475	84000
19	6268800010070	1	3	8500	430	1515	82000
20	6268800010120	3	3	8800	441	1697	87200
21	6268800030090	1	3	7700	451	1732	82000
22	6268800030060	3	3	8580	524	1613	90000
23	6473900110150	0	3	11000	419	1777	86000
24	6473900600020	3	3	7125	422	1512	77200
25	6473900300060	3	3	7500	421	1403	74600
26	6473900700120	1	3	8040	454	1703	87000
27	6473900300160	1	3	7763	469	1503	72000
28	6473900500140	3	3	7125	458	1577	91000
29	6473900500080	3	3	7600	430	1394	78000
30	6473900050060	2	2	7410	455	1372	88000
31	6473900010570	3	3	8036	477	1472	87400
32	6473900010020	1	2	7500	460	1321	76000
33	6473900010250	1	3	7995	466	2065	97000
34	6473900010290	3	3	7500	471	153⁵	87800
35	6473900020060	3	3	8000	471	153!	79000
36	6473900110100	1	3	11000	427	1640	79800

Figure B.4   Means, Standard Deviations, and Simple Correlation Coefficients of Variables—First Analysis

```
MEANS

VARIABLE NO.  1 - PORCH =        1.8055
VARIABLE NO.  2 - BDRMS =        2.9444
VARIABLE NO.  3 - LT SZ =    8,978.5555
VARIABLE NO.  4 - GAR A =      455.5000
VARIABLE NO.  5 - LIV A =    1,670.4722
VARIABLE NO.  6 - PRICE =     86988.9000


STANDARD  DEVIATIONS

VARIABLE NO.  1 - PORCH =        1.0642
VARIABLE NO.  2 - BDRMS =        0.3333
VARIABLE NO.  3 - LT SZ =    2,277.2125
VARIABLE NO.  4 - GAR A =       25.0855
VARIABLE NO.  5 - LIV A =      199.4894
VARIABLE NO.  6 - PRICE =      6828.0200


SIMPLE  CORRELATION  COEFFICIENTS

     1        2       3       4       5     DEP VAR
   PORCH    BDRMS   LT SZ   GAR A   LIV A    PRICE

  1.0000  -0.0313 -0.1746 -0.0069 -0.2225  0.0224
           0.9999  0.1511  0.2596  0.5082  0.2909
                   1.0000 -0.0168  0.3232  0.0686
                           0.9999  0.0720  0.3210
                                   1.0000  0.6598
                                           0.9999
```

Figure B.5   Summary of Comparable Sales—First Analysis

```
STEP NUMBER 1   ENTER VARIABLE 5

STANDARD ERROR OF ESTIMATE:    5205.38
ADJ COEFF DETERM:              .418814
DEGREES OF FREEDOM:       34
F RATIO:                  26.2216
CONSTANT TERM:            49260.5

VARIABLE        COEFFICIENT     S.D. OF COEFF.     T VALUE
 5 LIV A          22.5855         4.41062          5.1207

STEP NUMBER 2   ENTER VARIABLE 4

STANDARD ERROR OF ESTIMATE:    4919.33
ADJ COEFF DETERM:              .480935
DEGREES OF FREEDOM:       33
F RATIO:                  17.2144
CONSTANT TERM:            16311.5

VARIABLE        COEFFICIENT     S.D. OF COEFF.     T VALUE
 4 GAR A          74.8245        33.2339          2.25145
 5 LIV A          21.9069         4.17913         5.24197

STEP NUMBER 3   ENTER VARIABLE 1

STANDARD ERROR OF ESTIMATE:    4843.79
ADJ COEFF DETERM:              .496755
DEGREES OF FREEDOM:       32
F RATIO:                  12.5162
CONSTANT TERM:            12236

VARIABLE        COEFFICIENT     S.D. OF COEFF.     T VALUE
 1 PORCH        1126.44         789.177           1.42737
 4 GAR A          74.3876        32.7249          2.27312
 5 LIV A          23.2482         4.22089         5.5079

STEP NUMBER 4   ENTER VARIABLE 2

STANDARD ERROR OF ESTIMATE:    4808.05
ADJ COEFF DETERM:              .504154
DEGREES OF FREEDOM:       31
F RATIO:                  9.89659
CONSTANT TERM:            12661.4

VARIABLE        COEFFICIENT     S.D. OF COEFF.     T VALUE
 1 PORCH        1220.57         787.172           1.55058
 2 BDRMS       -3580.89        2945.92           -1.21554
 4 GAR A          85.0186        33.6402          2.52729
 5 LIV A          26.3048         4.88641         5.38325
```

B.5   Continued

```
STEP NUMBER 5   ENTER VARIABLE 3

STANDARD ERROR OF ESTIMATE:   4803.71
ADJ COEFF DETERM:             .505047
DEGREES OF FREEDOM:           30
F RATIO:                      8.14275
CONSTANT TERM:                14710.9

VARIABLE         COEFFICIENT    S.D. OF COEFF.    T VALUE
  1 PORCH          1130.22        791.362         1.4282
  2 BDRMS         -3563.51       2943.32         -1.21071
  3 L1 S7          -.389959        .379485        -1.0276
  4 GAR A           83.5747        33.6393         2.48444
  5 LIV A           27.6346         5.05062        5.47153
```

Figure B.6   Comparison of Actual and Estimated Sale Prices of Comparables Showing Residuals and Percentages of Error—First Analysis

```
                         RESIDUAL ANALYSIS


OBSERVATION   PREDICTED Y    ACTUAL Y   RESIDUAL  % ERROR  # STD DEV
```

OBSERVATION	PREDICTED Y	ACTUAL Y	RESIDUAL	% ERROR	# STD DEV
1	87144.10	91000.00	3855.87	4.24	0.56
2	82705.70	85800.00	3094.30	3.61	0.45
3	93187.00	93800.00	612.98	0.65	0.09
4	89310.80	97200.00	7889.22	8.12	1.16
5	87787.70	93800.00	6012.30	6.41	0.88
6	97474.20	98800.00	1325.84	1.34	0.19
7	87790.80	90600.00	2809.18	3.10	0.41
8	87412.40	97200.00	9787.64	10.07	1.43
9	84638.80	85600.00	961.21	1.12	0.14
10	92775.80	87800.00	-4975.78	-5.67	-0.73
11	90756.20	90000.00	-756.19	-0.84	-0.11
12	92866.20	87800.00	-5066.20	-5.77	-0.74
13	94280.10	90000.00	-4280.09	-4.76	-0.63
14	87380.40	89800.00	2419.65	2.69	0.35
15	91518.60	90000.00	-1518.55	-1.69	-0.22
16	93803.60	96600.00	2796.44	2.89	0.41
17	84110.40	79800.00	-4310.43	-5.40	-0.63
18	79184.00	84000.00	4816.04	5.73	0.71
19	79639.50	82000.00	2360.52	2.88	0.35
20	87731.80	87200.00	-531.75	-0.61	-0.08
21	87703.20	82000.00	-5703.23	-6.96	-0.84
22	92432.90	90000.00	-2432.95	-2.70	-0.36
23	83855.30	86000.00	2144.70	2.49	0.31
24	81684.60	77200.00	-4484.62	-5.81	-0.66
25	78442.60	74600.00	-3842.64	-5.15	-0.56
26	87020.00	87000.00	-19.96	-0.02	-0.00
27	82854.70	72000.00	-10854.70	-15.08	-1.59
28	86489.60	91000.00	4510.45	4.96	0.66
29	78907.10	78000.00	-907.10	-1.16	-0.13
30	82895.90	88000.00	5104.11	5.80	0.75
31	84820.60	87400.00	2579.41	2.95	0.38
32	80739.10	76000.00	-4739.09	-6.24	-0.69
33	98044.10	97000.00	-1044.13	-1.08	-0.15
34	86269.10	87800.00	1530.87	1.74	0.22
35	86074.20	79000.00	-7074.16	-8.95	-1.04
36	81868.20	79800.00	-2068.18	-2.59	-0.30

Figure B.7   Residuals Percentage of Error—First Analysis

```
                      RESIDUALS  AS  A  PERCENT  OF  ACTUAL
6358500000230  ■                     4.23                                              ■   1
6358500000290  ■                    3.60                                               ■   2
6358500000110  ■        0.65                                                           ■   3
6358500000270  ■                                            8.11                        ■   4
6358500000120  ■                               6.40                                     ■   5
6358500000150  ■            1.34                                                         ■   6
6358500000100  ■                 3.10                                                    ■   7
6358500000070  ■                                                  10.06                  ■   8
6358500000140  ■            1.12                                                         ■   9
6594300000220  ■                              -5.66                                      ■  10
6594300000150  ■         -0.84                                                           ■  11
6594300000300  ■                              -5.77                                      ■  12
6594300000250  ■                         -4.75                                           ■  13
6594300000010  ■                 2.69                                                    ■  14
6594300000100  ■          -1.68                                                          ■  15
6594300000110  ■                 2.89                                                    ■  16
6594300000080  ■                         -5.40                                           ■  17
6268800040010  ■                    5.73                                                 ■  18
6268800010070  ■                 2.87                                                    ■  19
6268800010120  ■         -0.60                                                           ■  20
6268800030090  ■                                  -6.95                                  ■  21
6268800030060  ■              -2.70                                                      ■  22
6473900110150  ■                 2.49                                                    ■  23
6473900600020  ■                             -5.80                                       ■  24
6473900300060  ■                         -5.15                                           ■  25
6473900700120  ■     -0.02                                                               ■  26
6473900300160  ■                                                         -15.07  ■  27
6473900500140  ■                         4.95                                            ■  28
6473900500080  ■          -1.16                                                          ■  29
6473900050060  ■                    5.80                                                 ■  30
6473900010570  ■                 2.95                                                    ■  31
6473900010020  ■                             -6.23                                       ■  32
6473900010250  ■         -1.07                                                           ■  33
6473900010290  ■            1.74                                                         ■  34
6473900020060  ■                                       -8.95                             ■  35
6473900110100  ■              -2.59                                                      ■  36
```

Figure B.8   Selected Sales—Second Analysis

```
STEPWISE  MULTIPLE  REGRESSION
ANALYSIS

OBSERVATIONS


                       INDEPENDENT VARIABLE        DEP
OBS    PROPERTY     1      2      3      4      5    VAR.
NUM     I.D. #    PORCH  BDRMS  LT SZ  GAR A  LIV A PRICE
***  *************  *****  *****  *****  *****  *****  *****
  2  6358500000290    1      3    8100    484   1457  85800
  3  6358500000110    1      3    7575    520   1720  93800
  6  6358500000150    3      4   10002    501   2014  98800
  7  6358500000100    1      3    7560    459   1709  90600
  9  6358500000140    4      2    9033    421   1479  85600
 11  6594300000150    1      3   13040    444   1939  90000
 14  6594300000010    1      3    8400    459   1706  89800
 15  6594300000100    1      3   11085    444   1939  90000
 16  6594300000110    3      3   11022    444   1939  96600
 19  6268800010070    1      3    8500    430   1515  82000
 20  6268800010120    3      3    8800    441   1697  87200
 22  6268800030060    3      3    8580    524   1613  90000
 23  6473900110150    0      3   11000    419   1777  86000
 26  6473900700120    1      3    8040    454   1703  87000
 29  6473900500080    3      3    7600    430   1394  78000
 31  6473900010570    3      3    8036    477   1472  87400
 33  6473900010250    1      3    7995    466   2065  97000
 34  6473900010290    3      3    7500    471   1535  87800
 36  6473900110100    1      3   11000    427   1640  79800
```

Figure B.9 Means, Standard Deviations, and Simple Correlation Coefficients of Variables—Second Analysis

```
MEANS

VARIABLE NO.  1 - PORCH =        1.8421
VARIABLE NO.  2 - BDRMS =        3.0000
VARIABLE NO.  3 - LT SZ =    9,098.3157
VARIABLE NO.  4 - GAR A =       458.6842
VARIABLE NO.  5 - LIV A =    1,700.6842
VARIABLE NO.  6 - PRICE =     88589.5000


STANDARD  DEVIATIONS

VARIABLE NO.  1 - PORCH =        1.1672
VARIABLE NO.  2 - BDRMS =        0.3333
VARIABLE NO.  3 - LT SZ =    1,605.3780
VARIABLE NO.  4 - GAR A =       31.2908
VARIABLE NO.  5 - LIV A =      202.1781
VARIABLE NO.  6 - PRICE =      5479.8900


SIMPLE  CORRELATION  COEFFICIENTS

     1        2        3        4        5     DEP VAR
   PORCH    BDRMS    LT SZ    GAR A    LIV A    PRICE

  1.0000  -0.1427  -0.1895   0.1232  -0.2878   0.0431
           0.9999   0.1005   0.4261   0.4410   0.4014
                    0.9999  -0.3764   0.5334   0.1066
                             0.9999   0.0870   0.5390
                                      1.0000   0.7721
                                               1.0000
```

Figure B.10   Summary of Comparable Sales— Second Analysis

```
STEP NUMBER 1   ENTER VARIABLE 5

STANDARD ERROR OF ESTIMATE:   3583.14
ADJ COEFF DETERM:                .572451
DEGREES OF FREEDOM:          17
F RATIO:                     25.1005
CONSTANT TERM:               52997

VARIABLE         COEFFICIENT    S.D. OF COEFF.    T VALUE
  5 LIV A          20.9283         4.17728        5.01004

STEP NUMBER 2   ENTER VARIABLE 4

STANDARD ERROR OF ESTIMATE:   2462.36
ADJ COEFF DETERM:                .798089
DEGREES OF FREEDOM:          16
F RATIO:                     36.5742
CONSTANT TERM:               16714.5

VARIABLE         COEFFICIENT    S.D. OF COEFF.    T VALUE
  4 GAR A          83.2604        18.6186         4.47189
  5 LIV A          19.8066         2.88159        6.87348

STEP NUMBER 3   ENTER VARIABLE 1

STANDARD ERROR OF ESTIMATE:   2222.09
ADJ COEFF DETERM:                .835571
DEGREES OF FREEDOM:          15
F RATIO:                     31.4899
CONSTANT TERM:               14425.3

VARIABLE         COEFFICIENT    S.D. OF COEFF.    T VALUE
  1 PORCH         1022.45        474.292          2.15573
  4 GAR A           77.5591       17.0087         4.55996
  5 LIV A           21.5828        2.72783        7.91208

STEP NUMBER 4   ENTER VARIABLE 3

STANDARD ERROR OF ESTIMATE:   2100.97
ADJ COEFF DETERM:                .853006
DEGREES OF FREEDOM:          14
F RATIO:                     27.1136
CONSTANT TERM:               22393.8

VARIABLE         COEFFICIENT    S.D. OF COEFF.    T VALUE
  1 PORCH         1051.87        448.789          2.3438
  3 LOT SZ          -.703438       .421954       -1.6671
  4 GAR A           62.0166       18.5888         3.33624
  5 LIV A           24.8207        3.22866        7.68762
```

```
STEP NUMBER 5   ENTER VARIABLE 2

STANDARD ERROR OF ESTIMATE:   2025.46
ADJ COEFF DETERM:              .863383
DEGREES OF FREEDOM:          13
F RATIO:                     23.751
CONSTANT TERM:               22030.7

VARIABLE        COEFFICIENT    S.D. OF COEFF.    T VALUE
 1 PORCH         990.254        434.779          2.2776
 2 BDRMS        -2559.79       1782.04          -1.43644
 3 LOT SZ        -.670822        .407421        -1.64651
 4 GAR A          73.7264       19.6877          3.7448
 5 LIV A          26.2837        3.275           8.02554
```

Figure B.11   Comparison of Actual and Estimated Sale Prices of Comparables Showing Residuals and Percentages of Error—Second Analysis

```
                  RESIDUAL ANALYSIS


OBSERVATION   PREDICTED Y    ACTUAL Y   RESIDUAL  % ERROR  # STD DEV
-----------   -----------    --------   --------  -------  ---------
          1     83886.90    85800.00    1913.15     2.23      0.35
          2     93805.80    93800.00      -5.80    -0.01     -0.00
          3     97925.00    98800.00     874.97     0.89      0.16
          4     89029.40    90600.00    1570.57     1.73      0.29
          5     84725.00    85600.00     874.99     1.02      0.16
          6     90292.70    90000.00    -292.68    -0.33     -0.05
          7     88387.10    89800.00    1412.91     1.57      0.26
          8     91604.10    90000.00   -1604.13    -1.78     -0.29
          9     93626.90    96600.00    2973.09     3.08      0.54
         10     81161.80    82000.00     838.25     1.02      0.15
         11     88535.60    87200.00   -1335.63    -1.53     -0.24
         12     92594.70    90000.00   -2594.67    -2.88     -0.47
         13     84569.80    86000.00    1430.23     1.66      0.26
         14     88181.10    87000.00   -1181.09    -1.36     -0.22
         15     80565.70    78000.00   -2565.67    -3.29     -0.47
         16     85788.50    87400.00    1611.54     1.84      0.29
         17     98610.70    97000.00   -1610.70    -1.66     -0.29
         18     87361.50    87800.00     438.46     0.50      0.08
         19     82549.00    79800.00   -2748.98    -3.44     -0.50
```

Figure B.12   Residuals Percentage of Error—Second Analysis

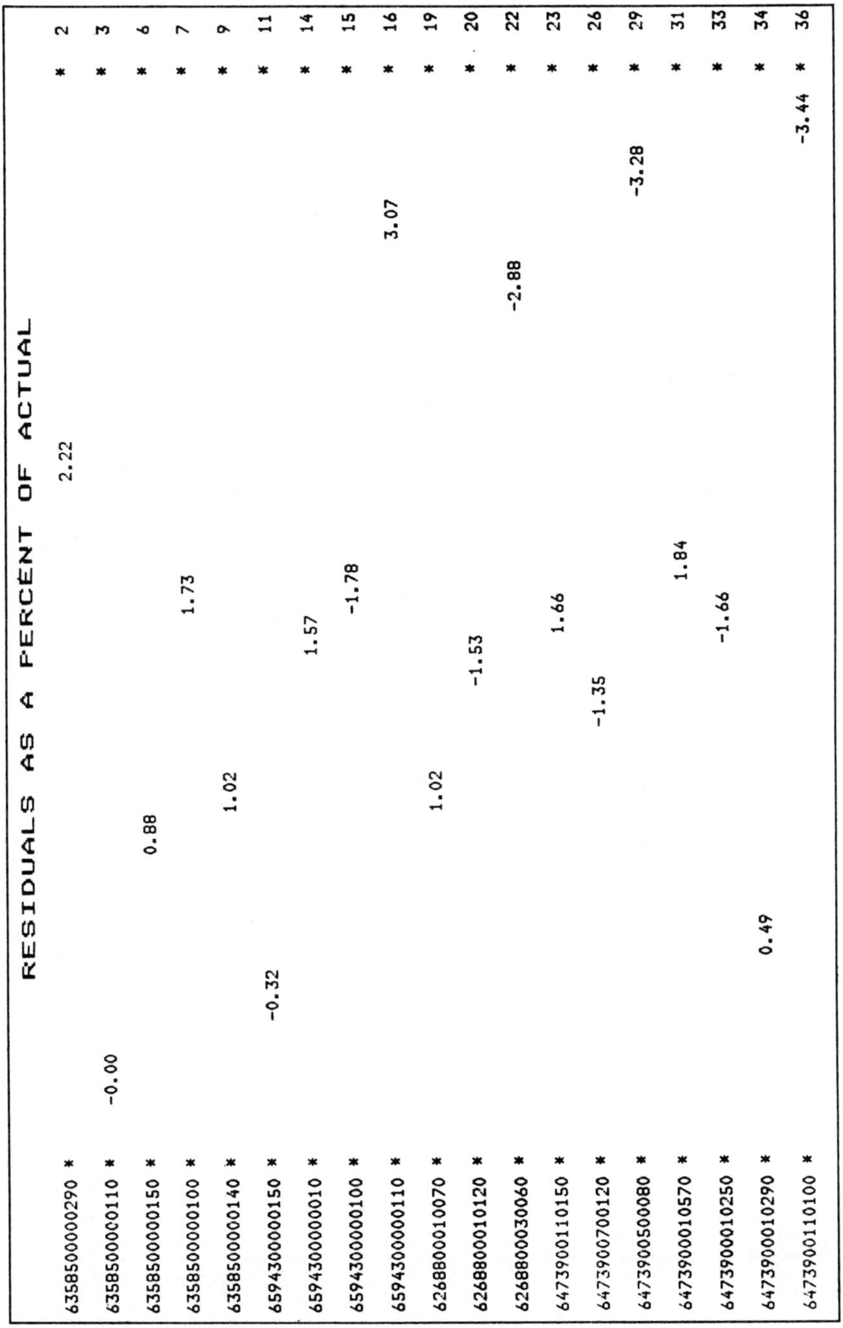

RESIDUALS AS A PERCENT OF ACTUAL

ID	Value	Index
6358500000290 *	-0.00	2
6358500000110 *	2.22	3
6358500000150 *	0.88	6
6358500000100 *	1.73	7
6358500000140 *	1.02	9
6594300000150 *	-0.32	11
6594300000010 *	1.57	14
6594300000100 *	-1.78	15
6594300000110 *	3.07	16
6268800010070 *	1.02	19
6268800010120 *	-1.53	20
6268800030060 *	-2.88	22
6473900110150 *	1.66	23
6473900700120 *	-1.35	26
6473900500080 *	-3.28	29
6473900010570 *	1.84	31
6473900010250 *	-1.66	33
6473900010290 *	0.49	34
6473900110100 *	-3.44	36

Figure B.13   Final Summary of Data Analyzed

```
            HOME  FEDERAL  SAVINGS  AND  LOAN

                  MARKET  DATA  ANALYSIS

    PROPERTY ADDRESS    9290  132 ST   NO

    APPRAISER                                  DATE -

    PARAMETERS FOR COMPARABLES SEARCH:

    PORCHES      GENERAL      BEDROOMS    GENERAL     LOT SIZE    GENERAL
    GARAGE AREA GENERAL       LIVING AREA GENERAL


    COMPARISON GRID:
                                             COMPARABLE PROPERTIES
                         PROPERTY   ************************************
          ITEM           APPRAISED      #1          #2          #3
    ***************      *********   **********  **********  **********
    DATE SOLD              10 82       9 82        10 82       10 82
    LOT SIZE               7,575       8,400       11,000      11,000
    CONSTRUCTION DATE      1978        1976        1972        1972
    PORCHES               NONE        NONE         UNKWN       NONE
    BEDROOMS              THREE       THREE        THREE       THREE
    BATHS                 TWO         TWO          TWO         TWO
    LIVING AREA           1,720       1,706        1,777       1,640
    POOL                  NONE        NONE         NONE        NONE
    PARKING               2 GR'GE     2 GR'GE      2 GR'GE     2 GR'GE
    COOLING               CNTRL       CNTRL        CNTRL       CNTRL
    FINANCING             CNVTL       CNVTL        UNKWN       UNKWN
    EXTRAS               N           N            N           N
    SALES PRICE          $   93800   $   89800    $   86000   $   79800

    ADDRESSES            # 1   9002  127LANE NO
                         # 2  11455  131 AVE   N
                         # 3  11450  132 AVE  N




                              (Continued)
```

STEPWISE MULTIPLE REGRESSION
VALUATION ANALYSIS

SUMMARY DATA FOR ALL COMPARABLE SALES ANALYZED:
       TOTAL NUMBER OF SALES ANALYZED   19
       MEAN SALES PRICE FOR ALL SALES . . . . $ 88590
       STANDARD DEVIATION IN PRICE FOR ALL SALES . . . . . . $ 5480

SUMMARY DATA FOR THE MULTIPLE REGRESSION ANALYSIS:
       ADJ COEFF DETERM 0.8634
       STANDARD ERROR OF THE ESTIMATE 2025.46
       NUMBER OF VARIABLES IN REGRESSION EQUATION   5
       DEGREES OF FREEDOM   13
       F RATIO 23.7492

APPLICATION OF REGRESSION RESULTS FOR PROPERTY VALUATION:

VARIABLE NAME	SIGNIFICANCE (T VALUE)	MULTIPLIER CALCULATED	DATA FOR SUBJECT	EXTENSION FOR SUBJECT
********	************	**********	********	***********
PORCH	2.2775	990.254	1.0000	$ 990
BDRMS	-1.4363	- 2559.79	3.0000	$- 7679
LT SZ	-1.6463	0.670822	7575.0000	$- 5081
GAR A	3.7445	73.7264	520.0000	$ 38338
LIV A	8.0251	26.2837	1720.0000	$ 45208

       CONSTANT TERM OF THE REGRESSION EQUATION . . . . . $ 22031
       INDICATED VALUE FOR THE PROPERTY APPRAISED . . . . . $ 93807

CONFIDENCE INTERVALS FOR THE VALUE ESTIMATE:

DEGREE OF CONFIDENCE	RANGE OF CONFIDENCE IN PERCENT	IN DOLLARS	REASONABLE VALUE INTERVAL MINIMUM	TO MAXIMUM
**********	**********	**********	**************************	
68.26%	+/- 0.0228	+/- $ 2025	$ 91782	$ 95832
95.44%	+/- 0.0457	+/- $ 4050	$ 89757	$ 97857

Appendix C
Financial Tables

The following material is from financial tables and formulas designed for and used in the American Institute of Real Estate Appraisers' courses, *Capitalization Theory & Techniques*, Parts I, II, and III.[1] Some discussion on the development of the factors used in the tables has been added.

Although the tables were created as an educational tool for appraisers, they should prove useful to other students of the mathematics of finance, as well as practicing appraisers, lenders, investment consultants, and other financial analysts. Each sample table from the nine sets of tables of financial factors is prefaced by its formulation, a brief explanation, and examples of use.

The selection and arrangement of tables illustrated in the follow-

[1]James J. Mason, MAI, ed. and comp., *American Institute of Real Estate Appraisers Financial Tables*, rev. ed. (Chicago: American Institute of Real Estate Appraisers, with tables computed by Financial Publishing Company, 1982).

ing pages is unique. Special features are continuous compounding and discounting factors; annuities changing in constant amount; annuities changing in constant ratio; sinking fund factors for annual payments with daily interest; part paid off for monthly, direct reduction loans; and straight-line *J*-Factors for income adjustment in mortgage-equity analysis.

The straight-line *J*-Factor should be of particular interest with respect to inflation studies. It works within the standard Ellwood formula, yet unlike the Ellwood *J*-Factor, the overall rate reflects the relationship between the anticipated first-year income and the present value; in addition, this adjustment contemplates the change in income *after* the first year. On the other hand, it is similar to the Ellwood *J*-Factor in that a constant overall capitalization rate will result from those situations in which the rate of change in both income and value are assumed to be the same.

SUMMARY OF BASIC FORMULAS
CAPITALIZATION THEORY AND TECHNIQUES, PART I

Where:

I = Income
R = Capitalization Rate
V = Value
M = Mortgage Ratio
DCR = Debt Coverage Ratio
F = Capitalization Factor (Multiplier)
GIM = Gross Income Multiplier
$EGIM$ = Effective Gross Income Multiplier
NIR = Net Income Ratio

Subscript:

0 = Overall Property
M = Mortgage
E = Equity
L = Land
B = Building

Basic Income/Cap Rate/Value Formulas:

$$I = R \times V$$
$$R = I/V$$
$$V = I/R$$

Basic Value/Income/Factor Formulas:

$$V = I \times F$$
$$I = V/F$$
$$F = V/I$$

Adaptations for Mortgage/Equity Components:

Band of Investment (using Ratios):

$$R_0 = M \times R_M + [(1 - M) \times R_E]$$
$$R_E = (R_0 - M \times R_M)/(1 - M)$$

Equity Residual:

$$V_0 = [(I_0 - V_M \times R_M)/R_E] + V_M$$
$$R_E = (I_0 - V_M \times R_M)/V_E$$

Mortgage Residual:

$$V_0 = [(I_0 - V_E \times R_E)/R_M] + V_E$$

Debt Coverage Ratio:

$$R_0 = DCR \times M \times R_M$$
$$DCR = R/(M \times R_M)$$
$$M = R/(DCR \times R_M)$$

Adaptations for Land/Building Components:

Land Residual:

$$V_0 = [(I_0 - V_B \times R_B)/R_L] + V_B$$
$$R_L = (I_0 - V_B \times R_B)/V_L$$
$$R_B = (I_0 - V_L \times R_L)/V_B$$

Building Residual:

$$V_0 = [(I_0 - V_L \times R_L)/R_B] + V_L$$

Cap Rate/Factor Relationships:

$$R = 1/F$$
$$R_0 = NIR/GIM$$
$$R_0 = NIR/EGIM$$

Note:

NIR may relate to Scheduled Gross or Effective Gross Income and care should be taken to ensure consistency.

SUMMARY OF BASIC FORMULAS
CAPITALIZATION THEORY AND TECHNIQUES, PART II

Where:
  PV = Present Value
  CF = Cash Flow
  Y = Yield Rate
  R = Capitalization Rate
  Δ = Change
  a = Annualizer
  $1/S_{\overline{n}|}$ = Sinking Fund Factor
  $1/n$ = 1/Projection Period
  CR = Compound Rate of Change
  V = Value

Subscript:
  n = Projection Periods
  0 = Overall Property
  I = Income

Discounted Cash Flows/Present Value (DCF/PV):

$$PV = \frac{CF_1}{1 + Y} + \frac{CF_2}{(1 + Y)^2} + \frac{CF_3}{(1 + Y)^3} + \ldots + \frac{CF_n}{(1 + Y)^n}$$

Basic CAP Rate/Yield Rate/Value Change Formulas:

$R = Y - \Delta a$

$Y = R + \Delta a$

$\Delta a = Y - R$

$\Delta = (Y - R)/a$

Adaptations for Common Income/Value Patterns:

Pattern	Premise	Cap Rates (R)	Yield Rates (Y)	Value Changes (Δ)
Perpetuity	($\Delta = 0$)	$R = Y$	$Y = R$	
Level Annuity*	($a = 1/S_{\overline{n}|}$)	$R = Y - \Delta 1/S_{\overline{n}|}$	$Y = R + \Delta 1/S_{\overline{n}|}$	$\Delta = (Y - R)/1/S_{\overline{n}|}$
St. Line Change	($a = 1/n$)	$R = Y - \Delta 1/n$	$Y = R + \Delta 1/n$	$\Delta = (Y - R)/1/n$
Exponential Change	($\Delta_0 a = CR$)	$R_0 = Y_0 - CR$	$Y_0 = R_0 + CR$	$\Delta_0 = (1 + CR)^n - 1$

*Inwood Premise: $1/S_{\overline{n}|}$ at Y Rate; Hoskold Premise: $1/S_{\overline{n}|}$ at Safe Rate

St. Line Change* in Income:	**St. Line Change* in Value:**	**Compound Rate of Change:**
$\$\Delta_I = V \times \Delta 1/n \times Y$	$\$\Delta 1/n = \$\Delta_I/Y$	$CR = \sqrt[n]{FV/PV} - 1$
$\Delta_I = (Y \times \Delta 1/n)/(Y - \Delta 1/n)$	$\Delta 1/n = (Y \times \Delta_I)/(Y + \Delta_I)$	$CR = Y_o - R_o$

*Δ_I in these formulas is the ratio of one year's change in income related to the first-year income.

SUMMARY OF BASIC FORMULAS
CAPITALIZATION THEORY AND TECHNIQUES, PART II

Table Relationships:

Conversion of the Annual Constant (R_M) for a monthly payment loan to the corresponding monthly functions.

Function for Monthly Frequency:	Formula:
Amount of $1	$S^n = R_M/(R_M - I)$
Amount of $1 per month	$S_{\overline{n}|} = 12/(R_M - I)$
Sinking Fund Factor	$1/S_{\overline{n}|} = (R_M - I)/12$
Present Value of $1	$1/S^n = (R_M - I)/R_M$
Present Value of $1 per month	$a_{\overline{n}|} = 12/R_M$
Partial Payment	$1/a_{\overline{n}|} = R_M/12$

(In these formulas, I = Nominal Interest Rate)

Present Value of Increasing/Decreasing Annuities:

Straight Line Changes:

To obtain the present value of an annuity that has a starting income of **d** at the end of the first period and *increases h dollars* per period for **n** periods:

$$PV = (d + hn)a_{\overline{n}|} - \frac{h(n - a_{\overline{n}|})}{i}$$

To obtain the present value of an annuity that has a starting income of **d** at the end of the first period and *decreases h dollars* per period for **n** periods, simply treat **h** as a negative quantity in the foregoing formula.

Constant Ratio (Exponential Curve) Changes:

To obtain the present value of an annuity that starts at $1 at the end of the first period and *increases each period* thereafter at the rate **x** for **n** periods:

$$PV = \frac{1 - (1 + x)^n/(1 + i)^n}{i - x}$$

Where **i** is the periodic discount rate and **x** is the ratio of the increase in income for any period to the income for the previous period.

To obtain the present value of an annuity that starts at $1 at the end of the first period and *decreases each period* thereafter at rate **x**, simply treat rate **x** as a negative quantity in the foregoing formula.

SUMMARY OF BASIC FORMULAS
CAPITALIZATION THEORY AND TECHNIQUES, PART III

Where

r	=	Basic Capitalization Rate
Y	=	Yield Rate
M	=	Mortgage Ratio
C	=	Mortgage Coefficient
P	=	Ratio Paid Off — Mortgage
$1/S_{\overline{n}}$	=	Sinking Fund Factor
R	=	Capitalization Rate
$S_{\overline{n}}$	=	Future Value of \$1 Per Period
Δ	=	Change
J	=	J Factor (Changing Income)
n	=	Projection Period
NOI	=	Net Operating Income
B	=	Mortgage Balance
I	=	Nominal Interest Rate

Subscript:

E	=	Equity
M	=	Mortgage
P	=	Projection
0	=	Overall Property
I	=	Income
1	=	1st Mortgage
2	=	2nd Mortgage

Mortgage/Equity Formulas:

Basic Capitalization Rates (r):

$$r = Y_E - MC$$

$$r = Y_E - (M_1C_1 + M_2C_2)$$

$$C = Y_E + P\, 1/S_{\overline{n}} - R_M$$

$$P = (R_M - I)/(R_{MP} - I)$$

$$P = 1/S_{\overline{n}} \times S_{\overline{n}}\, P$$

Capitalization Rates (R):

Level Income:

$$R = Y_E - MC - \Delta 1/S_{\overline{n}}$$

$$R = r - \Delta 1/S_{\overline{n}}$$

J Factor Changing Income:

$$R_0 = \frac{Y_E - MC - \Delta_0\, 1/S_{\overline{n}}}{1 + \Delta_I J}$$

$$R_0 = \frac{r - \Delta_0\, 1/S_{\overline{n}}}{1 + \Delta_I J}$$

Required Change in Value (Δ):

Level Income:

$$\Delta = \frac{r - R}{1/S_{\overline{n}}}$$

$$\Delta = \frac{Y_E - MC - R}{1/S_{\overline{n}}}$$

J Factor Changing Income:

$$\Delta_0 = \frac{r - R_0\,(1 + \Delta_I J)}{1/S_{\overline{n}}}$$

$${}^*\Delta_0 = \frac{r - R_0}{R_0 J + 1/S_{\overline{n}}}$$

Note: For multiple mortgage situations, insert M and C for each mortgage.

*This formula assumes Value and Income change at the same Ratio.

SUMMARY OF BASIC FORMULAS
CAPITALIZATION THEORY AND TECHNIQUES, PART III

Equity Yield (Y_E):

Level Income: **J Factor Changing Income:**

$$Y_E = R_E + \Delta_E \, 1/S_{\overline{m}}$$

$$Y_E = R_E + \Delta_E \, 1/S_{\overline{m}} + \left[\frac{R_0 \, \Delta_I}{1 - M} \right] J$$

Change in Equity:

$$\Delta_E = (\Delta_0 + MP)/(1 - M) \text{ or}$$

$$\Delta_E = [V_0 (1 + \Delta_0) - B - V_E]/V_E$$

Assumed Mortgage Situation:

Level Income: **J Factor Changing Income:**

$$V_0 = \frac{NOI + BC}{Y_E - \Delta_0 \, 1/S_{\overline{m}}}$$

$$V_0 = \frac{NOI (1 + \Delta_I J) + BC}{Y_E - \Delta_0 \, 1/S_{\overline{m}}}$$

Mortgage/Equity Without Algebra Format:

1. Loan Ratio × Annual Constant   =   _____

2. Equity Ratio × Equity Yield Rate   =   + _____

3. Loan Ratio × Paid Off Loan Ratio × SFF   =   − _____

                     Basic Rate (r)   =   _____

4. + Dep **or** − App × SFF   = + / − _____

                     Cap Rate (R)   =   _____

Note: SFF is sinking fund factor at equity yield rate for projection period.
Dep/App is the change in value from depreciation/appreciation during the
projection period.

SUMMARY OF BASIC FORMULAS
CAPITALIZATION THEORY AND TECHNIQUES, PART III

Where:

			Subscript:
PV	=	Present Value	
NPV	=	Net Present Value	
CF	=	Cash Flow	0 = At Time Zero
i	=	Discount Rate in NPV Formula	1 = End of 1st Period
n	=	Projection Period	2 = End of 2nd Period
IRR	=	Internal Rate of Return	3 = End of 3rd Period
PI	=	Profitability Index	n = End Period of Series
MIRR	=	Modified Internal Rate of Return	
$FVCF_j$	=	Future Value of a Series of Cash Flows	
i	=	Re-investment Rate in MIRR Formula	

Net Present Value (NPV):

$$NPV = CF_0 + \frac{CF_1}{1 + i} + \frac{CF_2}{(1 + i)^2} + \frac{CF_3}{(1 + i)^3} + \ldots + \frac{CF_n}{(1 + i)^n}$$

Internal Rate of Return (IRR):

$$\text{Where: } NPV = 0; IRR = i$$

Profitability Index (PI):

$$PI = PV / CF_0$$

Modified Internal Rate of Return (MIRR):

$$MIRR = \sqrt[n]{\frac{FVCF_j}{CF_0}} - 1$$

$$MIRR = \sqrt[n]{\frac{CF_1(1 + i)^{n-1} + CF_2(1 + i)^{n-2} + CF_3(1 + i)^{n-3} + \ldots + CF_n}{CF_0}} - 1$$

Note: In these formulas . . . . individual CF's may be positive or negative for PV and NPV solutions, however, CF_0 is treated as a positive value for PI and MIRR solutions.

Table 1. Compound Interest (Future Value of $1)

The amount to which an investment or deposit will grow in a given number of time periods including the accumulation of interest at the effective rate per period. This factor is also known as the *amount of one*.

$$S^n = (1 + i)^n$$

Where $\quad S^n$ = Future Value Factor

$\quad\quad\quad\quad$ i = Effective Rate of Interest

$\quad\quad\quad\quad$ n = Number of Compounding Periods

AND $\quad\quad S^n = (e)^{in}$ for Continuous Compounding

Where $\quad S^n$ = Future Value Factor

$\quad\quad\quad\quad$ i = Nominal Rate of Interest

$\quad\quad\quad\quad$ n = Number of Years

$\quad\quad\quad\quad$ e = 2.718282

This Table is used in solving problems dealing with compound growth.

Example 1:
What is the Future Value of $10,000 assuming interest at 6%, compounded annually, for 10 years?

$10,000 × 1.790848 = $17,908.48

Example 2:
What is the Future Value of $10,000 assuming interest at 6%, compounded annually, for 10 years and 7 months?

$10,000 × 1.790848 × 1.035000 = $18,535.28

(Assumes simple interest for time less than one conversion period).

Example 3:
A property sold for $135,000. Five years previously it sold for $100,000. What is the trend in sales price expressed as a monthly compound rate of growth?

$135,000 ÷ $100,000 = 1.350000 (Future Value Factor)

Scan tables of Future Value Factors, monthly frequency, for 1.350000 at 5 years. Closest match is found at 6% nominal and monthly rate of growth is therefore approximately 0.5%.

Example 4:
How long will it take prices to double assuming a 6% rate of inflation?

2.00 ÷ 1.00 = 2.000000 (Future Value Factor)

Scan tables of Future Value Factors at 6% nominal interest for 2.000000.

Assuming annual frequency, the target is bracketed between the Factors for 11 and 12 years. Visual interpolation indicates an answer of slightly less than 12 years. Mathematical straight-line interpolation calculates 11.9 years:

(2.000000 − 1.898299)/(2.012196 − 1.898299) + 11 = 11.9 years

---

When money is invested or deposited at the beginning of a period in an account bearing interest at a fixed rate, it grows according to the interest rate and to the number of compounding (conversion) periods it remains in the account. To illustrate how and why this growth occurs, assume an investment of $1.00, a nominal interest rate of 10% with annual compounding, and an investment or holding term of five years.

Original investment	$1.00
Interest, first year at 10%	.10
Accumulation, end of 1 year	$1.10
Interest, second year at 10%	.11
Accumulation, end of 2 years	$1.21
Interest, third year at 10%	.121
Accumulation, end of 3 years	$1.331
Interest, fourth year at 10%	.1331
Accumulation, end of 4 years	$1.4641
Interest, fifth year at 10%	.14641
Accumulation, end of 5 years	$1.61051

One dollar grows to $1.61051 in five years with interest at 10% (the future value of one factor at 10% annually for 5 years is 1.610510) and $1,000 would grow 1,000 times this amount to $1,610.51, over the same 5 years at the same 10% annual rate. When interest is not collected or withdrawn as earned but is added to the capital account on which additional interest accumulates in subsequent periods, the procedure is called compounding.

The same results are obtained by the formula $(1+i)^n$, where n is the number of compounding periods and i is the interest rate per period (10% or .10), as follows:

(n)		
1	$1.10 \times 1 = 1.10^1$	= 1.10
2	$1.10 \times 1.10 = 1.10^2$	= 1.21
3	$1.10 \times 1.10 \times 1.10 = 1.10^3$	= 1.331
4	$1.10 \times 1.10 \times 1.10 \times 1.10 = 1.10^4$	= 1.461
5	$1.10 \times 1.10 \times 1.10 \times 1.10 \times 1.10 = 1.10^5$	= 1.61051

Thus, the factors in this table, the amount of one or the future value of one, reflect the growth of $1.00 accumulating at interest for the number of compounding periods shown at the left and right of each page of tables. Reference to a 10% annual column reveals a factor 2.593742 for 10 periods. This means that $1.00 deposited at 10% interest compounded annually for 10 years will grow to $1.00 × 2.593742, or just over $2.59. In other words, $1.10^{10} = 2.593742$. Reference to the factors for seven years and eight years indicates $1.00 (or any investment earning 10% per year) would double in value in approximately 7.5 years. Similarly, an investment of $10,000 made 10 years ago, earning no periodic income during the 10-year holding period, must be liquidated in the current market at $10,000 × 2.593742, or $25,937.42, to realize a 10% return on original investment.

This factor reflects the growth of the original deposit measured from the *beginning deposit period*. Thus, at the end of the first period at 10% the original $1.00 has grown to $1.10, and the factor is 1.100000, as shown above.

COMPOUND INTEREST   6%
(Future Value of $1)

Base: 2.718 282   1.005 000   1.015 000   1.030 000   1.060 000

Frequency of Conversion

Months	Continuous	Monthly	Quarterly	Semiannual	Annual	Months
0	1.000 000	1.000 000	1.000 000	1.000 000	1.000 000	0
1	1.005 013	1.005 000	1.005 000	1.005 000	1.005 000	1
2	1.010 050	1.010 025	1.010 000	1.010 000	1.010 000	2
3	1.015 113	1.015 075	1.015 000	1.015 000	1.015 000	3
4	1.020 201	1.020 151	1.020 075	1.020 000	1.020 000	4
5	1.025 315	1.025 251	1.025 150	1.025 000	1.025 000	5
6	1.030 455	1.030 378	1.030 225	1.030 000	1.030 000	6
7	1.035 620	1.035 529	1.035 376	1.035 150	1.035 000	7
8	1.040 811	1.040 707	1.040 527	1.040 300	1.040 000	8
9	1.046 028	1.045 911	1.045 678	1.045 450	1.045 000	9
10	1.051 271	1.051 140	1.050 907	1.050 600	1.050 000	10
11	1.056 541	1.056 396	1.056 135	1.055 750	1.055 000	11

Years						Years
1	1.061 837	1.061 678	1.061 364	1.060 900	1.060 000	1
2	1.127 497	1.127 160	1.126 493	1.125 509	1.123 600	2
3	1.197 217	1.196 681	1.195 618	1.194 052	1.191 016	3
4	1.271 249	1.270 489	1.268 986	1.266 770	1.262 477	4
5	1.349 859	1.348 850	1.346 855	1.343 916	1.338 226	5
6	1.433 329	1.432 044	1.429 503	1.425 761	1.418 519	6
7	1.521 962	1.520 370	1.517 222	1.512 590	1.503 630	7
8	1.616 074	1.614 143	1.610 324	1.604 706	1.593 848	8
9	1.716 007	1.713 699	1.709 140	1.702 433	1.689 479	9
10	1.822 119	1.819 397	1.814 018	1.806 111	1.790 848	10
11	1.934 792	1.931 613	1.925 333	1.916 103	1.898 299	11
12	2.054 433	2.050 751	2.043 478	2.032 794	2.012 196	12
13	2.181 472	2.177 237	2.168 873	2.156 591	2.132 928	13
14	2.316 367	2.311 524	2.301 963	2.287 928	2.260 904	14
15	2.459 603	2.454 094	2.443 220	2.427 262	2.396 558	15
16	2.611 696	2.605 457	2.593 144	2.575 083	2.540 352	16
17	2.773 195	2.766 156	2.752 269	2.731 905	2.692 773	17
18	2.944 680	2.936 766	2.921 158	2.898 278	2.854 339	18
19	3.126 768	3.117 899	3.100 411	3.074 783	3.025 600	19
20	3.320 117	3.310 204	3.290 663	3.262 038	3.207 135	20
21	3.525 421	3.514 371	3.492 590	3.460 696	3.399 564	21
′22	3.743 421	3.731 129	3.706 907	3.671 452	3.603 537	22
23	3.974 902	3.961 257	3.934 376	3.895 044	3.819 750	23
24	4.220 696	4.205 579	4.175 804	4.132 252	4.048 935	24
25	4.481 689	4.464 970	4.432 046	4.383 906	4.291 871	25
26	4.758 821	4.740 359	4.704 012	4.650 886	4.549 383	26
27	5.053 090	5.032 734	4.992 667	4.934 125	4.822 346	27
28	5.365 556	5.343 142	5.299 034	5.234 613	5.111 687	28
29	5.697 343	5.672 696	5.624 202	5.553 401	5.418 388	29
30	6.049 647	6.022 575	5.969 323	5.891 603	5.743 491	30
31	6.423 737	6.394 034	6.335 622	6.250 402	6.088 101	31
32	6.820 958	6.788 405	6.724 398	6.631 051	6.453 387	32
33	7.242 743	7.207 098	7.137 031	7.034 882	6.840 590	33
34	7.690 609	7.651 617	7.574 984	7.463 307	7.251 025	34
35	8.166 170	8.123 551	8.039 812	7.917 822	7.686 087	35
36	8.671 138	8.624 594	8.533 164	8.400 017	8.147 252	36
37	9.207 331	9.156 540	9.056 789	8.911 578	8.636 087	37
38	9.776 680	9.721 296	9.612 546	9.454 293	9.154 252	38
39	10.381 237	10.320 884	10.202 406	10.030 060	9.703 507	39
40	11.023 176	10.957 454	10.828 462	10.640 891	10.285 718	40

COMPOUND INTEREST

10%

(Future Value of $1)

Base:	2.718 282	1.008 333	1.025 000	1.050 000	1.100 000	
			Frequency of Conversion			
Months	Continuous	Monthly	Quarterly	Semiannual	Annual	Months
0	1.000 000	1.000 000	1.000 000	1.000 000	1.000 000	0
1	1.008 368	1.008 333	1.008 333	1.008 333	1.008 333	1
2	1.016 806	1.016 736	1.016 667	1.016 667	1.016 667	2
3	1.025 315	1.025 209	1.025 000	1.025 000	1.025 000	3
4	1.033 895	1.033 752	1.033 542	1.033 333	1.033 333	4
5	1.042 547	1.042 367	1.042 083	1.041 667	1.041 667	5
6	1.051 271	1.051 053	1.050 625	1.050 000	1.050 000	6
7	1.060 068	1.059 812	1.059 380	1.058 750	1.058 333	7
8	1.068 939	1.068 644	1.068 135	1.067 500	1.066 667	8
9	1.077 884	1.077 549	1.076 891	1.076 250	1.075 000	9
10	1.086 904	1.086 529	1.085 865	1.085 000	1.083 333	10
11	1.095 999	1.095 583	1.094 839	1.093 750	1.091 667	11

Years						Years
1	1.105 171	1.104 713	1.103 813	1.102 500	1.100 000	1
2	1.221 403	1.220 391	1.218 403	1.215 506	1.210 000	2
3	1.349 859	1.348 182	1.344 889	1.340 096	1.331 000	3
4	1.491 825	1.489 354	1.484 506	1.477 455	1.464 100	4
5	1.648 721	1.645 309	1.638 616	1.628 895	1.610 510	5
6	1.822 119	1.817 594	1.808 726	1.795 856	1.771 561	6
7	2.013 753	2.007 920	1.996 495	1.979 932	1.948 717	7
8	2.225 541	2.218 176	2.203 757	2.182 875	2.143 589	8
9	2.459 603	2.450 448	2.432 535	2.406 619	2.357 948	9
10	2.718 282	2.707 041	2.685 064	2.653 298	2.593 742	10
11	3.004 166	2.990 504	2.963 808	2.925 261	2.853 117	11
12	3.320 117	3.303 649	3.271 490	3.225 100	3.138 428	12
13	3.669 297	3.649 584	3.611 112	3.555 673	3.452 271	13
14	4.055 200	4.031 743	3.985 992	3.920 129	3.797 498	14
15	4.481 689	4.453 920	4.399 790	4.321 942	4.177 248	15
16	4.953 032	4.920 303	4.856 545	4.764 941	4.594 973	16
17	5.473 947	5.435 523	5.360 717	5.253 348	5.054 470	17
18	6.049 647	6.004 693	5.917 228	5.791 816	5.559 917	18
19	6.685 894	6.633 463	6.531 513	6.385 477	6.115 909	19
20	7.389 056	7.328 074	7.209 568	7.039 989	6.727 500	20
21	8.166 170	8.095 419	7.958 014	7.761 588	7.400 250	21
22	9.025 013	8.943 115	8.784 158	8.557 150	8.140 275	22
23	9.974 182	9.879 576	9.696 067	9.434 258	8.954 302	23
24	11.023 176	10.914 097	10.702 644	10.401 270	9.849 733	24
25	12.182 494	12.056 945	11.813 716	11.467 400	10.834 706	25
26	13.463 738	13.319 465	13.040 132	12.642 808	11.918 177	26
27	14.879 732	14.714 187	14.393 866	13.938 696	13.109 994	27
28	16.444 647	16.254 954	15.888 135	15.367 412	14.420 994	28
29	18.174 145	17.957 060	17.537 528	16.942 572	15.863 093	29
30	20.085 537	19.837 399	19.358 150	18.679 186	17.449 402	30
31	22.197 951	21.914 634	21.367 775	20.593 802	19.194 342	31
32	24.532 530	24.209 383	23.586 026	22.704 667	21.113 777	32
33	27.112 639	26.744 422	26.034 559	25.031 896	23.225 154	33
34	29.964 100	29.544 912	28.737 282	27.597 665	25.547 670	34
35	33.115 452	32.638 650	31.720 583	30.426 426	28.102 437	35
36	36.598 234	36.056 344	35.013 588	33.545 134	30.912 681	36
37	40.447 304	39.831 914	38.648 450	36.983 510	34.003 949	37
38	44.701 184	44.002 836	42.660 657	40.774 320	37.404 343	38
39	49.402 449	48.610 508	47.089 383	44.953 688	41.144 778	39
40	54.598 150	53.700 663	51.977 868	49.561 441	45.259 256	40

Table 2 - REVERSION FACTORS (Present Value of $1)

The present value of one to be collected at a given future time when discounted at the effective interest rate for the number of periods from now to the date of collection. This factor is reciprocal to the corresponding factor in Table 1.

$$1/S^n = \frac{1}{(1 + i)^n}$$

Where $1/S^n$ = Present Value Factor

                 i = Effective Rate of Interest

                 n = Number of Compounding Periods

AND $1/S^n = \frac{1}{(e)^{in}}$ for Continuous Compounding

Where $1/S^n$ = Present Value Factor

                 i = Nominal Rate of Interest

                 n = Number of Years

                 e = 2.718282

This Table is used in solving problems dealing with compound discounting.

Example 1:
What is the Present Value of $10,000 to be received in 10 years, assuming an interest rate of 6% and annual compounding?

$10,000 × .558395 = $5,583.95

Example 2:
What is the Present Value of $10,000 to be received in 10 years and 7 months, assuming an interest rate of 6% and annual compounding?

$10,000 × .558395 × .966184 = $5,395.12

(Assumes simple interest for time less than one conversion period.)

Example 3:
Assuming a 6% rate and annual compounding, what is the Present Value of the following cash flows: $1,000 in 1 year; $2,000 in 2 years; and $3,000 in 3 years?

Cash Flows		Present Value Factor		Present Value
$1,000	×	.943396	=	$ 943.40
2,000	×	.889996	=	1,779.99
3,000	×	.839619	=	2,518.86
	Present Value		=	$5,242.25

Example 4:
A property sold for $100,000. Five years previously it sold for $135,000. What is the depreciation in sales price expressed as a monthly compound rate?

$100,000/$135,000 = .740741 (Present Value Factor)

Scan tables of Present Value Factors, monthly frequency, for .740741 at 5 years. Closest match is found at 6% nominal and therefore monthly rate is approximately 0.5%.

Example 5:
How long will it take $1 to be worth 50 cents assuming a 6% rate of inflation?

.50/1.00 = .500000 (Present Value Factor)

Scan tables of Present Value Factors at 6% nominal interest for .500000.

Assuming annual frequency, the target is bracketed between the Factors for 11 and 12 years. Visual interpolation indicates an answer of slightly less than 12 years. Mathematical straight-line interpolation calculates 11.9 years:

(.526788 − .500000)/(.526788 − .496969) + 11 = 11.9 years

As demonstrated in the discussion of the future value of one, $1.00 compounded annually at 10% would grow to $1.610151 in five years. Accordingly, the amount that would grow to $1.00 in five years is $1.00 divided by 1.61051, or $0.62092 (10% Table, present value of one factor for five years is precomputed at 0.620921). In other words, $1.00 to be collected five years from today would have a present value of $0.620921 when discounted at 10% per annum. And $10,000 to be collected five years from today, when discounted at the same 10% annual rate, would have a present value of $10,000 × .620921 = $6,209.21. The $10,000 sum to be received in five years is called a *reversion.*

6%   REVERSION FACTORS
(Present Value of $1)

Base: 2.718 282   1.005 000   1.015 000   1.030 000   1.060 000

Frequency of Conversion

Months	Continuous	Monthly	Quarterly	Semiannual	Annual	Months
0	1.000 000	1.000 000	1.000 000	1.000 000	1.000 000	0
1	.995 012	.995 025	.995 025	.995 025	.995 025	1
2	.990 050	.990 075	.990 099	.990 099	.990 099	2
3	.985 112	.985 149	.985 222	.985 222	.985 222	3
4	.980 199	.980 248	.980 320	.980 392	.980 392	4
5	.975 310	.975 371	.975 467	.975 610	.975 610	5
6	.970 446	.970 518	.970 662	.970 874	.970 874	6
7	.965 605	.965 690	.965 833	.966 044	.966 184	7
8	.960 789	.960 885	.961 051	.961 261	.961 538	8
9	.955 997	.956 105	.956 317	.956 526	.956 938	9
10	.951 229	.951 348	.951 559	.951 837	.952 381	10
11	.946 485	.946 615	.946 849	.947 194	.947 867	11

Years						Years
1	.941 765	.941 905	.942 184	.942 596	.943 396	1
2	.886 920	.887 186	.887 711	.888 487	.889 996	2
3	.835 270	.835 645	.836 387	.837 484	.839 619	3
4	.786 628	.787 098	.788 031	.789 409	.792 094	4
5	.740 818	.741 372	.742 470	.744 094	.747 258	5
6	.697 676	.698 302	.699 544	.701 380	.704 961	6
7	.657 047	.657 735	.659 099	.661 118	.665 057	7
8	.618 783	.619 524	.620 993	.623 167	.627 412	8
9	.582 748	.583 533	.585 090	.587 395	.591 898	9
10	.548 812	.549 633	.551 262	.553 676	.558 395	10
11	.516 851	.517 702	.519 391	.521 893	.526 788	11
12	.486 752	.487 626	.489 362	.491 934	.496 969	12
13	.458 406	.459 298	.461 069	.463 695	.468 839	13
14	.431 711	.432 615	.434 412	.437 077	.442 301	14
15	.406 570	.407 482	.409 296	.411 987	.417 265	15
16	.382 893	.383 810	.385 632	.388 337	.393 646	16
17	.360 595	.361 513	.363 337	.366 045	.371 364	17
18	.339 596	.340 511	.342 330	.345 032	.350 344	18
19	.319 819	.320 729	.322 538	.325 226	.330 513	19
20	.301 194	.302 096	.303 890	.306 557	.311 805	20
21	.283 654	.284 546	.286 321	.288 959	.294 155	21
22	.267 135	.268 015	.269 767	.272 372	.277 505	22
23	.251 579	.252 445	.254 170	.256 737	.261 797	23
24	.236 928	.237 779	.239 475	.241 999	.246 979	24
25	.223 130	.223 966	.225 629	.228 107	.232 999	25
26	.210 136	.210 954	.212 585	.215 013	.219 810	26
27	.197 899	.198 699	.200 294	.202 670	.207 368	27
28	.186 374	.187 156	.188 714	.191 036	.195 630	28
29	.175 520	.176 283	.177 803	.180 070	.184 557	29
30	.165 299	.166 042	.167 523	.169 733	.174 110	30
31	.155 673	.156 396	.157 838	.159 990	.164 255	31
32	.146 607	.147 310	.148 712	.150 806	.154 957	32
33	.138 069	.138 752	.140 114	.142 149	.146 186	33
34	.130 029	.130 691	.132 013	.133 989	.137 912	34
35	.122 456	.123 099	.124 381	.126 297	.130 105	35
36	.115 325	.115 947	.117 190	.119 047	.122 741	36
37	.108 609	.109 212	.110 414	.112 214	.115 793	37
38	.102 284	.102 867	.104 031	.105 772	.109 239	38
39	.096 328	.096 891	.098 016	.099 700	.103 056	39
40	.090 718	.091 262	.092 349	.093 977	.097 222	40

10%

REVERSION FACTORS
(Present Value of $1)

Base:	2.718 282	1.008 333	1.025 000	1.050 000	1.100 000	
			Frequency of Conversion			
Months	Continuous	Monthly	Quarterly	Semiannual	Annual	Months
0	1.000 000	1.000 000	1.000 000	1.000 000	1.000 000	0
1	.991 701	.991 736	.991 736	.991 736	.991 736	1
2	.983 471	.983 539	.983 607	.983 607	.983 607	2
3	.975 310	.975 411	.975 610	.975 610	.975 610	3
4	.967 216	.967 350	.967 547	.967 742	.967 742	4
5	.959 189	.959 355	.959 616	.960 000	.960 000	5
6	.951 229	.951 427	.951 814	.952 381	.952 381	6
7	.943 335	.943 563	.943 948	.944 510	.944 882	7
8	.935 507	.935 765	.936 211	.936 768	.937 500	8
9	.927 743	.928 032	.928 599	.929 152	.930 233	9
10	.920 044	.920 362	.920 925	.921 659	.923 077	10
11	.912 409	.912 756	.913 376	.914 286	.916 031	11
Years						Years
1	.904 837	.905 212	.905 951	.907 029	.909 091	1
2	.818 731	.819 410	.820 747	.822 702	.826 446	2
3	.740 818	.741 740	.743 556	.746 215	.751 315	3
4	.670 320	.671 432	.673 625	.676 839	.683 013	4
5	.606 531	.607 789	.610 271	.613 913	.620 921	5
6	.548 812	.550 178	.552 875	.556 837	.564 474	6
7	.496 585	.498 028	.500 878	.505 068	.513 158	7
8	.449 329	.450 821	.453 771	.458 112	.466 507	8
9	.406 570	.408 089	.411 094	.415 521	.424 098	9
10	.367 879	.369 407	.372 431	.376 889	.385 543	10
11	.332 871	.334 392	.337 404	.341 850	.350 494	11
12	.301 194	.302 696	.305 671	.310 068	.318 631	12
13	.272 532	.274 004	.276 923	.281 241	.289 664	13
14	.246 597	.248 032	.250 879	.255 094	.263 331	14
15	.223 130	.224 521	.227 284	.231 377	.239 392	15
16	.201 897	.203 240	.205 908	.209 866	.217 629	16
17	.182 684	.183 975	.186 542	.190 355	.197 845	17
18	.165 299	.166 536	.168 998	.172 657	.179 859	18
19	.149 569	.150 751	.153 104	.156 605	.163 508	19
20	.135 335	.136 462	.138 705	.142 046	.148 644	20
21	.122 456	.123 527	.125 659	.128 840	.135 131	21
22	.110 803	.111 818	.113 841	.116 861	.122 846	22
23	.100 259	.101 219	.103 135	.105 997	.111 678	23
24	.090 718	.091 625	.093 435	.096 142	.101 526	24
25	.082 085	.082 940	.084 647	.087 204	.092 296	25
26	.074 274	.075 078	.076 686	.079 096	.083 905	26
27	.067 206	.067 962	.069 474	.071 743	.076 278	27
28	.060 810	.061 520	.062 940	.065 073	.069 343	28
29	.055 023	.055 688	.057 021	.059 023	.063 039	29
30	.049 787	.050 410	.051 658	.053 536	.057 309	30
31	.045 049	.045 632	.046 799	.048 558	.052 099	31
32	.040 762	.041 306	.042 398	.044 044	.047 362	32
33	.036 883	.037 391	.038 410	.039 949	.043 057	33
34	.033 373	.033 847	.034 798	.036 235	.039 143	34
35	.030 197	.030 639	.031 525	.032 866	.035 584	35
36	.027 324	.027 734	.028 560	.029 811	.032 349	36
37	.024 724	.025 105	.025 874	.027 039	.029 408	37
38	.022 371	.022 726	.023 441	.024 525	.026 735	38
39	.020 242	.020 572	.021 236	.022 245	.024 304	39
40	.018 316	.018 622	.019 239	.020 177	.022 095	40

Table 3 - ORDINARY LEVEL ANNUITY (Present Value of $1 per Period)

The present value of a series of future installments or payments of one per period for a given number of periods when discounted at an effective interest rate. This factor is commonly referred to as the *Inwood Coefficient.*

$$a_{\overline{n}|} = \frac{1 - 1/S^n}{i}$$

Where

$a_{\overline{n}|}$ = Level Annuity Factor

$1/S^n$ = Present Value Factor

i = Rate of Interest/Yield

This Table is used in solving problems dealing with the compound discounting of cash flows that are level or effectively level.

Example 1:
What is the Present Value of an ordinary annuity of $1,000 per month for 10 years, assuming an interest rate of 6%?

$1,000 × 90.073453 = $90,073.45

Same example assuming payments in advance.

$1,000 × 90.073453 × 1.005000 = $90,523.82
                         OR
$1,000 × 90.073453/.995025 = $90,523.81

Example 2:
What is the Present Value of an ordinary annuity of $1,000 per month for 10 years and 7 months, assuming an interest rate of 6%?

$1,000 × 90.073453	=	$90,073.45
$1,000 × 6.862074 × .549633*	=	3,771.62
		$93,845.07

* Reversion Factor for 120 months.

Example 2 (Cont.)
Same example assuming payments in advance.

$93,845.07 × 1.005000 = $94,314.30
                OR
$93,845.07/.995025 = $94,314.28

Example 3:
What is the Present Value of an ordinary annuity consisting of the following cash flows at a 6% annual discount rate: $1,000 per year for 5 years; then $2,000 per year for 5 years; then $3,000 per year for 5 years?

$1,000 ×   4.212364   = $ 4,212.36
  2,000 × (7.360087 − 4.212364)   =   6,295.45
  3,000 × (9.712249 − 7.360087)   =   7,056.49
                                                        $17,564.30

Same example assuming payments in advance.

$17,564.30 × 1.060000 = $18,618.16
                OR
$17,564.30/.943396 = $18,618.16

Example 4:
A 10-year level ordinary annuity of $1,000 per month has a Present Value of $90,000. What is the indicated interest/yield rate?

$90,000/$1,000 = 90.000000 (Present Value Factor)

Scan Ordinary Level Annuity tables at 10 years, monthly frequency, for 90.000000.

Closest match is at 6% nominal.

Finding the present value of a future income stream is a discounting procedure in which future payments may be treated as a series of reversions. The present value of a series of future receipts may be quickly ascertained through use of the precomputed present value of one per period factors for the selected discount rate provided the receipts are all equal in amount, equally spaced over time, and receivable at the end of each period.

For example, if the amount to be received one year from today is $1.00, and if 10% per year is a fair rate of interest (or discount), it would be justifiable to pay $0.909091 (10% annual present value of one factor) for the right to receive $1.00 one year from today. Assuming the cost of this right is $0.909091, the $1.00 received at the end of the year would be divided between principal and interest as follows:

Return of principal	$0.90909
Interest on principal for one year @ 10%	0.09091
Total received	$1.00000

If approximately $.091 is the present value of the right to receive $1.00 of income that is to be paid one year from today, coupled with 10% interest, the present value of the right to receive $1.00 two years from today is less. By reference to the present value formula, the present value of that $1.00 to be received two years from today is shown as the factor .826446. The present value of $1.00 payable at the end of two years may be confirmed as follows:

Return on principal	$0.82645[a]
Interest for first year at 10% on 0.82645	0.08264
	$0.90909
Interest for second year at 10% on 0.90909	0.09091
Total principal repayment & interest received	$1.00000

[a]Present value factor, 0.826446 × $1.00 = $0.82645 (rounded).

Similarly, the present value of the right to receive $1.00 at the end of three years is $0.751315, at the end of four years is $0.683013, and at the end of the fifth year is $0.620921. The present value of these rights to receive income at one-year intervals for five years is accumulated as the present value of $1.00 per annum. This is known as the compound interest valuation premise, also referred to as the ordinary annuity factor. Therefore, the sum of the five individual rights to receive $1.00 each year, payable at the end of the year, for five years is $3.790787 (10% annual present value of one per period factor for five years):

Sum of Individual Present Values of $1.00
Payable at the End of the Period

Present value of $1.00 due in 1 year	$0.909091[a]
Present value of $1.00 due in 2 years	.826446[a]
Present value of $1.00 due in 3 years	.751315[a]
Present value of $1.00 due in 4 years	.683013[a]
Present value of $1.00 due in 5 years	.620921[a]
Total (present value of $1.00 per year for 5 years)	$3.790785[b]

[a]10%   Present value of one factor.

[b]10%   Present value of one per period factor is 3.790787 (difference is due to rounding).

Reference to the present value of one per period table for five annual discounting periods (n = 5) gives a factor representing the total of the present values of a series of periodic amounts of $1.00, payable at the end of each period. Thus, the need for the above addition is eliminated, since multiplying $1.00 by the factor for the present value of one per year for five years develops the same present value ($1.00 × 3.790787 = $3.790787).

Restated for appraisal practice, the present value of one period factor may be used to multiply periodic income with the characteristics of an ordinary annuity to derive a present value (investment value) of the right to receive that income stream. The future payments of income provide for recapture of, and interest on, this present value. These present value factors are multipliers and perform the same function as capitalization rates.

The 10% ordinary annuity factor for five years (3.790787) represents the present value of each $1.00 of annual end-of-year collection on the basis of a nominal (annual) discount rate of 10%. Tables or calculations for semiannual, quarterly, and monthly payments are also available. The ordinary annuity factor for semiannual payments in the 10% nominal annual rate table is 7.721735. If payment continues for five years, each $1.00 of semiannual payment represents $10.00 received, but reflects only $7.72 of discounted present value of monthly payments for five years in the monthly table at a 10% nominal rate is 47.065369, indicating that the present value of an ordinary annuity income stream of 60 monthly payments of $1.00 each discounted at a nominal rate of 10%, is 47.065369 × $1.00, or about $47.065.

On the basis of five years at a 10% nominal rate, the semiannual payments involve an effective rate of 5%. In the 5% annuity table, the factor for 10 periods is 7.721735, the same factor as in the 10% semiannual table for a five-year period. Thus, when tables are unavailable at the effective rate, annuity factors for less-than-annual payment periods can be derived using only nominal annual rate tables. Preprogrammed financial calculators can be used to facilitate these calculations.

In computing the present value of an annuity income stream, it may be desirable to assume periodic payments at the beginning instead of the end of each payment period. This is known as an annuity payable in advance, and the present value of such an annuity is equal to the present value of an ordinary annuity (in arrears) multiplied by the base (1 plus the effective interest rate for the discounting period: [1 + i]). Thus, the present value of semiannual payments in advance over a five-year period discounted at a nominal rate of 10% becomes $1.00 × 7.721735 × 1.05 = $8.107822, $8.11 (rounded) instead of $7.72 as computed for payments received at the end of each payment period.

6%

ORDINARY LEVEL ANNUITY
(Present Value of $1 per period)

Base: 1.005 000   1.015 000   1.030 000   1.060 000

Frequency of Payments

Months	Monthly	Quarterly	Semiannual	Annual	Months
1	.995 025	—	—	—	1
2	1.985 099	—	—	—	2
3	2.970 248	.985 222	—	—	3
4	3.950 496	—	—	—	4
5	4.925 866	—	—	—	5
6	5.896 384	1.955 883	.970 874	—	6
7	6.862 074	—	—	—	7
8	7.822 959	—	—	—	8
9	8.779 064	2.912 200	—	—	9
10	9.730 412	—	—	—	10
11	10.677 027	—	—	—	11

Years					Years
1	11.618 932	3.854 385	1.913 470	.943 396	1
2	22.562 866	7.485 925	3.717 098	1.833 393	2
3	32.871 016	10.907 505	5.417 191	2.673 012	3
4	42.580 318	14.131 264	7.019 692	3.465 106	4
5	51.725 561	17.168 639	8.530 203	4.212 364	5
6	60.339 514	20.030 405	9.954 004	4.917 324	6
7	68.453 042	22.726 717	11.296 073	5.582 381	7
8	76.095 218	25.267 139	12.561 102	6.209 794	8
9	83.293 424	27.660 684	13.753 513	6.801 692	9
10	90.073 453	29.915 845	14.877 475	7.360 087	10
11	96.459 599	32.040 622	15.936 917	7.886 875	11
12	102.474 743	34.042 554	16.935 542	8.383 844	12
13	108.140 440	35.928 742	17.876 842	8.852 683	13
14	113.476 990	37.705 879	18.764 108	9.294 984	14
15	118.503 515	39.380 269	19.600 441	9.712 249	15
16	123.238 025	40.957 853	20.388 766	10.105 895	16
17	127.697 486	42.444 228	21.131 837	10.477 260	17
18	131.897 876	43.844 667	21.832 252	10.827 603	18
19	135.854 246	45.164 138	22.492 462	11.158 116	19
20	139.580 772	46.407 323	23.114 772	11.469 921	20
21	143.090 806	47.578 633	23.701 359	11.764 077	21
22	146.396 927	48.682 222	24.254 274	12.041 582	22
23	149.510 979	49.722 007	24.775 449	12.303 379	23
24	152.444 121	50.701 675	25.266 707	12.550 358	24
25	155.206 864	51.624 704	25.729 764	12.783 356	25
26	157.809 106	52.494 366	26.166 240	13.003 166	26
27	160.260 172	53.313 749	26.577 660	13.210 534	27
28	162.568 844	54.085 758	26.965 464	13.406 164	28
29	164.743 394	54.813 133	27.331 005	13.590 721	29
30	166.791 614	55.498 454	27.675 564	13.764 831	30
31	168.720 844	56.144 153	28.000 343	13.929 086	31
32	170.537 996	56.752 520	28.306 478	14.084 043	32
33	172.249 581	57.325 714	28.595 040	14.230 230	33
34	173.861 732	57.865 769	28.867 038	14.368 141	34
35	175.380 226	58.374 599	29.123 421	14.498 246	35
36	176.810 504	58.854 011	29.365 088	14.620 987	36
37	178.157 690	59.305 706	29.592 881	14.736 780	37
38	179.426 611	59.731 286	29.807 598	14.846 019	38
39	180.621 815	60.132 260	30.009 990	14.949 075	39
40	181.747 584	60.510 052	30.200 763	15.046 297	40

10%

ORDINARY LEVEL ANNUITY
(Present Value of $1 per period)

Base:	1.008 333	1.025 000	1.050 000	1.100 000	
		Frequency of Payments			
Months	Monthly	Quarterly	Semiannual	Annual	Months
1	.991 736	—	—	—	1
2	1.975 275	—	—	—	2
3	2.950 686	.975 610	—	—	3
4	3.918 036	—	—	—	4
5	4.877 391	—	—	—	5
6	5.828 817	1.927 424	.952 381	—	6
7	6.772 381	—	—	—	7
8	7.708 146	—	—	—	8
9	8.636 178	2.856 024	—	—	9
10	9.556 540	—	—	—	10
11	10.469 296	—	—	—	11

Years					Years
1	11.374 508	3.761 974	1.859 410	.909 091	1
2	21.670 855	7.170 137	3.545 951	1.735 537	2
3	30.991 236	10.257 765	5.075 692	2.486 852	3
4	39.428 160	13.055 003	6.463 213	3.169 865	4
5	47.065 369	15.589 162	7.721 735	3.790 787	5
6	53.978 665	17.884 986	8.863 252	4.355 261	6
7	60.236 667	19.964 889	9.898 641	4.868 419	7
8	65.901 488	21.849 178	10.837 770	5.334 926	8
9	71.029 355	23.556 251	11.689 587	5.759 024	9
10	75.671 163	25.102 775	12.462 210	6.144 567	10
11	79.872 986	26.503 849	13.163 003	6.495 061	11
12	83.676 528	27.773 154	13.798 642	6.813 692	12
13	87.119 542	28.923 081	14.375 185	7.103 356	13
14	90.236 201	29.964 858	14.898 127	7.366 687	14
15	93.057 439	30.908 656	15.372 451	7.606 080	15
16	95.611 259	31.763 691	15.802 677	7.823 709	16
17	97.923 008	32.538 311	16.192 904	8.021 553	17
18	100.015 633	33.240 078	16.546 852	8.201 412	18
19	101.909 902	33.875 844	16.867 893	8.364 920	19
20	103.624 619	34.451 817	17.159 086	8.513 564	20
21	105.176 801	34.973 620	17.423 208	8.648 694	21
22	106.581 856	35.446 348	17.662 773	8.771 540	22
23	107.853 730	35.874 616	17.880 066	8.883 218	23
24	109.005 045	36.262 606	18.077 158	8.984 744	24
25	110.047 230	36.614 105	18.255 925	9.077 040	25
26	110.990 629	36.932 546	18.418 073	9.160 945	26
27	111.844 605	37.221 039	18.565 146	9.237 223	27
28	112.617 635	37.482 398	18.698 545	9.306 567	28
29	113.317 392	37.719 177	18.819 542	9.369 606	29
30	113.950 820	37.933 687	18.929 290	9.426 914	30
31	114.524 207	38.128 022	19.028 834	9.479 013	31
32	115.043 244	38.304 081	19.119 124	9.526 376	32
33	115.513 083	38.463 581	19.201 019	9.569 432	33
34	115.938 387	38.608 080	19.275 301	9.608 575	34
35	116.323 377	38.738 989	19.342 677	9.644 159	35
36	116.671 876	38.857 586	19.403 788	9.676 508	36
37	116.987 340	38.965 030	19.459 218	9.705 917	37
38	117.272 903	39.062 368	19.509 495	9.732 651	38
39	117.531 398	39.150 552	19.555 098	9.756 956	39
40	117.765 391	39.230 442	19.596 460	9.779 051	40

Table 4 - ORDINARY ANNUITIES CHANGING IN CONSTANT AMOUNT
(Present Value of Annual Payments Starting at $1 and Changing in Constant Amounts)

$$PVF = (1 + hn)a_{\overline{n}|} - \frac{h(n - a_{\overline{n}|})}{i}$$

Where PVF = Present Value Factor

               h = Annual Increase or Decrease after 1st Year

               n = Number of Years

               $a_{\overline{n}|}$ = PVF for Ordinary Level Annuity

               i = Rate of Interest/Yield

               (h is positive for increase; negative for decrease)

This Table is used in solving problems dealing with the compound discounting of cash flows that are best represented by a straight-line pattern of change (increase/decrease).

Example 1:
Assuming a 15% interest/yield rate, what is the Present Value of an ordinary annuity of ten annual cash flows that start at $10,000 and increase $1,000 per year?

$10,000 × 6.7167 = $67,167

Same example assuming payments in advance.

$67,167 × 1.150000 = $77,242
                OR
$67,167/.869565 = $77,242

Example 2:
Assuming a 15% interest/yield rate, what is the Present Value of an ordinary annuity of ten annual cash flows that start at $10,000 and increase $300 per year?

$10,000 × (5.3584 + 5.6979)/2 = $55,282
                       OR
$10,000 × (5.018769 + 16.979477 × .03) = $55,281.53

Example 3:
There are 5 years remaining on a lease that provides a level income of $1,000 per year. Inflation over this period will cause purchasing power to decline an average of 10% per year (straight-line basis). What is the value of the income expressed in constant dollars and discounted at 6%?

$1,000 × (.90 × 4.212364 − 7.934549 × .10) = $2,997.67

PROOF:

Year	Income	×	Inflation Factor	×	PVF @6%	=	Value
1	$1,000	×	.90	×	.943396	=	$ 849.06
2	1,000	×	.80	×	.889996	=	712.00
3	1,000	×	.70	×	.839619	=	587.73
4	1,000	×	.60	×	.792094	=	475.26
5	1,000	×	.50	×	.747258	=	373.63
							$2,997.68

This table is similar to the ordinary level annuity table, except that the annual receipts must be changed in constant dollar amounts. For instance, if the amount to be received one year from today is $10,000 and additional future receipts are expected to increase $1,000 per year for the next nine years and 15% per year is a fair rate of interest, it would be justifiable to pay $67,167 (15% annual present value of one factor) for the right to receive $10,000 one year from today and nine additional payments growing at $1,000 per year for nine additional years. The factor to be applied to the initial receipt as found in this table is 6.7167. The proof is as follows:

Year	Income	×	Present Value Factor	=	Present Value
1	$10,000	×	.869565	=	$ 8,695.65
2	11,000	×	.756144	=	8,317.58
3	12,000	×	.657516	=	7,890.19
4	13,000	×	.571753	=	7,432.79
5	14,000	×	.497177	=	6,960.48
6	15,000	×	.432328	=	6,484.92
7	16,000	×	.375937	=	6,014.99
8	17,000	×	.326902	=	5,557.33
9	18,000	×	.284262	=	5,116.72
10	19,000	×	.247185	=	4,696.50
Present Value					$67,167.17

$$\frac{\text{Present Value}}{\text{Initial Receipt}} = \text{Factor}$$

$$\frac{\$67,167.17}{\$10,000.00} = 6.7167$$

10%
ORDINARY ANNUITIES CHANGING IN CONSTANT AMOUNT
(Present Value of Annual Payments Starting at $1 and Changing in Constant Amounts)

Base: 1.100 000

Annual INCREASE of:

Years	Slope	.00	.02	.04	.05	.10	Years
1	.000 000	.909 091	.9091	.9091	.9091	.9091	1
2	.826 446	1.735 537	1.7521	1.7686	1.7769	1.8182	2
3	2.329 076	2.486 852	2.5334	2.5800	2.6033	2.7198	3
4	4.378 116	3.169 865	3.2574	3.3450	3.3888	3.6077	4
5	6.861 802	3.790 787	3.9280	4.0653	4.1339	4.4770	5
6	9.684 171	4.355 261	4.5489	4.7426	4.8395	5.3237	6
7	12.763 120	4.868 419	5.1237	5.3789	5.5066	6.1447	7
8	16.028 672	5.334 926	5.6555	5.9761	6.1364	6.9378	8
9	19.421 453	5.759 024	6.1475	6.5359	6.7301	7.7012	9
10	22.891 342	6.144 567	6.6024	7.0602	7.2891	8.4337	10
11	26.396 281	6.495 061	7.0230	7.5509	7.8149	9.1347	11
12	29.901 220	6.813 692	7.4117	8.0097	8.3088	9.8038	12
13	33.377 193	7.103 356	7.7709	8.4384	8.7722	10.4411	13
14	36.800 499	7.366 687	8.1027	8.8387	9.2067	11.0467	14
15	40.151 988	7.606 080	8.4091	9.2122	9.6137	11.6213	15
16	43.416 425	7.823 709	8.6920	9.5604	9.9945	12.1654	16
17	46.581 939	8.021 553	8.9532	9.8848	10.3507	12.6797	17
18	49.639 539	8.201 412	9.1942	10.1870	10.6834	13.1654	18
19	52.582 683	8.364 920	9.4166	10.4682	10.9941	13.6232	19
20	55.406 912	8.513 564	9.6217	10.7298	11.2839	14.0543	20

Annual DECREASE of:

Years	Slope	.00	.02	.04	.05	.10	Years
1	.000 000	.909 091	.9091	.9091	.9091	.9091	1
2 —	.826 446	1.735 537	1.7190	1.7025	1.6942	1.6529	2
3 —	2.329 076	2.486 852	2.4403	2.3937	2.3704	2.2539	3
4 —	4.378 116	3.169 865	3.0823	2.9947	2.9510	2.7321	4
5 —	6.861 802	3.790 787	3.6536	3.5163	3.4477	3.1046	5
6 —	9.684 171	4.355 261	4.1616	3.9679	3.8711	3.3868	6
7 —	12.763 120	4.868 419	4.6132	4.3579	4.2303	3.5921	7
8 —	16.028 672	5.334 926	5.0144	4.6938	4.5335	3.7321	8
9 —	19.421 453	5.759 024	5.3706	4.9822	4.7880	3.8169	9
10 —	22.891 342	6.144 567	5.6867	5.2289	5.0000	3.8554	10
11 —	26.396 281	6.495 061	5.9671	5.4392	5.1752	—	11
12 —	29.901 220	6.813 692	6.2157	5.6176	5.3186	—	12
13 —	33.377 193	7.103 356	6.4358	5.7683	5.4345	—	13
14 —	36.800 499	7.366 687	6.6307	5.8947	5.5267	—	14
15 —	40.151 988	7.606 080	6.8030	6.0000	5.5985	—	15
16 —	43.416 425	7.823 709	6.9554	6.0871	5.6529	—	16
17 —	46.581 939	8.021 553	7.0899	6.1583	5.6925	—	17
18 —	49.639 539	8.201 412	7.2086	6.2158	5.7194	—	18
19 —	52.582 683	8.364 920	7.3133	6.2616	5.7358	—	19
20 —	55.406 912	8.513 564	7.4054	6.2973	5.7432	—	20

15%
ORDINARY ANNUITIES CHANGING IN CONSTANT AMOUNT
(Present Value of Annual Payments Starting at $1 and Changing in Constant Amounts)

Base: 1.150 000

Annual INCREASE of:

Years	Slope	.00	.02	.04	.05	.10	Years
1	.000 000	.869 565	.8696	.8696	.8696	.8696	1
2	.756 144	1.625 709	1.6408	1.6560	1.6635	1.7013	2
3	2.071 176	2.283 225	2.3246	2.3661	2.3868	2.4903	3
4	3.786 436	2.854 978	2.9307	3.0064	3.0443	3.2336	4
5	5.775 143	3.352 155	3.4677	3.5832	3.6409	3.9297	5
6	7.936 781	3.784 483	3.9432	4.1020	4.1813	4.5782	6
7	10.192 403	4.160 420	4.3643	4.5681	4.6700	5.1797	7
8	12.480 715	4.487 322	4.7369	4.9866	5.1114	5.7354	8
9	14.754 815	4.771 584	5.0667	5.3618	5.5093	6.2471	9
10	16.979 477	5.018 769	5.3584	5.6979	5.8677	6.7167	10
11	19.128 909	5.233 712	5.6163	5.9989	6.1902	7.1466	11
12	21.184 888	5.420 619	5.8443	6.2680	6.4799	7.5391	12
13	23.135 223	5.583 147	6.0459	6.5086	6.7399	7.8967	13
14	24.972 496	5.724 476	6.2239	6.7234	6.9731	8.2217	14
15	26.693 019	5.847 370	6.3812	6.9151	7.1820	8.5167	15
16	28.295 990	5.954 235	6.5202	7.0861	7.3690	8.7838	16
17	29.782 805	6.047 161	6.6428	7.2385	7.5363	9.0254	17
18	31.156 492	6.127 966	6.7511	7.3742	7.6858	9.2436	18
19	32.421 267	6.198 231	6.8467	7.4951	7.8193	9.4404	19
20	33.582 173	6.259 331	6.9310	7.6026	7.9384	9.6175	20

Annual DECREASE of:

Years	Slope	.00	.02	.04	.05	.10	Years
1	.000 000	.869 565	.8696	.8696	.8696	.8696	1
2	—.756 144	1.625 709	1.6106	1.5955	1.5879	1.5501	2
3	—2.071 176	2.283 225	2.2418	2.2004	2.1797	2.0761	3
4	—3.786 436	2.854 978	2.7792	2.7035	2.6657	2.4763	4
5	—5.775 143	3.352 155	3.2367	3.1211	3.0634	2.7746	5
6	—7.936 781	3.784 483	3.6257	3.4670	3.3876	2.9908	6
7	—10.192 403	4.160 420	3.9566	3.7527	3.6508	3.1412	7
8	—12.480 715	4.487 322	4.2377	3.9881	3.8633	3.2392	8
9	—14.754 815	4.771 584	4.4765	4.1814	4.0338	3.2961	9
10	—16.979 477	5.018 769	4.6792	4.3396	4.1698	3.3208	10
11	—19.128 909	5.233 712	4.8511	4.4686	4.2773	—	11
12	—21.184 888	5.420 619	4.9969	4.5732	4.3614	—	12
13	—23.135 223	5.583 147	5.1204	4.6577	4.4264	—	13
14	—24.972 496	5.724 476	5.2250	4.7256	4.4759	—	14
15	—26.693 019	5.847 370	5.3135	4.7796	4.5127	—	15
16	—28.295 990	5.954 235	5.3883	4.8224	4.5394	—	16
17	—29.782 805	6.047 161	5.4515	4.8558	4.5580	—	17
18	—31.156 492	6.127 966	5.5048	4.8817	4.5701	—	18
19	—32.421 267	6.198 231	5.5498	4.9014	4.5772	—	19
20	—33.582 173	6.259 331	5.5877	4.9160	4.5802	—	20

Table 5 - ORDINARY ANNUITIES CHANGING IN CONSTANT RATIO
(Present Value of Annual Payments Starting at $1
and Changing in Constant Ratio)

$$PVF = \frac{1 - (1 + x)^n/(1 + i)^n}{i - x}$$

Where   PVF = Present Value Factor

               x = Constant Ratio Change in Income

               n = Number of Years

               i = Rate of Interest/Yield

               (x is positive for increase; negative for decrease)

This table is used in solving problems dealing with the compound discounting of cash flows that are best represented by an exponential-curve pattern of change (increase/decrease).

Example 1:
Assuming a 15% interest/yield rate, what is the Present Value of an ordinary annuity of ten annual cash flows that start at $10,000 and increase 10% per year compounded?

$10,000 × 7.1773 = $71,773

Same example assuming payments in advance.

$71,773 × 1.150000 = $82,539
                 OR
$71,773/.869565 = $82,539

Example 2:
Assuming a 15% interest/yield rate, what is the Present Value of an ordinary annuity of ten annual cash flows that start at $10,000 and decrease 3% per year compounded?

$10,000 × 4.5429 = $45,429

Example 3:

There are 5 years remaining on a lease that provides a level income of $1,000 per year. Inflation over this period will cause purchasing power to decline 10% per year (compound basis). What is the value of the income expressed in constant dollars and discounted at 6%?

$1,000 × .90 × 3.4922 = $3,142.98

PROOF:

Year	Income	×	Inflation Factor	×	PVF @6%	=	Value
1	$1,000	×	.900000	×	.943396	=	$ 849.06
2	1,000	×	.810000	×	.889996	=	720.90
3	1,000	×	.729000	×	.839619	=	612.08
4	1,000	×	.656100	×	.792094	=	519.69
5	1,000	×	.590490	×	.747258	=	441.25
							$3,142.98

6%

ORDINARY ANNUITIES CHANGING IN CONSTANT RATIO

(Present Value of Annual Payments Starting at $1 and Changing in Constant Ratio)

Base: **1.060 000**

Annual Percentage INCREASE of:

Years	7%	8%	9%	10%	11%	12%	Years
1	.9434	.9434	.9434	.9434	.9434	.9434	1
2	1.8957	1.9046	1.9135	1.9224	1.9313	1.9402	2
3	2.8570	2.8839	2.9110	2.9383	2.9658	2.9934	3
4	3.8273	3.8817	3.9368	3.9926	4.0491	4.1062	4
5	4.8068	4.8984	4.9916	5.0867	5.1835	5.2821	5
6	5.7956	5.9342	6.0763	6.2220	6.3714	6.5245	6
7	6.7936	6.9896	7.1917	7.4002	7.6153	7.8372	7
8	7.8011	8.0648	8.3386	8.6229	8.9179	9.2242	8
9	8.8181	9.1604	9.5180	9.8916	10.2820	10.6897	9
10	9.8447	10.2766	10.7308	11.2083	11.7104	12.2382	10
11	10.8810	11.4139	11.9779	12.5747	13.2061	13.8743	11
12	11.9270	12.5727	13.2603	13.9926	14.7725	15.6030	12
13	12.9829	13.7533	14.5790	15.4640	16.4127	17.4296	13
14	14.0488	14.9562	15.9350	16.9909	18.1302	19.3596	14
15	15.1247	16.1818	17.3294	18.5755	19.9288	21.3988	15
16	16.2108	17.4305	18.7632	20.2199	21.8123	23.5534	16
17	17.3072	18.7028	20.2376	21.9263	23.7846	25.8301	17
18	18.4138	19.9990	21.7538	23.6971	25.8499	28.2355	18
19	19.5309	21.3198	23.3129	25.5347	28.0126	30.7772	19
20	20.6586	22.6654	24.9161	27.4417	30.2773	33.4627	20

Annual Percentage DECREASE of:

Years	7%	8%	9%	10%	11%	12%	Years
1	.9434	.9434	.9434	.9434	.9434	.9434	1
2	1.7711	1.7622	1.7533	1.7444	1.7355	1.7266	2
3	2.4973	2.4728	2.4486	2.4245	2.4006	2.3768	3
4	3.1344	3.0896	3.0455	3.0019	2.9590	2.9166	4
5	3.6934	3.6250	3.5579	3.4922	3.4278	3.3647	5
6	4.1838	4.0896	3.9978	3.9085	3.8215	3.7367	6
7	4.6141	4.4929	4.3755	4.2619	4.1520	4.0456	7
8	4.9916	4.8429	4.6997	4.5620	4.4295	4.3020	8
9	5.3228	5.1466	4.9781	4.8168	4.6625	4.5149	9
10	5.6134	5.4103	5.2170	5.0331	4.8581	4.6916	10
11	5.8684	5.6391	5.4222	5.2168	5.0224	4.8383	11
12	6.0921	5.8377	5.5983	5.3728	5.1603	4.9601	12
13	6.2883	6.0101	5.7495	5.5052	5.2761	5.0612	13
14	6.4605	6.1597	5.8792	5.6176	5.3733	5.1452	14
15	6.6116	6.2896	5.9907	5.7131	5.4550	5.2148	15
16	6.7441	6.4023	6.0863	5.7941	5.5235	5.2727	16
17	6.8604	6.5001	6.1685	5.8629	5.5811	5.3207	17
18	6.9624	6.5850	6.2390	5.9213	5.6294	5.3606	18
19	7.0520	6.6587	6.2995	5.9710	5.6700	5.3937	19
20	7.1305	6.7226	6.3514	6.0131	5.7040	5.4212	20

10%

ORDINARY ANNUITIES CHANGING IN CONSTANT RATIO

(Present Value of Annual Payments Starting at $1 and Changing in Constant Ratio)

Base: 1.100 000

Annual Percentage INCREASE of:

Years	1%	2%	3%	4%	5%	6%	Years
1	.9091	.9091	.9091	.9091	.9091	.9091	1
2	1.7438	1.7521	1.7603	1.7686	1.7769	1.7851	2
3	2.5102	2.5337	2.5574	2.5812	2.6052	2.6293	3
4	3.2139	3.2586	3.3037	3.3495	3.3959	3.4428	4
5	3.8601	3.9307	4.0026	4.0759	4.1506	4.2267	5
6	4.4533	4.5539	4.6570	4.7627	4.8710	4.9821	6
7	4.9981	5.1318	5.2697	5.4120	5.5587	5.7100	7
8	5.4982	5.6677	5.8435	6.0259	6.2151	6.4115	8
9	5.9575	6.1646	6.3807	6.6063	6.8417	7.0874	9
10	6.3791	6.6253	6.8837	7.1550	7.4398	7.7388	10
11	6.7663	7.0526	7.3548	7.6738	8.0107	8.3664	11
12	7.1218	7.4487	7.7958	8.1644	8.5557	8.9713	12
13	7.4482	7.8161	8.2088	8.6281	9.0759	9.5542	13
14	7.7479	8.1568	8.5955	9.0666	9.5724	10.1158	14
15	8.0230	8.4726	8.9576	9.4811	10.0464	10.6571	15
16	8.2757	8.7655	9.2967	9.8731	10.4989	11.1786	16
17	8.5077	9.0371	9.6142	10.2436	10.9307	11.6812	17
18	8.7207	9.2890	9.9115	10.5940	11.3430	12.1656	18
19	8.9163	9.5225	10.1898	10.9252	11.7365	12.6323	19
20	9.0959	9.7390	10.4505	11.2384	12.1121	13.0820	20

Annual Percentage DECREASE of:

Years	1%	2%	3%	4%	5%	6%	Years
1	.9091	.9091	.9091	.9091	.9091	.9091	1
2	1.7273	1.7190	1.7107	1.7025	1.6942	1.6860	2
3	2.4636	2.4406	2.4177	2.3949	2.3723	2.3498	3
4	3.1264	3.0834	3.0410	2.9992	2.9579	2.9171	4
5	3.7228	3.6561	3.5907	3.5266	3.4636	3.4019	5
6	4.2596	4.1664	4.0755	3.9868	3.9004	3.8162	6
7	4.7428	4.6210	4.5029	4.3885	4.2776	4.1702	7
8	5.1776	5.0259	4.8798	4.7390	4.6034	4.4727	8
9	5.5689	5.3867	5.2122	5.0450	4.8848	4.7312	9
10	5.9211	5.7082	5.5053	5.3120	5.1277	4.9521	10
11	6.2381	5.9946	5.7638	5.5450	5.3376	5.1409	11
12	6.5234	6.2497	5.9917	5.7484	5.5188	5.3022	12
13	6.7801	6.4770	6.1927	5.9259	5.6754	5.4401	13
14	7.0112	6.6795	6.3699	6.0807	5.8105	5.5579	14
15	7.2192	6.8599	6.5262	6.2159	5.9273	5.6586	15
16	7.4063	7.0207	6.6640	6.3339	6.0281	5.7446	16
17	7.5748	7.1639	6.7855	6.4369	6.1152	5.8181	17
18	7.7264	7.2914	6.8927	6.5267	6.1904	5.8809	18
19	7.8629	7.4051	6.9872	6.6051	6.2553	5.9346	19
20	7.9857	7.5064	7.0705	6.6736	6.3114	5.9805	20

15%

ORDINARY ANNUITIES CHANGING IN CONSTANT RATIO

(Present Value of Annual Payments Starting at $1 and Changing in Constant Ratio)

Base: 1.150 000

Annual Percentage INCREASE of:

Years	7%	8%	9%	10%	11%	12%	Years
1	.8696	.8696	.8696	.8696	.8696	.8696	1
2	1.6786	1.6862	1.6938	1.7013	1.7089	1.7164	2
3	2.4314	2.4531	2.4750	2.4969	2.5190	2.5412	3
4	3.1319	3.1734	3.2154	3.2579	3.3010	3.3445	4
5	3.7835	3.8498	3.9172	3.9858	4.0557	4.1268	5
6	4.3899	4.4850	4.5824	4.6821	4.7842	4.8887	6
7	4.9541	5.0816	5.2129	5.3481	5.4874	5.6308	7
8	5.4790	5.6418	5.8105	5.9851	6.1661	6.3534	8
9	5.9674	6.1680	6.3769	6.5945	6.8212	7.0573	9
10	6.4219	6.6621	6.9137	7.1773	7.4535	7.7427	10
11	6.8447	7.1261	7.4226	7.7348	8.0638	8.4103	11
12	7.2381	7.5619	7.9049	8.2681	8.6529	9.0605	12
13	7.6042	7.9712	8.3620	8.7782	9.2215	9.6937	13
14	7.9447	8.3556	8.7953	9.2661	9.7703	10.3104	14
15	8.2616	8.7165	9.2060	9.7328	10.3000	10.9110	15
16	8.5565	9.0555	9.5952	10.1792	10.8113	11.4959	16
17	8.8308	9.3739	9.9642	10.6062	11.3048	12.0656	17
18	9.0861	9.6729	10.3139	11.0146	11.7812	12.6204	18
19	9.3235	9.9537	10.6453	11.4053	12.2410	13.1607	19
20	9.5445	10.2173	10.9595	11.7790	12.6848	13.6870	20

Annual Percentage DECREASE of:

Years	7%	8%	9%	10%	11%	12%	Years
1	.8696	.8696	.8696	.8696	.8696	.8696	1
2	1.5728	1.5652	1.5577	1.5501	1.5425	1.5350	2
3	2.1415	2.1217	2.1021	2.0827	2.0634	2.0442	3
4	2.6014	2.5670	2.5330	2.4995	2.4664	2.4338	4
5	2.9733	2.9231	2.8739	2.8257	2.7784	2.7319	5
6	3.2740	3.2081	3.1437	3.0810	3.0198	2.9601	6
7	3.5173	3.4360	3.3572	3.2808	3.2066	3.1347	7
8	3.7140	3.6184	3.5261	3.4371	3.3512	3.2683	8
9	3.8730	3.7643	3.6598	3.5595	3.4631	3.3705	9
10	4.0017	3.8810	3.7656	3.6552	3.5497	3.4487	10
11	4.1057	3.9744	3.8493	3.7302	3.6167	3.5086	11
12	4.1898	4.0490	3.9155	3.7888	3.6686	3.5544	12
13	4.2579	4.1088	3.9679	3.8348	3.7087	3.5895	13
14	4.3129	4.1566	4.0094	3.8707	3.7398	3.6163	14
15	4.3574	4.1949	4.0422	3.8988	3.7639	3.6368	15
16	4.3934	4.2254	4.0682	3.9208	3.7825	3.6525	16
17	4.4224	4.2499	4.0888	3.9380	3.7969	3.6645	17
18	4.4460	4.2695	4.1050	3.9515	3.8080	3.6737	18
19	4.4650	4.2852	4.1179	3.9620	3.8166	3.6808	19
20	4.4804	4.2977	4.1281	3.9703	3.8233	3.6862	20

Table 6 - SINKING FUND FACTORS (Periodic Payment to Grow to $1)

The level periodic investment or deposit required to accumulate one in a given number of periods including the accumulation of interest at the effective rate. This is commonly known as the *amortization rate* and is reciprocal to the corresponding factor from Table 7.

$$1/S_{\overline{n}|} = \frac{i}{S^n - 1}$$

Where $1/S_{\overline{n}|}$ = Sinking Fund Factor

             i = Effective Rate of Interest

             n = Number of Compounding Periods

             S^n = Future Value Factor

This table is used in solving problems dealing with the calculation of required sinking fund deposits and/or the provision for change in capital value in investment situations where the income/payments are level.

Example 1:
Assuming a 6% interest rate, what monthly, end-of-period deposit is required to provide $10,000 in 10 years?

$10,000 × .006102 = $61.02

Same example except deposits at the beginning of the period.

$10,000 × .006102/1.005 = $60.72

Example 2:
Assuming a 6% interest rate, what monthly, end-of-period deposit is required to provide $10,000 in 10 years and 7 months?

$10,000/(1/.006102 + 1.819397*/.140729) = $56.56

* Future Value Factor for 120 months.

Same example except deposits at the beginning of the period.

$56.56/1.005 = $56.28

Example 3:
What is the annual constant for a direct reduction loan, 12% interest, monthly payments for 25 years?

.12 + 12 × .000532 = .126384*

*Actually, loan payments are rounded up to the nearest penny or more and published tables of annual constants will reflect this practice. One common table of annual constants is calculated for $1,000 of loan, which means that the sinking fund factor is rounded up in the 5th decimal place. On this basis, the constant for a 12%, 25-year loan would be:

.12 + 12 × .000540 = .126480

Example 4:
Assuming a 12% interest/yield rate, what monthly payment will provide for interest and 40% amortization of a $100,000 loan in 10 years?

$100,000 × (.12/12 + .4 × .004347) = $1,173.88

Example 5:
A property has an anticipated net operating income of $10,000 per year for the next 5 years and the trend in prices indicates a 15% increase in value over that period of time. What is the calculated value, assuming that a 12% yield rate is appropriate?

$10,000/(.12 − .15 × .157410) = $103,747

Assuming deposits made at the end of each compounding period, as in the future value of one per period, these factors reflect the fractional portion of $1.00 that must be deposited periodically at specified interest to accumulate to $1.00 by the end of the series of deposits.

Assuming that $10,000 is to be accumulated over a 10-year period and that annual deposits will be compounded at 10% interest, the factor on the 10-year line in the sinking fund column of the 10% annual table reveals that each annual deposit must be in the amount of $10,000 × .062745, or $627.45.

This table is used in solving problems dealing with the calculation of required sinking fund deposits and the provision for change in capital value in investment situations in which the income or payments are level.

6%

SINKING FUND FACTORS
(Periodic Payment to Grow to $1)

Base:

	1.005 000	1.015 000	1.030 000	1.060 000	1.061 831	
		Frequency of Payments and of Conversions				
					Annual Payment Daily	
Months	Monthly	Quarterly	Semiannual	Annual	Conversion	Months
1	1.000 000	—	—	—	—	1
2	.498 753	—	—	—	—	2
3	.331 672	1.000 000	—	—	—	3
4	.248 133	—	—	—	—	4
5	.198 010	—	—	—	—	5
6	.164 595	.496 278	1.000 000	—	—	6
7	.140 729	—	—	—	—	7
8	.122 829	—	—	—	—	8
9	.108 907	.328 383	—	—	—	9
10	.097 771	—	—	—	—	10
11	.088 659	—	—	—	—	11
Years						Years
1	.081 066	.244 445	.492 611	1.000 000	1.000 000	1
2	.039 321	.118 584	.239 027	.485 437	.485 006	2
3	.025 422	.076 680	.154 598	.314 110	.313 547	3
4	.018 485	.055 765	.112 456	.228 591	.227 971	4
5	.014 333	.043 246	.087 231	.177 396	.176 749	5
6	.011 573	.034 924	.070 462	.143 363	.142 703	6
7	.009 609	.029 001	.058 526	.119 135	.118 471	7
8	.008 141	.024 577	.049 611	.101 036	.100 374	8
9	.007 006	.021 152	.042 709	.087 022	.086 365	9
10	.006 102	.018 427	.037 216	.075 868	.075 218	10
11	.005 367	.016 210	.032 747	.066 793	.066 152	11
12	.004 759	.014 375	.029 047	.059 277	.058 646	12
13	.004 247	.012 833	.025 938	.052 960	.052 340	13
14	.003 812	.011 521	.023 293	.047 585	.046 977	14
15	.003 439	.010 393	.021 019	.042 963	.042 367	15
16	.003 114	.009 415	.019 047	.038 952	.038 369	16
17	.002 831	.008 560	.017 322	.035 445	.034 875	17
18	.002 582	.007 808	.015 804	.032 357	.031 799	18
19	.002 361	.007 141	.014 459	.029 621	.029 077	19
20	.002 164	.006 548	.013 262	.027 185	.026 654	20
21	.001 989	.006 018	.012 192	.025 005	.024 487	21
22	.001 831	.005 541	.011 230	.023 046	.022 541	22
23	.001 688	.005 112	.010 363	.021 278	.020 787	23
24	.001 560	.004 723	.009 578	.019 679	.019 201	24
25	.001 443	.004 371	.008 865	.018 227	.017 762	25
26	.001 337	.004 050	.008 217	.016 904	.016 452	26
27	.001 240	.003 757	.007 626	.015 697	.015 258	27
28	.001 151	.003 489	.007 084	.014 593	.014 166	28
29	.001 070	.003 244	.006 588	.013 580	.013 165	29
30	.000 996	.003 019	.006 133	.012 649	.012 247	30
31	.000 927	.002 811	.005 714	.011 792	.011 402	31
32	.000 864	.002 620	.005 328	.011 002	.010 624	32
33	.000 806	.002 444	.004 971	.010 273	.009 906	33
34	.000 752	.002 281	.004 642	.009 598	.009 243	34
35	.000 702	.002 131	.004 337	.008 974	.008 630	35
36	.000 656	.001 991	.004 054	.008 395	.008 062	36
37	.000 613	.001 862	.003 792	.007 857	.007 535	37
38	.000 573	.001 742	.003 548	.007 358	.007 046	38
39	.000 536	.001 630	.003 322	.006 894	.006 592	39
40	.000 502	.001 526	.003 112	.006 462	.006 170	40

10%   SINKING FUND FACTORS

(Periodic Payment to Grow to $1)

Base: 1.008 333   1.025 000   1.050 000   1.100 000   1.105 156

Frequency of Payments and of Conversions

Months	Monthly	Quarterly	Semiannual	Annual	Annual Payment Daily Conversion	Months
1	1.000 000	—	—	—	—	1
2	.497 925	—	—	—	—	2
3	.330 571	1.000 000	—	—	—	3
4	.246 897	—	—	—	—	4
5	.196 694	—	—	—	—	5
6	.163 228	.493 827	1.000 000	—	—	6
7	.139 325	—	—	—	—	7
8	.121 400	—	—	—	—	8
9	.107 459	.325 137	—	—	—	9
10	.096 307	—	—	—	—	10
11	.087 184	—	—	—	—	11

Years						Years
1	.079 583	.240 818	.487 805	1.000 000	1.000 000	1
2	.037 812	.114 467	.232 012	.476 190	.475 024	2
3	.023 934	.072 487	.147 017	.302 115	.300 614	3
4	.017 029	.051 599	.104 722	.215 471	.213 843	4
5	.012 914	.039 147	.079 505	.163 797	.162 125	5
6	.010 193	.030 913	.062 825	.129 607	.127 932	6
7	.008 268	.025 088	.051 024	.105 405	.103 749	7
8	.006 841	.020 768	.042 270	.087 444	.085 821	8
9	.005 745	.017 452	.035 546	.073 641	.072 059	9
10	.004 882	.014 836	.030 243	.062 745	.061 212	10
11	.004 187	.012 730	.025 971	.053 963	.052 481	11
12	.003 617	.011 006	.022 471	.046 763	.045 334	12
13	.003 145	.009 574	.019 564	.040 779	.039 404	13
14	.002 749	.008 372	.017 123	.035 746	.034 427	14
15	.002 413	.007 353	.015 051	.031 474	.030 211	15
16	.002 126	.006 482	.013 280	.027 817	.026 609	16
17	.001 879	.005 733	.011 755	.024 664	.023 511	17
18	.001 665	.005 084	.010 434	.021 930	.020 831	18
19	.001 479	.004 520	.009 284	.019 547	.018 500	19
20	.001 317	.004 026	.008 278	.017 460	.016 464	20
21	.001 174	.003 593	.007 395	.015 624	.014 679	21
22	.001 049	.003 212	.006 616	.014 005	.013 108	22
23	.000 938	.002 875	.005 928	.012 572	.011 722	23
24	.000 841	.002 577	.005 318	.011 300	.010 495	24
25	.000 754	.002 312	.004 777	.010 168	.009 407	25
26	.000 676	.002 076	.004 294	.009 159	.008 440	26
27	.000 608	.001 867	.003 864	.008 258	.007 579	27
28	.000 546	.001 679	.003 480	.007 451	.006 811	28
29	.000 491	.001 512	.003 136	.006 728	.006 126	29
30	.000 442	.001 362	.002 828	.006 079	.005 512	30
31	.000 398	.001 227	.002 552	.005 496	.004 963	31
32	.000 359	.001 107	.002 304	.004 972	.004 471	32
33	.000 324	.000 999	.002 081	.004 499	.004 029	33
34	.000 292	.000 901	.001 880	.004 074	.003 632	34
35	.000 263	.000 814	.001 699	.003 690	.003 276	35
36	.000 238	.000 735	.001 536	.003 343	.002 955	36
37	.000 215	.000 664	.001 390	.003 030	.002 667	37
38	.000 194	.000 600	.001 257	.002 747	.002 408	38
39	.000 175	.000 542	.001 138	.002 491	.002 174	39
40	.000 158	.000 490	.001 030	.002 259	.001 963	40

12%

SINKING FUND FACTORS
(Periodic Payment to Grow to $1)

Base: 1.010 000   1.030 000   1.060 000   1.120 000   1.127 474

Frequency of Payments and of Conversions

Months	Monthly	Quarterly	Semiannual	Annual	Annual Payment Daily Conversion	Months
1	1.000 000	—	—	—	—	1
2	.497 512	—	—	—	—	2
3	.330 022	1.000 000	—	—	—	3
4	.246 281	—	—	—	—	4
5	.196 040	—	—	—	—	5
6	.162 548	.492 611	1.000 000	—	—	6
7	.138 628	—	—	—	—	7
8	.120 690	—	—	—	—	8
9	.106 740	.323 530	—	—	—	9
10	.095 582	—	—	—	—	10
11	.086 454	—	—	—	—	11

Years						Years
1	.078 849	.239 027	.485 437	1.000 000	1.000 000	1
2	.037 073	.112 456	.228 591	.471 698	.470 041	2
3	.023 214	.070 462	.143 363	.296 349	.294 233	3
4	.016 334	.049 611	.101 036	.209 234	.206 957	4
5	.012 244	.037 216	.075 868	.157 410	.155 090	5
6	.009 550	.029 047	.059 277	.123 226	.120 922	6
7	.007 653	.023 293	.047 585	.099 118	.096 862	7
8	.006 253	.019 047	.038 952	.081 303	.079 114	8
9	.005 184	.015 804	.032 357	.067 679	.065 568	9
10	.004 347	.013 262	.027 185	.056 984	.054 959	10
11	.003 678	.011 230	.023 046	.048 415	.046 479	11
12	.003 134	.009 578	.019 679	.041 437	.039 592	12
13	.002 687	.008 217	.016 904	.035 677	.033 925	13
14	.002 314	.007 084	.014 593	.030 871	.029 210	14
15	.002 002	.006 133	.012 649	.026 824	.025 253	15
16	.001 737	.005 328	.011 002	.023 390	.021 907	16
17	.001 512	.004 642	.009 598	.020 457	.019 060	17
18	.001 320	.004 054	.008 395	.017 937	.016 624	18
19	.001 154	.003 548	.007 358	.015 763	.014 530	19
20	.001 011	.003 112	.006 462	.013 879	.012 724	20
21	.000 887	.002 733	.005 683	.012 240	.011 159	21
22	.000 779	.002 404	.005 006	.010 811	.009 800	22
23	.000 686	.002 117	.004 415	.009 560	.008 617	23
24	.000 604	.001 866	.003 898	.008 463	.007 585	24
25	.000 532	.001 647	.003 444	.007 500	.006 683	25
26	.000 470	.001 454	.003 046	.006 652	.005 892	26
27	.000 414	.001 285	.002 696	.005 904	.005 199	27
28	.000 366	.001 136	.002 388	.005 244	.004 590	28
29	.000 324	.001 005	.002 116	.004 660	.004 054	29
30	.000 286	.000 890	.001 876	.004 144	.003 583	30
31	.000 253	.000 788	.001 664	.003 686	.003 168	31
32	.000 224	.000 698	.001 476	.003 280	.002 802	32
33	.000 198	.000 619	.001 310	.002 920	.002 479	33
34	.000 176	.000 548	.001 163	.002 601	.002 194	34
35	.000 155	.000 486	.001 033	.002 317	.001 942	35
36	.000 138	.000 431	.000 918	.002 064	.001 719	36
37	.000 122	.000 383	.000 815	.001 840	.001 523	37
38	.000 108	.000 339	.000 725	.001 640	.001 349	38
39	.000 096	.000 301	.000 644	.001 462	.001 195	39
40	.000 085	.000 267	.000 573	.001 304	.001 059	40

Table 7 - SINKING FUND ACCUMULATION FACTORS (Future Value of Periodic Payments of $1)

The total accumulation of principal and interest of a series of deposits or installments of one per period for a given number of periods with interest at the effective rate per period. This factor is also known as the *amount of one per period*. It is reciprocal to the corresponding factor from Table 6.

$$S_{\overline{n}|} = \frac{S^n - 1}{i}$$

Where

$S_{\overline{n}|}$ = Sinking Fund Accumulation Factor

i = Effective Rate of Interest

S^n = Future Value Factor

This table is used in solving problems dealing with the growth of sinking funds and/or the calculation of capital recovery in investment situations where the income/payments are level.

Example 1:
Assuming a 6% nominal interest rate, how much money would be accumulated if month-end deposits of $100 were made for a period of 10 years?

$100 × 163.879347 = $16,387.93

Same example except deposits made at the beginning of each month.

$16,387.93 × 1.005 = $16,469.87

Example 2:
Assuming a 6% nominal interest rate, how much money would be accumulated if month-end deposits of $100 were made for a period of 10 years and 7 months?

$100 × (163.879347 + 7.105879 × 1.819397*) = $17,680.78

* Future Value Factor for 120 months
OR
$100 × (7.105879 + 163.879347 × 1.035529*) = $17,680.77

* Future Value Factor for 7 months

Example 3:
Assuming a 6% nominal interest rate and daily compounding, how much money would be accumulated in a Keogh Retirement Plan if year-end deposits of $1,200 were made for 10 years?

$1,200 × 13.294699 = $15,953.64

Same example except deposits made at the beginning of each year.

$15,953.64 × 1.061831 = $16,940.07

Example 4:
Given a $100,000 loan with monthly payments of $908.71 including nominal interest at 10%, how much will be paid off in 10 years?

[$908.71 − ($100,000 × .10/12)] × 204.844979 = $15,440.53

These factors are similar to the amount of one (future value of one) except that deposits are periodic (a series) and are assumed to be made at the *end* of the first compounding period and periodically thereafter at the *end* of each period. Thus, the initial deposit, made at the end of the first period, has earned no interest and the factor for the first period is 1.000000.

If compounding is at 10% annually for 10 years, the factor of 15.937425 reveals that a series of 10 deposits of $1.00 each made at the end of each of the 10 years will have accumulated to $1.00 × 15.937425, or almost $15.94.

6%   SINKING FUND ACCUMULATION FACTORS
(Future Value of Periodic Payments of $1)

Base:	1.005 000	1.015 000	1.030 000	1.060 000	1.061 831	

Frequency of Payments and of Conversions

Months	Monthly	Quarterly	Semiannual	Annual	Annual Payment Daily Conversion	Months
1	1.000 000	—	—	—	—	1
2	2.005 000	—	—	—	—	2
3	3.015 025	1.000 000	—	—	—	3
4	4.030 100	—	—	—	—	4
5	5.050 251	—	—	—	—	5
6	6.075 502	2.015 000	1.000 000	—	—	6
7	7.105 879	—	—	—	—	7
8	8.141 409	—	—	—	—	8
9	9.182 116	3.045 225	—	—	—	9
10	10.228 026	—	—	—	—	10
11	11.279 167	—	—	—	—	11

Years						Years
1	12.335 562	4.090 903	2.030 000	1.000 000	1.000 000	1
2	25.431 955	8.432 839	4.183 627	2.060 000	2.061 831	2
3	39.336 105	13.041 211	6.468 410	3.183 600	3.189 317	3
4	54.097 832	17.932 370	8.892 336	4.374 616	4.386 516	4
5	69.770 031	23.123 667	11.463 879	5.637 093	5.657 740	5
6	86.408 856	28.633 521	14.192 030	6.975 319	7.007 565	6
7	104.073 927	34.481 479	17.086 324	8.393 838	8.440 851	7
8	122.828 542	40.688 288	20.156 881	9.897 468	9.962 760	8
9	142.739 900	47.275 969	23.414 435	11.491 316	11.578 769	9
10	163.879 347	54.267 894	26.870 374	13.180 795	13.294 699	10
11	186.322 629	61.688 868	30.536 780	14.971 643	15.116 727	11
12	210.150 163	69.565 219	34.426 470	16.869 941	17.051 413	12
13	235.447 328	77.924 892	38.553 042	18.882 138	19.105 723	13
14	262.304 766	86.797 543	42.930 923	21.015 066	21.287 053	14
15	290.818 712	96.214 652	47.575 416	23.275 970	23.603 258	15
16	321.091 337	106.209 628	52.502 759	25.672 528	26.062 677	16
17	353.231 110	116.817 931	57.730 177	28.212 880	28.674 164	17
18	387.353 194	128.077 197	63.275 944	30.905 653	31.447 123	18
19	423.579 854	140.027 372	69.159 449	33.759 992	34.391 538	19
20	462.040 895	152.710 852	75.401 260	36.785 591	37.518 009	20
21	502.874 129	166.172 636	82.023 196	39.992 727	40.837 794	21
22	546.225 867	180.460 482	89.048 409	43.392 290	44.362 846	22
23	592.251 446	195.625 082	96.501 457	46.995 828	48.105 855	23
24	641.115 782	211.720 235	104.408 396	50.815 577	52.080 300	24
25	692.993 962	228.803 043	112.796 867	54.864 512	56.300 489	25
26	748.071 876	246.934 114	121.696 197	59.156 383	60.781 618	26
27	806.546 875	266.177 771	131.137 495	63.705 766	65.539 821	27
28	868.628 484	286.602 288	141.153 768	68.528 112	70.592 229	28
29	934.539 150	308.280 125	151.780 033	73.639 798	75.957 034	29
30	1004.515 042	331.288 191	163.053 437	79.058 186	81.653 552	30
31	1078.806 895	355.708 115	175.013 391	84.801 677	87.702 292	31
32	1157.680 906	381.626 531	187.701 707	90.889 778	94.125 033	32
33	1241.419 693	409.135 393	201.162 741	97.343 165	100.944 900	33
34	1330.323 306	438.332 297	215.443 551	104.183 755	108.186 449	34
35	1424.710 299	469.320 826	230.594 064	111.434 780	115.875 751	35
36	1524.918 875	502.210 922	246.667 242	119.120 867	124.040 492	36
37	1631.308 097	537.119 271	263.719 277	127.268 119	132.710 069	37
38	1744.259 173	574.169 720	281.809 781	135.904 206	141.915 697	38
39	1864.176 824	613.493 716	301.001 997	145.058 458	151.690 520	39
40	1991.490 734	655.230 772	321.363 019	154.761 966	162.069 733	40

10%   SINKING FUND ACCUMULATION FACTORS
(Future Value of Periodic Payments of $1)

Base:	1.008 333	1.025 000	1.050 000	1.100 000	1.105 156	
			Frequency of Payments and of Conversions			
Months	Monthly	Quarterly	Semiannual	Annual	Annual Payment Daily Conversion	**Months**
1	1.000 000	—	—	—	—	1
2	2.008 333	—	—	—	—	2
3	3.025 069	1.000 000	—	—	—	3
4	4.050 278	—	—	—	—	4
5	5.084 031	—	—	—	—	5
6	6.126 398	2.025 000	1.000 000	—	—	6
7	7.177 451	—	—	—	—	7
8	8.237 263	—	—	—	—	8
9	9.305 907	3.075 625	—	—	—	9
10	10.383 456	—	—	—	—	10
11	11.469 985	—	—	—	—	11
Years						**Years**
1	12.565 568	4.152 516	2.050 000	1.000 000	1.000 000	1
2	26.446 915	8.736 116	4.310 125	2.100 000	2.105 156	2
3	41.781 821	13.795 553	6.801 913	3.310 000	3.326 524	3
4	58.722 492	19.380 225	9.549 109	4.641 000	4.676 327	4
5	77.437 072	25.544 658	12.577 893	6.105 100	6.168 069	5
6	98.111 314	32.349 038	15.917 127	7.715 610	7.816 676	6
7	120.950 418	39.859 801	19.598 632	9.487 171	9.638 643	7
8	146.181 076	48.150 278	23.657 492	11.435 888	11.652 200	8
9	174.053 713	57.301 413	28.132 385	13.579 477	13.877 493	9
10	204.844 979	67.402 554	33.065 954	15.937 425	16.336 789	10
11	238.860 493	78.552 323	38.505 214	18.531 167	19.054 693	11
12	276.437 876	90.859 582	44.501 999	21.384 284	22.058 401	12
13	317.950 102	104.444 494	51.113 454	24.522 712	25.377 964	13
14	363.809 201	119.439 694	58.402 583	27.974 983	29.046 599	14
15	414.470 346	135.991 590	66.438 848	31.772 482	33.101 010	15
16	470.436 376	154.261 786	75.298 829	35.949 730	37.581 766	16
17	532.262 780	174.428 663	85.066 959	40.544 703	42.533 698	17
18	600.563 216	196.689 122	95.836 323	45.599 173	48.006 353	18
19	676.015 601	221.260 504	107.709 546	51.159 090	54.054 489	19
20	759.368 836	248.382 713	120.799 774	57.274 999	60.738 620	20
21	851.450 244	278.320 556	135.231 751	64.002 499	68.125 624	21
22	953.173 779	311.366 333	151.143 006	71.402 749	76.289 413	22
23	1065.549 097	347.842 687	168.685 164	79.543 024	85.311 670	23
24	1189.691 580	388.105 758	188.025 393	88.497 327	95.282 667	24
25	1326.833 403	432.548 654	209.347 996	98.347 059	106.302 170	25
26	1478.335 767	481.605 296	232.856 165	109.181 765	118.480 436	26
27	1645.702 407	535.754 649	258.773 922	121.099 942	131.939 313	27
28	1830.594 523	595.525 404	287.348 249	134.209 936	146.813 467	28
29	2034.847 258	661.501 133	318.851 445	148.630 930	163.251 721	29
30	2260.487 925	734.325 993	353.583 718	164.494 023	181.418 550	30
31	2509.756 117	814.711 013	391.876 049	181.943 425	201.495 721	31
32	2785.125 947	903.441 034	434.093 344	201.137 767	223.684 118	32
33	3089.330 596	1001.382 375	480.637 912	222.251 544	248.205 750	33
34	3425.389 447	1109.491 289	531.953 298	245.476 699	275.305 967	34
35	3796.638 052	1228.823 303	588.528 511	271.024 368	305.255 923	35
36	4206.761 236	1360.543 518	650.902 683	299.126 805	338.355 284	36
37	4659.829 677	1505.937 989	719.670 208	330.039 486	374.935 228	37
38	5160.340 305	1666.426 280	795.486 404	364.043 434	415.361 756	38
39	5713.260 935	1843.575 325	879.073 761	401.447 778	460.039 359	39
40	6324.079 581	2039.114 724	971.228 821	442.592 556	509.415 060	40

Table 8 - DIRECT REDUCTION LOAN FACTORS (Monthly Payment and Annual Constant per $1 of Loan)

Payment: $1/a_{\overline{n}|} = \dfrac{i}{1 - 1/S^n}$

Annual Constant: $R_M = 12/a_{\overline{n}|}$

Where $1/a_{\overline{n}|}$ = Direct Reduction Loan Factor

                         $1/S^n$ = Present Value Factor

                         i = Effective Rate of Interest

                         R_M = Annual Constant

Part Paid Off: $P = \dfrac{R_M - 12i}{R_{Mp} - 12i}$

Where R_M = Actual Annual Constant

                         R_{Mp} = Annual Constant for Projection Period

                         i = Effective Rate of Interest

This table is used in solving problems dealing with monthly payment, direct reduction loans. (Payments and constants for quarterly, semiannual, and annual payment loans can be obtained by calculating reciprocals of factors from Table 3.)

Example 1:
What is the level monthly payment and annual debt service for a direct reduction loan in the amount of $100,000 assuming nominal interest at 10% and full amortization over 25 years?

$100,000 × .0090870 = $ 908.70*
$100,000 × .1090441 = $10,904.41*

*In actual practice, the payment would be rounded up to $908.71 and the debt service would be: $908.71 × 12 = $10,904.52

Example 2:
In ten years, how much would be paid off of the loan in Example 1?

$100,000 × .1544 = $15,440

                              OR

$100,000 × [($10,904.52/$100,000 − .10)/(.1585809 − .10)] = $15,440.53

Example 3:
For the loan in Example 1, what discounted price would achieve a 14% yield?

Assuming Full Term:

$10,904.41/.1444513 = $75,488.49

Assuming a 10-Year Call:

$10,904.52/.1863197   = $58,525.86
($100,000 − $15,440.53) × .248603* =   21,021.74
                                      $79,547.60

* Present Value Factor for 120 months.

Example 4:
What is the level monthly payment and annual debt service for a direct reduction loan in the amount of $100,000 assuming nominal interest at 10% and full amortization over 25 years and 7 months?

$100,000/(1/.0090870 + .082940*/.1476586) = $904.09

$904.09 × 12 = $10,849.08

* Present Value Factor for 300 months.

Example 5:
In 10 years, how much would be paid off of the loan in Example 4?

$100,000 × [($10,849.08/$100,000 − .10)/(.1585809 − .10)] = $14,494.14

These factors reflect the amount of ordinary annuity payment that $1.00 will purchase. Also known as mortgage constants for loan amortization, they reflect the periodic payment that will extinguish a debt and include interest on the declining balance of the debt over the life of the payments. The mortgage constant may be expressed on a basis related to the periodic payments. Thus, a mortgage constant related to a monthly payment is the ratio of the monthly payment amount to the original amount of the loan. Whether payments are monthly or less frequent, the mortgage constant is usually expressed in terms of the total payments in one year as a percentage of the original loan amount. This is called the annual constant, represented by the symbol R_M. Alternatively, as the loan is paid off and the outstanding balance is reduced, a new annual mortgage constant may be calculated as the ratio of total annual payments to the unpaid balance of the loan at that time.

A loan of $10,000 to be amortized in 10 annual end-of-year payments at a mortgage interest rate of 10% would require level annual payments of $10,000 × .162745 (10% direct reduction annual factor for 10 years). If payments were monthly at 10% over 10 years, the amount of each payment would be $132.15 ($10,000 × .013215). The annual mortgage constant in this case would be .158580 (12 × .013215).

Direct reduction factors consist of the interest rate plus the sinking fund factor at the same time. These factors are also reciprocals of corresponding ordinary level annuity factors.

10% DIRECT REDUCTION LOAN FACTORS
(Monthly Payment and Annual Constant per $1 of Loan)

Base: 1.008 333

Months	Payment	Annual Constant	1 Year	5 Years	10 Years	15 Years	Months
			Part Paid Off Projection				
1	1.008 3333	—	—	—	—	—	1
2	.506 2586	—	—	—	—	—	2
3	.338 9043	—	—	—	—	—	3
4	.255 2299	—	—	—	—	—	4
5	.205 0277	—	—	—	—	—	5
6	.171 5614	—	—	—	—	—	6
7	.147 6586	—	—	—	—	—	7
8	.129 7329	—	—	—	—	—	8
9	.115 7920	—	—	—	—	—	9
10	.104 6404	—	—	—	—	—	10
11	.095 5174	—	—	—	—	—	11

Years	Payment	Annual Constant	1 Year	5 Years	10 Years	15 Years	Years
1	.087 9159	1.054 9906	1.0000	—	—	—	1
2	.046 1449	.553 7391	.4751	—	—	—	2
3	.032 2672	.387 2062	.3007	—	—	—	3
4	.025 3626	.304 3510	.2140	—	—	—	4
5	.021 2470	.254 9645	.1623	1.0000	—	—	5
6	.018 5258	.222 3101	.1281	.7893	—	—	6
7	.016 6012	.199 2142	.1039	.6402	—	—	7
8	.015 1742	.182 0900	.0860	.5297	—	—	8
9	.014 0787	.168 9442	.0722	.4449	—	—	9
10	.013 2151	.158 5809	.0613	.3780	1.0000	—	10
11	.012 5199	.150 2385	.0526	.3242	.8576	—	11
12	.011 9508	.143 4094	.0455	.2801	.7410	—	12
13	.011 4785	.137 7418	.0395	.2436	.6443	—	13
14	.011 0820	.132 9843	.0345	.2129	.5631	—	14
15	.010 7461	.128 9526	.0303	.1868	.4942	1.0000	15
16	.010 4590	.125 5082	.0267	.1646	.4354	.8810	16
17	.010 2121	.122 5453	.0236	.1455	.3849	.7787	17
18	.009 9984	.119 9812	.0209	.1289	.3411	.6901	18
19	.009 8126	.117 7511	.0186	.1145	.3030	.6131	19
20	.009 6502	.115 8026	.0165	.1020	.2698	.5458	20
21	.009 5078	.114 0936	.0148	.0909	.2406	.4868	21
22	.009 3825	.112 5895	.0132	.0812	.2149	.4348	22
23	.009 2718	.111 2618	.0118	.0727	.1922	.3890	23
24	.009 1739	.110 0866	.0106	.0651	.1722	.3484	24
25	.009 0870	.109 0441	.0095	.0584	.1544	.3124	25
26	.009 0098	.108 1172	.0085	.0524	.1386	.2804	26
27	.008 9410	.107 2917	.0076	.0471	.1245	.2519	27
28	.008 8796	.106 5552	.0069	.0423	.1119	.2264	28
29	.008 8248	.105 8972	.0062	.0381	.1007	.2037	29
30	.008 7757	.105 3086	.0056	.0343	.0906	.1834	30
31	.008 7318	.104 7813	.0050	.0309	.0816	.1651	31
32	.008 6924	.104 3086	.0045	.0278	.0735	.1488	32
33	.008 6570	.103 8843	.0041	.0251	.0663	.1342	33
34	.008 6253	.103 5033	.0037	.0226	.0598	.1210	34
35	.008 5967	.103 1607	.0033	.0204	.0540	.1092	35
36	.008 5710	.102 8526	.0030	.0184	.0487	.0985	36
37	.008 5479	.102 5752	.0027	.0166	.0440	.0889	37
38	.008 5271	.102 3254	.0024	.0150	.0397	.0803	38
39	.008 5084	.102 1004	.0022	.0136	.0359	.0725	39
40	.008 4915	.101 8975	.0020	.0122	.0324	.0655	40

14%   DIRECT REDUCTION LOAN FACTORS
(Monthly Payment and Annual Constant per $1 of Loan)

Base:	1.011 667	Annual		Part Paid Off Projection				
Months	Payment	Constant	1 Year	5 Years	10 Years	15 Years	Months
1	1.011 6667	—	—	—	—	—	1
2	.508 7669	—	—	—	—	—	2
3	.341 1412	—	—	—	—	—	3
4	.257 3340	—	—	—	—	—	4
5	.207 0541	—	—	—	—	—	5
6	.173 5380	—	—	—	—	—	6
7	.149 6011	—	—	—	—	—	7
8	.131 6513	—	—	—	—	—	8
9	.117 6928	—	—	—	—	—	9
10	.106 5283	—	—	—	—	—	10
11	.097 3957	—	—	—	—	—	11

Years							Years
1	.089 7871	1.077 4454	1.0000	—	—	—	1
2	.048 0129	.576 1546	.4653	—	—	—	2
3	.034 1776	.410 1316	.2882	—	—	—	3
4	.027 3265	.327 9177	.2005	—	—	—	4
5	.023 2683	.279 2190	.1485	1.0000	—	—	5
6	.020 6057	.247 2689	.1144	.7705	—	—	6
7	.018 7400	.224 8801	.0905	.6097	—	—	7
8	.017 3715	.208 4580	.0730	.4917	—	—	8
9	.016 3337	.196 0044	.0597	.4023	—	—	9
10	.015 5266	.186 3197	.0494	.3327	1.0000	—	10
11	.014 8867	.178 6399	.0412	.2775	.8342	—	11
12	.014 3713	.172 4553	.0346	.2331	.7007	—	12
13	.013 9510	.167 4124	.0292	.1969	.5918	—	13
14	.013 6049	.163 2588	.0248	.1671	.5021	—	14
15	.013 3174	.159 8090	.0211	.1423	.4277	1.0000	15
16	.013 0770	.156 9239	.0181	.1216	.3654	.8544	16
17	.012 8748	.154 4971	.0155	.1041	.3130	.7318	17
18	.012 7038	.152 4460	.0133	.0894	.2687	.6283	18
19	.012 5588	.150 7051	.0114	.0769	.2311	.5404	19
20	.012 4352	.149 2225	.0098	.0662	.1991	.4656	20
21	.012 3297	.147 9561	.0085	.0571	.1718	.4016	21
22	.012 2393	.146 8715	.0073	.0494	.1483	.3469	22
23	.012 1617	.145 9408	.0063	.0427	.1283	.2999	23
24	.012 0950	.145 1405	.0055	.0369	.1110	.2595	24
25	.012 0376	.144 4513	.0047	.0320	.0961	.2247	25
26	.011 9881	.143 8570	.0041	.0277	.0833	.1947	26
27	.011 9453	.143 3439	.0036	.0240	.0722	.1688	27
28	.011 9084	.142 9004	.0031	.0208	.0626	.1464	28
29	.011 8764	.142 5167	.0027	.0181	.0543	.1270	29
30	.011 8487	.142 1846	.0023	.0157	.0472	.1103	30
31	.011 8247	.141 8969	.0020	.0136	.0410	.0958	31
32	.011 8040	.141 6475	.0018	.0118	.0356	.0832	32
33	.011 7859	.141 4313	.0015	.0103	.0309	.0723	33
34	.011 7703	.141 2436	.0013	.0089	.0268	.0628	34
35	.011 7567	.141 0808	.0012	.0078	.0233	.0546	35
36	.011 7450	.140 9394	.0010	.0067	.0203	.0474	36
37	.011 7347	.140 8166	.0009	.0059	.0176	.0412	37
38	.011 7258	.140 7100	.0008	.0051	.0153	.0358	38
39	.011 7181	.140 6173	.0007	.0044	.0133	.0312	39
40	.011 7114	.140 5368	.0006	.0039	.0116	.0271	40

Table 9 - J-FACTORS (Adjustment Factors for Changes in Income)

Ellwood: $J = 1/S_{\overline{n}} \, [n/ \, (1 - 1/S^n) - (1/Y_E)]$

Straight-Line: $J = (1/n - 1/S_{\overline{n}})/Y_E$

Where J = Factor

$1/S_{\overline{n}}$ = SFF at Equity Yield Rate for Projection

n = Projection

$1/S^n$ = Reversion Factor at Y_E for Projection

Y_E = Equity Yield Rate

This table is used in solving mortgage/equity problems dealing with changing income: specifically, the factors can be substituted in any of the "J-Factor, Changing Income" formulas which solve for Overall Rates, Change in Property Values, or Equity Yield Rates.

The Ellwood Premise J-Factors reflect curvilinear income that changes from time zero in relation to a Sinking Fund Accumulation curve; the Straight-Line premise J-Factors reflect income changing in equal annual amounts after the first year.

Facts for the examples: Change in both Income and Value = +25% in 5 years; Mortgage terms = 70% ratio, 12% nominal interest, and 25-year term; desired Equity Yield = 18%.

$$C = Y_E + P \, 1/S_{\overline{n}} - R_M$$

$$C = .18 + .0435 \times .139778 - .1263869$$

$$C = .05969344 \text{ say, } .0597$$

Example 1:

Assuming income at time zero is $10,000, what is the calculated value using the Ellwood premise?

$$R_0 = (Y_E - MC - \Delta_0 \, 1/S_{\overline{n}})/(1 + \Delta_I J)$$

$$R_0 = (.18 - .70 \times .0597 - .25 \times .139778)/(1 + .25 \times .4651)$$

$$R_0 = .092509$$

$$V_0 = I_0/R_0$$

$$V_0 = \$10,000/.092509$$

$$V_0 = \$108,098$$

PROOF: Debt Service = $108,098 × .70 = $75,668
$75,668 × .1263869 = $9,563

Reversion = $108,098 × 1.25 − $75,668 × (1 − .0435) = $62,746

Equity = $108,098 × .30 = $32,429

Time	Income	−	Debt Service	=	Cash to Equity	×	PVF @18%	=	Value
1	$10,349	−	$9,563	=	$ 786	×	.847458	=	$ 666
2	10,762	−	9,563	=	1,199	×	.718184	=	861
3	11,248	−	9,563	=	1,685	×	.608631	=	1,026
4	11,823	−	9,563	=	2,260	×	.515789	=	1,166
5	12,500	−	9,563	=	2,937	×	.437109	=	1,284
Reversion:					62,746	×	.437109	=	27,427
Total Equity									$32,430

Example 2:

Assuming Income at the end of year one is $10,000, what is the calculated value using the Straight-Line premise?

$$R_0 = (Y_E − MC − \Delta_0\, 1/S_{\overline{n}})/(1 + \Delta_I J)$$

$$R_0 = (.18 − .70 × .0597 − .25 × .139778)/(1 + .25 × .3346)$$

$$R_0 = .095294$$

$$V_0 = I_0/R_0$$

$$V_0 = \$10,000/.095294$$

$$V_0 = \$104,938$$

PROOF: Debt Service = $104,938 × .70 = $73,457
$73,457 × .1263869 = $9,284

Reversion = $104,938 × 1.25 − $73,457 × (1 − .0435) = $60,911

Equity = $104,938 × .30 = $31,481

Time	Income	−	Debt Service	=	Cash to Equity	×	PVF @18%	=	Value
1	$10,000	−	$9,284	=	$ 716	×	.847458	=	$ 607
2	10,500	−	9,284	=	1,216	×	.718184	=	873
3	11,000	−	9,284	=	1,716	×	.608631	=	1,044
4	11,500	−	9,284	=	2,216	×	.515789	=	1,143
5	12,000	−	9,284	=	2,716	×	.437109	=	1,187
Reversion:					60,911	×	.437109	=	26,625
Total Equity									$31,479

If income is expected to change by +25% in five years and the yield rate is 16%, the *J*-Factor would be .4790 on the Ellwood (sinking fund) premise or .3412 on the straight-line basis. The appropriate factor would then be inserted into the mortgage-equity formula.

J - FACTORS

(Adjustment Factors for Changes in Income)

YEARS	16.0% ELLWOOD	16.0% STRAIGHT LINE	16.5% ELLWOOD	16.5% STRAIGHT LINE	17.0% ELLWOOD	17.0% STRAIGHT LINE	17.5% ELLWOOD	17.5% STRAIGHT LINE	YEARS
1	1.0000	.0000	1.0000	.0000	1.0000	.0000	1.0000	.0000	1
2	.7116	.2315	.7104	.2309	.7093	.2304	.7082	.2299	2
3	.5986	.3005	.5966	.2995	.5946	.2986	.5926	.2977	3
4	.5298	.3289	.5270	.3276	.5242	.3263	.5215	.3250	4
5	.4790	.3412	.4755	.3395	.4720	.3379	.4685	.3362	5
6	.4374	.3455	.4333	.3435	.4291	.3415	.4250	.3395	6
7	.4015	.3453	.3968	.3430	.3921	.3406	.3874	.3384	7
8	.3695	.3423	.3642	.3397	.3590	.3371	.3538	.3345	8
9	.3403	.3377	.3345	.3348	.3289	.3319	.3233	.3290	9
10	.3134	.3319	.3072	.3287	.3012	.3255	.2952	.3224	10
11	.2884	.3253	.2820	.3219	.2756	.3185	.2694	.3152	11
12	.2652	.3182	.2585	.3146	.2519	.3110	.2454	.3074	12
13	.2435	.3109	.2366	.3070	.2299	.3032	.2233	.2995	13
14	.2233	.3033	.2163	.2993	.2095	.2953	.2028	.2914	14
15	.2045	.2957	.1974	.2915	.1905	.2873	.1838	.2832	15
16	.1870	.2880	.1799	.2837	.1730	.2794	.1663	.2752	16
17	.1707	.2804	.1636	.2759	.1568	.2715	.1502	.2672	17
18	.1555	.2729	.1486	.2683	.1419	.2638	.1354	.2594	18
19	.1415	.2656	.1347	.2609	.1281	.2563	.1219	.2518	19
20	.1286	.2583	.1219	.2535	.1155	.2489	.1095	.2443	20
21	.1166	.2513	.1101	.2464	.1040	.2417	.0981	.2371	21
22	.1056	.2444	.0994	.2395	.0934	.2347	.0879	.2301	22
23	.0955	.2377	.0895	.2328	.0838	.2280	.0785	.2233	23
24	.0862	.2312	.0805	.2263	.0751	.2215	.0700	.2168	24
25	.0778	.2249	.0723	.2200	.0672	.2152	.0624	.2105	25
26	.0700	.2188	.0648	.2139	.0600	.2091	.0555	.2044	26
27	.0630	.2130	.0581	.2080	.0535	.2032	.0493	.1986	27
28	.0565	.2073	.0519	.2024	.0477	.1976	.0437	.1930	28
29	.0507	.2018	.0464	.1969	.0424	.1922	.0387	.1876	29
30	.0455	.1965	.0414	.1917	.0377	.1870	.0343	.1825	30
31	.0407	.1915	.0369	.1866	.0334	.1820	.0303	.1775	31
32	.0364	.1866	.0328	.1818	.0296	.1772	.0267	.1728	32
33	.0325	.1819	.0292	.1771	.0262	.1726	.0236	.1683	33
34	.0290	.1773	.0259	.1727	.0232	.1682	.0208	.1639	34
35	.0258	.1730	.0230	.1684	.0205	.1639	.0183	.1597	35
36	.0230	.1688	.0204	.1642	.0181	.1599	.0161	.1557	36
37	.0205	.1648	.0181	.1603	.0160	.1560	.0141	.1519	37
38	.0182	.1609	.0160	.1565	.0141	.1522	.0124	.1482	38
39	.0162	.1572	.0142	.1528	.0124	.1486	.0109	.1447	39
40	.0143	.1536	.0125	.1493	.0109	.1452	.0095	.1413	40

J - FACTORS

(Adjustment Factors for Changes in Income)

	18.0%		19.0%		20.0%		21.0%		
YEARS	ELLWOOD	STRAIGHT LINE	ELLWOOD	STRAIGHT LINE	ELLWOOD	STRAIGHT LINE	ELLWOOD	STRAIGHT LINE	YEARS
1	1.0000	.0000	1.0000	.0000	1.0000	.0000	1.0000	.0000	1
2	.7070	.2294	.7047	.2283	.7025	.2273	.7002	.2262	2
3	.5906	.2967	.5866	.2949	.5827	.2930	.5787	.2912	3
4	.5187	.3237	.5132	.3211	.5078	.3186	.5024	.3160	4
5	.4651	.3346	.4582	.3313	.4514	.3281	.4448	.3249	5
6	.4210	.3375	.4129	.3336	.4050	.3298	.3971	.3260	6
7	.3828	.3361	.3736	.3316	.3647	.3272	.3558	.3228	7
8	.3487	.3320	.3386	.3269	.3288	.3220	.3191	.3171	8
9	.3177	.3262	.3069	.3206	.2963	.3152	.2861	.3098	9
10	.2894	.3194	.2779	.3133	.2668	.3074	.2561	.3016	10
11	.2632	.3118	.2513	.3054	.2398	.2990	.2288	.2928	11
12	.2391	.3039	.2269	.2970	.2152	.2903	.2039	.2838	12
13	.2168	.2958	.2044	.2885	.1926	.2815	.1814	.2747	13
14	.1963	.2875	.1838	.2800	.1720	.2727	.1609	.2656	14
15	.1773	.2792	.1649	.2714	.1533	.2639	.1423	.2567	15
16	.1599	.2711	.1477	.2630	.1363	.2553	.1256	.2479	16
17	.1439	.2630	.1319	.2548	.1209	.2469	.1106	.2394	17
18	.1292	.2551	.1176	.2467	.1070	.2388	.0972	.2311	18
19	.1159	.2474	.1047	.2389	.0944	.2308	.0851	.2232	19
20	.1037	.2399	.0929	.2313	.0832	.2232	.0744	.2155	20
21	.0926	.2326	.0824	.2240	.0732	.2159	.0650	.2082	21
22	.0826	.2256	.0729	.2170	.0642	.2088	.0566	.2011	22
23	.0735	.2188	.0643	.2102	.0563	.2021	.0491	.1944	23
24	.0653	.2123	.0567	.2037	.0492	.1956	.0426	.1880	24
25	.0579	.2060	.0499	.1974	.0429	.1894	.0369	.1819	25
26	.0513	.2000	.0438	.1915	.0374	.1835	.0319	.1761	26
27	.0454	.1942	.0385	.1857	.0326	.1779	.0275	.1705	27
28	.0401	.1886	.0337	.1802	.0283	.1725	.0237	.1652	28
29	.0354	.1833	.0295	.1750	.0245	.1673	.0204	.1602	29
30	.0312	.1782	.0258	.1700	.0213	.1624	.0175	.1554	30
31	.0274	.1733	.0225	.1652	.0184	.1578	.0150	.1509	31
32	.0241	.1686	.0196	.1606	.0159	.1533	.0129	.1466	32
33	.0212	.1641	.0171	.1563	.0137	.1491	.0110	.1424	33
34	.0186	.1598	.0148	.1521	.0118	.1450	.0094	.1385	34
35	.0163	.1557	.0129	.1481	.0102	.1412	.0081	.1348	35
36	.0142	.1517	.0112	.1443	.0088	.1375	.0069	.1312	36
37	.0125	.1480	.0097	.1406	.0075	.1340	.0059	.1278	37
38	.0109	.1443	.0084	.1372	.0065	.1306	.0050	.1246	38
39	.0095	.1409	.0073	.1338	.0056	.1274	.0043	.1215	39
40	.0083	.1376	.0063	.1306	.0048	.1243	.0036	.1186	40

Interrelationships among the Tables

As can be noted from the formulas for the various tables, mathematical relationships exist among them. These relationships are useful both in understanding the tables and in solving appraisal problems. For example, it is often helpful for appraisers to know that the ordinary level annuity and the direct reduction tables are reciprocals, and the factors in the ordinary level annuity table can be used as multipliers instead of direct reduction loan divisors.

Reciprocals

Reciprocals are numbers divided into 1 (one). Thus, the reciprocal of 10 is 1/10; the reciprocal of .5 is 1/.5. The numbers in some of the tables are reciprocals of numbers in other tables, as indicated by their formulas:

a. Future Value of $1.00 and Reversion Tables

$$S_{\overline{n}|} \text{ and } \frac{1}{S_{\overline{n}|}}$$

Thus, the reversion factor at 12% for 10 years (annual compounding) is .321973, which is the reciprocal of the future value of the factor $\left(.321973 = \dfrac{1}{3.105848}\right)$.

b. Sinking Fund Accumulations and Sinking Fund Factors Tables

$$S_{\overline{n}|} \text{ and } \frac{1}{S_{\overline{n}|}}$$

Thus, the sinking factor at 12% for 10 years (annual compounding) is .056984, which is the reciprocal of the sinking fund accumulations factor $\left(.056984 = \dfrac{1}{17.548735}\right)$.

c. Ordinary Level Annuity and Direct Reduction Tables

$$a_{\overline{n}|} \text{ and } \frac{1}{a_{\overline{n}|}}$$

Thus, the direct reduction factor at 12% for 10 years (annual compounding) is .176984, which is the reciprocal of the ordinary level annuity factor $\left(.176984 = \dfrac{1}{5.650223}\right)$.

Summations

a. Ordinary Level Annuity Table

Ordinary level annuity factors are summations of reversion factors for all periods up to and including the period being considered. For example, the ordinary level annuity factor for five years at 12% (annual compounding) of 3.604776 is the sum of all the reversion factors for years one through five:

$$
\begin{array}{r}
.892857 \\
.797194 \\
.711780 \\
.635518 \\
\underline{.567427} \\
3.604776
\end{array}
$$

b. Direct Reduction Factors

Direct reduction factors are the summation of the interest (yield, discount) rate (stated at the top of the page) and the sinking fund factor. For example, the direct reduction factor number at 12% for 10 years (monthly compounding) of .1721651 is the sum of .12 plus the monthly sinking fund factor of .0643471 times 12 (.12 + .0521651) = .1721651).

Conversely, the sinking fund factor can be obtained by subtracting the interest rate from the direct reduction factor. Thus, the sinking fund factor at 12% for 10 years (monthly compounding) is .1721651 − .12 = .0521651. In addition, the interest rate can be obtained by subtracting the sinking fund factor from the direct reduction factor. Thus, the interest rate, given a mortgage constant of .1721651 with monthly compounding for 10 years, is .1721651 − .0521651 = .12000, or 12.0%.

Suggested Readings

Books

Akerson, Charles B. *Capitalization Theory and Techniques: Study Guide.* Chicago: American Institute of Real Estate Appraisers, 1980.

Albritton, Harold D. *Controversies in Real Property Valuation: A Commentary.* Chicago: American Institute of Real Estate Appraisers, 1982.

American Association of State Highway Officials. *Acquisitions for Right of Way.* Washington, D.C., 1962.

American Institute of Real Estate Appraisers. *The Appraisal Journal Bibliography, 1932-1969.* Chicago, 1970.

_____. *The Appraisal of Rural Property.* Chicago, 1983.

_____. *Condemnation Appraisal Practice.* Vol. 2. Chicago, 1973.

_____. *Guidelines for Appraisal Office Policies and Procedures.* Chicago, 1981.

_____. *Readers' Guide to the Appraisal Journal, 1970-1980.* Chicago, 1981.

_____. *Readings in the Appraisal of Special Use Properties.* Chicago, 1981.

_____. *Readings in Highest and Best Use.* Chicago, 1981.

_____. *Readings in the Income Approach to Real Property Valuation.* Chicago, 1977

_____. *Readings in Market Value.* Chicago, 1981.

_____. *Readings in Real Estate Investment Analysis.* Chicago, 1977.

_____. *Readings in Real Property Valuation Principles.* Chicago, 1977.

_____. *Real Estate Appraisal Bibliography.* Chicago, 1973.

_____. *Real Estate Appraisal Bibliography, 1973-1980.* Chicago, 1981.

American Society of Appraisers. *Appraisal and Valuation Manual.* Washington, D.C., 1956-1972. 9 vols.

Andrews, Richard N. L. *Land in America.* Lexington, Mass.: D. C. Heath, 1979.

Babcock, Frederick M. *The Valuation of Real Estate.* New York: McGraw-Hill, 1932.

Barlowe, Raleigh. *Land Resource Economics.* 3rd ed. Englewood Cliffs, N.J.: Prentice-Hall, 1978.

Bierman, Harold, Jr., and Seymour Smidt. *The Capital Budgeting Decision.* 5th ed. New York: Macmillan, 1980.

Bish, Robert L., and Hugh O. Nourse. *Urban Economics and Policy Analysis.* New York: McGraw-Hill, 1975.

Bloom, George F., and Henry S. Harrison. *Appraising the Single Family Residence.* Chicago: American Institute of Real Estate Appraisers, 1978.

Bonright, James C. *The Valuation of Property.* Vol. I. New York: McGraw-Hill, 1937.

Boyce, Byrl N., ed. *Real Estate Appraisal Terminology.* Rev. ed. Chicago: American Institute of Real Estate Appraisers and Society of Real Estate Appraisers, 1981.

Burton, James H. *Evolution of the Income Approach.* Chicago: American Institute of Real Estate Appraisers, 1982.

Clark, Louis E., and F. H. Treadway. *Impact of Electric Power Transmission Line Easements on Real Estate Value.* Chicago: American Institute of Real Estate Appraisers, 1972.

Conroy, Kathleen. *Valuing the Timeshare Property.* Chicago: American Institute of Real Estate Appraisers, 1981.

Desmond, Glenn M., and Richard E. Kelley. *Business Valuation Handbook.* Llano, Calif: Valuation Press, 1980.

Dilmore, Gene. *Quantitative Techniques in Real Estate Counseling.* Lexington, Mass.: D. C. Heath, 1981.

Dombal, Robert W. *Residential Condominiums: A Guide to Analysis and Appraisal.* Chicago: American Institute of Real Estate Appraisers, 1976.

Eaton, James D. *Real Estate Valuation in Litigation.* Chicago: American Institute of Real Estate Appraisers, 1982.

Ellwood, L. W. *Ellwood Tables for Real Estate Appraising and Financing.* 4th ed. Chicago: American Institute of Real Estate Appraisers, 1977.

Foreman, Robert L. *Communicating the Appraisal: A Guide to Report Writing.* Chicago: American Institute of Real Estate Appraisers, 1982.

Friedman, Edith J., ed. *Encyclopedia of Real Estate Appraising.* 3rd ed. Englewood Cliffs, N.J.: Prentice-Hall, 1978.

Garrett, Robert L., Hunter A. Hogan, Jr., and Robert M. Stanton. *The Valuation of Shopping Centers.* Chicago: American Institute of Real Estate Appraisers, 1976.

Gibbons, James E. *Appraising in a Changing Economy: Collected Writings.* Chicago: American Institute of Real Estate Appraisers, 1982.

Gimmy, Arthur E. *Tennis Clubs and Racquet Sport Projects: A Guide to Appraisal, Market Analysis, Development and Financing.* Chicago: American Institute of Real Estate Appraisers, 1978.

Graaskamp, James A. *A Guide to Feasibility Analysis.* Chicago: Society of Real Estate Appraisers, 1970.

Greer, Gaylon E. *The Real-Estate Investment Decision.* Lexington, Mass.: D. C. Heath, 1979.

Haggett, Peter. *Locational Analysis in Human Geography.* New York: St. Martin's, 1965.

Harrison, Henry S. *Houses—The Illustrated Guide to Construction, Design and Systems.* Rev. ed. Chicago: Realtors National Marketing Institute, 1976.

Heuer, Karla L. *Golf Courses: A Guide to Analysis and Valuation.* Chicago: American Institute of Real Estate Appraisers, 1980.

Hoover, Edgar M. *The Location of Economic Activity.* New York: McGraw-Hill, 1963.

Institute on Planning, Zoning, and Eminent Domain. *Proceedings.* Albany, New York: Matthew Bender.

International Association of Assessing Officers. *Assessing and the Appraisal Process.* 5th ed. Chicago, 1974.

————. *Property Assessment Valuation.* Chicago, 1977.

Jevons, W. Stanley. *The Theory of Political Economy.* 5th ed. New York: Augustus M. Kelley, 1965.

Kahn, Sanders A., and Frederick E. Case. *Real Estate Appraisal and Investment.* 2nd ed. New York: Ronald Press, 1977.

Kinnard, William N., Jr. *Income Property Valuation: Principles and Techniques of Appraising Income-Producing Real Estate.* Lexington, Mass.: D. C. Heath, 1971.

————, and Byrl N. Boyce. *An Introduction to Appraising Real Property.* Chicago: Society of Real Estate Appraisers, 1978.

————, Stephen D. Messner, and Byrl N. Boyce. *Industrial Real Estate.* 3rd ed. Washington, D.C.: Society of Industrial Realtors, 1979.

Kratovil, Robert, and Raymond J. Werner. *Real Estate Law.* 7th ed. Englewood Cliffs, N.J.: Prentice-Hall, 1979.

Lukens, Reaves C. *The Appraiser and Real Estate Feasibility Studies.* Chicago: American Institute of Real Estate Appraisers, 1972.

Mason, James J., ed. and comp. *American Institute of Real Estate Appraisers Financial Tables.* Chicago: American Institute of Real Estate Appraisers, 1981.

National Cooperative Highway Research Program. *Reports.* Washington, D.C.: National Academy of Sciences Highway Research Board.

Olin, Harold B., John L. Schmidt, and Walter H. Lewis. *Construction—Principles, Materials & Methods.* 4th ed. Chicago: Institute of Financial Education and Interstate Printers and Publishers, 1980.

Ratcliff, Richard U. *Modern Real Estate Valuation: Theory and Application.* Madison, Wis.: Democrat Press, 1965.

————. *Urban Land Economics.* New York: McGraw-Hill, 1949.

Reynolds, Judith. *Historic Properties: Preservation and the Valuation Process.* Chicago: American Institute of Real Estate Appraisers, 1982.

Ring, Alfred A. *Valuation of Real Estate.* 2nd ed. Englewood Cliffs, N.J.: Prentice-Hall, 1970.

Rohan, Patrick J., and Melvin A. Reskin. *Condemnation Procedures and Techniques; Forms.* Albany, N.Y.: Matthew Bender (looseleaf service).

Rushmore, Stephen. *Hotels, Motels, and Restaurants: Valuations and Market Studies.* Chicago: American Institute of Real Estate Appraisers, forthcoming.

Sackman, Julius L., and Patrick J. Rohan. *Nichols' Law of Eminent Domain.* 3rd ed. rev. Albany, N.Y.: Matthew Bender (looseleaf service).

Schmutz, George L. *The Appraisal Process.* 3rd ed. rev. Manhattan Beach, Calif., 1959.

————. *Condemnation Appraisal Handbook,* rev. and enlarged by Edwin M. Rams. Englewood Cliffs, N.J.: Prentice-Hall, 1963.

Shenkel, William M. *Modern Real Estate Appraisal.* New York: McGraw-Hill, 1978.

Smith, Halbert C. *Real Estate Appraisal.* Columbus, Ohio: Grid Publishing, 1976.

————, Carl J. Tschappat, and Ronald L. Racster. *Real Estate and Urban Development.* 3rd ed. Homewood, Ill.: Richard D. Irwin, 1981.

Sutte, Donald T., Jr. *Appraisal of Roadside Advertising Signs.* Chicago: American Institute of Real Estate Appraisers, 1972.

Vane, Howard R., and John L. Thompson. *Monetarism—Theory, Evidency and Policy.* New York: Halsted, 1979.

Weimer, Arthur M., Homer Hoyt, and George F. Bloom. *Real Estate.* 7th ed. New York: Wiley, 1977.

Wendt, Paul F. *Real Estate Appraisal Review and Outlook.* Athens: University of Georgia Press, 1974.

Wolf, Peter. *Land in America: Its Value, Use, and Control.* New York: Pantheon, 1981.

Building Cost Manuals

Boeckh Building Valuation Manual. Milwaukee: American Appraisal Co., 1967. 3 vols.
Vol. 1—Residential and Agricultural; Vol. 2—Commercial; Vol. 3—Industrial and Institutional. 1967 cost database; wide variety of building models; built up from unit-in-place costs converted to cost per square foot of floor or ground area. Boeckh Building Cost Modifier, published bimonthly for updating with current modifiers.

Building Construction Cost Data. Duxbury, Mass.: Robert Snow Means Co., annually.
Average unit prices on a variety of building construction items for use in making up engineering estimates. Components arranged according to uniform system adopted by American Institute of Architects, Associated General Contractors, and Construction Specifications Institute.

Dodge Building Cost Calculator & Valuation Guide. New York: McGraw-Hill Information Systems Co. (looseleaf service; quarterly supplements).
Building costs arranged by frequently occurring types and sizes of buildings; local cost modifiers and historical local cost index tables included. Formerly Dow Building Cost Calculator.

Marshall Valuation Service. Los Angeles: Marshall and Swift Publication Co. (looseleaf service; monthly supplements).
Cost data for determining replacement costs of buildings and other improvements in the United States and Canada; includes current cost multipliers and local modifiers.

Residential Cost Handbook. Los Angeles: Marshall and Swift Publication Co. (looseleaf service; quarterly supplements).
Presents square-foot method and segregated-cost method; local modifiers and cost trend modifiers included.

Sources of Operating Costs and Ratios

Only a few published sources are cited below. Attention is directed to the first item listed, the annotated bibliography issued by Robert Morris Associates.

Robert Morris Associates. *Sources of Composite Financial Data—A Bibliography.* 3rd ed. Philadelphia, 1971.
An annotated list of 98 nongovernment sources; arranged in manufacturing, wholesaling, retail, and service categories; subject index to specific businesses; publishers' names and addresses given for each citation.

Building Owners and Managers Association International. *Downtown and Suburban Office Building Experience Exchange Report.* Washington, D.C.
Annually, since 1920; analysis of expenses and income (quoted in cents per square foot); national, regional, and selected city averages.

Dun & Bradstreet, Inc. *Key Business Ratios in 125 Lines.* New York.
Annually; balance sheet, profit-and-loss ratios.

Pannell, Kerr, Forster & Co. *Clubs in Town & Country.* New York.
Annually, since 1953; income-expense data and operating ratios for city and country clubs; the geographical data given are listed according to four U.S. regions.

————. *Trends in the Hotel-Motel Business.* New York.
Annually, since 1937; income-expense data and operating ratios for transient and resort hotels and motels; the geographical data given are listed according to five U.S. regions.

Institute of Real Estate Management. *Income/Expense Analysis: Apartments, Condominiums & Cooperatives.* Chicago.
Annually, since 1954; data arranged by building, then by national, regional, metropolitan, and selected city groupings; operating costs per room, per square foot, etc. Formerly Apartment Building Experience Exchange.

_____*Income/Expense Analysis: Suburban Office Buildings.* Chicago.
Annually, since 1976; data analyzed on basis of gross area, gross and net rentable office areas; dollar-per-square-foot calculations; national, regional, and metropolitan comparisons and detailed analyses for selected cities.

Laventhol & Horwath. *Lodging Industry.* Philadelphia.
Annually, since 1932; income, expense, and profit data; includes historical trend tables.

_____ and National Restaurant Association. *Table-Service Restaurant Operations.* Philadelphia.
Annually, since 1976; income-expense data and operating ratios; superseded the Laventhol & Horwath Restaurant Operations report that began in 1959.

National Retail Merchants Association, Controllers' Congress. *Department Store and Specialty Store Merchandising and Operating Results.* New York.
Annually, since 1925; merchandise classification base used since 1969 edition (1968 data); geographical analysis by Federal Reserve districts. Known as the "MOR" report.

_____. *Financial and Operating Results of Department and Specialty Stores.* New York.
Annually, since 1963; data arranged by sales volume category. Known as the "FOR" Report.

Realtors National Marketing Institute. *Percentage Leases.* 13th ed. Chicago, 1973.
Based on reports of 3,100 leases for 97 retail and service categories in 7 U.S. regions. Data broken down by type of operation, area, center, and building; with regional and store averages given for average minimum rent, rent per square foot, average gross leaseable areas, and sales per square foot.

Urban Land Institute. *Dollars and Cents of Shopping Centers.* Washington, D.C., 1978.
First issued in 1961; revised every three years; income and expense data for neighborhood, community, and regional centers; statistics for specific tenant types given.

Periodicals

American Right of Way Proceedings. American Right of Way Association, Los Angeles.
Annually. Papers presented at national seminars.

Appraisal Digest. New York State Society of Real Estate Appraisers, a Division of the New York State Association of Real Estate Boards, Inc., Albany, N.Y.
Quarterly. Primarily articles published elsewhere; some original material included.

Appraisal Institute Magazine. Appraisal Institute of Canada, Winnipeg, Manitoba.
Quarterly. General and technical articles on appraisal and expropriation in Canada; includes information on institute's programs, news, etc.

The Appraisal Journal. American Institute of Real Estate Appraisers, Chicago.
Quarterly. Oldest periodical in the appraisal field, published since 1932; technical articles on all phases of real property appraisal; section on legal decisions included as regular feature. Consolidated index covering 1932-1969 available.

Editor and Publisher Market Guide. Editor and Publisher, New York.
Annually. Standardized market data for more than 1,500 areas in the United States and Canada; information includes population estimates for trading areas. List of principal industries, transportation, climate, chain store outlets, etc.

Journal of the American Real Estate and Urban Economics Association. New Brunswick, N.J.
Quarterly. Focuses on research and scholarly studies of current and emerging real estate issues.

Journal of the American Society of Farm Managers and Rural Appraisers. Denver.
Semiannually. Appraisal articles included.

Just Compensation. Sherman Oaks, Calif.
Monthly; reports on condemnation cases.

Land Economics. University of Wisconsin, Madison.
Quarterly. Subtitle: A Quarterly Journal Devoted to the Study of Economics and Social Institutes. Good source of reports on university research; covers trends in land use; frequent articles on developments in other countries.

The Real Estate Appraiser. Society of Real Estate Appraisers, Chicago.
Bimonthly. Technical articles and society news; section on legal cases included as regular feature. Consolidated bibliographies for 1935-1960 and 1961-1970 available. Previously published as The Review *and as* Residential Appraiser.

Real Estate Issues. American Society of Real Estate Counselors. Chicago.
Semiannually.

Right of Way. American Right of Way Association, Los Angeles, Calif.
Bimonthly. Articles on all phases of right-of-way activity; condemnation, negotiation, etc.; pipelines, electric power transmission lines, and other uses as well as highways; includes association news.

Small Business Reporter. Bank of America, San Francisco.
Irregularly. Each issue devoted to a specific type of small business; has covered, for instance, coin-operated laundries, greeting card shops, and restaurants.

Survey of Buying Power. Sales Management, New York.
Annually. Population totals and characteristics, income and consumption data presented in various categories: national, regional, metropolitan area, county, city; separate section of Canadian information. A source for population estimates between the decennial United States censuses.

Valuation. American Society of Appraisers, Washington, D.C.
Three issues per year. Articles on real property valuation included with articles on the appraisal of personal and intangible property; includes society news. Previously published as Technical Valuation.

Index